They Call Me Cat

By Jan Crossen

They Call Me Cat is the amalgamation of the three books in the
9 LIVES Trilogy by Jan Crossen.

A Gold Level Mom's Choice Award Winning Young Adult Series

9 LIVES: I Will Survive
9 LIVES: Cat Tales
9 LIVES: Full Circle

This is a fictionalized series inspired by my son, Joshua.

Cimarron Pines Publishing
Lopez Island, WA 98261
Cover Photo: Claudia Paulussen

They Call Me Cat

JAN CROSSEN

The Mom's Choice Awards Named The 9 Lives Trilogy

Among the Best Products of 2009

The Mom's Choice Awards has named Jan Crossen's *9 LIVES Trilogy,* among the best in family-friendly media products and services of 2009. The Mom's Choice Awards (MCA) is an annual awards program that recognizes authors, inventors, companies, parents and others for their efforts in creating quality family-friendly media, products and services. Parents, educators, librarians and retailers rely on MCA evaluations when selecting quality materials for children and families.

The Mom's Choice Awards seal helps families and educators navigate the vast array of products and services and make informed decisions. Jan Crossen's *9 LIVES* series earned the Gold Award for a Young Adult Series.

This fictional work was inspired by Crossen's adopted son, Joshua, who suffers from Fetal Alcohol Spectrum Disorders, which are brain disabilities caused by prenatal exposure to alcohol. The trilogy targets preteens, teenagers, reluctant readers, foster, adoptive and birth parents, teachers, social workers, therapists, and those working with the special needs population. The series includes: **9 LIVES: I Will Survive; 9 LIVES: Cat Tales; and 9 LIVES: Full Circle.**

For more information on the Mom's Choice Awards program and the honorees, visit www.MomsChoiceAwards.com.

High Praise

"When Jan gave me the manuscript, I sat down and read the first book in the series in just one day. I really didn't want to put it down. I was so absorbed in the experiences of this little boy. The series is inspired by Jan's own adopted son, and is told from his point of view. This child went through so much in his childhood, and has to cope with the difficulties of prenatal alcohol exposure.

This touching story has a therapeutic effect. It has the potential to heal the emotional wounds carried by adopted children, birth parents, and adoptive parents. I would recommend this book for all children, teens, and parents. This series was a joy to read."

Teresa Kellerman, Former Director,
Fetal Alcohol Syndrome Community
Resource Center, Tucson, AZ

"It is truly an uplifting adoption story, but also very realistic. I love the 'voice' you used, meaning Joshua's. That gives it credibility, plus an easy writing style to read – especially for adolescents and even younger. You have quite a story to tell and you are telling it so well! If all of that happened to YOUR Joshua, then he is some amazing kid for sure, and so are his parents! I mean, he really DOES have nine lives! It's great, Jan – Congratulations!"

Pam Sweetser, Executive Director
Cultural Heritage Camps, Denver, CO

"My boys, ages 10 and 7, and I read the series aloud as a family and we loved it! Your style of writing, explaining technical or social work terms to kids was perfect for even my youngest son. Almost each time we read one of those parts he would say, 'I was just about to ask what that meant, and then it was explained to me.' You tell this story with tremendous tenderness, and bring to life Joshua's gentle spirit and his resilience. This is a lovely way to educate children about the foster care system, and the diversity of families."

Susan Fule, Former Social Worker
and Mother, Albuquerque, NM

"What an enjoyable read! I think this book should appeal to a wide audience."

Cheri Scott,
Adoptive Mother of Justin, AK

"WOW! These books deeply touched so many emotions and I am in awe of all that you have done, and of your wonderful family. Congratulations on capturing the story of Josh in such a remarkable way. Your work will surely help so many others who live similar lives."

Diane Reid, Founder, Whispering
Hope Ranch, Payson, AZ

Foreword

Our children with FASD can be so endearing, as we find in Jan's first two books in her 9 LIVES series. Perhaps it is enjoying their endearing qualities during those early years that helps us form a secure bond with them, a bond that sustains us through the troubled times to come – adolescence and young adulthood.

For most of us who parent children with FASD, the teen years means a loss – a loss of those high spirited years of cuteness, intelligence and creativity. Our dreams for our children, once fresh and full of hope, begin to cave into the depressed and agitated states that can characterize this period. This loss greets us each morning and follows us to bed each night. However, humans are very adaptable, and we learn along with Jan, as she adapts to this roller coaster of adolescence and FASD.

Through a mother's loving eyes, we learn that, in a day, some of the things Josh will do are wonderful, full of generosity and respect, and some of the things he will do – in the very same day – will be dangerous and oblivious to the sensitivities of others. We learn, from Jan's telling, that artful parenting and caring community support can provide a stable foundation for what's to come next.

It's important to read Jan's first two books, because we see in them how this mother's responses to her son have preserved their relationship and his sense of nobility. Josh is happy and honest and, on his good days, responsible, and he is always caring. His mother is learning the importance of disciplining in order to educate, being careful not to condemn or shame. She is learning to pause and listen to understand, and to grab the winning moments and quiet her fears.

9 LIVES: Full Circle is the enchanting story about family and community walking, often running, with Josh through his teen years and into early adulthood. It is a well crafted story in which otherwise ordinary life events are extraordinarily lived by someone with FASD.

Through Jan's storytelling, we make the critical paradigm shift from believing that Josh's actions are willful misbehaving, to knowing that they are behavioral manifestations of organic brain damage. We learn that patience and perseverance can win out and that troubled life stories can have fulfilling, happy moments.

Jan ends her story with Josh going off to a new adventure. But we know, after living through years with Jamie and Joshua that theirs is a never-ending pattern of trials and victories. And so we ask, how will Jamie celebrate this latest victory with her son, and how will she support him through his next trial?

We know she will be there, forever, as Joshua, full of joy and hope, albeit naïve to the perils that accompany him, continues his worthy pursuit of himself. I feel Jan has shown us the important lessons many parents come to from different paths, that staying in relationship is the essential ingredient for both.

Sally Caldwell, LPC, Mother,
author, therapist, Fairbanks, AK
Foreword in Fantastic Antone Grows Up
Chapter author in Fantastic Antone Succeeds!

Contents

9 LIVES: Full Circle

For Joshua and my Honey B.
And for all families created through adoption.

A Note From the Author

I wrote the original three books in the 9 LIVES Trilogy to raise awareness of Fetal Alcohol Spectrum Disorders, especially the 'Invisible Disorder' known as Alcohol Related Neurological Disorder (ARND) formerly known as Fetal Alcohol Effect (FAE). I targeted young people because I felt it important to educate them about the dangers of mixing alcohol with being sexually active or pregnant. The series was written for teens and adults with FASD, those living in foster, adoptive, and interracial homes, or with same sex parents, and those with low reading abilities.

In book one; I wanted you to fall in love with young Joshua. In the second book, I wanted you to see that just like every other kid on the planet Joshua wanted to be "normal" and fit in with his peers. I chose the third book to share some of the daily challenges of parenting a child on the spectrum.

Over the years I have heard that many parents and caregivers have read and utilized the series so I thought it might be easier if all three books were contained within the same binding. Hence this revised book, They Call Me Cat. I'm hoping the eBook format will assist with ease of distribution as well.

I appreciate you taking the time to read our fictionalized story and hope that you have benefited from reading about our journey. If you are a parent of a child on the spectrum, I want you to realize that you are not alone. Take heart; there are many kindred spirits walking a similar path.

If you enjoyed this book, I encourage you to share it with others and to please consider writing a review on Amazon.com.

Jan Crossen

Feel free to drop me an email at: jancrossen20@yahoo.com and please write They Call Me Cat in the subject line. I'd love to hear from you! Thanks for taking the time to read and share your thoughts. It takes a village.

Jan Crossen

9
LIVES
I Will Survive

CHAPTER

1

A Time of Innocence

I've been told that I'm like a cat. People say that cats are lucky because they have nine lives. Somehow, they can survive eight brushes with death. If it's true that I'm like a cat, then I'm eighteen years old and already had several brushes with death. My very existence is a miracle. This book is about my early years. My life has been pretty amazing so far and I want to share some of my experiences with you.

A lot of wonderful things happened to me too. Like when I was eight years old and first met my mom. That may sound kind of weird to you, but you see, I'm adopted. My name is Joshua and I'm black. My mom, Jamie Carson, is white. We're an inter-racial family. Mom says that's part of our strength.

Starting at the beginning means that you need to hear about what happened even before I was born. My birth parents are DeShona and Randall Radford Sr. They're both black and were 28 years old when I was born.

My folks had been married two years when I came along. I'm the middle child. My older brother is Randall Jr, or RJ, and my baby sister is Amanda. We sometimes called her Mandy.

My family didn't have a lot of money. Dad was a cook and Mom was an aide who took care of old people. Even though they had jobs, with three kids, it was always a struggle to pay the rent and other bills.

My parents had serious relationship problems and they fought a lot. They were not a good match for each other. My parents tried to avoid their pain and instead of making things better, everything got worse.

My mother was insecure, so she turned to other men to make her feel pretty and wanted. As a result, RJ and Mandy are really my half-brother and half-sister. They each have different fathers than I do. My dad is Randall Sr.

DeShona also partied in her attempts to try to feel better. She smoked crack and drank alcohol, and it made her really sick. It also made her mean and violent.

My father was living a lie. He was married to my mom, but knew he wasn't the father of two of her children. And, my dad was attracted to other men. He was gay but afraid that if he came out and told people he was gay, that his family would reject him. And he was right about that, a few years later, when he came out to his family, they did turn away from him. Man, what's with that?

Dad was messed up on drugs and Mom on drugs and alcohol. They didn't mean to, but they neglected us kids. Things were awful! Lies, drugs, and alcohol broke my birth family apart. Alcohol damaged RJ, Amanda, and me even before we were born. Mom drank booze while she was pregnant with me. I'm eighteen now and didn't know about her drinking until a few months ago. It sure explains a lot of things. I'll tell you about all of that later.

You see, whatever the mother eats or drinks, her baby does too. So if a woman drinks alcohol, smokes cigarettes, or does drugs, so does her fetus. A fetus is another name for a baby before it's born.

Did you know that the fetus gets its food from the mother's blood supply? Can you imagine feeding beer to a baby? Me neither. But that's what happened.

DeShona didn't drink just one beer; she drank two or three six-packs, or a bottle of wine, or a bottle of booze, by herself, and all in one night. And she wasn't picky about what she drank. She was a sneaky drinker and would hide her liquor. She'd swallow whatever alcohol she could get.

Alcohol causes birth defects and permanent brain damage to the innocent unborn child. And a woman doesn't need to be an alcoholic to hurt her fetus. It only takes a small amount of liquor to harm a baby for life.

No amount of alcohol, not one beer, one glass of wine, or one shot of whiskey, is safe to drink when a woman is pregnant. Because of DeShona's drinking, RJ, Amanda, and I will never reach our full potential. It isn't fair. We were screwed out of normal lives, even before we took our first breaths of air.

CHAPTER

2

A Time of Consequences

My dad had just returned home from work and was in the kitchen fixing himself a quick snack, when he heard my mom's frantic cries for help.

"Randall, help me!" DeShona screamed as she dropped to the bathroom floor. "I'm bleeding, Randall...Randall, where are you? I need you!"

DeShona was pregnant with me. I was a tiny, twenty-six week old fetus, developing in her womb. My mom's placenta was tearing away from the uterine wall. The placenta is the lining of the uterus or womb that cushions and feeds the fetus before it is born. The blood, flowing through her placenta, brought food and oxygen to me. It kept me alive. Right now, I was in grave danger of dying.

"Randall," she yelled. "The blood is just gushing out of me. I'm afraid we'll lose the baby, help me, please!" she shouted as loudly as she could.

"Hold on, Honey," Dad said. "I've called 911 and an ambulance is on the way. Nothing bad is going to happen to you or our baby," my dad tried to reassure her.

"What about RJ?" DeShona asked about my older brother.

"He's still napping," Dad said. "I'll get him up when the EMTs arrive. Everything's going to be all right. Have faith, Woman." Randall said. He knelt down beside her and reached for her slender hand. Together they waited anxiously for help to arrive.

Most women carry their babies for between 37-40 weeks. DeShona was only 18 weeks into her pregnancy when she started bleeding heavily. This meant that she had been in danger of losing me for two months now. Her doctor was very concerned and ordered her to stay in bed. DeShona left her bed to go to the bathroom. That's when she discovered how badly she was bleeding. She was losing a lot of blood very quickly.

"The ambulance is here, Honey," Dad said. "You and the baby are in good hands now," my dad assured her. "I'll wake up RJ and we'll meet you at the hospital."

A taxi cab took Dad and my brother to the hospital. Dad ran down the halls, carrying RJ in his arms. He stopped at the emergency room desk long enough to find out where they had taken my mom. When my birth mom arrived at the hospital she was immediately examined by a doctor.

"We need to do an emergency C-Section, DeShona," the doctor said, "if we hope to have any chance of saving this baby's life."

Within minutes DeShona was in surgery having a Caesarean or C-Section. That means they cut open her belly and took me from her uterus. Her physician was desperately trying to save my life.

"It's a boy," the doctor said as he gently lifted me from the womb. "But he's an extreme preemie and awfully tiny." An extreme preemie is a baby that is born at or before 28 weeks of pregnancy. I was born at just 26 weeks.

The doctor wanted me to breathe, so he slapped me on my bare butt. He needed me to cry because that would cause oxygen to be sucked into my lungs. At first I was silent, so he spanked again.

"Come on baby boy;" he said. "Let's hear what you're made of."

"Waaaaaaaaaaaaaaa, Waaaaaaaaaaaaaaaa!" This time I protested the smack on my tender tush. Everyone smiled with relief. They knew my crying was a good sign because it meant that I was breathing and alive. The nurse reached for me and put me on the scale.

"2 pounds, 2 ounces," she said, as she took a tape measure and began to measure my body. "He's just under the length of a ruler from head to toe. Wow, I think a baseball is bigger than this little fellow's head. And check out these skinny little arms and legs. They're not even as thick as my index finger. Look here, his whole hand is no bigger than my thumb. This newborn wasn't ready to join the world just yet."

Suddenly, the room became strangely quiet.

"He's stopped crying, and he's turning blue," the doctor said. "Get him on oxygen and take him to the NICU. You close up the mother and I'll focus on the little guy," the doctor said.

He turned the surgery over to his assistant and went with me to the NICU. The NICU is where very sick newborns are treated and monitored. NICU stands for Neonatal Intensive Care Unit. Each infant in the NICU gets extra special care and attention.

"Because he is extremely premature, he is at the very lower limits of viability," the doctor said. "If he does survive, he may have multiple medical issues affecting his brain and learning, vision, hearing, lungs, kidneys, bowels, every organ and system. He could have problems anywhere in his body and these issues can last a lifetime. He's still having trouble getting enough air. Let's continue to help him breathe."

The doctor handed me to the nurse who positioned my body for a life-saving procedure. The doctor inserted a tube in my little mouth and down my narrow throat. Someone hooked me up to a machine called a respirator. It made the oxygen flow in and out of my lungs. It helped keep me alive.

In addition to my lungs, my heart was having problems. It was beating way too fast. Instead of having a steady pace of 'lub-dub; lub-dub; lub-dub,' the beats were fast and irregular. The rhythm sounded like a drummer who was showing off during his spotlight solo on stage. Eventually, I was stable and resting in a small bed in the NICU.

My dad was scared so he called his mother, Grandma Jodie. She came to the hospital. She was sitting with Dad and RJ when the doctor went to talk with them.

"Mr. Radford, you and your family need to prepare yourselves for the worst," the doctor said. "Your son came very early and isn't fully developed. There's a chance that he won't make it through the night. Does your son have a name?"

"Yes," Dad said. "His name is Joshua." Dad wiped a tear from his eye. "Joshua Nelson Radford is his name. May I please see my son now?"

"Not just yet," the doctor said. "We'll let you know when it's OK to visit Joshua. The nurses have put him an incubator. His body temperature was too low, so they are warming him with a special heater."

"Thank you, Doctor," Dad said. "Thanks everyone," Dad said to the medical staff that was caring for Mom and me.

"You're welcome, Mr. Radford," the doctor said. "Um, there's another thing. Joshua can't suck yet. He needs his mother's breast milk, but he can't take it. He will need to go back into surgery so that we can put a feeding tube in his body," the doctor said. "He needs calories and to gain weight."

"OK, then," Dad said. "Please do it. Take care of my boy!"

They whisked me back into the surgery and sewed a feeding tube to the inside of my stomach. The tube was used to nourish me for several weeks. A couple of hours later a nurse found my father and grandmother in the waiting room. My brother, RJ, was asleep on Grandma Jodie's lap.

"You may visit your son now, Mr. Radford," a nurse told my father. "You'll need to scrub up before entering the NICU. The sink is over there. Scrub your hands and arms really well. Dry them, and then put on a sterile gown, mask, and cap. Cover your shoes with these slippers."

My father did as he was told, then walked into the neonatal nursery where I lay in a small clear box.

"Why is he so restless?" Dad asked. "May I hold him?"

The nurses answered his questions. They didn't want me out of my incubator yet.

"You can't hold him yet," the nurse said. "But it would be fine if you were to gently stroke him with your fingers, like this." The nurse showed my dad what to do. Dad hummed a song as he softly brushed my head, arms, back, and legs.

"Daddy loves you, Joshua," he whispered. "You're going to be fine, Son. You listen to your papa now, you hear me?" Dad put his index finger against the palm of my right hand and I curled my fingers around it. "That's right, Joshua. Take all of the energy you need, Son, to get strong."

Grandma Jodie had been taking care of RJ but she wanted to see me too. Dad went out to stay with RJ and Grandma Jodie scrubbed and put on a sterile gown too. She sang soft lullabies to me. My family prayed for me to get better.

For several hours my mom was still in the recovery room. It wasn't until later in the day that she was able to visit me.

That's when she learned that I might die. She absolutely refused to accept that possibility.

"Hello, beautiful baby boy," DeShona cooed as she laid eyes on me for the first time. "I do believe that you're going to be handsome and look just like your Papa. You've got to be strong, now. I know you can do this. I love you, Baby Joshua."

For weeks my dad, mom, or grandmother would visit me in the hospital. Finally, I was allowed out of my incubator for short periods of time, and they were able to hold and rock me. The doctor wanted my mother to try to nurse me. But so far I hadn't been able to suckle.

"Let's see if Joshua is able to nurse yet," he said. "DeShona, please sit down over here and try nursing him again. Your milk has been really good for him and nursing would be great bonding experience as well."

"Nope," she said. "He still can't suck."

They used a pump to get my mother's milk so they could bottle feed me. I continued to develop and get stronger. I stayed in the hospital for two months before the doctor would let me go home.

"You may take Joshua home when you can operate his breathing monitor," the doctor told my parents. "If he has a crisis and stops breathing, the alarm will sound, and you need to know what to do to save his life."

My folks listened carefully as the nurse explained the monitor and what to do if it went off and I stopped breathing. They learned what to do in an emergency. Finally, I went home with my parents. I was still very small and hooked up to monitors. Luckily, the alarm never sounded and I continued to breathe on my own. My entry into this world was the first of my cat like nine lives. One serious brush with death down, eight to go.

CHAPTER

3

Two
Photographs

There wasn't much meat on my bones when I finally left the hospital. Gaining weight wasn't easy for me, and I was a small fry for a long time. As time passed I learned to roll over, sit-up, and crawl, like other infants.

RJ is only ten months older than I am, and we played together. We had a lot more fun once I learned to walk, run, and talk. RJ thought it was especially fun to bully and beat up on me.

"RJ, get off of me," I said. "Let me up or I'll tell Dad."

"You'd better not, little brother," he said. "Now, give me your cookie, I'm hungry!"

I gave him my cookie, but I wasn't happy. He picked on me a lot until our baby sister came along. About two years after I was born Amanda May joined our family. She was a cute little thing, and always feisty. I liked having a big brother and baby sister. I loved having a family.

My folks were still having problems getting along and they were distracted and not taking good care of us. One summer evening, my folks really got into it with each other. Dad came home from work to find Mom drunk and sitting on the sofa. It should have been time for our baths, but we hadn't even eaten supper yet. Mom and Dad started screaming and yelling at each other. It sounded like two angry cats in an alley.

Within minutes, their arms were locked around each others heads. Losing their balance, they fell with a thud to the living room floor. The whole room shook from the force. My mother was just as big and strong as my father. They gasped for breath as they wrestled one another.

Breathing hard and cussing at one another, they squirmed and rolled until somebody's foot kicked a table lamp. It flew into the air and shattered against the television. Large sharp chunks of glass lay on the blue shag rug. My folks moved into the kitchen, slamming the high chair which tipped over. Luckily, Mandy was in her playpen by now and no longer sitting her highchair. Pictures fell off the walls; their frames lay broken on the gray linoleum floor.

One of our neighbors must have heard the fight and called the police. Within a few minutes we heard the wail of a siren and a patrol car arrived at our apartment. The cops had been to our place two other times before when my folks' fighting had gone out of control.

The Tucson police officers realized that it was not safe for us to live with our parents. That night we kids were removed from our home. RJ was four years old, I was three, and Amanda was just a baby.

For a couple of weeks we lived in a shelter called Casa De Los Ninos. There were a lot of other kids there. It was a safe house where grown-ups didn't yell or fight. Living there was the beginning of our time in foster care.

About a year later, a judge decided DeShona could no longer be our mother. A caseworker from the state of Arizona asked my father to give up his legal rights to be our dad. She tried to convince him that it would be better for us kids if we were raised by someone who was equipped to care for three small children.

My parents were separated and Dad was trying to care for us as all by himself. He was also a closeted gay man who had a drug problem. My dad felt very alone, frightened, and helpless. He worried about providing the proper care for his kids. Dad was very sad the day that he agreed to turn us over to the state of Arizona. He was no longer my legal Dad.

I don't remember much from those early days with my birth family. I do have a couple of photographs that were taken back then. One picture is of my mother and us kids at the zoo.

We were standing in front of the giraffe area. My birth mom was a tall, slender, and stylish black woman. She was very pretty with a friendly smile and sparkling eyes. You could tell that she liked posing for the camera. I think maybe I can even remember having that photo taken. Or maybe I've just looked at that photograph so many times that it feels as though I remember that day.

"You boys go stand by your momma," my father said. "Now, everybody look this way and smile."

Mom was holding Amanda in her arms. Mandy was a pretty little girl. That day she wore a fancy red dress with a matching coat and shoes. She looked so sweet and innocent, and had a big smile on her face.

RJ was standing next to Mom and he was trying to look tough in the snap shot. RJ's a teenager now, and he looks just the same as he did in that picture. RJ is a tank; he's solid and built like a Mack truck. If I were ever in a fist fight, I'd want to have him on my side!

I was still a skinny little kid. In the picture, I was standing on a fence rail, looking towards Papa who held the camera. He must have been our family photographer.

I have a picture of my dad too. He's tall and thin like I am. We have the same big old teeth-showing grin. Our ears are similar too. I think Dad's handsome and that we look alike. Maybe when I'm a little older, I'll look just like he does in that picture. I'm glad I have these two photos because they help me understand my history. Those pictures connect me to my beginnings.

I spent just three short years living with my birth family, and I don't have many memories of that time. It feels like it was a lifetime ago and that it all happened to someone else.

CHAPTER

Please Hurry!

RJ, Amanda, and I needed someplace safe to live. We needed new parents, and to start our lives over. We were sent to California to live with some relatives that we had never met before.

"Hi Randall Jr., Joshua, and Amanda," said the small black woman as she knelt down to see us face-to-face. "I'm your Aunt Suzette and this is your Uncle Joey. Your uncle here is your mom's big brother."

Shyly we looked into the eyes of these strangers. Aunt Suzette gave us a slight smile. She had a small space between her two front teeth, and seeing that made me smile back at her.

"They call me RJ," my brother said. "And we call her Mandy May." He tossed his head towards our sister.

"We don't have any children of our own," my aunt said. "So you're coming to live with us. That way your parents will get to see you and you'll still be part of our family. Come over here now and give your Aunt Suzette a big hug."

RJ and I looked at each other. We didn't know what to think of all of this. Mandy walked right up to our aunt and jumped into her open arms.

"Do these kids have any bags?" Uncle Joey asked the social worker who had taken us to California.

"Just this one," the case worker said indicating the black garbage bag in his left hand. He handed it to my uncle, had them sign a release form, and said a quick goodbye.

Aunt Suzette was really nice to us. She took good care of us and said that she wanted to adopt us. But Uncle Joey drank too much and he wasn't nice when he drank.

On the night before Halloween, Uncle Joey had been drinking beer and smoking cigarettes all day long. The more he drank, the meaner he got. Our aunt had spent the day helping us put together our costumes for trick-or-treating. We were excited about dressing up and collecting our loot of goodies the next evening. We were already tucked in bed for the night when the trouble started.

Uncle Joey started picking a fight with Aunt Suzette. They were in the kitchen when he began yelling. His words grew louder and he started to cuss. Uncle Joey picked up a dinner plate and threw it, like a Frisbee, at our aunt. The edge of the plate smacked into her back and Uncle Joey laughed. He began hurling the rest of our dirty dinner dishes in her direction.

"Grunt, crash...grunt, crash!" We heard our uncle's grunting followed by the shattering of dishes. He threw glasses, plates and bowls, some still filled with food, as hard as he could across the kitchen. They fell in tiny pieces on the floor. RJ climbed down from his bunk and I sprang to my feet.

"We've got to stop him!" RJ growled.

We bolted down the hall to help our aunt. Bright red meat sauce and spaghetti noodles stained the wall behind the kitchen table. Broken glass, forks and spoons decorated the floor. Uncle Joey's face was puffed up. His eyes were full of hate, and his nostrils flared. The veins in his neck and temples were bulging. Spit sprayed out of his mouth when he screamed.

"Stop, Uncle Joey, stop!" RJ begged.

"Please don't hurt Aunt Suzette," I pleaded, "Please!" But he wouldn't listen.

"You kids better get back in your room now, if you know what's good for you!" he threatened.

Uncle Joey loosened his belt and came after us. RJ and I flew down the hall and ran into our room. We slammed and locked the door to our bedroom. Diving under the bed, our hearts pounded against the bare wooden floor.

"You leave those kids alone, Joe!" Aunt Suzette yelled.

Once again Uncle Joey focused his attention on his wife. Amanda was awake by now, and hiding under some blankets in our closet. We all tried not to breathe too loudly for fear that he might hear. We couldn't risk him breaking down our door and venting his anger on the three of us.

I heard him yelling again at my aunt. Thinking it was safe, I crawled out from my hiding spot and quietly tip-toed into the room next door. It was Uncle Joey and Aunt Suzette's bedroom. Carefully, I picked up the telephone, and then eased my way back to my safe spot, under our bunk beds.

Crack...hummmmmmmmmmmmmmm. I had a dial tone. I studied the numbers and slowly dialed 9-1-1, Beep, Beep, Beep.

"911 what is your emergency?" The lady operator asked.

Hugging the phone to my ear, I whispered, "Uncle Joey's crazy mad! He's yelling and throwing things at Aunt Suzette."

"What is your name, son?" the operator asked.

"Joshua, ma'am," I said. "Joshua Radford."

"How old are you Joshua?" she asked me.

"I'm seven years old, ma'am," I said.

"Is there anyone else in the house besides you and your aunt and uncle?"

"Yes," I said, "RJ and Mandy are here too."

"And who are RJ and Mandy?"

"RJ is my brother and Mandy is my little sister," I said. "We're hiding in our bedroom, with the door locked."

"Good, Joshua. You stay right where you are," the lady said. "Do you know your address, Honey?"

I nodded my head and my voice quivered as tears welled up in my eyes. I told her the address and tightened my grip on the phone

"Just stay on the line with me, Joshua," the operator said. "I'm sending the police to help you right now."

"Please hurry," I said. "We're really scared."

I tried not to cry and prayed that help would come soon. RJ, Amanda, and I strained to hear the wail of the approaching sirens.

Aunt Suzette was sobbing and Uncle Joey was still screaming when the police car crunched to a halt in the gravel in front of the house. I watched the pattern of the blue and red lights as they danced around the walls of our room. Those lights were a very welcome sight. RJ unlocked and opened the door just a crack so that we could see what was happening.

Boom, Boom, Boom. "Police, open up!" commanded the men in blue. Uncle Joey held the stub of a filtered cigarette in his mouth. He clutched a half-empty bottle of beer in his hand as he staggered to the door and turned the brass knob.

"Well, hello, officers," my uncle greeted the cops with a sly smirk on his face. He took a long swig from his brown bottle. Finding it was now empty, he tossed it outside. The glass shattered as it smashed against a gray concrete wall.

The police entered the house. Using calm voices, with respectful words, they began talking with my uncle. He began to calm down.

"I need you to turn around, sir, and put your hands behind your back," a young cop said to my uncle.

Uncle Joey did as he was told. The officer locked the cuffs around his wrists. They walked him carefully out the door and put him in the back of their car. We watched as they drove him away in their black and white cruiser. Not until then, did I believe that we were truly safe.

"RJ, Josh, Mandy, are you kids all right?" Aunt Suzette asked us.

We responded by running to her and crying as she rocked us in her arms. We dried our tears and snotty noses on the sleeves of her pink Mickey Mouse sweatshirt. It was clear to everyone that living with my uncle wasn't safe. This wasn't the first time he had been mean to Aunt Suzette or us. And this wasn't our only telephone call for help. But tonight would be the last.

The police told the Department of Children and Families, DCF, about us. The next day a nice lady, driving an old red Volkswagen bug, came to talk with Aunt Suzette. Our aunt told the social worker about our uncle's drinking and his nasty temper. Aunt Suzette admitted that he beat us with his belt. He even whipped the leather across her bare back at least two times. Our aunt said that when he was really angry, she was powerless to stop him.

One at a time, the DCF lady asked RJ, Amanda, and me what our uncle had done to us. He hurt me, and I didn't want to talk about it. I started crying when it was my turn to meet with the lady.

"Joshua, I know that your uncle hurt you with his belt. Did he hurt you in any other way?" she asked.

"I don't want to talk about it." I said defiantly and turned my back to the stranger.

"Honey, you didn't do anything wrong," she said. "We need to stop your uncle from hurting you or anybody else ever again. Josh, you can trust me. I need to know what your uncle did to you."

I was quiet for a long time. Finally I said, "He touched me."

"Did your uncle touch your private parts?" she asked.

Keeping my face away from hers I nodded. With the back of my hand, I wiped the tears off my cheeks.

"Oh, sweetheart," she said, "I'm so sorry. What your uncle did to you was wrong. It wasn't your fault," she explained. "He'll never hurt you again, I promise."

The next day the DCF lady took me to see a lady doctor. She talked with me and we sat on the floor and played with some puppets. Then the doctor told the case worker that I was telling the truth about my uncle.

A few months ago I learned that my aunt and uncle had split up. It's better this way. I hope Uncle Joey has stopped drinking and smoking. I pray Aunt Suzette isn't afraid of him any more.

To this day, I hate the smell of beer and cigarettes because they remind me of Uncle Joey. Living through hell with Uncle Joey was another close call for my safety and well being. That's a lot of scary stuff for a seven years old kid.

CHAPTER

5

The Owens Family

That was the last time that RJ, Amanda, and I lived together. The social worker couldn't find a home that would take all three of us, so we had to split up.

"Give your brother and sister a hug," the case worker said. "You're all going to be living with different families now, so say good-bye and tell them you love them."

I did as I was told, then burst into tears. "No, no, don't leave me," I screamed as RJ and Amanda were escorted into two different cars. "I want RJ and Mandy," I sobbed, my heart broken. My small body shook with grief at our separation from one another.

"It's going to be all right, Joshua," the adoption worker tried to comfort me. "Amanda already has two new wonderful parents who will love and adore her. She'll be just fine, and so will you and Randall."

An older married couple wanted to adopt Amanda. My birth parents' legal rights had been severed, so Amanda was available. The family was black and had two grown sons. They wanted a little girl, so Amanda moved immediately into their home. A lot of people want to adopt babies and little kids.

Amanda is loved, safe, and happy with her new family. I'm glad about that now.

"RJ is going to live in a foster home with an African American family," the agent said. "He'll be living near Amanda and her new home."

RJ's foster parents were a married couple with one biological child and three adopted kids. His foster home was just six houses away from where Mandy's new family lived. They got to see a lot of each other back then.

"What about me?" I asked, sniffling through my tears.

"I heard that you like animals," the case worker said. "Is that right, Joshua?"

"Yes ma'am," I said as I stopped crying. "I especially like dogs and cats."

"Well, you're going to live with a very nice lady who loves children and animals. I'm sure that you'll like living with her, Josh."

The case worker drove me across town to meet LaTisha Owens and her family. Her house was sort of out in the country, and she had two acres of land. We drove into the driveway and the social worker cut the engine. Taking my hand she gave it a squeeze. She escorted me to the front door, which opened before we could knock or ring the bell.

"Well, you must be Joshua," an attractive black woman greeted me with a smile. "I'm LaTisha, Honey, please come in and make yourself at home," she said. LaTisha stepped aside and gestured for us to enter.

LaTisha Owens was a single black woman who already had seven kids living in her home. She had three biological babies from her marriage. Those kids were already grown and no longer living with her. After LaTisha and her husband divorced, she took in foster children. It wasn't unusual for her to adopt some of them.

The walls of her family room were covered with pictures of her big family. Some of those kids were grownups by then, with children of their own. LaTisha knelt down beside me so that we were eye level with one another.

"My name is LaTisha Owens but my kids all call me 'Mom.' You can call me whatever feels right for you, OK?"

I nodded in understanding.

"Let me introduce you to the family and we'll get you settled in," she said.

LaTisha had adopted her oldest children when they were three, five, and six years old. Now they were teenagers. She pointed to each one and told me their names.

"Kids, this is Joshua," she introduced me to the crowd of friendly faces. "And this is Jabar, Lulu, and Adrianna."

"Hi, Joshua," Jabar said.

"Nice to meet you," said Lulu.

"Welcome to the family, Joshua," said Adrianna.

"This is Benjamin, my eight year old foster child," LaTisha said. She rested her hands on his shoulders. "The two of you will be sharing a room."

"Hi," we spoke to one another.

"And this is Mitchell, who is five," LaTisha said, "and Roberto, who just turned four and little Maria, who is only two years old." She continued. "I've adopted them too."

Mitchell and Roberto waved at me. Maria ran to her mother and buried her face in LaTisha's neck. I managed a weak "Hi," and quick wave of my hand. The case worker excused herself and left.

"Joshua, I hear that you like animals, is that right?" LaTisha asked.

"Yes, ma'am," I answered quietly.

"We have quite a few around here," LaTisha said. "Would you like to see some of our animals now?"

"Sure, that would be great," I said, beginning to relax.

"Jabar, would you please get Britches and bring him to us?" LaTisha asked. "Joshua, would you mind sitting on the edge of this couch? When Britches arrives he'll want to meet you. He gets to know you by smelling you."

Jabar returned to the room carrying a fat, little, tan dog with a smashed in nose.

"This is Britches," Jabar announced. "He's a pug and very friendly. Don't worry, he won't bite you. First let him smell the back of your hand and then you can pet him."

I extended my arm and his whiskers ticked my flesh. Reaching for his little velvet ears I started talking softly to him.

"I like the way you're petting Britches, Joshua," LaTisha said. "You have a gentle way with animals."

I grinned at her. Meeting Britches was fun!

"Would you like to meet our Doberman?" LaTisha asked. "His name is Dakota. Some people are afraid of him because of his size, but I promise you, he won't hurt you either," LaTisha assured me.

"Well, OK," I said, cautiously. "If you promise that he isn't mean."

Jabar handed Britches to me and left the room once again. The pug curled up next to me and quickly fell asleep. Because he had a squished in nose, he began to snore. I thought that was hilarious. The rest of the family laughed along with me.

This time Jabar returned with a very large, black and tan Doberman walking calmly by his side. Dakota didn't look like the Dobermans that I had seen before. His ears hung down. They hadn't been cropped to make them stand up and point towards the sky. His ears were left natural and that made him look friendly. I liked Dakota right away.

"Dakota, sit," Jabar commanded, and the dog obeyed. I extended my hand and he checked it out with his long nose.

"Is it OK to pet him now?" I asked.

"Yes," Jabar said. I stroked his head and scratched behind his ears. Dakota stretched to lay his head in my lap. I took it as a good sign.

"He likes me," I said with pleasure.

"Indeed he does," LaTisha agreed.

"Would you like to meet my kitten?" Jabar asked. I nodded and followed him to his room where I found a gray, male, tabby kitten named Tyler.

"You can play with him if you like," Jabar said. "He loves to chase this green feather that I got from our bird." He handed me the feather which had been tied to the end of a long blue string.

"Here kitty, chase the feather," I said. I teased and dragged the feather along the ground. It wiggled and Tyler pounced on it and made me laugh. We played like that for a few minutes.

"He's great, thanks for letting me play with him," I told Jabar.

"You're welcome, Joshua," Jabar said. "Do you want to see the rest of our pets?"

I nodded and followed Jabar back to the family room where everyone had been waiting for us.

"How do you feel about snakes, Joshua?" LaTisha asked. "Do you like them?"

"Snakes?" I asked, not sure that I had heard her correctly.

"Yep, that's right," Lulu confirmed. "I have a corn snake."

Lulu walked towards a large cage that was sitting on a table at the other end of the room. The teenage girl opened the door and confidently lifted out the yellow and white reptile.

"This is Slim," Lulu said, draping him around her shoulders like a feather boa.

"Wow," I said laughing nervously as Lulu carried him back to where I was sitting. "He's big," I said as Lulu held him by his tail with his head almost touching the ground.

"He's as long as I am tall!" I said.

Slim was yellow on top and white on the bottom. His quick tongue flicked in and out of his mouth. His black eyes stared at me.

"Do you want to hold him, Joshua?" Lulu asked. "It's OK, he isn't poisonous or anything."

I thought this was some kind of a test. I felt as though I had to hold the snake in order to prove myself to these kids. I didn't really want to hold the snake, but I mustered up my courage.

"OK," I said.

"Don't squeeze him, just relax," Lulu said as she placed the serpent in my open palms. The rest of the kids exchanged looks and nodded their approval. I felt Slim's long body move. It was like a wave of dominoes collapsing in sequence in my hands. It was amazing! I smiled, marveling at this amazing creature.

"Wow!" I said, "This is tight!"

"It's time for his dinner," Lulu said. "Do you want to watch me feed him?"

I nodded and Lulu took Slim from me and returned him to his cage. The rest of us followed. Opening a much smaller cage, Lulu lifted a live mouse by its tail. She dropped the rodent into Slim's private quarters. Lulu had bought the mouse at a pet store the day before. Slim needs to eat one live mouse every week. The snake attacked the mouse with his mouth wide open. He swallowed it whole. His muscles contracted as he pushed his dinner slowly down his body.

"Eeeeewwwww, gross!" I said. "Look, you can still see the shape of the mouse inside of him."

"Speaking of dinner," LaTisha said, "That reminds me. It's time for us to eat too."

We all returned to the family room and everyone pitched in to make the evening meal.

CHAPTER

6

Brothers and Sisters

With such a big family and so many animals, we each had chores to do. One of mine was to feed the pig.

"Come on, Joshua, grab those food scraps and we'll go feed the pig," LaTisha told me after dinner that first night. She took me out to the barn to meet Stinkerboy. She showed me how to feed him and get fresh water for his trough. Stinkerboy was a huge, black pig. I swear he was the size of our bathtub! He didn't smell nice either, so I guess that's how he got his name. He had a long snout that wiggled a lot.

"Have you ever petted a pig, Joshua?" LaTisha asked. "The hair on his body is long and stiff. Would you like to feel?"

I reached over the rail and felt his wiry hair.

"That's weird," I said.

A horse nickered at the other end of the barn. She was greeting her owner and asking for her supper.

"Do you like horses?" LaTisha asked.

"I guess so, but I've never ridden one," I said.

"Come and meet Doll-girl. She's a twenty year old quarter horse."

"Oh," I said, "Does that mean that she's young or old?"

"Well, that's a good question," LaTisha said. "I guess by horse standards she's on the old side. But she still has plenty of get-up-and-go when she needs it."

Doll-girl came over to where we stood. She lifted her head over the rail and LaTisha began stroking her.

"May I pet her?" I asked.

"I think she'd like that," LaTisha said as she guided my hand gently down the mare's nose.

"I can feel her breath," I almost whispered, "Its warm and her nose feels so soft. Look at those long hairs on her nose."

"Her nose is called a muzzle, and you're right, it's very soft like velvet. I appreciate the way you behave around animals, Joshua. It's very calm and gentle."

"Thank you, ma'am," I said as I beamed with pride.

Doll-girl is a bay mare. That means that her body is brown and her mane and tail are black."

"She's pretty," I said. "And I like the way she smells."

"I like that horsey smell, too," LaTisha agreed. "Let's get her some food and fresh water before it gets too dark, OK?"

We took care of our chores and returned to the house. The dishes and kitchen had been cleaned by the kids after dinner. Now they were all settled down together to watch the movie 'Stewart Little' on DVD.

"Joshua, why don't you go watch the movie with the other kids?" LaTisha said. "I'll show you our bird later. You'll have the job of changing the newspaper in the bottom of his cage."

I settled on the floor to watch the movie which was about a little mouse that got adopted. After the movie I went to LaTisha who was working on some paperwork.

"Excuse me, ma'am," I said. "May I please meet your bird now?"

"Certainly," she said smiling. "This is Jade and he's a Quaker Parrot. He's smart and he talks."

Just then he greeted me, "Good-morning, good-morning, squawk, beautiful bird, beautiful bird."

I chuckled, "Its night time, silly bird! But he's right about being beautiful. What gorgeous feathers! I can see why Jabar used one of these feathers to make a toy for Tyler the cat."

I admired Jade's vibrant blue and green markings. He was strikingly handsome but very messy. He'd throw his birdseed outside of the cage and it would get all over the kitchen floor. It became my job to sweep it up.

"AHHHHHHHCCCChhhheeeewwwww!" I sneezed.

"God bless you!" LaTisha said smiling.

"Excuse me, ma'am," I said. "But the way Jade smells makes my nose tickle."

"I understand what you mean," LaTisha said. "A lot of people sneeze when they are around birds. Shall we put him to bed for the night?" LaTisha asked as she covered his cage with a sheet. "Nighty-night," she told the bird. "Sometimes Jade gets very loud," LaTisha said. "It gets annoying. Sometimes he'll start talking and then begin squawking. When he gets carried away, it's hard to get him quiet. That's when we put him in a 'time out.' Do you know what a time out is, Joshua?"

"Yes, ma'am," I said. "A 'time-out' is when you sit quietly by yourself until you get your emotions under control. It gives you time to cool off and think about what you've done, and how you've been acting," I explained.

"Excellent, Joshua," LaTisha said. "I can tell that you and I are going to get along just fine. When Jade needs a 'timeout,' we cover him with the sheet like this and tell him, 'Nighty-night.' Sometimes it's the only way to have a little peace and quiet in this house."

LaTisha touched my shoulder. I was starting to feel comfortable with my new foster mom. She was a pretty woman with big, brown, friendly eyes. She smiled and laughed a lot, and seemed happy.

LaTisha was nice to me and I liked living with her. After a couple of days, I started calling her "Mom." I secretly hoped that she would adopt me too, but she never did.

I got used to being part of a mixed race family. LaTisha and Adrianna were black. They wore their hair in corn rows and braids. Jabar was biracial and his skin was a little lighter than mine. One of his parents was black and the other one was white.

Lulu, Roberto and Maria were Hispanic. Roberto and Maria were biological brother and sister. They had the same birth parents and they looked alike. Benjamin and Mitchell were each white. Benjamin was thin and had short, spiked red hair. His face was covered with red freckles.

The night before I moved to the Owens house, Ben had lost his two front teeth. Lucky for him, the tooth fairy had paid him a visit. Ben liked to jingle his four new shiny quarters in his pocket.

Mitchells' face looked a little odd. I could tell that something was different about him. LaTisha explained to me that Mitchell's birth mother drank a lot of alcohol when she was pregnant with him.

Mitch didn't talk very well. A lot of grown-ups couldn't understand what he was saying. He was old enough to use the restroom but he still had accidents. He still needed to wear a diaper. Mitchell laughed and smiled a lot. He was a fun kid and we all got along with him.

When I stayed with the Owens' family, I practically lived in the same pair of comfortable old blue jeans. They were size 6 slim. I'd yank on my favorite blue t-shirt, pull up some mismatched socks, and grab my size 3 basketball shoes. I was built for speed but dressed for comfort.

At first LaTisha kept my black nappy hair clipped short. After a few months, I convinced her to let me grow an afro. I liked that it felt soft and puffy to my touch. Having an afro made me feel like the brothers I saw on TV. I wanted it to grow long enough for LaTisha to braid it for me.

"You have the most beautiful smile, Joshua," LaTisha would say. "And your pearly white ivories just light up the room," LaTisha used to tell us, "Even though you don't look alike; you're all my kids and are brothers and sisters in God's eyes."

CHAPTER
7

A Miracle

"Mom, I don't feel well," I complained one Sunday evening in early spring.

"What's the matter, Honey?" LaTisha said as she turned her attention to me.

"I keep coughing," I said. "I can't breathe, and my tummy hurts." I moaned and doubled over in pain.

"Lulu, get Joshua's coat for him. Jabar, you're in charge of the house. I'm taking him to Urgent Care."

She grabbed her purse and keys, and rushed me outside and into the van. I flopped across the back seat and closed my eyes. I must have quickly fallen asleep. Before I knew it, we were parked at the medical center and LaTisha was shaking me awake.

Slowly I crawled out of the car and dragged myself to the front door of the Urgent Care Medical Clinic. Once inside, my legs gave out and I collapsed. Luckily, LaTisha caught me just before I hit the hard tile floor. A male nurse scooped me up and carried me quickly into an exam room. He laid me on the table. Someone paged the doctor to hurry into the room.

"Dr. Bee, Dr. Bee, emergency in room #2; Dr Bee, emergency in room #2."

The message filled the hallways. Medical staff and patients paid attention to the announcement. They were curious to know what was going on.

I was alert now, but having difficulty breathing. I was sucking air as if I had just run a 100 yard dash. My heart was racing. The nurse began taking my vital signs; my temperature, pulse, and blood pressure. A pretty lady doctor entered room #2 and took charge of things. She was Dr. Bee, and she began asking LaTisha and me a lot of questions.

"What's your name, son?" the doctor asked. "How old are you? Are you his mother? What are his symptoms? Where does it hurt? How long has he not felt well? Did he lose consciousness? How long was he out? Does he take any medication? Which ones and for what medical issues? Is he allergic to any medicines? Did he eat anything unusual last night or today?"

Dr. Bee fired questions at us, trying to figure out why I was so sick. She ordered x-rays of my chest. When she saw them, she realized that I was in big trouble.

"Ms. Owens, Joshua has serious problems with his lungs," the doctor said. "He needs to be admitted to the hospital immediately. We'll send him by ambulance, and call ahead so they'll be expecting you," Dr. Bee said. "Good luck, Ms. Owens. Be well, Joshua."

They wrapped me in a blanket and loaded me into a red ambulance. Even the wailing of the sirens didn't keep me from falling asleep on the way to the hospital emergency room.

When we arrived, I was immediately taken to the ICU, that's the Intensive Care Unit, for kids. I had just entered the building, and was already one of the sickest patients in the hospital.

Dr. Martin was my doctor in ICU. He was a young guy with a long brown pony tail and an easy smile. He ordered a bunch of tests on me that checked my blood and urine. He also took more x-rays. It was obvious to everyone that I was in very bad shape and that I was rapidly getting worse.

Dr. Martin told my mom that I had something called Strep Pneumonia. The pneumonia made it hard for me to breathe. The doctor put me on a machine called a ventilator. It's like a respirator, and helped me get the oxygen I needed to stay alive.

While all of this was happening, my heart was still racing. It wasn't getting enough air, and I had a slight heart attack. That means that part of my heart muscle wasn't working. Thank God the respirator helped my heart get more oxygen, because I could have died! Dr. Martin told my mom that I also had a very bad infection. It was called Septicemia. He started me on antibiotics to fight the infection.

"Ms. Owens, Josh is a very sick little boy. His kidneys are shutting down," the doctor explained to LaTisha. "The kidneys clean the blood, and his have stopped working."

LaTisha was shaken by this news. She sat down on a chair in the ICU waiting room. Someone handed her a cup of water. She was stunned and stared into space for a moment. My physician took a seat beside her. The bad news wasn't over yet. He leaned forward and very calmly gave her an update on my serious condition.

"Joshua is suffering a multiple system shutdown. His heart, lungs, and kidneys need assistance in order to work. His whole body is starting to shut down. We've given him drugs to put him into a medical coma. This is a very deep sleep. We hope that by doing this, his body can stay alive with the least amount of effort possible. But I must prepare you for the worst. He could die at any time," the doctor warned.

"We will continue to do all that we can for him, but it doesn't look good. I'm sorry, but I recommend you call your family together to say good-bye. You may want to start making funeral arrangements," Dr. Martin told my foster mom.

LaTisha sat paralyzed in her seat. She began to weep quietly. A nurse came to comfort her.

"Is there someone we can contact for you?" the nurse asked.

LaTisha jerked back to reality and sprang into action. "Joshua is my foster child. I need to call his caseworker and I need to get in touch with his attorney."

During the next three days, my foster brothers and sisters came to the hospital to see me. They each wanted to say "good-bye." There was a lot of crying and sadness.

Someone found my birth father, Randall Radford Senior. They reached him by telephone and explained what was happening to me. My dad and Grandma Jodie came to the hospital to see me. By then, dad and my birth mother, DeShona, had separated and she had moved to Tennessee. Dad and Grandma Jodie shuffled quietly into my hospital room. My father staggered weakly to my bedside. He gently lifted my little hand and rested it in his own.

"You're my son, Joshua. In my heart you always have been, and always will be. I love you, baby boy. Please be strong and stay with us. We need you to live, Son." My dad was crying as he pleaded with me. He prayed for me to survive.

"Jesus loves you, this I know, for the Bible tells me so. Little ones to Him belong. They are weak, but He is strong," Grandma quietly sang.

A hospital aide remembered that I was in foster care. The nurse realized that Dad's parental rights had been severed and my blood relatives were told they had to leave.

"I'm sorry, but the law no longer recognizes your connection to Joshua. You won't be allowed in his room. You aren't even supposed to have information on how he is doing. I'm sorry, but you'll have to leave now," the nurse sadly informed them. Dad and my grandmother kissed me and left my room.

That night my foster mom, caseworker, and court appointed lawyer were all sitting together in the waiting room. They had all come to the hospital to check on me.

"Josh needs to be on a kidney machine, and we don't have one here," Dr. Martin told the group. "We've located one at a different hospital. It's twenty miles away on the other side of town. Josh needs to be transferred immediately."

The grown-ups listened carefully. "Josh could die while he is being moved to another hospital. It's going to take a miracle to save him, but it's the only chance that he has to live."

They agreed that I should go to another hospital. LaTisha kissed me on the forehead. Together my foster mom, my caseworker, and my attorney watched as the medical team loaded me into the waiting ambulance. With flashing lights and blaring sirens, we sped into the darkness of the night.

I survived the transport to the new hospital. Within an hour I was hooked up to the kidney machine. Immediately it started working and cleaning my blood. I was still in a deep sleep, but my condition was improving.

I stayed in the ICU of this second hospital for a month. During that time I continued to have a tube down my throat to help me breathe. There were two other tubes in my body that supplied food to my stomach. I had needles in my arms giving me medicines and fluids. There were dozens of wires and tubes surrounding my body. I looked like fresh prey caught in the giant web of a spider.

During the week of my eighth birthday, the breathing tube was removed from my throat. LaTisha brought a chocolate sheet cake to the hospital to celebrate. She shared it with all of the doctors, nurses, and technicians who had been taking care of me. She thanked them for all that they had done, and were still doing to make me well again.

My foster sister, Adrianna, had come to visit. She was sitting by my bed, quietly reading to herself. There was a piece of cake sitting on a plate on the tray table in front of me. Adrianna decided she wanted the cake, so she reached for it.

"Don't even think about it," I said, and threatened her with my hoarse voice.

"AAAAYYYY!" Adrianna jumped to her feet, throwing her book to the floor.

LaTisha heard the scream and ran into my room followed by several nurses. Adrianna stood across the room pointing to me on the bed.

"He's alive," she said. "He's awake, Josh just spoke to me!" she insisted. "Look at him!"

I was awakening. My eyes were half-opened. The nurses could tell that I was more alert than I had been earlier in the day. My medically induced coma had lasted for four long weeks and now it was finally over. A miracle had happened, and I had survived another near death experience. My recovery from this coma marks another one of my nine cat lives.

CHAPTER

8

The Angel Kiss

To prevent patients from getting bed sores, hospital workers usually move their patients around in the bed. Because everyone thought that I was going to die, nobody bothered to adjust me or change the position of my head anymore.

As a result, I got a pressure sore on the back of my head. It came from lying in the same position for four weeks while I was in a coma. The hair stopped growing at this spot on my head, and now it was bald. My bald spot is oval like an egg. If you touch your thumb to your first finger, you can see the shape. That's about the size of it too.

"Hey baldie," kids would say, "What's wrong with the back of your head?" The mean kids would tease me. Even some grown-ups asked me what happened. I was self-conscious about my bald spot. I got mad and embarrassed whenever anybody asked about it.

When I was in the fourth grade some guys at school were teasing me. I wanted them to stop so I made up a wild story about how I got my bald spot.

"I'm from a tribe in Africa," I told them. "This mark is from my tribal initiation ceremony. Every male child from my tribe has a bald spot like mine. It means that we're accepted as men in our tribe. Are you a man yet?"

The guys believed me, too! Ha! They left me alone and never teased me again. I was pretty proud of myself.

Later on, when I met my adoptive mom, she kissed the back of my head where my bald spot is and explained it this way. "Well, Josh. I call this spot your angel kiss. I think it's where the angel kissed you to awaken you, so that you could be my son, and I could be your forever mom." From then on we always called my bald spot, my angel kiss.

CHAPTER

Winterhaven

It was winter when I first met my forever mom. A forever mom can be different from your biological mother. A forever mom chooses you to be her child. She legally adopts you to make you her own. She loves and takes care of you. She is a mother that keeps you forever.

"It's almost Christmas and school is out for the winter break," LaTisha said. "What do you say we all go to Winterhaven some night this week?" LaTisha asked her family.

"What's Winterhaven?" I asked.

"That's a neighborhood in town where every house is decorated for the holidays," she said.

"The Winterhaven streets are filled with colored lights," Lulu said. "There are scenes of the first Christmas with stables, Baby Jesus, Mary and Joseph. Some houses even have the Three Wise Men, shepherds and their sheep."

"Of course, there are plenty of Santa Clauses and reindeer on display too," Adrianna said. "Last year there was one house that had it all. It had the manger scene, Santa and his workshop, snowmen, and even giant candy canes."

"Hey, don't forget there was a railroad train that traveled all around the front yard," Jabar added.

"And they had music blaring and gave away free candy canes and hot chocolate," Adrianna said. "It was great!"

"Winterhaven is a big deal every year and a lot of people visit it," LaTisha said. "And almost everyone brings a can or box of food to donate to the local food bank."

"What's a food bank?" I asked.

"The food bank gives food to people who need it," LaTisha said. "Nobody should ever have to go to bed hungry, especially kids!" she said as she rubbed my afro.

"There will be a lot of people and cars going to this event," LaTisha said. "So I have a plan. We'll park our van at a mall and ride the free bus over to the entrance. That way we can walk the streets and enjoy the sights, then get back on the bus and return to our van. And we can avoid all of that traffic," LaTisha said, pleased with herself.

On the evening of our outing, the sky was filled with dark gray clouds. The temperature was dropping and we could smell the possibility of snow in the air. The day turned into night as we waited at the mall for the bus. We were bored just standing around waiting.

"Got-cha, you're it!" Lulu yelled. She brushed Adrianna on the back with her hand, and took off running.

Some of the kids were playing tag. The game was fun and might even help them get warm. We were all eager to get on the bus and out of the harsh wind.

I had forgotten to wear my hat and gloves and was already cold. Instead of playing tag, I knelt down to conserve my heat. I pulled up my jacket collar, tucked my chin against my chest, and shoved my hands into the pockets of my coat.

LaTisha was chatting with a couple of white women that I didn't know. Apparently, she had talked with one of them on the phone about adoption. That lady had told LaTisha that she wanted to adopt a little boy. LaTisha invited her to join us at Winterhaven. That way she and LaTisha could talk in person and the potential adoptive mom could meet LaTisha's kids.

I had overheard LaTisha's conversation on the phone a couple of days earlier. I heard my foster mom say, "One of my foster boys needs a forever home. He's eight years old and available for adoption. He is very sweet, and his name is Joshua."

"Kids, come over here please," LaTisha said.

We gathered around her and she introduced each of us by name. Finally, she pointed to me and said, "And this is Joshua."

Poking my head out from inside of my collar I gave a little nod. I looked briefly at the women, but didn't smile. Like a turtle, I ducked my head back into my cover. I was trying to be cool.

"These women are friends of mine," said LaTisha. "This is Jamie and this is her sister Julie."

"Hi," my brothers and sisters said in unison. "Nice to meet you."

I kept my head down and remained silent.

"Bus!" Jabar yelled, and we all scrambled to get on and take our seats.

"You sit with me, Joshua," LaTisha said. She positioned herself next to the window, and wrapped her arm around me. I buried myself in her cloak, and snuggled up against her to get warm.

The sisters we had just met were sitting across from LaTisha and me. Feeling shy, yet curious, I peeked at them every now and then. Every time I looked, one of them was watching and smiling at me. It was a short ride to Winterhaven. The bus turned onto a brightly illuminated residential street. The brakes moaned and the bus sighed, as we eased to a stop.

"Watch your step folks and enjoy your visit," our bus driver said. He was a thin black man with a shaved head and a thin moustache. "Buses depart from this location every half hour, to take you back to the mall." He winked and handed me a candy cane as I passed his seat. "Have fun, young man," he said.

The trees were draped with strands of glimmering lights. Red, yellow, blue, and green globes hung like precious stones from a necklace. Even the rooftops and windows of the houses glowed with thousands of twinkling sparkles. It reminded me of sparklers on the Fourth of July; each one being lighted by a match at the same time.

"Come on, kids," LaTisha said, "Let's hustle off this bus and get moving."

Shivering with excitement, I hopped down from the bus onto the frozen earth.

"Wow!" I said. "I've never seen so many Christmas lights in one place before. Let's go!" I pleaded, grabbing her hand and pulling her into the street.

We followed the crowd into the festive night air. Jabar, Lulu, and Adrianna led the way. They joined arms and sang Christmas carols. Jabar is a very good singer. It was comforting to hear his strong voice carry the melodies and messages of each song.

"Turn right at this corner, kids," LaTisha said.

We strolled up one street and down another. By the end of the night, I was worn out from our hours of walking. We probably wore down five miles worth of shoe leather that evening.

"Should we take this bus, Mom?" Lulu asked.

"Yes, if everyone is here."

My foster mom did a head count. When she was satisfied that her brood was intact, she stepped up into the vehicle and found a seat. Following her lead, I pulled myself onto the bus and dropped down next to her.

Wondering who else was riding with us, I leaned forward to scope out the rows of faces. Immediately, I spotted the sisters that we had met earlier. One of them spotted me too, so I jumped back in my seat and pretended to hide. Slowly inching forward, I peeked again. Busted! She caught me looking. I giggled and pressed my back against the seat. For the rest of the ride we played a silly game of hide-and-peek.

"This is where we get off," LaTisha announced to the family. She and I climbed down from the bus.

I turned to her, tugged on her coat sleeve and said, "I want to give that lady a hug."

She looked puzzled. "What lady, Joshua?"

"Your friend, that white lady in the purple jacket," I said.

The sisters stepped off the bus. The one who played the peeking game with me wore a purple coat. I looked up at her and lifted my arms in the air. This was my invitation for her to pick me up. She gave me a small welcoming smile, put her hands under my arms and said, "Jump."

I did and she lifted me into her arms. She held me for a long time. Her grip felt safe and confident. Her soft cheek warmed my frozen face. I turned my nose to her skin and breathed in her smell. It was foreign, yet pleasant to my nostrils. Then she lowered me back to the ground.

"I guess I'd better introduce myself again, Joshua," she said. "My name is Jamie and this is my sister, Julie."

She motioned towards her sister who was standing nearby. I could tell that they were sisters, because they looked a lot alike.

"Hi," I greeted them, flashing my pearly whites. I shivered from exposure to the cold temperatures. My fingers felt like they had turned into icicles. Jamie took both of my hands in hers.

"Oh, my goodness, Joshua," Jamie said. "Your little hands are frozen."

As she blew warm air on them, my hands began to thaw. I liked that she was caring for me and giving me special attention.

"Shall we walk with you to your car?" Jamie asked.

The sisters escorted us to the van. All of the time, Jamie held both of my hands in hers. When we reached the car, she turned towards me. "Jump," she said, and I did. She lifted me up for another hug.

"That's what I call a jump hug, Joshua," Jamie said.

I nodded in agreement then she put me down.

"See ya later alligator," she said. "Good night, LaTisha, bye kids. Thanks for inviting us to come along tonight."

"See ya!" I shouted climbing into the van and taking my seat in the back.

When everyone was settled, LaTisha honked her horn and drove quickly away. Looking out of the back window, I saw that Jamie was still watching me. I waved and she waved back; we each smiled. I felt a shock of electricity flash through my body. It reached all the way down to my toes. I was happy, and for the first time that night, I felt warm all over.

CHAPTER
10

Two New Friends

"Are you hungry?" LaTisha asked me as we entered the golden arches of McDonalds.

"Yes, ma'am!" I said with a grin. "And I want to play on the playground!"

I skipped to keep up with her long strides. We were having one of our special one-on-one outings. Every week, my foster mom made a date to spend time alone with one of her kids. Today was my turn for her undivided attention.

"What would you like to eat, Joshua?" she asked.

"A kid's meal," I answered.

"Excuse me?" LaTisha said. "I don't think I heard you correctly."

"May I have a kid's meal, please?" I rephrased my words, this time remembering my manners.

"That's much better, Joshua, I heard you clearly that time."

"What's the prize anyway?" I asked, eager to know what toy I would be getting.

"It's a glow-in-the-dark ball. I don't think you have one."

LaTisha placed my order with the clerk, and ordered her favorite. She loved her salad with mandarin oranges and strong black coffee. Within minutes we were seated in a booth with our food.

"Mummmmmmm, this is great!" I said. "Thank you for lunch, Mom, and for spending time with me."

"It's such a pleasure dining with a young man who remembers his manners," LaTisha said proudly.

I grinned, delivering a salty potato stick into my mouth. LaTisha was quiet; she always paused in prayer before eating her meal. For a few minutes we sat quietly together, focused on our food.

"Hey, LaTisha. Hi Joshua!" came a greeting from someone entering the restaurant.

We looked at the door, and saw Jamie, the woman we had met at Winterhaven last week. Jamie smiled, waved, and came over to our table. She had someone with her and began the introductions.

"LaTisha, Joshua, I'd like you to meet my partner, Brooke," Jamie said. "Brooke, these are the folks I was telling you about. This is Joshua, and his foster mom, LaTisha Owens. I met them last week at Winterhaven."

Brooke shook hands with LaTisha and me. "It's nice to meet you both. I heard you had a great time the other night," Brooke said. "I'm sorry I missed it."

We talked a while about Winterhaven. Then Jamie and Brooke excused themselves to get in line to order something to eat.

"Would you like them to join us?" LaTisha asked me.

"Sure!" I said with a smile.

The grown-ups talked while we ate. We learned that Brooke is a veterinarian. That means that she is a doctor for animals. Brooke and Jamie own an animal hospital and work together. It's called the Family Cat and Dog Clinic.

"May I please be excused?" I asked my foster mom. "I've finished my burger."

She nodded 'Okay' and I ran to the play area. The room was filled with bright yellow, green, and red tunnels. To me it looked like a giant octopus. I was eager to explore inside of its body and climb throughout the legs.

Six ladders gave me access to this monstrous creature. Four small round windows became his eyes. I threw off my shoes and climbed into the beast.

"Hey, everybody," I called. "Look up here!" I yelled to the adults as I peered out one of his eyes.

I stuck my head through a portal and waved. They spotted me, smiled, and waved back. Dropping to my hands and knees, I pulled myself higher into one of the tubes. I was headed for this guy's guts. At each window I poked my head out to see if anyone was watching. Brooke and Jamie always were and we waved. Then I'd disappear again, only to find my way to another body part and a different window. I came to a slide that landed in a tub filled with squishy spongy balls.

"Ahhhhhhhhhhhhhhhhhhh   Ahhhhhhhhhhhhhhhhhhh Ahhhhhhhhhhhhhhhhhhhh," I filled my lungs and exhaled hard as I belted out my loudest Tarzan call ever.

"Joshua," scolded LaTisha, "not so loud!" LaTisha giggled and shook her head. "He's got a great imagination, that boy," LaTisha told our guests.

I jumped onto the slide and landed in the tub of balls. Swooshhhhhhh. I was almost buried under the soft round spheres.

"G G G G R R R R O O O O W W W W L L L L ! SSSSNNNNAAAARRRRLLLL!" I became the monster exploding from under the blanket of balls. I tossed them into the air in all directions and laughed with delight.

"OK," announced LaTisha, "it's time to go, Joshua. Please find your shoes and put them back on your feet."

After a bit of searching, I found mine in the pile of cast off shoes. I stuck my favorite sneakers on my feet. I had them on the wrong feet but didn't care. I stuffed the laces down into the sides.

"It was nice seeing you again," LaTisha said to Jamie, "and a pleasure meeting you, Brooke."

"Thank you," Brooke answered. "I really enjoyed meeting each of you."

LaTisha took my hand and we said goodbye. We began walking toward the parking lot. "Wait a sec," I begged and ran back to give Jamie and Brooke each a hug.

"See ya later, alligator!" I said.

"After while, crocodile," Jamie and Brooke smiled and said together.

I ran to catch up with LaTisha and reached for her hand. We walked together to the van.

"It looks like you've made some new friends, Joshua," LaTisha said.

"Yeah, now I have two new friends," I announced with pride.

CHAPTER

11

Quality Time

The phone rang and Adrianna answered. "Hello? Just a minute please. Joshua, telephone."

I stopped playing tag with Benjamin and Mitchell, and ran to her. I looked puzzled as she handed the phone to me.

"Hello?" I spoke timidly. I never got any phone calls and wondered who was on the line.

"Hi, Josh," came a familiar voice. "It's Jamie. How are you?"

"Good," I said.

"I'm so glad to hear that," Jamie said. "Hey, Honey, I was wondering if you wanted to go to a movie with me this weekend?"

I asked LaTisha if it was OK and she thought it was a great idea. We saw the movie, "Flubber," and had a good time. Jamie, Brooke and I started doing things together every week.

"Mom, can we go to Mt. Lemmon and play in the snow today?" Jabar asked LaTisha on Sunday morning. "It's been snowing and the TV weatherman says there's at least a foot of snow at the summit."

LaTisha thought it was a grand idea so she invited Jamie and Brooke to go too. Brooke had plans and couldn't make it, so Jamie went with me.

"Mom, is it OK if I ride up the mountain with Jamie?" I asked.

It was fine with her, so Jamie picked me up at my foster home. We headed up the mountain road with me belted into the back seat. I'd never been up the mountain before, so this was a new and exciting experience for me. The road was winding and it curved back and forth like a snake. Each turn took us closer to the top.

"Duck your head," Jamie said. "We're headed for a tunnel." She laughed.

We dropped our heads and I didn't lift mine until we exited the other side of the small tube.

"Wow!" I said lifting my head and looking around. "This looks just like Heaven!"

Everywhere I looked there were tall evergreen trees. Their branches were heavy with fresh white powder.

"This looks like a scene from a Christmas card," I told Jamie. "Hey look. There's my mom's van."

We spotted LaTisha's van parked in the lot up ahead and pulled off the road and parked beside her. My foster brothers and sisters were already having fun. The teenagers carried their sleds up the hill, while the little kids made snow angels.

"Do you know how to make a snow angel, Josh?" Jamie asked.

"No ma'am," I said laughing. "I've never even seen snow until today."

"Let's get you started then," she said. "I think you'll make excellent snow angels."

Jamie lay down on the bed of white down and showed me how to move my arms and legs. I followed her lead and was proud of my first snow angel. Jabar threw a snowball, hitting Adrianna in the leg.

"Oops," he said. "Are you all right? I'm sorry if I hurt you."

"You're dead meat, Jabar!" she said laughing, and fired a snowball back at him.

Within minutes things had erupted into a full scale battle. Luckily, the snow was dry and powdery and most of the balls fell apart before they found their marks. We fell into the snow drifts laughing. It was a blast.

"I'll race you down the hill," said Jabar to anyone who would listen.

Always up for a challenge, Adrianna and Lulu each grabbed a sled and started down the mountain.

"Last one down is a rotten egg!" Adrianna shouted.

I watched as they bounced over the moguls and landed in the snow. Eager to give it another try, they hurried back up the hill, only to race back down again and again.

"Come on, Josh," said Jabar. "Jump on."

I sat down in front of him and away we flew, the snow hitting me in the face, stinging my cheeks. I closed my eyes and trusted Jabar's steering. I was grateful when we slowed to a stop.

"How about I ride behind you next time?" I asked.

Jabar nodded in agreement and we trudged our way back to the top of the run. Three more times down the hill and I had enough of the cold.

"Jamie, I'm ffffrrreeeezzzziiiinnnngggg," I said through chattering teeth.

"Let's get you warmed up, then," Jamie said. "We're heading for the car," she called to LaTisha.

Jamie turned on the motor of her red Subaru. "Hurry up, little engine," she said. "We need to get some heat in this car to warm Josh. Honey, take off your wet boots and drop them in the back, on the floor then come over here and get into this blanket," she said, laying a kid-sized, blue 'Smokey the Bear' sleeping bag in the empty seat. "It has a zipper there on the side," she said.

Eagerly, I kicked off my wet shoes and climbed into the front seat. It felt great snuggling into the comforter.

"Do you like hot chocolate, Joshua?" Jamie asked. "I made this thermos full of it just for you."

I nodded and Jamie handed me a cup of the sweet beverage. The warm cup felt good in my hands. The drink was hot and good and it warmed me from the inside out.

"Would you like me to read to you while we wait for the others?" She asked.

"Sure," I said. "LaTisha reads to the little kids, but nobody reads stories to me."

Jamie adjusted her seat to make room for me on her lap. I snuggled in and she read the story Balto, The Sled Dog. She finished the book just as everyone else arrived at LaTisha's van ready to go home. I was glad to get off the mountain and back into some warm, dry, clothes. I had enough of the snow and hated being cold!

"I thought maybe you'd like to go with me to visit my parents tonight, Josh." Jamie told me after I had changed my clothes. "My mom makes the best hamburger in the state, and my folks are looking forward to meeting you. What do you say; would you like to go meet my folks?"

I agreed and we drove over to her parents' house. Compared to me, they were old, maybe even ancient. Jamie's mother made me a hamburger with ketchup only, because that's the way I like them. My burger was perfect.

"Would you like a bowl of Cookies-n-Cream ice cream, Josh?" Jamie's dad asked me after dinner.

"Oh, yes, please!" I said. "Cookies-n-Cream is my favorite!"

Before the night was over, her dad had dipped me two bowls of the sweet treat. I was in seventh heaven. Before we left their house, Jamie's dad showed me how to juggle with three tennis balls. I had fun visiting them.

I started spending even more time with Jamie and Brooke. We saw each other during the week instead of just on weekends now.

"Do you like basketball, Josh?" Brooke asked me one day. "We have tickets to the University of Arizona women's game on Thursday. Would you like to go with us?"

"Sure!" I said with a smile. "As long as LaTisha says it's OK."

We went to a game and I was impressed by the players. They were really good. Jamie says that I'm a good player, too. I like dribbling and scoring three pointers the best.

"This team is called the Wildcats," Jamie said. "Look over there, do you see her?" Jamie said, pointing to the creature standing on the sideline of the basketball court. "That's Wilma Wildcat," she said.

A person, dressed in a wildcat costume, was walking upright along the side of the basketball court. Wilma paraded all around the court and went up into the stands to interact with the fans.

"The University of Arizona is also called the U of A," Brooke said. "Their team's colors are red and blue, and that's why Wilma wears a little red skirt with a blue top, like the cheerleaders."

"Do you see the red bow that she wears over her ear?" Jamie asked. "It matches her red and blue polka-dotted shoe laces."

Wilma had a big head and a long tail. She didn't talk, but I understood what she wanted when she came over to our seats.

She motioned for me to join her in the aisle. I climbed over Jamie and Brooke and moved to the stairway. Wilma put her arm around me and Brooke took our photo.

I slapped her paw for a high five, laughed and went back to my seat. From that day on, Wilma came to see me at each home game. We'd meet in the stairs, give each other a hug and high five, and finally bump fists.

Half-time was my favorite part of every game. That's when kids from the crowd got invited to play games on the basketball floor. One time they asked me if I wanted to participate.

"Heck, yes!" I said.

It was hard for me to sit still during the first half. I was nervous and excited to get onto the court. With three minutes left in the first half Jamie turned to me.

"OK, it's time for you to head on down to the floor," Jamie said. "Have fun and good luck."

I gave Jamie and Brooke a high five and scooted out of my seat. When the buzzer sounded, ten tired college players exited the floor heading for their locker rooms. At the same time, ten energetic kids immediately replaced them at center court. The college students set-up nine folding chairs and explained the rules for the game we would play.

"We're going to play a basketball version of musical chairs," one guy with long sideburns and a shaggy beard said. "Each of you will have a basketball. When the music starts you need to split up. You five will dribble down court and shoot at that basket," he said pointing to one end of the court. "And the rest of you will dribble and shoot at the other goal." He swung around and indicated the opposite side of the floor.

"You need to keep shooting until you score, and then dribble back to the chairs as fast as you can. When the music stops, grab a chair and sit down. If you don't find a chair, you're out. After each round, a player and a chair will be taken away. Does everybody understand?"

Ten heads went up and down with eager nods and anticipation. It was time for him to stop talking and let us do our thing. I was on that night. My ball handling was controlled and my shots were hitting. I was one of three kids still playing after several rounds.

There were two of us guys and one girl left. The other guy was about a head taller than I was. I'd guess that he was maybe ten. The girl was about my age and size. She was fast and really good, too! Remember now, I was only eight years old when this happened.

The music started and we were off. I raced down the court and shot a three pointer. It swished through the net and I was the first kid back to the chairs.

"Whooo-hooo!" Jamie and Brooke cheered from the stands. "Way to go, Joshie!"

The other boy missed his shot twice and the girl beat him back to the seats. He was eliminated so now there were only two of us left and we were down to only one chair. The crowd was on their feet, cheering and clapping. My heart pounded.

The music played again and I took off in a fast break towards my hoop. I tried a bank shot, no good. I grabbed the rebound and hit a lay-up then sprinted back to the chair. The girl and I bumped our hips together as we each tried to sit at the same time. We each had half a cheek on the chair. It was a tie!

I was really pumped! I took a deep breath and tried to settle myself before we started our tie-breaker. At the sound of the very first note I was on my feet. My shoes were pounding against the floor as quickly as I could move.

My first shot missed and so did my second. Lucky for me, my opponent was also having difficulty finding the hole. I snatched my rebound and tried a left handed lay-up. It dropped through the net and I sprinted towards center court. I arrived just after she took possession of the folding metal seat. She won - game over.

"Congratulations," I said. "You were great!" I smiled at her as we shook hands.

"You're really good, too," she said.

"Thanks," I said.

We panted to catch our breath as we walked off the court together. The crowd gave us a standing ovation. It felt as though each of us had won.

"Nice job, you two," I heard people say.

"Well done, young man."

"Congratulations, young lady."

Strangers told me what a great sport I was. They patted me on the back. Men, women, and other kids gave me high fives. It was tight! I made my way back to Jamie and Brooke.

"You were awesome, Josh!" they said, hugging me tightly.

"We're so proud of you," Brooke said as she slapped my hand with a high five, a low five, and a fist punch.

"I'm so impressed with your sportsmanship," Jamie said. "That was outstanding."

She shook my hand then punched fists with me too. The people sitting around us were grinning from ear to ear. I felt like a hero that night and I loved it!

CHAPTER

12

The Question

I didn't pay much attention to what happened during the second half of the game. I guess I was too pumped up from my half-time activities. After the final buzzer sounded, I took hold of Jamie's and Brooke's hands and led them to the car. Brooke drove the Subaru and Jamie sat in the back seat with me.

"Joshua," Jamie said. "Do you know what it means to be adopted?" She looked at me and held my hand in hers.

"Sure," I answered, "It means that you're a family and you keep someone forever and ever."

"That's right, Honey," Jamie said. "And I'd like to adopt you and be your forever mom. I want you to be my son. What do you think of that idea?"

"Yes!" I said. "I love it!" I said, cheering. I reached out and gave Jamie a hug. "Now can I call you Mom?"

"That works for me, Son," Jamie said.

"Beeeeeeeeeeep, Beeeeeeeeeeep, Beeeeeeeeeeeep, Beeeeeeeeeeep!" Brooke celebrated on the car horn. She flashed the caution lights too. We were celebrating!

"Honey, look at our hands," Mom said to me.

"I know, black, white, racial," I said as I looked at the back of my small black hand resting on top of her white palm.

"Some people may not like that you have a white mother," Jamie said. "Some folks might be mean to you because of it."

"It doesn't bother me," I said, "We'll deal with it."

"Honey, do you know what it means if someone is gay?" Jamie asked.

"I think so," I said. "It means that boys like boys and girls like girls."

"That's right. And a gay couple means that two men or two women understand, love, and support one another. They relate better to each other than to someone of the opposite sex. They are partners and are happiest when they are together. Does that make sense?"

I nodded that I understood. Brooke stopped the car at a red light and turned around to look at us in the back seat.

"If I adopt you," Jamie said, "then you'll have two moms, Brooke and me, because we're a couple. How do you feel about that?"

"I love you and Brooke," I said. "So if you're a couple, it's fine with me. Having two moms would be great. What should I call you, Brooke?"

"What feels right to you?" Brooke asked.

"How about Momma B?" I asked.

"That's perfect," she said, taking my hand. I squeezed her hand quickly before the light turned green and she drove off.

"So when are you going to 'dopt me?" I asked.

"Well, it takes a while to get all of the paperwork done. In Arizona it isn't legal for an unmarried couple to adopt a child. And two men or two women can't legally marry in this state, so we can't adopt you together," Mom said.

"That's stupid!" I said. "I want both of you to be my moms."

"We agree with you, Honey, and we don't understand that way of thinking," Brooke said. "We love you and want to be your parents."

"So what do we do?" I asked.

"I'll be your legal parent," Jamie said, "and Brooke will be your second mom."

"How do we do that?" I asked.

"Well, I need to attend classes about adopting an older child," Jamie said, "because that's what you are, an older child. A lot of people only want to adopt babies. I know that you've had some rough times, Joshua, and I need to learn what to expect, and how to help you. Does that make sense?"

"I guess so," I said. "I'm just glad that you're going to 'dopt me."

"You know, Honey," Jamie said. "There are so many kids, of all ages, who need loving homes. And I'll tell you this; to me you are the pick of the litter."

"What does that mean?" I asked.

"The pick of the litter means that of all the kids in the world who need a mom, you're the best. And you're the one that I choose for me."

"Wow, I'm the pick of the litter," I said. "So when you finish your classes, will I be your son then?"

"I need to do more than just attend classes," Jamie said. "Some social workers will come out to my house."

"Why do they come to your house?"

"Because they need to see if my home is a safe place for you to live," Jamie said. "And they'll ask me a lot of questions."

"How come?" I asked.

"It's their job to make sure that I'd be a good mother for you," she said.

"Heck, all they have to do is ask me," I said. "I'll tell them that you'll be the greatest mom!"

"Thanks for the support, Honey," Jamie said smiling. "Some people who know me really well will write letters for me. They'll explain why they think I would be a good mother. And the state will run a background check on me."

"What's a background check?" I asked.

"They look into my life. It's their responsibility to make sure I'm a good person, and not a criminal or someone who would hurt you. The state is very careful about making sure children are adopted into good loving homes."

"That's a lot of stuff to get done," I said.

"Yes, it is, Josh," Jamie said. "But you're worth it."

Six months later, Jamie's application to adopt was accepted and I finally got to move in with her. I liked calling her "Mom" and we started making up our own routines. Whenever we wanted to hug, I'd jump up into her arms for what we called a "jump hug." We'd squeeze each other tight. It was one of our favorite things to do. I knew that I was going to love being 'dopted.

CHAPTER

13

The Pool Party

"Hi, Jamie," LaTisha said, into the phone. "We're having a pool party next Sunday afternoon and we'd love for you all to join us."

"That sounds great, what shall we bring?" Mom asked.

"How about dessert?" LaTisha said.

"You got it," Mom said. "See you then."

The party started at 3:00 p.m. As soon as we got to LaTisha's house, I ran to the bathroom to change into my swimming trunks.

"Joshie, please be careful and stay in the shallow end," Mom said. "We need to be able to see you at all times."

Most of my former foster brothers and sisters were already in the pool. I quickly jumped into the shallow end to join them. Splash!

"Hi, guys!" I called to them.

"Hey, Josh," Lulu said. "Good to see you."

There were a lot of adults sitting around the pool supervising their kids in the water. Mom and Momma B were standing at the end of the pool. They were watching me, and talking with Jabar, who was wearing his street clothes.

"Where's Josh?" Momma B asked. "I just saw him a few seconds ago. I keep looking for his angel kiss, but now I can't find it."

She had been looking for my angel kiss on the back of my head. It's my special bald spot identification, and she got worried when she couldn't find it.

"There he is," Jabar said, pointing to me. I was on the bottom of the deep end of the pool.

"Jabar, get ready to go in," Mom said.

Jabar jumped in the water and swam over to where I was. Mom and Momma B came around to the side of the pool. Momma B was already dialing 911 on her cell phone, calling an ambulance for help.

Jabar pulled me from the bottom of the pool, and laid me across my mom's lap. I was limp. My eyes were big, white, and rolled back into my head. I was unconscious and not breathing.

"Joshie, NO!" Mom yelled trying to stop what was happening. She stared at me in disbelief. Mom froze in confusion and shock. She couldn't think of what she should do next. A lady that she had met just a few minutes ago ran up to her. That lady suspected that I wasn't breathing and that my heart wasn't beating either.

"Who knows CPR?" she asked.

"I do!" Mom said as she snapped into action. "I'll breathe, you do the chest compressions." They started doing CPR on me. The lady was pushing on my chest to make my heart beat, and my mom was blowing air into my lungs. After a few seconds, I started to throw up some water. Mom turned my head to the side, so that I wouldn't choke.

The lady stopped pushing on my chest and Mom stopped breathing into my mouth. I was breathing on my own and opened my eyes. Mom looked at LaTisha's daughter, Adrianna.

"Adrianna, please get my purse from out of our car," Mom said. "It's not locked and my purse is on the floor of the front passenger side, bring it to me." She turned her attention to Lulu.

"Lulu, Josh's dry clothes are on the hamper of the guest bathroom. They are a pair of green sweat pants and a shirt. Please get them for me now."

Adrianna and Lulu did as they were asked. Mom dried me with a towel, and put dry clothes on my shivering body. By then the emergency medical technicians, or EMTs, had arrived at the pool. They took over caring for me. They covered me with a blanket and put me in the back of an ambulance.

"Are you his mom?" one EMT asked. "Why don't you jump in the cab with me?"

Mom nodded "yes," and jumped into the front of the ambulance.

"I'll follow in our car," Momma B said. "Which hospital?"

"St. John's is the closest," the driver said. "We'll go there."

Mom rode in the cab with the driver. We quickly traveled to the emergency room, or ER, of St. John's Hospital. Momma B arrived as we pulled up to the door. The EMTs pulled me from the ambulance and wheeled me into the exam room. They quickly told the doctor what had happened.

"How long was he under water? Did someone perform CPR? How long did you do that?" The ER doctor began firing questions at my parents. She was trying to determine how much damage had been done to my brain. The longer I was without oxygen, the worse my chances for making a full recovery.

"It's hard to say," Momma B said. "I'd guess he was under water for only a few seconds. We did CPR for about 20 seconds before he regained consciousness."

"Let's get some x-rays and test his blood," the ER doctor ordered, "Has he been a patient here before? Somebody pull his records."

My hospital records told the doctor that I had recently been a coma patient. The x-ray films showed a lot of gas caused from the CPR.

"Because of the coma Joshua experienced a few months ago, I'd like him to stay in the hospital tonight for observation," the doctor said. "We'll put a cot into his room for you, Ms. Carson."

"Thank you," Mom said. "I'd appreciate that."

Eventually, Momma B left the hospital to go home and take care of our animals. Mom stayed overnight with me. Momma B came to the hospital early the next morning.

"Good morning, Joshie," Momma B said. "How are you feeling, Sweetheart?" She kissed Mom and me on the cheek. "How are you doing, Honey?" she asked my mom.

"I didn't sleep very well," Mom said. "Every time I closed my eyes I had flashbacks of the near drowning. I'd see Jabar handing Josh's limp body to me and laying him across my lap. It was a rough night."

"Oh, that's terrible," Momma B said. "I'm so sorry. What's the word from the doctors?"

"They've ordered more tests," Mom said. "They want to be absolutely sure that he's all right." Then the doctor came to see me. She listened to my heart and lungs.

"Josh is improving," she said. "But just as a precaution, I'd like him to spend a second night in the hospital."

So my mom decided she would stay in the hospital with me the second night too. After lunch, a short Hispanic woman walked into my room.

"I thought Joshua might be getting a little bored," the nurse said. "Would you like to play a little Nintendo?" she asked, handing the game to me.

"Yes! And thank you, ma'am!" I said, my eyes getting big with anticipation. My folks sat at the edge of my bed and watched me play. After a little while my mom spoke to me.

"Joshie, what happened to you in the pool?" she asked.

"Well, I was in the deep end, holding onto the side of the pool with my hands," I said. "I used to do that a lot when I lived here with LaTisha. My hands slipped and I started going down under the water."

"But, Honey," Mom asked, "why didn't you kick and splash and call for help?"

"I did call for help," I defended myself. "I yelled 'MOM!' But you couldn't hear me, 'cause I was under water."

"Oh, Sweetheart," Mom said as she hugged and kissed me. Momma B gave my hand a squeeze, and kissed my forehead. They had tears in their eyes.

"Do you remember anything from when you were under the water, Honey?" Momma B asked.

"Well," I said softly. "It was very quiet and peaceful."

"May I go back to playing my game now, please?" Mom nodded and I picked up the game controls and focused on the action on the screen.

"You two will probably think this is weird," Mom said to us, "but I had a premonition about this accident."

"What's a prem-a, prem-a...?" I asked her.

"Premonition," Mom said, helping me with the word. "That's when you sort of know that something is going to happen before it does. It's kind of a warning. On the drive over to LaTisha's house that day, I had a feeling there was going to be a near drowning. I even wondered how serious an accident would have to be to justify calling 911," she said.

"Really?" Momma B asked looking surprised.

"Yes, somehow I knew that Josh would be involved. I thought I might need his insurance information. So when I got out of the car, I intentionally put my purse in a spot where anyone could easily find it if need be."

"That's amazing," Momma B said.

"I even watched to see where Josh put his sweat clothes after he changed into his swim trunks," Mom said. "I noticed that they were on the hamper in the guest bathroom. I felt like he might need them in a hurry. And when we were talking with Jabar, something kept drawing my attention to the bottom of the pool. If I tried to ignore it, the feeling persisted. I could see a black spot at the bottom of the pool, but I thought it was a marking on the pool floor."

"I wore my black swim trunks," I said. "They were the trunks that I begged you buy for me."

Mom pulled me to her and held me as she continued to tell her story. "If I looked away from that spot, my attention was immediately drawn back to it," Mom said. "I believe one of two things happened. One is that Josh and I have an extremely strong bond to each other. Somehow, in my mind, I heard him calling me and I knew he needed help even though he was under water."

"That makes sense," Momma B agreed.

"The second explanation is that you have a guardian angel, Josh, and that angel saved you. Your angel tried to warn me of the accident on the way to the party. Then she kept trying to get my attention when you were in trouble in the water."

"Don't forget that Jabar is also your hero, Joshua," Momma B said. "He jumped into the water and pulled you out before you drowned."

"Joshie, please don't ever scare us like that again," Mom said to me. "We were so afraid that we'd lost you."

"I'm sorry," I answered softly. "I didn't mean to scare you."

"Joshie, Honey," Mom said, "When you were born nine years ago, you didn't come from my body. But two days ago I breathed my air into your lungs." Mom looked me straight in the eyes. "There's no question that you are my son."

Mom was crying as we rocked together in silence for a few seconds. She kissed my cheeks, nose, and my forehead, and then she kissed my bald spot.

"Thank you, God and Guardian Angel," Mom said. "Thank you, Jabar, and Brooke, and CPR lady. Thank you, EMTs, and all of the wonderful doctors and nurses, and thank you beautiful angel kiss," she whispered.

Not everybody recovers from a near downing experience and I'm very grateful that I have the luck of a cat.

CHAPTER

14

Facing My Fears

The day after I got out of the hospital, I had a swimming lesson at the YMCA. I had been taking lessons before I nearly drowned.

"Maybe we should get you a life jacket to wear in the pool," Mom said. My folks were worried that I would be afraid of the water.

"No way!" I said. "I'm not afraid of the water."

My moms took me to my swimming lessons and told the teacher about what had happened. My teacher was impressed to see me back at the pool. She said that I was brave.

"Josh, I'd like for you to sit at the edge of the pool today," she said, "and dangle your feet in the water."

That's what my teacher asked me to do, so that's what I did. A couple of days later I had another swimming lesson. By that time, Mom had bought me some bright yellow swim trunks. No more black trunks for me.

During this class I got in the water and participated with the other kids. Three weeks later was the last day of our swimming classes. Everyone was supposed to do a couple of challenges to pass the course. The first challenge was to go down the slide where the water would be over our heads. It wasn't very deep, just a couple of inches over my head.

My folks were watching me as I stood at the bottom of the slide. I took a deep breath, and slowly climbed to the top. Sitting down, I held onto the sides. Slowly, I eased my way go down the slope and dropped into the cool liquid. My teacher was waiting for me in the water in case I needed help but I was fine and quickly swam to the edge of the pool.

As a final test, we had to jump off of the diving board at the deep end of the pool. I was proud of myself for going down the slide and had gained back some of the confidence. Now it was time for the diving board.

I'll be honest. I was scared about going under water in the deep end of the pool. I was afraid of drowning. I was in no hurry to get in the water so I stood at the back of the line behind my classmates. Finally, they had all jumped off of the diving board. Now it was my turn.

I stepped onto the 12' plank and just stood there. I took a deep breath and pretended to blow out 100 candles on a birthday cake. I blew my breath out long and hard. This gave me fresh oxygen in my lungs. I took another big breath and this time I slowly allowed the air to escape from my lips. I walked to the edge of the board and looked down at my teacher who was treading water in the deep end. She was there in case I panicked and got into trouble.

"You can do this, Josh," she said to me. "I'm here if you need me, but you won't."

I didn't bounce, but simply stepped off the end and dropped into the pool. My head went under water once and I quickly came to the surface. Grinning from ear to ear, I yelled, "Yeah!"

My teacher grabbed me and turned me towards the pool ladder. I swam to the edge and climbed up to the deck. "I did it!" I yelled to my parents. "I faced my fears and I conquered them!"

They cheered and clapped and came towards me carrying a huge blue beach towel. Mom wrapped me in it and hugged me. Momma B gave me a high five. I was so proud of myself. I felt fantastic!

CHAPTER

15

A Full Heart

At bedtime Mom would tuck me in. We had a whole routine that we did every night. First, she'd kiss me. "I love you, Joshie, see you in the morning," she'd say. Then we'd puff out one of our cheeks, and pop them against each other. It was something silly that Mom and Grandpa did, so we did it too.

We'd make our hands into the American Sign Language symbol for "I love you," and we'd touch fingers. Finally, we'd blow kisses to each other and pretend to catch them from the air and touch them to our own cheeks. One of us would say, "See you tomorrow!" The other one would answer, "You've got a date."

Sometimes we'd just keep doing that over and over again. I liked it when Mom would put me to bed and we'd finish our whole routine. Sometimes I'd say, "Would you rock me for a little while?" She always did. Then we'd get to go through our good night routine all over again.

Another fun thing that we liked to do was give each other "Blurbles." That's our family name for a "Raspberry." Mom gave me blurbles by putting her mouth on my bare belly or neck and blowing hard. It tickled and made a funny sound. Blurbles always made me laugh! Mom and I lived in her house for about six months. Then she sold it and we moved into a bigger house that she and Momma B bought together.

The first night that we stayed in our new home, my bed had already been set up in my new room. I noticed my room had a very big window and that there were no curtains up yet.

"Ok, Honey," Mom said. "It's time for bed. Hit the bathroom and brush your teeth, please. Your bed is all ready for you."

"Mom," I said. "I don't want to sleep in that room without curtains. The window is too big and it's really dark outside."

"You're absolutely right, Josh," she said. "I'm sorry that we didn't think of that. How about if we take a bunch of pillows and blankets and make you a temporary bed in the guest bedroom tonight? That room already has curtains. Will that work for one night?"

"That would be great!" I said. "I never knew anybody wanted to take such good care of me like that. Thanks, Mom," I said, and I meant it too. As my mom was tucking me in that night I asked a question.

"So am I 'dopted yet?" I asked.

"Well, not officially," Mom answered, "but in my heart you're already my son."

"Well, then when are you going to 'dopt me?" I asked.

"Josh, you know that next Sunday we're having your Naming Ceremony," Mom said. "And on Monday, we'll go to the courthouse and talk with the judge."

"Then will I be yours forever?"

"You're already mine forever, Josh, but yes, the judge will legally make you my son."

It was the weekend just before our adoption became final. My parents had invited Mom's parents, Grandma and Grandpa, and my mom's sister, Aunt Julie, to my Naming Ceremony. Momma B's sister, Aunt Lynette, drove all the way from California to attend. LaTisha and her family came, and a few of my parents' closest friends. One friend was a minister and she performed my Naming Ceremony in our back yard.

Mom had written the Naming Ceremony just for me. It had special messages about new beginnings and my being part of this forever family. We had music and it ended with singing. My mom had one thing to say during the whole thing and that was when the minister asked her, "Jamie, what name do you give your son?"

"Joshua Radford Carson," she said with a quivering voice and tears running down her cheeks. Mom had decided to keep my old last name and make it my new middle name. She did that because I had already been Joshua Radford for nine years so Mom added her last name to the end of my old name.

At one point Momma B, Mom, and I gave each other jewelry pins to wear. The pins were in the shape of little hands forming 'I love you' in American Sign Language.

We had given the guests the words to "Joshua's Song" which we sang at the end of the ceremony. We sang my words to the tune of "Barney's Song" from the kids' television show about the purple dinosaur. The words are: "I love you, you love me, we're the perfect family, with Mom, Momma B, and Joshua too, happy Naming Day to you!"

We finished the day by eating Cookies-n-Cream ice cream and German Chocolate cake. Momma B took a lot of pictures and it was a great celebration!

My adoption became official the next day. Being adopted is a really big deal. We got dressed up to go to court and appear in front of the judge. I like to get spiffed up, so I wore a suit and a tie. We all stood at attention when the judge entered the room.

"You may be seated," I heard somebody say. So we sat back down.

"We have an adoption petition from Jamie Carson requesting to formalize her adoption of Joshua Radford," the judge began. "Are all parties present?"

"Yes, your Honor," Mom said. "And are you Jamie Carson? Is this Joshua?" he asked and we answered. "I'm assuming by the tears running down your cheeks that you would like for me to grant this petition. Is that correct, Ms. Carson?"

"Yes, please, your Honor," Mom said, nodding her head and trying not to cry. Mom explained happy tears to me a long time ago. She told me, "Josh, sometimes my heart is so happy and full of so much love, that it makes tears overflow and spill out of my eyes. Those are my happy tears, Honey, and it's very good when I cry those tears."

Mom had cried happy tears on my "Naming Day," too and now she was doing it on our official adoption day. Mom must have been really happy about my adoption.

"Joshua, do you want Jamie Carson to be your forever mom?" I quickly nodded and quietly whispered, "Yes, please and thank you."

The judge smiled and said, "OK, then. I hereby legally declare you to be Mother and Son from this day forth. That entitles you to all of the rights and responsibilities, as if you were related via a natural birth."

Our friends and family cheered, cried, and hugged. Mom and I had our picture taken with the judge. Afterwards, Mom, Momma B, Aunt Lynette, and I went out to celebrate by eating at my favorite restaurant which serves my favorite food – pancakes! After we ate my mom asked me a question.

"Josh, shall we go to your school and share the news with your classmates and teacher?" Mom asked.

"Yeah, that'd be tight!" I answered excitedly.

Mom and I had a short drive in the car to my school. She and I smiled as we walked in the classroom door holding hands. My teacher, Mrs. Jones, stopped writing on the blackboard, and everyone turned to look at us.

"I have an announcement to make," I told my classmates.

I walked up to the black board and picked up a piece of chalk. Very carefully, I printed this on the board:

"My name is Joshua Radford Carson."

I turned to face the class and gave them a smile with a whole lot of teeth showing.

"Today, Joshua was adopted," Mrs. Jones said. "He and his mom became a forever family."

Mrs. Jones hugged me and then she hugged my mother. Everyone cheered. I was happy and I knew Mom was, too, because happy tears spilled out of her eyes again. A couple of them landed on the back of my head, on my angel kiss. And that's how I started my life; as part of my forever family.

Mom says that my future is bright and that I have a lot to offer the world. I'm really happy about being 'dopted and excited about my new life. I don't know if it's true that I'm like a lucky cat with nine lives. But I do know that my name is Joshua Radford Carson, and that I have a forever family, and that I will survive.

The End of 9 LIVES:
I Will Survive

9

LIVES
Cat Tales

CHAPTER

1

Meeting Alexi

"Come on, Mom," I pleaded, "can we go now, please?"

"Honey, we can't check in until 9:00 a.m., and it's only 7:30 a.m.," she said. "It will only take us twenty minutes to get to the YMCA Camp pick-up location. You have about an hour before we need to leave. Did you get enough breakfast? Would you like some more toast?"

"No, thank you," I said, "I'm too excited to eat or do much of anything else. I just want to go to camp."

It was summertime, and I was scheduled to spend a week at the YMCA overnight camp. The night before, Mom helped me pack my suitcase and camp gear.

"Honey, do you want to take these shorts and jeans?" she asked, holding up four pairs of shorts and two pairs of old jeans.

"Yes, please," I answered.

"Why don't you grab a couple of sweatshirts, and I'll get your underwear and pajamas?"

"How many is a couple?"

"Two."

I selected my red hoodie and my navy blue pullover sweatshirts.

"All set, Mom."

"Josh, make sure you have your toothbrush and toothpaste, and here's a washcloth, towel, and soap."

"OK," I said, as I headed to the bathroom to get the items. I wasn't planning to use them, however. Whoever heard of brushing your teeth and taking a bath when you're camping?

At 8:30 a.m. we headed downtown to the YMCA building. There were a lot of kids and parents already there. We checked in at the registration table, and then sat down on the sidewalk to wait for the bus that would take me to the mountain camp.

"Excuse me, young man; are you going to camp this week?" A woman asked me.

"Yes, ma'am," I smiled, showing a lot of teeth. "I sure am!"

"Oh, great," she said. "I want you to meet my son, Alexi. He's going to camp, too."

"Hi," I said. "I'm Josh."

Alexi and I shook hands and bumped fists.

"Alexi is from Russia," the woman said. "I recently adopted him, and he's only been in the United States for a few weeks. He doesn't know much English yet."

"I'm adopted too!" I said. "This is my mom." I pointed towards my mom and the women shook hands.

"Josh, I'm wondering if you'll pal around with Alexi while he's at camp. It's pretty rough when you don't know anyone. And it's even worse when you don't understand the language very well. He could sure use a nice friend like you," she said.

"Sure," I said. "I can do that."

Alexi and I began communicating using body and hand motions. Sometimes we understood each other but most of the time we just laughed.

"May I have your attention please?" the YMCA leader said, using a loud speaker system. "It's time for all campers to get on the buses."

"Have a great time, honey, I'll see you in a week," Mom said, as she kissed me.

Alexi said goodbye to his mom and we boarded the bus together.

"Find a seat, kids," the bus driver said, "we have plenty of room for everybody. Just in case you need it, we have a restroom in the back of the bus."

Alexi and I found two seats and sat down together. I waved once more to Mom from the window. We said "I love you" in sign language. Mom blew me a kiss, which I pretended to catch. I sent her a kiss too as the bus began to move. That was one of the routines we did whenever Mom tucked me in at night, or when we said 'good-bye.'

The bus was much nicer than any bus I had ever ridden. There were only two seats in each row, and they tilted back like my mom's Lazy-Boy recliner.

"Want some of my Cheese Doodles, Alexi?" I asked as we picked up speed.

He gave me a puzzled look so I showed him the bag of snacks. He broke into a grin and pulled out his package of trail mix. We shared our snacks and began our friendship.

It was a long two hour ride to Y-Camp and a lot of the kids were rowdy. They sang, told jokes and made a lot of noise. Everyone was excited.

Finally, we turned off the main road onto the Y-Camp driveway. The driver slowed the bus to about 15 miles per hour. The tires crunched on the gravel, as if they were eating the new stones on the road.

"Smell that fresh air," I said as I inhaled the scent of the evergreen trees.

Alexi closed his eyes and took a deep breath of air. He smiled. In front of us was a dark green building with 'Mess Hall' written above the double wide screened doors.

Large black screens covered the windows to let in the fresh mountain air. The 'Mess Hall' became our primary meeting place. We ate most of our meals there and it was also an indoor recreation center. We played ping pong and board games and one night we even had a dance there.

CHAPTER

2

Y-Mountain Camp

"Welcome to the Y-Mountain Camp!" said the tall, white man standing next to the American flag. "We're going to have a wonderful and fun week together."

Everyone clapped and cheered in agreement.

"Let's get things started. My name is John Hart, and I'm the Camp Director. This building is the Mess Hall where we'll eat our meals. There are 10 cabins for boys and an equal number for the girls," the Camp Director said. "Each cabin has a counselor who is in charge of the campers in that bunk-house. When I call your name, the counselor in charge of your cabin will raise his or her arm high up in the air. Please go stand beside your counselor. Are there any questions?"

Nobody had a question so the director began calling the girls' names. He assigned each one to a cabin and counselor.

"The girls and their counselors are excused from the Mess Hall," the director said. "Now, I'll read the cabin assignments for the boys."

Alexi was assigned to a different cabin than the one I was in. He and I talked to the Camp Director and explained his situation.

"Hello, I am Alexi from Russia, I no speak English very good yet," he said.

"Would you please put Alexi in my cabin so that he won't be so alone?" I asked.

The Camp Director thought that was a great idea so he reassigned Alexi to my cabin.

"Campers, follow your counselors to your cabins," the director said. "We'll see you all back here for lunch. You'll hear the food bell ring in about an hour."

My counselor was a black guy named Hermie J. Flick. He was a big guy who wore his hair in corn-rows. We followed Herm to our cabin, picked out our bunks, and put away our gear.

"Bongggg, Bongggg, Bongggg, Bongggg."

A loud bell signaled that it was time for lunch.

"Race you to the Mess Hall," I said to Alexi and then sprinted in the direction of the sound. He broke into a run and was by my side every step of the way. We arrived at the front door smiling and panting for air.

We sat down at our assigned tables and waited for our turn at the buffet. For lunch, I picked two fat and juicy Ballpark hot dogs. They were glistening with moisture as I stuck them with my fork and put them on my plate. I added a drop of Catsup and two perfectly toasted buns, and my Ballparks were ready to eat. I topped off my meal with a grape Popsicle. This is my kind of food!

Two of the girl counselors took the floor. One was the most beautiful black girl I'd ever seen in my life. I immediately had a crush on her. She was probably 20 years old, thin and about 5'10" tall. Her black hair was straight and hung to her shoulders. She had deep brown eyes and was really hot!

The other girl was a perky, little, short, white, blonde, and I couldn't help smiling every time she looked at me. She walked with a bounce and you could tell she was fun to be around.

These counselors taught us some funny songs with hand and arm motions. One song was called, 'Boa Constrictor.' It went like this:

(Chorus)
I'm being eaten by a boa constrictor, a boa
constrictor, a boa constrictor,
I'm being eaten by a boa constrictor,
Oh, no; it's nibbling at my toe.'

I'm being eaten by a boa constrictor, a boa
constrictor, a boa constrictor,
I'm being eaten by a boa constrictor,
'Oh, gee, he's up to my knee.'

I'm being eaten by a boa constrictor, a boa
constrictor, a boa constrictor,
I'm being eaten by a boa constrictor,
Oh, my, he's wrapping 'round my thigh.'

The song goes on and ends with…nah; I'm not going to tell you how it ends. You'll have to go to camp and learn that song for yourself. After singing we listened as our camp director told us about the activities we would get to do over the next week.

"An activity schedule is posted outside of the Mess Hall on the bulletin-board," he said. "You'll each have a chance to swim in our outdoor pool, go horseback riding and hiking on the mountain trails, play soccer, tetherball, ping-pong, basketball and volleyball. We'll have a camp dance on the last night before you all return home."

A thunderous applause erupted from the crowd of listeners. Alexi and I covered our ears with our hands to reduce the noise.

The director said, "In your crafts classes you'll make lanyards and sit-upons. You can use your sit-upons every night at your private cabin campfires."

I really liked my craft classes. Alexi and I went to crafts the next morning after breakfast.

"You're very good with your hands, Joshua," the crafts lady said.

"Thanks," I said. "I like making things. I've already finished my sit-upon." I showed her my newspaper pillow. "I made it first thing this morning."

"Wow, that's great, Josh," she said. "Would you like to be my assistant and help the other campers with their projects?"

"Sure, can I help Alexi make his sit-upon now?"

"You bet. Let me know if you need any more supplies."

Alex and I trotted over to the columns of newsprint that were stacked on the floor. He selected his papers and I showed Alexi how to weave it into a pillow. By the time the class was over Alexi was ready for the evening campfire.

CHAPTER

3

The Campfire

Alexi and I played basketball after dinner so we were always tired and hungry in the evenings. Herm was a miracle worker and managed to get a pack or two of marshmallows and hot dogs for us to roast at our campfire.

Each cabin had its own spot for the nightly events. Herm would light our fire right after our recreation time ended at 8:00 p.m. Then eight happy and dirty kids would eagerly huddle around the flame.

"Tube steaks taste better when they're cooked over a campfire," Herm would say every night. That was our cue to grab a stick and a wiener and start roasting. Herm called hot dogs, tube steaks. He said "It makes them sound more expensive."

At night, we'd usually talk about what happened that day. Then Herm would play his guitar and we'd sing songs. You could tell that Alexi liked the music because he usually drummed softly on a hollow stump.

"Alexi, you have a good sense of rhythm," I said, listening to him tap out the beat on the log. Trying to make him understand, I nodded my head to the beat and joined in the drumming. Alexi smiled and pounded even harder on his wooden drum.

Sometimes Herm would tell us scary stories. Alexi wasn't scared because he had no idea what Herm was saying. He would watch our reactions though and try to get a feel for what was happening in the stories.

One night Herm was telling us about the time his Jeep broke down in the desert.

"It was a cool and quiet Sunday night. The fall moon was full and it shined brightly on the two lane road ahead," Herm began his story.

"I had spent a long weekend visiting my folks in Sedona, Arizona. I was alone in my Jeep and headed back to college at the University of Arizona. I was running late, so I decided to take a short cut back to school. "

We sat motionless and listened to his words.

"My engine sputtered, choked, and died." He made the sounds of the dying engine.

"The Jeep slowly drifted to a stop along the side of the road. I realized, too late, that I was out of gas and I was stranded."

"I looked around and saw no other cars in sight. I was easily 20 miles from the nearest little town. I could clearly see the desert landscape around me in the moonlight."

Herm used his arms and body to act out the scene.

"Giant saguaro cacti were silhouetted against the night sky like an army of soldiers standing at attention."

Herm paused and slowly looked each of us in the eye.

"Suddenly, I heard a loud scream," his voice quickened and his eyes grew large with alarm.

"It happened again and I could tell that the sound was coming towards me. I looked around, anxious to know what it was."

I nervously looked at Alexi, then quickly back at Herm.

"A dark shadow was flying directly at me. It was coming from above my head and was just ten feet away. In order to save myself, I dove under my jeep."

All eight of us were leaning forward with our eyes wide open. Alexi could sense the tension in the story and he sat perfectly still.

"A huge bird swooped to the road in front of my Jeep. It snatched a small rodent from the ground, and effortlessly carried the prey in his sharp, deadly talons."

With dramatic arm movements Herm mimicked the behavior of the large predator bird. Our eyes followed his every movement.

"It was a massive bird, a Great Horned Owl, out hunting for food. I sighed and laughed at myself."

Relieved, we chuckled and readjusted our seats.

"The night was once again peaceful. Off in the distance I saw headlights so I stood in the road ready to flag down the approaching driver."

I looked at Alexi and smiled, confident now that the story would soon have a happy ending.

"An awesome, red, 1986 Corvette Stingray convertible zipped around the curve in the road. The top was down and a very attractive white woman sat behind the wheel. She was traveling alone and I waved my arms signaling for her to stop. She glanced at me, but didn't slow down. Her engine roared as she sped away."

I shook my head in disbelief wondering why anyone would leave Herm stranded in the desert alone at night. Was she afraid of him? Was she afraid because he was a big guy, a black man?

"I shook my head and dropped my waving arms," Herm said.

We moved uneasily on our sit-upons.

"There was a rustling in the bushes and I held my breath to listen more clearly," Herm said.

"Rattttttttttttttttttttttttttttttttttttttttle, Rattttttttttttttttttttttttttt tttttttttttle…"

"It was the distinct rattle of a vibrating snake." he whispered.

"Rattttttttttttttttttttttttttttttttttttttttle, Rattttttttttttttttttttttttttt tttttttttttle…"

"The snake sent his warning message once again..."

I held my breath and sat perfectly still as I waited for Herm to tell us what happened. Just then a single trumpet broke the tension and the spell that had surrounded our campfire.

"Da-da-daaaaaaaaaaaaaaaaaaaaaaaaaaaaaaaaaaaaaaaaaa, Da-da-daaaaaaaaaaaaaaaaaaaaaaaaaaaaaaaaaaaaaaaaaaa, Da-da-daaa aaaaaa, Da-da-daaaaaaaaaaaa, Da-da-daaaaaaaaaaaaaaa, Da-da-daaaaaaaaaaaaaaaaaa, Da-da-daaaaaaaaaaaaaaaaaa, Da-da-daaaaaaaa aaaaaaaaaaaaaaaaaaaaaaaaaaaaaaaaaaaaaa."

A camp bugle sounding "Taps" interrupted Herm's story. The horn signaled that it was time to drown our fire and head for our bunks. In thirty minutes it would be time for lights out.

"Sorry guys, that's it for tonight," Herm said.

"Ahhhhhhhhhhhhhhhhhhh, come on, Herm, finish the story," we said to him.

"You know the rules, hit the can and then your bunks," he said.

We slowly got to our feet and stretched. Herm poured a bucket of water on the fire. With the hiss of a snake and a puff of black smoke, the campfire was out.

We picked up our gear and turned towards the restroom and shower cabin. That's when we heard the rattle of a nearby snake.

"Rattttttttttttttttttttttttttttttttttttttttle; Rattttttttttttttttttttttttt ttttttttttttle;"

"Shhhh!" Herm said. "Freeze!"

We stopped in our tracks, unable to identify the source of the noise.

"Rattttttttttttttttttttttttttttttttttttttttle; Rattttttttttttttttttttttttt ttttttttttttle;" it warned again.

We held our breath and watched the 6' viper cross the path that lead to our cabin and slither deeper into the woods.

"Gospodi!" Alexi exclaimed, once the serpent had left our immediate area.

"Gospodi!" he repeated, shaking his head, his eyes huge with fright.

"What does that mean," I asked.

"I'm not sure but I think it's Russian for, 'Oh my God!'" Herm said.

"I can't believe you were just talking about a rattlesnake and one appeared in our camp!" I said. "Oh, my God is right!"

"Watch carefully where you're walking," Herm said. "And make your footsteps heavy. Snakes feel the vibrations and should stay out of our way."

We quickly hit the restroom and were safely in our beds within minutes. Nobody wanted to risk being out and about with poisonous reptiles in the area.

The next morning camp was buzzing with stories of our night time reptile visitor. Some kids didn't believe that our story was true, but we knew what we saw and heard was no campfire tale.

CHAPTER

4

Call Me 'Cat'

On the third day of camp I got to spend some time alone with Herm. We started talking about things and found out we shared a lot in common.

Herm had a scar near his left eye. He said he got it when he was a little kid. He and his family were at his uncle's house. The grown-ups were inside and he went outside to play. He saw a wooden ladder leaning up against the garage, and decided to climb it.

Herm got almost to the top when he lost his balance. He fell onto the gravel driveway and the ladder landed on top of him knocking the breath out of his lungs.

"I must have smashed my face against a rock because blood started pouring out of me," he said. "I couldn't breathe and I couldn't see because there was blood all over my eye."

"Wow, that's scary!" I said.

"Finally, I was able to yell for my mom. She ran outside to where I was lying, under the ladder."

"Then what happened?" I asked.

"Mom tossed that ladder off of me like it was no heavier than a baseball bat," Herm said laughing. "She held a cold wet rag to my head and took me to the hospital emergency room. I ended up having eight stitches right next to my eye."

"Wow," I said.

"Yeah, the doctor said I was lucky I didn't poke my eye out. If I had landed on that stone any differently, I'd be staring at you through a glass eye for sure."

We sat quietly for a while, tossing little pebbles at a fallen tree.

"I had some scary accidents too," I said. "Want to hear about them?"

"Sure," Herm said.

I told him about being born too early and how I almost died as a baby. I shared about the fights I saw when my siblings and I lived with my aunt and uncle. Then I shared the story about my month long coma and how the doctor told my foster mom to plan my funeral, because I was going to die.

I showed him my angel kiss and explained how it happened while I was in the hospital in a coma. I told him how my adopted mom explained that my bald spot was really an "angel kiss" to wake me up so that I could be her son, and she could be my forever mom.

Finally, I told him about my near drowning, and how my Guardian Angel, my foster brother, Jabar, my moms, and the EMTs all helped to save my life.

"Man, you're a miracle kid!" he said. "You're like a lucky cat, man, a cat with nine lives."

I nodded my agreement.

"You should have a nickname," Herm said. "You're a cool kid and one very lucky cat, so I think I'll call you 'Cat,' if that's OK with you?"

"That would be tight," I said, beaming with pride. "Thanks, man."

We bumped fists and did a cool handshake. From that night on, Herm and my cabin mates called me 'Cat.' I started telling kids to call me by my nickname, 'Cat.'

CHAPTER

5

Coming Home

While I was away at camp, my parents had been busy shopping for me. I knew nothing about the wonderful surprises my moms had waiting for me at home.

"Josh's wardrobe is in sad shape," Mom said to Brooke as they entered the 'Boys' section of the Target store. "He needs new everything; shirts, jeans, shorts, underwear, shoes, pajamas…"

"This is going to be fun!" Brooke said with a laugh. "And expensive."

"It sure is!" Mom said. "He wears a size 6 slim jean."

"Let's get three pair, two blue and one black," Brooke answered as she began sorting through the stacks of jeans on the shelves.

"You get those and I'll pick up some shorts," Mom said. "I have a feeling this will be one shopping trip we'll never forget!"

My parents bought me an entire new wardrobe that day. And that was just the beginning. In addition to the new clothes, my folks had decorated my room with all sorts of cool things.

They were excited to see my reaction to all of their efforts while I was away at summer camp.

Mom met the bus from camp and I greeted her with a jump-hug. During the drive home I told her the campfire and rattlesnake story. I also told her about my new nickname.

"Well, Honey, the name 'Cat' does seem to fit," she said. "And you know how much we love cats around our house. I'm sure Brooke will think it's a pretty good nickname too."

We pulled into our garage and I quickly jumped out of the car.

"Cat-Honey, would you please drop your dirty clothes at the laundry room, and then take your empty suitcase back to your room and put it in your closet?" Mom asked.

I dropped my dirty clothes and started calling for my other mother as I walked back towards my room.

"Momma B, I'm home!" I said.

"I'm in your room, Joshie," Momma B yelled back.

I walked into my bedroom and couldn't believe my eyes. Momma B was sitting on the bed waiting for me. She jumped to her feet and greeted me with a hug and kiss.

"Oh, my gosh," I said. "Check out my room. I love it! Look at this dresser. It's my favorite color, and a new blue blanket on my bed!"

I dove onto the bed and laughed as I wrapped myself in the warm comforter.

"How do you like your pillow, Josh?" Momma B asked holding up a pillow with Bugs Bunny's face. His big toothy grin smiled at me and his long gray ears poked out from the side of the blue fabric. Bugs Bunny has always been my favorite cartoon character.

"He's great!" I said, taking him in my arms and hugging the pillow. My folks had also hung my Bugs Bunny kite in one corner of the room. It looked great and I was thrilled. Taking my time to look around, I noticed that my walls had been decorated with posters and pictures of black people.

"Do you recognize any of these people?" Mom asked.

"Sure, that's Martin Luther King, Jr., and that's Michael Jordan," I said pointing to the correct images.

"Very good," she said. "Do you know any of the others?"

I shook my head from side to side, "No."

"This is Arthur Ashe, he was a famous tennis player," Mom said, "and over here is Frank Robinson. He was my favorite baseball player when I was your age. He wore uniform #20 and played for the Cincinnati Reds professional baseball team."

I walked over to examine the faces.

"Hey, do you know who this handsome guy is?" Mom asked.

"No, but he's a football player," I said.

"You're right," Mom said. "He's Lynn Swann and he played for the World Champion Pittsburgh Steelers. I've always had a big crush on him."

"Ah, Mom," I said.

"Well, it's true," she said. "I think he's gorgeous."

"I bet that before long you'll be able to name the famous African Americans on this poster," Momma B said, referring to a poster with the faces of about 30 black people on it.

"Who are they?" I asked.

"I know a few but not all of them," she said. "Here's a guide to tell us who's who," she said, handing me a paper.

"You know how I love history," Mom said. "It'll be fun learning more about these important people."

Then I spotted four framed photographs of some children. I walked over to get a better look. They were black and white pictures of some kids who were playing in a park.

One photo had five young girls playing together on a swing set. Three of them were black and two white. The next photo had the same five kids on a 'Jungle Jim' set.

Another photo was of a young black boy standing on the sidewalk. He was holding a string that was tied to a helium balloon. The last picture was of three white girls standing in front of a wall. The girl in the middle had a smirk on her face, while her friends covered their mouths to keep from giggling.

"These are tight, Mom," I said. "Thanks!"

"You're welcome," she said. "Do you have a favorite photo?" Mom asked.

"Yes, ma'am, I like this one the best," I said pointing to the three girls.

"That's my favorite too," she said. "It's called 'The Secret.' Do you think the girl in the middle has a secret?"

"Yes, ma'am, and she's not telling," I said.

We laughed at that because we all know that I am not good at keeping a secret. I always promise not to tell, but somehow I just can't help myself.

"Josh, you might want to check out your closet," Momma B said.

I opened my closet door. "Wow!"

I saw all new clothes and shoes. I dropped to the floor and grabbed a brand new pair of basketball shoes. I smelled them and then held them up in the air. I love to smell things.

"These are tight!" I said. "Thank you!"

I put them back in their box and picked up a pair of brown shoes with laces on the top.

"Those are for school," Momma B said.

I smelled them and held them up to admire. Next I examined a pair of black loafers.

"I've never worn shoes like these before," I said.

"They're called loafers," Mom said. "You just slide your feet into them like slippers. With loafers you don't have to worry about tying any laces."

The leather smelled great and I knew that I'd like wearing them. My dress shoes came last.

"Wow, look at these," I said. "They're so shiny that I can see my own reflection!"

I love shiny things and these shoes were polished black dress shoes. They were for special occasions. I put them on and strutted like a proud rooster into the kitchen. There I danced all over the tile floor.

My folks followed me into the kitchen and clapped as I showed them my fancy footwork.

"You get your dancing ability from your Mom," Momma B said, laughing.

"May I try on my new clothes?"

"Sure, but let's have you take a bath first," Mom said. "You have an acre of camp dirt on you."

I ran to the bathroom and started running water in the tub. Within fifteen minutes I was washed, dried, and ready to model my new threads. I'd never had so many new clothes and shoes before.

The state of Arizona gives each kid in foster care a little money each year to buy clothes and shoes. It isn't much money, so most foster parents go to thrift stores to get clothes for their foster kids. I was thrilled to have brand new clothes that nobody else had ever worn before. I ran to mom and gave her a jump-hug. Then I gave Momma B a jump-hug too.

"Thank you both so much for my room and new clothes and my shoes." I said.

"You're welcome, honey, it's our pleasure," they said.

"Thank you for 'dopting me," I said.

"Thanks for being our son, Joshie, we love you very much."

"I love you too!" I said with a smile and skipped down the hall.

CHAPTER

6

Mom's School

"Honey, I need to talk with you," Mom said. "Please come over here and sit by me."

Joining her on the couch I looked into her face. Mom looked serious.

"I know that you have been angry because you were neglected and abused by adults in the past. And nobody blames you for what happened, or for being mad at the grown-ups in your life. I'd be angry too."

She had my full attention.

"But because of your anger, Honey, you haven't been able to focus much on your school work. For the past three years, your teachers have been helping you handle your emotions. They've been trying to teach you to have more appropriate behaviors. Do you understand what I've said so far?"

I nodded that I understood, "Yes, ma'am."

"Because you've been dealing with your anger, Josh, you're behind in what you should have already learned in school. Does that make sense?"

Again I nodded my head up and down, "Yes, ma'am."

"Good. Well, I was thinking that we should take advantage of your summer vacation. I think that we should work together, for about an hour every day, on your school work. I'm hoping that we can get you caught up a little. Will you do that with me? Will you work with me to help you get caught up with your school work?"

"OK," I said. "If that's what you think I should do."

"I do, Honey, and thanks for agreeing to work with me. I'll get some workbooks and we'll get started."

Mom had my summer school program all planned out for me. She used to be a school teacher, so she thought that working with me would be easy. She was wrong. It was hard, especially for me.

"Josh, I'm not exactly sure where we should start. I'm going to ask you to do things that you may already know how to do. I just need to figure out where to begin. Is that OK?"

"Uh, huh, I mean, yes ma'am."

"OK," she smiled, "I don't mean to bore or insult you, but I need to find out what you do and don't know. Can you say the alphabet for me?"

"Sure!" I said, and quickly rattled off the letters.

"Good, now do you know which letters are called vowels?"

"Hummmm…I'm not sure."

"Let's look at your name." Mom printed 'J-O-S-H-U-A' on a piece of paper. "One example of a vowel would be the letter 'A.'"

"I remember now, A, E, I, O, U."

"Great job," Mom said. "So what are the other vowels in your name?"

"O and U."

"Excellent. Now have you learned about 'Phonics'?"

"I don't think so. What's Phonics?"

"Well, it's a great way to help you read and learn how to pronounce new words. You start by learning the different sounds that vowels and consonants make. Do you know what a consonant is?"

"Yes, those are the letters that are not vowels. Like in my name the consonants are 'j, s, and h," I said, pointing to each letter in my name.

"Exactly," Mom said. "Do you know the sounds that each vowel can make?" Mom asked. "Let's look at the word 'skate.' Do you see the 'e' on the end of the word?"

"Yes, ma'am," I said.

"Good," she said. "Well that 'e' on the end of this word tells you that the vowel in front of it, says its own name. What is the vowel in front of the 'e?'"

"It's the letter 'a."

"Exactly, so for this word the 'a' says its' own name. We say, skate. Do you hear the 'A' sound?"

"Yes, ma'am."

"When a vowel says its own name, we call that a long vowel sound. Like 'a' in skate. OK?"

"I think so."

Mom wrote some different words on the paper. Each one had an 'e' on the end of it. We practiced words that had long vowel sounds. After about ten minutes Mom said that we were done for the day.

"OK, that's all for today, Joshie, school's out for the day, great job. Now let's go shoot some hoops."

We had a good time making baskets and I almost beat Mom at the game of "horse." One of these days I know that I'll beat her. I'm going to practice my shooting until I do!

Later that night my parents were sitting at the kitchen table talking. I was already in bed, but still awake. I could hear voices but I couldn't make out any of the words.

"So how did the school lesson go today?" Brooke asked.

"Brooke," Mom said, "I'm shocked at how low Josh's reading level is. He's nine years old and in the fourth grade but he can barely read even the easy words. He knows his alphabet and a little bit about Phonics. This is going to be much harder than I had planned. It's going to take a lot of hard work for him to catch up to his age and grade level."

Mom and I worked together every day that summer, even though I didn't like it much. Whenever I'd finish a workbook my folks always made a big deal out of my accomplishment.

"DAH-da-da-DAH! Ladies and germs, I mean gentlemen," Mom said, pretending to be an announcer in front of a crowd.

"I'd like to call your attention to the outstanding achievement of Mr. Joshua Carson. Today he successfully completed another workbook. Mr. Carson, would you please step forward?"

My parents would clap and cheer as they presented me with an achievement award certificate. I liked getting my awards and kept them in a three ring binder.

When I got better at phonics, my parents asked me to read to one of them for half an hour every day. Mom picked out most of my books. They were often about famous black people or black history and black families. My folks didn't want me to forget that I was black.

CHAPTER

7

Discovering Girls

I had my first girlfriend in the fourth grade. She was white and had pretty blonde hair that she wore in a ponytail. Her name was Peggy, and I called her Pretty Peggy. She wasn't in my class, but we played tag during recess.

"Class, tomorrow is Grandparents' Visitation day," Mrs. Jones, my teacher said. "Joshua's grandparents are the only ones coming to school this year. This is a very special occasion, so I've order a flower for Joshua to give to his grandmother."

"Thank you, Mrs. Jones," I said. "I'm sure that Grandma will like the flower."

"I'm sure she will too," Mrs. Jones said. "Your guests will arrive at 10:30 a.m. and visit our classroom first. Then Josh, you are to take them to the cafeteria and eat lunch with them. They are guests of the school so they won't need to buy their lunches. Just go through the line and when you finish, your grandparents will leave the school, and you'll come back to class. OK?"

I nodded that I understood. The next day Mrs. Jones sent me to the office to pick up my flower. It was a red carnation and it had something called 'Baby's Breath' with it. 'Baby's Breath' is a bunch of little dainty white flowers all on the same stem.

I wanted to impress my girlfriend, Peggy, so I quickly ran down the hallway to her classroom door. Standing outside, I waved to get her attention.

"May I please use the restroom?" Peggy asked her teacher.

The teacher gave her approval, and Peggy stepped into the hallway to talk with me.

"Hi Pretty Peggy," I said smiling. "I got his flower for you." I said handing her the red carnation.

Her deep blue eyes lit up with surprise. "Thank you so much, Joshua!"

Peggy kissed me on the cheek and I blushed. Then she returned to her classroom, forgetting all about her excuse to use the rest room. Feeling very pleased, I skipped down the hall to the front door. My grandparents were just arriving so I handed the 'Baby's Breath' to Grandma.

"This flower is for you, Grandma," I said and gave her a hug.

"Well, thank you, Joshua," my grandmother said. "How lovely."

I walked my grandparents to my classroom and held the door while they walked in. I introduced them to my teacher, Mrs. Jones, and then showed them all of the schoolwork displayed on the walls.

"This is my drawing," I said pointing to some artwork on the wall. "It's a picture that I drew of myself."

"That's a fine looking boy in that picture," Grandpa said, "you did a nice job, Josh; he looks a lot like you." He patted me on the back.

"It is a good drawing, Joshua," Grandma said. "I wish that I could draw that well."

"The only thing I can draw is flies in the summertime," Grandpa said and then he laughed.

I looked at him, confused as to why he was laughing.

"Joshua, it's time for you to escort your guests to the lunchroom," Mrs. Jones said. "Thank you so much for visiting us today. It meant a great deal to Joshua."

I took my grandmother's hand and led the way to the cafeteria. We had pizza that day. I handed each of my grandparents a tray and then took one for myself. We each took a plate with one slice of pepperoni pizza, some salad, and a container of applesauce.

"Let's sit over here," I said, pointing to my usual table.

We sat down and my grandparents noticed the other children with their grandparents. Each of the other women had been given a red carnation and a sprig of Baby's Breath. I focused on my lunch and began taking the pepperoni off of my pizza.

"Why, Joshua, don't you like the meat?" Grandpa asked.

"No, would you like it?" I asked, picking it up and offering it to him with my bare hands.

"Why, sure, thanks, Josh," Grandpa said. "I hate to see good food going to waste." He smiled when I used my fingers to put the round, red meat slices on his plate.

I gobbled down my pizza, but didn't touch my salad or my applesauce.

"May I please be excused?" I asked.

"Are you finished eating?" Grandpa asked. "There's still a lot of food on your plate."

"I'm full, you can have it," I said. "May I please be excused?"

"Well, OK…" Grandma said.

She wondered what I was planning. I stood up from my seat, left my tray on the table, and gave each of them a quick kiss on the cheek.

"Thanks for coming," I said, as I ran outside to play tag with Peggy.

My grandparents laughed.

"No wonder that boy is so thin," my grandmother said, "he sure doesn't eat much. It wasn't too long ago Jamie told me she used to find crackers, fruit, half eaten sandwiches, all kinds of food hidden under his pillow, in his drawers, and tucked behind shoes in the back of his closet. I understand foster children are sometimes food insecure and worried about when they might eat again. He doesn't seem too worried about food now."

"No, and that's a good thing. It looks to me like he's more interested in that little blonde than he is in his lunch," Grandpa said. "That little girl with the pony tail and holding that red carnation is a real pretty little girl."

They finished their meals, took the empty trays and dishes to the drop off counter, and left the school. Later that evening they called Mom on the phone. Mom wasn't too pleased when she found out what I had done with the carnation and Baby's Breath. My grandparents didn't seem to mind.

"Oh, cut him a break," Grandma said to my mother, "He's only in fourth grade. I thought it was cute."

"I think he's a pretty clever kid," Grandpa said. "He was pretty smart to think of splitting the flowers between his girlfriend and his grandmother."

"I can't believe he left you in the lunchroom and went out to play tag with that little girl," Mom said shaking her head.

"That boy's got good taste, Jamie," Grandpa said, "He'll be OK."

"You know," Grandma said to my mom, "His teacher, Mrs. Jones, told us that no child from her class has ever had grandparents visit before. Now that's a shame."

"It certainly is and thank you for doing that for Josh," Mom said. "I'm sure that he appreciated your visit."

And she was right, I did!

CHAPTER

8

Nightmares

"Mom!" I awoke with terror and cried out for her in the middle of the night. "Mom!" I sounded a second blood-curdling scream. Before the word was out of my mouth, the light was on and my mother was at my bedside.

"It's OK, Honey, I'm here," she assured me as she wrapped me in her arms. "Shhhhhhhh, shhhhhhhhh, you're safe now, Sweetheart, nobody's going to hurt you."

"He tried to kill me," I sobbed to my mom. "In my dream Uncle Joey was trying to shoot me with a pistol."

When I was younger I lived for a while with Uncle Joey and Aunt Suzette. She was nice, but Uncle Joey was really mean when he was drunk. He abused my brother and me, and I'm still really mad about what he did to me.

"Oh, Joshie," Mom said. "I'm so sorry. It's OK now, Baby, you're safe now."

"Does Uncle Joey know where I am?" I asked. "Can he find me? Will he hurt me?"

"No, Josh, he doesn't have any idea where you are," Mom said as she looked me in the eyes. "He'll never find you or hurt you again, I promise."

My mom was worried about the weekly nightmares that I had. She and Momma B took me to a psychiatrist. That's a doctor who helps you when you have emotional problems. Mom asked him to figure out how to help me.

"Hi, Joshua, I'm Doctor French," the doctor said shaking my hand. "Your mother asked me to talk with you to see if I can figure out some ways to help you feel better. We're going to step into this room next door and talk for a while today. Your moms will be waiting right here for you when we finish. OK?"

"OK," I said.

Mom had told me that Dr. French was going to try and help us put an end to the nightmares. I was all for that.

"I'd like your help answering some questions. Will you do that for me?" Dr. French asked.

"I guess so," I said.

Dr. French let me play with some dump trucks while we talked about my past. He asked me a lot of questions about my birth parents and Uncle Joey and Aunt Suzette. We spent a long time together. When we were finished he talked with my folks while I played on the floor.

"Joshua has a diagnosis with a couple areas of concern," he said. "He is ADHD which stands for Attention Deficit Hyperactivity Disorder. That means that he has difficulty focusing his attention and needs to move around frequently. We can help his ADHD with some prescription medications."

"You said 'a couple areas of concern.' What else is there?" Mom asked.

"He suffers from 'PTSD' which stands for Post Traumatic Stress Disorder. It means that he remembers and relives the abuse from when he was much younger. The PTSD is causing his nightmares and he could continue to have these for quite some time."

"How do we help him?" Momma B asked.

"I'd suggest Play Therapy. It would be good for him to work through his anger towards his uncle. There are a couple of places in town that work with young kids like this," he said handing a sheet of paper to my mother. "Good luck."

Mom got me connected with a woman who did Play Therapy. After several sessions of working with me, the therapist met with my folks.

"There is nothing else that I can do for Joshua," she told them. "Josh is making nice with the bad guys. He's serving coffee and donuts to them. I'm sorry, but I've done all that I can for him."

"What else do you think we can do to help him?" Mom asked. "He's still angry and he's still acting out at school and at home. He still has an occasional nightmare."

"I'm sorry, but I don't know what to tell you. I wish I did," the therapist said shaking her head. "Good luck," she said and walked away from us.

"We need to find additional therapy services for Josh," Momma B said. "He's not over his issues if he's still acting out."

"I agree," my mom said. "We'll keep looking for help. In the meantime, let's see what we can do to improve his self-esteem. Skating lessons were great for Josh. Let's get him enrolled in some other activities that will build his skills and confidence."

"Great idea," Momma B agreed. "And let's see what else we can do to promote his identity as an African American. I sure wish Big Brothers and Big Sisters would find us a black role model. He's been on their waiting list for months now. Having a positive black role model would really help him, I think."

"It sure would," Mom said.

CHAPTER

Therapy

Mom asked LaTisha, my former foster mom, for the name of a good child therapist. She suggested a woman named Katy Wilson. My moms and I went together to our first meeting with Katy. She asked me a few questions and then let me play with the stuff in her toy box.

"It seems that Josh is very angry because of the neglect and abuse he suffered as a youngster," Katy told my parents. "He's insecure and desperate for attention, any kind of attention. It doesn't matter to him if people are praising or scolding, as long as they see him. He wants someone to know that he exists."

"We've worked hard at improving his self-esteem and praising him when he has appropriate behaviors," Mom said. "It's difficult to reward him when he acts out, lies, and steals."

It's true that I did those things. I lied about stuff because I didn't want to get caught and get in trouble at home. Then my parents would be mad at me and I'd have consequences and my TV, Game Boy, and computer privileges would be taken away.

I stole because I wanted things. I used to take things from my parents, teachers, and kids at school, stores, and even the veterinary clinic that my folks owned. It was easy to steal things, but I usually got caught sooner or later.

"Maybe he steals as a result of the neglect he experienced as a young child," Katy said.

"But he has everything he needs now," Mom said. "How long will this go on? We have a rule, 'Nothing comes into this house without my approval.' We have that rule because he's always showing up with toys and pens and things that he's taken from someone. I make him return the item and apologize, but he just keeps stealing."

"And sometimes he's defiant at home," Momma B said. "We knew that Josh would have a "Honeymoon" period, a time when he would be on his best behavior at home. Well, that time is definitely over."

"It seems that Joshua is testing our love," Mom said. "Every day he pushes the limits to see if we are really committed to him."

"Josh isn't ready to trust the adults in his life," Katy said. "That's going to take a lot of time and consistency."

"Josh was diagnosed with ADHD," Momma B said. "I understand that he has difficulty staying focused and sitting still, but what about the disruptions that he causes in class?"

"Because of his anger issues, Josh's teachers decided that he needed to be in special education classes," Mom said. "His IQ is in the normal range, but he may have learning disabilities. Special education classes are smaller and give him more one-on-one attention. Josh is in a self-contained classroom because of his anger and emotional problems."

"EEEEaaaaaaaaaawwwwwwwwwwwwwwww," a loud noise came from my lips and I giggled.

"Joshua, why did you do that just now?" Katy asked.

"I guess 'cuz I felt like it," I said.

"Do you make those noises in school?" Katy said.

"Sometimes," I said.

"What happens when you do that?"

"My teacher says, 'Joshua, stop disrupting class,'" I said mimicking my teacher's female voice.

"But I like making weird noises, it makes the kids laugh."

"So you enjoy being the class clown?" Katy asked.

"Yeah, it's fun."

"That brings up another issue," Mom said. "Josh claims to have a lot of friends, but he usually doesn't even know his classmates' first names, let alone their last names."

"And no one calls or invites him to do anything. His relationships are all very surface. It's really very sad," said Momma B.

"EEEEaaaaaaaawwwwwwwwwwwwwwwwww," I went again.

"OK, Josh, no one is laughing here. I need you to stop making those noises," Mom said.

Katy and my folks continued talking.

"EEEaaaaaaaaawwwwwwwwwwwwwwwwww," I yelled again.

"Joshua that is not acceptable behavior. Take a time out in that corner," Mom said pointing to the area farthest from the toy box. "And leave all of the toys here."

I walked over and sat down on the floor. I began picking at the carpet. It sounded like a cat sharpening its nails on a rug. Then I lifted myself off the floor with my arms and dropped back to the ground with a 'huff.' I did that several times before getting bored and losing interest. Closing my eyes, I took a nap.

"Joshua's teacher sends home notes about his behaviors," Mom said. The school calls and asks me what they should do. Shoot, they're supposed to be the experts on dealing with kids who have emotional issues. I've suggested they move his desk right next to their desk or try moving him far away from the other students. Nothing works."

"His teachers have taken recess away from him, given him detention, lectured and threatened him," Brooke added. "They've tried rewarding Josh with toys and food. Nothing makes an impact and he continues to disrupt the class. It's like he doesn't care."

"And it takes him a very long time to get his work done," Mom said. "Special education teachers don't give much homework. I asked why he never had homework and was told, 'Why cause another battle for the parents at home?' If they do give an assignment, it's usually some sort of a project. And Josh doesn't finish his projects. His teacher told me that even in class he doesn't finished his work or turn it in. He just doesn't seem to care."

"Josh's teacher said that he tries to be the first student finished with his test papers," Momma B said. "He doesn't bother reading the directions or checking his answers. He just wants to hand his test in first. It's like he thinks it's all a game and the person who finishes first wins."

"And he never studies for his quizzes or tests," Mom added. "We'll ask him about homework, projects, and tests and he'll say he doesn't have any. Then we get his report card and find out that he's not doing anything in class except acting out and socializing."

"Does Josh have any dreams for his future?" Katy asked.

"Oh yes," Mom said, "But they aren't realistic. One day he wants to be a magician, then a business man, then a veterinarian, then a chef. It's fine that his goals change, but he doesn't understand that he needs to study and do well in school in order to get into college."

"Let me recap," Katy said, "Joshua has a normal IQ and is in a self-contained classroom, which he disrupts frequently. He has outbursts in class and doesn't stop when he is asked. He enjoys the attention of being a class clown, thinks everyone is his friend, yet he doesn't have any close friends. Nobody calls to invite him to play. Is that correct so far?"

"Yes, and the fact that sometimes he tries to push every button we have in an effort to drive us crazy," Mom said.

"Josh lies, steals, and is defiant. He doesn't seem to be able to follow directions. It's like he thinks the rules don't apply to him," Katy said.

"Exactly," Mom said.

"Let me discuss Joshua's behaviors with my supervisor and see what we might be able to put in place to help all of you."

"Thank you," my folks said at the same time.

"Joshie, wake up, Honey, it's time to go now," Mom said.

"See you next week, Joshua," Katy said. "Goodbye."

"Goodbye, Katy, thanks for letting me play with your toys," I said as we walked out the door.

CHAPTER
10
Helpful Ideas

At our next meeting, my therapist, Katy, told us about several suggestions she had to help my family and me.

"You told me that Joshua recently had a physical examination, right?" Katy asked. "And that his physical health is fine?"

"Yes," Mom said.

"And Dr. French gave him an IQ test and a psychological evaluation.

You said that Josh has a normal IQ, and that he has a diagnosis of PTSD and ADHD?"

"That's correct."

"OK, I just wanted to make sure. Is he taking medications to help with his ADHD?"

"Yes, he's on 'Strattera and Risperdal," Mom answered.

"Do you think the medications are helping?"

"Yes, we noticed an immediate improvement when he started the Risperdal. He isn't as combative now." Momma B said.

"Good, I think that we should schedule a regular program of monthly weekend respite for Joshua," Katy said.

"What's a respite?" I asked.

"That's when you spend a weekend with someone other than your parents taking care of you," Katy said. "It gives you and your moms a little break from each other."

"That sounds good, let's make it happen," Momma B said.

"It would be good if Josh had a black man to hang out with," Katy said next. "What about enrolling him in a program like Big Brothers and Sisters?"

"He's already registered," my mom told her. "He's been waiting for a match with an African American man for several months already."

"That's great, I hope that he finds a match soon," Katy said. "In the meantime, I could schedule one of our interns to come out once a week and spend a couple of hours with Josh. They could shoot baskets or something. It wouldn't be a black male, but it would bring a male presence into his world. What do you say, Josh? Would you like to hang with one of our guys once a week?"

"That'd be tight," I said. "Excuse me, may I use the restroom?"

Katy pointed to the men's room door and away I went.

"Since Josh has difficulty in social settings and in making friends, I'd like to invite him to participate in a weekend program that I run. It's called 'Saturday Group' and we spend three hours working on social skills. We play games, eat lunch, work on appropriate behaviors, and at the end of the day, everyone gets a prize. It would be perfect for Josh."

"That sounds great," Mom said, as I walked back into the room. "Is it OK if I tell him about it now?"

Katy smiled and nodded, "Please do."

"Josh, you've been invited to join a group of kids that get together every Saturday. They play games and eat lunch together and you'll even get a prize at the end of the day. Katy will be there too. What do you say?"

"Hey, that sounds cool, thanks!"

"I'll put these plans into action and we'll see how things are going," Katy said.

On Saturday, my mom took me to Saturday Group. It was kind of fun because I got to play with other kids and pick a toy at the end of the morning. They even had a graduation ceremony when I successfully completed the program and I had my picture taken wearing a long black robe.

I started going on respite for one weekend a month. Somebody told my folks about a black man who did respite, so I started spending my respite weekends with him. He was nice but there were way too many kids at his house for me to get any of his time and attention.

A college guy started coming to my house and we played basketball together. He came every week and we'd shoot hoops. It was fun hanging out with him. Sometimes we'd talk a little bit about my anger towards my Uncle Joey. The college guy suggested that I write my uncle a letter and tell him about my feelings.

"Go ahead and tell your uncle how angry you are and why," he said.

"I bet you'll feel better once you get some of that off your chest."

After a couple of months the college guy graduated from college so he stopped coming around.

I did write my uncle a letter and then I asked my mom to mail it for me. In my letter I told Uncle Joey about how mean he was to me and to my brother and sister. I told him that it wasn't right for him to treat us that way. I told him that he shouldn't have hurt me. Then I said that now I was adopted and that he couldn't find me or hurt me ever again. I signed my letter:

> "Love,
>> Joshua Radford Carson."

CHAPTER

11

First Christmas

It was my first Christmas with my new family and Mom and I were at the mall. I spotted Santa Clause sitting on a big red chair and pointed him out to my mom.

"Look, Mom," I said, "its Santa!"

"Do you want to go see him?" she asked.

"Yes, please."

We walked to the end of the line and within a few minutes Santa was greeting me with a smile and motioning for me to come closer to him.

"Come on up here," Santa said, "so we can have a little talk."

I moved so that I was standing in front of him.

"Would you like to sit on my lap?" Santa asked.

"It's okay, Josh, if you want to." Mom said. So I climbed onto his ample thighs.

"So Joshua, how's it going for you?" he asked.

"Really well," I answered.

"Glad to hear that. What's been happening since the last time I saw you?"

"I got adopted and that's my mom."

"Well that's wonderful news, Josh. I can tell by the smile on your mom's face that she's happy about it."

"Yeah, I have a great family now, with two moms and a lot of dogs and cats."

"I'm so happy to hear that. Now tell me what you would like for Christmas this year."

I whispered into his ear. Santa gave me a puzzled look.

"Tell me more about that, Son."

I leaned closer and explained again what I wanted. I turned my head around and showed him my angel kiss.

"Well, Josh, that's a very unusual request," he said. "I can't promise you'll get your wish for Christmas this year, because Christmas is only a few days away. But I'll see what I can do for next year, OK?"

I nodded, "OK, and thank you, Mr. Clause."

"Call me Santa. After all, we've known each other for quite a while now."

"OK, Santa," I said.

"Shall we take a photo together?" he asked, looking at my mom.

"Yes, please," she said. I looked at my mom and she had tears in her eyes. She calls those her 'happy tears.' She explained to me that sometimes her heart gets so full of joy that tears spill out of her eyes. Happy tears are a good thing.

Santa gave me a candy cane and said goodbye. Another boy was waiting to talk with this important man.

"So what did you tell Santa you wanted for Christmas, Josh?" Mom asked, while we waited for our photo to print.

"Is it okay if I tell you some other time?" I asked. "Santa told me that I had an unusual wish, and that he'd try to get it for me next Christmas."

"Hmmmmm, well, all right," Mom said.

Santa's helper handed Mom my picture and she showed it to me.

"Nice photo, Honey," she said with a smile.

"Thanks."

I took her hand and we headed home. That evening, Momma B, Mom, and I all went out together to pick out our Christmas tree. I knew right away which tree I wanted. It was very round with lots of branches.

"We'd like that tree," Momma B said, pointing to the one that I had selected. "The tree that's about as wide as it is tall."

Mom paid for the tree and soon it was in our living room surrounded by boxes of holiday decorations. My mom found a cassette tape of some old Christmas music and put it on to play.

"When I was growing up," she said, "my family always played this Christmas music when we decorated our trees."

She began singing the songs along with the people on the tape.

"Josh, do you like to decorate the Christmas tree?" Momma B asked.

"I don't know, I've never done it before."

"Well, we'll have to do something about that now, won't we?" she said, smiling.

I helped my folks untangle the strings of lights and test them before they went on the tree. Then it was time for ornaments.

"Josh, we have a special early present for you," Mom said, with her hands behind her back.

"What is it?" I asked.

"It's your very own Christmas ornament," she said, as she held a small box out to me. "Open it."

Inside was a figurine of a little black boy sitting on the lap of a black Santa.

"Is this really for me?" I asked.

"It sure is, Sweetheart," Mom said. "And every year you'll get another ornament to add to your collection."

Mom lifted me up so that I could hang my Santa high on the tree.

"Thanks, Moms, I love it," I said.

"You're welcome, Honey," my moms said together.

"Josh, would you please help me hang these little wooden stars, trees, and angel ornaments that Grandpa made for us?" Mom asked.

"Sure," I said. "But how did he make them?"

"Grandpa makes things out of wood," Mom told me.

"I want to make things out of wood, too."

"Well, maybe you and Grandpa can make some things together."

"That'd be tight."

"We have a few items that go around the bottom of the tree, Josh," Mom said, handing me three wooden reindeer.

"Did Grandpa carve these reindeer out of wood, too?"

"He sure did."

"Hey look, it's Rudolph!" I said holding up the animal with the bright red nose.

We found the angel and Mom lifted me up so that I could place her at the top of the tree. Momma B plugged her in and her face began to glow.

"That's nice," I said.

"Yes, it is," Momma B said. "It's nice to have our Guardian Angel keeping watch over us."

"Josh, would you get the little manger out of that box, and put it under the tree?" Mom asked. "This baby doll goes in it."

I found the wooden manger and reached for the doll that Mom was holding.

Jan Crossen

"Is that supposed to be Baby Jesus?" I asked.

"Yes." Momma B said.

"But, that baby has dark skin," I said.

"Well, what makes you think Jesus didn't have dark skin?" Mom asked. "He certainly wasn't white. He came from a part of the world where people have dark skin."

I'd never seen a dark skinned Jesus before. I cradled the baby doll in my arms and then gently placed it in the bed.

"Sleep tight, Baby Jesus," I whispered. "Sweet dreams."

"Sleep tight is right, Joshie," Mom said. "It's time for you to go to bed, too."

"I need to get a snack for Santa first, OK?"

I found some home made chocolate chip cookies that Momma B had baked. I filled a plate and poured a glass of milk. I put ice in the glass to keep the milk nice and cold for when Santa arrived.

I kissed Momma B goodnight and then Mom tucked me into bed. That night I slept very well. I trusted that Santa would find me living with my new family, and that our Guardian Angel would watch over us. I was right about both things. I had a wonderful Christmas with my forever family.

CHAPTER

12

Buffalo Soldiers

"Josh, do you know what tomorrow is?" Mom asked.

"Monday," I answered.

"That's right, and it's Martin Luther King Jr. Day," she said. "Brooke has to work, but you and I are going to City Park to take part in the celebration."

"What are we going to celebrate?" I asked.

"Well, tomorrow is a national holiday to honor Dr. King. There will be speakers and music, dancing, and food. It'll be fun. Before we go, I want to read that book I gave you on Dr. King. Would you get it for us please?"

"OK," I said and I handed her the book.

Mom and I sat on the couch and took turns reading pages from the book about Dr. King.

"I have a dream!" I read the words the way I had heard Dr. King say them on a video that Mom bought for me.

"Wow, Josh, you did that very well," Mom said. "It really brings the story to life when you read it that way. I bet you'd be a good actor."

"Thank you," I said with a smile.

We finished the story and talked about how important it is for everyone to have equal rights.

"You know, Honey, if Dr. King and his supporters hadn't done the work they did for civil rights, you probably would not be my son."

"What do you mean?" I asked.

"People, like Dr. King, were responsible for African Americans to finally have the legal rights and opportunities they deserve," Mom said. "Black people were denied these rights in the past. Dr. King was killed because he fought for equality. He knew that the color of someone's skin wasn't important. He wanted all people to have the same rights and privileges. He led the way to change through peaceful, non-violent methods. If it weren't for Dr. King and his efforts for civil rights, I never could have adopted you. The law and society would never have allowed it."

"Wow," I said. "I never knew that."

The next day Mom and I attended the celebration for Dr. King. It was held outdoors at a park. There were at least a thousand people sitting on benches and blankets. They were listening to the speakers and enjoying the people who were singing and dancing.

The mayor spoke for a few minutes. Then some gospel singers sang some songs, and then a high school band played something called the steel drums. After that we heard some Hip-Hop music and then some black tap dancers gave a performance.

A bald, black man with a gray beard talked about Dr. King and said some of Dr. King's "I Have a Dream" speech. Finally, we watched about a dozen black soldiers give a marching demonstration. Mom told me they were the Buffalo Soldiers.

"Josh, do you know who the Buffalo Soldiers were?" Mom asked.

"No, ma'am," I said. "I've never heard of them."

"Well, around the time of the Civil War, the United States government established an all black cavalry," Mom said.

"What's a cavalry?" I asked.

"That's a good question. A cavalry is a military troop that rides horses. They used to travel all over the Southwestern United States on horseback."

"What did they do?" I asked.

"They kept the peace, built roads, protected the mail carriers, and fought in the Indian Wars. And the Buffalo Soldiers were even our nation's first Park Rangers."

"That's pretty cool," I said. "But why were they called Buffalo Soldiers?"

"That name was given to them by the Native Americans from the Cheyenne Nation. The Cheyenne warriors respected the black soldiers as fierce fighters. And the soldiers' dark, curly, black hair reminded the Natives of the fur on a buffalo. The name 'Buffalo Soldier' was a term of admiration and honor."

"That's tight," I said, in appreciation.

"Yes it is, Josh, yes it is."

CHAPTER

13

Skate World

The next fall, I was in the fourth grade at Lineweaver Elementary School and my school was having a skating party as a way to raise money.

"Mom, may I please go to our school skating party?" I asked. "It sounds like fun and I really want to go."

"Do you know how to skate, Honey?" Mom asked.

"No, but I can learn," I said confidently. "Pretty please?"

Mom laughed and agreed to take me to Skate World later that night. I could hardly wait to get in the door. Popular music blasted from the DJ stand. A lot of kids from my school were already on the floor.

"You'll need some rental skates," Mom said, leading the way to the counter. "Size 3 please," she said to the teenage boy working the area.

I lifted the heavy boots from the counter top and we headed for the benches. Mom helped me lace the skates so that they were tight. Hoping to learn this new skill, I studied the other kids as they skated past.

"Wish me luck," I said, holding onto the wall and inching my way onto the rink.

"Good luck," Mom said. "Have fun!"

Slowly I shuffled around the floor. It wasn't exactly skating but I was still on my feet and moving around the oval floor. The kids who had skated before blew past me. Some could skate forwards, backwards, and even dance to the music. They were good.

"OK, it's time for some skating games," the DJ said from atop his perch. His booth was at least four feet above the crowd so he had a good view of everything that was going on. I watched the games and races and I knew that they were way above my skill level. It was fun watching and being part of the school event.

The next day at breakfast mom asked, "Josh, are you interested in taking skating lessons? They offer them at Skate World and you could start this Saturday morning."

"That would be awesome!" I said, "Thanks, Mom!"

Saturday morning I was up, dressed, and eager for my first lesson. There were eight kids in my class. My teacher was an older woman who must have been skating since it was invented. She was very patient and worked with each of us by ourselves, while the other kids practiced.

Saturday morning at Skate World became a regular part of my schedule. I would rent my skates and carefully go onto the floor. Mom always waited during my lesson. Then she'd let me skate for a while and practice on my own when the rink opened to the public.

Skating lessons went on for eight weeks. I was skating well and my confidence grew as my skills improve.

CHAPTER

14 On Your Mark...

That spring my school sponsored another skate party and this time I was ready. It turned out the event was scheduled on the same day as my tenth birthday.

My folks took me to Skate World. I got my skates from the rental stand and confidently took to the floor. I was zipping along with the other kids, grooving to the music, and having a good time.

"OK, kids, it's time for the games and races," the DJ said.

The races were divided into boys and girls by age group. Because it was my birthday I would compete against the boys in the 10-12 age group. They called for the younger girls to race first.

Next, it was competition for the younger boys. Finally, they called my group and I joined the older boys at the start line. All of them were taller and bigger than I was. That wasn't going to scare me. Finding my spot near the front of the pack, I was ready to race.

"On your mark, get set, GO!" the DJ shouted.

I took off with my arms and legs pumping. I moved closer to the inside of the track. 'Skate, skate, skate, skate' I kept telling myself. We were half-way around the rink and I was one of six guys in the lead.

'Faster, faster,' I told myself, 'go, go, go, go."

I pushed harder. One boy slipped and fell. He knocked over two other skaters with him. Now there were only three of us left.

"Go Josh, go!" I could hear my moms cheering for me. A lot of kids were cheering and yelling too. It was so exciting! Then, it seemed like there was total silence and everything began to move in slow motion.

Looking over my right shoulder, I saw a tall, white, kid with long, brown hair skating next to me. He was about to throw an elbow in my direction. Using a cross-over step, I avoided his jab and moved out in front of him. I grunted, leaned forward, and crossed the line first. I HAD WON THE RACE!

I threw my arms up into the air in victory. It felt so good! Showing all of my pearly whites, I skated over to my parents.

"I've never won a race before in my life!" I shouted to them.

Kids gave me high fives and slapped me on the back. My folks were excited and hugged and congratulated me.

"It's time to award the prizes to our winners," the DJ said. "Would the winner from each race please come to the DJ stand to get your trophy?"

Joining the other three winners, the DJ gave each of us a small gold trophy. On top was a roller skater with his arms up in the air. It was the same victory sign that I used after winning the race. Turning ten years old was an awesome birthday, and one that I'll never forget.

CHAPTER

15

Karate Kid

"Mom, I want to take karate lessons," I said one day in early September. "I think they teach karate at the YMCA and it would be really cool if I could learn how to do that."

"We had recently watched the Karate Kid movie and I pictured myself being like Daniel LaRusso, the star of the show. 'Wax on, wax off, paint the fence.' I dreamed of doing that famous one-legged crane kick and winning the girl and the tournament at the same time. My parents decided that taking skating lessons had been good for my self-esteem so they agreed to let me take karate lessons.

"OK," Mom said, "you can give karate a try. We'll need to find you a gi to wear."

"What's a gi?" I asked.

"A gi is the karate uniform," Momma B said. "It's those white baggy pants with the big shirt that you tie with a belt. Everyone in your class will wear one."

We got my gi and I was ready for my first class. My folks dropped me off and then went to workout in the fitness room at the YMCA. An hour and a half later they picked me up at my classroom door.

"So how did it go, Josh?" Mom asked.

"Great," I said. "Karate is really fun!"

"Do you like your teacher?" Momma B asked.

"You mean Sensei," I said. "That means teacher or master."

Just then my Sensei walked out into the hall. He waved to us and we waved back.

"Wow," Momma B said. "He's a Black Belt."

"What does that mean?" I asked.

"It means you'd better pay attention in class because he's really good at karate," she teased me.

"I see that most of the kids in your class have white belts like you," Mom said. "But look at those kids. That boy and girl are wearing different colored belts. The boy has on a yellow belt and the girl's belt is green."

"That's because they're assistants to Sensei," I said. "They aren't beginners like the rest of us. You can tell that they've taken karate before. Sensei said the boy has already earned the first level belt with color, and the girl has earned her second level belt."

"Cool," Mom said.

"Way cool," said Momma B.

"So what'd you learn today?" Mom asked.

"We learned to bow," I said. "We bow to Sensei to show respect. We also bow before class starts and to each opponent before we fight. Then we bowed to Sensei again at the end of the lesson."

"That's impressive," Momma B said.

"Sensei wants us to do ten push-ups at the beginning of every class. That was too easy for me so I did twenty instead. See my muscles?" I flexed my right arm and then my left.

"Those are some nice looking biceps, Josh," Mom said.

"Thanks," I said, and then kissed each of my arms.

"Tonight we learned how to fall and hit the ground without getting hurt. We did a lot of tumble rolls and slapped our hands down hard on the mat. I even learned some moves to take my opponent down."

"It sounds like you had a good workout tonight."

"Yes, ma'am," I said. "And now I'm starving!"

My folks laughed as we climbed in the car.

"I'm hungry too," Mom said. "Let's see if we can find something to eat around here.

"Hey," I said, "how about pancakes?"

My karate lessons lasted for three months.

"Class, this week we have our final two practices before the competition," Sensei said. "The competition is on Saturday, starting at 9:00 a.m."

"What competition?" I asked.

"What do we do?" Another student asked. "How does this work?"

"Each of you has been learning a certain routine," Sensei said. "Now it is time for you to perform it in front of the judges. I'll be a judge and so will three other master Senseis. Do you have any other questions?"

No one spoke or raised a hand. We sat on the floor shaking our heads.

All week long I practiced my routine. I'd put on my gi and go into the backyard to practice. If it was dark or raining, Mom let me move the furniture in the living room and practice in there.

Mom got me up early on Saturday morning so that I could have a good breakfast before the competition. I put on my gi and was ready.

My parents were a little nervous and very excited for me. They found two seats in the front row so that they could take a lot of pictures of me when I did my routine.

"Good luck, Josh!" they said when Sensei called my name.

I walked to the center of the floor looked at Sensei and bowed. "Begin," he said. Then he sat down next to the other judges.

I focused my mind on the routine and did my moves with power and confidence. I finished and bowed at the judges. Sensei excused me from the floor. My folks cheered, clapped, and whistled. I smiled with embarrassment.

At the end of the day, Sensei gave out awards.

"Joshua Carson," he said.

I walked to where he was standing and bowed. He bowed back at me and handed me a Certificate of Achievement. I had accomplished my goal and was proud of myself and of my success in karate. Momma B framed my karate certificate and hung it on my bedroom wall.

Driving home that afternoon I told my folks, "Thank you for giving me karate lessons. I liked karate but I don't really want to do that anymore."

My parents sighed and then smiled, shaking their heads.

CHAPTER

16

Ms Bianca

"Mom, I want to tap dance," I said.

"I take it you liked the movie 'Tap' that we watched the other night?" Momma B said. Gregory Hines and Sammy Davis Jr. were tap dancers in this old movie. They were great.

"Yeah, it was the bomb!" I said. "I bet I can dance like that."

My folks decided that tap dancing would be another good way to build my confidence. They agreed to look for a teacher and a few days later my mom told me the good news.

"Josh, I've located that African American woman whose dance class performed at the Martin Luther King celebration. Her name is Bianca Wheeler and she teaches dance. She has a new tap class starting this coming Saturday morning," Mom said. "Do you still want to dance?"

"Yes, ma'am, thank you," I said with a smile. "I need tap shoes."

"You're right. We'll see about getting some today," Momma B said.

It took a while, but we found a store that sold kids' tap shoes. They cost $75.

"Josh, these are very expensive shoes," Mom said. "If we're going to spend this kind of money, I need you to tell me that you aren't going to quit after a month or two."

"I won't quit, I really want to dance," I said.

We bought the shoes and I couldn't wait to try them out. As soon as we returned home, I grabbed my boom-box and new tap shoes and ran to the garage. I started dancing, just like Gregory Hines, all over the cement floor.

On Saturday morning Mom and I headed to Miss Bianca's class together. Her studio was on the second floor of an old building on the other side of town.

There were a dozen other black kids in my class. It was nice for me to be around other black people. My world was filled with white faces and this was a nice change.

An attractive black woman entered the room. She was about 5'5", with a thin build, and strong arms and legs. Her hair was long and wild. She wore it on top of her head, held back with a yellow elastic band. She greeted us with a warm smile.

"Welcome everyone," she said, "My name is Bianca Wheeler, you may call me Miss Bianca. I've been teaching dance lessons in this town for thirty years. I recognize some of you parents as former students of mine. It's nice to see you again, and to see so many wonderful new young faces. I'm looking forward to dancing with you."

I could tell Miss Bianca was a respected teacher. Everyone was quiet and paying attention when she spoke.

"Do you all know who started the art of tap dance?" she asked the class.

I looked around the room, but no one had an answer.

"Well, tap dance was started by African slaves a long time ago," Miss Bianca said. "You're going to learn a dance that was started by your ancestors. What do you think of that?"

"Tight," I answered.

"And who are you, young man?" she asked me.

"I'm Joshua Carson, ma'am. That's my mom over there." I said, pointing to where my mother was sitting. Mom waved at the introduction.

"It's nice to meet you Joshua," she said. "So who else do we have in this class?"

Miss Bianca listened while each student said his or her name.

"OK, everybody," she said. "Let's dance!" Miss Bianca walked over to the tape player and starting the music.

She clapped to the beat and then started doing some dance moves. We followed her lead. The rhythm of the metal taps sounded against the wooden floor.

'Tap, tap, clap, clap, tap, tap, clap, clap.'

"That's called a shuffle ball change," Miss Bianca said as she demonstrated the dance step.

For an hour and a half, I worked hard following her example and learning my tap steps. When class was over and we got home, I showed Momma B what I had learned in class.

"That's very impressive, Josh" Momma B said. "You've got great sense of rhythm. You must get that from your mom," she said with a smile.

The next week Miss Bianca told us that she had an announcement.

"We'll be learning a routine and giving a performance in a couple of months," she told us. "Your parents, family, and friends will be in the audience. So let's really focus and see what we can accomplish today."

We worked hard that day and every Saturday. Every night during the week I practiced on the cement floor of the garage at home. Before I knew, it was time for our show. My folks dropped me at the stage door and took a front row seat. They planned to video tape my dance.

Several other acts went on before it was time for our class of beginners. Finally, it was our turn.

"Clap-clap; clap-clap; clap-clap, clap-clap," our steps announced our arrival on stage as we jogged into position. Proudly we stood and smiled at the audience as we waited for our music to begin. I danced my very best and had a great time! Our time on stage went by quickly. It was hard to believe the music had stopped and we needed to leave the floor.

The audience erupted with applause as we left the stage. I smiled and threw kisses to them. It was great being on stage and the center of attention.

My parents had spent a lot of money on my tap shoes and dance lessons. Gas was expensive and mom had driven me across town every weekend for my classes. I had my moment in the spotlight. I wasn't sure how to tell them that I no longer wanted to continue with my tap dance lessons.

CHAPTER
17
Piano Guy

Momma B played piano when she was a young girl and her piano sat in the living room of our home. Sometimes I'd ask her if I could play it and most of the time she said "Yes."

"Moms, I want to take piano lessons," I said, one Sunday evening.

"Someone told me that playing a musical instrument helps kids do better in math," Mom said to her partner. "What do you think?"

"Well, Josh doesn't abuse my piano," Momma B said. "When he sits down to play, he usually comes up with pleasant sounds. Josh, you may practice on my piano as long as you continue to be respectful of it."

Mom found a piano teacher, Judy Kimutis, who was accepting new students. She was a petite woman who had been teaching children how to play piano for a long time. For a whole year I went to her house once a week for my lessons.

"We have two piano recitals each year," Mrs. Kimutis told Mom and me. "Our first one is scheduled in three months.

"What's a recital?" I asked.

"A recital is when you play the piano for an audience," said Mrs. Kimutis. For my students, the audience is usually just friends and family who come to hear you play."

"OK," I said. "I can do that."

"For our recitals, we play on a big, beautiful, black, grand piano. It belongs to the parents of one of my students. They graciously allow us to use it and their home for our recitals."

"Wow, I get to play on a grand piano?" I asked. "Sweet!"

"Well, you need to practice every day and memorize your music first," said Mrs. Kimutis. "You'll play one number by yourself, and then you and I will play a duet together. How does that sound?"

"Great!" I said.

"We have a lot of work to do to prepare for it," she said. "Let's get busy."

I practiced a lot so that I could memorize my musical pieces for the recital. My teacher expected us to perform without looking at the music, but it was always on the piano just in case we forgot.

Some days when I was supposed to be practicing I'd just sit at the piano and make up my own creations. I thought that was more fun.

"Josh, that was very nice," Mom said from the kitchen. "But it doesn't sound like either of the songs you're playing in the recital."

"I made it up," I said.

"Maybe you need to rehearse your recital songs first, and when you're finished practicing you can spend some time creating your own music."

"OK," I said. And I went back to practicing for my performance.

On the day of the recital I wore a nice shirt and my dress slacks. Our family friend, Jillian Johnson, went with my parents to see and hear me play. Jillian had attended my Naming Ceremony several months ago and was a special friend of our family.

"Are you nervous, Josh?" Jillian asked.

"No," I said shaking my head. "I'm ready."

"Break-a-leg," she said. "That's what you say to an actor before he goes on stage. I'm not sure what you're supposed to say to a musician to wish him good luck."

She smiled and gave me a hug. My moms hugged me too, and then I walked over to sit with the rest of the kids. Mrs. Kimutis had about six other kids play before she called my name. I walked to the front of the group to introduce myself and my music.

"Hello, my name is Joshua Radford Carson," I said, "and it is my pleasure to play for you today. I hope you enjoy my music."

I sat down and began to play. I didn't even think about the audience because I was really into my music. When I finished the song the people clapped and my teacher walked over to the piano. I stood up and announced that we would now play a duet. We sounded good together and it was fun.

After my second recital, I told my moms that I didn't want to take piano lessons anymore. I still liked the piano, but was tired of taking lessons. For a while I just wanted to make my own music.

That Christmas my parents surprised me with an electric keyboard. It was tight! It had 63 keys and I could add in 100 different background instruments. The keyboard came with a stand and a stool. I spent hours in my bedroom creating beats on my keyboard. I had found my groove.

CHAPTER

18

Hoops

"Mom, I want to play basketball," I said.

"OK, let me finish tossing the laundry in the machine and then I'll join you in the driveway," Mom said.

For my tenth birthday my folks had given me a new basketball and hoop. They asked a neighbor to install the backboard to the garage so our driveway became my court.

Mom used to be the head coach for high school girls' basketball team and an assistant coach for a college team. She taught me some ball handling skills and how to shoot and dribble. I liked shooting a lot and was a better offensive player than a defensive one. I spent hours outside in the driveway perfecting my long shot.

"I want to do more than just shoot, Mom," I said. "I need to play on a team. And play real games. Can you please find me a basketball team?"

"The City Recreation Department has youth basketball leagues," Mom said. "We'll find out when their leagues start."

Two weeks later I was registered for the upcoming season. We had practice or games every Tuesday and Friday evening.

On the first night of practice I had difficulty catching my breath after I ran down the floor a few times.

"Momma B, I'm having trouble breathing," I said. "Every time that I sprint down the floor, I start wheezing."

"Maybe you have exercise induced asthma," Momma B said.

"Coach has to take me out of the action so that I can catch my breath," I said. "I miss too much of the action just sitting on the sidelines!"

Mom took me to the doctor who said that I had a breathing problem which was caused by hard running.

"Joshua has asthma brought on by exercise," he said. "Let's try using this inhaler and see if it helps when he's playing sports. Joshua, take two puffs a few minutes before you play. And let me know if it doesn't help."

The next day at practice I used the inhaler. My breathing was a lot better and I was able to stay on the floor. I could play my games now and not get winded.

"Josh would you like to go to a summer basketball camp?" Mom asked. "It's Lute Olson's camp; he's the coach of the U of A men's basketball team."

"Duh…I know who Coach Olson is, Mom," I said. "And, yes, I'd love to go!"

Every day, for a week, my mom drove me to McKale Center on the University of Arizona campus. There were a lot of kids there, maybe as many as 300 or 400! Late in the afternoon, my mom came to pick me up.

"How was camp, Honey?" Mom asked when I got in the car.

"Good," I said.

Mom waited a couple of minutes hoping that I would say more. Finally she said, "Well, tell me about your day, Josh."

"I don't know what to say," I said.

"Well, tell me what you learned." Mom asked.

"I don't know." I said.

"Well, what did you do?"

"We played basketball."

"I know that, Josh. Can you tell me anything specific that you did?"

"I don't remember."

"Josh, you just left the gym after spending the entire day there. How can you not remember what you did?"

"I don't know."

"Hmmmmm. Did you have any trouble breathing?"

"A little."

"Did you use your inhaler?"

"Yes, ma'am."

"Do you still have it with you?"

"I don't know."

"Would you please look in your bag for it?"

I searched my backpack. "It's not here. It must be in the gym someplace."

"Oh, Josh," Mom said. "Let's go see if we can find it now. If we wait until tomorrow to look for it, you may never see it again."

Mom parked the car and we returned to the gym floor. Mom talked with one of the coaches and explained our problem. He asked some other kids to help us look for my inhaler. We looked all over the gym, the locker room, and where we ate lunch. Finally, a tall kid with short red hair walked up to us. He handed me my inhaler.

"I found this on the floor of one of the stalls in the restroom," he said.

"Thank you so much!" Mom said.

"Yeah, thanks, man," I said.

"No problem," he said, and he walked away.

"Honey, you need to keep better track of your things. It could be dangerous for you if you needed your inhaler, but couldn't find it."

"Okay," I said.

Mom and I returned to our car and headed home. She tried again to learn more about what happened at camp.

"Did you see Coach Olson today?" Mom asked.

"Yes, I even had my picture taken with him. He's going to autograph it for me."

"Wow, that'll be nice to have," Mom said.

At the end of the week the coaches handed out the photographs. Momma B framed mine and hung it on my bedroom wall.

"Josh, this is a nice photo of you and Coach Olson," Mom said. "He's a basketball legend, Honey; he's one of the best."

"Sweet," I said admiring the newest picture on my wall.

"Very sweet," Mom said, smiling.

CHAPTER

19

Whispering Hope Ranch

My parents discovered a wonderful place called Whispering Hope Ranch. It's way out in the country near Payson, AZ. My folks took me there for a visit. It was a long ride but definitely worth it. There are lots of beautiful Ponderosa Pine trees. Their trunks smell like vanilla, and I thought that was great. And this is elk country so we kept our eyes open for them along the road.

My mom is an excellent critter spotter. Grandpa taught her how to spot animals and she was teaching me. We knew that if there were any elk or deer around, my mom would point them out for us.

There is an electric gate at the entrance to the Ranch. Momma B pushed the button and the gate slowly swung away. Our car made a crunching sound as we drove the long driveway to the parking area.

"Hi, and welcome to Whispering Hope Ranch," a pretty, dark haired woman said as she stepped off the porch to meet us. "I'm Diane Reid, the founder of the Ranch."

My folks shook her hand and introduced each of us. A beautiful brown tabby cat ran towards us and rubbed against my leg. I reached down to pet her.

"That's Strawberry," Diane said. "She lives here along with a dozen other cats."

"I love cats," I said. "She's beautiful. Hi, Strawberry."

"We noticed the horses along the driveway," Momma B said. "What other animals do you have here?"

"Whispering Hope Ranch is home to over one hundred animals," Diane said. "We have horses, cows, goats, burros, pigs, emus, and llamas. We also have peacocks, ducks, dogs, cats, sheep, deer, and bunnies."

"Why are there so many animals?" I asked.

"Well, because this Ranch is a safe place for animals that have been abused or neglected," Diane said. "It is a forever home for those that have physical deformities. These animals never did any thing to hurt anyone, but they've been hurt by people. Now they have a safe place to live and they are learning to trust again. And at the same time, they are helping people heal, too."

"May we have a look around?" Mom asked.

"Of course," Diane said. "Let me get a golf cart and I'll take you on a tour myself. We have a lot of acres here so with the cart we can ride in style."

We climbed into the cart and Diane began her tour. She told us the name and story of each animal that we saw.

"People visit the Ranch to see and interact with the animals," Diane said. "Being with the animals helps them feel better and enjoy themselves."

"Can anybody come to the Ranch?" Mom asked.

"Yes, everyone is welcome, but we are especially helpful to someone who is grieving, going through a difficult time, or has an illness like diabetes, autism, Down syndrome, or cancer."

We came to a large pen which was the home to four llamas. Getting out of the cart Diane called "Tony, Tony, come here Sweetheart, come and meet Josh and his moms."

Four wooly llamas walked over to the fence.

"This handsome guy is Tony Llama," Diane said. "He really likes to give kisses. If you go stand by him, Joshua, I bet he'll give you a kiss."

I walked to the fence and looked at the large beast. He leaned his face over the wooden bar and tickled my cheek with a kiss.

"Oh, my goodness!" I said, rubbing my cheek. "That's funny!"

I touched my cheek to show him that I wanted another kiss. He quickly gave me a second one. We climbed back into the cart and continued our tour. Soon we arrived at some Indian tipis.

"What are the tipis for?" I asked Diane.

"When kids come for the Diabetes Camp, we use those for sleeping tents," she said.

"This place is amazing," Momma B said. "Who's your veterinarian?"

Diane talked with my folks about health care for the animals while I went off into the woods exploring by myself.

"We'd like to do something for the Ranch," Momma B said. "Would it help if we brought our hospital staff up here and examined and vaccinated the dogs and cats? We would donate our services and the vaccine."

"Wow," Diane said, "that would be wonderful!"

Momma B made arrangements for us to do just that. My folks had their first veterinary staff retreat at Whispering Hope Ranch that fall. Of course, I got to go too.

It was snowing when we arrived there on a Saturday afternoon for our retreat. It was the elk mating season and that evening we could hear the males bugling as they tried to attract females.

At dusk we took a ride in the car and saw at least a dozen elk. They're really big, and they came so close to our car. It was amazing!

The next day Momma B examined each dog and cat, and then she vaccinated them. I had a great time taking care of the animals and playing in the snow. Before we left to return to Tucson, I helped to make a snow-cat. I really liked being at the Ranch and could hardly wait for our next trip.

CHAPTER
20

Do You Believe in Magic?

When I was nine years old, my folks took me to Las Vegas, Nevada.

It was awesome! We got tickets to see Lance Burton, a professional magician, do his show. I was really into magic, and sat on the edge of my seat for the entire performance. That's when I knew that I wanted to do magic, too.

There was a magic shop in Vegas and my folks bought me a card trick. I studied and practiced that trick until I could do it perfectly. I asked everybody I knew if they wanted to see it.

My folks found a magician who also lived in Tucson. His name was George Cage and he and his wife, Colette, did a show at a local dinner theatre. They were also barbers so I started having George cut my hair. I'd ask Mom for a haircut even when I didn't need one, just so I could spend time with George.

"You like magic, huh?" George said to me on our first meeting.

"Yes, sir, I do!" I answered with a big grin.

He took out a quarter and bit it in half. He showed it to me and I could see that half of it was gone. Then he spit on it and the other half of the coin reappeared. It was tight!

"Do you know any magic?" he asked.

"I sure do," I said.

"Okay, then," he said. "Show me."

I did the only card trick that I knew.

"Very good, Josh. How would you like to work with me at my magic show on Saturday night? I perform at a dinner theatre every week and I'd love to include you in my act."

"Oh my, gosh, yes!" I said.

"You'll do what we call close-up magic."

"What's that?"

"It's magic that you perform with your audience sitting at a table right in front of you. You'll go up to a table while the people are waiting to be served their dinner. You ask them, 'May I please do some magic for you?' If they say 'Yes,' then you do your card trick. When it's over you bow, say 'Thank you,' and go to another table."

"That sounds great," I said.

"OK, Josh," he said, "but I have a couple of rules that you must follow."

I listened carefully to what he was about to say.

"Do you have a pair of dress slacks, white long sleeved shirt and a tie?" He looked at my mom who nodded her head.

"He has a black suit if you'd like him to wear that," Mom said.

"Perfect," George answered. "And you've got to have short clean fingernails. A magician always has manicured nails and clean hands."

Mom found out where I needed to be and at what time. She made reservations for Momma B and her to have dinner and see the magic show.

I had a blast doing up-close magic. Some of the people even tipped me. At the end of the night I had $10.00 in tip money in my pocket. Mom said since I was getting paid, I was a professional magician.

I started saving my weekly allowance money to buy more tricks at the magic store in town. Mom bought me books and a video on magic. I practiced and got pretty good.

My grandpa made me a magician's table and when I visited them, I would perform magic for my grandparents.

"How does he do that?" Grandma always used to say as she clapped for me.

"Will you do that again, Josh," Grandpa said, "but a little slower this time?" Grandpa would shake his head in amazement.

"I'm sorry, Grandpa," I said, "but a magician only does each trick one time," I'd tell them with delight.

My parent's had a good friend named June Murphy. Sometimes I was invited to go to lunch with June and my folks. One day she told me that she bought something for me on a recent trip that she took to Las Vegas. She handed me a large square box which I quickly opened.

"Josh, I saw this top hat, with these flashy gold sequins on it, and I just knew that you should have it," June said. "I thought you could use it for your magic."

"Wow!" I said admiring my gift and giving her a kiss on the cheek. "This is awesome! Thank you!"

June knew that I was dreaming of a career as a famous magician who performed in Las Vegas. Her gift was perfect for me.

CHAPTER

21

Martin Luther King III

A few months later my mom got a phone call from Diane Reid whom we met at Whispering Hope Ranch. Diane invited my family to go there for a special weekend. She said that she wanted us to meet Martin Luther King III. He's the son of the famous civil rights leader, Dr. Martin Luther King Jr., and he was going to be at the Ranch.

At the time, Mr. King had a cable television program called, "Wisdom of Dreams." He was doing a story about Whispering Hope Ranch.

It was Diane's dream to have a safe place where abandoned, abused, and neglected animals could live. It would also be a place where people who were sick or in pain could come. There they could spend time with the animals and the magic that happened between them would help to heal the pain of the people and of the animals.

My parents took me to the Ranch and I got to meet Mr. King. Diane introduced my parents and me to him. He was a really nice guy and I liked spending time with him.

"Mr. King, would you please autograph these two books that I brought with me?" I asked. "They're books about your dad."

"It would be my pleasure, Joshua," he said, as he wrote in my books.

"Thank you, Mr. King," my mom said. "Those are very special books and we'll keep them forever."

Mr. King asked my moms how we met and the story of how we became a family. Mom explained about me being a miracle baby because I was born two months early. She also told him about how I survived a coma and about my near drowning.

"You're one lucky guy, Joshua," he said, "you remind me of a lucky cat."

"'Cat's' my nickname," I said proudly.

"Well it certainly seems to fit you," Mr. King said.

I had my picture taken with Mr. King and then he asked my mom a question.

"I do a television program called 'Wisdom of Dreams," he said. "I'd like to interview you and Joshua about your adoption. And I'd like to talk about what Whispering Hope Ranch means to you. We'd include the interview in our segment about the Ranch. What do you say?"

"Josh would you like Mr. King to interview us?" Mom asked.

"Sure," I said.

So Mr. King, Mom, and I all sat down in front of the tipis. The camera man started shooting, and Mr. King asked questions.

"Joshua, why do you like coming to the Ranch?" he asked me.

"I love the freedom," I said. "I get to explore all over and play with the animals. I help feed and water them, and sometimes I get to drive the golf cart."

"Do you have a favorite animal here at the Ranch?" Mr. King asked.

"Well, yes, I have two favorites," I said, "Strawberry Cream Pie who is a beautiful cat; and Tony Llama, who is a llama. I like him because he gives kisses."

"Ms. Carson, why do you like to bring your son to Whispering Hope Ranch?"

"It's such a peaceful place with so many wonderful animals," Mom said. "Josh has a great time and it's so good for his self-esteem."

"How is coming here good for his self-esteem?" Mr. King asked.

"The Ranch is a safe place, the animals are gentle, and the staff and volunteers are welcoming. They make everyone feel important and valued," Mom answered. "Josh hangs with the men, helps them with the farm chores, and interacts with the animals and people. It's a great experience for him and for all of us."

Mom and Mr. King talked about my mother's dream of adopting a son. Mom said that the work done by Mr. King's father helped to make that dream come true.

At the end of the filming, I walked over to one of the tipis and I painted on the side of the tent with red paint. Other kids had written on them or made drawings. I wrote, 'Wisdom of Dreams.' My painting has been on that tipi ever since.

When we shook hands and said goodbye Mr. King handed me his business card and said, "If I can ever do anything for you, Josh, here is where you can find me. I'd love to help you in any way that I can."

"Sweet," I said. "Thank you, sir."

We said goodbye to Mr. King, Diane, the staff, and volunteers who work at the Ranch and headed back to Tucson. I never thought that I'd get to meet somebody as famous and important as Martin Luther King III.

CHAPTER

22 Heritage Camp

When I was thirteen, my family drove to Denver, Colorado so that I could attend the African American Cultural Heritage Camp. My parents thought it was important for me to experience more of my African American culture.

This was a camp for black or biracial kids who've been adopted by parents who aren't black. 'Biracial' means that a person has parents who are from two different races. Like maybe one parent is black and the other is white, Asian, or Indian. At the camp, I wasn't the only kid who had two white parents. But I was the only kid who had two moms.

"Josh, there will be African American kids at this camp," Mom said, "and there are also some kids who were adopted from Africa."

"And there are camps all summer long," said Momma B. "They have camps for kids who are adopted from Korea, China, Vietnam, India, Russia, and probably other countries too."

"Sweet," I said. "This should be fun!"

I had a blast at camp. The parents went to meetings while the kids did cool things. We beat on African drums, listened to rap music and got down with some hip-hop dancing. We even learned about some famous black people.

Each kid was given the name of an important black person. We found out about our person and then pretended to be him or her. The adults and other campers tried to guess who we were supposed to be.

I was Louie Armstrong. He was a famous jazz trumpet player. His nickname was 'Satchmo,' and he carried a white handkerchief with him to wipe the sweat from his face. When it was my turn, I jumped on the stage carrying a white Kleenex. I turned to the crowd with a big smile. I used a gravelly voice and said,

"Hey you cats, welcome to my gig. Ha, ha, ha. I was born in New Orleans, Louisiana back in 1901. My sweet Grandmother raised me 'til I was 12 years old. As a kid, I learned to play the trumpet, and later I started something called 'scat' singing. Some famous singers like Billie Holiday and Ella Fitzgerald followed this style of singing. One of my famous hit recordings was a song titled, "Hello Dolly." Can you guess who I am?"

Then I dabbed my forehead and pretended to play the trumpet. The grown-ups called out, "Satchmo, Louie Armstrong," they yelled. It was fun pretending to be somebody famous.

One day we had a picnic in the park. We ate fried chicken and played games. I had a great time.

"Parents, campers," the camp director said. "May I please have your attention?"

We all stopped what we were doing and came over to where she was standing so that we could hear what she was about to say.

"Tomorrow night is our last night," she said.

Everyone said, "Boooooooooooooooooooooo." We didn't like that camp was almost over.

"So we have a special party planned that should be a lot of fun."

The 'boos' turned into cheers.

"Yeahhhhhhhhhhhhhhhhhhhhhhhhhhhhhhhhhhh," we all cheered.

"We're having a themed party and our theme is the Roaring Twenties," she said. "The girls will come as flappers, those were flashy dancers from a long time ago, and the boys will be the handsome gentlemen."

The next evening everyone got dressed up. The girls wore short dresses and long beads. I put on my black suit, a white shirt, white socks, and black tie. I wore my shiny black dress shoes and a black hat.

The party room was decorated with a lot of little round tables that were covered with sheets. It was supposed to look like a night club. We had a DJ who played a lot of music from the 1920's. After a while I got tired of the old time music, so I asked him to play some music so that we could dance. I asked for something by Michael Jackson. The DJ played 'Billy Jean, Thriller, and Beat It' for me.

"Come on, Cat, do Michael Jackson for us," the kids said at the party. "Michael, Michael, Michael, Michael," they chanted.

It didn't take much coaxing for me to jump onto the stage. I took off my tie and jacket, unbuttoned several buttons of my shirt, and pulled a sparkling silver glove out of my front pocket and put it on my right hand.

The sounds of "Beat It" pulsed and I started with my moves. I did a head nod, then jerked and twitched. I did the moon walk, spun around, and kicked. By now my shirt was partly off my shoulders. I grabbed my crotch then held my hat and went up on my toes. The crowd went wild cheering for me and I beamed with pride. It felt so good!

CHAPTER

23 Christmas Wish

It was fall and Halloween was fast approaching. Already, I was dreaming about Christmas.

"Moms, I want something very special for Christmas this year," I said to my parents one Saturday morning in mid-October.

"What's that, Cat-Honey?" Mom asked.

"I'd like my angel kiss to disappear," I said. "I'm tired of people always asking me about it and making fun of me."

My folks looked at each other and then Mom said, "We'll see what we can do about that Josh."

My mom made an appointment for me to meet with a plastic surgeon. He examined by scar and then said, "I can't make your angel kiss disappear completely, Josh, but I can make it a lot smaller. After you have surgery, it will just look like a thin line. Will that work for you?"

"Yes, sir, thank you!" I told him.

My surgery was scheduled for the Thursday before we started our Christmas break from school. My folks and I got up while it was still dark outside in order to drive to the hospital on the far northwest part of town.

"Good morning," Mom said to the woman behind the hospital desk. "This is my son, Josh Carson. He's here for surgery this morning."

The lady had Mom sign a bunch of papers and then my parents and I were taken to a room where I changed into a stupid looking hospital gown. Dr. Gibbs, my surgeon, and another doctor came by to see me. They explained what they were going to do to fix my head and asked me if I were ready.

"Yes, sir, I'm definitely ready," I said.

My mom kissed my angel spot and then she kissed my cheek.

"See you in a little while, Honey, I love you," Mom said.

Momma B kissed my forehead and said, "See you later, alligator."

"After while, crocodile," I said back.

Mom and I signed "I love you" in sign language, and then we touched fingers. Mom blew me a kiss, which I pretended to catch, and I blew one back to her. She caught it, and we each touched our "kiss" to our cheeks at the same time. Then my parents left the room.

"I'm going to put this mask over your nose and mouth, Joshua," a man said to me. "You'll start to smell the gas which will help you go to sleep. You won't feel a thing during your surgery, Son. I promise. OK?"

"OK," I said.

He placed the mask over my face.

"I want you to count out loud to me. Count backwards from 10 to 1, Joshua, and just breathe normally."

I began to count for him. I could hear my voice.

"Ten, nine, eight, sev..."

That was the last thing I remember. Then I heard someone calling me and telling me to wake up.

"Joshua, wake up. It's all over and it's time for you to wake up now," a nurse said to me as I slept in the Recovery Room.

"Huh?" I said slowly.

"Wake up, Josh," she said.

"What?" I said. I was confused and didn't know where I was.

"That's it, Joshua, good boy. It's time for you to wake up now, Sweetie, you're all finished," the nurse said.

"I am?" I asked. "Where are my moms?"

"They're in the next room. They've been waiting for you. I'll get them right now," she said, and she left me.

My parents entered the room and they smiled and kissed me.

"That's quite a bandage you have on your head, Joshie," Momma B said.

"Your head won't get cold this winter with that wrapped around it," Mom said.

I stayed in the recovery room for about two hours and then Dr. Gibbs told my parents they could drive me home. I slept the whole way. I woke up when we pulled into our garage. Mom helped me walk into the house because I wasn't very steady on my feet.

"I want to go to the bathroom," I said. "And I want to see myself in the mirror."

Mom led me to the bathroom and turned on the lights. I was amazed at what I saw.

"Oh, my gosh!" I said. "I look like a giant Q-tip! How long do I have to wear this bandage?"

"Dr. Gibbs wants to see you in three days," Mom said. "He'll see how well you're healing, and he will probably change your bandage then."

"Do I have to go back to school looking like this?" I asked.

"No, Sweetheart," Mom said. "Your bandages will be long gone by the time school starts again after the holidays. Remember, you'll just have a thin little scar where your Angel Kiss used to be."

"Good," I said. "Can I go back to sleep now?" And I was off to bed.

Three days later we went to see Dr. Gibbs for my follow-up appointment. He was pleased with how I was healing. And just like Mom said, the bandages were all gone by the time school started in January.

"Moms," I said a few days later during dinner. "I know that some people don't believe in Santa Clause, but I know that he's real."

"Well, I believe in him," Momma B said.

"Me too!" said my mom. "Why do you believe in Santa, Joshie?"

"Do you remember last Christmas when I talked to Santa at the mall?" I asked.

"Yes," Mom said. "You wouldn't tell us what you asked for last year."

"That's because Santa told me that he couldn't get me what I wanted last year. He said that I'd have to wait until this Christmas for my wish to come true."

"I remember that," Momma B said. "So what was your wish, Josh?"

"I asked Santa to make my Angel Kiss disappear," I said. "I was tired of people always asking about it and teasing me."

"Well, it looks like Santa came through for you," Mom said.

"He sure did," I said nodding my head.

School started again in early January and I was excited about sharing my Christmas story with the teachers and the kids in my class. When someone asked me if I had a good Christmas or what Santa brought me, I'd smile and turn around to show them the back of my head.

"This year my Christmas was perfect," I said. "I got exactly what I asked Santa for; a normal looking head. Now nobody's going to tease me about my bald spot ever again."

The End of 9 LIVES:
Cat Tales

9

LIVES

Full Circle

CHAPTER

1

First Kiss

When I was eleven years old I started sixth grade at New Phoenix Charter School. There were maybe 200 kids in the entire school. It was the first year for this school, and they were having some problems getting started.

I had a girlfriend there and her name was Joyce. She was black and as tall as my mom. Joyce was very mature for her age. She even wore a bra.

In the mornings, before school, my mom and I always stopped at the veterinary hospital. We went there to say 'good morning' to Momma B, and to drop off a couple of our dogs who always spent the day in my mom's office. Then Mom would take me on to school.

One day I was in Momma B's office when I saw some pretty jewelry lying on her desk. It was a gold pin with a red bird sitting on a red flower. No one was around me, so I took it and put it in my pocket. I wanted to give it to Joyce.

Pretty soon Mom and I left for school. She dropped me off at the New Phoenix front door and I immediately went looking for Joyce.

"Hi Joyce," I said when I found her standing next to the water fountain. "This is for you," I said as I dug into my pocket and pulled out the brooch.

"Why, thank you, Baby," she said. "It's beautiful."

Joyce took the pin from me and put it on her light blue, V-neck blouse. She leaned over and kissed me on the lips. Her lips touched mine for a long time. Her mouth was soft and full. I'd never been kissed on the lips by a girl before. Kissing her sent butterflies off in my stomach. Joyce smelled really good, like a sweet flower

"It's my pleasure, Sugar," I said smiling.

All day long I kept thinking about that kiss and hoping for a lot more kisses from Joyce. I wondered what else I might give to her. That afternoon, Mom came by the school to pick me up. I was waiting in front of the building talking with Joyce and we were holding hands.

Mom parked the car and walked over to where we were standing. She looked at Joyce's blouse and saw that she was wearing Momma B's bird pin. Mom recognized it at once.

"Hi Joyce," Mom said. "I'm Joshua's mother. I'm sorry, but the jewelry that Josh gave you doesn't belong to him. And he didn't have permission to give it to you. I need you to give it back please."

Mom held out her hand and Joyce looked at my mom and then at me. Slowly, she took off the pin and handed it to my mom. Joyce glared into my mother's eyes and gave Mom a mean look.

"Josh is welcome to purchase jewelry for you, but he isn't allowed to give you something that belongs to someone else," Mom said. "Josh, you need to say 'good-bye' now and get in the car."

I said goodbye and walked to the car. I felt so embarrassed and humiliated. I was angry with my mother for doing and saying what she did. I knew that she was mad at me too.

"Joshua, we've talked about stealing before," Mom said. "Why did you take that pin from Momma B?" Mom asked as soon as the car doors were closed.

"I wanted to give it to Joyce," I said.

"But Joshua, it wasn't yours to give," Mom said. "Taking something without asking is stealing and that isn't allowed… remember?"

I didn't say anything. I just stared angrily at the floor of the car.

"Joshua, I'd appreciate an answer. Do you know that stealing is wrong?"

"Yes."

"This stealing behavior has got to stop, Josh, and it must stop NOW!" she said. "You'll need to talk with Momma B about this when we get home."

Mom started the engine and began to pull out of her parking spot.

"Well, it was wrong for you to embarrass me in from of my girlfriend and the other kids," I said trying not to raise my voice. "You made me mad."

"I hear what you're saying, Josh, but I couldn't think of any other way to deal with the situation," Mom said. "I got really angry when I saw that you had stolen that pin from Brooke."

We pulled out of the parking lot in silence. Each of us was trying to calm down. Soon Mom spoke again.

"That girl, Joyce, is way too old for you, Josh" Mom said. "She's two years older and very mature for her age. Why don't you find a girlfriend from your own class? What about that nice girl, Johnnie, over there?"

Mom nodded her head towards a small black girl who was getting onto a school bus. "She has a nice smile." Mom said. "Do you know her?"

I ignored her and we rode home in silence.

When Brooke got home from work, Mom made me tell her about what I had done. Momma B was not happy about me stealing from her either.

"Thank you for telling me, Josh," Momma B said. "I'm very angry and disappointed that you're still stealing. Your mother and I will discuss what your consequences will be for this."

My parents decided to search their jewelry boxes to see if anything else was missing.

"Joshua," my mother called with alarm in her voice. "My good gold necklace and my matching silver chain are both missing. Do you have them? Where are they?"

"I don't know," I said.

"Did you take them?" Mom asked.

"No."

"Joshua, it's important that you tell me the truth," Mom said. "I really need to know if you took them."

"I said I didn't."

Mom didn't believe me. She began searching my room for her chains. Mom looked in every drawer, under the bed, in my closet, and in my desk.

"What did you do with them?" she asked.

"I don't remember," I finally said.

"How could you not remember?"

"It happened a long time ago," I said.

Mom found a little red box that I had hidden in the back of my closet. It was under a pile of shoes. Inside of it she found her gold chain. I had tied it into little knots and it was ruined.

"Oh, Joshua," she said. "You've ruined my good gold chain. This was an expensive piece of jewelry. It cost over $400! Where's the silver chain?"

"I don't know."

Mom never did find out what I did with the matching silver necklace. I certainly didn't remember.

Mom was pissed. "Josh, why did you do this? What were you thinking?"

"I don't know," I said.

"For Heaven's sake, Joshua, these were two of my favorite necklaces. Now one is missing and the other is ruined. You had no right to take them. Just who do you think you are?"

"Joshua Radford Carson," I said looking at her seriously.

Mom paused. She looked surprised by my response.

"That's right, Joshua, and Carsons don't steal. Taking things that don't belong to you is wrong. You're going to end up in jail and we don't want that for you. Is that what you want?"

"No," I said.

"Then you need to stop these behaviors because stealing will send you there."

CHAPTER

2

Suspended

My folks weren't happy about the way things were going at the charter school, so after only two months of going there, my mom withdrew me. She enrolled me in the sixth grade class at Magee Middle School.

"Ms. Carson?" a man's voice came through the telephone at the veterinary hospital that my parents own.

"Yes," Mom said.

"This is Mr. Webster, the principal at Magee Middle School. Your son, Joshua, is in my office. I'd appreciate it if you'd come down and take him home. He's been suspended for three days."

"What did he do?" Mom asked.

"I'd prefer to discuss it when you arrive. Can we expect to see you soon?"

"I'll be right there," Mom said.

I was sitting on a chair next to the door when my mother walked into Mr. Webster's office. Although she was trying to be calm, I could tell that she was upset. Mr. Webster and Mom shook hands.

"Please have a seat," the principal said.

Mom sat down next to me.

"Joshua has been suspended because he was trying to sell what he said was marijuana. He offered the substance to two students just before his fourth period gym class," Mr. Webster said.

Mom looked at me in shock.

"It was actually some parsley flakes that he was trying to sell," the principal said. "I suspect they came from your kitchen. The school district has a 'No Tolerance Policy' when it comes to use or selling of illegal substances, or even fake illegal substances, on campus."

"Thank you for bringing this to my attention, Mr. Webster," Mom said. "We'll address this at home."

I could tell that Mom wanted to breathe fire like a dragon. She nodded her head to indicate that we were leaving. Standing up I grabbed my backpack and we left the building. Mom didn't say a word to me the entire ride back to the animal clinic. She ignored me and began working at her desk until it was time to close for the day.

"Follow me," she said, as she headed down the hallway to Momma B's office.

"Hi," Momma B greeted us as she looked up from her computer. "Uh-oh, I'm sensing trouble here, what's up?"

"Josh, please tell Brooke what happened at school today," Mom said.

"I got suspended," I said.

"Why? What happened?" she asked.

I didn't answer. I just looked at the floor.

"He tried to sell parsley flakes to two students before gym class," Mom said. "He told them it was marijuana and apparently they were smart enough to turn him in."

"What in the world were you thinking?" Momma B asked.

I shrugged.

"Josh, we've talked to you a hundred times about the dangers of illegal drugs. Now you're trying to be a drug dealer? What's that all about?" Mom asked.

Again, I shrugged.

"If you had actually sold any of those parsley flakes to kids who wanted to buy the real thing, you'd be in deep trouble with them, too. As it is, you're in deep trouble with the school and with us. Do you want the reputation of being a drug dealer?" Mom asked.

"I don't know," I said.

"Joshua, what in the world is wrong with you? Don't you remember that drugs and alcohol destroyed your birth parents lives?" Mom said.

I shrugged.

"What part about the dangers of illegal drugs, and the selling of illegal drugs don't you understand?" Mom asked, shaking her head in frustration. "Do you want to end up in prison?"

I didn't say anything.

"You're grounded and have no privileges," Momma B said, "No TV, telephone, Nintendo, basketball, nothing. Is that understood?"

"I don't care," I said defiantly.

"Joshua, your behaviors scare me," Mom said. "We never know what you're going to do to get into trouble. We love you, Josh, and we worry when you do these dangerous things."

I shrugged and walked out of the room. My parents didn't understand how desperate I was to fit in at school. I was willing to do just about anything to be accepted, to be cool, have friends, and feel like I belonged.

CHAPTER

3

Busted

Mom was always looking for books on parenting and ones about black people that she thought might interest me. We went into one of the major bookstores in town and she headed towards the Children's Department.

"May I please go look in the Music Department?" I asked. "I won't wander off and make you come looking for me, I promise."

"OK, but stay there," Mom said. "I won't be long."

About ten minutes later my mom had bought two books and came to the music area to get me. The department manager approached her.

"Is Joshua your son?" he asked.

"Yes," she said, spotting me sitting on the floor. She waved at me to stand up and join them. I got up and walked to where they were talking.

"A few minutes ago I caught Joshua trying to shop-lift a CD."

"Really?" Mom asked.

"Yes," the manager answered. "Josh took the cellophane off of a Michael Jackson CD and stuffed it in his jeans. The security buzzer sounded when he tried to leave the area."

"Josh, what in the world were you thinking?" Mom asked.

"I don't know," I said with a shrug.

"Would you please call the store manager over here?" Mom asked.

Using her cell phone, Mom called Brooke to discuss the situation. Then she spoke with my therapist Katy Wilson. Katy suggested that it might do me good to be arrested. Katy knew that my mothers had tried everything else to stop me from stealing, but that I continued to steal. Katy thought that I needed to understand that my actions had consequences.

The store manager shook hands with my mother. Mom and the manager moved away from me so that I couldn't hear them talking. I knew that they were talking about what should be done with me.

"I just spoke with Joshua's therapist and she thinks that it would be good for him to be arrested," Mom told her. "He needs to be held responsible for his actions. Josh doesn't connect his behaviors with their consequences. He needs to finally make that association before it's too late."

"Well," the store manager said, "it's our store policy not to press charges for incidents like this."

Mom tried to convince her that I needed to understand what happens when I steal, but the woman refused to call the police. The manager walked up to me.

"Joshua, what you did was wrong," she said. "I'm not going to call the police on you this time, but I don't ever want you to come back into this store again. If you do, I will call the police and you'll be arrested for trespassing. Is that understood?"

"Yes, ma'am," I said.

Mom and I left the store. Mom shook her head and quietly cried during the fifteen minute ride home.

CHAPTER

4

Bling

One spring day, Mom and I were running errands together. She stopped in a department store that was having a sale on women's under-garments.

"I need to pick up some bras," Mom said.

Being in that department always embarrasses me, but Mom insisted that I stay with her. She hurried into the dressing room to try on some bras. Five minutes later, she had purchased her items and we were out of the store.

The next day my parents and I were having lunch at a local café. We had just given our food orders when Mom looked at me and the smile on her face vanished.

"Josh, I didn't give you those earrings," she said. "I would never buy you huge fake diamonds like that. Where did you get them?"

I had pierced ears and usually just wore silver studs in them. I looked at her but said nothing.

"You took them from the department store yesterday while I was in the dressing room, didn't you?" Mom asked.

Taking a drink of water, I knew that I was busted but I remained silent.

"Please take them off and hand them to me."

I removed the cheap jewelry from my ears and handed them to my mother.

"Geez, Joshua, using erasers from your school pencils to hold them onto your ears is a dead give-away."

"Did you take them from the display card and leave the earring backs in the store?" Momma B asked.

"Yes," I finally said.

"How many pair of earrings did you steal, Josh?" she asked.

"Three," I said, digging the others out of my pocket and handing them to my mother.

"Josh," Mom said. "I don't get it. Why do you continue to steal like this?"

I shrugged my shoulders and mumbled, "I don't know."

Our lunch came and we ate in silence. When we had finished our meal Brooke went back to work and Mom and I drove to the department store.

Mom had me tell the store manager what I had done and I apologized. The manager turned me over to the store's Head of Security. He was a tall white guy who was probably in his 60's. He put his arm around my shoulder like we were buddies. We walked around the store together talking.

Like the first time that I got busted for shop-lifting, the store didn't call the police or press charges. And I'm never allowed in that store again, either. Mom shook her head in frustration and disbelief at what I had done. She couldn't understand why I continued to steal and get into trouble.

CHAPTER

5 Mom's Birthday

My mom's birthday is in August and to celebrate, she and Momma B were going out to a birthday luncheon. I didn't want to go so I asked if I could go to Skate World instead. They dropped me off at the skating rink and went to a nearby restaurant.

I quickly put on some skates and took to the floor. The music was fine and I was having a great time. I skated up to a white kid who had stopped along the wall of the rink. I had business to conduct.

"Hey, Buddy," I said. "Do you want to buy some crack?"

I showed him a brown vial in my hand. He shook his head and skated away. So then I approached a black girl who was sitting on a bench and I asked her the same question.

"No, you idiot," she said, and she escaped into the Girls' Room.

Spotting a boy that I knew from my school, I stood beside him at a video game for a while. When he finished playing, I made him the same offer. Like the first two kids, he wasn't interested and moved away. Pretty soon, I heard my name called over the loud speaker.

"Joshua Carson, please come to the DJ's stand, Josh Carson."

I skated over to the music station and the DJ said, "Hey, man, you're wanted in the office."

I knocked on the office door and the manager invited me inside.

"Hey, Josh," the manager said. "I hear that you've been trying to make a little money here today. Are you selling 'Crack' to my skaters?"

"Well, yes and no," I said. "It isn't really 'Crack,' I was just pretending that it was. It's just my Strattera medication," I explained, holding up the brown vial to show him.

"Well, thanks for explaining that to me," the manager said. "Why don't you leave the vial with me and go back out there and skate?"

I handed him my prescription medicine and went out to the rink. About ten minutes later two police officers walked into the noisy building. They called me over and asked me what was going on. I told them what I had said to the manager.

"Joshua Carson, you are under arrest for possession with the intent to distribute a controlled substance," the older male officer said to me. "Please turn around and put your hands behind your back."

I turned my back to him and he slapped the handcuffs on me. We started walking out the door. Once I was inside their car the young female cop began reading me my rights.

"You have the right to remain silent. Anything you say, can and will be used against you in a court of law. You have the right to an attorney. If you cannot afford an attorney, one will be appointed for you by a court of law. Do you understand your rights as I have read them to you?" she asked.

"Yes ma'am," I answered. I was quiet for the short ride to the police station. Inside, the officers asked me a lot of questions. They asked for my name, address, and date of birth. I gave them telephone numbers where they could reach my parents.

When they started asking questions about drugs I said, "I want a lawyer."

The lady cop stayed in the room with me while the older man left the room and called my parents.

"Hello?" Mom said into the phone.

"Mrs. Carson?" the male officer asked.

"This is Ms. Carson," Mom said.

"This is Sergeant Reilly of the Tucson Police Department. Ma'am, your son, Joshua, has been arrested."

"Oh, my God, what for?" Mom asked.

"He's been charged with possession, with the intent to distribute a controlled substance. This is a Class Four Felony, ma'am. I need you to come down to the station and pick him up. He's at the station on Golf Links."

"Thank you, Officer Reilly," Mom said, and hung up the phone. She looked at Brooke, sighed and shook her head. "Well, this is one birthday present from Joshua that I'll never forget…he's been arrested."

My folks came to the police station to get me. I could tell that they were very mad at me. There was silence in the car as we drove home. Both of my moms looked like they were going to cry. It felt as though a deep sadness had settled over our home. I know that a dark sadness had settled over my parents' hearts.

CHAPTER

6

Juvenile Court

A public defender was assigned to my case and a date was set for my hearing. My case was to be heard by a Juvenile Court judge. My mom asked me to wear my dress slacks with my good shoes, a white shirt, and a tie.

"It's important to dress up for the judge," she said. "We want you to make a good impression."

"I don't see what the big deal is or why I should get dressed up for the judge," I said. "But since I look cool in a tie, I'll put one on."

I finished getting ready and joined Mom who was already in the car. She drove me to the Juvenile Court building which was across town. The parking lot was full and it took us a while to find a parking space.

Mom pulled the car into a spot and we walked across the parking lot together. There was a line of people waiting to go through the security screening. For some reason, I set off the alarm as I walked through the door with the metal detector.

"Stand over here with your arms out to your sides," a Security Officer said.

I did as he asked and he ran a wand over my body.

"OK, you can go on in," he said.

There are thirteen different courtrooms in that one building. The last time my mom and I were in that building was to finalize my adoption. That was about four years ago. My mom was a lot happier that day.

She was not happy going to court with me this time. Mom found the right courtroom and I was introduced to my court appointed attorney. Her name was Ona Black and she moved me away from my mother. Ms. Black wouldn't let Mom listen to what she was saying to me.

"I'm sorry, Ms. Carson, but my conversation with Joshua is private," she said.

"But I'm his mother and he's a minor." Mom said.

"Sorry," she said, "but you're not my client, he is."

My attorney explained to me how things would go, once we went into the next room and I was sitting in front of the judge. Someone called my case and Ms.

Black, Mom, and I walked into the courtroom. I sat next to my attorney and Mom had to sit in the chairs behind me.

The judge entered the room and we all stood up to show our respect. Someone read the charge against me. Ms. Black had told me what to say when I was asked, "How do you plea?"

"Guilty, your Honor," I said looking at the judge.

"Tell me what happened, Joshua," the judge said.

"You see, Your Honor, I was really only pretending to sell 'Crack.' It was really just my medicine in that vial. I was just trying to look cool to the other kids."

"Joshua, did you realize that if those kids had taken your medicine, it might have made them really sick?"

"No, sir," I said.

"Did you know that those children may even have died, if they had taken your medicine?" the judge asked me.

"No, sir," I said, "I didn't think my medicine would hurt anyone. I'm supposed to take it, and it doesn't hurt me."

"I believe you, son," the judge said. "How old are you, Joshua? What grade are you in?"

"I'm 14 and will be in the 9th grade when school starts, sir."

"I can see by the way you're dressed that you're a nice young man," the judge said. "And, because this is your first offense, I'm putting you on six months probation."

I sighed with relief.

"You'll do twenty hours of 'Community Service,' attend a class where you'll learn about illegal substances, and in school you'll need to maintain a 'C' average in all of your classes. Is that understood?"

"Yes, sir," I said. "And thank you, your Honor, sir."

"So be it," the Judge said, and he slammed a wooden hammer on his desk.

A lady came up to me after court and said that she was my Probation Officer and that her name was Amy Presley.

"Here are the conditions of your parole," Officer Presley said to my mom and me. "You'll need to call my office every Monday," she said. "Here's my card with my phone numbers."

She handed me a small piece of paper.

"And I'll be dropping by the school, unannounced, to check on you," Officer Presley said. "You need to be where you're supposed to be, and not somewhere goofing off. OK?"

"OK," I said.

"And you'll be doing unscheduled drug drops," Officer Presley said.

"What's that?" I asked.

"That's a urine test to see if you're using drugs. You just pee in a cup, and they send me the results. Do you have any questions?"

"No, ma'am," I said.

"OK, now where will you be going to school?"

I gave her the information and Mom and I left juvenile court. I knew that the next six months weren't going to be a lot of fun.

My parents had grounded me and now I'd have a Probation Officer checking up on me. I needed to put in my hours of community service, so every Saturday morning, I cleaned litter boxes at a local cat shelter. Then I gave the cats fresh water and food. I like cats, so that was OK.

I also worked as a volunteer at the Susan G. Komen Race for the Cure. That's a fund raising event to fight breast cancer. Momma B's mother, and my mom's younger sister, Jesse, both died from breast cancer.

My family always participated in the annual event, but this time I handed out water to the runners. After the race I helped clean up the mess of paper cups, carried trash bags to the dumpsters, and helped put away tables and chairs. I actually enjoyed myself. Doing my community service work was a good thing.

CHAPTER

7

City Bus

School was about to start and I would begin my freshman year. My folks thought that since I was into music, photography, and dance, that maybe I'd do better at a school that offered the arts. They enrolled me in City High School for the Arts, or 'Arts High."

It was there that I began my high school career. Arts High was about eleven miles from my home, so I rode a school bus most mornings and afternoons.

"Mom, I missed the school bus," I said into a cell phone that I borrowed from some kid.

"I'm tied up with work this afternoon, Josh. Can you catch the city bus and take it to the clinic?" Mom asked. "It'll cost $1.00. Do you have any money with you?"

"Yes, Mom, I have two dollars."

"OK, then. You should get to the clinic about 90 minutes later than you usually do. Be careful and I'll see you later."

It turns out that Mom had some errands to run that afternoon. She was sitting in her car at a red light when she spotted the city bus that I was riding. The bus had stopped to drop off and pick up passengers. The bus was about two miles away from the animal hospital when I decided that I wasn't ready to go to the clinic just yet. I got up from my seat and stepped off the bus. Mom watched me from her car.

I was in a hurry to cross the busy street. I could have walked 50 steps to the crosswalk, but I didn't. Instead, I jaywalked. Jay walking is crossing the street from someplace other than the crosswalk. It's not safe and it's illegal. I bolted across six lanes of busy traffic.

A huge yellow Hummer and a green Dodge truck each slammed on their brakes to avoid hitting me. Then a guy riding a motorcycle swerved so that he wouldn't run over me either. They all blasted their horns at me. The guy on the motorcycle was really mad. He yelled and then flipped me off.

I shrugged and ignored him. I had made it safely to the other side of the road and was proud of my speed. I sauntered across the parking lot and entered the lobby of a furniture store. I knew that this store had free cookies and drinks for its customers. I was hungry and wanted a snack. I helped myself to a soda and then wolfed down several cookies. My stomach was happy, at least for a little while.

Deciding to drop in on a friend who lived in an apartment complex next to the furniture store, I crossed the parking lot and scrambled up a retaining wall. I wandered around from building to building and finally found my friend's apartment. I knocked on the door but there was no answer. I headed back towards the street.

Then I felt the urge to pee. I walked over to the bushes and let it fly. Feeling much better now, I turned around and headed out of the apartment complex. That's when I spotted my mom's car. She had seen what I was doing and had followed me into the parking lot. The passenger door was open for me to get into the car.

"Hi, Mom," I said, as I fastened the seat belt.

"Hi, Josh," she said. "Why did you get off of the bus here?"

"I just wanted to," I said.

"Honey, I saw you bolt across six lanes of traffic," Mom said. "You could have been killed or caused an accident."

"I'm sorry," I said. "I didn't think about that. But I'm fine, nothing happened."

"My heart nearly stopped beating when I watched you running in front of those trucks and that motorcycle," Mom said. "I'm relieved that you're safe, but upset at your reckless actions."

"I'm sorry, Mom, I didn't mean to scare you. But seriously, I'm fine."

"What were you doing in the furniture store?"

"I was hungry and they have cookies."

"Oh, Josh," she said, shaking her head. "Those cookies are for the store's customers. Do you think I'd be happy if some kid got off of the bus in front of our clinic, and came into our reception area to help himself to the refreshments that I buy for our clients?"

"No."

"And what were you doing at the apartment complex?"

"I went to visit a friend."

"What friend?" she asked. "And how did you know which is your friend's apartment?"

"You don't know him, but I've been to his place before."

"Josh, I don't know anything about you ever being at this apartment complex. When were you here?"

"One other time when I rode the bus home," I said "That's why I was late getting home. I stopped here for a while."

"You told me that you were late because the bus was late."

"Oops, sorry," I said.

"Josh, I need you to stop telling lies," Mom said. "And I need you to be where you're supposed to be. Do you understand?"

"Yes, ma'am," I said.

"And what's with you urinating in the bushes?"

"I had to go."

"Can you think of other options for that besides going in the bushes?"

"I don't know."

"You could have used the restroom at the furniture store or that fast food restaurant, couldn't you?"

"I guess so."

"Josh, did you know that it is against the law to urinate in public?"

"No, I'm sorry. It won't ever happen again, Mom."

"I certainly hope not. Let's go, I need to get back to work."

CHAPTER

8

Hit and Run

About two months later I called my mother on another borrowed cell phone. I used to have my own cell phone but I kept losing it. After I'd lost my third replacement phone, my folks said I couldn't get another one until I was more responsible.

"Hi, Mom," I said. "I've missed my bus again. Can I ride the city bus to the clinic?"

"Can I trust you to get off at the correct stop this time?" Mom asked.

"Yes," I said.

"OK, then," Mom said. "See you in a little while."

About ten minutes later I called her back again.

"Hi, Josh, what's up?" she asked.

"Um, Mom, I've been hit by a car," I said.

"You what?" she asked.

"I was hit by a car."

"Are you OK?"

"Well, my hip is scraped and bruised, and my ankle hurts. But I think I'm okay."

Mom found out where I was and appeared on the scene within a few minutes. By then I was waiting inside the back of a police cruiser. Mom parked her car and ran to where I was sitting.

"Honey, are you all right?" Mom asked.

I nodded my head.

"Are you Joshua's mother?" the police officer asked.

"Yes, I am," Mom said. "Josh, please tell me what happened."

"Well, I missed my bus and was walking down the sidewalk to catch the city bus," I began. "At the cross-walk I decided to cross the street. I looked both ways and then stepped off of the curb."

I knew my mom wanted to hear that I had followed the rules, but we both knew that I was lying. I really hadn't looked both ways or tried to cross at the cross-walk.

"Then out of nowhere came this big black van and WHAM it hit me. I went flying in the air and landed on my hip in the middle of the street."

I rubbed my hip to show her where it hurt.

"I flew at least fifty feet from the van," I said.

Mom and I both knew that I had no idea how far fifty feet really was. It was probably more like ten feet, but I thought fifty feet sounded better.

"Oh, Josh," Mom said. "What did the driver do? Did he stop and help you?"

"Well, an Hispanic woman got out of the car. She came over to me and said, 'Hey, kid, are you OK?'

I said, "NO, my leg hurts."

She said, "Sorry." Then she got back in the van and drove away."

"You mean it was a 'hit and run'?" Mom said. "She just left you there?"

"Yes!" I said, getting into the story. "Then another woman, and her daughter, ran over to see if I was OK. They saw the whole thing from their table at that Mexican restaurant," I said pointing to the eatery. "The mother let me use her cell phone to call you. Then she called the police."

"Where do you hurt, Josh?" Mom asked.

"I have a big scrape on my hip," I said pointing to the sore spot. "I cleaned it up in the bathroom at that restaurant."

"Did you hurt anything else?" Mom asked.

"The palms of my hands were bleeding from when I landed on them and skidded in the street," I said, showing Mom my injured hands. "I cleaned them up a little too."

"Do you have any other injuries?" Mom asked.

"Well, my left leg hurts near my ankle, and my hip is sore."

"Is that where the van hit you?" Mom asked. "There on your hip?"

"Uh-huh."

"We have a description of the van and a partial on the license plate," the officer said, "but quite frankly, the driver is probably long gone by now. Since your son isn't seriously injured, there's no point in pursuing this."

Mom shook her head in disbelief. The officer gave Mom a copy of the police report. Mom thanked the officer and he left. Then we got into her car.

"Let's get you to the hospital Josh and get you checked."

Mom used her cell phone to call Momma B. Then she called my regular doctor to tell him about my accident. We drove to the Emergency Room at St. Joseph's Hospital.

"Honey, you are so lucky to be alive," Mom said.

"I know," I said. "I'm lucky like a cat with nine lives, remember?"

"Yes, I do remember. And you're using up too many of your lives much too quickly!"

"Josh, you weren't really at the cross-walk when you were hit, were you?"

"No," I said. "I told you that so you would think I had followed the rules."

"And you didn't look both ways, did you?" Mom asked.

"No," I confessed.

"Oh, Honey, sometimes I'm afraid for you."

We arrived at the emergency room and waited six hours before the doctor could see me. By that time, Momma B had joined us there.

The hospital staff took x-rays, but the doctor wasn't sure if my leg was bruised or broken. They decided that I should see a doctor who specializes in bones. We waited another two hours for the bone specialist because it was his day off and he was at home.

Finally, the doctor came to talk with my folks and me. He examined my legs and compared one to the other. He looked at my x-rays.

"I've determined that your leg isn't broken, Joshua, but it is very badly bruised." The bone specialist doctor said. "Just to be safe, we'll splint your leg and give you some crutches. Come and see me next Wednesday for a follow-up."

He handed Mom his business card and left the room. A nice woman put a splint on my leg and showed me how to walk using crutches. It had been a very long night and we finally went home.

The next day I went back to Arts High. Because I had crutches, I got special permission to use the elevator at school. The crutches also helped me get extra attention from the girls. I wasn't supposed to, but I gave the girls rides with me in the elevator. I think using crutches had its benefits after all.

CHAPTER

The Bloods

I was hanging with a rough crowd at school. Mom didn't know that the reason I kept missing my school bus was because I was hanging with my homies. They were a gang called the 'Bloods.'

My folks tried talking with me about how dangerous gangs were but I didn't listen. At school I'd get into trouble a lot because I was late to my classes. I didn't care. I was hanging with my friends. We'd get together before school, between classes, and during lunch. Sometimes we'd even skip class and just hang out at the corner store.

Most of these guys were older than I was. They smoked cigarettes, chewed tobacco, and got high on weed. I wanted to fit in but didn't have any money to buy cigarettes or grass. So I rolled fake joints and stuffed them in my socks.

I thought they were cool and I wanted to be cool too. One day I missed the school bus because I stayed for my gang initiation. I was told to meet the gang down under the bleachers of the old brick football stadium.

The members formed a circle around me. Then the leader, his name was Blade, stepped into the middle of the circle. Blade had his hair shaved and wore a red baseball cap turned down on the right. He wore black, baggy jeans. They rode low on his hips and showed his under shorts.

Although it didn't do much good, he wore a red rope as a belt. Blade's right pant leg was rolled up and the tongues of his tennis shoes stuck straight up. He had a red lace in his right shoe, but it hung loose and was tucked into his shoes.

"We down with this associate?" he asked the members.

"We down wit-it," they said.

"OK, you know the rules, no blows to the head; easier to hide the bruises that way," he said.

Blade turned to look at me. "Don't try to block the blows. You down?"

I nodded. Then it began. It started from behind me. Somebody kicked the back of my right thigh. I immediately fell to the cement smacking my knees on the hard surface.

Fists and feet came at me from every angle. I curled into a ball, trying to protect myself as best I could. They kicked my butt and my back. They stomped on my arms, calves, and thighs. I was punched in my side, and in my ribs, and in the middle of my back. After what seemed like an hour, Blade called for them to stop. I lay on the ground for a while wondering if it was really over.

"Stand," he said.

Slowly, I got to my feet. Nobody helped me up.

"It's all about respect, dude, and now we respect you. You got a new name too. We'll call you 'Gato.' That means 'Cat' in Spanish."

When I first started Arts High in the fall, I told the guys that my nickname was 'Cat.' I guess he remembered. Blade handed me a red rubber band and I put it on my right wrist and that was it. I was in. I was a Blood.

Somehow I managed to make my way to the bus stop which was two blocks away. I was in a lot of pain and I ached all over. The bus arrived just as I hobbled to the stop. It stopped and the doors flew open. I slowly pulled myself up the steps and stood by the driver.

I found four quarters in my jeans pocket and took a seat in the back of the bus. Every bump in the road hurt. It felt like someone was kicking me again. Finally, I made it home. Mom was upset with me.

"Honey, where have you been?" Mom asked. "We've been worried sick."

"I'm sorry," I said. "I missed my bus and had to take the city bus. I couldn't find anyone with a cell phone so I couldn't call you. If you'd just get me another phone…"

"Don't go there." Mom warned, cutting me off. "Are you OK? You look awful."

"I'm just really tired," I said. "I'm going to go lie down for a while."

When dinner was ready, Momma B tried to awaken me to join them.

"I'm not hungry," I mumbled, then pulled the quilt over my head.

I slept clear through 'til morning. The next day was Saturday so I could sleep late. I sure needed it. Except for a couple of times when I got up to eat and use the restroom, I slept all weekend. I never told my folks that my pee was red. I think there was blood in it, and that was kind of scary.

"What do you think is going on with Josh?" Mom asked Momma B.

"I don't know," Momma B said. "I've heard that teenage boys only want to eat and sleep. Neither of us grew up with brothers so we have no comparisons for his behavior. We'll see how he acts tomorrow and take it from there."

By Monday, I was feeling and acting more like myself. I didn't tell my parents about the Bloods. I knew that they would not approve of me being in a gang. But I didn't care because I finally fit in.

CHAPTER
10

Probation

The week after my trial, my Probation Officer, Amy Presley, paid me a surprise visit at school.

"The conditions of your probation state that you are to be in class on time," she said. "How are you doing with that?"

"OK, I guess," I said, telling her a lie.

"Good," she said. "And how are your grades? You're supposed to have a 'C' average in all of your classes. How are you doing?"

"OK except for my Business Skills class. I need to officially drop that class because the teacher just has it in for me," I said.

"Hmmm, then you'll need to take that up with your teacher. I'll need a copy of your grades in a few weeks. You need to have everything in order before you go back in front of the judge in six months."

"OK," I said.

"I need you to go to this lab and do a drug screening test before Friday. They'll send me the results. If you don't drop clean, Josh, your probation time will probably be extended. Understand?"

"Yes, ma'am," I said.

She handed me a paper with the lab address on it. The next afternoon Mom took off work so that she could drive me to the lab. It was located in a part of town that was unfamiliar to us.

We drove around the block several times until we finally found the building. It was small and square and was painted an ugly brown color on the outside. The inside wasn't any better.

There were four rows of metal folding chairs facing the reception desk window. I walked to the window and a woman opened the sliding glass window. I gave her my name and the window slammed shut.

I could tell my Mom wasn't very comfortable being there with me. There were tough looking characters all around us. We were surrounded by people who were also on probation. Some of them were teenagers, but they all looked worn and tired.

Every seat was taken. Mom and I stood by the door and waited for my name to be called. After about twenty minutes it was finally my turn. I picked up a little cup and a heavy set Hispanic woman walked me to the restroom. She waited outside for me to do my thing. I wrote my name on a label and put the lid on the cup. I handed it to her. That was it and I was free to go.

Mom and I walked outside, happy to be out of that place. That time I managed to 'drop clean.' That means that no illegal drugs showed up on my urine test.

Six months after I first went to Juvenile Court, I had to reappear before the judge. Mom made me get dressed up, wear a tie, and get a haircut, but I didn't want to.

This was the follow-up for my Class Four Felony Charge. My Probation Officer was there and she testified that I had successfully completed the conditions of my probation.

Officer Presley didn't know that I had fake weed in my backpack and another fake joint in my sock when I appeared in court that day.

Mom was upset with my Probation Officer because she didn't think the Officer held me accountable to the conditions of my probation. I usually forgot to check in with Officer Presley every week. I only called when Mom reminded me.

I was still late for classes and hung around with my homies. By being on probation, I was respected by the Bloods. I would have earned even more respect if the judge had sentenced me to 'House Arrest,' and if I had worn an ankle monitor. Some of my gang brothers wore them, and that was a real badge of honor among my homies.

I still didn't do homework or study for tests. I managed to drop the Business class that I was failing. My grades were 'C's 'and I had two 'Incompletes.' I was really lucky that my Probation Officer cut me some slack.

I did put in my Community Service hours and attend the drug education classes. Those classes were really stupid. Hearing and talking about drugs so much only made me more interested in them.

The judge didn't know I had fake joints on me that day in court. He must have figured that I'd learned my lesson and was through with drugs. The judge accepted Officer Presley's recommendation and he took me off probation. I was once again a free man.

CHAPTER

11

It's Up to Me

That evening at home my mom decided to go through my backpack. She did that sometimes and usually found something that I wasn't supposed to have.

That's when she found the fake joint that I had hidden in it. Mom showed it to Momma B and together they came into my room.

"Josh, you were in court today to resolve your Class Four Felony drug charge," Mom said. "And just now I found this fake joint in your backpack."

"Josh, what on earth are you thinking?" Momma B asked.

I sat there staring at them.

"Take off your shoes and socks, Joshua," Mom said.

I did and a fake joint rolled onto the floor.

"Josh, what do you think the judge would have said if he knew about these fake joints?"

I shrugged.

"Joshua, it's time for you to stop this sort of thing and to focus on turning your life around," Momma B said.

"But, Mom, I just want to be normal and fit in," I said.

"We know, Honey," Mom said. "We want that for you too. But kids who sell and use drugs are not the kids you should be hanging around. They are the wrong crowd. They'll lead you down a dangerous path."

"But those are the kids I fit in with," I said. "They like me."

"They don't even know you, Josh," Momma B said. "We love you, and we don't want you to end up in prison, living on the streets, or getting yourself killed."

"Josh, you're part of the steel drum band and you're on the Hip-Hop dance team at school," Mom said. "Why can't you fit in with those kids?"

"I don't know," I said. "They aren't cool."

"Well being involved with criminal activity isn't cool," Momma B said.

"You've already been arrested once," Mom said. "Didn't you learn anything from that experience?"

I shrugged again.

"You're old enough to know right from wrong, Josh," Momma B said, "and to make the right choices for yourself and your future."

"What kind of a person do you want to be?" my mother asked. "When people talk about you, what do you want them to say about you?"

"I don't know," I said, "I haven't thought about that. I really don't care."

"Well, Josh, everyday you show the world who you are," Momma B said. "You show them by what you say, what you do, and who your friends are."

"Do you want to be known as a liar, a drug dealer, a thief?" Mom asked looking me in the eyes.

I didn't answer; I just stood against the wall staring at my parents.

"You define yourself by the friends you keep," Momma B said. "Do you want a reputation as a gang member and a criminal?"

Still, I said nothing.

"Remember the Kwanzaa principle?" Mom said. "If it's to be, it's up to me…"

I looked up at her.

"Well, it's up to you, Son," Mom said. "Who you are and what you want for your life is all up to you, Josh. You make the choices."

My parents walked out of the room leaving me alone to think. I sank down to the floor and hugged my knees to my body. I pulled the hood of my sweatshirt so that it covered my face. I rested my head on my arms and tears fell from my eyes.

CHAPTER

12

Fresh Start

"We've got to do something about Josh," Mom said to Brooke. "We can't let him continue down this path of crime."

"I agree," Momma B said. "We need to get him away from that crowd, and the sooner, the better."

"What do you think about moving to the San Juan Islands?" Mom said. "We love it up there."

"And the small rural community would give him the chance to make a fresh start away from those bad influences," Brooke said.

"Let's take Lynette and Josh up to Washington State and see what they think about the idea of moving there."

Lynette is my aunt, Momma B's sister. A few years ago, Lynette was in a terrible car accident in California. She broke a bunch of bones. Her lung collapsed, and she was in a coma for two months.

Just like with me, the doctors didn't think that she would survive. But Momma B drove to California every weekend to see and take care of her.

When she finally got out of the hospital, Lynette came to Tucson to live with us. She needed someone to take care of her while she continued to recover. Aunt Lynette has lived with us ever since.

"OK, I'll look into airline tickets," Momma B said. "Maybe we can go next month during Spring Break."

My folks bought the tickets and we flew to Seattle. We rented a car and drove 45 minutes north to Anacortes, WA. We drove the rental car onto the ferry and rode another 45 minutes to Lopez Island.

Lopez Island is a rural island with a population of about 2200 full time residents. The islanders are friendly and actually wave to one another when they pass on the two lane roads. There are a lot of small farms and we saw bald eagles and deer almost every day that we were there.

There's a small village on the island, with a grocery store, post office, doctor's office, barber shop, some churches, a few restaurants, and a drug store with a hamburger shop in the back. There's not a signal light anywhere on the island.

"Let's stop by the school," Mom said. "It looks like the high school, middle and elementary schools are all together on one campus."

We walked into the office of the high school and a kid my age walked up to me.

"Hi," he said, shaking my hand, "I'm Angus. Are you moving here?"

"Maybe," I said.

"Do you play football?" he asked.

"Yeah, you got a team?" I said.

"Yeah we do. Hey, here comes our coach, come on, I'll introduce you."

I met Coach Brown and a couple of other kids. They were cool and said they hoped I'd move there and join the team.

We left the school and looked at some houses that were for sale. My folks liked a little house that sat on eight acres. It had a meadow in the center of it, and was surrounded by trees.

"If we buy this house, Josh, you can explore all over the island," Momma B said.

"You mean that I can explore by myself?" I asked.

"Yep, it's very safe here," she said. "You can even hitch-hike because the people who live here know the kids."

"Wow, that's tight!" I said.

"So, what do you think of Lopez, Josh?" Mom asked me.

"I like it," I said.

"Would you like to live here?" Mom asked. "It would be a chance for you to make a fresh start. Nobody here knows about the problems you've had in Tucson. You can be the person that you want to be. What do you say?"

"I'm down with that," I said. "Can I play football?"

"Yes, you can," Mom said.

"Tight!" I said.

"Lynette, what are your thoughts?" Momma B asked.

"I think it's absolute paradise," Lynette said. "I'd love to live here."

My parents sold our house in Arizona and bought the small house with eight acres. They put our veterinary business in Tucson on the market. Because my parents still owned the veterinary hospital, Momma B and Lynette stayed in Tucson to run it while we waited for someone to buy it.

Football practice started in mid-August, so Mom took me to the doctor to get a sport's physical. A few days later, we loaded the car to make the three day drive to Washington.

We took two of our small dogs and two cats with us in the car. We arrived on Lopez the day before the start of football practice. The moving van with our furniture and other things didn't arrive until a week later, so Mom and I had to sleep on the floor until it got there. I definitely prefer sleeping on a bed to sleeping on the floor.

CHAPTER

13

Football

I'd never played football in my life and really didn't know much about the rules. Mom taught me how to throw a football when I was younger. She says I'm a natural athlete. That's a good thing because I didn't have any football skills when I showed up for the first day of practice.

My coaches and teammates were cool though. They tried to help me learn the game. We lived in a small community with only a limited number of students and players. As a matter of fact, there were only eight other kids in my entire sophomore class. Since we didn't have a lot of athletes we played in a league that needed only eight players on a team.

It was sprinkling one day at practice. I went to tackle a kid and must have done something wrong. I heard a loud 'SNAP' and then landed flat on my back on the ground.

"Come on, Josh, get up," Coach Brown said. "We're running the next drill."

"I can't move, Coach," I said. "I'm trying, but I can't move my arms or legs."

The coaches and players gathered around me.

"Don't play with me, Josh," Coach said. "Can you move or not?"

"I'm dead serious, Coach, I can't feel or move anything," I said.

"Somebody run to the office and have them call 911," Coach said. "Then notify his mother."

One of my teammates ran into the building and burst into the principal's office.

"Mr. McVey, we need to call 911," the kid said. "Josh is hurt and can't move his arms or legs."

Mr. McVey called the emergency squad and then dialed my home number.

"Jamie? This Principal McVey from the school. Joshua's been hurt in an accident during football practice. Can you come to the field?"

"I'll be right there," Mom said.

They were afraid to move me because they thought it might make things worse. The ambulance arrived and someone checked me over.

"Josh, we're going to slide this flat white board under your back," the man in charge said. "It won't be very comfortable for you, but it'll keep you from having additional injuries."

"OK," I said.

They strapped me down to the board. I had straps around my head, my chest, my hips, and my legs. Mom drove onto the practice field and sprinted to where I was lying.

"Honey, are you OK?" she asked.

"I can't feel anything in my arms or legs," I said.

"Oh, Joshie," she said.

"We're taking him to the clinic," the man said to my mom. "Doctor Ben has already left for the day, but they're calling him back in. Do you want to meet us there?"

"Sure."

It was a short ride to the medical clinic in the village. Mom pulled into the parking lot right behind the ambulance. The EMT squad left the board under me and put me onto a bed to be examined. Someone got me a blanket.

"Josh, we need to remove your practice jersey. We're going to cut it off of you," the nurse said.

"OK," I said.

"We need to cut off your shoulder pads too."

"OK, but then can you please cover me up again? I'm cold," I said.

"Sure, Honey," Mom said. She covered my bare chest as soon as the equipment was removed. "Is that better?"

"Yes, thanks, Mom."

"Do you think we should remove his helmet?" one of the nurses asked.

"Let's wait until Dr. Ben gets here."

"What about his football pants and pads? Should we cut those off now?"

"Yes, let's get him ready for the doctor."

I couldn't believe they were cutting off my leg pads. They were brand new pads that Coach B had special ordered for me. Coach gave them to me just yesterday and now they were going to be ruined. They cut off my clothes and now all that I had on were my socks and my under shorts. I was grateful to have the blanket over me.

Dr. Ben arrived and examined me. He decided that I needed to go to the hospital on the mainland. The nearest one is in Anacortes, Washington, which is a 45 minute boat ride.

"It's raining pretty hard, and it's getting really foggy," one of the ambulance people said. "There's no way the helicopter can fly him out of here in that soup."

"He just missed the ferry to the mainland," someone else said.

"Let's call the sheriff. His new boat might be able to get Josh and his Mom to the mainland," Dr. Ben said.

"I'm on it," the nurse said and picked up the phone.

"The sheriff has agreed to transport Joshua to the mainland," the nurse said. "You're to meet him at the dock at Odlin Park as soon as you can get there."

Mom called Momma B in Tucson to let her know what was going on. She followed the ambulance to the meeting site. By now it was pitch black, raining hard, and very foggy. Two men carried me through the rain onto the Sheriff's new boat. Mom left her car at the dock and went with me. The men put me on a bed inside the boat. I still couldn't feel anything and I was still lying on the flat white board.

"Everything will be OK, Honey," Mom said. "I love you."

"I love you too, Mom," I said.

The driver started the engine and we took off across the black waters of the Salish Sea.

CHAPTER
14
I Feel Nothing

I closed my eyes and wondered if I would be paralyzed. Would I spend the rest of my life in a wheelchair? Mom gently stroked my cheek. At least I could still feel her loving touch on my face.

Our boat had a small fog light on it which helped the driver see where he was going. A couple of times he cut the engine and we just drifted in the water.

The Sheriff's Department had purchased the boat just a week ago. The pilot wasn't used to the navigational system. He wasn't always sure where in the water we were. He didn't want to go any farther and find out we were way off our course.

"Look at those flashing orange lights," one of the EMT's said. "Do you think that's the ambulance waiting to meet us?"

"Let's hope so," the pilot said. "In this fog it's impossible to see anything and tell where we're going."

The pilot headed the boat towards the flashing beacons.

"Yes, it's the ambulance!" the pilot said.

By now it was 9:00 p.m. and starting to rain even harder.

"Thank you all so much," Mom said to the boat pilot and Lopez EMT crew. "We appreciate all that you've done for us. Have a safe trip home."

"Good luck to you, Joshua," they said. "Bye for now."

The Anacortes EMT's loaded me into their ambulance. Mom sat up front with the driver. When we arrived at the hospital I told the doctors what had happened during football practice. A doctor examined me, and he ordered some x-rays. I had been lying on that white flat board now for three hours.

"Can I get off of this board please? It's hurting my back," I said.

"Sorry, Josh," the nurse said. "For now, it needs to stay where it is."

Mom was concerned about our little dogs at home that needed to be fed and let out. She called one of the few people that she knew on Lopez. My football accident happened in September and we had only been on the island for about a month. Luckily, Mom was able to reach someone who said that she would take care of our pets for us.

"That's a relief," she said. "Now, we need to focus on taking care of you, Honey."

"These x-rays aren't telling me enough," the doctor said. "I'm ordering a CAT scan. We should know something more in the next 30 minutes."

After the CAT scan the doctor walked up to where Mom and I were waiting. We were still in the hospital emergency room.

"Ms. Carson, I'm still not satisfied and I'd like Joshua to have an MRI. Unfortunately, we don't have that equipment at this hospital," the doctor said. "He needs to be transported to Bellingham tonight."

Once again, I was loaded into the ambulance. Mom sat in the co-pilot seat. The rain continued to pour. Mom and I rode another 45 minutes in the ambulance up to the hospital in Bellingham, Washington. There we were cared for by another team of doctors and nurses. At 1:30 in the morning, I had the MRI. When the procedure was finished, they moved me into a regular hospital room for the rest of the night.

"Let's get this board out from under him," a male nurse said. "He's been lying on this hard wood for almost eight hours now."

Two people gently took the board from under my back. I was so relieved and happy to have that thing gone!

"There's a recliner," the nurse said to my mom. "Maybe you can get a little rest in it."

At 8:00 AM a nurse came into my room.

"Joshua, we need to do another MRI this morning," she said.

This time they pushed my bed, with me in it, down the hall. We went back to the room that I was in just a few hours before. While I was in there, Mom called Momma B again in Tucson. She wanted to update her on what was going on.

"He's having another MRI now," Mom said. "We haven't seen the doctor yet this morning, but I'm hoping he'll be by soon."

The test was finished and I was returned to my hospital room. When we were alone I said, "Mom, I can feel my toes, and I can move them too."

"What?" Mom said. "Show me."

Mom lifted the blankets off of my feet, and I showed her that I could wiggle my toes. She called the nurse and told her the news. The nurse notified the doctor who came to my room and examined me.

"Josh, you're a very lucky young man," the doctor said. "You have a very unique football injury called a 'Stinger.' I've never seen this type of football injury before. I've only heard about it."

"Will I be OK?" I asked.

"Yes, you should be getting feeling back in both arms and legs," he said. "Let me know when you feel normal again, and we'll send you home."

CHAPTER

15

Butt Naked and Stranded

"Does this mean that we can go home now?" I asked Mom.

"Well, I need to find you some clothes first," she said. "We can't have you walking out of here buck naked or butt naked either."

"Huh?" I said.

"Never mind," Mom said. "I just mean that you need some clothes. I'll talk with the hospital social worker about finding you something. I'm sure that she'll help us."

Mom spoke with the social worker and explained what had happened to me. She told her that my football uniform had been cut off of me at the medical clinic on Lopez, and that the only clothes I had were my socks and under shorts.

"We'll have to find that young man some clothes," she said. "Will sweatpants, a sweatshirt, and some flip-flops work?"

"Perfect," Mom said, "and thanks."

"OK, that problem is being handled," Mom said. "Now we need to figure out how to get from Bellingham, Washington to Anacortes so that we can catch the ferry to the island."

Once again, Mom called the few people that she knew on the island. Peggy, at the bookstore, had some friends who lived in Bellingham. They were willing to pick us up at the hospital and drive us to the ferry landing in Anacortes.

"These people are amazing," Mom said. "The call for 'Help' goes out, and perfect strangers are there to lend a hand. That sense of community is one of the great things about living on this small island. That type of caring is very special."

With the help of our new friends, we returned to our home on the island. Our dogs and cats were happy to see us, and greeted us with squeals of delight and full body wiggles. The feeling was mutual.

My accident pretty much ended my football career. The season was almost over when I got hurt, and the doctor told me to 'take it easy, and not play any football for another two weeks.'

By the time those two weeks were up, it was time for basketball season to begin. I tried out for the team, and the coach selected me for the squad. I still didn't feel like I fit in with the other guys on the team. I wanted friends. I wanted to feel like I belonged.

Although I spent two hours with the jocks every day after school at practice, they didn't invite me to sit with them during lunch. I still felt different and left out. I was lonely and tired of feeling different and alone.

CHAPTER

16

Girls, Girls, Girls

I didn't have a lot of guy friends at school, but I was pretty popular with some of the girls. Three of them followed me around the campus every day. They came to my football and basketball games. The really funny thing is that Brittany, Shannon, and Tina were all best friends. Sometimes I wasn't sure which one I was going out with. They were sort of a package deal.

Brittany was a senior. She was white, about my height, and had shoulder length brown hair. She had a great smile and a wonderful laugh. Britt was a lot of fun and I liked her a lot.

"Joshua would you like to have one of my senior yearbook pictures?" she asked one morning before school started.

"Sure," I said.

Brittany handed me the photo. It was a casual pose where she was smiling at the camera while sitting on the limb of a tree.

"Wow, you look beautiful, Brittany," I said.

"Thanks, Josh, do you really think so?"

"Yeah, this is a great photo of you. Thanks."

It was easy for me to talk with Brittany. She'd call me every night, and we'd talk about the problems that I was having with my girlfriend of the day. I was a player and changed girlfriends pretty often.

Even before Britt and I were dating, she used to give me a good luck hug before every football game. Heck, we'd hug just about every time I saw her. She's a good person and a friend.

Then there was Tina, who was a sophomore and a close friend to Brittany.

Tina was also a white girl. She was cute and had brown hair that she wore in a shag haircut. She had the most beautiful blue eyes. They reminded me of the ocean because they'd change color with the light in the sky.

Tina was into music and we were in the school band together. Our band wasn't your typical high school band. We didn't march or perform at football games. We only had six members; a drummer, three guitar players, a singer, and me. I played the keyboard. Tina was our lead vocalist and the only girl in our group.

Tina and I started dating one fall day when we went to a band gig in Seattle. Since our group was small the parents drove us places for our field trips and performances. Tina and I rode with my mom in our car while the rest of the band rode in two other cars.

Tina and I got together during the drive down to the Seattle Center. By the time we reached the city, we were holding hands. We dated off and on until she gave me the bad news. We were talking on the phone when she told me.

"I'm sorry, Josh, but I have to break up with you," she said.

"How come?" I asked. "You said that you loved me."

"I do, but my dad says that I can't date you."

"Why not?" I asked. "Is it because I'm black?"

"Hmmmmm...yes," she said.

I was quiet for a minute then finally said, "It's OK, I understand. Talk with you later. Bye."

"Bye," she said through tears, and then hung up the phone. I told Tina that I understood and respected what her father had said. But deep down inside I didn't understand at all. I thought it sucked!

After Tina broke up with me I wanted to do something really special for her. I picked a perfect rose from my parents' garden at home. I selected the prettiest and sweetest smelling blossom that I could find.

The petals were a deep peach color and they felt like velvet when I touched them to my lips. I cut off the flower leaving a long stem, and wrapped it in a wet paper towel. Then I put aluminum foil around the bottom of the flower to hold in moisture. The village is about eight miles from our house. I hitched a ride and went to the restaurant where Tina worked as a server.

"Hi," I said to the owner. "Is Tina here? May I please see her for a minute?" The restaurant didn't have many patrons right then, so Tina was able to go on a break.

"A beautiful rose for a beautiful lady," I said, handing my gift to her.

Tina had tears in her eyes and she gave me a hug.

"Thank you Josh," she said. "That's the nicest thing anyone has ever given me. I'll never forget you."

I turned around and left the restaurant. Giving her the rose made me feel better. I hope that she doesn't forget me because I won't forget her either.

The third girl in the group was Shannon. Shannon and Tina were best friends and Shannon was also white. She was twelve and in the eighth grade, but she looked and acted a lot older. She was a little shorter than I, and the top of her head came up to my eyebrows. Shannon was pretty and had shoulder length blonde hair.

Shannon always came to my games and band gigs. Somehow she'd manage to show up wherever I was. She was the first girl to give me a French kiss. It happened one Saturday when I was at the Skate Park. Shannon was there watching me roller blade. I'd rather roller blade than ride my skate board.

"Josh, can you take a break and go for a walk with me?" she asked. "There's a little path in the woods not far from the park. Want to check it out?"

"Sure, OK," I said, as I sat down on the bench and removed my skates. "We'll be back in a few minutes, guys," I yelled to the other kids at the park. Nobody responded.

The path was soft and wide and covered with bark. We walked side by side holding hands. The trail wound back and forth, turning left and then right. We came to a small clearing and Shannon stopped and turned her body facing mine. I put my arms around her back and pulled her close to me. She wrapped her arms around my neck. I could feel my heart pounding under my shirt.

Shannon lifted her face, closed her eyes and gently touched her lips to mine. Her lips were soft, moist, and tender. They parted just a little so I opened my mouth to match hers. Then I felt the moist tickle of her tongue touching mine. It sent an electric charge through my body. Our tongues danced for a moment and then Shannon slowly pulled away.

She looked at me and smiled. She gave me a little kiss on my mouth and then on my cheek. Then we stood for a moment in the woods, just holding each other. I thought for sure that I must be in love. About a week later, Shannon and I were talking on the phone just like we did every day. She said she wanted to break up with me.

"Josh, I'm sorry, but I'm not ready for a relationship," she said. "I'm breaking up with you and am going to be single for a while."

"Yeah, OK," I said with a cool tone. "I'm going to be single, too." I didn't know what to think about our break-up. I was confused, hurt, and angry.

My mom had gone into the village and had left me home to do some chores. I was supposed to separate the recycling items and get them ready to take to the recycling center the next day. The sun was beginning to set and I decided to ride my bike instead. I needed to blow off some steam.

My bike had 20 gears, hand brakes, and a narrow seat. I yanked it out of the barn and jumped on. I pedaled as fast as I could down our driveway and onto the country road.

I didn't stop and look for oncoming traffic. Instead, I peddled hard and moved onto the wrong side of the road. Lucky for me, nobody else was on the road coming towards me. I tossed the handlebars from side to side, pumping the pedals as hard as they would go. I was mad and the madder I got, the harder I pumped. The harder I pumped, the faster I went and the better I began to feel.

Within minutes, however, I became winded and started sucking for air. I have exercise induced asthma. That means that sometimes I have trouble breathing when I exercise too hard. I began wheezing as my lungs began to close, cutting off my air supply. I didn't have my inhaler with me, so I had to stop riding. I hoped that by resting I could end the asthma attack.

I stood on the double yellow line, which was painted down the center of the road. About 20 feet from me was the top of a hill. I straddled my bike and tried to catch my breath. Off in the distance I heard the distinct rumble of a large diesel truck. The road made an "S" curve, and I couldn't tell from which direction the sound was coming. Frozen in place, I listened as the roaring engine approached.

Suddenly, two bright headlights were shining on my face. The front grill of a huge, red Mack truck appeared at the crest of the hill. The driver's eyes locked on mine as he swerved to avoid hitting me. His heavy load passed inches from my bike and body. I watched him disappear around the next bend in the road. I shook my head, climbed back onto the seat and headed home. That truck driver should have been more careful. He was lucky he didn't hit me!

CHAPTER 17

The Gun

Getting dumped by my girlfriends wasn't fun, but I got over it pretty quickly. I figured that I was a cool guy and could have another girlfriend any time I wanted. I decided to stay single and remove all of that drama from my life for a while.

Monday morning I went to school and was hanging out by the gym when a ninth grader told me that a friend of mine wanted to see me. He pointed to the back of the building and I went over to see what was happening.

"Hey, man, what's up?" I asked.

"Look," he said, and he pulled a pistol out from under his jacket.

"Whoa!" I said, "Let me see it."

"Not here, somebody could see us," he said.

"OK, then let's go into the restroom."

We casually walked into the boys' restroom and made sure that no one else was in there.

"Let me see it, man," I said.

He handed the gun to me. It looked old and was a little rusty.

"Sweet," I said. "Where'd you get it?"

"Not saying," he said.

I turned to look at myself in the mirror.

"Does it work?" I asked.

"Don't know, maybe," he said.

Just then the bell rang to announce the beginning of first period.

"Give it back, Josh," he said. "I gotta go."

I handed the weapon back to him and he walked out of the room. I followed behind and watched as he walked off the school property and headed towards the village. I made it to class and had just sat down when the school secretary appeared at the classroom door.

"Joshua, please come with me," she said, as she motioned for me to follow her.

I shrugged, stood up and walked behind her to the principal's office. Mr. McVey was the principal and he had already heard about the gun. He started asking me questions about it and the boy who had brought it to school. He asked me if I had held the pistol and I told him the truth.

"Yes, sir," I said. "I held it in the restroom."

"Do you know where the boy was going when he left the school campus, Josh?"

"No, sir, I honestly don't know. But he was walking towards town."

Mr. McVey picked up the phone and dialed my home number.

"Jamie?" he said into the telephone. "This is Ron McVey down at the school. There's been an incident and I'm suspending Joshua."

"What's he done?" Mom asked.

"I'd prefer to talk about it when you get here. Can you come down here now?"

"Of course," Mom said. "I'll be right there."

Mom arrived at the principal's office within ten minutes. The school secretary brought her into the principal's office. I was sitting in a chair with my legs stretched out, my arms folded across my chest, and my head down.

"Hi, Josh," Mom said. She sounded worried.

"Hi," I said, not looking up.

Mom sat down and looked at the principal and then me.

"What happened?" Mom asked.

"Apparently, one of Joshua's friends brought a hand gun to school today," the principal said. "He told Josh about it and they went into the boy's restroom so Josh could see it. Josh has admitted to holding the pistol while they were in the bathroom."

"Oh, my, gosh!" Mom said. "Is everyone okay?"

"Nothing happened," the principal said. "The student ended up leaving the school campus and taking the gun with him. Another student came forward and told me about the gun.

Just then there was a knock at the door. The secretary asked to speak with Mr. McVey in private. He stepped out of the room and then quickly returned.

"With the help of the Sheriff's Department, we were able to locate the student and obtain the weapon without any problems."

"Thank God," Mom said.

"Yes, the young man claims that he found the gun along the side of the road. And that it was rusty and not in good working condition," the principal said. "He said that it probably wouldn't even fire, and that he wasn't intending to use it, he just wanted to show it off to his friends."

"Well, a school certainly isn't the place to be showing off a gun," Mom said.

"No, it's not. The student with the gun will be suspended for the rest of the year. And technically, since Josh was in possession of the hand gun while on school property, I need to suspend him too. He'll be suspended for three days."

"Josh, why didn't you tell a teacher or the principal about the gun?" Mom asked.

"I don't know," I said.

"Why did you hold the gun?" Mom said.

"I wanted to see what it felt like," I said.

"Josh, you know that guns are dangerous, and it's terrible to have a gun at school. Don't you remember watching the news and hearing about all of those horrible school shootings where kids, teachers, and staff were slaughtered by gun violence? "

"Nobody was going to shoot anybody," I argued.

"I'm glad to hear that, but accidents happen. You need to use your head, Josh. And you need to pick different friends. These kids could get you into some very serious trouble," Mom said.

I shrugged and looked away from her. I didn't see why she was making such a big deal of it.

"Is there anything else, Mr. McVey?" she asked.

"Yes, sometime in the next day or two Josh needs to go to the Sheriff's Office and fill out some paper work."

"All right, we'll do that. Thank you," Mom said.

"So who was the boy?" Mom asked as soon as we got in the car.

"You don't know him," I said.

"Probably not, but I'd like to know his name."

"It doesn't matter. You don't need to know his name."

"Josh, you've got to stay away from situations and people who can get you into trouble. Do you understand that?"

I didn't answer her.

"Shall we go to the Sheriff's Office now and take care of the paperwork?"

"I guess."

So that's what we did. The Deputy took my sworn statement about what happened. He didn't think that I'd be called to testify, but said that it was a possibility. I felt sorry for my friend. He's an okay guy. He just got caught bringing that gun to school.

I stayed home for three days and Mom put me to work around the farm. I would much rather have been at school with my friends than doing manual labor at home.

CHAPTER

18

A Business Proposition

After my three day suspension I returned to school. Two months later the school year ended and I had completed my sophomore year. I had also turned sixteen and wanted to get my driver's license.

"Mom, can I get my driver's permit?" I asked.

"What have I always said about driving and dating?" she said.

"You said that I had to wait until I was thirty to drive or date. But that's dumb."

"I know you may think it's dumb," Mom said, "But I've always thought that thirty sounded about right for you." She winked at me.

I gave her a look that said, 'I'm not buying that idea.'

"OK, you get the driver's manual and study the laws. I'll look into a driver's education class that you can take."

I smiled and asked her if I could go to the Skate Park for a while. She thought about it for a minute and finally said, "OK." I grabbed my skates and walked down the gravel driveway.

Instead of heading towards the village, where the park was, I turned in the opposite direction. I was hoping to find some friends and hang with them at their place. Nobody was home at my friend's house, so I headed for the house where this older guy, Charlie, lived. He was a cool dude. Charlie was in his late thirties. I had met him a few days earlier when he picked me up when I was hitch-hiking. He gave me a ride home in his old Chevy truck.

I stepped onto the porch and yelled for him, "Charlie? You home?"

"Back here, c'mon in," he said.

I opened the door and let the screen door slam. Walking into the kitchen, I found Charlie was seated at a table. He was petting his cat, Whiskers, drinking a beer and smoking a cigarette.

"Hey, man, good to see you," Charlie said. "Grab yourself a beer, my man."

I opened the refrigerator and reached for a beer. The cold can stung like a snowball in the palm of my hand.

"Man, this is cold!" I said.

Charlie laughed, "I had them in the freezer for a little while. I wanted cold beer in a hurry."

The feel of the cold can sent a shiver down my spine. I pulled on the tab and beer bubbled up onto the top of the can. I took a swig even though I didn't really like the taste of beer, but I drank it anyway.

"So, Josh," Charlie said, "What brings you to my place?"

"I'm supposed to be at the Skate Park," I said. "But I decided to come hang here instead."

"Good move, my man," he said. "I have a business proposition for you."

"Oh, yeah, what's that?" I asked.

"I know where there's a piece of land here on the island that we can buy together. It's on the water and the owner is selling it for only $135,000. If we buy it now and sell it in the future, we'll make a fortune."

"Sweet!" I said, "I'm down with that."

"Do you think your mom will sign the loan with us?" Charlie asked.

"I don't know," I said. "Let's go find out."

We got in Charlie's truck and drove to my house. Mom was outside working in the garden.

"Hi, Mom," I said. "You know Charlie, right?"

"Yes, Hi, Charlie," Mom said. "How was the park, Honey?"

"I didn't make it there. My blades needed some repairs, so I stopped at Charlie's so he could help me fix them."

"Hummmm," Mom said.

"Hummmm, can we talk to you a minute?" I asked.

"OK," Mom said. "Let's go sit in the shade."

Charlie, Mom, and I sat down in the shade of the evergreen trees.

"Mom, I want to go into business with Charlie," I said. "He knows about some property that's for sale that we can buy for $135,000. The land is on the water, and if you'll sign the loan for us, we can sell the land in the future and make a fortune."

"Excuse me a minute," Charlie said. "I'll let you two discuss this in private." He walked towards his truck.

"Josh, there is something wrong with a grown man who wants to go into the real estate business with a sixteen year old boy," Mom said. "He's trying to use you and me, and there's no way that I'm going to sign a loan with him."

After a few minutes, Charlie came back from the truck and sat down in the grass with us.

"Charlie, my mom said 'No.' She won't sign the loan with us," I said.

"Man, that's a bummer," Charlie said. "This is a prime real estate opportunity and we'd be super business partners."

"Charlie, nobody is going to loan that kind of money to a teenage boy," Mom said. "He's under-age, he doesn't have a job, and he isn't a good credit risk."

"I don't know," Charlie said. "Josh has two jobs lined up for the summer. He looks like a good risk to me."

"Then you're not thinking clearly," Mom said as she shook her head. "Well, if that's all you wanted to discuss, then I'm going back to my garden. Josh I need you to stay here and give me a hand."

Charlie stood up, walked to his truck and drove away. I was mad, but I followed Mom towards the vegetable garden.

"Mom, I don't know why you can't sign that loan for me. Why won't you support me?"

"Josh, I already told you. That guy, Charlie, is bad news. He's trying to take advantage of you; he's trying to use you. You shouldn't trust an adult who thinks it's a good idea to go into business with a teenager. I want you to stay away from him."

I started to argue but stopped myself. Instead, I simply turned around and walked out of the garden. Mom called after me but I ignored her and walked to Charlie's place.

CHAPTER
19

Charlie

A few hours later I returned home. It was time for dinner time and I knew that my mom was making spaghetti. She makes the best spaghetti and I didn't want to miss out on eating it. I walked into the kitchen and dropped my backpack on the floor. Mom came over to me.

"It's nice of you to come home," she said.

I just looked at her.

"Let me see your backpack," Mom said.

"Why?" I asked.

"Because I want to see what you have in there."

She lifted my bag off of the floor and placed it on the counter. She opened it and found three full bottles of beer.

"Where did these come from?" she asked.

"I found them along the side of the road," I said.

"Sure you did."

Mom unzipped the side pocket of my bag.

"And I suppose you found this open pack of Marlboros and this lighter along the road too?"

I shrugged.

"While you were gone this afternoon I took some of your clean clothes up to your room. While I was there, I noticed that the small ceiling door that leads to the attic space was slightly open so I decided to investigate."

I felt uneasy and shifted my weight from one foot to another.

"I got the step stool and a flashlight and had a look inside the attic. Guess what I found?"

I didn't answer. I just stared at my mother. Mom reached into a brown grocery bag and pulled out several items.

"I found these eight rolled joints and these two lighters. I also found these rolling papers and this empty vile that smells like it has held marijuana. What are you doing with these things, Josh? You know that you aren't allowed to have any of this stuff. Where did you get it?"

"It doesn't matter," I said angrily.

"Yes, it does. Somebody is selling or giving you illegal substances. This has to stop, and it has to stop now!"

"It's no big deal, just leave me alone," I shouted.

"Josh, I've had it with you. You won't listen to a word I say. You don't respect me and you refuse to follow the rules. I'm tired of you lying to me. If you're going to continue to disobey me, then you can just leave. Get out now!"

Mom was yelling now too. She pointed to the stairs and the front door. I walked toward the door.

"And don't let the door hit you in the butt on the way out," she said called after me.

I turned around and walked out into the evening air.

After I left, Mom called the Sheriff's Office and spoke with the Deputy. She told him that she suspected Charlie had given me some beer, cigarettes, marijuana, and a lighter. She told him about the things that she had found in my room. Mom asked the Deputy to look for me. She said that if he found me with Charlie, to deliver a message to the man. Tell him to, "Stay away from my son!"

The Deputy found us as we were about to get into a kayak. He talked with Charlie and delivered my mother's message. Then he drove me home. I walked into the house. I didn't say anything to my mom, nor did she talk to me. I just went up the stairs to my room where I stayed until morning. I didn't get my spaghetti.

CHAPTER

20

My People

For the next few days Mom and I didn't have much to say to each other. We were polite but I stayed out of her way. One morning Mom was sitting on our back deck drinking her morning coffee. She liked to listen to the birds and watch the bunnies play in the yard.

"Mom, I love you," I said. "I'm sorry that I've cause so much trouble. I'm not happy living here. This island is just too white for me. I don't fit in anywhere. I need to be around black people. I want to go live with my people."

"Well, Josh, I'm sorry that you are blaming race as the cause of your problems. It's never been an issue with us. But I'll see what I can do to help you connect more with 'your people.'"

My mother has always been amazing at making things happen. Within a month I was living with the Cage family on the mainland in Washington State.

Everyone in the house was African American.

The family was made up of the mother, Roberta, and her mother, Gayle, and four kids. Two of the kids, Jabar and Jamall, were guys my own age. Jabar was in foster care and Jamall was Roberta's nephew. The oldest girl was Georganne. She was

Roberta's biological daughter. The youngest girl was Kamisha and she was adopted. Roberta told my mom that she knew how to handle me and raise a black child.

It was September and I enrolled in Avonworth High School for my junior year. The plan was for me to stay with the Cages until the first semester was over. Then, depending on how things were going, I would either finish the year with this family or return home to live with my mom.

Since I wasn't around to take care of anymore, my mother decided to temporarily return to Tucson, Arizona to help sell our family veterinary business. She and Momma B had been living apart for over a year now and they were tired of it. So Mom drove the two little dogs and cats back to Arizona. In November Mom got a phone call from Roberta Cage.

"I'm sorry, but Joshua has to go," she said. "He won't follow the rules, he comes and goes as he pleases, and he's disrespectful to me. He won't do his homework, and I've caught him smoking marijuana in the park. I can't do this anymore. You need to get this child out of my house! You need to send him an airplane ticket because he's out of here come Thanksgiving."

Mom sent me a ticket. I packed a suitcase and my keyboard and flew from Seattle, Washington to Tucson. My parents met me at the airport.

"Hi Josh," Momma B said, as she gave me a hug. "It's nice to see you."

"Hi Moms," I said. "It's good to see you too."

"I'm sorry that living with 'your people' didn't work out for you," Momma B said. "Apparently, black folks have rules and expect them to be followed, just like white folks do. It isn't about race, is it, Josh?"

"No," I said.

"Nothing has changed here, Joshua," Mom said. "When you are living under our roof, you need to obey our rules, 'Capeesh?"

'Capeesh' means 'understand.'

"Capeesh," I said.

We got into the car and headed for Momma B's little apartment. That is where she and my mom had lived after selling our house over a year ago.

"I'd like to call my friends and just hang out for a few days," I said. "I haven't seen them in over a year."

"Oh, no, Josh," Momma B said, "Your mom has already enrolled you in a charter high school. You start on Monday."

"Geez," I said, and sank down in the back of the car.

CHAPTER

21

Reunited

I arrived back in Tucson a week before Thanksgiving. My big brother, Randall Jr., or R.J. had turned eighteen and aged out of foster care. He was living in a group home. He had called my mom, and she told him that I was back in town.

"Yo, Josh, what's up little brother?" he asked.

"Not much, what's up with you?" I said.

"Good stuff, listen, I've been talking with our dad. He sent me a couple of letters and we've talked on the phone. He lives in Phoenix and wants to see us. Can you ask your mom if you can meet him?"

"Yeah, just a minute. Hey, Mom, R.J.'s been talking to my dad! He wants to meet me. Can I meet him?" I asked.

"Yes, but I have some conditions for the meeting. I want to make sure the experience will be a positive one for you."

Mom's conditions for my dad and me to meet were:

- That my moms would meet him too.
- We would meet in a restaurant.
- For Dad to only talk about positive things.

Dad agreed to the conditions and we set up the meeting for the Saturday after Thanksgiving. Dad would drive from his home in Phoenix, AZ down to Tucson. That's about a two hour drive.

I was nervous and excited about seeing my birth father. I hadn't seen him in fourteen years. My parents and I drove to the restaurant and I walked into the dining room ahead of them. Immediately, I spotted a tall, thin, black man standing next to a large circular booth. He smiled at me and called my name.

"Joshua," he said, smiling and holding out his arms.

"Dad," I said running to him.

We hugged and smiled for a long time. Then I introduced him to my parents and he hugged them too.

"Thank you so much for taking such great care of Joshua," he said to my mom. "Thank you, thank you, thank you!"

Dad had a friend, Sarah, with him who was video taping our reunion. Sarah had been a friend of my dad's for years, and was so thrilled that his dream of reuniting with his kids was finally coming true.

We nervously laughed and talked until my brother, RJ, arrived at the restaurant. Then we started hugging and laughing all over again. Our baby sister, Amanda May, wasn't with us that day. She'd been adopted and had a new family. We weren't sure if her parents would let her come to the reunion, so we didn't tell her about it. We thought she'd have to meet our dad another time.

Dad, RJ, my moms and I sat down in the booth. We started to talk and make up for lost time. Mom had written down questions for my father, so he began by answering those. Mom took notes on what he said. She wanted to have a record of the information for me.

My dad told us about his birth family and his parents. He talked about his siblings and about his life. He told us how he met my birth mother, DeShona, and about their struggles and their difficult life together. He showed us a photo of her.

"She's pretty," I said.

"Yes, she is, Josh," my dad said.

"Here are some old pictures of RJ, Amanda, and Joshua," he said.

"I remember that little blue car!" RJ said, as he looked at a photo of the three of us standing next to a little toy car.

"Yeah, we rode that thing all over the yard!" I said.

"I've never forgotten my kids," Dad said. "I've been trying to get my children back ever since I signed the papers to give up my parental rights. That was fourteen years ago. I felt pressured by the state social workers to sign the papers. Signing those papers really tore me up inside. It was the biggest mistake of my life."

"I'm sure that was a very difficult time for you," Mom said.

"Yeah," Dad said. "DeShona and I divorced and she moved to Tennessee. I didn't think that I could take care of three kids and hold down a job. Not all by myself. I was a young, scared, gay, black man. I felt alone in the world. My family rejected me because I was gay. I didn't have a support system. I thought the kids would be better off with somebody else, so I signed those papers."

"Wow, that must have been rough," Momma B said.

"My life has really improved now that I'm with my partner, Gabriel. He's a tailor and he used to make all of my clothes. We had a commitment ceremony and have been together for almost fourteen years now."

"Congratulation!" my moms said at the same time, "That's wonderful!"

A few years ago my moms had a commitment ceremony too. A commitment ceremony is like a wedding. I got to dress up and be part of it. It was fun.

Dad told us that both he and Gabriel were HIV positive. That means that they have a serious disease. Dad said that they had been sick for many years, but that he and Gabriel had learned how to live with and manage their disease. Dad said that was why he was so thin. He's even skinnier than I am.

"Gabriel has two sons that I helped to raise. Their names are Gabriel Jr. and Malcolm. They're adults now. From the beginning, we were actively trying to get my kids back. One time we came close to being approved to adopt RJ but that didn't work out. We've been planning this reunion forever. Gabriel and I even bought a house with five bedrooms so that there would be enough bedrooms for everybody."

"Wow, that's a long time to hold onto a dream," Mom said.

"Yeah, but it's what kept me going. Four years ago, Gabe and I adopted a baby boy together. Our son's name is Gemini."

"You mean I have another brother?" I asked.

"Yes, Joshua, and you also have a sister named Kameo. She and her baby live in Mississippi."

"Wow, that's tight!" I said.

When Dad was telling us about Gabriel, Gabriel Jr., and Malcolm, Momma B got a strange look on her face.

"You look like you've seen a ghost," Dad said to Momma B.

"I think that I know Gabriel and his sons," Momma B said. "Did he used to live in Tucson and raise Boston Terriers?"

"Yes, he did," Dad said.

"I was their veterinarian," Momma B said.

"I went to your animal hospital once with Gabriel," Dad said. "I thought you looked familiar."

"Talk about a small world..." Momma B said.

"Randall, can you tell us about when DeShona was pregnant with Joshua?" Mom asked. "Did she drink alcohol while she was pregnant with him?"

"Oh, yes ma'am," Dad said. "DeShona liked beer the best but she'd drink just about any type of alcohol she could get. And she had a very difficult pregnancy when she was carrying Joshua."

"What do you mean?" Mom asked.

"Well, a few months into her pregnancy, DeShona's placenta began to tear," Dad said.

"Josh, you remember that a fetus develops in its mother's womb for about nine months, right?" Mom asked.

"Yes," I said.

"Well, the placenta is sort of like a blanket that surrounds a developing baby. It is a lifeline that connects the fetus and the mother. The fetus gets oxygen and food from its mother through the placenta. Everything that the mother eats, drinks, or smokes passes into the developing baby's brain and body. If a woman drinks alcohol, smokes cigarettes, marijuana, or crack cocaine, or takes other drugs while she is pregnant, these substances can damage her developing baby. The infant can be born with physical disabilities and brain damage. Alcohol, tobacco and drugs can cause physical, mental, and emotional problems for that baby from the moment he is born until the day he dies," Mom explained.

"Wow," I said, "I never knew that."

"Unfortunately, a lot of people don't realize how potentially dangerous the combination of alcohol, tobacco, drugs and pregnancy can be," Mom said.

"DeShona started bleeding heavily because of her torn placenta. The doctor ordered her to stay in bed and rest," Dad said. "Joshua ended up coming almost three months early, and he was delivered by an emergency Cesarean Section. He almost didn't make it. He was so tiny and fragile. The doctors had him in the Newborn's Intensive Care Unit of the hospital. He was hooked up to all kinds of machines so that he could survive. He stayed in the hospital for three or four months before he could come home."

"Oh, my gosh!" said Mom.

"Yeah, Joshua only weighed 2 pounds and 2 ounces when he was born."

"How much alcohol did DeShona drink?" Mom asked.

"Well, she liked to party. DeShona drank throughout the pregnancy. As a matter of fact, she even drank wine coolers when she was in the hospital for her emergency C-Section."

"You're kidding," Mom said.

"No, ma'am, I'm not kidding," he said. "She had permission from the doctors to drink wine coolers because she was so agitated without the alcohol. They hoped the coolers would help calm her nerves."

"Well, that certainly explains a lot," Mom said, as she looked at me and smiled.

We sat quietly for a few minutes then Momma B asked, "Randall is Gabriel in town with you today?"

"Yes, ma'am," Dad said. "He and Gemini are visiting Gabriel's son, Malcolm. He doesn't live far from here."

"Can you call him and ask him to meet us here? I'd love to see him again."

"Yes, ma'am!" Dad said with a big grin.

Dad called Gabe and he agreed to come to the restaurant. He brought Gemini, and his adult son, Malcolm, with him. It was great to meet this part of my family. We talked in the parking lot for half an hour. Finally, we said 'goodbye' and went our separate ways. I was so happy to see my father again!

CHAPTER

22

Time With Dad

It had been a great day for me. My dad promised that we would see each other again soon. I climbed into the back seat of our car and was lost in my thoughts about our reunion. That evening I asked Mom if I could call my dad on the phone. She said, "OK," so Dad and I spent another half an hour talking.

"Mom, Dad wants to know if I can go up to Phoenix sometime and visit him," I asked as soon as we hung up the phone.

"That would be fine, Josh," Mom said.

"Can I call Dad back and let him know?"

"OK, and find out when he would like for you to come."

I called my dad back. He was thrilled that my mom said that I could visit him at his home.

"Joshua, you are always welcome here," he said. "Can you come this weekend?"

Mom said that was fine and she made arrangements for me to ride the Greyhound bus from Tucson to Phoenix. Mom started giving me bus fare so that I could spend every weekend with my dad. It felt great to spend time with him. We were a lot alike.

Mom even let me spend Christmas with Dad and his family that year. It was the first time that he and I were together for the holiday since I was three years old. My brother, R.J., was there, and Dad's partner, Gabriel, and Gemini. I got to meet my Dad's mother, Grandma Jody, too. I hadn't seen her since I was three years old.

"Joshua, you have no idea how wonderful it is for me to see and hug you again," Grandma Jody said. "I've prayed for you every day since you left. Being able to hold you in my arms again is the answer to my prayers."

After the holiday, I returned to Tucson. I told my parents what I was thinking and feeling.

"Moms, when I turn eighteen, I want to go live with my father," I said.

"OK, Josh," Mom said, "If that's what you want and if Randall wants that too."

That was exactly what my dad wanted. We started planning and counting down the days 'til I would be eighteen. That's when I could move to Phoenix and we could live together again.

CHAPTER

23

My Invisible Disabilities

Two days after my reunion with my dad, Mom called a woman named Teresa Kellerman. She's the director of the Fetal Alcohol Syndrome Community Resource Center in Tucson. They set an appointment to talk in person the next day.

"Hi, I'm Jamie Carson," Mom said. "We spoke yesterday on the phone about my son, Joshua."

"Yes, I'm Teresa Kellerman," she said. "It's nice to meet you. Please sit down."

Mom took a seat and looked around the room. She saw several photos of a young Native American man.

"That's my son, John," Teresa said. "I adopted him when he was just a few days old."

"I was reading about him on your website," Mom said.

"John has a diagnosis of Fetal Alcohol Syndrome," Teresa said. "He has the facial characteristics of FAS, and people can see that he has a disability. The term Fetal Alcohol Spectrum Disorder or FASD is not a diagnosis. It is an umbrella term used to describe the many physical, mental, emotional, behavioral and learning challenges caused by prenatal exposure to alcohol."

"I see," Mom said. "My son, Joshua, has had many possible diagnoses over the years. We've been told that he may have Attention Deficit Hyperactivity Disorder or ADHD, Post Traumatic Stress Disorder or PTSD, maybe Reactive Attachment Disorder or RAD, possibly Conduct Disorder, Oppositional Defiance, and even Bipolar Disorder. The list of possibilities goes on but none of the experts told us that he probably suffers from FASD. I've been reading a lot about these disabilities and the behaviors seem to describe my son."

"Kids with FASD fall into a wide range of behaviors, abilities, and disabilities. That's why it's called a spectrum. There are a lot of disorders that seem to occur with FASD. Some children have normal, above normal or even genius intelligence. Others have below normal intelligence."

"Josh has a normal IQ," Mom said.

"Many kids with FASD are talented in art or music. My son, John, for example is a talented drummer."

"Josh is athletic, good with his hands, and he has an aptitude for music," Mom said. "But I've been reading about FASD on the internet and about some of the struggles these children face growing up," Mom said.

"Oh, yes," Teresa said. "FASD causes many serious challenges. Some FASD babies are physically small, like my son, John. You can see from his baby picture that he was little and looks different from most babies," Teresa said as she handed my mother a photograph of her son. "Alcohol exposed babies may have permanent brain damage causing mental and emotional disabilities. Behavioral issues are the biggest problem."

"I've certainly experienced behavioral issues with Joshua," Mom said. "I used to think that he misbehaved on purpose just to push my buttons."

"Kids with FASD don't intentionally cause trouble," Teresa said. "They're doing the best they can under the circumstances. These kids have poor impulse control. They say and do things without thinking. Often their actions are careless and risky, causing them to get into trouble. Their brains are damaged, and they aren't able to learn from their mistakes. They can't connect their behaviors to the outcome."

"That sure describes Joshua," Mom said. "I could never understand why he was so reckless or why he kept repeating the same mistakes over and over."

"People with this type of brain damage have difficulty with organization, sequencing, and planning," Teresa said. "They have difficulty managing money, working with abstract concepts such as time, logical reasoning, and making good decisions. They are very literal thinkers."

"Josh is a terrible money manager," Mom said. "He can't save a dime. As soon as he has a couple of bucks, it's gone. He either spends it or gives it away. And Josh totally lives in the moment. He has no concept of time or planning for the future. And he thinks very literally. He gets frustrated if we use common phrases that don't make sense to him. One time he had done something and I was extremely angry with him. I said, 'Just who do you think you are?' and he answered, 'Joshua Radford Carson.' That's when it hit me that he really has a literal understanding of language."

"Individuals who struggle with FASD have poor memories and often have learning disabilities," Teresa said. "They may understand something one day and have no recollection of it the next."

"That fits Josh, too," Mom said. "His high school music teacher used to tell me that one day he'd play his keyboard in class and really know what was going on. Then a couple of days later she'd ask him to play the same music and he wouldn't know where to put his fingers in order to start the song."

"Would you like me to do an FASD screening for Josh?" Teresa asked. "The results are based on your answers to questions about Josh and his behaviors, and about what he can and can't do."

"Yes, please," Mom said. "That would be wonderful."

Teresa got out a form and began asking my mom a series of questions about me.

"Does he have a poor memory?" Teresa asked.

"Yes."

"Does he get distracted easily?"

"Oh, yes," Mom said. "He was diagnosed with Attention Deficit Hyperactivity Disorder."

"Does Josh have trouble with impulse control?"

"Yes."

"Does he respect personal boundaries?"

"No. He assumes what is yours is his as well," Mom said. "And we know that he used to walk into neighbor's houses uninvited."

"Does he steal?"

"Yes, at least he used to. I don't think that he steals as much as he used to. At least I hope he doesn't."

"Does he lie?"

"Yes, but he's improved in his ability to tell the truth as well. Either that or I'm just really good at knowing when he's lying to me."

"Does he have inappropriate social behavior?"

"Yes, at least sometimes he certainly used to. But he can also be a perfect gentleman. Even when he was much younger, if we'd go out to dinner he'd hold the door for me, and sit quietly and make conversation during the meal. The servers often commented how respectful and polite he was."

"Is he overly friendly with strangers?"

"Oh, my yes, he hugs everybody, even people he just met."

"Does he have many friends?"

"No, not really. Unfortunately, his relationships are very superficial."

"Does he repeat the same mistakes?"

"Yes, time and again."

"Does he have difficulty following directions?"

"Yes."

"Does he know what your rules are?"

"Absolutely."

"Does he have difficulty following the rules?"

"Absolutely."

"Does he engage in risky behaviors?"

"Yes, sometimes he scares me to death. When he was little we'd ride bikes together as a family. I'd turn around to check on him and he'd be riding down the middle of the road or even on the wrong side of the street facing oncoming traffic."

"Does he have difficulty with the concept of time?"

"Yes."

"Is he able to manage money?"

"No."

"Is he irritable?"

"Oh, yes. He certainly can be. He's especially grouchy in the morning. Sometimes he seems angry all day long for no apparent reason. One time he told me that he just 'wakes up mad every day.'"

"Does he have an exaggerated reaction to being startled?"

"Yes."

"Is he uncomfortable with loud noises?"

"Yes. He used to cover his ears when we'd be at U of A basketball games. He told me that the noise of the crowds and pep band were too loud."

"Is he physically sensitive to things, perhaps heat or cold or touch of water on his skin?"

"Yes. As a child he would wear sweatshirts in the summer time when it was over 100 degrees here in Tucson. And he used to do everything he could to avoid taking a bath or shower. He would go into the bathroom, turn the water on, and let the shower run for ten minutes or so. He'd pretend to bathe, but would never actually get in the water. It never occurred to me that the water might be uncomfortable to him."

"Is he a literal thinker?"

"Yes, very."

"Is he good at abstract thinking?"

"No."

"Is he good at problem solving?"

"No. If I ask him, 'how else might you solve that problem?' he'd say, 'I don't know.' and let it go at that."

"Does he frequently lose things?"

"Oh, my, yes. Somehow he's lost three cell phones and six pairs of glasses within two years."

"Is he good at organizing?"

"No."

"Is he good at sequencing?"

"No, not at all."

"Does Josh have an aptitude for music or the arts?"

"Yes, Josh is very good with his hands and he likes to make things. He enjoys crocheting, drawing, painting, weaving, and working with clay. He's got a great sense of rhythm and was on the high school Hip Hop Dance team, and in the Steel Drum Band. Josh plays the keyboard, writes rap lyrics and even creates and records his own 'beats' on the keyboard."

"Was Josh a full term baby?"

"No. I recently learned that he was born by C-section at just 26 weeks gestation. He spent several months in the Neonatal ICU before he was strong enough to go home."

"So he was he an underweight baby?"

"Yes. He weighed only two pounds and two ounces."

"Was he a 'failure to thrive' baby?"

"Yes, I remember one of the social workers using that term to describe his inability to grow and gain weight."

"Does he have a thin upper lip?"

"Hmmmmm, his upper lip gets thin when he smiles, but I think his mouth is perfect and beautiful."

"Does he have a smooth, wide, philtrum? That's the little groove between his nose and mouth."

"Now that you mention it, yes, he does."

The questions continued and within a few minutes Teresa had finished the screening evaluation.

"Jamie, based on the answers you've given me," Teresa said, "there is a strong probability that Joshua has brain damage as a result of being exposed to alcohol while he was developing in the womb. He falls within the range of Fetal Alcohol Spectrum Disorders."

"That's what I suspected," Mom said. "It's such a shame, but it certainly explains why he's had so many problems, and why we have struggled so much as a family. I certainly wish that I had known about this from the beginning. It would have saved us all a lot of grief and stress."

There was a silence in the room for several seconds.

"So, Teresa, does this screening qualify Josh as having a diagnosis of Fetal Alcohol Spectrum Disorders?

"No, remember, FASD is an umbrella term describing several disabilities. The screening that we just did is an instrument to detect the possibility of FASD behaviors. The only way to know for sure if Josh had fetal exposure to alcohol is to have a diagnosis from a specially trained professional, or obtain confirmation, from a reliable source, that his birth mother drank alcohol during her pregnancy with him.

"Well, we have that. Josh reunited with his birth father this past weekend, after not seeing him for fourteen years. His dad is clean and sober, and I liked him a lot. He confirmed that Josh's birth mother drank throughout her pregnancy with him."

"That pretty well confirms it then, doesn't it?" Teresa agreed. "Jamie, do you have a picture of your son?"

"Sure, I have several," Mom said proudly, as she dug them out of her purse. "Josh is a beautiful child with a wonderful smile."

Mom handed each photo to Teresa who took time to examine each one.

"Yes, Josh is a very handsome young man," Teresa said. "And he certainly has a beautiful smile."

Teresa returned the photos to my mother.

"The fact that Joshua looks so normal, and the fact that his disability is invisible actually works against him," Teresa said.

"What do you mean?" Mom asked.

"Josh looks like other kids his own age, so people expect more of him. But kids with FASD are not as mature at their peers. Their thinking and behaviors are more like someone who is half their age. Josh's brain has been damaged by his prenatal exposure to alcohol. He wants to but isn't capable of doing the things that most other kids can do. He can't deliver what others expect of him and that causes problems."

"You're right," Mom said. "That has happened several times."

"Josh is smart. And because he is, and because his disability is invisible, he doesn't qualify for a lot of services that are available to other people with FASD disabilities," Teresa said. "My son, John, for example has full Fetal Alcohol Syndrome or FAS. He's eligible for all kinds of help and support. He's living now in a group home where he is supervised twenty four hours a day, seven days a week."

"Wow!" Mom said.

Again, there was silence in the room.

"Jamie, I know that you weren't aware of or prepared for these disabilities when you adopted Joshua. It is important for you to grieve the loss of your dreams for your son. Once you have processed that grief, you can go on with your life, and once again enjoy parenting your precious child."

"Yes, you are absolutely right," Mom said. "It helps that you recognize and validate the emotional pain that I, as a parent with an FASD child, feel when I realize that my son has special needs and isn't ever going to be capable of living a happy, 'normal,' independent life."

"Joshua needs to understand and to accept his disability," Teresa said. "If you would like for me to talk with him about it, I'd be happy to do that."

"Would you?" Mom asked. "That would be great, Teresa. Thank you so much! I'll talk with Josh first and then bring him in to meet and talk with you later this week. Will that work?"

"That sounds perfect," Teresa said.

Mom stood and gave Teresa a hug. Mom and she had formed a bond over these past two hours. They were kindred spirits walking similar paths as mothers loving children who suffer with FASD.

Mom left Teresa's office and drove back towards the animal hospital. She was eager for the work day to be over and to spend time with her family. She needed to share the information about my FASD with Momma B and with me.

CHAPTER

24

Forgiveness

The work day was over and we were at home. As soon as Mom had the chance she grabbed Momma B by the hand and led her to their room. Mom wanted privacy for their conversation.

"We need to talk," Mom said, as she closed the bedroom door behind them.

About twenty minutes later, my moms came out of their room and walked over to where I sat watching television.

"Honey, would you please turn of the TV?" Mom said.

I was into the program and didn't hear her.

"Josh," she said. "I need you to turn off the TV please."

This time I realized that she had asked me to do something.

"Pardon me?" I said, putting the sound on 'mute.'

"Please turn off the television, Josh," Momma B said. "We need to talk with you."

I turned off the set and looked at my parents.

"Joshua, we want to apologize to you," Mom said. "We used to think that you lied, and stole things, and disobeyed us on purpose just to be difficult."

"We're so sorry that we thought those things about you, Honey," Momma B said.

"They weren't true and you weren't intentionally trying to make us frustrated or angry. We were wrong and we made mistakes in how we were parenting you," Mom said.

"We expected too much from you," Momma B said. "We expected you to do things that you aren't capable of doing."

"Joshua, will you please forgive us?" Mom asked.

"I accept your apology, Moms," I said, and stood up to give them each a hug.

"Thank you, Honey," my parents said, as they wrapped their arms around me.

"Josh, we now know that you have disabilities that affect your brain and behaviors. These disabilities are called Fetal Alcohol Spectrum Disorders. Your birth father confirmed it when he talked about your birth mother, DeShona, drinking alcohol while she was pregnant with you," Mom said.

"Do you remember that part of the conversation?" Momma B asked.

"I remember Mom asking my dad about that," I said.

"I'm glad that you do," Mom said. "Because now we know that you couldn't control those behaviors that were getting you into trouble. We're so sorry, Josh, for being hard on you and for not understanding what the problems really were."

Mom had tears in her eyes but I don't think they were happy tears.

"It's OK, Mom," I said. "I forgive you."

"Thank you, Honey," Mom said.

"Thank you, Sweetheart," Momma B said.

My moms and I talked for a long time about my disabilities.

"Your birth parents used to like to party, Josh," Mom said. "Drinking alcohol was something that they did a lot when they were together."

"Well it sucks that DeShona drank while she was pregnant with me," I said. "It isn't fair and I'm really mad at her!"

"I understand that you're upset, Josh, and you have every right to be," Momma B said. "But being angry with your birth mother isn't going to make things any better."

"DeShona and your dad are responsible for you being alive," Mom said.

"Together they created you and gave you life. I'm very grateful to them for that."

"I think that you would feel better if you forgave them for drinking alcohol while they were pregnant with you," Mom said. "They love you, Joshua, and I'm sure they never meant to harm you. They probably didn't even realize that what they were doing could hurt you."

"Well, it still stinks!" I said.

"Yes, it does, Honey, it stinks that you have these disabilities, but those are the facts and you need to accept them and move on," Momma B said.

"Now that we know that you have FASD, we need to find ways to help you manage it," Mom said. "Can you find it in your heart to forgive DeShona and Randall for what they did to you before you were born?"

I was quiet for a few seconds as I thought about that request. Then I softly said, "Yes, I forgive them."

"Thank you, Josh," Mom said. "I'm sure they would feel better knowing that you have forgiven them."

"I'd like to go to my room and be alone for a while if you don't mind," I said.

I got up from the couch and walked to my room. I closed the door, fell onto my bed and cried myself to sleep.

Later that week my mom took me over to the FAS Community Resource Center where Teresa was waiting to meet me. Mom and I walked into her office. I was nervous when we shook hands.

"Hi, Josh, it's a pleasure meeting you," Teresa said.

"Thank you," I said. "It's nice meeting you, too," I said, smiling cautiously.

"Joshua, I understand that you were adopted. I have an adopted son too. His name is John and this is his picture."

She handed me a photo of a young, dark haired man standing with a young woman who was wearing a fancy dress. They were smiling at the camera.

"That's John and his girlfriend, Becky. Both of their birth mothers drank alcohol while they were pregnant. As a result, John and Becky each have Fetal Alcohol Syndrome. John's birth mother drank heavily during the first few months of her pregnancy with him. He has the facial characteristics associated with Fetal Alcohol Syndrome, and he has a legal diagnosis of FAS," Teresa said.

"In a way, John is lucky because people realize, when they meet him, that he has a disability and they cut him a break."

"How old is John?" I asked.

"Well, he is twenty eight years old, but he is emotionally and mentally much younger. John thinks and acts very immaturely and his behaviors are more like someone who is less than half his age. He has poor impulse control and poor decision making abilities. He isn't able to live on his own and has been living in a group home for four years."

"Hmmm," I said.

"Teresa, you told me the other day that John is a talented drummer," Mom said.

"Yes, most kids with fetal alcohol exposure have wonderful talents. Do you have talents Josh?"

"Yes, ma'am, I like music and I create beats on my keyboard," I said.

"Josh is also a hip-hop dancer," Mom said, as she smiled. "And he is very skilled with his hands. He works well with various media such as paint, clay, and yarn. And he is a skilled athlete. You should see him play basketball!"

"That's wonderful," Teresa said.

"It has always amazed me that Josh can remember dialogue from a movie that he has only seen once. And that he can deliver it, word for word, just like the actor in the film," Mom said. "But sometimes he can't remember what I asked him to do five minutes earlier."

"That's very typical of kids with fetal alcohol exposure," Teresa said. "They have brain damage and memory problems."

Teresa looked at my mother and then she turned towards me and leaned forward.

"Josh, I bet you get into trouble for things that you know you really shouldn't do," she said. "Things like talking out in class, stepping out into traffic, or even shop lifting. Am I right?"

"Yes, ma'am," I said.

"That's because you have Fetal Alcohol Spectrum Disorders or FASD. These are disabilities that cause mental, physical, emotional, and behavioral problems. It can also cause learning disabilities. People with FASD have difficulty controlling their impulses. They often act before they think about the consequences of their actions."

"Yeah," I said. "People are always telling me to stop and think before I do or say something. But I don't, I just do it."

"And I bet you repeat the same mistakes over and over," Teresa said.

I nodded my head in agreement.

"Well, that's because the nerve paths in your brain are damaged from the alcohol your birth mother drank while she was pregnant with you. The alcohol went into her body and it also went into your tiny, developing body. As a matter of fact, every time that your birth mom had a beer, you were swimming in alcohol."

"I was swimming in alcohol?" I asked. "What do you mean?"

"Let me explain," Teresa said. "Did you know that a developing fetus is surrounded by something called amniotic fluid while in its mother's womb?"

"No. What's enemy fluid?"

"Amniotic fluid," Teresa said, correcting the word for me. "Amniotic fluid is a nourishing and protective liquid that surrounds a fetus. It cushions the developing baby and helps it stay warm. It also promotes the development of muscles and bones, and helps the fetus move around easily inside the mother's uterus."

"So the baby must feel kind of like I do when I'm swimming under water," I said.

"I suppose it does," Teresa agreed. "Did you know, Joshua, that a fetus even urinates when it is inside of his mother's womb?"

"Ewww, that's gross!" I said.

"The fetus swallows the fluid and then urinates," Teresa said.

"Wow!" I said.

"That's interesting," Mom said. "I didn't know that, but it makes sense when you think about it."

"It does seem a little weird to think about a fetus urinating while it is inside of its mother's body, doesn't it?" Teresa said.

"Uh, huh," I said.

"Do you know how alcohol affects the body, Josh?" she asked.

"Well, I know it can make you drunk," I answered.

"That's true," Teresa said. "When a person drinks beer, wine, or any alcoholic beverage, it's rapidly absorbed into the bloodstream. The alcohol is carried through all of the organs in the body, including the uterus where the fetus is developing. About 20% of the alcohol is absorbed through the stomach."

"What happens to the rest of it?" I asked.

"The rest is mostly absorbed from your small intestine. The liver is the organ in the body that breaks down most of the alcohol, about 90-98% of it. The liver processes the alcohol so that it can be eliminated from the body when you urinate or exhale."

"How long does it take for the liver to do its thing?" I asked.

"That depends on several factors," Teresa said. "But it takes about an hour for the average adult to process one alcoholic drink."

"Hmmm," I said.

"The liver in a fetus isn't developed yet so it doesn't function like the liver in an adult. So, if a pregnant woman drinks alcohol, it passes through her body and into the fetus by way of the umbilical cord. The baby's liver can't process the alcohol so the baby absorbs the alcohol into its tiny body and then it urinates it back into the amniotic fluid. So really, the baby is floating in the alcohol for about an hour, even longer if the woman has more than one drink in a day."

"That's just gross," I said.

"As a result," Teresa said, "the baby's developing central nervous system, which includes the brain, doesn't develop correctly or connect the way it should. The cells become damaged and the nerve pathways aren't right. So that is why people who have been exposed to prenatal alcohol don't process information the way that people who were not exposed to alcohol process things. Does that make sense to you, Joshua?"

"Sort of," I said.

"I'll bet, Josh, that sometimes in school you'll know something one day, and the next day you have no idea what the teacher is talking about. Is that right?"

"Yeah, in high school last year my music teacher used to get frustrated with me. One day I'd know the music and be jamming like crazy. The next time I was in music class she'd have to tell me what notes to play just to start the song. It was embarrassing."

"That's your disability again, Josh. And prenatal exposure to alcohol disables one out of every one hundred babies born in North America," Teresa said.

"Wow, that sounds like a lot of babies," I said.

"Yes, unfortunately that is a lot of babies," Teresa said. "If women would avoid drinking alcohol when they are sexually active, it would greatly reduce the number of FASD babies."

"What do you mean?" Mom asked.

"Often a woman may be several weeks along in her pregnancy before she realizes she is pregnant," Teresa said. "These are crucial developmental weeks for the fetus. Just think of how many parties that woman and her fetus may have attended, and how many drinks she and her baby might have shared during those first few weeks. Remember, if the woman has a drink, then so does her baby."

"Hmmm, I guess I never thought about that," Mom said.

"And as soon as a woman knows that she is pregnant, she must stop drinking alcohol altogether," Teresa said. "No amount of alcohol is safe to drink during pregnancy. That is why we want pregnant women to adhere to the message, '9 Months and Not a Single Drop.'"

"That sounds like an important message," Mom said.

"It's a vital message," Teresa said, "if we are going to reduce or eliminate FASD. Are you aware that the extent of damage done to the fetus depends on multiple factors?"

"What factors do you mean?" Mom asked.

"The amount of damage done to the fetus depends on: how much alcohol the woman drank, how often she drank, and the developmental stage of her fetus when she was drinking," Teresa said. "That's why some people, like my son, John, have full blown FAS, and others, like Joshua, are on the spectrum but look normal."

"Wow!" Mom said.

"And it's also important that nursing moms don't drink either," Teresa said. "Studies show that drinking while nursing is bad for the development of the children," Teresa said.

"That's a lot of important information," Mom said.

"Well, I just want to know if the doctors can fix me." I said.

"Unfortunately, no, Josh. The damage caused by fetal alcohol exposure is a permanent condition. These disabilities last a lifetime. That's why it is so important for you to understand and accept your disabilities. And it would be best if your family and friends understood your disabilities, too," she said. "It's nothing to be ashamed of, Josh. It's just part of who you are."

Mom reached over and touched my hand. She looked lovingly at me.

"If you were blind, deaf, or needed a wheelchair, people would understand those disabilities and make accommodations to support you," Teresa said. "Because your disabilities are invisible people won't understand unless you tell them. When you have a job, you should explain your FASD to your boss so he or she can understand how you think and process information. I'm sure that you don't want to be fired because you didn't understand something that you were told to do, or for being asked to do something that you aren't capable of doing," Teresa said.

"Yeah, that's already happened," I said.

"Joshua, you're going to need help in making the best decisions and behavioral choices for the rest of your life," Teresa said.

I looked at her. I was confused and starting to get angry at the same time.

"I don't want to talk about this anymore," I said.

"I can understand that you are upset by this information, Joshua. It's difficult to hear. But you need to realize that your brain is damaged because of alcohol. It isn't your fault, and it is nothing to be embarrassed about. That's just the way it is. Sometimes your brain works fine and sometimes it doesn't. Do you understand what I've said so far?" Teresa asked.

"Yes," I said.

"Good," she said.

We sat quietly for a few minutes while I tried to digest the information that Teresa had given me. Finally, Teresa spoke again.

"Because you have invisible disabilities, it would be best if you had someone, like a coach, to advise you and help you make good decisions. Your coach would also help keep you safe. I call this person your 'external brain.' But you may want to call him or her your life coach. It would be best if this person could be with you as much as possible."

"Where do I get a life coach?" I asked.

"Well, that depends," Teresa said. "Your coach may change from time to time. Sometimes your coach can be one of your moms, maybe your birth father, another relative, your boss, a minister, a trusted friend, or maybe a girlfriend or spouse. But your coach must be someone that you trust. And it must be someone that you can turn to, to help you make good choices. And it is important that your coach doesn't also have FASD."

"That sounds like a baby sitter to me," I said. "I don't need a baby sitter."

"No, Josh, you don't need a baby sitter," Teresa said. "You need a good strong support system. That's what we are talking about creating for you."

Again, we sat quietly for a few minutes.

"Josh, when you were a little boy, did you ever play a game called, Ring Around the Rosie?" Teresa asked.

"Maybe, I'm not sure," I said.

"Well, in that game everyone joins hands and makes a circle around the person who stands in the middle of the group. Can you picture that?" Teresa asked.

"Yes."

"Good. Now imagine that your family and friends are the people who are holding hands and that they've formed a circle around you."

"OK."

"Your family and friends are there to catch you if you start to stumble and fall. That's what a circle of support is. It's a group of people forming a safety net around someone they love," Teresa said. "These people are there to help you when you need help making decisions."

"I think I get it," I said.

"You may need to talk about this again, Joshua," Teresa said. "Here's my card," she said, as she handed me her business card. "Please call me any time if I can help you."

"Thank you, Teresa," Mom said.

"It's my pleasure. Good luck, Joshua," Teresa said. "I have great hope for you and for a bright future. Your parents have given you a wonderful start in life and in forming two strong points in your circle of support. They obviously love you very much. Please keep in touch and let me know how you're doing. I'd love to do a story about your success for our website."

"OK, thank you," I said. We shook hands and Mom and I left her office.

"Mom, do you think that maybe my brother and sister have FASD too," I asked as we got into the car.

"It's certainly possible, Josh," she said. "You know that R.J. has been in trouble at school, in his foster homes, and with the law. It would be good if he knew about FASD. He needs to understand and accept that he may have these disabilities too. He needs a support group and some life coaches to help keep him safe and out of trouble."

"Man, why did my birth mom have to drink?" I asked. "It's not fair."

"No, Honey, it isn't fair," Mom said. "And there's a pretty good chance that your birth mom may have FASD also. You don't know much about her life history, or if her mother, that would be your birth grandmother, drank alcohol while she was pregnant with DeShona. I know in my heart, Josh, that DeShona would never do anything on purpose to hurt you or any of her children."

"Yeah, I know," I said.

We were quiet for the ride home.

"Josh, your Dad needs to know about and understand your disabilities if you're going to be living with him."

"I know," I said. "Will you explain it to him for me?"

"Of course, Honey," Mom said.

"Thanks, Mom. I love you."

"I love you more," she said.

"I know."

CHAPTER

26

Full Circle

Mom spent a long time talking with my dad about Fetal Alcohol Spectrum Disorders. At first Dad didn't really understand my disabilities. He kept thinking that I was just immature and that I would outgrow my irresponsible behaviors.

To demonstrate to my parents that he was sincere about wanting to be a positive influence in my life, Dad finally agreed to attend an FASD training program in Phoenix. Teresa Kellerman, the woman who had talked with Mom and me about FASD, was holding a training session and she would be Dad's trainer.

Dad arrived at the training room about ten minutes before class was scheduled to start. He wanted to make sure that he got to meet Teresa. Confidently, he walked up to the woman standing in the front of the room. He stuck out his hand, gave her a big toothy grin and said, "Are you Teresa? I'm Randall Radford, and I understand that you have met my son, Joshua. He lives in Tucson with his adoptive moms."

"Of course," she said. "Jamie and Brooke attended a training that I gave in Tucson a couple of weeks ago. They are wonderful parents and Joshua is a delightful young man. I have high hopes for him. I'm so glad that you're here for the training as well. I understand Joshua is planning on moving to Phoenix to live with you."

"Yes, that happens next month, I'm very excited about it," Dad said.

"Well, good luck to you both," Teresa said. "Let me know if I can help in any way. It looks as though it is time to start class. If you'll excuse me and take a seat, we'll get started." She turned away and greeted the rest of her students.

My dad sat down and listened to what Teresa had to say. He knew that my birth mother drank while she was pregnant with me, but he still wasn't convinced that I had any disabilities. After all, I looked normal and seemed healthy in every other way. Even though Dad had gone through the FASD training, he really didn't think that there was anything wrong with me or my brain. It wasn't until later, when we were actually living together, that he could see the struggles that I faced on a daily basis.

About a month later, I turned eighteen. Since I was now a legal adult, I dropped out of high school so I could move to Phoenix to live with my dad. I'd been dreaming about living with him ever since we'd reunited five months earlier.

Dad and Gemini traveled from Phoenix to Tucson to get me so that I could move in with them. They arrived at our veterinary clinic around 8:00 Friday morning. I was eager to go and was standing in front of our animal hospital watching for them to arrive. Dad's car pulled into the parking lot and I ran out to greet them.

"Hi, Dad!" I said, grinning from ear to ear.

"Hi, Joshua," Dad said as he jumped out of the car and gave me a big hug.

"Are you about ready?"

"Yes, sir!" I answered excitedly.

Dad put his arm around my shoulder and we walked over to the passenger side of the car. Dad needed to get Gemini out of his car seat which was in the back seat.

"Hey there, little man," I said.

"Hi, Joshua," Gemini said, as he held up his arms asking me to pick him up.

I lifted him from the car and lead the way inside the building.

"Good morning," Dad said. "How are my 'wives' this morning?" Dad asked playfully.

"Hi Randall," Mom said, giving him a hug, "We're glad you had a safe trip down here."

Momma B hugged my dad. Gemini wiggled so I put him down and he ran to my mom.

"Hi Momma J," he said as he lifted his arms up. She told him to jump as she hoisted him into the air. Gemini gave her a tight squeeze.

"I like you, Momma J," he said.

"I like you, too, Gemini," Mom said.

My parents talked about the schedule for the day. Mom said that I had a couple of appointments. Dad wanted to go with us so that he would have a better understanding as to my needs. He left his car at the clinic, and Mom, Dad, Gemini and I all climbed into mom's car. Momma B couldn't come because she had to see her veterinary patients.

First Mom drove us to see my psychiatrist. The purpose of the meeting was to close out my file with them and start the transition process with another agency in Phoenix. Since I was taking medication to help manage my behaviors my mom wanted to make sure that I wouldn't run out of medications once I moved in with my father.

Mom, Dad, and I talked with my doctor while Gemini played with a truck from the toy box. Finally, the doctor shook our hands, said 'goodbye and good luck' and we stood up to leave.

"That was easy enough," Dad said, as we left the office.

"Yes, I wish all of our meetings were that easy," Mom said.

"Momma J, I'm hungry," Gemini said, looking at my mom with his big brown eyes.

"Well, we'll just have to do something about that now, won't we?" Mom asked.

"How about we hit McDonalds?" Mom said. She knew that it was his favorite place for breakfast. "Will that work, Gemini?"

He nodded his approval and we headed for the fast food restaurant. While we ate, Mom told Dad a story about when she and I first went to Mickey D's together.

"The first time Josh and I came here together he was eight years old. I think he only weighed 52 pounds and was a little bitty thing," Mom said. "I was surprised when Josh ordered a Big Mac, Biggie Fries, and a Biggie Coke."

"Did he eat it all?" Dad asked.

"He ate every last bite!" Mom said, with a laugh. "And then he wanted to go into the play area and climb around those tubes. I would have been too full to move after all of that food."

"Oh, me too," Dad said holding his stomach.

"Look at Gemini," Mom said. "He's eaten his pancakes and scrambled eggs, and he drank his juice. That's a lot of food for a four year old."

"He's always hungry," my dad said. "He's always been a good eater."

"Josh is too, these days. He's really filled out nicely," Mom said as she looked at me and smiled.

"What time is his eye appointment?" Dad asked.

"Not until 11:00 a.m.," Mom said.

"Is it OK if Joshua goes with us to visit some of my family and friends until his appointment? If you give me the address I could take him there and save you a trip," Dad said.

"Sounds like a plan to me," Mom said.

We rode back to the animal hospital so that Mom could go back to work and Dad could get his car. We were all full from our breakfasts so we didn't talk much.

We dropped my mom off at the clinic and got into Dad's car. Dad, Gemini, and I left to meet some of his friends and family before it was time for my eye appointment.

I had a great time meeting all of these people. They said things like, "We're so happy that you and your father are back together. He loves you, Joshua, and he has never stopped thinking about you, praying for you, or looking for you. Your Dad is the happiest that I've seen him in years."

Their words made me feel good. Every time someone would talk like that I'd grin and hug my dad. We were all happy about our reunion.

At 5:00 p.m. I called Mom and told her we'd be at the clinic soon to get my things. I had packed my suitcases and keyboard, and taken them to the clinic earlier in the day. Mom and Momma B were waiting outside for us when we arrived. I loaded my stuff into the back of my father's car and then turned to my parents.

"I'm going to miss you," I said to Momma B, giving her a hug and a kiss.

"I'll miss you too, Honey," she said, as tears started to well up in her eyes.

I went to Mom and we held each other for a long time.

"You take good care of yourself, Honey," she said.

"I will," I said.

"I love you, Joshua Radford Carson," Mom said. Momma B put her arms around both of us.

"I love you, too, Mom. I love you, Momma B. Thank you both for everything, I mean that," I said.

"It's our pleasure, Sweetheart," Momma B said.

Dad came over and our group hug got bigger. Then my moms and my dad held hands and formed a circle around me.

"Me too," Gemini said, and he grabbed Mom's hand and Momma B took his other little hand.

"Joshie, you have family and friends who love you. You have a full circle of support," Mom said. "Please trust us and come to us. We love you and are here to help and support you. If you stumble and fall, we're here to catch you."

My folks squeezed hands and then let go. Mom hugged and kissed my dad and Gemini. Momma B said good-bye to them too. Then it was time for me to go.

I walked back to my Mom and put my arms around her again. She held me and kissed me on the cheek and I kissed her back. We blew air into our cheeks and popped them against each other.

"I love you, Joshie," Mom said.

"I love you more," I said.

"No, I love you more," Mom said.

"I know."

Then we made our hands into 'I love you' in sign language. We touched fingers, and then I climbed into Dad's car. My moms held hands and waved as Dad drove the car out of the clinic parking lot. Mom blew me a kiss and I pretended to catch it. I blew her one too, and she caught it with ease.

THE END

Epilogue

Three months after Joshua moved to Phoenix to live with his father, Jamie and Brooke successfully sold their veterinary business in Tucson. Jamie, Brooke, and Brooke's sister, Lynette, finally made the permanent move from Tucson, Arizona to their small farm in the San Juan Islands of Washington State.

Joshua spent seven months living with his birth father, Randall, and his father's adopted son, Gemini. During those months they went through difficult times because of Joshua's FASD, and Randall's continued denial of Josh's disabilities.

Eventually, Josh called his mothers and asked if he could return to live with them on the island. Josh moved back to the farm and soon submitted his application to attend The Job Corps program.

The Job Corps is a free program available through the United States Department of Labor. It provides youth between the ages of 16 and 24 the opportunity to complete their high school education and learn the skills necessary to work at a trade upon completion of the program.

Through the Job Corps, Joshua, who dropped out of high school when he turned eighteen, would have the opportunity to complete his diploma or earn a GED. He would also learn the skills needed for a career in culinary arts. Joshua's birth father was a cook, and Josh had enjoyed helping his parents in the kitchen since he was a little boy.

Upon successful completion of the nine-month Culinary Arts Program, the Job Corps will allow him to train in two additional fields, or assist him in finding employment as a professional cook. Six months following his return to Washington state, Josh entered the Job Corps. His parents drove him to the campus where he now lives in a dormitory room with seven other young men.

Joshua talks with his parents weekly and visits them during vacation breaks. He also communicates with Randall Sr. on a regular basis. He and Gemini are planning to travel to Washington state to join the graduation celebration when Joshua completes the Job Corps.

Acknowledgements

Thanks to LeJana Olague and her family for all that they did for Joshua. A special thanks to Jason Olague for rescuing him from the bottom of the pool. Thank you to St. Nicholas Adoptions in Tucson, AZ; to our case workers and the many social workers, therapists, doctors, EMTs, respite caregivers and teachers whose time, knowledge, guidance, and expertise have helped Josh throughout the years.

Thank you, Teresa Kellerman, of Tucson, AZ for sharing your knowledge of Fetal Alcohol Spectrum Disorders with so many families, and for your belief in this project. Special thanks to Sally Caldwell, Cheri Scott, Pam Sweetser, Susan Fule, and Diane Reed for your contributions to this book and for validating my efforts as a mother and author.

Thank you author Karen McQuestion for your encouragement via my reading of your book, Write That Novel. It gave me the boost I needed to create this one.

A special note of gratitude goes to my Honey B, Barbara Swahlen, DVM, for being my editor, and more importantly for being my rock throughout our many years together. I couldn't have done any of this without you, nor would I want to try.

Meet Jan

Jan Crossen's interest in the welfare of children began years ago. As a high school teacher and coach, Jan was a mentor to many of her players. She is thrilled to be in contact with many of her former students and athletes today.

She has been a sponsor of children living in developing countries, and served as a court appointed surrogate parent for two young siblings in the Arizona foster care system. For seven years, Jan served as a mentor to a child in her island community. The strong connection formed during that relationship continues even though this child has moved to another city and is now a senior in high school.

Jan had always dreamed of creating her family through adoption and her vision became a reality in 1999, when she adopted her son, Joshua. The three books in the 9 LIVES series were inspired by their journey together.

Her son, Joshua, is now thirty one and living in California in order to be near his daughter, Brooklyn. She is kind, smart, funny, brave and beautiful; and she is absolutely adored by her grandmothers. Brooklyn is the same age that Josh was when he met his forever mother. Josh recently graduated from an auto mechanics certification program and is also an entrepreneur. He plays the keyboard, creates beats, and produces music for local Hip Hop artists.

On 12/12/2012, Jan was delighted to finally legally put a ring on it and marry her "chosen one, Honey B." She and Barbara are happiest when they are together and have been partners for over twenty six years. They recently retired from their mobile veterinary house call practice and are grateful every day to live on their beautiful island paradise. Life is great, blessed be!

This photo of Jan and Joshua was taken a few months after they met.

Also by Jan Crossen

FOREVER A Children's Book published in 2020

Everyone needs and deserves a family. We all want to be loved, to feel we belong with someone, and to have a home. This is the true story of a young African American boy who was living in foster care, and the magical Christmas holiday night when he met the white woman who would become his adoptive mother. It is the heartwarming tale of connection and the beginnings of a forever family. It is a story of hope.

ISBN: 9798653581748

9 LIVES Trilogy

9 LIVES: I Will Survive first published in 2007

ISBN: 13: 978-0-9793981-9-3
ISBN: 10: 0-9793981-9-3

9 LIVES: Cat Tales first published in 2008

ISBN: 13: 978-0-9798686-3-4
ISBN: 10: 0-9798686-3-7

9 LIVES: Full Circle first published in 2008

ISBN: 13: 978-0-978686-4-1
ISBN: 10: 0-9798686-4-5

Resources

Fetal Alcohol Spectrum Disorders (FASD):
www.fasstar.com

National Organization on Fetal Alcohol Syndrome
www.nofas.org

FASD State Resource Directory
www.nofas.org/resource/directory

University of Washington Fetal Alcohol Drug Unit
Seattle, WA
206-543-7155
http://depts.washington.edu/fadu

Adoption:
Adoptive Families
www.adoptivefamilies.com

North American Council on Adoptable Children
www.nacac.org

National Adoption Center
www.adopt.org

National Resource Center for Special Needs Adoption
www.spaulding.org
Come Unity
www.comeunity.com

LGBTQ+ Families:
www.familypride.org
www.rainbowfamilies.org
www.proudparenting.com

The Job Corps:
The Job Corps Program
1-800-733-JOBS
http://jobcorps.dol.gov/

Printed in Great Britain
by Amazon

15755387R00180

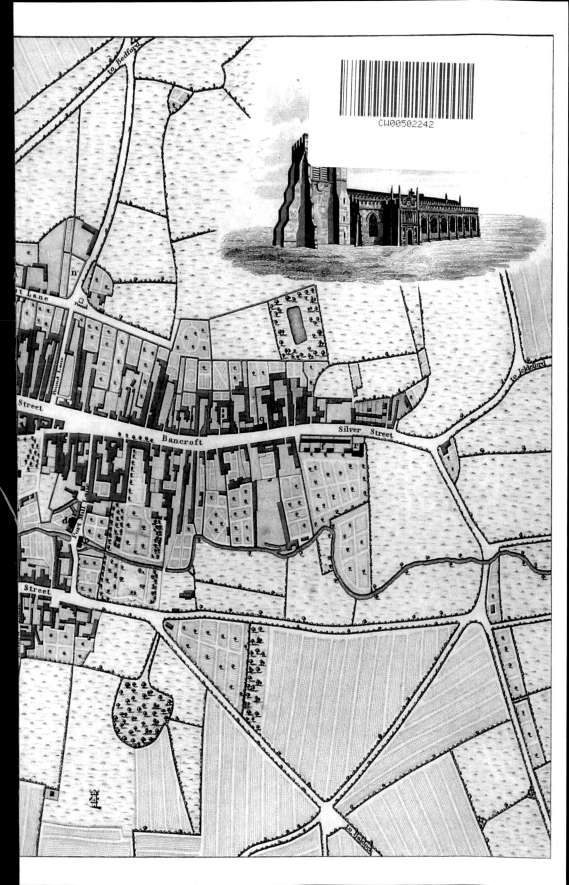

William Wilshere Esquire (*North Hertfordshire Museum: Lawson Thompson Scrapbooks Vol 1A p3*).

Hertfordshire Record Publications Volume 39

WILLIAM WILSHERE'S

HITCHIN FARM AND GARDEN,

1809-1824

Edited by Bridget Howlett and with an Introduction
by Bridget Howlett and Tom Williamson

Hertfordshire Record Society
Volume for the membership year 2023/24

Hertfordshire Record Society

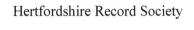

ISBN 978-0-9501741-6-7

Printed and bound in the UK by
P2D Books Ltd, Westoning,
Bedfordshire MK45 5LD

Contents

Illustrations

Colour Section (between pages xl and xli)

INTRODUCTION

Wilshere Family Tree (Only those family members mentioned in the text are shown)

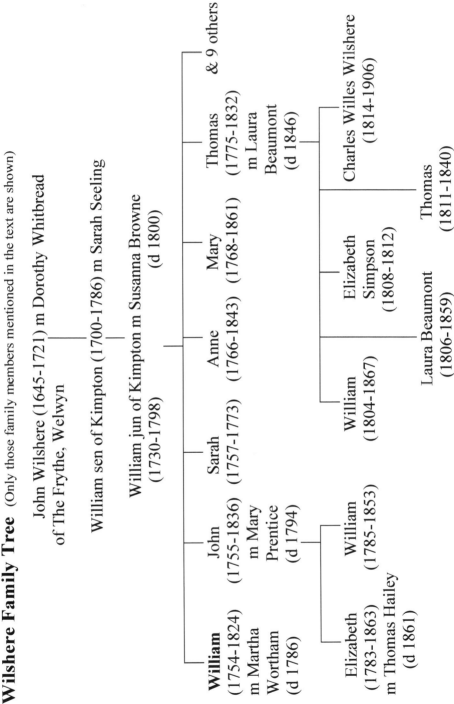

John Wilshere (1645-1721) m Dorothy Whitbread of The Frythe, Welwyn

William sen of Kimpton (1700-1786) m Sarah Seeling

William jun of Kimpton m Susanna Browne (1730-1798) (d 1800)

William (1754-1824) m Martha Wortham (d 1786)

John (1755-1836) m Mary Prentice (d 1794)

Sarah (1757-1773)

Anne (1766-1843)

Mary (1768-1861)

Thomas (1775-1832) m Laura Beaumont (d 1846)

& 9 others

Elizabeth (1783-1863) m Thomas Hailey (d 1861)

William (1785-1853)

William (1804-1867)

Elizabeth Simpson (1808-1812)

Thomas (1811-1840)

Charles Willes Wilshere (1814-1906)

Laura Beaumont (1806-1859)

Introduction

1. William Wilshere and Hitchin

By Bridget Howlett

The Wilshere family

William Wilshere was born on 6 September 1754, the eldest of 15 children of William and Susanna Wilshere of whom ten died in childhood or early adulthood. The Wilshere family were minor gentry who had owned the property known as The Frythe in Welwyn in Hertfordshire since the sixteenth century. Wilshere's great grandfather, John Wilshere (1645-1721) and his wife, Dorothy Whitbread, lived at The Frythe, but William Wilshere's grandfather, also called William (1700-1786), married Sarah Seeling who inherited property in the nearby village of Kimpton where they made their home. Their only son, yet another William (1730-1798), moved with his rapidly growing family to the north of the county to Hitchin where he became a maltster. In 1759 William Wilshere junior of Kimpton, described as a gentleman, leased a messuage in Bancroft near the gate into the churchyard (later known as Church House) and the malthouse and kiln behind it. By 1760 he was malting in partnership with William Leak, a well known maltster in Ware. His father, William Wilshere senior of Kimpton, bought another house and malthouse in Bancroft in the 1770s or 1780s.[1]

In 1725 Daniel Defoe described Hitchin 'as a large market town particularly eminent for its being a great corn market for wheat and malt, but especially the first, which is brought here for London market'. Hitchin had been supplying London with malt since at least the sixteenth century and by the eighteenth century, with other Hertfordshire towns, it was one of the main sources of malt for London's breweries. Samuel Whitbread rented a malthouse in Hitchin for a

---

[1] M Pieris, *Take 6 Carrots, 4 Heads of Celery, 8 large Onions - - - The Receipts of a Hertfordshire Family* (Hitchin, 1994) pp11-15; will of John Wilshere of Welwyn 1721 [HALS: 143HW53]; Wilshere family tree [HALS: ACC/6412]; lease of Church House, 1759 [HALS: 57765]; will of William Wilshere of Kimpton, 1787 [TNA: PROB11/1151/142].

INTRODUCTION

few years from 1748 and Hitchin continued to supply his brewery. Almost every house of any size in Hitchin's main street, Bancroft, had a maltings behind it.[2]

Another reason for the Wilshere family's coming to Hitchin was the Back Street Independent Church. While still living in Kimpton, William Wilshere junior was received into the communion of that church and baptised on 4 December 1756. His daughter Sarah was born in Kimpton on 7 June 1757 and baptised two weeks later at the Back Street Meeting House. In 1764, after the move to Hitchin, Wilshere became a deacon. Only two of his daughters, Sarah and Mary were admitted full members of the church, but he and his wife and most of their children were buried in Back Street burial ground and four of his son Thomas's children were baptised there.[3]

His eldest son, William, was educated at the Hitchin Free School in Tilehouse Street. In January 1769 at the age of 14 William was articled to Richard Tristram whose legal practice in Hitchin had been established in the late sixteenth century by John Skynner. William's father had also found employment in Richard Tristram's office after his business as a maltster is said to have run into difficulties.[4] However the family continued their involvement in malting. In 1780 William's brother John, described as a merchant, bought Church House and its maltings and entered into partnership with his father whereby John was doing the malting. John Wilshere also set up a joint enterprise farming and malting with his elder brother William who was now the tenant of Richard Tristram's maltings behind his house in Bancroft. William was also in partnership with his father. All these Wilshere enterprises used William Leak's services in Ware. However it was his legal career which was to provide the foundation for the younger William Wilshere's wealth. His partnerships with his brother and father were both wound up in 1787. John Wilshere continued his involvement in malting together with other businesses.[5]

---

[2] D Defoe, *A Tour through the Whole Island of Great Britain* (Penguin edition 1971, repr 1983) p435; P Mathias, *The Brewing Industry in England 1700-1830* (Cambridge, 1959) pp418, 438-441, 467.
[3] Back Street Independent Church Book [HALS: NR8/1/1]; Wilshere family tree [HALS: ACC/6412].
[4] Note by Reginald Hine in Wilshere's school exercise book 1766-1767 [HALS: 61171]; Pieris, *Take 6 Carrots - - - ,* pp11-15.
[5] Mathias, *The Brewing Industry in England,* pp440-441; Hitchin manor court book, 1780 [TNA: LR3/29 p56]; Ledger A [HALS: 61542]. Mathias consulted records of the Wilshere family's malting businesses and William Wilshere's involvement in Whitbread's brewery which were then held by the Hertfordshire County Record Office

INTRODUCTION

Back Street Independent Church. Built in 1690, it was demolished in 1855 and replaced by Queen Street Congregational Church. Wilshere Court now stands on the site of the church and burial ground (*NHM: Lawson Thompson Scrapbooks Vol 1A p33*).

William Dunnage, Hitchin postmaster, in 1815 wrote, 'this Place was formerly noted for its great Trade in Malt, but that of late years has considerably diminished, partly in consequence of the heavy expense of Land Carriage to the Town of Ware, and the large establishments for manufacturing the Article in that Neighbourhood, and the advantage of a Navigation from thence to London'. Dunnage continued, 'The Market here in Tuesdays for Corn, Cattle and Pedlary is very considerable and ranks as high as any other in the County; the Market for Straw Plat which is now arrived at a great height, also contributes much to the trade of the Town in several branches.' He commented, 'it would also greatly increase the Trade of the Town by a Navigation or Railway from Biggleswade in Bedfordshire, both of which have been in contemplation, but there is little prospect of either being carried out'. Coal was usually brought to Hitchin by

---

(61083-61716). These were subsequently handed over to Whitbread's Brewery on the depositor's instructions. Their present whereabouts are unknown. They were not included with the records of Whitbread's Brewery now held by London Metropolitan Archives (LMA/4453), nor have they been returned to Hertfordshire Archives.

road from Biggleswade, where Hitchin merchants Crabb and Chapman had a wharf on the Ivel Navigation. William Wilshere on at least one occasion in 1811 purchased 2 tons of Wedgebrook coal which was brought by cart from Boxmoor on the Grand Union Canal. The population of the town of Hitchin in 1811 was 3,044 and that of the parish (including the hamlets of Walsworth, Charlton, Preston and Langley) was 3,809.[6]

William Wilshere (1754-1824)

Richard Tristram was evidently impressed by Wilshere's ability and application. At the age of 21 Wilshere was admitted as an attorney of the Court of Common Pleas and as a solicitor of the Court of Chancery. He remained in Tristram's office managing his business until in January 1781 he became his partner taking one third of the profits of their joint business. He lived in Tristram's house until his marriage in August 1785 to Martha Wortham. Wilshere now owned property worth £1,500 and expected to inherit another £1,000 when his father died. His wife, who came from a wealthy family in Royston, brought him a dowry of £1,700. Richard Tristram, a childless widower, died on 10 November 1785 leaving William Wilshere his house in Bancroft. Wilshere returned here with his wife, but Martha died in September 1786 after only 13 months of marriage. There were no children. Wilshere never remarried.[7]

William Wilshere succeeded Richard Tristram as Steward of the Manor of Hitchin. He was appointed Deputy Registrar of the Archdeaconry of Huntingdon which brought him fees for proving wills and other church business. He managed estates in Hertfordshire and Bedfordshire for several local landowners including the Radcliffes of Hitchin Priory, the Honourable George, then Thomas Bowes of St Paul's Waldenbury, and William Maurice Bogdani and his heir, Anthony Rhudde, lessees of the Manor of Hitchin. He held manor courts, collected rents, organised the repair of farm buildings and cottages, and supervised woodland including Hitch Wood owned by Thomas Dashwood. In 1790 he reckoned the profits of his profession were £2,000 per annum for the previous five years while his housekeeping and personal expenditure amounted to £550 a year. Evidence of his activities is provided by his Ledgers A and D started in 1782 (Ledgers B and C have not survived) and his cash books for 1789-1824. Wilshere administered the estate and arranged the funeral of Richard Lytton, the owner of the Knebworth estate, who died in December 1810 at St

[6] Dunnage's manuscript History of Hitchin [NHM: 1203 pp10-13]; bill from Crabb & Chapman, 1805 [HALS: 61480/106]; cash book 1810-1811 [HALS: 61503 p70].
[7] William Wilshere's Minutes of Property [HALS: 61613 pp6, 20-22].

INTRODUCTION

Lawrence in Kent. He was then sued by Lytton's daughter, Mrs Elizabeth Bulwer-Lytton, for the repayment of nearly £2,000.[8]

In 1789, with Joseph Margetts Pierson a Hitchin grocer, Daniel Chapman, builder and distributor of stamps, and John Crabb a brewer, Wilshere established the Hitchin and Hertfordshire Bank, which he claimed was the first bank in the county.[9] He and his partners purchased from the Duke of Bedford the lease from Trinity College Cambridge of the Rectories of Hitchin, Ippollitts and Great Wymondley. In August 1799 Wilshere became Captain of the Hitchin Loyal Volunteers celebrating with a dinner in his garden.[10]

Another landowner for whom Wilshere acted was Samuel Whitbread, the politician, whose father had founded the Whitbread Brewery in London. His country estate was at Southill in Bedfordshire. Both served as Justices of the Peace for Bedfordshire (Wilshere was also JP for Hertfordshire). Wilshere loaned Whitbread money and in 1801 entered into an agreement with Whitbread to take £33,333 6s 8d of his share in the stock and trade of the Chiswell Street Brewery. This gave him a substantial annual income from the brewery of 5% of his capital plus a share of the profits. After Samuel Whitbread's death in 1815 Wilshere became a partner in the brewery. In 1817 he gave up £10,000 of his share to Whitbread's younger son Samuel Charles in return for a payment of £10,000 from his elder son, William Henry Whitbread.[11]

Wilshere became a member of Lincoln's Inn in 1803 and was called to the Bar in 1808. He had his name struck off the Roll of Attornies in 1805, his former

---

[8] Appointment as steward of manor of Hitchin [HALS: 60994]; British Schools Museum, *Educating Our Own. The Masters of Hitchin British School 1810 to 1929* (Hitchin, 2008) pp19-21; Minutes of Property [HALS: 61613 p34]; ledgers 1782-1825 [HALS: 61542-61543]; cash books 1789- 1814 [HALS: 61482- 61506], cash books 1814 – 1823 [HALS: 61525-61532]; cash book 1823-1824 [HALS: 61535]; diary 1810-1811 [HALS: 61173]; J Preston, *That Odd Rich Old Woman. Elizabeth Barbara Bulwer-Lytton of Knebworth House, 1773-1843* (1998) p108.

[9] See J Parker, *'Nothing for Nothing for Nobody' A History of Hertfordshire Banks and Banking*, (Stevenage, 1986), pp14-15.

[10] Minutes of Property [HALS: 61613 pp28-30]; S Flood ed, *John Carrington, Farmer of Bramfield, His Diary, 1798-1810 Volume 1, 1798-1804* HRS Vol 26 (Hertford, 2015) p28; R L Hine, 'Hitchin and the Threatened Invasion of 1806' in *Relics of an Un-Common Attorney* (1951) pp102-114.

[11] Minutes of Property [HALS: 61613 pp54-96]; Mathias, *The Brewing Industry in England*, pp301, 310, 327, 441; R Fulford, *Samuel Whitbread 1764-1815. A Study in Opposition.* (1967) pp94-96.

clerk, Joseph Eade, taking over his practice in the Common and Crown law and Court of Chancery.[12]

Wilshere invested much of his wealth in mortgages and in purchases of land in Hitchin and in the neighbouring parishes of Pirton and Shillington (then known as Shitlington which was just across the county boundary in Bedfordshire). On his father's death in 1798 he inherited The Frythe at Welwyn, as well as a house in Hitchin, a farm in Great Wymondley and another farm in Shillington. In 1806 he bought the Manor of Wymondley, though not the manor house, Wymondley Bury. Wilshere recorded that by 1813 'The value of the real estate has been very considerably increased by the Inclosure of Shitlington, Wymondley & Pirton, the high prices of Grain & other agricultural produce and the consequent advance of rents.' In 1817 he acquired the lease of the Manor of Hitchin. In 1819 he bought St Julian's Farm near St Albans and in 1822 he purchased two farms, including Highover, in Walsworth, a hamlet in the parish of Hitchin. Walsworth's open fields had been enclosed in 1767, but the open fields of Hitchin remained open, subject to a gradual process of piecemeal enclosure by Wilshere and other landowners.[13]

Wilshere was concerned about the increase in poverty and assisted Samuel Whitbread in devising a scheme for reforming the Poor Law. Whitbread introduced his Poor Laws Reform bill to the House of Commons in February 1807. He was persuaded to replace this with four separate bills of which he considered his Parochial Schools Bill the most important. This would have compelled magistrates to build a school and appoint a school master in any parish funded by the rates where there were a number of the poor who could not afford to pay for the education of their children. Whitbread praised the methods advocated by Joseph Lancaster. The bill was defeated in the House of Lords. Joseph Lancaster visited Hitchin in January 1808 to see Wilshere where he also met Samuel Whitbread who was passing through the town on his way to London. In 1810 Wilshere founded the Hitchin British Schools in a house and maltings which he had inherited from William Crawley. In 1811 he spent £750 on 'building (principally school rooms in Hitchin)'.[14]

---

[12] Minutes of Property [HALS: 61613 pp56-66].
[13] Minutes of Property [HALS: 61613]; B Howlett 'The Fields Beneath' in B Howlett & P Humphries ed, *Discovering More About Hitchin* (Hitchin, 2018) pp6-10.
[14] Fulford, *Samuel Whitbread,* pp176-180; D Rapp, *Samuel Whitbread (1764-1815) A Social and Political Study* (1987) pp216-219, 232-240; British Schools Museum, *Educating Our Own,* pp22-25; Minutes of Property [HALS: 61613 p72].

INTRODUCTION

In Wilshere's Commonplace Book in 1815 he noted an account in a report of the Society for Bettering the Condition of the Poor of a charitable fund at Mortlake 'one of the objects of which is to supply the poor with coals at a reduced price. The plan is that a 1/- subscribed in summer shall entitle the subscriber to as many bushels of coals (not exceeding 1 bushel per week) in the winter months.' Wilshere became involved in a similar scheme in Hitchin subscribing £10 10s to the Coal Fund. In March 1816 he was paid for the carriage of 1,000 bushels of coal from the River Ivel Navigation at Biggleswade to be retailed to the poor.[15]

Another idea promoted by the Society for Bettering the Condition of the Poor was the provision of cottage gardens or allotments. In 1810 Wilshere converted the Chalk Dell, which was manorial waste, into 13 'potatoe gardens' for which a rent of 1d a year was paid to the Lord of the Manor. The tenants were reported many years later to have 'made a soil from scrapings from the road & horse dung'.[16] More gardens had been created on the manorial waste by 1818. By 1823 part of his own land, Lower Benslow Hill, was rented as 15 gardens of 20 poles each for rents of 12s a year each. Wilshere also subscribed to the Irish School Society, the Refuge for the Destitute, the Refuge for Juvenile Offenders, Bedford Infirmary and the Hitchin Lying In Charity.[17]

Wilshere's Memoranda and Commonplace Book shows that he was a man of wide ranging interests and extensive reading. He belonged to the Hitchin New Book Society. As well as the *Monthly Review* and Parliamentary Papers, he read Madame de Stael's *Considerations on the French Revolution* and Lady Caroline Lamb's *Glenarvon* the month it was published in 1816. His bequest from Richard Tristram included all his 'optical and philosophical instruments whatsoever'. Wilshere was a Fellow of the Society of Antiquaries and a member of the Hertfordshire and Bedfordshire Agricultural Societies, the Horticultural Society, the Society for Promoting Christian Knowledge and the Dissenting Ministers Benevolent Society. In 1814 he paid a subscription to the African Society. When in London in 1792 he visited Vauxhall and Ranelagh Gardens and a museum. He and his brothers and sisters remained members of the Back

---

[15] Commonplace Book [NHM: 1216 p81]; cash book 1816 [HALS 61626: pp21, 84].
[16] M Willes, *The Gardens of the British Working Classes* (Yale, 2014) pp61, 115; cash book 1814-1815 [HALS: 61525 p7]; cash book 1818-1819 [HALS: 61528 p123]; letter from John Hawkins, 14 Oct 1861 [Trinity College Cambridge: 42 Hitchin 74].
[17] Cash book 1823-1824 [HALS: 61535 pp43, 51]; Later addition to plan of land occupied by Wilshere, 1819 [HALS: 67196]; eg cash books [HALS: 61528 pp122-126, 61531 pp78-84].

INTRODUCTION

Street Independent Meeting, though Wilshere and his wife were buried in St Mary's Church, Welwyn.[18]

As Lord of the Manor of Great Wymondley William Wilshere had the duty of presenting the first cup of wine to King George IV at his coronation feast in 1821; the cup became a family heirloom and is now on display in North Hertfordshire Museum.[19]

By the time of his death on 2 September 1824 William Wilshere possessed assets worth almost £230,000 (over £200 million today). In the last year of his life he enjoyed an income of £11,500, more than Jane Austen's Mr Darcy's £10,000 a year (over £7 million today) of which he spent £3,700. He adopted as his heir his nephew William, the eldest son of his brother Thomas.[20]

According to Reginald Hine's unfinished history of Hawkins Solicitors, the legal practice formerly owned by Wilshere, he was a tough and enterprising business man known as 'Devil Wilshere' on account of his willingness to lend money and to foreclose where necessary.[21] However, in contrast, William Lucas, a Quaker brewer and farmer, entered in his diary on 2 September 1824 the following tribute:

> 'This evening abt ¼ past 8 died our neighbour Wm Wilshere aged 70 years all but a few days - the most eminent public character of this town & neighbourhood. He began life with but little property but by his address, assiduity & superior abilities soon rose into great practice in his profession as an attorney & steward to copyhold courts, by which he acquired much wealth & influence. For several years past he had relinquished practice - & being appointed a magistrate, he distinguished himself by his sound judgement & usefulness in that station & was of late Chairman to the Quarter Sessions of Bedford. He was a man of great prudence & sagacity – of polished manners & kept an elegant

---

[18] Commonplace Book [NHM: 1216 pp88, 137-140]; Richard Tristram's will 1785 [TNA: PROB11/1136/42]; election to fellowship 1817 [HALS: 61101]; cash books 1814 – 1823 [HALS: 61525-61532]; cash book 1792 [HALS 61484 p54]; Wilshere family tree [HALS: ACC/6412].
[19] N Farris, *The Wymondleys* (Hertford, 1989) pp56-57, 134.
[20] Minutes of Property [HALS: 61613 pp96-97]; R Floud, *An Economic History of the English Garden* (2019) pp63, 126.
[21] Pieris, *Take 6 Carrots - - -,* pp15, 19.

INTRODUCTION

establishment both in house & gardens & was very kind to the poor who have in him lost a good friend.'[22]

William Wilshere's house and garden

The house which Wilshere inherited from Richard Tristram and where he lived for almost 40 years was situated on the east side of Bancroft (formerly Bancroft Street), the broad road which runs through the centre of Hitchin leading to the Market Place. Adjoining it to the south was the house and maltings bought by his grandfather which he inherited on his father's death in 1798. Behind the house extensive gardens stretched as far as Back Street (now Queen Street) comprising 3 acres 3 roods and 27 perches. The little River Hiz ran northwards through the centre of the garden roughly parallel with the roads. Wilshere's nephew and heir named the house 'the Hermitage'. Although anachronistic, 'the Hermitage' will be used as a convenient way of identifying the house. The southern part of the house was demolished in 1874 for the construction of Hermitage Road between Bancroft and Queen Street. The remaining part of the house was described in 1911 as 'a building of irregular plan which incorporates a large barn, probably of the 16th century, converted into part of a dwelling house in the 18th century, the rest of the house being re-built or added at the same time. The barn is of plastered timber with two large disused archways.'[23] This too was demolished in the 1920s. The site of Wilshere's house and most of his garden is now occupied by Hermitage Road and the shops, offices and other buildings adjoining it with the car parks behind.

---

[22] William Lucas' diary [NHM: 492/7].
[23] Map of Hitchin 1816 [NHM; colour section No 5]; Pieris, *Take 6 Carrots - - -,* p19; Royal Commission on Historical Monuments (England), *Inventory of the Historical Monuments in Hertfordshire* (1911) p123.

xvii

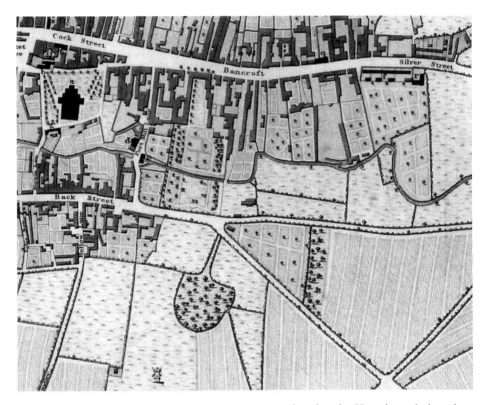

Detail from map of Hitchin 1820 by Henry Merrett showing the Hermitage below the trees on Bancroft (*North Hertfordshire Museum*).

The first documentary reference to the property which became the Hermitage is in the will of John Emmyng the elder of Hitchin, yeoman, made in 1524. He was obviously wealthy as he was able to leave each of his four sons a house in Bancroft. His son Thomas also received his tanhouse which suggests the source of his wealth. John Emmyng left the Hermitage to his wife Agnes for her life. He described it as 'the place that she dwelleth in with four rentalles longing about the place'. After Agnes' death, the property was to go to his son Robert and his male heirs, failing which to the next male heir of the Emmynges.[24] A survey of the Manor of Hitchin dated 1556 described the Hermitage as two burgages in Bancroft Street held by John Hemmynge. Burgages were substantial town houses – each of these would have had a frontage to Bancroft of between 90 and 100 feet. John Hemmynge had no sons. When he died, his property in

---

[24] John Emmyng's will proved 1525 [TNA: PROB11/21/519].

Hitchin was inherited by his daughter, Anne, and her husband Thomas Gaddesden, a lawyer, who lived in the Hermitage.[25] In 1584 Thomas bought land to the rear making possible the eventual extension of the garden as far as Back Street. This was the large orchard belonging to The Bury Barns which fronted on to Portmill Lane. It occupied the land behind the Hermitage and the adjoining houses and the River Hiz. Gaddesden also bought the field between the river and Back Street.[26]

By 1615 Thomas Gaddesden had moved to Newnham in Hertfordshire and he and his son John sold the Hermitage.[27] The purchaser was John Skynner, a lawyer, who had moved from Norwich to Hitchin where he established the legal practice which was later acquired by Richard Tristram. John Skynner lived to the great age of 91 dying in 1660. His elder son John, also a lawyer, inherited the Hermitage. When he died in 1669 he left most of his extensive property to his only surviving child, his daughter Mary, who had married Sir Thomas Byde of Ware Park. After her death it was to go to her second son, Ralph Byde, on condition that he took the additional name of Skynner. An exception was the Hermitage which John Skynner left to his younger brother Ralph for his life. On his death it was to go to Mary Byde and her son Ralph. The Hermitage now comprised the main house where Ralph Skynner lived, a cottage on the south side occupied by Thomas Wilkinson who had been John Skynner's servant, and another cottage and a house on the north side let to tenants.[28]

Ralph Skynner never married. Like his father he was very long lived, dying at the age of 89 in 1697. The house then passed to his great nephew, Ralph Skynner Byde, but although both he and his first wife were buried in Hitchin Parish Church, it is not clear whether the younger Ralph ever lived in Hitchin. When he died aged 47 in 1705 his home was in London. He bequeathed most of his property in Hitchin to the son of his first marriage, John Byde. He left the Hermitage to his second wife Sarah for her life, then it was to go to her stepson,

---

[25] Survey of the Manor of Hitchin 1556 [TNA: E315/391]; deed of partition 1583 [HALS: 87679]; C W Brooks, *Pettyfoggers and Vipers of the Commonwealth. The 'Lower Branch' of the Legal Profession in Early Modern England* (Cambridge 1986, paperback edition 2004) p167.

[26] Deeds to The Grange House, 1584-1620 [HALS: 60356-60362]; rental of the Manor of Hitchin 1591 [TNA: SC12/8/29].

[27] Deeds [HALS: 60315-60318, 60359, 87685, 87687].

[28] John Skynner's will proved 1669 [TNA: PROB11/330/40]; B Howlett ed, *Survey of the Royal Manor of Hitchin 1676,* HRS Vol 16 (Hertford, 2000) p72.

INTRODUCTION

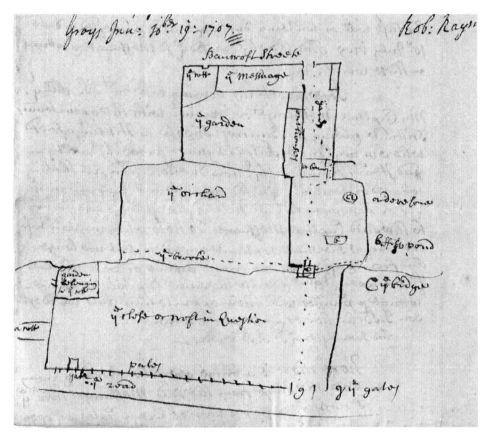

Plan of the grounds of Sarah Byde's House, 1707 (*HALS: 60325*).

The house (later owned by William Wilshere) is on the east side of Bancroft Street, with the garden behind. Beyond are the orchard, dove house and fish pond separated from 'the close or croft in Question' by the River Hiz. The road at the bottom is Back Street.

John. Uncertainty over what exactly was included in his bequest to Sarah led to the drawing of a plan of the grounds of the Hermitage in a legal document of 1707. This concerned the field between the river and Back Street where Ralph Skynner used to graze his horse, but 'being grown old and having no occasion for horses' he had let the field to a tenant. The legal opinion was that the field was part of the Hermitage. By now the cottage to the north of the Hermitage had been converted into a wash house and brewery for the main house, while the cottage on the south side which had been occupied by Ralph Skynner's gardener, was incorporated into the house. The plan shows a relatively small garden immediately behind the house. Beyond it, extending behind the neighbouring house to the south and stretching as far as the river was the orchard. North of the orchard was a dove house and fish pond. A carriage drive crossing a bridge over the river led to a gateway into Back Street.[29]

Hitchin's famous old box trees beside Hermitage Road, 1906 (*Gerry Tidy Collection*).

Although Sarah Byde came from Hitchin (she was the daughter of the lawyer, George Draper), she continued to live in London during the 40 years of her widowhood. The Hermitage was occupied by a succession of tenants. In 1728 she became embroiled in another legal dispute, this time with her next door neighbour about an overgrown hedge. He was Richard Tristram, a lawyer (father of William Wilshere's later partner and benefactor), whose house was on the south side of the Hermitage. Early one morning in May 1728 Tristram employed two men to break down his garden wall and to go into the garden of the Hermitage to cut down six of the largest trees in the hedge which had grown over 10 feet tall and was within 6 inches of his wall. What is notable about this dispute is that the hedge was described as consisting of box trees which were over 100 years old. In 1819 Wilshere recorded that there were 56 box trees on the south side of his garden. The tallest trees were 35 feet high while the girth of the largest was 2 feet 11 inches. The other trees varied in height from 1 to 4 feet.

---

[29] Ralph Skynner Byde's will proved 1705 [TNA: PROB11/482/402]; case for opinion, 1707 [HALS: 60325].

INTRODUCTION

In 1795 Elizabeth Simpson, a wealthy widow, left most of her property in
Hitchin and Great Wymondley to her kinsman and fellow member of Back
Street Independent Meeting, William Wilshere's father. He was to enjoy it for
his life, then her Hitchin property was to go to his youngest son, Thomas.
William Wilshere immediately exchanged land with his father and brother so he
could acquire seven acres of arable land in Purwell Field next to Walsworth
Road. Some of this lay between Walsworth Road and The Dell while the rest
formed a triangle between Walsworth Road and Whinbush Road. Here Wilshere
created a nursery, which later became his new kitchen garden (1 acre 3 roods 8
perches in extent). This garden was never enclosed by high brick walls though
part may have been bounded by lower walls.[37] At the apex of the triangle he
built a thatched lodge with a semi-circular front facing towards Back Street. The
lodge still stands though much enlarged and no longer thatched.

Ornamental thatched cottage built by Wilshere in his kitchen garden, *c*1900 (*Gerry Tidy
Collection*).

In 1801 Wilshere bought a house called The Grange on the north side of
Portmill Lane west of the River Hiz which he let to his business partner, Joseph
Eade. The Grange had an additional garden east of the River Hiz surrounded by
high brick walls which Wilshere appropriated as his Frame Yard or Garden (2

---

[37] Deeds [HALS: DE/Ha/T111]; map of Hitchin 1816 [NHM].

roods, 32 perches in extent). It was probably here that he constructed a peach house in 1813 at a cost of £200. His gardeners successfully cultivated large quantities of pineapples, peaches, grapes, melons and cucumbers. Wilshere's house and gardens now occupied a total of 6 acres, 1 rood, 27 perches.[38] By 1802 he also possessed that essential prerequisite for fine dining, an ice house, but where it was situated is unknown. The first reference to it in his cash books was in November 1802. The coincidence of dates and lack of reference in his cash books to constructing the ice house suggests he may have acquired it when he purchased The Grange in 1801. On 25 November 1819 the ice house was filled with 30 cart loads of ice from Mr Pierson's pond at Ickleford.[39]

Tree Nursery

Wilshere established a highly productive tree nursery on his triangle of land between Walsworth and Whinbush Roads. In 1811 he sold trees and shrubs from his nursery to Lord Tavistock, the eldest son of the Duke of Bedford, and Mr Lee Antonie of Colworth, Bedfordshire. These comprised 4,000 spruce firs, 1,000 Scotch pines or firs, 100 larches, 1,000 laurels, 250 lilacs, syringia, and laurentinas, 200 limes and planes, 4 large firs, 100 Chinese roses half in pots, 20 weeping birches, 50 roses, 20 honeysuckles, 2 hickories, 20 rosemary, 22 box, 100 laburnums, 2 large cypress, 30 sugar maples, 100 hornbeams, 12 Persian lilacs, 12 large abele, and 20 large white poplars. In November 1822 he supplied over 3,000 trees including 1,000 oaks for Lady De Grey, the owner of Wrest Park.[40]

Great Wymondley was enclosed in 1811 and Wilshere acquired a compact block of land in the north west of the parish adjoining Walsworth. He immediately started planting trees in some of his new fields. Two of his plantations now form part of Wymondley Wood where the trees are congested and many have grown very tall. The Upper Plantation includes mature oak, beech, lime, horse chestnut, and ash, while the Lower Plantation, where there are springs and a pond, has in addition willows and poplars. One of the oaks near the edge of the Lower Plantation had a circumference of 10 feet 6 inches in 2020 and was probably

---

[38] Hitchin Manor court book [TNA: CRES5/37 p125]; cash book [HALS: 61505 pp68, 94]; map of Hitchin 1816 [NHM].
[39] Cash book 1802-1803 [HALS 61495 p56]; See p129.
[40] See pp19-20, 155.

planted by Wilshere, while five oaks in the Upper Plantation ranged between 7 feet 2 inches and 8 feet 8 inches. Oak trees were also planted in the hedgerows.[41]

Rawlings Hill and the Dell

Between 1799 and 1804 Wilshere ended John Ransom's tenancy and converted the former arable land on the steep slope of Rawlings Hill into meadow. He planted oaks and elms in the hedges.[42] In 1814 he purchased grass seed for Dimsey's Close which adjoined the hill from Thomas Gibbs & Co of London, a seedsman recommended by the Honourable George Villiers of Aldenham for obtaining 'by infinite labour and attention, all the most valuable grasses both for pasture and hay ground'. He bought the windmill from John Ransom and let it to John Farmer, a corn merchant. From back of his house the grass covered hill bordered by trees would have given the impression of park like surroundings beyond the garden. The top of the hill gave a panoramic view over his garden and the town of Hitchin and the hills beyond. Here he built a thatched summer house in 1819.[43]

To the north of Rawlings Hill was the Dell, a sand pit with steeply sloping sides dug into the hillside. Formerly known as Rawlings Dell, this was one of the communal quarries owned by the Lord of the Manor where the tenants of the manor had the right to dig sand and gravel. A map of Purwell Field dating from about 1770 shows it as a Sand Dell. From 1792 Wilshere paid an annual rent of 10s 6d to the Foreman of the Jury of Hitchin Manor Court for Rawlings Dell which he surrounded by a hedge and planted with trees. These became a valuable source of timber and fire wood.[44]

The management of the garden

Wilshere paid his gardener regular sums of money on account. Most of this was used to pay wages, but it also covered minor incidental expenses. When John

---

[41] Great and Little Wymondley enclosure award and map [HALS: QS/E80-81]; See pp39, 62, 127.
[42] Cash book October 1799 [HALS: 61492 p5]; plan of estate [HALS: 58869]; See p62.
[43] See Appendix Two [HALS: 61479/29]; A Young, *General View of the Agriculture of Hertfordshire* (1804, reprint 1971) p137; cash books [HALS: 61525 pp92, 110; 61526 pp47-48; 61529 p8].
[44] Deeds [HALS: 87597, DE/Ha/T111]; terrier of Manor of Hitchin 1727 [HALS: 64356 f.56]; plan of Purwell Field [HALS: DZ/72/P121605]; cash book [HALS: 61484 pp32, 68].

INTRODUCTION

Fells was in charge of the garden from 1790 to 1806, Wilshere sometimes recorded the details of the money spent by Fells in his cash books. A typical example is given below:

1805 May 1 Self Garden. Paid John Fells as under from 23 March to 27 April both inclusive:

		£ - s - d
John Fells senior	5 weeks	2 – 10 – 10
Phipp	Ditto	2 – 12 - 6
Abbis	Ditto	2 – 12 - 6
Fells junior	Ditto	0 – 15 - 0
Digging up close for potatoes		2 – 19 - 0
Garden pots		0 – 14 - 0
Picking potatoes		0 - 1 - 0
Soot		0 - 0- 6
Catching mole		0- 0- 6
Weeding		0 - 3 - 0
		12 – 8 – 10[45]

Other payments by John Fells included picking twitch 4s, brooms, skip & baskets 11s 10d, sieve, rub stones, bricks and paper 5s 11d, mats 15s, cabbage seed 4s, dressing trees 10s and filling fish pond 10s.[46]

Wilshere's normal practice after 1806 was to pay his gardener £10 on account, usually about once a month, less often in winter, more frequently in summer, but not to record how the money was spent, other than the occasional note that the £10 was on account of wages. Periodically he would draw up a balance (but usually without any details) when any outstanding money would be paid to the

---

[45] Cash book [HALS: 61497 p75].
[46] Cash books 1798-1806 [HALS: 61490-61497].

gardener, or occasionally refunded to Wilshere. For instance in the year October 1808 to September 1809 he paid his gardener, Thomas Grant, a total of £105 including his own wages of £35 a year. In the year October 1821 to September 1822 he paid his gardener Daniel McIntosh £165 on account including his wages of £35.[47]

Other costs, including bills for plants were paid by Wilshere directly. In the 1790s surviving bills for plants, trees, seeds and bulbs record Wilshere's purchases from the London nursery and seedsmen Hairs, Hairs & Co, Grimwood and Wykes, and Gordon Dermer & Co, as well as from Isaac and Thomas Emmerton of Barnet. Other purchases of plants, bulbs and seeds for which no bills survive are recorded in his cash books as well as a payment of 15s in November 1796 for the hire of two horses with a cart to go to London to fetch plants. Hitchin gardeners were able to supply some of his needs; in November 1796 he paid Henry Bentley £1 15s for seeds, 17s 6d for plants and £1 17s 6d for 'work'. A bill from Henry Bentley survives for November 1797 to August 1798 for seeds for beans, peas, onions, cabbages, lettuce, radishes and mustard and cress and 20½ days' work at 2 shillings a day. One of the Dimsey family provided him with quick thorn for hedging Rawlings Dell in 1792.[48] During the period covered by the memoranda books Wilshere's purchases of plants were mainly from Hertfordshire nurserymen, Henry Hodgson and John Bentley of Hitchin and Robert Murray and William McMullen of Hertford, though he did buy dahlias from Tate while on a visit to London in 1821 plus more dahlias from Wood the same year. Two bills from Robert Murray dated 1813-1814, one from Thomas Gibbs & Co of London for grass seed in 1814, and one from Henry Hodgson for 1823 have been transcribed as Appendix Two.[49]

Wilshere also paid directly for building work and maintenance in the garden, often as part of bills for similar work at his house and farm. For instance he paid £10 3s to Robert Newton plumber of Hitchin for garden lights in January 1823. Other payments included gravel. When he purchased coal and coke for his

---

[47] Cash books [HALS: 61501, 61531-61532].
[48] Bills [HALS: 61480/138, 170, 172-3, 184-187]; cash book [HALS: 61489 pp6, 8]; bill [HALS: 61479/19]; cash book 1792 [HALS: 61484 p68].
[49] Wood may have been John Wood of Huntingdon while Tate was probably James Edward Tate who took over the London Botanic Garden in Chelsea in 1822 [L J Drake, *Wood & Ingram: Huntingdon Nursery, 1742–1950* (Cambridge, 2008); *VCH* Middlesex vol 12 pp150-155]; cash books [HALS: 61535 p70, 61530 p76, 61531 pp80, 82]; bills [HALS: 61479/31, 61479/44].

house, usually he did not state what quantity was intended for garden use, but in October 1823 he paid Samuel Allen £3 12s (including £1 for carriage) for 3 chaldrons of coke for the garden. He also paid for garden tools, gravel for paths, flints to edge path, pebbles for the river, and for tan, soot, malt dust and compost.[50]

Wilshere's gardeners were:

John Fells	Jan 1790	-	July 1806
Thomas Grant	July 1806	-	July 1810
James Carter	July 1810	-	Feb 1811
Daniel McIntosh	Feb 1811	-	Dec 1812
James Bowie	Dec 1812	-	Aug 1814
John Downing	Oct 1814	-	Aug 1818
James Gray	Aug 1818	-	June 1820
Daniel McIntosh	July 1820	-	May 1823
John Carter	June 1823	-	Sept 1824

After Wilshere's death John Carter was employed by his nephew and heir until his own death in 1857, moving with him to The Frythe in 1846.[51]

Wilshere bequeathed £15 each to two of his garden men, James Abbis and William Knightley. Every other garden man, who had been in his employ for a year, was to receive £5. James Abbis and his wife lived in the ornamental thatched lodge in the new kitchen garden where they cared for some of Wilshere's poultry. There is no evidence that Wilshere provided a cottage specifically for his head gardeners, many of whom were unmarried, while they were in his employment. The exception was John Fells who in 1801 lived in Bridge Street with his family. In 1824 Wilshere bequeathed £10 to his principal gardener 'whether residing in my house or not so residing'. His nephew later

---

[50] Cash books [HALS: 61532 p68, 61535 p42, 61493-61505, 61525-61535, 61525 p10].
[51] Cash books [HALS: 61482-61506; 61525-61532; 61535. 61512]; 1851 census; John Carter's will [HALS: 31HW94].

built a gardener's cottage in the Frame Garden. For more information about Wilshere's gardeners see the Biographical Notes.[52]

William Wilshere's Farm

Hitchin lies in that part of northern Hertfordshire where the land was cultivated in open fields. Unlike many of the neighbouring parishes in both Hertfordshire and Bedfordshire, Hitchin was not enclosed by Act of Parliament except for the hamlet of Walsworth where the open fields were enclosed in 1767. By the 1790s the former nine or ten open fields of Hitchin township had been reduced to six. Each of the three larger fields was paired with one of the smaller fields in a three yearly rotation. Two years after Wilshere bought the lease of the Manor of Hitchin in 1817, the manor court drew up a statement of the customs of the manor regulating the open fields and commons. These allowed owners of land in the open fields (except for Bury Field and Welchman's Croft, two smaller fields near the River Hiz which were cow commons) to enclose their land and withdraw it from the general cultivation and common grazing of the fields. Wilshere took full advantage of this long established practice to build up by a process of gradual purchase and exchange a compact block of land in Purwell Field, one of the three large open fields. Other landowners were similarly enlarging and consolidating their holdings at the same time, notably the Quaker Ransom and Lucas families.[53]

Opportunities for acquiring a substantial area of land in Hitchin were limited. The two largest sales of land at this period by Thomas Byde of Ware Park in 1783 and by the Reverend Thomas Whitehurst in 1791, both as a result of financial difficulties, occurred before Wilshere was in a position to benefit. Sir Francis Willes, a government code breaker, bought 200 acres from Thomas Byde. Wilshere's youngest brother, Thomas, managed Sir Francis Willes' property. Sir John Henniker, a London merchant trading with Russia, bought Whitehurst's 605 acres in Walsworth. These three farms were inherited by his

[52] William Wilshere's will [TNA: PROB11/1692/97]; photocopy of 1801 census [NHM]; 1838 rate assessment [HALS: DP/53/18/9].
[53] Howlett, 'The Fields Beneath' and J Lucas, 'Oughtonhead, Oakfield and the Lucas Family' in Howlett & Humphries, *Discovering More About Hitchin* pp1-9, 51-54; F Seebohm, *The English Village Community* (1883) pp443-453.

grandson, Sir Francis Sykes, during whose long minority they were managed by Wilshere. In 1822 they were sold to Wilshere and his brother, John.[54]

In 1785, as well as his house and garden, Wilshere inherited seven acres of land from Richard Tristram comprising Rawlings Hill, Home Close at its foot, and the Linces (the steep hillside above Rawlings Dell). After Elizabeth Simpson's death in 1795 Wilshere acquired by exchange with his father and brother (in addition to the site of his nursery and kitchen garden) 5½ acres of enclosed land on the opposite side of Walsworth Road adjoining his existing property. After their father's death in 1798, Thomas Wilshere agreed to exchange almost 26 acres of land with his brother, though the legal formalities remained uncompleted at the time of William's death in 1824. This land was all in the vicinity of Walsworth Road and Benslow Hill.[55]

Wilshere gradually acquired more land, varying from purchases of strips of one acre to two closes of 12 acres, 2 roods exchanged with Sir Francis Willes in 1808. This gave him the remainder of what became Great Wimbush (or Wimbush Field) and enabled him to amalgamate three small pieces into Little Wimbush Field in 1815. He also rented adjacent land. By 1806 he occupied Thomas Brown's arable close of just under seven acres. In 1812 he agreed to rent in addition Brown's two meadows of five acres. He rented another meadow from John Ransom. By 1806 he was the tenant of the 18 acres, 1 rood, 2 perches of Great Benslow Hill owned by the Reverend Wollaston Pym. By 1820 he occupied a compact block of 122 acres, 2 roods, 13 perches of which 36 acres, 3 roods, 4 perches were rented. In addition by 1816 he owned over 60 acres of land scattered in strips throughout the open fields of Hitchin rented to tenants.[56]

The land farmed by Wilshere was on the west facing slope of the chalk spur immediately to the east of Hitchin town centre. Rawlings Hill, the Linces, and the upper part of Benslow Hill were on a steep incline. Lower Benslow Hill,

---

[54] B Howlett, 'Sir Francis Willes and Frederick Lovell – from code breaker to landowner' and B Howlett & J Walker, 'Highover and Farming in Walsworth' in Howlett & Humphries, *Discovering More About Hitchin*, pp111-112, 117, 119.
[55] Richard Tristram's will 1785 [TNA: PROB11/1136/42]; deeds [HALS: DE/Ha/T111]; William Wilshere's will [TNA: PROB11/1692/97].
[56] Sale particulars for Thomas Plumer Byde's estate 1783, Lovell Papers [Wiltshire & Swindon Archives: 161/57]; plan of an estate of William Wilshere *c*1808 [HALS: 58869]; cash book [HALS: 61499 p28]; See p48 [HALS: 61181 p113]; plans of fields occupied by Wilshere 1806 and 1819 [HALS: DE/Ws/P15-16]; map of Hitchin 1816 [NHM].

INTRODUCTION

Brown's Twelve Acres, Starlings Bridge Close, and Great Wimbush sloped more gently down towards the River Hiz. Beyond Rawlings Hill was the gentle dip of Nettledell (called Nettledale by Wilshere) before the land rose again. The chalk is often close to the surface while elsewhere it is overlain by glacial deposits of sand and gravel of varying thickness. The steep slope of Rawlings Hill is covered by sand and Rawlings Dell was shown as a sand dell on a map of *c*1770. Gravel from Benslow Hill was used to make paths in Wilshere's garden.[57]

The management of the farm

Between 1782 and 1787 Wilshere was farming and malting in partnership with his brother John, though it is not clear what land he was cultivating apart from Home Close. In 1782 he harvested 27 acres of barley. In 1784-5 he sold 62 loads of wheat for £92 4s 6d as well as selling hay for £50 5s 5d. However in 1784-5 he had to buy 500 quarters of barley for £629 8d. The partnership was dissolved in 1787 and Wilshere appears to have given up any direct interest in malting. His farming activities for the next 15 years were limited to keeping a few cows and pigs and making hay, presumably for consumption by his household and stables. In 1792 he purchased from his brother John a row of cottages with land behind them at the north end of Back Street next to Rawlings Hill. The area behind the cottages became his farmyard supervised by his gardener, John Fells.[58]

John Fells' first itemised accounts in 1794 include payments for haymaking. As the area of land farmed gradually increased, so did Fells' farming expenditure which from 1802 is often distinguished from his payments for the garden. An example of his account for the farm from 21 August to 13 November 1802 is as follows:

	£ - s - d
Haybinding	0 - 8 – 4
Catching mole	0 – 0 – 6
Cow	0 – 1 – 9

---

[57] Plan of Purwell Field [HALS: DZ/72/P121605]; cash book [HALS: 61525 p74].
[58] Ledger A [HALS: 61542]; cash books 1789-1803 [HALS: 61482-61495].

Pollard[59]	1 - 16 – 6
Grains	0 – 18 - 6
Sow	0 – 1 – 0
Malt grinding	0 - 2 - 3

His account for the following year included haymakers' bread, cheese & beer £4 ½d and sow to the boar 1s. This suggests a very limited operation.[60]

In 1803 barley was grown and thrashed, then sold in February 1804 to Richard Smith who from November 1803 had shared responsibility for the farm with John Fells. By the following year wheat and oats were also being cultivated and a Harvest Home celebrated. In late 1804 William Wren took over management of the farm. On 2 October 1804 Wilshere bought two horses for the farm at Baldock Fair paying £50. The same month he paid John Clark, blacksmith, £2 3s 5d for ironwork for a plough. The following June he settled a bill for £6 5s 6d for a drill, plough and barrows.[61] By 1805 John Kingsley was paying Wilshere for turnips, which, presumably as in later years, were eaten by his sheep in the fields. In 1807 Wilshere bought the houses on the corner of Back Street and Portmill Lane, part of a former tanhouse, and used the land and buildings behind as his lower farm yard.[62]

Wilshere's method of managing his farm was similar to that he used for managing his garden (and indeed his household, stables, office and the British Schools.) He paid Wren regular sums of money on account. The difference was that periodically Wren paid Wilshere money which he presumably had received for the sale of produce. In the year October 1808 to September 1809 Wilshere made no payments to Wren, but received from him £75. In addition he received £39 5s in January 1809 for the sale of clover hay. Wilshere paid rent for Great Benslow Hill of £20. He also paid local and national taxes and tithes.[63]

William Wren became seriously ill then died in the autumn of 1809. This prompted Wilshere to take a closer interest in the management of his farm. In

---

[59] Here meaning the bran sifted from flour.
[60] Cash book [HALS: 61495 pp12, 90].
[61] Cash books 1803-1805 [HALS: 61495-61497].
[62] Cash book [HALS: 61500 p7]; deed [HALS: 60536].
[63] Cash book 1808-1809 [HALS: 61501].

INTRODUCTION

August 1809 he bought 'Grigg's book on the management of a farm'.[64] In October he started his first Farm and Garden Memoranda Book. On 15 October 1809 he recorded the appointment of James Robinson 'as farming man to live in the farm cottage, to go with the horses & with his wife to milk & take care of the cows, pigs & poultry. Wages 12s per week with the usual addition in harvest'.[65] The cottage was probably part of the late medieval timber framed house with a hammer beam roof on the corner of Back Street and Portmill Lane which Wilshere bought in 1807 together with the farmyard behind. As with Wren, he paid periodic sums of money to Robinson on account and received from him the balance from produce he had sold.

His usual rotation of crops was wheat followed by turnips which were eaten in the field by John Kingsley's sheep during the following winter. In the spring barley was sown. After harvest the fields were sown with clover or sometimes trefoil or sanfoin in preparation for wheat the following year. Sometimes peas, beans or tares were grown usually after wheat and before turnips. Occasionally oats were grown. Great Wimbush or Wimbush next to Wilshere's kitchen garden and plantation was sown each year with a variety of crops, usually between half an acre and two acres each, including wheat, tares, potatoes, turnips, carrots, mangel-wurzels and cabbages.

In the autumn of 1816 William Wilshere starting recording in his memoranda books far more details of crops sown, wages paid, and sales of produce. James Robinson ceased to be bailiff in September 1818, though he was employed for harvest work in 1820. Wilshere placed the day to day management of the farm in the care of his gardener, James Gray who was paid £52 a year and lived in the farm cottage.[66]

Some of the produce from the farm was consumed by Wilshere's household which in 1801 comprised four males and two females. The cash books indicate that his indoor staff had not much increased comprising a butler, male servant, housekeeper, cook, housemaid and sometimes a kitchen maid. Many payments were made months if not years in arrears. Increasingly in the early 1820s crops were stored rather than being sold the year they were harvested. This makes it difficult to estimate whether his farming enterprise was profitable. In the year October 1817 to September 1818 Wilshere recorded in his cash books receipts of £369 14s 9¼d from his farm of which £215 0s 7d were payments from

---

[64] See p7; Cash book [HALS: 61501 p74].
[65] See p6.
[66] See pp106-7, 135; cash books [HALS: 61528-61529].

Robinson and another £107 19s was received from Thomas Hailey for clover seed. Excluding rates and rent to Brown and Ransom, he paid out £338 10s of which the largest sums were a total of £71 3s to Robinson between July and September 1818, £112 5s to George Beaver for malting and carriage to Ware, £22 10 4d to William Clark, blacksmith, £27 to Thomas Hailey for peas, £30 to Edward Burr for barley and pollard, and £31 10s rent to the Reverend Wollaston Pym.[67]

The following year, October 1818 to September 1819, he did not receive any payments from James Gray. The receipts in total came to £431 1s 0d. The largest payments were £24.9 9s 6d for malt, £90 for wheat from James Nash, a local miller, £60 for the sale of six heifers, and £22 10 for the sale of straw to John Marshall. Excluding rates and rent to Brown and Ransom, his total expenditure (including £225 to Gray for the farm) came to £491 3s 7d. Larger payments were £31 10s rent to the Reverend Wollaston Pym, £56 19s to John Croft for oats and beans, £20 19s 6d to William Clark the blacksmith, £15 9s 7½d to Henry Asplin for peas and £15 13s 9d to William Watson, wheelwright.[68]

When Gray left Wilshere's service in June 1820, responsibility for the farm passed to John Willding aged 22, who had been employed in Wilshere's office since 1814. Wilshere's memoranda book records his active involvement in the management of his farm throughout 1819 and 1820. He made no entries in his memoranda book between December 1821 and June 1822.[69]

In the year from October 1821 to September 1822 Wilshere paid John Willding £170. He also made payments during the year of over £200 including rent, seed and meal, oats, peas and beans, soot, and paid bills from a blacksmith, wheelwright, ironmonger, collarmaker, plumber, brickmaker, bricklayer and cooper and brewer. He employed his own carpenter, William French. Wilshere also paid £39 19s 6d tithes. He received on 19 September 1822 £193 18s from James Nash for wheat from October 1818, but set against this were payments already made to Robinson of £96 11s 1d and debts for flour of £133 14s 0d.[70] In October 1822 Wilshere was owed £180 by John Kingsley for turnips eaten in the

---

[67] Photocopy of 1801 census [NHM]; eg cash books [HALS: 61506 p124, 61530 p94, 61531 p82]; cash books 1817-1818 [HALS: 61527-61528].
[68] Cash books 1818-1819 [HALS: 61528-61529].
[69] Cash book 1820 [HALS: 61530 p20].
[70] Cash books 1821-1823 [HALS: 61531-61532].

INTRODUCTION

field by Kingsley's sheep dating back to 1819. Kingsley paid him £360 on account in June 1823.[71]

William Wilshere's death and legacy

By the spring of 1824 Wilshere appears to have been aware he might not have long to live. The last extract in his Commonplace Book is from the Edinburgh Review of March 1824. He ceased making regular entries in his Farm and Garden Memoranda Book after March 1824, though a loose note made at the end of June 1824 was presumably intended to be entered in the book later. Instead he concentrated on putting his affairs in order. On 29 February 1824 he completed his 'Minutes of Property'. His will and its first two codicils were dated 26 March 1824. In a further codicil to his will dated 31 July 1824 he stated that when he made his will 'he was at that time engaged in the revision of all my accounts and I then gave directions in regard thereto in case I should not live to complete the revision in which I have made considerable progress but I still find old unclosed accounts' on which balances appeared against him of about £3,700. William Bentley was now examining and making up these accounts to facilitate which William Wilshere had allocated £5,000.[72] After Wilshere's death William Lucas recorded 'Altho his health had for some months been almost imperceptibly declining yet his decay at last was rather rapid'.[73]

William Wilshere died on 2 September 1824. He bequeathed his estates in trust to Thomas Lord Dacre and the Reverend Joseph Parsons for their use for 15 years after his death, then to the use of his nephew and adopted heir, William, the eldest son of his brother Thomas, for his life, then to his male heirs, failing which to Thomas's younger sons and their heirs, then to his other nieces and nephew and their children, and, if there were none, to 'his highly esteemed cousin Elizabeth wife of the Honourable William Waldegrave' and her heirs. The term of 15 years was determinable when his nephew William reached the age of 25 when his uncle's household goods were to become his personal property.[74]

At the time of his uncle's death the younger William was aged 20 and a student at Wadham College, Oxford. His father Thomas took over the management of

---

[71] Cash book 1823-1824 [HALS: 61535 p23].
[72] Minutes of property [HALS: 61613 pp2, 96-98]; William Wilshere's will 1824 [TNA: PROB11/1692/97].
[73] William Lucas' diary [NHM: 492/7].
[74] William Wilshere's will 1824 [TNA: PROB11/1692/97].

the house, garden and farm reporting to the trustees. As Thomas had his own farm, he presumably had no use for all his brother's livestock and implements and put up the surplus for auction. He gave up the tenancy of Thomas Brown's 12 acres, but retained Great Benslow Hill. Young William in due course took up residence in his uncle's house which he named 'The Hermitage' and in 1837 was elected Member of Parliament for Yarmouth. However the desirability of the Hermitage as a residence with the River Hiz running through its gardens must have been much diminished by the increasingly overcrowded and insanitary Back Street slums upstream. On the far side of Portmill Lane 17 houses built about 1820 were crammed into Chapman's Yard between Back Street and the river. Here lived 90 people who shared two privies built over the River Hiz.[75] In 1845-1846, William Wilshere rebuilt part of the original Wilshere family home, The Frythe, in Welwyn and moved there. He took with him his gardener, John Carter, who had been in charge of the Hermitage garden since 1823. The house and garden were let to Charles Prime, though the Frame Garden was reunited with the Grange House occupied by John Hawkins who now owned William Wilshere's legal practice.[76]

In 1850 the Great Northern Railway opened its mainline from London to Doncaster cutting through the far end of Great Benslow Hill and built a station at Hitchin. Landowners including William Wilshere started selling land between the town centre and the station for development. Hitchin's main drainage scheme was completed in 1854. Though not without its problems, it must have done much to restore the River Hiz as an attractive garden feature. Prime bought the Hermitage in 1864. In 1865-1866 he also bought Windmill Hill.[77]

When Charles Prime left Hitchin in 1874, the Hermitage (with Windmill Hill) was bought by his next door neighbour, the Quaker banker and historian, Frederic Seebohm. He also bought the Dell. As he and his family continued to live mainly in their existing home, he gave the site of part of William Wilshere's

---

[75] Estate account books [HALS: 61512, 61515]; W Ranger, *Report to the General Board of Health on a preliminary inquiry into the sewerage, drainage, and supply of water and the sanitary condition of the inhabitants of the Town of Hitchin* (1849) pp8-9.

[76] Obituary of William Wilshere 1867 [NHM: Lawson Thompson Scrapbooks Vol 1A p2]; 1851 census; draft lease [HALS: 60618]; copyhold lands of William Wilshere [HALS: 60637].

[77] V Taplin & A Stewart, *Two Minutes to the Station. The tale of Hitchin's Victorian Triangle* (Hitchin, 2010); A Foster & L M Munby, *Market Town. Hitchin in the Nineteenth Century* (Hitchin, 1987) pp40-52; schedule of title deeds 1864 [HALS: 60649]; plans 1865-1866 [HALS: DE/Ws/P22-P23].

INTRODUCTION

house and garden to the town for the construction of Hermitage Road as an improved route from the town centre to the station. A tunnel under the road next to the river provided private access to the remaining part of the garden on the south side of Hermitage Road. Frederic Seebohm died in 1912. His daughters, Esther and Hilda, sold the Hermitage in 1926. The remaining part of William Wilshere's house was then demolished to make way for the construction of shops, offices and a ballroom. All that survive are some old brick walls in the rear and the much altered lodge which William Wilshere built in his new kitchen garden.[78]

On William Wilshere's death in 1867, the estate inherited by his younger brother, Charles Willes Wilshere, included only four of the fields formerly farmed by his uncle: Waby's Field, Nettledell, the Four Acres next Wymondley Road, and Mount Garrison. The development of the first three fields was already under consideration though most of the Nettledell estate was built in the 1890s and early 1900s. Almost all William Wilshere's farm and garden are now covered by bricks, concrete and tarmac. However the grass covered slope of Windmill Hill (Rawlings Hill and Home Close) which was given to Hitchin Urban District Council by Esther and Hilda Seebohm in 1919 'as an open space for the recreation of the inhabitants' and, enlarged by the purchase of Mount Garrison from Miss Wilshere, still dominates the view from Hermitage Road. The Dell with the steep wooded hillside above (The Linces and Dimsey's Slipe) was bequeathed to the town in 1938 by Mrs Constance Gainsford as a bird sanctuary. In 1951 an open air theatre was created in the Dell as part of the celebrations of the Festival of Britain.[79]

William Wilshere's main legacy to Hitchin was the British Schools, which he founded in 1810 and bequeathed to Lord Dacre in 1824 together with other property intended as an endowment. Lord Dacre set up a trust in 1826 which

---

[78] Newspaper cutting 14 March 1874 [NHM: Loftus Barham Scrapbooks Vol 4 p609]; George Beaver's Journal [NHM: M265]; S Walker, *Underground Hitchin. A look at what's under our feet* (Hitchin, 2000) pp2-5; HUDC minutes 23/6/1926 p18, HUDC minutes 13/10/1926; Housing, Development and Town Planning Committee 9/11/1926 p67 [HALS: UDC/10/1/14]; HUDC minutes 24/7/1929 p5, General Purposes Committee 7/10/1929 p77 [HALS: UDC/10/1/17].
[79] Map of C W Wilshere's estate 1868 [HALS: 61047]; P Douglas & P Humphries, *Discovering Hitchin* (Hitchin, 1995) pp141-142, 146-148; HUDC minutes 20/8/1919 p48 [HALS: UDC/10/1/10]; Gainsford Papers [HALS: DE/Ha/B570]; R Whitmore, *Didn't you used to be Richard Whitmore? Memoirs of a TV newsreader and reluctant drawing room lady killer* (Mattingley Press, 2015) pp52-54.

owned the whole site and managed the boys' school. Hertfordshire County Council took over responsibility for the schools in 1903 and in 1926 the trustees conveyed the site and the endowment land in Storehouse Lane to the County Council. The schools finally closed to pupils in 1969. They are now the British Schools Museum.[80]

The Farm and Garden Memoranda Books

These are two small leather bound note books with the binding at the top deposited in Hertfordshire Archives with the Wilshere papers. The first one measures 6¼ inches by 4 inches (158mm by 100mm) and contains 166 pages. The second is slightly larger at 7½ inches by 4½ inches and contains over 170 pages, the last few of which are unused. Wilshere started the first volume on 1 October 1809 and continued making entries until June 1824, six months before his death. A catalogue of the sale of his farm stock in December 1824 has also been transcribed.

The transcript of the Memoranda Books and sale catalogue is followed by a transcript of the two gardening books started by Wilshere's new gardener, James Bowie, in December 1812 and January 1813. The first comprises 'Lists of Trees, Seeds etc Sown and Planted etc' in William Wilshere's garden. It has a leather binding and measures 7 inches by 4½ inches (173mm by 113mm). The second is a garden journal kept in a stouter vellum bound volume measuring 8 inches by 6 inches (200mm by 154mm). The journal breaks off in June 1813, but was resumed on 1 January 1814 until May 1814. James Bowie had previously been employed in the Royal Botanic Gardens at Kew. He left William Wilshere's service in August 1814 and by that autumn was on his way to Brazil with Allan Cunningham to collect plants for Sir Joseph Banks for Kew. He was sent from there to Cape Colony arriving in November 1816. The garden journal was continued by his successors, John Downing, from October 1814 to August 1815, and by Daniel McIntosh, from November 1821 to January 1822. Another of William Wilshere's gardeners, James Gray, added a few entries of the List of Trees, Seeds etc in November 1818. These are also deposited in Hertfordshire Archives.[81]

William Wilshere also kept Commonplace Books, one of which, a similar small leather bound note book dating from 1814 to 1824 containing about 300 pages has survived. This was given by Wilshere's great niece, Miss Alice Wilshere, to

---

[80] British Schools Museum, *Educating Our Own*, pp29-31, 98, 108, 115.
[81] R Drayton, 'James Bowie', *ODNB*.

INTRODUCTION

Reginald Hine, Hitchin's local historian, in the 1930s and is now in the collection of North Hertfordshire Museum.[82] Selected entries of agricultural and horticultural interest have also been transcribed as Appendix One.

Finally three bills from nurserymen dating from 1813 to 1823 have been transcribed as Appendix Two. Earlier bills from London nursery and seedsmen Hairs, Hairs & Co, Grimwood and Wykes, and Gordon Dermer & Co, as well as from Isaac and Thomas Emmerton of Barnet dating from the 1790s also survive in Hertfordshire Archives.[83]

[82] Commonplace Book [NHM: 1216].
[83] Bills [HALS: 61480/138, 170, 172-3, 184-187].

1 The garden front of William Wilshere's house at Hitchin by H G Oldfield, *c*1800 (*HALS: DE/Of/4/153*).

2 Sketch of the modernised garden front of Richard Tristram's house and plan of his garden from a map of Purwell Field *c1770* (*HALS: DZ/72/P121605*).

This was inherited by William Wilshere in 1785. The River Hiz separated the garden from the pasture enclosed by a fence bordering Back Street.

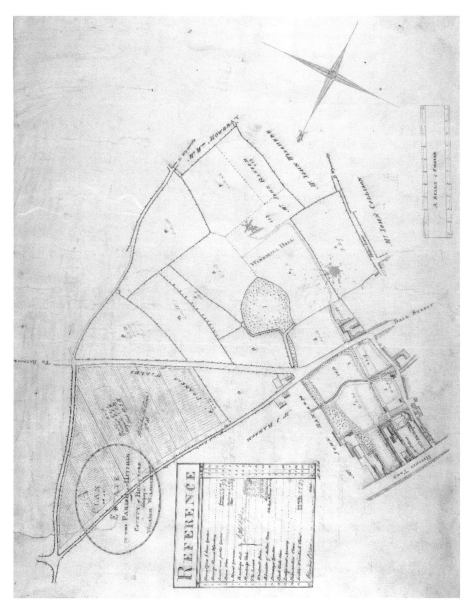

3 Plan of an estate in Hitchin belonging to William Wilshere *c*1801-1807 (*HALS: 58869*).

This extended as far as what are now Verulam and Highbury Roads. At their junction with the road to Baldock (now Walsworth Road) was Joan Biggs' Grave. Windmill Hill was then usually known as Rawlings Hill.

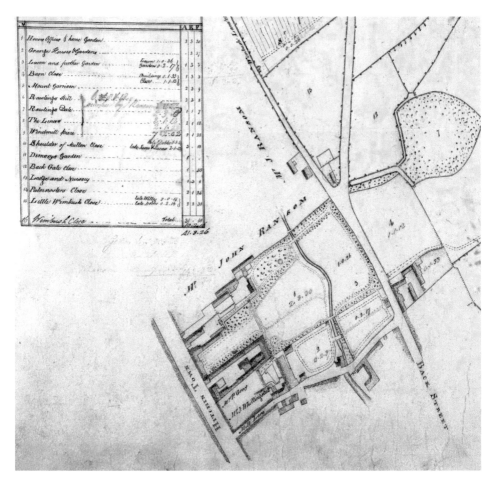

4 William Wilshere's garden (nos 1 & 3) and the garden of the Grange (no 2): excerpt from the plan of an estate in Hitchin belonging to William Wilshere *c*1801-1807 (*HALS: 58869*).

The Frame Yard was the area of 2 roods 17 perches bounded by the River Hiz, Mill (or Portmill) Lane, Back Street and Wilshere's garden. On the far side of Back Street was Wilshere's farmyard. The wooded enclosure (no 7) is The Dell or Rawlings Dale. On the opposite side of the road the triangular piece of land (no 13) is described as 'Lodge and Nursery'.

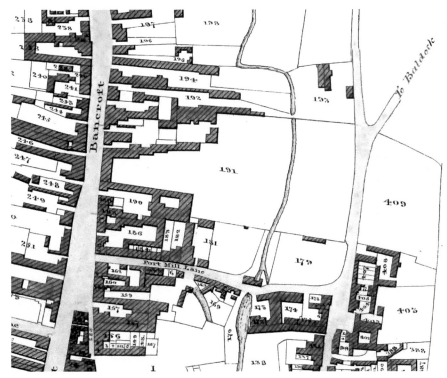

5 Excerpt from Henry Merrett's copy of a Plan of the Town of Hitchin 1816 (*North Hertfordshire Museum*).

Wilshere's house and garden was 191, his Frame Yard 179, and 181 was the Grange House on the other side of the river and the Port Mill. Wilshere's Back Street farmyard was 408; the cottages in front (407) also belonged to him. His Portmill Lane farmyard was 174; he also owned the houses and workshops 175-178. On the other side of Portmill Lane next to the Grange House was the house used by his legal practice (182) with Joseph Eade's brewhouse (166) opposite.

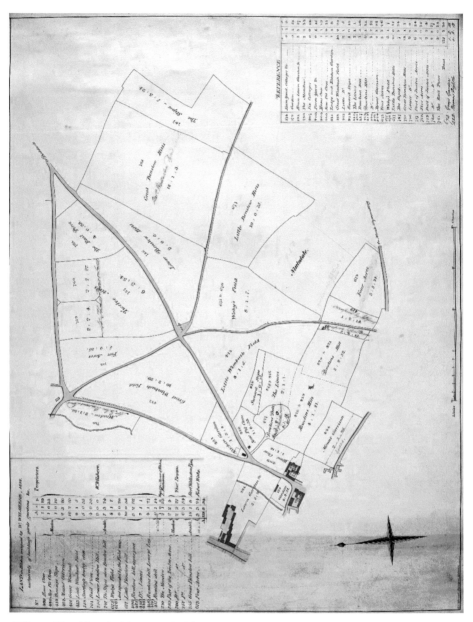

6 Plan of land in Hitchin occupied by William Wilshere 1818 (*HALS: DE/Ws/P16*).

This extended beyond Joan Biggs' Grave to Nightingale Road and the top of Benslow Hill. Much of the additional 78 acres of land was either rented or secured by exchange with his brother. See Appendix 3 Table of William Wilshere's Fields. The nursery (411 on this map) has become the Kitchen Garden.

7 Excerpt from Henry Merrett's copy of Map of part of the Township of Hitchin 1816 (*North Hertfordshire Museum*).

By 1820 Wilshere had also acquired the seven strips of Nettledeall or Nettledale nos 667-672.

8 View from Windmill Hill by Samuel Lucas *c*1827 (*North Hertfordshire Museum*).

Windmill Hill (or Rawlings Hill) was owned by William Wilshere. At the top he built a thatched summer house where he could enjoy the view of his house and garden. St Mary's Church can be seen on the left beyond the huddled roofs of Wilshere's Back Street farmyard and cottages.

2. Wilshere in Context; farming and gardening in the early nineteenth century

By Tom Williamson

Introduction

Farming diaries, journals and memorandum books from the eighteenth and nineteenth centuries constitute a vitally important source for agricultural history and a number of examples have been transcribed, in whole or part, and published by county records societies or record offices.[84] They display a measure of variation, in purpose, scope and content, which cuts across the particular description of the volume in question, whether given by the author himself or attributed by later archivists. All focus on farming activities and their outcomes, in terms of yields and profits, and some, like the 'Farming Journal' kept by Randall Burroughes of Wymondham in Norfolk between 1794 and 1799, do so almost exclusive of anything relating to family or social life. Others, in contrast, such as the 'Farming Diary' maintained by Thomas Pinniger of Avebury in Wiltshire between 1813 and 1847, contain rather more extraneous information, while still maintaining a firm agricultural focus. Wilshere's memorandum books are more like the first of these sources than the second – we learn next to nothing about the author's family or friends – but in marked contrast to both, and indeed to any other example of the *genre* known to us, also include copious information about the author's horticultural endeavours.

The individuals who produced these documents were not struggling to make a living on a few rented acres. Some, indeed, were well-educated 'gentleman' farmers – Burroughes for example came from a wealthy background, had been educated at Cambridge and uses Latin quotations in his 'journal'.[85] Wilshere came from a family of minor gentry and was a wealthy and successful lawyer and businessman; his active involvement in farming came quite late in life and continued alongside these other activities. The latter, we should note, are hardly

---

[84] J James and J H Bettey (eds) *Farming in Eighteenth-Century Dorset: James Warne's Diary, 1758 and George Boswell's Letters 1787-1805* (Dorset Record Society Vol 13, Dorchester, 1993); A Wadsworth, *The Farming Diaries of Thomas Pinniger, 1813-1847* (Wiltshire Record Society Vol 74, Gloucester, 2021); S Wade Martins and T Williamson (eds) *The Farming Journal of Randall Burroughes of Wymondham, 1794-99* (Norfolk Record Society Vol 58, Norwich, 1995); J Jones, *Seedtime and Harvest: the Diary of an Essex Farmer, William Barnard of Harlowbury, 1807-23* (Chelmsford, 1992).
[85] *Farming Journal of Randall Burroughes*, p7.

hinted at in the two memorandum books, which are firmly focused on matters agricultural and horticultural: on his farm, kitchen garden, ornamental garden, orchards and tree nursery. It is clear that farming, and to an extent these other activities, were treated as serious businesses. Wilshere was no hobby farmer. But his wealth did not primarily depend on the activities recorded in the memorandum books. Living in a large and fashionable house fronting on one of Hitchin's main streets, with elaborate gardens, a peach house and an ice house, owning an extensive portfolio of property and even employing a gamekeeper, Wilshere, like Burroughes, clearly falls into the category of 'gentleman farmer'.

Men like this, and indeed the kinds of people more generally who produced farming journals and memorandum books, were not entirely representative of the wider farming community. Careful monitoring of agricultural procedures and outcomes suggests individuals unusually keen to improve performance, and most of those responsible for producing such documents appear to have had a particular enthusiasm for the latest farming methods, often keeping abreast of developments through reading available publications. Wilshere himself records on a number of occasions the results of agricultural experiments, as in 1820 when he sowed a late crop of turnips in Benslow Hill with 'oil dust … drilled with the seed, a small patch being drilled with crushed salt & ashes with an interval on each side with[ou]t any manure'; he also notes tips and techniques received from aquaintances or acquired from his reading. But on the other hand, there is no reason to believe that these men were members of a tiny minority of obsessives and enthusiasts, or that most of their basic farming practices were not more widely shared.

The Farming Landscape.
Wilshere's farm changed in size over time, as we have already described, but while not large by national standards was above average in a county in which, as the agriculturalist Arthur Young observed in 1804, 'the farms are not large'.[86] In 1820 he cultivated 122½ acres. When the tithes for Hitchin were commuted just over two decades later there were around 30 farms in the parish, ignoring numerous part-time enterprises and smallholdings of less than 20 acres, of which perhaps a third were larger than this.[87] But in a number of ways the farm appears unusual for its time. We say 'appears' because, while it deviates in important respects from text-book models of an early nineteenth-century farm run on 'modern' lines, it probably represents a reasonably common type of

---

[86] A Young, *General View of the Agriculture of Hertfordshire* (1804), p18.
[87] In 1844: Tithe Award Map and Apportionment for Hitchin [HALS: DSA4/53/2].

enterprise, one of a number of farm types neglected by agricultural historians. Two unusual aspects are immediately noticeable. Firstly, the new methods of farming developed in the eighteenth century raised cereal yields by increasing the numbers of livestock providing manure for the arable fields, but while Wilshere certainly kept cattle and pigs, he had no sheep, and much of the dung applied to his fields came from animals owned by others. Secondly, and more importantly, while most of the farm was cultivated on fairly conventional modern lines a small area – the field called Great Wimbush - was farmed more intensively, in small unenclosed plots, producing in addition crops like potatoes, carrots and cabbages. In some ways the field resembled a market garden, and it is striking that it is depicted on the undated map of Wilshere's farm, drawn up between 1801 and 1807, as a series of hatched strips, reminiscent of the way in which some of the nineteenth-century Ordnance Survey 6-inch and 25-inch maps represent kitchen gardens, market gardens and allotments.[88] Although the land here was sometimes ploughed there are also references to trenching, indicating spade cultivation.

Much of the land farmed by Wilshere lay on the light, well-drained calcareous soils which characterise the chalk escarpment running all along the northern edge of Hertfordshire, from Barley to Offley, and which were said by Chauncy just over a century earlier to produce 'the choisest wheat and barley, such as makes the best mault that serves the King's Court or the City of London'.[89] Loamy, calcareous soils of the Swaffham Prior Association, directly overlying chalk, were to be found on the higher ground, in the north-eastern part of the farm, particularly in the fields called Great, Little and Lower Benslow Hills, Rail Piece and The Slipes.[90] They are well drained and easy to cultivate but they leach nutrients rapidly, and fertility was traditionally maintained by folding sheep on the land – that is, penning them up at night on the harvest stubbles, fallows or fodder crops, so that they trod dung and urine into the soil. But other kinds of soil were also found on Wilshere's farm, the local geology and topography of the Hitchin Gap being complex, and while the differences were not great they had a significant influence on Wilshere's farming. The generally smaller fields towards the south-west of the farm – on the lower ground closer to Wilshere's home and to Hitchin town – Home Close, Saw Pit Close, The Linces,

[88] Plan of An Estate in the Parish of Hitchin and County of Hertford belonging to William Wilshere Esq c1801-1807 [HALS: 58869; colour section No 3].
[89] H Chauncy, *The Historical Antiquities of Hertfordshire* (1700), p2.
[90] C Hodge, R Burton, W Corbett, R Evans and R Scale, *Soils and their Uses in Eastern England* (Soil Survey of England and Wales, Harpenden, 1984), pp316-9.

INTRODUCTION

Rawlings Hill, Mount Garrison, Sweard Slipe and much of Little Wimbush –
overlay glaciofluvial gravels and here the soils of the Sonning 1 Association
were sandier and more acidic.[91] Much of this land was also farmed as arable but
it was here that most of Wilshere's few, small pasture fields were located, some
apparently managed as hay meadow.[92] Even today, as the Soil Survey notes,
large areas of the Sonning soils, in Hertfordshire as elsewhere, are under
pasture. Further to the north – that is, in the north-western section of the farm –
the superficial geology became more clayey, producing rather stiffer, more
moisture retentive loams of the Hornbeam 3 Association.[93] One of the fields,
Starlings Bridge Close, was farmed as arable; part of The Twelve Acres was
meadow; but Great Wimbush was subdivided in the manner described and it
was here, on soils well suited to growing vegetables as well as more
conventional arable crops, that Wilshere's most unusual farming was to be
found. Lastly, the farm eventually came to include a small (*c*2½-acre) floodplain
hay meadow, on alluvial soils beside the river Hiz.

In medieval times, the chalk escarpment, and the land lying immediately below
it, in north Hertfordshire had been 'champion' or open-field countryside.[94]
Farms comprised large numbers of scattered strips and agricultural routines
operated on highly communal lines. But the character of the open fields was, in
a number of respects, different from those, familiar from text books, found
across much of Midland England. Instead of there being two or three great
'fields' in each village, one of which lay fallow each year, Hertfordshire
townships lying on or below the escarpment usually had more. Ickleford had
four named fields when mapped in 1771 (West Field, Home Field, Mildens and
North Field), as had Great Wymondley in 1811 (Roxley, Middle, Little Middle
and Purwell) while Pirton had no less than seven when enclosed in 1818 (Dane,
Highdown, White, Hambridge, Windmill, North Mead and Green Ley Hill).[95]
Hitchin itself had nine or ten open fields listed in a survey of 1676 (the precise
number is uncertain due to ambiguities in nomenclature): by 1819, however,
there were six, which were grouped into three 'seasons' for the purposes of

---

[91] Hodge *et al.*, *Soils and their Uses*, p312.
[92] Home Close, Saw Pit Close, Dimsey's or Sweard Slipe, Mount Garrison and Rawlings
Hill.
[93] Hodge *et al.*, *Soils and their Uses*, pp221-4.
[94] A Rowe and T Williamson, *Hertfordshire: a Landscape History* (Hatfield, 2013),
pp32-44.
[95] Plan of the Manor and Parish of Ickleford and other Lands, 1771 [HALS: DE/Ha/P1];
Great Wymondley Inclosure Map and Award, 1811 [HALS: QS/E80–QS/E81]; Pirton
Enclosure Map, 1818 [HALS: PC528].

cropping.[96] The furlongs, and often the individual strips, were defined by unploughed grassy banks or 'balks', locally described as 'walls', where there were steep slopes, and the strips were laid out along the contours, they were sometimes cut into the hillside as terraces which early maps and documents call *lynchets, lynces* or *linces*. The management of the fields displayed much variation, over space and over time, but of central importance – and a key structuring principal – were the communal folding arrangements, which ensured that all the arable strips received a reasonable share of the manure required to keep the land in heart.[97]

A few of the scarpland parishes were enclosed in their entirety at an early date, and in most of the others the open fields were whittled away by gradual, 'piecemeal' enclosure. Owners bought and sold land until they had a number of contiguous strips, which they could then fence or hedge and remove from the routines of communal cultivation. The new field boundaries, established on the edges of former strips, perpetuated their slightly sinuous outline.[98] But for the most part north Hertfordshire was characterised by remarkably late enclosure. In most parishes the remaining open fields were removed by parliamentary enclosure acts and in several cases at a very late date (Sandon in 1842, Therfield in 1849 and Ashwell in 1863); while in Hitchin, Bygrave, Wallington and Clothall, large areas of open arable survived, unenclosed, into the twentieth century, and were widely noted by historians and antiquarians as intriguing survivals from the medieval past. Gilbert Slater discussed Clothall and Bygrave in his *The English Peasantry and the Enclosure of Common Fields* of 1907; while Hitchin formed a major part of Frederic Seebohm's discussion of open-field farming in *The English Village Community* of 1883.[99]

Even in these parishes the extent of open arable had usually been much reduced by piecemeal enclosure. In Hitchin, at least by the seventeenth century, the manorial court freely granted tenants permission to enclose portions of the

---

[96] B Howlett (ed.), *Survey of the Royal Manor of Hitchin, 1676* HRS Vol 16, (Hertford, 2000), ppxv–xvi.

[97] For the central importance of folding in the organisation of open fields on light, freely-draining soils, see J Belcher, *The Foldcourse and East Anglian Agriculture and Landscape, 1100-1900* (Woodbridge, 2020) and E Kerridge, *The Common Fields of England* (Manchester, 1993).

[98] S R Eyre, 'The Curving Plough-Strip and its Historical Implications', *Agricultural History Review* 3, 2 (1955), pp80-94.

[99] G Slater, *The English Peasantry and the Enclosure of Common* Fields (1907); Seebohm, *English Village Community* (1883).

fields. The customs of the manor of Hitchin, as set out in 1819 but almost certainly recording ancient practice, noted that:

> Every owner and every occupier of land in any of the common fields of this township may at his will and pleasure enclose and fence any of his land lying in the common field of this township (other than and except land in Bury Field and Welshman's Croft), and may, so long as the same shall remain so enclosed and fenced, hold such land … exempt from any right or power of any other owner or occupier of the land in the said township to common or depasture his sheep on the land so enclosed and fenced (no right of common on other land being claimed in respect of land so enclosed and fenced).[100]

Wilshere, as we have seen, was fully involved in the process of enclosure and consolidation but he was continuing a long process, and virtually all of the 122½ acres that he farmed in 1820 had originally been open - field land, as is clear both from the sinuous character of the field boundaries shown on the various maps of his farm, and from the numerous small kinks they exhibit. The name of the field called 'The Linces' is also noteworthy. The fields, as noted, varied greatly in size, reflecting the piecemeal character of their creation, but in general the largest were on the chalk soils, the smallest on the lower ground near to Hitchin town (where some, as we have noted, were under pasture). One striking feature of the farm was the manner in which fields were regularly subdivided for cropping, with different sections planted with different crops. This probably reflects the difficulty of growing similar proportions of crops each year, following regular rotations, where arable fields varied so much in size (Great Benslow Field was around eight times the size of The Linces, for example). This same problem also largely accounts for the progressive amalgamation of the smaller fields which occurred on the farm over time. The practice may also, however, reflect the continuing existence in the local landscape of open fields, and thus the apparent normality of farming in unhedged land parcels. But neither of these factors explains the extreme subdivision of the 10½ acre Great Wimbush into parcels ranging from half an acre to two acres.

Where land was farmed as open field, it lay fallow or uncropped every third year, to be grazed and fertilised by communal sheep flocks. The customs of Hitchin manor, drawn up in 1819, noted that the fields had 'immemorially been and ought to be kept and cultivated in three successive seasons of tilthgrain,

---

[100] Seebohm, *English Village Community*, pp443–53.

etchgrain and fallow'.[101] But enclosure allowed the land to be farmed in new ways and Wilshere, like many contemporary farmers in south-east England and East Anglia, employed some kind of 'improved' rotation. Rather than letting the land lie fallow every third year, courses of cereals were interspersed with years in which root crops, especially turnips, and clover or some similar plant, were grown. These were either fed off in the field by livestock which dunged the land directly, or they were lifted and taken to a farmyard and fed to stalled animals, especially cattle, the manure from which - combining dung with bedding straw, rotted by urine – was taken to the fields by cart during the winter months, and spread by hand.[102] The Chiltern Hills, lying immediately to the south-west of Hitchin, had been one of the earliest areas in England to embrace such rotations, at least on enclosed land. The agricultural writer William Ellis suggests they were standard practise here by the 1730s.[103] We should not, it is true, exaggerate the importance or universality of such rotations, especially on heavier land. Arthur Young makes it clear that many Hertfordshire farmers in the early nineteenth century did not grow turnips, and still left their fields fallow every third year.[104] But by this time, the cultivation of crops like turnips and clover was ubiquitous on the lighter lands of southern and eastern England, at least where this lay in enclosures, and fallows had been largely abolished.

Although Wilshere's farm was now enclosed, it thus continued to be dunged using folded sheep. They were now grazed, not on fallow weeds, but on courses of field crops in the arable rotation – usually turnips or swedes, occasionally cabbages – and sometimes at least on the young barley, to 'tiller' it. Yet Wilshere did not keep his own flock but instead used the sheep of others, mainly those of his neighbour John Kingsley. Although Wilshere benefitted from the manure he also charged for the feed, usually at so much per acre. He sometimes calculated the number of sheep grazed on particular parcels of land, per acre, per week, as well as noting the money received from Kingsley (and on occasions, what the arrangement had cost Kingsley himself, in terms of feed per head). Stocking densities were high. In 1809 Wilshere stated, in general terms, that

---

[101] Howlett, *Survey of Hitchin,* pxvii.
[102] J V Beckett, *Agricultural Revolution* (Oxford, 1990): M Overton, *Agricultural Revolution in England* (Cambridge, 1996), pp117-21; S Wade Martins and T Williamson, *Roots of Change: Farming and the Landscape in East Anglia, c1700-1870* (British Agricultural History Society, Exeter, 1999), pp99-103.
[103] W Ellis, *The Practical Farmer: or, the Hertfordshire Husbandman* (1736), pp24-5, 54, 74, 137.
[104] Young, *General View*, pp61-71.

INTRODUCTION

'100 Western or about 120 South Down sheep will fold an acre of land in 14 days', but the rates he actually recorded were usually higher, at 140 per acre in 1819 and 180 in 1817. Sheep folding was not the only way in which Wilshere maintained fertility, however. It was a particular feature of the fields on the chalk hills in the east of the farm. It was used, but perhaps more sparingly, on the heavier land in the north-west – on Starlings Bridge Close and on various of the small parcels making up Great Wimbush. On the sandier land in the southwest, Little Wimbush is mentioned only once in relation to folding and the two other arable fields, The Linces and Rawlings 'beyond the mill', not at all. They lay closer to Wilshere's farmyards than the other arable fields and were presumably mainly manured with yard dung, produced by Wilshere's cows and other livestock, brought in his 'dung cart'. Great Wimbush, divided into a number of small plots, was also mainly manured in this way, apparently quite intensively, although it was sometimes folded. But even the arable fields on the higher and more calcareous ground were not solely manured by the sheep flocks. Wilshere refers to the application of yard dung to these more distant fields, on a number of occasions, although in all cases prior to the turnip course. This may have been standard practice, as it certainly was on most farms following 'improved' rotations at the time.

Given that most of the fields on the farm were under arable cultivation and that these were grazed, at particular phases of the cropping cycle, only by sheep, contained within folds of hurdles, some of their perimeter hedges probably only had limited use as barriers to livestock. But all had another important function, one often neglected by historians. Coal had long been available in Hitchin, usually brought by road from wharfs on the Ivel Navigation at Biggleswade, some 10 miles to the north, but as in the rest of Hertfordshire prior to the advent of the railways most people used wood as a domestic fuel, for their hearths and bread ovens. Some of this was supplied by the county's numerous coppiced woods but, as Arthur Young explained in 1804, the demand had also 'induced the farmers to fill the old hedges everywhere with all sorts of plants more generally calculated for fuel than for fences'.[105] In 1820, in one of the most interesting passages contained in the memorandum books, Wilshere described his hedgerow management, apparently distinguishing wood for domestic fires and material destined for bread ovens.

> The wood of my hedges when cut for sale is divided into fire wood & faggot wood, the fire taking all the strait & lower parts of the wood cut

---

[105] Young, *General View*, p39.

INTRODUCTION

into lengths of 4½ to 5 feet then made into bundles. The remainder of the wood is made into bush faggots. They are sold at 15/- for 120 called an hundred, that is 1½[d] each faggot. A bundle of fire wood is considered as equal to & sold at the price of 2 faggots. I found them when made up to weigh the fire wood per bundle about 28 lbs & the faggots about 18 lbs. The length of the fire wood 4½ feet, circumference of the bundle 2 feet 3 inches. Length of the faggot 4½ - circumference about 3 feet.

There is no indication that the hedges were being plashed or layed. Instead, as in many areas of southern England by the early nineteenth century, they were probably managed as linear coppices, cut on a long rotation of perhaps ten years.[106]

Farming: Crops and Rotations

For a number of reasons, not least the frequent subdivision of fields for the purposes of cropping, it is difficult to reconstruct in detail the rotations followed on Wilshere's farm. It is, however, clear that much of his land – and especially that on the higher chalkier soils – was farmed under the most popular of the 'improved', turnip-based rotations, the so-called 'Norfolk four-course'. This was a regular cycle of wheat, followed by turnips, followed by barley and then clover. Wheat was normally planted in the autumn – usually between early October and early November on Wilshere's farm, a comparatively late sowing reflecting the well-drained character of the local soils. There are, however, a few references to it being spring-sown. Wilshere refers to 'red' and 'brown' wheat, types used to make strong flavoured general purpose flour; but more often to 'white', with no major bran gene and producing a milder flour; usually he doesn't distinguish. Occasionally specific varieties are mentioned, some – like Talavera – familiar from other sources, others - like 'Dantzick' (?Danzig?) or 'American' – less certainly identifiable. The crop was harvested between late July and the start of September.

The field then lay uncropped until late spring or early summer, when it was sown with turnips, usually as noted following an application of muck brought from Wilshere's yards. They matured over the summer and early autumn and were then mainly eaten in the field, as already discussed, by Kingsley's sheep, with some being lifted by Wilshere's men and taken back to his yards and used

---

[106] G Barnes and T Williamson, *Trees in England: Management and Disease Since 1600* (Hatfield, 2017), pp65-8.

xlix

INTRODUCTION

to feed his own livestock. Wilshere distinguishes - although not consistently –
between a number of different kinds of 'turnip'. 'Swedish' turnips, what we
usually call 'swedes', were not strictly a turnip *Brassica rapa rapa* at all but a
separate although related species, *Brassica napus*.[107] The Swedish turnip was
more winter hardy than the true turnip and its cultivation was for long a
particular feature of Hertfordshire farming.[108] First grown in England as a field
crop in the middle decades of the eighteenth century, Young described in 1804
how:

> In other parts of the kingdom, these turnips are met with in the farms of
> gentlemen, rarely in those of tenants; but in Hertfordshire, they have so
> rapidly made their way, as to be found in the usual management of the
> common farmers; no trivial proof of their observation, knowledge, and
> good sense.[109]

Some farmers thought that they were unsuitable for feeding sheep, in spite of the
fact that they relished them, because they tended to break their teeth on the
roots, which were harder than ordinary turnips (Swedes contain significantly
more dry matter). But they were widely praised as cattle fodder and could, in
particular, be safely fed to milking cows as, unlike turnips, they did not taint the
taste of the milk. Wilshere's swedes were certainly eaten in the field by
Kingsley's sheep, as in 1816, but they were probably also used to feed his
bullocks and probably his cows. Like other Hertfordshire farmers, Wilshere
seems to have sown his swedes in May, slightly earlier than his 'true' turnips.

Wilshere also refers to 'Red', 'Green', 'White', 'Bullock', 'Yellow' and
'Yellow Scotch' turnips. Nineteenth-century writers usually distinguished
between white-fleshed turnips, fast-growing and heavy-cropping, but with a low
percentage of dry matter; and yellow-fleshed turnips, less watery, more resistant
to frost and with better keeping qualities. Wilshere's 'Yellow' and 'Yellow
Scotch' are presumably turnips of the latter type, while his 'green' and 'red'
were white turnips, which came in green-, purple- and red-topped forms.[110]
Overall, Wilshere seems to have shown a preference for the hardier yellow type,
in 1817 growing them alone. He also cultivated the mangel-wurzel – a root crop
Beta vulgaris related to beetroot and sugar beet, but (in common with other

---

[107] G M de Rougemont, *A Field Guide to the Crops of Britain and Europe* (1989), p170.
[108] N Harvey, 'The Coming of the Swede to Great Britain: an Obscure Chapter in
Farming History', *Agricultural History* 23, 4 (1949), pp286-88.
[109] Young, *General View*, p105.
[110] J C Loudon, *An Encyclopedia of Agriculture* (1825), p786.

1

contemporary farmers) not as part of a standard four-course rotation. It was, instead, one of the many crops grown in the small plots in Great Wimbush Field.

Barley, as noted, was a key crop on the light chalk soils of north Hertfordshire, mainly turned to malt for the brewing industry in local malthouses. It was sown after the last of the turnips had been lifted or eaten off and on Wilshere's farm usually quite early, in February and March, again reflecting the well-drained nature of the soil. It was harvested earlier than the wheat, mainly before the end of August. Wilshere does not distinguish different varieties of barley, beyond making a handful of references to 'Egyptian' and 'Siberian' barley. The former, planted in small quantities in 1815 and 1816, may be the 'purple Egyptian' barley, a six-roll hulless variety with a purplish-black layer, used to make flour with specialised baking uses, and to produce high quality malt; in 1804 members of the Society of Arts, Manufactures and Agriculture reported successful trials of the crop.[111] Siberian barley, in contrast, was a naked (beardless) variety grown on a small and largely experimental scale following its introduction to England in the late eighteenth century.[112] The Egyptian barley may have been grown as a normal field crop, as part of Wilshere's four-course, but Siberian demanded 'a fertile, rich and well-tilled soil' and thus only appears to have been cultivated on the small plots in Great Wimbush.[113] The cultivation of both, of course, reflects Wilshere's particular interest in agricultural innovation and experiment.

As was normal practice, clover or some similar 'grass' crop was generally sown with the barley, growing on after it had been harvested. In the following spring and summer this might be grazed but Wilshere usually cut it as a hay crop, to feed to his cows and other livestock over the winter. Clover (*Trifolium pratense*) was Wilshere's favourite 'grass' crop in the four-course rotation, as was usual, but he sometimes used sanfoin (*Onobrychis sativa*) in its place, an erect plant with leafy stems, small paired lanceolate leaves and pink-red flowers.[114] He also sometimes planted trefoil (*Lotus corniculatus*), a low-growing, near prostrate plant with thick stems and yellow flowers, but perhaps usually where the 'grass' course was extended, as it occasionally was, to two years, as a 'ley'.[115] Lucerne

---

[111] *The Repertory of Arts, Manufactures and Agriculture* 4 (1804), p237.
[112] *Letters and Papers on Agriculture, Planting &c. Selected from the Correspondence of the Bath and West of England Society for the Encouragement of Agriculture, Arts, Manufacture and Commerce* (Bath, 1802), pp200-201.
[113] A D Thaer, *The Principles of Agriculture*, 2 Vols. (1844), Vol. 2, pp430-431.
[114] de Rougemont, *Field Guide to Crops*, pp42-5.
[115] de Rougemont, *Field Guide to Crops*, p44.

INTRODUCTION

(*Medicago sativa*) was another 'grass' cultivated by Wilshere but only on a small scale, and perhaps mainly, again, in the small plots within Great Wimbush Field.

Other variations on the basic 'four course', in addition to extending the 'grass' course for a second year or more, could be found on Wilshere's farm. These involved the addition to the rotation of crops other than wheat, barley, 'roots' and 'grasses'. Sometimes, and especially on the sandier soils of Nettledell and Shoulder of Mutton, peas were intruded into the rotation, usually after wheat and before turnips, while on the more clayey soils of Starlings Bridge Close a course of 'Heligoland beans', or broad beans *Vicia faba*, was added in the same position. Both crops were destined for animal feed, rather than human consumption. In addition, oats were sometimes substituted for barley, again in particular on the lower, sandier land, while small parcels of summer or winter tares or buckwheat might be sown in particular fields as part of the clover course, both crops threshed for their seeds which were used for livestock and, in particular, poultry feed.

The most remarkable deviations from conventional 'improved' practice were, however, to be found in the small plots in Great Wimbush. Here Wilshere grew some conventional field crops (barley, wheat, turnips, tares, swedes and buckwheat). But he also grew mangel-wurzel, lucerne, cabbages, beet, and in particular large quantities of potatoes and carrots. It is impossible to reconstruct courses of cropping here as the various small plots are not individually named, but Wilshere notes on a number of occasions that wheat was planted after potatoes, and carrots after mangel-wurzels, although successive courses of carrots were sometimes taken.

Some of the crops grown on these small plots were used by Wilshere to feed his own pigs, cows and bullocks, together with the farm horses; some were sold to others for animal feed; but some, especially turnips, mangel-wurzel, peas and carrots were grown for seed. This was used by Wilshere himself but also sold to others, as a commodity. Indeed, he even grew and sold small amounts of canary seed (*Phalaris canariensis*), probably to be used by purchasers to feed game birds or even, perhaps, domestic pets. Much of the potato and some of the carrot crop, however, was intended for human consumption; some of the small parcels were described as 'garden beds'; while the peas and beans grown here included varieties usually destined for human rather than livestock feed, such as marrowfat peas (dried peas, used to make 'mushy peas'); and 'crown' peas (an old garden variety, now seldom grown, its particularly wide and succulent stems ensuring that it was once classed as a different species (*Pisum umbellatum*) to

INTRODUCTION

the common pea (*Pisum sativa*)).[116] Such essentially horticultural cropping was not entirely restricted to this part of the farm. Small areas of potatoes and cabbages were, in particular, sometimes planted in fields like Nettledell, where the soils were clayey or sandy rather than calcareous. But it was in the unusual, subdivided Great Wimbush that crops of this kind were mainly to be found.

Of particular importance is the information that Wilshere provides about his potatoes, a crop of increasing importance in England in the early nineteenth century, although one which has been rather neglected in agricultural history. The potato had been grown in gardens in England since the sixteenth century and by the eighteenth century was widely cultivated, although seldom on any scale as a field crop, except on the more marginal, acidic soils of the north and west of England – especially in Cumberland, Cheshire and Lancashire. In 1801 the latter county boasted the most extensive acreage, around 8% of the cropped area; across England as a whole the figure was only around 2%.[117] Potatoes yield nearly twice as much nutritional value per acre as cereals. But 'they are less concentrated as a food source ... because of their high water content, their storage life is shorter, and the cost of transport much greater'. [118] Although in the 1820s William Cobbett could refer to the 'modern custom of using potatoes to supply the place of bread', until the arrival of the railways production was concentrated in emerging industrial areas (as in Lancashire) or close to major urban centres.[119] But a localised emphasis on the crop could also be found where soils were particularly suitable and – as here – in the immediate vicinity of the larger market towns.

Wilshere occasionally describes particular potatoes as 'bought', indicating that he usually planted his own tubers, held over from the previous year. Indeed, the stored potatoes itemised in his annual accounts of 'farming stock' are on one occasion said to be listed exclusive of those 'cut for planting'. He refers to no less than 28 different varieties, few of which can be identified and none of which appear to have survived into the twentieth century. [120] Most were presumably part of the great explosion in the number of varieties which

---

[116] See, for example, W Alton, *Hortus Kewensis; or, a Catalogue of the Plants Cultivated at the Royal Botanical Gardens in Kew*, Vol. 4 (1812), p302.
[117] M E Turner, 'Arable in England and Wales: estimates from the 1801 Crop Return', *Journal of Historical Geography* 7 (1981), pp291-302; p296.
[118] de Rougemont, *Field Guide to Crops*, p280.
[119] W Cobbett, *Cottage Economy* (1822), p48.
[120] R N Salaman, *Potato Varieties* (Cambridge, 1926); A Romans, *The Potato Book* (2005).

INTRODUCTION

occurred in the second half of the eighteenth and early nineteenth centuries, as nurserymen and growers carefully selected seedlings to produce tubers with particular qualities.[121] While in the 1730s Rye could only list five potato varieties and Miller discussed only three, early nineteenth-century writers like Knight could describe many.[122] The majority of these varieties were, in turn, swept away by further breeding programmes in the course of the nineteenth century, increasingly scientific in character and making more use of new introductions from the potato's south American homelands, which were aimed at both improving the quality and quantity of the crop and increasing its resistance to disease.[123] It is not surprising, then, that most of Wilshere's varieties are unidentifiable with those grown today, or in the recent past.

Indeed, only a handful can even be confidently identified with varieties known from eighteenth- and nineteenth-century sources. The 'common White Kidney' must almost certainly be the 'flat white kidney potato', one of the five types noted by Rye in the 1730s.[124] It was an early variety, cropping in July or August. An 'early' at this time was what we would today describe as a 'second early': early potatoes in our sense of the term did exist but, to judge from Knight's descriptions of 1807, 1810 and 1811, were small plants, closely planted in hot beds, frames or garden beds, producing low yields of small tubers which were treated as an upper class delicacy.[125] The 'red kidney' was a widely cultivated type in the early nineteenth century, as was the 'redfone or yam' which Wilshere planted on an acre in Great Wimbush in 1809. Also known as the Surinam, it was a heavy cropper with an indifferent taste, mainly used as animal feed.[126]

---

[121] R N Salaman, *The History and Social Influence of the Potato* (Cambridge, 1949; revised edn 1984), pp161-2.

[122] D R Glendinning, 'Potato Introductions and Breeding up to the Early 20th Century', *New Phytologist* 94 (1983), pp479-505; T A Knight, 'On Potatoes', *Transactions of the Horticultural Society of London,* 1 (1810), pp187-193: T A Knight, 'On the Culture of the Potato', *Transactions of the Horticultural Society of London* Series 2, 1 (1833), pp415-18; Salaman, *History*, p2.

[123] Glendinning, 'Potato Introductions'.

[124] Glendinning, 'Potato Introductions', p. 486.

[125] T A Knight, 'On the Raising of New and Early Varieties of the Potato *Solanum tuberosum*', *Transactions of the Horticultural Society of London,* 1 (1807), pp57-59; T A Knight, 'On the Culture of the Potato in Hotbeds', *Transactions of the Horticultural Society of London,* 1 (1810), pp213-4; T A Knight, 'On Some Early Varieties of the Potato and the Best Method of Forcing Them', *Transactions of the Horticultural Society of London of London,* 1 (1811), pp244—247.

[126] Glendinning, 'Potato Introductions', p489.

'Fox's Seedling was a round, yellowish-white early variety, while Shaw or Shaw's was another early, said by Loudon in 1835 to be 'much cultivated by the growers for the London market'.[127]

The other varieties planted – 'Old Redrup', 'Mr Maughan's', 'Blood Royal', 'Pear Cheshire', 'a black potato called the Emperor of Morocco', 'Golden Drop', 'Red Kidney', 'the Callico', 'German Kidney', 'Upright White', 'Apple', 'Dirk Handle', 'Asparagus', 'Frorroges Purple', 'Blood Red', 'Early King', 'Prince Regent', 'Blue Kidney', 'Painted Lady', 'Callico White', 'Black Read', 'Buntingford Kidney' and 'Black Kidney' – cannot be readily identified and do not appear to be referred to in published texts, although the 'Apple' may be the 'Devonshire Apple' described by Loudon.[128] Many were doubtless short-lived and local in character; 'Mr Maughan's' was presumably a type acquired from John Maughan, a local land surveyor (see Biographical Notes).[129] Loudon, writing in 1822, remarked that 'Every town and every district has its peculiar or favourite varieties, so that … any list, however extended, could be of little use'.[130] The Buntingford Kidney was clearly a fairly well-established Hertfordshire variety, long associated with the town of that name, given that Wilshere in 1812 describes the purchase of 'A few of *true* Buntingford Kidney', implying that imitations had developed. Some of Wilshere's potatoes might have been given a different name elsewhere for, as with apples (below, pp lxxix-lxxxv), nomenclature was often fluid and local, while the same name might be given in different places, and at different times, to different varieties. Loudon in 1835 described how 'The varieties of potatoes are innumerable, and they are continually under going change. The same variety also bears many different names in different parts of the country'.[131] Wilshere's 'Champion' cannot be the popular variety of that name developed by John Nichol in the 1870s and famous for its resistance to blight, but it may be the 'champion' which is mentioned in the anonymous *Hints Concerning the Cultivation and Use of the Potato* of 1795, and which was described by Loudon as large, round, white and very prolific.[132]

The development of potato varieties in the later eighteenth and early nineteenth centuries, especially at a local and regional level, remains under-researched and

---

[127] J C Loudon, *An Encyclopedia of Gardening*, revised edn (1835), p830.
[128] *Ibid.*
[129] William Wilshere, Ledger D [HALS: 61543], p98.
[130] J C Loudon, *An Encyclopedia of Gardening* (1822), p698.
[131] J C Loudon, *Encyclopedia of Gardening*, (revised edn 1835), p830.
[132] Romans, *Potato Book*, p117; anon., *Hints Concerning the Cultivation and Use of the Potato* (1795), p4; Loudon, *Encyclopedia of Gardening*, (revised edn 1835), p830.

anyone willing to take up this topic will find the memorandum books a useful source because Wilshere provides some descriptions of the appearance of particular types and experimented to assess their culinary potential. We thus know that the Callico was 'a spotted potato' which in 1810, cooked and compared with others, he found 'the most mealy & fit for immediate use'. Those others were the Blood Red, 'the fullest flavour & sufficiently mealy'; the White Kidney, 'rather waxy & not quite dry enough'; the Moroccan Black, 'still more waxy but very well tasted'; and the Golden Drop, which he found 'scarcely distinguishable from the White Kidney'. Further tests the following year, specifically involving boiling, led Wilshere to declare the Callico and the German Kidney both 'excellent mealy potatoes' but:

> The Callico rather more mealy to the middle. The Kidney remained harder but rather better flavoured. The Upright White was not sufficiently boiled but was a good potato. The Morocco very moderate (it is likely to be better towards the spring). The Blood Red watery & insipid.

He also experimented with the cultivation of new varieties, in 1821 planting '3 roots of a red potatoe sent from Holland called Lanckmann's Potatoe said to be from South America', a variety also referred to by the horticulturalist Thomas Knight.[133]

While Wilshere fed some of the crop to his pigs, his 'tasting notes', as well as the diversity of varieties cultivated each year, leave no doubt that most of the potatoes grown were destined for human consumption. On occasions he lists the individuals to whom they were sold or given; some he evidently used himself; some were destined 'for labourers' as part of their pay; but much of the crop was described as being 'disposed of', presumably to local grocers. It was stored prior to disposal in a 'potato cellar', in the 'Potato Hovel next Wood Barn', in a pit in Wilshire's 'Garden Plantation' (below, pp lxxvi), or in 'the buildings in the Dog Yard'. The Callico seems to have been the most frequently planted variety.

Nothing much is said about the types of carrot cultivated, beyond references which suggest heavy cropping and in some cases, the large size of the individual roots. In 1811 Wilshere recorded the average size of one crop at 14 oz, with individual examples as much as 3 feet 6 inches long and weighing 4½ pounds. The implication is that most of the field carrots were destined for animal feed,

---

[133] T A Knight, 'On the Potato', *Transactions of the Horticultural Society of London, Series 2,* 1 (1831), pp93-100.

but some were certainly used for cooking, in 'the house', and some of those sold to others were probably likewise used.

Farming: Livestock

We have so far emphasised Wilshere's role as an arable farmer. Most of his farm was in tilth and he owned none of the sheep upon which, to a significant extent, the fertility of his fields depended. But he kept some livestock as all farmers, well into the twentieth century, were obliged to do. Firstly, he kept farm horses, for pulling ploughs, carts and other equipment. The number varied from year to year, from three to five, but was usually four. This, on a farm of a little over 120 acres, is significantly less than Warde's estimated national average of 7.2 horses for every 100 sown acres in the early nineteenth century, but close to Young's estimates for various parts of Hertfordshire, made in 1804, of 4 horses per 100 acres.[134] They were fed in part on hay, partly cut from Wilshere's few hay meadows but mainly made from clover, trefoil or sanfoin growing in the arable fields; in part on carrots, mainly grown in the small plots in Great Wimbush; sometimes on oats; and occasionally on swedes. As was normal with working animals, not destined for slaughter, they were individually named ('Gilbert', 'Smug', Tommy', 'Dimond', 'Captain'). Wilshere also kept similar numbers of dairy cows, which were likewise individually named ('Gentle', Brown', 'Dun' and 'Kicker' in 1817). They were partly grazed in the small number of pasture fields, partly fed on hay and turnips, and partly on beet, cabbages and mangel-wurzels grown on the small plots in Great Wimbush. If all of his four, occasionally five cows were producing milk at the same time Wilshere would have had more than fifteen gallons a day at his disposal, more than even a large household could consume, suggesting that he sold the excess or gave it, perhaps, to workers. We should note, however, that in most years small numbers of suckling calves are also recorded, their presence on the farm reducing the quantity of milk available for human consumption. Rearing calves for sale was evidently a minor sideline, and in addition in 1817 Wilshere bought six steers (young bullocks) for fattening. These, too, were fed on crops grown on the farm, principally turnips.

More prominent, however, were the pigs which were kept on the farm, the number of which varied greatly from year to year but never fell below 10 and was often in excess of 30 or even 40. In those years when the total of 'hogs' was broken down and itemised, they included a boar, two or three sows, and varying

---

[134] P Warde, *Energy Consumption in England and Wales* (Consiglio Nazionale della Ricerche, Naples, 2007), p43; Young, *General View*, p197.

INTRODUCTION

numbers of 'pigs', or young stock. Wilshere was evidently breeding and then fattening; but he also bought in additional 'stores' for fattening, on occasions, as in November 1823 when he purchased 16 pigs which were 'immediately fed with peas and sold as they became sufficiently fat for market'. While he certainly consumed some of these animals himself – smoking some for bacon, 'pickling' or salting others as gammon, sometimes killing them at as young as ten weeks, presumably as suckling pig – he was thus also producing for sale. Wilshere fed his pigs on a range of food; peas, beans, the 'offal' from threshed beans, the chaff from threshed wheat, beet and ground barley. Pig farming is not much discussed by historians of farming in the 'agricultural revolution' period, and the memorandum books provide useful information about how it was integrated with other aspects of Wilshere's husbandry.[135]

Even more neglected has been the subject of poultry. Wilshere kept large numbers of hens, chickens, turkeys, guinea fowl and ducks, well over a hundred birds in most years, again indicating some production of meat, and perhaps eggs, for the market. The ratio of the different kinds of bird varied significantly over time but hens, chickens and unspecified 'fowl' were more numerous than turkeys or guinea fowl. Wilshere clearly bred turkeys (hence the references, in his list of farming stock, to small numbers of 'old' and larger numbers of 'young' birds). But, as with cattle and pigs, he sometimes bought in young poults for fattening, probably when his old breeding stock let him down; then, as now, turkeys are inconsistent breeders. The prominence of guinea fowl, a bird probably introduced into the country in the sixteenth century but only kept on a significant scale in the eighteenth, is noteworthy.[136] It was, by Wilshere's time, widely eaten (especially as a substitute for game birds, in the 'close' season) in upper-class and middle class households. Again, Wilshere maintained a small breeding population of 'old' birds, the numbers of their progeny in many years suggesting only domestic consumption but in others something more: in 1815 there were '42 Guinea chicks besides 10 young' on the farm. All the poultry seem to have been largely fed on barley or buckwheat, ground as meal.

Livestock was thus a significant if subsidiary aspect of Wilshere's farm. Much of the meat and other produce was probably consumed by Wilshere's household but a small surplus, of pigs and cattle especially, was sold, forming one of the

---

[135] They are, for example, mentioned only five times in Overton's *Agricultural Revolution*.

[136] D Newbold, 'A Historical Note on the Guinea Fowl', *Sudan Notes and Records* 9, 1 (1926), pp125-129; p128.

INTRODUCTION

many income streams in his complex farming business. The memorandum books allow us to see the importance of these activities, and also how they were integrated into, and help explain certain aspects of, his arable farming. Many of the crops grown in the small plots in Great Wimbush, for example, were evidently used as feed for livestock and poultry. What is less obvious from the books is the contribution that Wilshere's livestock made to his arable operations. Only scattered references indicate that the yard dung, produced by the cattle and horses and presumably the pigs, was applied to the turnip crop in the arable fields but in particular to the plots in Great Wimbush, described on several occasions as 'heavily dunged', where much of their feed was grown.

Farming: Productivity

Most agricultural historians agree that there was some kind of 'agricultural revolution' in the later eighteenth and nineteenth centuries, accompanying the 'industrial revolution'. Food production had to increase significantly, for the population of England rose rapidly from c6 million in 1750 to c9 million by 1800, reaching nearly 18 million by 1851, yet there were only low levels of food imports.[137] The 'revolution' featured a range of elements, in addition to the new crops and rotations already discussed, including the large-scale enclosure of open fields and common land, the improvement of livestock breeds, changes in the organisation of labour and the widespread adoption of land drainage and marling. Together, these developments allowed the growing cities of industrial England to be fed, both through increasing the amount of food produced per acre and by expanding the area under cultivation.[138]

Scholars debate the relative importance of these various factors in increasing the food supply, and there is no doubt that particular innovations were more important in some environmental contexts than others. Much attention has focused on the scale of improvement in crop yields on different kinds of farms, on different soils, farmed in different ways. Information on how much wheat, barley or other grain was produced comes from a range of sources, including the comments of contemporary agricultural writers, farm accounts and government surveys, but is often vague and generalised or patchy in nature.[139] Wilshere's memorandum

---

[137] B R Mitchell and P Deane, *Abstract of British Historical Statistics* (Cambridge, 1962), pp5-6.
[138] Overton, *Agricultural Revolution*; T Williamson, *The Transformation of Rural England: farming and the landscape 1700-1870* (Exeter, 1999).
[139] Overton, *Agricultural Revolution*, pp76-80.

lix

books, which frequently provide figures for the quantities produced by particular fields, are thus an important source of information.

In common with most contemporaries, Wilshere recorded quantities of grain by volume rather than by weight, using three main measures, the *bushel*, the *quarter* and the *load*. There are some occasions when the third of these terms is used in a literal sense, to mean a cart or waggon full of something, but when discussing his crop yields Wilshere clearly employed it as a measurement, sometimes combining it with one of the other two, as in 1809, when he recorded that the 3½ acres from 'the Corner close next Joan Bigg's grave' produced '15 loads 4 bushels of the best & 6 bushels of off[al] corn, together 17 loads, nearly 5 loads per acre'. A bushel was equivalent to 36.32 litres; a quarter was 8 bushels, or 290.5 litres; and in Hertfordshire, and as used by Wilshere, a load was equivalent to 5 bushels (726 litres) (in most counties it was 40 bushels).[140] Volumes of wheat are usually given in loads and bushels; those for barley usually in quarters and bushels, occasionally in loads.

The attention of agricultural historians has rightly focused on the yields of the two most important grain crops, wheat and barley. Wilshere estimated or recorded the yields of these two crops on numerous occasions and one of the most noticeable, but perhaps unsurprising feature of the figures, is the extent to which they varied both from year to year in individual fields, and on different fields within the same year, a clear indication of the dangers inherent in relying too much on isolated records as an indication of average productivity. Ignoring a couple of failed crops, explicitly described as 'bad' or 'very bad', the recorded yields for wheat range from 17.5 bushels an acre to as much as 35. The majority, however, fall in the range of 22 to 28 bushels per acre, with an average of around 24, although it must be emphasised that there is a measure of ambiguity and uncertainty about some of these records. Arthur Young in 1804 records some Hertfordshire wheat yields far higher than this, but when explicitly describing the *average* produce per acre in different parts of the county gives figures ranging from 17.5 to 25, and for the Hitchin area, 25 bushels an acre.[141] In 1800 average yields for the county as a whole were estimated by a House of Lords enquiry at 22 bushels an acre; the following year the Crop Returns

---

[140] As in 1810, when he recorded that 21 acres had produced 4½ loads per acre, and calculated the total at 473½ bushels. When yields are given as so many loads and so many bushels, the figure for the latter never exceeds four. This was different to the practice in the Midlands, East Anglia and much of southern England, where a Load was equivalent to 40 bushels; Young, *General View*, p67.
[141] Young, *General View*, pp87-9.

suggested 25 bushels; while the figure derived by Roger Kain from the tithe files of the 1830s was around 22 bushels.[142] Wilshere's wheat yields were thus around average for the locality, or perhaps only slightly below. They are also close to the average for the country as a whole which in the 1810s, according to the work of Turner, Becket and Afton, was 21.17 bushels and in the 1820s 23.6 bushels an acre.[143] In general, higher yields were produced on Wilshere's farm by the fields on the lower ground, poorer yields from those on the higher, more chalky land, but the pattern is neither striking nor consistent. The highest individual yields tended to be produced by plots in Great Wimbush, which on several occasions were well in excess of 30 bushels an acre. This probably reflects the intensive manuring and cultivation to which this area was subjected more than any intrinsic superiority of the Hornbeam soils, for in years of reasonable yields elsewhere those recorded here could fall to as low as 20 bushels, specifically when wheat followed a nutrient-hungry potato crop. Management could thus over-ride the influence of soils but, as noted, the differences in soil quality on Wilshere's farm were not great.

Wilshere provides fewer clear statements of the yield of his barley crop but these perhaps suggest an even greater degree of variation, with records ranging from as low as 20 to as high as 53 bushels an acre. As Young put it in 1804, barley was 'an uncertain crop on chalk soil', especially if sown late, because of its vulnerability to drought.[144] The compensation was that calcareous conditions produced a crop that was excellent for malting. Young estimated the average yield in Hertfordshire as a whole at a little over 32 bushels an acre and was informed that the usual yield around Hitchin was 28.[145] Wilshere's average appears significantly higher, at 38 bushels an acre. Although there are, once again, a number of ambiguous records and, as noted, this mean obscures a significant range, it is possible that he took particular care of his barley, on account of the buoyant local market for good malting grain. The majority of his crop appears to have gone for malting; as noted earlier, from 1817 he paid George Beaver to malt most of his barley.

---

[142] M E Turner, *Volume 190: Home Office Acreage Returns HO67. List and Analysis*, 3 parts, part 1 (List and Index Society, 1982); R J P Kain, *An Atlas and Index of the Tithe-Files of Mid Nineteenth Century England and Wales* (Cambridge, 1986).
[143] M E Turner, J V Beckett and B Afton, *Farm Production in England 1700-1914* (Oxford, 2001).
[144] Young, *General View*, p95.
[145] Young, *General View*, p95.

INTRODUCTION

Wilshere provides information about the yields of other crops, most notably carrots and potatoes, and these generally appear impressive; the carrot crop in 1809 was recorded as 7 tons per acre, not significantly below modern yields. He also provides much useful data on seeding rates - about the quantity of seed of different crops sown per acre. Students of agricultural history will, however, find less that is relevant to discussions of other measures of 'productivity', most notably labour productivity. Like many farmers in southern and eastern England by the early nineteenth century, Wilshere appears to have relied heavily on casual labour. Indeed, he retained only one permanent worker, contracted by the year and living in a tied cottage, to look after the livestock and do the milking, and to generally supervise the farm. The arable work was mainly undertaken by a 'flexible' workforce, hired for particular tasks (and, to a limited extent, paid in part with farm produce and, as was customary large quantities of beer at harvest).[146] He sometimes provides useful data about the numbers of individuals employed in specific activities, but not in a sufficiently consistent or comprehensive manner to allow the overall labour inputs of the farm to be calculated.

Wilshere's Farming Business

The value of Wilshere's farming memoranda is that they provide a holistic view of a complex business. They thus show how cautious we need to be with evidence that only captures fragments of a farm's activities, especially regarding crop yields, and they remind us that farms in the 'agricultural revolution' period displayed a measure of variety and sophistication which is not, perhaps, always fully recognised in academic texts. These tend to focus on a 'model' of a modern farm, cultivated under 'improved' rotations, on which the various elements worked together to produce grain and meat at higher levels than in earlier forms of farming without bringing in, from outside, much in the way of additional livestock feed, or additional sources of soil fertility. The roots and grasses grown on the farm allowed larger numbers of sheep and cattle to be fed than under earlier and less sophisticated systems, and thus more meat to be produced. More livestock also meant more manure and thus higher cereal yields. Even the straw from the cereal crops was largely recycled on the farm. Most was used to bed fatting bullocks, stalled in yards, and came back to the fields, mixed with dung and urine and rotted down, as manure. Some might be used to thatch hay or straw ricks but only a small proportion was usually sold beyond the farm

---

[146] S Wade Martins and T Williamson, 'Labour and Improvement: Agricultural Change in East Anglia c.1750-1870', *Labour History Review* 62, 3 (1997), pp275-295.

gates. The idea of the well-managed farm as a kind of 'closed system', recycling nutrients internally and only exporting meat, cereals and other arable produce, is not simply a modern fiction. Many contemporaries seem to have viewed farms in this way, especially the owners of large estates, keen to protect the long-term fertility of their farms. Agricultural leases accordingly often forbade the selling not only of hay and root crops off the farm, but in some cases even straw.[147]

In a number of important ways Wilshere's farming deviates from this familiar model. As we have seen, most of the turnips grown on the farm were consumed by, and much of the manure applied to the fields was produced by, sheep that did not reside on the farm but belonged to someone else. This is important because historians sometimes attempt to relate the yields produced on particular farms to the numbers of livestock kept there; if we only had at our disposal Wilshere's annual summaries of 'Farm Stock' we would greatly under-estimate their numbers, and thus the amounts of dung applied to the fields. Some of Wilshere's turnips were, moreover, lifted and sold off the farm, as was some of the clover hay, which on one occasion was taken as far afield as London. The capital, with its huge numbers of horses, had an insatiable appetite for hay, much of it grown in Hertfordshire, although it is surprising to see it being brought by waggon from as far away as Hitchin. Particularly striking is the fact that while much of Wilshere's straw was used as bedding, or for thatching ricks, a significant proportion of that from the wheat crop was similarly sold off the farm, most of it for a particular purpose.

As we noted earlier, straw plaiting was a significant industry in Hitchin, as it was in many parts of Hertfordshire and Bedfordshire.[148] Indeed, as late as 1861 no less than 1,939 people in the town, nearly 12 per cent of the adult population, were involved in producing plait, and straw hats and bonnets.[149] There was thus a ready market for plaiting straw, and the kind of well-drained, calcareous soils which predominated on Wilshere's farm were generally held to produce the best for the purpose: heavy or stony ground grew straw of poorer quality.[150] The straw was not simply a waste product, sold cheaply. It needed to be carefully laid in the stack, 'drawn' or split and flattened, and cut into the required lengths prior to sale, by men employed by Wilshere (although on one occasion they

---

[147] S Wade Martins and T Williamson, 'The Lease and East Anglian Agriculture, 1660-1870', *Agricultural History Review* 46, 2 (1998), pp127-141, p239.
[148] N Goose, 'Straw-Plaiting and Hat-Making', in D Short (ed.) *An Historical Atlas of Hertfordshire* (Hatfield, 2011), pp90-92.
[149] T G Austin, *The Straw Plaiting and Straw Hat and Bonnet Trade* Luton, 1871), p8.
[150] Young, *General View,* p224.

refused the proffered rate for the work, bought the straw and processed and sold it themselves). On a number of occasions Wilshere calculates the amount of money made from selling straw and while this evidently varied from year to year, and from field to field, it could be considerable. In 1815 he calculated that the wheat harvest from 12 acres of his lighter land was worth £150, once all costs had been accounted for, of which £60, or 40 per cent, or £5 an acre, came from the straw. Even what he considered a poor return, in 1818, brought in £4 an acre. In practice many farmers sold straw off the farm, especially in Hertfordshire, where much went to satisfy London's demand for stable bedding.[151] But straw production was evidently a significant if minor part of Wilshere's business portfolio and may even have been a factor in his decision to keep comparatively low numbers of livestock – stalled bullocks, in particular, required considerable quantities of bedding straw.

It is, however, the activities in Great Wimbush which deviate most from conventional models of 'improved', early nineteenth-century husbandry. The small, heavily-manured and intensively cultivated plots here produced some vegetables for human consumption; a range of seeds, both for Wilshere's own use and for sale to others; and a variety of fodder for the farm livestock. As we have noted, this part of the farm resembled in some ways a market garden, and the livestock kept by Wilshere – dairy cattle, pigs and poultry – are more reminiscent of those found on smallholdings than the flocks of sheep, and large numbers of store cattle, found on the classic 'agricultural revolution' farm. It may be relevant that Wilshere's farm in Hitchin lay only around 12 miles (20 kilometres) to the south of Sandy in Bedfordshire, in the vicinity of which a major market gardening industry had already developed by the end of the eighteenth century, and expanded significantly in the early nineteenth, following enclosure.[152] On the other hand, this aspect of Wilshere's farming activities may simply reflect the farm's proximity to Hitchin, and the market it offered for vegetables, pigs and the like. There may have been many enterprises like this in eighteenth- and nineteenth-century Hertfordshire, with its plethora of small towns.[153]

---

[151] Young, *General View*, pp86, 92-3 and 134.

[152] F Beavington, 'The Development of Market Gardening in Bedfordshire 1799-1939', *Agricultural History Review* 23, 1 (1975), pp23-47.

[153] T Slater and N Goose, 'Panoramas and Microcosms: Hertfordshire's Towns Through Both Ends of the Telescope', in T Slater and N Goose (eds), *A County of Small Towns: the Development of Hertfordshire's Urban Landscape to 1800* (Hatfield, 2008), pp1-26.

INTRODUCTION

We have, over the preceeding pages, tried to set William Wilshere's farming activities into their wider contexts, in terms of both the local landscape and environment and the more general development of agricultural practices in the later eighteenth and early nineteenth centuries. In so doing we have highlighted some of the ways in which the memorandum books can throw important new light on the history of English agriculture. But the purpose of this essay is to introduce, rather than to provide an exhaustive analysis, and agricultural historians, local and national, will find many other ways of using this wonderful source.

The Ornamental Gardens.

Although the bulk of the entries in the two memorandum books are concerned with farming, a substantial minority relate to Wilshere's horticultural interests and activities and of these, a significant number concern the ornamental grounds around his house. By great good fortune their meaning can be elucidated by a number of other surviving sources, documentary, visual and cartographic, which we also transcribe or reproduce in this volume. The picture of Wilshere's gardens that emerges is important because the attention of garden historians, especially those studying the eighteenth and nineteenth centuries, continues to be focused largely on the grounds of the country house, and with good reason.[154] The parks and gardens of the landed rich have left far more durable traces in the landscape than the more ephemeral creations of those lower down the social order. Smaller gardens in towns have been especially vulnerable, to successive waves of development. Landed estates tend, moreover, to be far better documented in surviving archives than other properties, even the residences of the wealthy upper middle classes, while famous designers like Capability Brown, between 1750 and the early 1780s, or Humphry Repton, between 1788 and 1816, were generally employed by those with broad acres at their disposal. Repton, it is true, also often worked for merchants and professionals who did not possess country estates; in Hertfordshire, for men like the banker George Stainforth at Woodhill in Essendon (1803), or the businessman William Towgood at Organ Hall in Radlett (c1804).[155] But his clients usually lived, as in these cases, in elegant 'villas' standing in extensive grounds and separate from other dwellings. Wilshere was, it is true, a wealthy man. But his gardens were

---

[154] Recent exceptions, examining gardens further down the social scale, include in particular C Hickman, *The Doctor's Garden: Medicine, Science, and Horticulture in Britain* (Yale University Press, 2022).

[155] S Flood and T Williamson (eds) *Humphry Repton in Hertfordshire: Documents and Landscapes* (Hatfield, 2018), pp207-26, 254-58.

INTRODUCTION

more typical of the middle class than those of Repton's clients, and especially of the many reasonably affluent people who, like him, lived in a country town, in a fine house but cheek-by-jowl with neighbours.

Wilshere's ornamental gardens were large by modern standards, if not by contemporary ones, covering nearly four acres and extending from the house, east across the river Hiz, as far as Back Street (now Queen Street). As is clearly shown on the undated estate map of 1801-7, they had an unusual shape.[156] The western section was narrow – around 20 metres in width, broadening to 30 metres – and was partly enclosed to the north by a wing of the house, a long service range and old maltings, and to the south by buildings attached to the adjacent property on Bancroft. After *c*70 metres they widened dramatically, and then more gradually as they extended beyond the river. Wilshere's land itself, however, expanded rather more at this latter point, for the 'Frame Yard' in which he grew fruit and vegetables, covering nearly three quarters of an acre, was here attached to and accessed from the southern side of the gardens.

The outline of the gardens reflected a history of piecemeal acquisition. Even in the sixteenth century the property, as we have seen, had been a large one. The will of the yeoman John Emmyng, drawn up in 1524, indicates that it then included, in addition to the main house, four smaller dwellings occupied by tenants, while a survey of the Manor of Hitchin made in 1556 described it as occupying two burgages (each with a frontage of between 90 and 100 feet (*c*27 – 30 metres).[157] But in 1584 the then owner, Thomas Gaddesden, extended it to the rear (the east) by purchasing a large area of land which continued beyond the river Hiz as far as Back Street.[158] It comprised an orchard to the west of the river and a pasture field to the east. A plan drawn up in 1707, soon after the property was inherited by Sarah Byde from her husband Ralph, shows a relatively small garden immediately behind the house, corresponding to the narrower western section of Wilshere's grounds.[159] Beyond it, extending behind the neighbouring house to the south and stretching as far as the river, was the orchard and beyond this, and running up to Back Street, was still an area of pasture. By 1770, when a sketch of the house and its grounds was included on a map of Purwell Field, the

---

[156] Plan of An Estate in the Parish of Hitchin and County of Hertford belonging to William Wilshere Esq, *c*1801-1807 [HALS: 58869].
[157] John Emmyng's will, proved 1525 [TNA: PROB11/21/519]; Survey of the Manor of Hitchin 1556 [TNA: E315/391].
[158] Deeds to The Grange House, Hitchin, 1584-1620 [HALS: 60356-60362]; Rental of the Manor of Hitchin 1591 [TNA: SC12/8/29].
[159] Case for opinion, 1707 [HALS: 60325].

orchard had largely gone and all the land as far as Back Street had been incorporated into the gardens.[160] The last significant addition to the property was made by Wilshere himself. In 1801 he purchased The Grange House in Portmill Lane, annexing part of its grounds, on which he established his 'Frame Yard'.

Wilshere's gardens are shown in some detail on the undated estate map of 1801-7, on an undated illustration by H G Oldfield showing the garden front of 'Mr Wilshere's at Hitchin' (complete with Venetian window), and on a painting made by Samuel Lucas in 1827, viewed from Windmill Hill to the east.[161] All suggest that the narrow, more enclosed area, close to the house, was rather 'formal' and symmetrical in appearance. It comprised a narrow rectangle of lawn, slightly wider than the central pediment of the house, which was flanked by lines of close-set shrubs. These in turn were flanked by straight gravel walks. Beyond, on the south side and on part of the north, narrow areas of shrubbery separated the walks from the walls of the adjacent buildings. This section of the garden was enclosed to the east by what was probably a hedge.

All this serves as a useful reminder of how the rules of mid and late eighteenth-century landscape and garden design adopted at country houses with rural estates – eschewing straight lines and symmetry, wholeheartedly embracing a 'naturalistic' irregularity – were not necessarily favoured on smaller plots, especially in urban contexts.[162] Indeed, it is hard to see how this particular narrow, rather enclosed space could have been treated in a convincingly naturalistic fashion and it is noteworthy that towards the east, as the gardens widened, the layout became more serpentine. Here a broad, central lawn was flanked, to north and south, by areas of ground planted with trees and shrubs, that to the north significantly wider than its southern counterpart. Paths meandered through and beside these areas, across the lawn and along the bank of the river.

---

[160] Plan of Purwell Field, 1770 [HALS: DZ/72/P121605; colour section No 2].
[161] Plan of An Estate in the Parish of Hitchin and County of Hertford belonging to William Wilshere Esq, [HALS: 58869; colour section No 3]; H G Oldfield drawing, c1800 [HALS: DE/Of/4/153; colour section No 1]; painting by Samuel Lucas [NHM; colour section No 8].
[162] S Spooner, *Regions and Designed Landscapes in Georgian England* (2018); T Williamson, 'Production, Power and the Natural: Differences between English and American Gardens in the Eighteenth Century', *Huntington Library Quarterly* 84, 3 (2021), pp467-90.

INTRODUCTION

Two bridges, placed close to the northern and southern boundaries of the garden, carried paths across the river and into a third section of the grounds lying beyond it. Here, too, there was a central area of lawn, rather wider than the previous one, surrounded to the north, south and east by narrow strips of planting, through and beside which a lone path continued, from bridge to bridge, forming a single circuit. The arrangement is reminiscent of a miniaturised version of a Capability Brown park, with a circuit drive threading through peripheral plantation belts. But, as the Lucas painting clearly shows, in the area beyond the garden boundary, on the west-facing slope of Windmill Hill on the far side of Back Street, Wilshere created a kind of full scale approximation to a fashionable parkland landscape. Home Close and the lower part of Rawlings Hill were laid to pasture and planted with groups of trees and, to accentuate the impression of parkland, the two fields were separated by – and Home Close was divided from the road by – wooden fences, rather than the kinds of hedges which bounded the fields elsewhere on his farm. Slightly higher up and further to the east, on Windmill Hill, Wilshere erected a thatched summer house in 1819, enabling him to sit and enjoy the view back towards his house and gardens so beautifully depicted on Lucas's painting.[163] The latter shows clearly how the central open lawns and peripheral areas of trees and shrubs in the gardens served to frame the prospect towards the park-like pastures on Windmill Hill, the planting in the terminal eastern belt featuring low growing plants to ensure that this was not obstructed.

Wilshere's gardens were not entirely his own creation; some features were inherited from their long previous history. We noted earlier the box trees, already well established in 1728, which continued as a feature of Wilshere's grounds, and latterly of Hitchin's townscape into the twentieth century. More importantly, much of the formal layout in the area near the house seems to be depicted on the sketch included on the Purwell Field map of c1770. It may have been laid out by Richard Tristram, perhaps soon after he acquired the property in the 1750s and raised and widened the pediment on the garden front, and provided it with the central Venetian window shown on the sketch and, more clearly, by Oldfield.[164] The more serpentine layout of the central and eastern parts of the grounds probably was the work of Wilshere – most of the features are not depicted on the (admittedly rather schematic) sketch on the map of c1770, which seems to suggest that this area was mainly occupied by a kitchen

---

[163] William Wilshere's cash book, 1819, p28 [HALS: 61529].
[164] 'Carpenters and Bricklayers work to be performed at Mr Tristram's House', 1763 [HALS: 60985]; Plan of Purwell Field, Hitchin [HALS: DZ/72/P121605].

INTRODUCTION

garden. But even here some older features seem to have persisted. The path which the 1801-7 map shows running along the southern edge of the central section of the grounds forms a precise circle at its western end which is also depicted on the *c*1770 sketch map, running through a well-planted area.[165] The wide area of trees shown in the northern part of this section of the gardens, probably what Wilshere described as his 'Old Orchard', seems to have been the truncated remnants of the much larger orchard shown on the 1707 map.[166]

The various maps, combined with the evidence of Samuel Lucas's painting, provide us with an unusual opportunity to reconstruct the essential layout of the kind of garden attached to a wealthy residence in a major country town at the start of the nineteenth century. The survival of formal, symmetrical elements was widely shared in urban contexts, where spaces for garden-making were often constricted and enclosed by walls and buildings. More unusual, perhaps – and reflecting Wilshere's wealth and ownership of farmland immediately adjacent to his residence – was the extent to which elements of the parkland fashions of the landed elite were embraced, so that the grounds featured a steady progression from symmetry and structure near the house, to irregular 'naturalism' on the slopes of Windmill Hill.

Gardens played an important role in late eighteenth and early nineteenth-century society. Like the houses they accompanied, they were powerful statements of status and provided arenas for social display and interaction. In August 1799, when he became Captain of the Hitchin Loyal Volunteers, Wilshere typically celebrated the event with a dinner in his garden.[167] Gardens were also places for private enjoyment, and many men and women, from the aristocracy downwards, were keen, active gardeners, themselves undertaking tasks like planting, weeding or pruning, or at least directly supervising those who carried them out.[168] The fact that Wilshere kept a record of garden 'memoranda' shows clearly that he was a member of this group. But so too, perhaps, does his choice of gardeners. James Bowie, who was appointed in December 1812, became a figure of some importance in the worlds of contemporary horticulture and botany. Before coming to Hitchin Bowie had been employed in Kew Gardens – Wilshere almost certainly met him through his membership of the Royal

---

[165] Plan of Purwell Field [HALS: DZ/72/P121605].
[166] Case for opinion, 1707 [HALS: 60325].
[167] S Flood (ed), *John Carrington, Farmer of Bramfield, His Diary, 1798-1810. Part 1, 1798-1804*, HRS Vol 26 (Hertford, 2015), p28.
[168] T Williamson, *The Archaeology of the Landscape Park: Garden Design in Norfolk, England, c1680-1840* (British Archaeological Reports, Oxford, 1998), pp162-66.

INTRODUCTION

Horticultural Society). He left in August 1814 when Sir Joseph Banks selected him to go on a plant hunting expedition to Brazil. In 1817 Bowie was sent to South Africa, undertaking horticultural expeditions far into the interior. Recalled to Kew in 1823, he returned to the Cape in 1827, where he was for a time gardener to Baron Ludwig of Ludwigsberg, while also continuing his botanical work. He corresponded regularly with the famous botanist William Harvey, who named a genus of bulbous perennial succulents found in eastern and southern Africa 'Bowiea' in his honour. Harvey described how Bowie's 'many years of patient labour in the interior of South Africa' had 'enriched the gardens of Europe with a greater variety of succulent plants than had ever been detected by any traveller'.[169] Bowie had health issues, however, and he died in poverty in 1853 (see 'Biographical notes'). Another of Wilshere's gardeners, Daniel McIntosh, later took charge of the great gardens at Wrest Park in Bedfordshire, a clear indication of unusual skill and ability.

Three of the four documentary sources transcribed here provide an unusual opportunity to flesh out some of the details of an early nineteenth-century garden shown in broad outline on a map and illustration, as well as throwing light more generally on the activities of an enthusiastic gardener. The memorandum books contain horticultural information and advice culled from publications and a variety of individuals; notes on the stock offered by London nurseries; lists of plants Wilshere had purchased or which he intended to purchase; and various notes relating to his gardens. Many of the latter, it should be emphasised, concern the cultivation of fruit and vegetables in his orchard and kitchen garden (see below, pp lxxiii-lxxix) and include descriptions of good and poor crops and the sizes attained by cucumbers, mushrooms, pineapples and the like. The second source, 'Lists of Trees, Seeds &c Sown, Planted &c, in the Garden of Wm Wilshere Esq. at Hitchin, Herts. by James Bowie', is a straightforward inventory of mainly ornamental plants, described by their Latin names (which often differ significantly from those of modern scientific nomenclature). The third source is the 'Journal kept in the Garden of William Wilshere Esq. Hitchin, Herts. By James Bowie gardener', between December 1812 and October 1814, and continued until August 1815 by John Downing and subsequently, in 1821 and 1822, by Daniel McIntosh. This essentially comprises notes on day-to-day activities which provide some useful insights into contemporary horticultural practice.

---

[169] R Drayton, 'James Bowie', *ODNB* (2004).

INTRODUCTION

We receive slightly different impressions of the gardens from these documents, for reasons that are not always clear. References to roses loom large in the memorandum books but they do not feature at all in Bowie's 'Lists'. Moreover, the trees and shrubs which map and illustration suggest were prominent in the garden only rarely appear in the written sources and are usually mentioned in passing, as in June 1801 when Wilshere notes of a particular rose, 'I think I have one in the upper garden immediately before the American ilex'. All this shows how cautious we need to be in circumstances where the planting of an individual garden is only described in a single source. Of particular interest is the way that the three documents all show us clearly what the map and painting, with their representations of trees and shrubberies, lawns and paths, do not – that Wilshere's garden contained an abundance of flowering herbaceous plants, although precisely where they were all growing remains unclear.

References to bulbs feature prominently in all three documents, especially to tulips, hyacinths, polyanthus, narcissus, jonquils, gladioli and lilys. These, together with the anemones, saxifrages and 'ranunculuses' – presumably *Ranunculus ficaria*, now known as *Ficaria verna*, the lesser celandine or pilewort – were probably planted in grass, on the edges of the shrubberies and beside paths running through them, to provide a mass of spring colour. The lower-growing flowers like anemone would be placed to the front and taller ones like tulips to the rear – common eighteenth-century practice which continued into the early nineteenth.[170] Some of the taller growing herbaceous plants referred to in the sources, especially those tolerant of partial shade, such as *Digitalis* (foxglove), Astrantia major, star gentian and bastard balm, may have formed a final tier in this progression, or may simply have been planted amongst the shrubs. Many of the flowers mentioned, however – half-hardy annuals like zinnias, perennials like campanula, rose campion, spigelia, delphinium – are sun loving, summer flowering varieties which would not have flourished if used in these ways and were clearly destined for beds or borders, as presumably were the roses mentioned by Wilshere in the memorandum books. Flower borders are, indeed, referred to in the gardening 'Journal'. In February 1813 Bowie noted 'Annuals on the borders of the grass plat sown'; in March 1814 he recorded 'Chief of the hardy annuals sown in the borders'; and in the following month his successor noted 'Zinnia revoluta planted on the borders' and 'Dahlias planted on the borders'. There is also a single telling mention in the first memorandum book, for June 1811, in which Wilshere writes of yellow lilys

---

[170] M Laird, *The Flowering of the Landscape Garden: English Pleasure Grounds, 1720-1800* (Pennsylvania, 1999), esp. pp142-4.

INTRODUCTION

in '2 fine bunches in the lower south border of the flower garden'. Precisely where the flower garden was located is uncertain, although presumably close to the house. Nor is it clear whether all the herbaceous borders were concentrated here or were more widely distributed through the grounds. What is clear is the sheer abundance of flowers, the documents providing a more reliable indication of contemporary taste than Repton's Red Books which, when dealing with smaller 'villa' residences especially, often scarcely mention them. The comments of other, less famous contemporaries indicate that Wilshere's floral displays were not unusual. Maria Jacson, for example, described in 1816 how 'A Flower-Garden is now become a necessary appendage of every fashionable residence', designed to exhibit 'a variety of colour and form so nicely blended as to present one whole'.[171] Bowies' 'List' alone names more than 40 varieties of herbaceous perennial present or planted in the garden in early 1813, over 30 hardy annuals and at least a dozen biennials.

All this is in addition to the 33 varieties of plants in the greenhouse and 28 in the 'stove', as well as the numerous varieties of peach and nectarine in the peach house, melons and other plants. Of particular interest is Wilshere's collection of West Indian specimens, some of which were probably sent to him by the son of a friend who was living on the island of Nevis, a reminder of the extent to which colonial connections permeated contemporary society.[172] Plants more generally, when not raised by Wilshere's own gardeners, were obtained from local nurserymen like Henry Hodgson, from friends or associates like the London lawyer John Desse, and from London companies - Lee & Kennedy of Hammersmith, Colville's on the Kings Road or Andrews of Lambeth, the latter otherwise unknown but perhaps the Henry Andrews who supplied heathers to Croome in Wiltshire in 1797.[173]

Although the written sources all, as we have noted, foreground the herbaceous elements of Wilshere's garden there are some references to the trees and shrubs which feature prominently in Lucas's painting and on the undated 1802-7 estate map. They include American ilex (presumably American holly *Ilex optica*), variegated holly, Laurustinus (*Viburnum tinus*), magnolia, azalea, probably

---

[171] M Jacson, *The Florist's Manual; or Hints for the Construction of a Gay Flower Garden* (1816), pp5, 11.
[172] For similar connections at the level of the large landed estate, see J C Finch 'A Transatlantic Dialogue: The Estate Landscape in Britain, the Caribbean, and North America in the Eighteenth Century', *Huntington Library Quarterly* 84, 3 (2021), pp491-515.
[173] J Harvey, *Early Nurserymen* (Chichester, 1974).

laurel and perhaps variegated elder. There was also a rhododendron border and a sweet briar hedge, although precisely where they were located remains uncertain. The documents also contain a number of references to Wilshere's peach house and 'stove' - that is, his heated greenhouse. Although in large measure associated with the production of exotic fruit, both appear to have been located somewhere in the grounds around the house, rather than within the larger area of kitchen garden that Wilshere possessed on the far side of Whinbush Road. Pineapples, nectarines and the like were valuable commodities which needed to be kept safe from theft. Moreover, the expensive technology required for their production was something to be displayed to guests, not hidden away in a remote spot. Nectarines as well as peaches were grown in the peach house, which was probably a masonry structure with large windows and probably, although not certainly, heated. Pineapples or 'pines' needed more heat and could either be grown in pits or 'frames' sunk into the ground and heated with tanners' bark (melons, gourds and cucumbers were similarly cultivated, but on beds of dung), or else in heated buildings called 'stoves'.[174] Wilshere employed both methods, noting in 1817 that he had 36 pines growing in pits and 69 in his 'stove'. Although he sometimes refers to the latter as his 'pine house' an impressive range of other exotic plants was also grown there. The peach house was constructed around 1813 and the 'stove' perhaps shortly before. The estate map of 1801-7 shows a single building on the eastern edge of the Frame Yard, perhaps the summer house beside the strawberry beds mentioned in a 'Journal' entry in 1814; the 1818 map shows one ranged against the north wall.[175] Long and thin, this may have comprised the stove and peach house, standing side by side.

The various documents also make references to a 'greenhouse', probably an unheated structure. This may not have stood in the Frame Yard but within the ornamental grounds proper: in June 1811 Wilshere refers to the 'Mottled Lilley immediately above the Althea nearest to the Greenho[use]: it is overshadowed by the Althea & the variegated holly next it'. It may have been somewhere near the 'Old Orchard', on the northern side of the central section of the garden. There are also references to a conservatory attached to the house, one of the several places where grapes were grown; and to a 'succession house', although where this stood is unclear. Likewise uncertain is the location of Wilshere's ice

---

[174] L Bellamy, *The Language of Fruit: literature and horticulture in the long eighteenth century* (Philadelphia, 2019), pp69-73; S Campbell, *A History of Kitchen Gardening* (2005).
[175] [HALS: 58869; HALS D/EWs/P16].

INTRODUCTION

house, which was filled in November 1819 with 30 cart loads of ice from a pond in Ickleford. In spite of these problems, the documents, maps and painting together provide a remarkably detailed picture of Wilshere's gardening activities and garden historians, especially those interested in urban and middle class gardens of the period, will find much to interest them here.

The Kitchen Garden

Wilshere, as we have already noted, appears to have had two areas of kitchen garden by the time the first memorandum book begins in 1809. The walled Frame Yard we have just discussed. Accessed directly from the ornamental gardens and covering a little under ¾ of an acre, it may have served a partly ornamental function. In addition, the 1818 estate map labels a much larger area as 'kitchen garden', lying quite separate from the grounds of the house, on the far side of Whinbush Road. It occupied a triangular area of just over 1¾ acres (0.7 hectares), bounded by Whinbush Road to the west and Walsworth Road to the south-east, and lay immediately to the south-west of the intensively-cultivated plots in Great Wimbush. It was at least partly bounded by a low brick wall, fragments of which still exist. The earlier, undated map of 1802-7 labels this same area as 'Nursery' and shows it as hedged rather than walled but the change in function may not have been quite as great as this contrast in nomenclature and representation suggest. There are indications that part of the 'Kitchen Garden' was still being used as a tree nursery; the building of walls and the change in name probably reflects a partial but not complete change of use, with the cultivation of vegetables now taking place alongside that of young trees.

A phenomenal range of vegetables was grown by Wilshere's gardener, to judge from scattered references in the two memorandum books and the 'Journal'. They included artichokes, asparagus, beans (French, broad and runner not distinguished: long-pod, Windsor, early yellow, black negro, scarlet runner, purple speckled, Mazagan, 'bog or fan' and white blossom), broccoli (Cape, early purple, late purple, white, Siberian and brimstone), Brussels sprouts, cabbage (red, savoy, 'hundred head' and York), 'Scots' kale, cauliflower, carrots, celery and red celery, cucumbers, endive, garlic, green beet, leeks, lettuce (Marseilles and green coss), onions (Reading, silver skinned, Strasbourg, Spanish and Black Spanish), parsnips, peas (dwarf Imperial, 'early', Hotspur, Knight's, Prussian, Spanish drop, Glory of England, marrowfat), pumpkin, radish, red beet (beetroot), shallots, spinach and turnips (including 'long turnips', 'early Dutch turnips' and 'curious stone turnips'). Some of the types and specific varieties given can be identified – a few are still regularly grown today – but others are more obscure. In the case of the onions, for example, 'silver skinned' is still widely employed as a term for the various kinds of small onion used for pickling, 'Spanish' is still used generically for a range of large, mildly flavoured and fine-grained onions while Strasbourg is an old variety, strongly flavoured with an oval bulb, a good keeper, which is still cultivated.[176] The 'Reading onion' is no longer grown but appears to have been a larger version of the Strasbourg; the character of the 'Black Spanish' remains uncertain.[177] In the case of the peas, the Prussian, also known as the Prussian Blue, was a popular type developed in Germany in the eighteenth century and noted for its dark blue-green seeds; the Hotspur was an old English variety, mentioned in Leonard Meager's *English Gardener* of 1683 as the earliest to fruit; 'early' might be any early variety; while marrowfat peas, as noted earlier, are still grown to make dried, yellow peas.[178] Some can be more cautiously identified. The Glory of England pea, for example, may be the 'Champion of England', recorded in catalogues from the mid nineteenth century and described by Johnson in 1854 but now lost; Spanish drop could be the then widely cultivated Spanish morotto pea (a large variety); and Knight's may be the Knight pea, a heavy cropping, fast-maturing variety still often grown.[179] The precise identity of the dwarf Imperial, however, remains obscure.

Potatoes were also grown, some the same varieties as in the plots in Great Wimbush – Black, Upright White, German Kidney, Blood Red – but also the Peach and the Large Kidney. It is unclear which of these, if any, were amongst the 'earlies' which, in the manner already discussed, were grown by the gardener in hot beds. The root vegetables 'scorzenera' and 'salsaffi', popular in nineteenth-century gardens but now rarely grown in the UK, were also cultivated together with herbs like marjoram, basil, parsley, Hambro (Hamburg) parsley and burnet and a range of soft fruit - strawberries, raspberries, blackcurrants, gooseberries and cranberries. Mushrooms were grown in a mushroom house and melons, cucumbers, American squash, gourd, and Patagonian cucumber (currently unidentified) in frames. The sheer range of

---

[176] All were described by Young in 1802: A Young, *Gleanings from Books on Agriculture and Gardening* (1802), p273.

[177] J Abercrombie, *The Complete Kitchen Gardener and Hot-Bed Forcer* (1789), p80.

[178] L Meager, *English Gardener* (1683), p68; T A Knight, 'Some Remarks *on the* supposed Influence of the Pollen, in cross breeding, upon the Colour of the Seed-coals of Plants, and the Qualities of their Fruits', *Transactions of the Horticultural Society* 5 (1824), pp377-80; Young, *Gleanings from Books*, p289.

[179] G W Johnson, *The Cottage Gardener and Country Gentleman's Companion* (1854), p455; Abercrombie, *Complete Kitchen Gardener*, p24, pp377-800.

produce is remarkable, comparable to that cultivated in the kitchen gardens of the country houses of the gentry and aristocracy. The area under cultivation seems rather large to have provided food solely for Wilshere's household and it is probable that surpluses were regularly sold (as they were from the kitchen gardens of many contemporary country houses), although there is no definite evidence.

On a number of occasions Wilshere refers to something called his 'Garden Plantation'. This contained some coniferous planting – larches are mentioned in 1809 and cypresses in 1813 – and featured eight 'quarters' and mown grass paths. There are references (in the 'Journal') to heavily manured beds sown with cabbages, garlic, shallots, peas and spinach. A significant number of fruit trees were also listed here in 1811. The 'Plantation' was, almost certainly, another name for the kitchen garden: Merrett's 1820 map of Hitchin shows that this was divided into eight areas each dotted with a few trees (and surrounded by a belt of trees which could be Wilshere's tree nursery).

Wilshere's Orchards and Fruit Trees

While the information about Wilshere's kitchen gardens is interesting, that which the memorandum books provide about his orchards and fruit trees will probably prove useful to a greater number of people. There is currently much popular interest in old orchards and historic fruit varieties, as indicated by the large number of books published on these subjects over the last few decades, and the popularity of 'apple days', organised by enthusiasts, at which individuals can have old varieties growing in their gardens and orchards identified.[180] Outside of western England, where cider was the main alcoholic beverage and apple orchards were correspondingly extensive, most orchards were comparatively small in the early nineteenth century. Attached to farms and

---

[180] See, for example, B Short, P May, G Vine and A-M Bur, *Apples and Orchards in Sussex* (Lewes, 2012); M Gee, *The Devon Orchards Book* (Halsgrove, Wellington, 2018); C Masset, *Orchards* (Princes Risborough, 2012); L Copas, *A Somerset Pomona: the Cider Apples of Somerset* (Wimbourne, 2001); P Brown, *The Apple Orchard: the Story of Our Most English Fruit* (2016); R Blanc, *The Lost Orchard: A French Chef Rediscovers a Great British Food Heritage* (2020); M Quinion, *Cider Making* (Princes Risborough, 2008); I D Rotherham (ed), *Orchards and Groves: their History, Ecology, Culture and Archaeology* (Sheffield, 2008); W Muggleton, *The Apples and Orchards of Worcestershire* (Malvern, 2017); J Morgan and A Richards, *The New Book of Apples* (Revised edn, 2002); P Blackburne-Maze, *The Apple Book* (1986); M Clarke, *Apples: a Field Guide* (revised edn Tewin, 2015); R Sanders. *The Apple Book* (2010); Common Ground, *Orchards: a Guide to Local Conservation* (1989).

the larger houses, they supplied fruit for the residents and sometimes, although not always, a modest surplus for sale. Some specialised areas of fruit production existed, notably in Kent and western Middlesex, in the northern Fenland on the boundary between Cambridgeshire and Norfolk, and in west Hertfordshire – in the area around Hemel Hempstead, Watford and St Albans, some 16 miles (25 kilometres) to the south-west of Hitchin. Here, as early as the seventeenth century, a major industry supplying cherries and apples to the London market had developed.[181] But even in such areas most orchards were run by farmers as one part, if a significant one, of their businesses.

Wilshere in fact had two orchards, to judge from the description he provides in 1811, following a survey of his fruit trees undertaken by his gardener, McIntosh, and the Hitchin nurseryman Henry Hodgson. One, as we have seen - the 'Old Orchard' - probably occupied the northern extremity of the ornamental gardens, the area shown as thinly scattered with trees on the map of 1801-7. Paths and a pond are also shown, and Wilshere describes trees growing 'next the Walk' and 'opposite the pond'. There may have been other partly ornamental, partly productive features here, for he refers to a 'White Nectarine next the fence of Herb Garden'. The other orchard was described as the 'Orchard of the Kitchen Garden'. The fruit trees growing in the 'border of the Kitchen Garden' are also itemised but neither name seems to reference the large kitchen garden that Wilshere established on the far side of Whinbush Road because the trees in the 'Plantation divided into 8 quarters' are also separately described, as are those growing in the Frame Yard. The location of this kitchen garden and its associated orchard are uncertain but the fact that one of the trees within the latter was growing 'in the border leading to the bridge next the sweet briar hedge', clearly suggesting proximity to the river, indicates that both lay somewhere near or within the main area of the grounds. It is possible that, although Grange House to the south was by this time leased to Joseph Eade, Wilshere took the opportunity to value the fruit trees there along with those on his own land, and that the kitchen garden was the name he gave to the grounds of that house – the enclosure which the 1801-7 map shows lying to the north of Portmill Lane and to the west of the Frame Yard. If so, the 'Kitchen Garden Orchard' would be either the group of trees shown between the Frame Yard and the river (also part of the Grange House property) or that lying immediately to the north of the boundary between the two properties, probably the former given the reference to

---

[181] G Barnes and T Williamson, *English Orchards: a Landscape History* (Oxford, 2022), pp84-93; G Barnes and T Williamson *The Orchards of Eastern England: History, Ecology, Myth* (Hatfield, 2021), pp45-53.

a bridge. An alternative explanation is that the names of both areas reference, not an existing kitchen garden, but the one which had formerly occupied, the *c*1770 Purwell Field map suggests, the central area of Wilshere's grounds, to the west of the river. Although by 1811, to judge from the evidence of the 1801-7 map, this was occupied by lawn and shrubberies, some of the fruit trees it had contained may have been retained within the latter. To the east of the river the lines of trees shown on the *c*1770 map may represent the 'Kitchen Garden Orchard', fragments of which, together with the name, may likewise have lived on in the peripheral planting shown here on the 1801-7 map. At the time of writing we are unable to decide between these alternatives and the issue remains unresolved.

In all, more than 120 trees were itemised by McIntosh and Hodgson in these various locations, of which around 60 per cent were apples. This, however, was 'exclusively of older trees' growing in the kitchen garden orchard, various references suggesting that these too were mainly apples. There were significant numbers of pear trees but rather smaller quantities of plums (including damsons) and still fewer cherries. There were also medlars, quinces and at least one outside nectarine. This balance of fruit was typical, outside areas of commercial production, and simply reflects the relative keeping properties of the fruit in question. Apples and to an extent pears can have an extended fruiting season, if the right range of varieties is planted, and stored in the right conditions they will keep for weeks or months. Plums and cherries fruit for only a short period and, unless turned into jam, bottled or otherwise preserved, will soon rot.

With such a large number of fruit trees it might seem obvious that Wilshere was not merely growing for his own household, but also for sale. He certainly did sell some of his fruit, but this may not be the main reason for such an abundance, and the details provided in the memorandum books perhaps explain more generally why orchards attached to farms and other residences often seem so large. The memorandum books make clear, in a way that few other sources do, the extreme variability of the fruit crop. Indeed, the extent of fluctuation seems unparalleled in recent records of orchard productivity, possibly suggesting that some of the varieties grown by Wilshere and contemporaries had lower resilience in the face of adverse growing conditions than those cultivated today. Some of the particularly good or poor crops correlate with extremes of weather known from other sources: the poor apple harvest in 1812 followed a notably cold summer in southern England; the 'exceedingly defective' apple crop of 1817, a very wet summer; while 1818, when the apples were 'very plentiful and mostly good', saw the hottest summer in living memory.[182]

The 'defective' apple crop in 1809 was 9 bushels; in 1812 the apple harvest 'failed in so great a degree' that it amounted to only 2½ bushels, while the 'exceedingly defective' crop of 1817 was only 1½ bushels. In contrast, in 1823 there were 41 bushels of apples and in 1820 no less than 44 (together with 16 bushels of pears). The average yield for the nine years for which Wilshere provides this information was around 19 bushels.[183] Given the extent to which the crop could fall short of this level, a supply of fruit for the household could only be assured by planting large numbers of trees, meaning in turn that there would be a saleable surplus in average and above-average years. Even in 1811, when the orchards produced 11 bushels of apples, Wilshere sold 1 bushel, but this figure rose to 12 of the 24 bushels in 1818 and to at least 26 of the 44 in 1820. Large orchards and an abundance of fruit trees, in other words, may have been intended primarily as an insurance against poor cropping years, rather than as a source of profit, although the latter would always be welcome. There are hints that on some occasions Wilshere may have purchased the surplus apples from neighbours to sell with his own; it is difficult to otherwise explain why in 1818, when his crop amounted to 24 bushels, he nevertheless recorded the purchase of half a bushel of golden pippins from 'Fossey' and a bushel of Norfolk beefings from 'Arlesey'.

It is, however, the lists of varieties, of apples and pears, which Wilshere provides which will perhaps be of greatest interest to students of the history of fruit-growing and orchards, not least because relatively few such lists have survived from the period before c1850 which relate to the orchards attached to farms, vicarages and urban residences, as opposed to country houses. Those from Hertfordshire and adjoining counties, moreover, generally list fewer varieties. That from the rectory at Westmill in north-east Hertfordshire, for example, drawn up in 1710, itemises only ten apple trees of six varieties, while that from the rectory at Ayot St Lawrence, compiled in 1807, lists fifteen varieties.[184] Of the apples which could be identified by McIntosh and Hodgson in their survey of 1811, albeit sometimes tentatively, there were, allowing for some ambiguities, around 36 different varieties (seven of the trees were described as 'unknown' or 'dead'). Elsewhere in the memorandum books a

---

[182] https://www.pascalbonenfant.com/18c/geography/weather.htm, accessed 3 Sep 2022.
[183] 1809 1812, 1816, 1817, 1818, 1819, 1820, 1821 and 1823.
[184] List of orchard trees, Westmill rectory, 1710 [HALS: DP/120/3/1]; list of orchard trees, Ayot St Lawrence rectory, 1807 [HALS: DP/10/1/3].

INTRODUCTION

further nine varieties are mentioned, presumably from amongst the older trees growing in the kitchen garden orchard which were not itemised in the survey.

As most readers will be aware, the majority of apple varieties will not 'breed true' so that a pip from, say, a Cox's Orange Pippin will not grow into a tree bearing fruit of this variety. Instead, every pip will represent a new genetic variation. Only by grafting wood from an existing Cox's tree, onto a rootstock, can a new tree of this variety be obtained.[185] Most of the chance variations arising from sown pips will be hard, bitter, or at best bland. But some seedlings will produce attractive and useful fruit, while new varieties also emerge from 'sports', that is, as genetic mutations on the tree itself. They might then be grafted, propagated and exchanged with friends or neighbours or marketed commercially. In addition, however, fruit breeders also deliberately developed novel types, by cross-pollinating established varieties with desirable characteristics. A vast range of varieties was developed in these ways over the centuries to fulfil particular functions in terms of storage or modes of consumption.

There are now many hundreds of apple varieties cultivated in England, a high proportion of which are routinely described as 'traditional', even 'ancient'. In reality, in spite of their evocative names varieties like Newton Wonder, Emneth Early, Beauty of Bath, Grenadier, Worcester Pearmain, Allington Pippin, Ellison's Orange are not in fact very old. Many are also described as 'local' to particular areas or regions but this, too, needs to be treated with a measure of caution.[186] There is much romanticism and nostalgia attached to our old apple varieties, but recent research in Hertfordshire and elsewhere has provided more evidence and suggests that they developed, over the last three centuries or so, in a series of stages.[187]

Before the early eighteenth century most people, even the wealthy, stocked their orchards with trees they had grafted themselves, using scion wood obtained from friends, neighbours or relatives, or they used young trees similarly acquired. In 1627, for example, Sir Henry Chauncy of Ardeley in Hertfordshire was asked by Sir John Butler of Woodhall near Watton-at-Stone to provide him

[185] Morgan and Richards, *New Book of Apples*, pp11, 18, 296-8.
[186] See, for example, A King and S Clifford, 'The Apple, the Orchard, the Cultural Landscape', in S Clifford and A King (eds) *Local Distinctiveness: Place, Particularity and Identity* (1993), pp37-46.
[187] For more detail see Barnes and Williamson, *Orchards of Eastern England*, pp171-215.

with 'some younge trees, of Apples, peares and wardens', as he was 'entendinge this winter (if God permit) to plant an orchyarde'.[188] It is often assumed, and to an extent correctly, that local propagation and exchange produced a plethora of very local varieties, which became traditional to particular areas or regions. Such exchanges were not necessarily local, however. In 1716 Ralph Freman of Hamels near Braughing was sent '3 litle cherry trees' from Northamptonshire, almost certainly by his mother-in-law.[189] Moreover, by the later seventeenth century commercial nurseries were already well established in London, and beginning to develop more widely, eroding any dependence on very local stock. By 1732 William Ellis, who farmed at Little Gaddesden, could describe how he obtained fruit trees from small local nurseries at Redbourne (Hertfordshire) and Brentford (Middlesex) as if this was a normal thing to do.[190].

The few surviving lists of fruit trees dating to the late seventeenth and early eighteenth centuries contain two broad kinds of name. On the one hand, there are obscure names which do not appear in other lists or old published sources, no longer exist, and are often simple, descriptive or whimsical in character, or reference named individuals or local villages. A list of apples growing in two orchards in Thwaite in Norfolk, compiled by Mary Birkhead in 1734, includes such names as Egypt Apple, Best Pearmain, Grey Pipen, White Apple, Sower Apple, Bloody Apple, the Good Housewife, Maid's Pippin, Lady's Longing, Jack Holland, 'Mr Walker's Apple', Thwaite, Free Thorpe, Corton and Halvergate, the last four referencing Norfolk or Suffolk villages lying within 20 kilometres of the orchards described.[191] None of these names appear in other sources. Some must represent very local or regional varieties, only a handful of which – such as the Norfolk Beefing, which Birkhead also lists – have survived to this day. On the other hand, early lists also include a range of standard, almost omnipresent varieties, found throughout the country, with rather vaguer, more generic names: Nonsuch, Nonpareil, Golden Pippin, Catshead, Golden Pearmain, Holland Pippin and the like. While the varieties growing in the grounds of Westmill parsonage in 1710 included obscurities like Spencer's

---

[188] W B Gerish, *Sir Henry Chauncy, Kt; Serjeant-at-Law and Recorder of Hertford* (1907), pp28-9.
[189] A Rowe (ed), *Garden Making and the Freman Family: a Memoir of Hamels*, HRS Vol 17 (Hertford, 2001), ppxlv and 8.
[190] W Ellis, *The Timber-Tree Improved* (1738), pp151-2.
[191] The orchard book of Mary Birkhead of Thwaite [Norfolk Record Office: BRA 926 122].

INTRODUCTION

Pippin and Girton Pippin, the most numerous types were Golden Pippin and Nonpareil.

While many of the names in this second group now denote defined varieties which are still cultivated, it is possible that in this period they may have been used more loosely, for groups of apples with broadly shared characteristics of appearance, flavour, use, fruiting season or storage. Nonpareil and Golden Pippin thus feature particularly prominently but the former may have been a general term for a small, yellow and russetted dessert apple, and the latter one for an early season, yellowish apple for culinary use. It is noteworthy that when William Ellis discusses some of these 'varieties' in his various publications he sometimes employs the plural, as when in 1732 he suggested that many existing orchard trees should be replaced by 'the Golden Rennets, Pippins, and Pearmains'.[192] The imprecision in nomenclature which causes problems for modern researchers perhaps reflects a lack of precise and narrow genetic definition at a time when many trees were bought from small local nurseries or were grafted from scion wood obtained from friends and relatives. In 1734 Mary Birkhead remarked that 'I have frequently had the same fruit from several persons by different names'.[193] The rector of North Runcton in Norfolk bemoaned in 1720 how 'The true Aromatick Golden Russeting is so scarse in this Countrey that I perceive they give the name to any ordinary fruit if it have butt a Russett coat.'[194]

As the eighteenth century progressed commercial nurseries steadily became more numerous, and often larger. Not only major London firms, but businesses like Rivers, established at Sawbridgeworth in 1735, or Mackie's of Norwich, marketed fruit trees (and other plants) widely, by the end of the century often advertising their stock in printed catalogues. Commercial expansion ushered in a second phase in the development of fruit varieties, which was well under way by Wilshere's time. The national, 'generic' types – Nonpareil, Golden Pippin and the like – remained popular but the unique and local 'varieties' disappear from lists of orchard trees. They were replaced by a few varieties which had formerly been restricted to particular parts of England, like the Norfolk Beefing, or by ones newly developed by provincial nurseryman, such as the Blenheim Orange, that were now marketed nationally. Of course, people still obtained fruit trees from local nurserymen or informally, from friends, acquaintances or neighbours.

[192] W Ellis, *The Practical Farmer, or, the Hertfordshire Husbandman* (1732), p179.
[193] Norfolk Record Office: BRA 926 122.
[194] Norfolk Record Office: PD 332/20.

INTRODUCTION

In 1812 Wilshere noted that Sir John Sebright of Beechwood was to 'direct his Gardener to send grafts of all the best sorts'. But these were not of local types, specific to the Chilterns around Flamstead, but new varieties recently developed by the horticulturalist Thomas Andrew Knight.

The subsequent development of varieties, after Wilshere's time, does not really concern us here but essentially falls into two further phases. Firstly, in the middle decades of the nineteenth century the old 'generic' types fell from favour, forming a smaller and smaller proportion of the trees recorded in orchard lists. In 1851 the pomologist Robert Hogg described how 'the Golden Pippin, and all the old varieties of English apple' had been 'allowed to disappear from our orchards' because they were 'not worth perpetuating, and their places supplied by others infinitely superior'.[195] Next, in the second half of the nineteenth century and the first decades of the twentieth, large commercial companies like River's, Mackie's, Lane's of Berkhamsted or Bunyards of Kent, their geographical reach extended by the spread of the rail network, competed vigorously for custom by expanding their offering with enticing novelties. Lane's catalogue for 1862 already included no less than 100 varieties of apple;[196] Daniels of Norwich were advertising 128 by 1878;[197] Rivers were supplying 113 in 1861, but this had risen to 132 by 1870 and to no less than 161 by 1914.[198] A flood of new varieties was developed to meet this demand, and it is this legacy of Victorian and Edwardian horticultural ingenuity that accounts for the overwhelming majority of 'heritage' fruit found in old orchards today, the oldest trees in which were generally planted around 1900.

The orchard and garden trees listed by Wilshere represent a large sample from what we have here characterised, in rather a bald and simplified account, as the second phase in the development of fruit varieties, embracing the later eighteenth and earlier nineteenth centuries. The names of his apples do not include many that are unusual or otherwise unparalleled, and thus suggestive of very local 'varieties'. Only five are hard to identify - the 'Bedford Seedling' (possibly a synonym for the old variety called 'Bedfordshire Foundling'), the 'Cheshire', the 'Northampton Creeper', the 'Duncan Apple' and the 'Peter Russet' - and the names of the first, second and third of these certainly preclude

---

[195] R Hogg, *British Pomology* (1851), p97.
[196] Lane's Fruit catalogue [Dacorum Heritage Centre, Berkhamsted, no catalogue number].
[197] Daniel Brothers, *The Illustrated Guide for Amateur Gardeners* (Norwich, 1878); consulted at Gressenhall Rural Life Museum, Norfolk.
[198] Rivers Fruit Catalogue [John Innes Library, Norwich].

a local origin. In a few cases, as with the 'Red Apple', Wilshere was clearly uncertain of the variety. Over half of the apples are the kind of widely-planted types found throughout England in the eighteenth and, in many cases, the seventeenth century: Hollow Crown Pippin ('a very good baking apple in November'), Lemon Pippin, Nonpareil and Russet Nonpareil, French Pippin and French Golden Pippin, Spice Russet, Margil, Catshead (also referred to by its other name, Tankard), Nonsuch, Royal Russet, Holland Pippin, Golden Pippin (as well as 'true' Golden Pippin), Golden Reinette, King of the Pippins, Monstrous Reinette, Winter Pearmain, Winter Pippin and 'Codlin'.[199] Space precludes a discussion of the uses and properties of these various apples, evidently a mixture of dessert and culinary varieties, but we might note that the Catshead, probably a general term for a large, oblong-conical cooking apple, while grown throughout England was particularly popular in Hertfordshire. William Ellis described in his *Modern Husbandman* of 1744 how it was 'a very useful apple to the farmer, because one of them pared and wrapped up in dough, serves with little trouble for making an apple-dumpling', for which purpose 'it has now got into such reputation in Hertfordshire … that it is become the most common food with a piece of bacon or pickle-pork for families'.[200]

A third of the varieties listed were either ones traditionally associated with other parts of Britain, or which had recently been developed there, but which were now marketed nationally: Hawthornden ('Hawthorndeaning', Midlothian, *c*1780), Ribston Pippin (Yorkshire, 1707), Downton Pippin (Shropshire, 1806), Kentish Fill Basket (Kent, 1782), Keswick Codling (Lancashire, 1793). The 'Whirle' is the Whorle, a Scottish variety probably developed in the eighteenth century, while the 'Minshaw Crab' is presumably the Minshull Crab, a late-season cooking apple that arose in the Cheshire village of that name, likewise in the eighteenth century. The Norfolk Buffon is the Norfolk Beefing, a culinary variety traditional in that county since at least the seventeenth century; the Oslin a Scottish apple of uncertain date first described in 1815. Two of the varieties listed had more distant origins. The New Town Pippin arose in New York in the 1750s, while 'Gilpin's Pippin' is probably the Gilpin apple, widely grown in North America in the nineteenth century.[201]

---

[199] Barnes and Williamson, *English Orchards*, pp176-8.
[200] W Ellis, *The Modern Husbandman or, the Practice of Farming* (1744), p139.
[201] For all of these identifications, see Morgan and Richards, *New Book of Apples*; and the website FruitID: https://www.fruitid.com/#main.

INTRODUCTION

It is easy to assume that the apples itemised in old lists, with their quaint and often unfamiliar names, were local and 'traditional' in character, specific to particular areas, an aspect of regional cultures. In the early eighteenth century this had been true, up to a point, although even then many apple trees came from commercial nurseries, rather than being obtained from friends and neighbours, and many types of apple appear, with monotonous regularity, in lists from throughout England. By Wilshere's time the steady growth in the number, and size, of nursery businesses had largely displaced very local varieties, leading to greater homogeneity, especially in the south and east of the country. The apples he lists are all essentially national rather than specifically local varieties, even if they had once been associated with particular localities. They were the products of a commercial nursery industry, even if some of the individual specimens had been obtained from friends or neighbours.

The development of apple varieties has received a fair amount of attention over the last few decades, but much remains unclear or debated, ensuring that Wilshere's memorandum books represent an important source. The history of other types of fruit has been less intensively studied and here the information provided by the books, especially concerning pear varieties, may prove useful to researchers, although fewer varieties of pears are listed and mostly ones – Swan's Egg, Buerre, Burgamot – which commonly appear in eighteenth- and early nineteenth-century lists.

The Nursery

Wilshere's memorandum books contain numerous references to his tree and shrub nursery. This was perhaps primarily intended to serve the needs of his own properties in Hitchin, Great Wymondley and Shillington, but it also provided substantial numbers of plants which were sold to others. The later eighteenth and nineteenth centuries saw an escalating demand for trees and shrubs throughout England. The area under woodland increased significantly, as landowners established new plantations on their estates for beauty, for profit and as game cover.[202] Thousands of kilometres of new hedge were planted, as open fields and commons were enclosed. In addition, vast numbers of specimen trees were required for new landscape parks, and ornamental shrubs for the pleasure grounds of the gentry and the gardens of the middle class, whose wealth and numbers were expanding steadily at this time. Research by a number of

---

[202] G Barnes and T Williamson, *Trees in England: Management and Disease Since 1600* (Hatfield, 2017), pp146-50; C Watkins, *Trees, Woods and Forests: a Social and Cultural History* (2014).

INTRODUCTION

individuals, most notably John Harvey, has thrown important light on the larger nursery companies which supplied these markets, those which produced printed catalogues and whose names appear frequently in the accounts preserved in the archives of landed estates; both the major London-based firms like Lee and Kennedy of Hammersmith, and the larger provincial concerns like Rivers of Sawbridgeworth.[203] But there were, in addition, a host of smaller commercial nurseries, often run by individuals who principally made their living in other ways, as gardeners, land surveyors or farmers; while the private nurseries maintained by large landed estates sometimes sold superfluous stock on a commercial basis. Wilshere's nursery activities appear to fall somewhere between these two categories.

We have already noted how the earliest map of Wilshere's lands in Hitchin, undated but drawn up some time between 1801 and 1807, describes an area of over 1.75 acres (0.7 hectares) on Walsworth Road, bounded by hedges, as 'Lodge and Nursery'; and how the second estate map of 1818 describes this same area as 'kitchen garden'. The function of this piece of land had evidently changed although not entirely. Young trees still seem to have been grown here, although perhaps on a reduced scale. This said, even in 1822 Wilshere was able to despatch no less than 20,000 'quicks' – hedging thorns, either hawthorn, blackthorn or a mixture of the two – to the Wrest Park estate in Bedfordshire, together with 1,000 oak, 1,000 larch and over 1,000 other trees, accompanied by a further 10,000 quick for Thomas Dimsdale, presumably destined for his properties at Willian. The largest commercial order recorded in the memorandum books, however, came in 1811, when the owners of Colworth House and Oakley Lodge in Bedfordshire were jointly provided, via the nurseryman Henry Hodgson, with 4,000 spruce, 1,000 Scots pine, 100 larch, 290 other trees and a variety of ornamental shrubs. Only one other sale is clearly recorded - in 1815, 550 trees and 180 ornamental shrubs were supplied to Baron Dimsdale's agent, partly destined for Lady Lucas at Wrest Park and partly for Dimsdale, probably for planting on his Willian estate – although there are hints of others.

---

[203] Harvey, *Early Nurserymen;* L Crawley, 'The Growth of Provincial Nurseries: Norwich Nurserymen, *c*1750-1860', *Garden History* 48, 2 (2020), pp119-34; L J Drake, *Wood & Ingram: Huntingdon Nursery: 1742–1950* (Cambridge, 2008); E Waugh, *Rivers Nursery of Sawbridgeworth: the Art of Pomology* (Ware, 2009); and E Waugh, Planting the Garden: the Nursery Trade in Hertfordshire in D Spring (ed), *Hertfordshire Garden History Vol 2: Gardens Pleasant, Groves Delicious* (Hatfield, 2012), pp177–201.

INTRODUCTION

Many, possibly the majority, of the plants grown in the nursery were thus used by Wilshere himself. In 1811, following the enclosure award for Wymondley, he sent 41,000 'quicks' from the nursery to hedge his new allotments there, with another 14,000 despatched the following year, although it is noteworthy that he was also obliged to source a further 92,000 from local nurserymen, mainly for hedging in that parish (the 'quick' used to plant new hedges on his Hitchin farm in 1809 also seems to have been purchased). Agricultural hedges at this time were usually planted with trees, both as timber and as pollards, and in 1815 the nursery provided '200 elms & 100 oak for the hedges in Rawlins'. Oak and elm, followed by ash, were the trees most commonly found in Hertfordshire hedges at this time.[204] The oaks and elms sent to Shillington in 1817 were also probably for hedgerow planting but were here augmented with smaller numbers of 'poplars'. Other trees were used in the small plantations that Wilshere established on his Wymondley lands, while larch, Scots pine, spruce and hedging thorn were sent to the Frythe, Wilshere's Welwyn property. In addition, apple trees and in one case filberts were provided for orchards he owned.

The most numerous trees by far grown in, and sent from, the nursery were fast-growing conifers - larch, spruce and Scots pine. Some plantations, and parkland clumps, were planted entirely with conifers in this period but this was fairly rare, in southern England at least. More usually, conifers were planted with deciduous trees, to act as their 'nurses', that is, to provide shelter and encourage straight, upward growth.[205] They usually outnumbered the 'forest' trees by some considerable margin and were thinned in stages, providing a regular supply of 'poles' which could be used for fencing, the construction or repair of farm buildings, and a host of other things. Eventually, in most cases, only the deciduous trees remained, which after further thinning might be felled for timber, or left to adorn the landscape and – perhaps now underplanted with shrubs like snowberry or rhododendron – provide game cover. The initial plantings were much denser than would be made today, with the trees spaced at intervals of a metre or less. This was in part because, in the absence of effective fencing, significant losses were expected from the depredations of hares and other wildlife, and in part because without chemical herbicides the dense shade produced by the tightly packed trees was the best way of controlling the growth of weeds. Young woods of this kind also afforded excellent cover for pheasants.

---

[204] Barnes and Williamson, *Trees in England*, pp101-107.
[205] J Brown, *The Forester* (1847).

INTRODUCTION

This approach to forestry required very large numbers of conifers, something clearly reflected in the quantities growing in Wilshere's nursery.

All this said, certain entries in the memorandum books seem to suggest that some of Wilshere's own plantations, in Wymondley, were entirely deciduous in character, while others were entirely coniferous. The 'minutes for planting at Wymondley' in 1819 record the establishment of only Scots pine, spruce and larch in Home Plantation, only 'fir' and larch in Furze Plantation, and black poplars alone in Willow Plantation, while in Hanging Plantation, Hill Plantation and Spring Grove oak, ash and elm were the only trees listed. But we need to treat this evidence with caution. Although these were all, to judge from later map evidence, relatively small woods, covering between 1 and 3 hectares, they would nevertheless have each required several thousand young trees. The trees listed in the 'minute' - ranging in number from 100 to 500 – thus represent only a fraction of the total planting, the rest of which is unrecorded, or not clearly recorded, in our source. More informative is the list of trees planted 'in that part of the Wymondley field which was called the Litler common' in 1812. In February this was planted with 150 larch, together with no less than 1,230 deciduous trees (620 oak, 300 ash, 200 poplar and small numbers of chestnut, birch and willow). But in March these were augmented with 30 more oaks, 30 willow sets and 'about 3,000 cuttings of sallow from Shitlington', evidently taking on the role of 'nurses' on a damp site where conifers were likely to fail – a not unusual practice in such circumstances. As noted earlier, some of the trees planted by Wilshere, or their descendants, may still survive in woodland in Wymondley and the presence of large numbers of willows, alongside black poplar, in what was originally Willow Plantation suggests that a similar scheme of planting was adopted here, but that only a limited amount of thinning was ever undertaken.

The most numerous deciduous trees grown and supplied by Wilshere were the two most widely planted in contemporary plantations and parks: oak, the main constructional timber and in high demand for ship building; and elm, the main source of high quality boards and planks. There are fewer references to ash and only one to maple. Other trees grown in rather small quantities were more ornamental in character, including American oak, lime, plane, oriental plane, beech, locust tree (*Robinia pseudoacacia*), Balm of Gilead fir, Weymouth pine, horse chestnut and 'spanish' (sweet) chestnut, sugar maple, weeping birch, hickory and cypress. The hornbeams included in the order for Colworth House and Oakley Lodge in 1811 may have been for garden hedging. The precise identity of some of these trees is uncertain, due to changes in (and contemporary

INTRODUCTION

looseness of) botanical nomenclature. Wilshere's 'American oak', for example, while probably what we now term scarlet oak (*Quercus coccinea*), could have been one of a number of species of *Quercus* introduced from the later seventeenth century from the eastern seabord of north America; his 'hickory' may be the bitternut (*Carya ordiformis*); while the term 'Balm of Gilead fir' did not necessary mean, as it did by the later nineteenth century, the balsam fir, *Abies balsamea*, but was sometimes more generally applied to silver firs (genus *Abies*). Overall, however, the trees grown in the nursery all appear to be native species or ones introduced before the middle of the eighteenth century, and all are familiar from texts published many decades earlier, such as James Gordon's *Planters, Florists and Gardeners Dictionary* of 1774.[206] Wilshere was not running a specialist nursery, dealing in novelties and rarities.

There is also some uncertainty concerning the species of poplar trees that Wilshere grew and supplied, the memorandum books referring to 'poplar', 'white poplar', 'black poplar' and 'abele'. Black poplar (*Populus nigra*) is a fast-growing tree of the working countryside rather than of gardens and parks, its wood valued for its mildly fire-resistant qualities which made it ideal for making doors in industrial premises like mills, or the floors of malthouses (which probably explains why Wilshere planted so many on his own lands).[207] Abele is an alternative name for the white poplar (*Populus alba*) but the memorandum books refer to the supply of both in a single order, in 1811, for Colworth House and Oakley Lodge. While white poplar was, like black poplar, essentially a tree of the countryside, it was sometimes used as structural planting in eighteenth- and nineteenth-century pleasure grounds, placed in such a way that its light foliage contrasted with the darker hues of plants like yew, as recommended by Thomas Whately in his *Observations on Modern Gardening* of 1770.[208] But why both names are used in the same order remains unclear. Equally uncertain is what Wilshere meant when he simply used the word 'poplar'. It is possible that on some occasions he was referring to the Lombardy poplar (*Populus nigra* Italica). Introduced in 1758, this rapidly became so popular that its familiar narrow profile appears in some numbers in Constable's

---

[206] M Campbell-Colver, *The Origins of Plants* (2001); A Mitchell, *Trees of Britain and Northern Europe* (1978); J Gordon, *Planters, Florists and Gardeners Dictionary* (1774).
[207] F Cooper, *The Black Poplar: History, Ecology and Conservation* (Oxford, 2006); G Barnes, P Dallas and T Williamson, 'The Black Poplar in Norfolk', *Quarterly Journal of Forestry* 103 (2009), pp31–8.
[208] T Whately, *Observations on Modern Gardening* (1770), pp25-35.

INTRODUCTION

paintings of the countryside around the Suffolk/Essex borders, made in the first two decades of the nineteenth century.[209]

The ornamental shrubs grown and supplied by Wilshere, like the trees, were typical of the period. Almost all had been used in English gardens, in a variety of ways, since at least the seventeenth century – laurel, lilac, Persian lilac, 'syringia' (philadelphus), laurestinus (*Viburnum tinus*), rose, honeysuckle, box, laburnum and rosemary.[210] But the 'Chinese roses' referred to in 1811 were presumably the China rose (*Rosa chinensis*), introduced in the second half of the eighteenth century, which gave rise through hybridisation with European roses to a range of repeat-flowering varieties. It is unclear whether the various trees and shrubs in the nursery were all grown from seed or layers by Wilshere himself (rather than being bought in as seedlings) but some evidently were, to judge from references in the 'Journal' to sowing acorns in drills (March 1814) and to planting 'fir seedlings' (February 1815). Young trees were planted out in the nursery ground when they were a foot or two in height (slightly larger in the case of poplar and lime) and despatched for sale when they were between 3 and 6 feet high, although trees for Wilshere's own use were sometimes smaller than this when sent for planting, as in general were elms.

Scots pine, larch and spruce were sold for around 6 shillings per hundred and 'quicks' for 8 shillings per thousand. In contrast, the '100 Chinese roses ½ potted' sent in 1811 were priced at £5. It is impossible to know how much money Wilshere made from his nursery as it is clear that we are only presented with a partial picture of his activities but the trees and shrubs sent to Wrest Park in 1822 brought in £20, equivalent to roughly £1,000 in modern money, while those sold to Colworth House and Oakley Lodge in 1811 brought in £51 4s 10d. The primary function of the nursery was probably to service Wilshere's own need for plants. It failed to entirely achieve this end – not only garden shrubs but also hedging plants and forest trees sometimes needed to be sourced from elsewhere. But on the other hand, it served as an additional if relatively minor income stream in Wilshere's complex portfolio of businesses.

Conclusion
What began as a brief essay, intended to place Wilshere in a wider historical context and to show some of the potential uses of the documents here transcribed, has grown – inexorably and unintentionally – into a more extended

---

[209] Mitchell, *Trees*, pp183-4; Barnes and Williamson, *Trees in England*, pp144-5.
[210] Laird, *Flowering of the Landscape Garden*.

INTRODUCTION

discussion. In part this simply reflects the inherent interest of the material, but in part it is a consequence of the complex character of Wilshere's activities, which also, as we emphasised at the outset, extended far beyond the essentially agricultural and horticultural matters recorded in the memorandum books. In many ways, not least in his apparently boundless energy, Wilshere was an atypical figure. Yet the memorandum books and associated documents nevertheless cast important light on more widely shared, more commonplace aspects of farming and gardening in the early nineteenth century, ones that most other sources describe only partially, or ignore altogether.

How this book came about

William Wilshere's farm and garden memoranda books, plus two small note books started by his gardener James Bowie, form part of the Wilshere Collection in Hertfordshire Archives and Local Studies. I came across them seven years ago when, as part of the Research Group of the Hertfordshire Gardens Trust, I was investigating the gardens of The Hermitage in Hitchin, which was William Wilshere's home for almost 40 years. Initially I was only interested in the garden content of the memoranda books. However in 2018 Professor Tom Williamson approached the Research Group to ask for assistance with the Orchards East Project based at the University of East Anglia. In response I sent him a copy of William Wilshere's 1811 inspection of fruit trees and estimates of his annual yields of apples and pears. This led to my transcribing in full the first few pages of the farm and garden memoranda books. Tom recognised their wider significance and drew up a proposal for their publication by the Hertfordshire Record Society.

INTRODUCTION

Acknowledgements

My thanks are due first and foremost to Tom Williamson for his unfailing support and encouragement and for contributing an introductory essay placing Wilshere's agricultural and horticultural activities in their broader context; Tom's expertise also provided additional footnotes to the transcripts. I must thank too Anne Rowe and the members of the Hertfordshire Gardens Trust Research Group for their advice and interest throughout this project. In addition the help and experience of Susan Flood, General Editor of the Hertfordshire Record Society, was central to the preparation of the book for publication. I must thank the staff of Hertfordshire Archives and Local Studies for their help always willingly given over many years. I am most grateful to Alan Fleck and to the staff of North Hertfordshire Museum, Hitchin; extracts from William Wilshere's Commonplace Book in the possession of the museum have been transcribed as Appendix 1. Gillian Hannington and Richard Luscombe have kindly provided key information about Daniel McIntosh's employment at Wrest Park for which I am most grateful. Sigi Howes and Terry Ransome, through the Friends of the British Schools Museum, Hitchin, have provided details of James Bowie's career in South Africa. Dr Susan Walker has enhanced my knowledge of later members of the Wilshere family. I owe thanks to my husband, David, for his advice and patience throughout. Finally I must record gratitude for the informal discussion with many local historians and others during the project and, of course, note that responsibility for any errors or omissions rests with me.

Bridget Howlett, Hitchin, June 2023

INTRODUCTION

Editorial method – Wilshere Farm and Garden Memoranda

- Abbreviations for ing [g], about (abt), adjoining (adjg), between (bet.), continued (contd), ditto (do), estimated (estd), page (pa, pg), part (pt), per (pr), remained (remd), remainder (remr), remaining (remg), together (togr), vide (v) which (wch), yard (yd), names such as Edward, George, Michael and William, and points of the compass have been silently extended.
- Where they appear in body of a memorandum, the names of the months and abbreviations for measures such as acre (a), rood (r), peck (p), bushel (B or b), load (L or Ld), and qtr (quarter) have been silently extended, but when they appear in a table, the original abbreviations have been retained.
- Spelling (including inconsistencies such as in the number of 'l's in mangel wurzel) is as in the original.
- Punctuation and capitalisation have been modernised to assist ease of reading.
- William Wilshere added later comments using red ink. These are in bold.
- Round brackets are as used in the original; square brackets indicate words or letters inserted by the editor.
- Editorial notes are given in Italic text within round brackets.
- A question mark before a word signifies the most likely reading of that word.
- Pages 1-20 of the first memoranda book 61181 are numbered and all the pages of the second memoranda book 61182 are numbered except the last few pages. The page numbers are given on the right hand side in square brackets as Wilshere refers to particular pages in his note books. Numbers have been assigned to the unnumbered pages in both memoranda books.
- William Wilshere uses the initials TW to refer to his brother, Thomas Wilshere. This usage has been retained.
- Money: twelve old pennies (12d) = one shilling (1s); twenty shillings = one pound (£1); one guinea = £1 1s 0d. One shilling equates to five new pence (5p). £, s and d symbols have been added on occasion for the sake of clarity.
- Where sums of money are expressed in the form 12/6 or 5/- this has been changed to the equivalent of 12s 6d and 5s.

INTRODUCTION

Abbreviations used in the text and footnotes

BLARS	Bedfordshire and Luton Archives and Records Service
HALS	Hertfordshire Archives and Local Studies
HRS	Hertfordshire Record Society
HUDC	Hitchin Urban District Council
LMA	London Metropolitan Archives
NHM	North Hertfordshire Museum
ODNB	*Oxford Dictionary of National Biography* (online edition)
TNA	The National Archives
VCH	*Victoria County History* followed by county
TW	Thomas Wilshere, William Wilshere's brother

Weights and Measures

Area
40 poles or perches (p) = 1 rood (r)
4 roods = 1 acre (a) (0.405 hectares)

Linear
12 inches (ins) = 1 foot (ft) (30.48 cms)
3 feet = 1 yard
22 yards = 1 chain
10 chains (220 yards) = 1 furlong
8 furlongs (1760 yards) = 1 mile (1,608.8 metres)

Volume
Wheat
4 pecks (p) = 1 bushel (B) (36.32 litres)
5 bushels = 1 load (Lo)

Barley, Malt and Oats
4 pecks = 1 bushel (B) (36.32 litres)
8 bushels = 1 quarter (qu)

Liquid
2 pints = 1 quart (qu)
4 quarts (8 pints) = 1 gallon (4.54 litres)

54 gallons of beer = 1 hogshead

Weight (Avoirdupois)
16 ounces (oz) = 1 pound (lb) (0.55 kgs)
14 pounds = 1 stone (st)
2 stones (28 pounds) = 1 quarter
4 quarters (112 pounds) = 1 hundredweight (cwt)
20 hundredweight = 1 ton (1232 kgs)

Weight (Troy Weight)
24 grains = 1 pennyweight (dwt)
12 pennyweights = 1 Troy ounce
20 Troy ounces = 1 Troy pound

WILLIAM WILSHERE'S
HITCHIN FARM AND GARDEN,
1809-1824

Farm and Garden Memoranda: list of farming stock 1 October 1809 (*HALS: 61181*).

NO 1 FARMING & GARDENING MEM[ORAN]D[U]MS FROM 1ST OCTOBER 1809 TO 1 OCTOBER 1817 [HALS 61181]

(*Note inside cover*) Garden pots. Banks, Hale Weston near Cross Hall, recommended by Grant, Southill, particularly his blanching pans which are a sort of bells of pottery in the form of small bell glasses.[1]

Farming Stock 1 October 1809 [p1]

	£	s	d
3 horses	50		
3 cows	30		
A weaned calf	3		
A fatting calf	4		
14 hogs & pigs (i.e. 1 boar, 2 sows, 11 pigs)[2]	20		
3 carts	30		
3 ploughs, 3 harrows, drill[3] & hoe	10		
Harness	5		
Various implements barn tackle etc	5		
Poultry - 24 old fowls at the farm and 12 at Abbis's[4],40 young fowls & chickens, 4 old turkies, 14 young, 5 old Guinea fowls, 4 young, 6 ducks	8	-	-
10 sacks	1	-	-
3 doz[e]n hurdles & a doz[en] of timber	1	10	-
	167	10	-
Cottage furniture not valued.[5]			

---

[1] Hail Weston is about 7 miles south of Huntingdon. Cross Hall or Crosshall was north west of St Neots on the Great North Road at the junction with a road to Hail Weston. Joseph Banks, farmer of Hail Weston, made his will in 1832 [TNA: PROB11/2003/32]. James Grant was Samuel Whitbread's gardener at Southill in Bedfordshire. See Biographical Notes.

[2] A boar was a male pig, sows female, 'pigs' were the young.

[3] Arthur Young in 1804 commented that seed drills were little used in Hertfordshire [Young, *General View,* pp126-132]. Wilshere kept one but seems to have used it mainly on his intensively-cultivated plots in Great Wimbush, although in 1820 he also hired the use of one to sow much of his turnip crop. Most of his crops were sown broadcast or 'dibbled', i.e. with individual seeds dropped into holes made with a stick.

[4] James Abbiss was one of William Wilshere's farming men who lived in the ornamental cottage in his kitchen garden. See Biographical Notes.

Farming Stock 1 October 1809 continued [p2]

		£		
B[rough]t over		£167	10	0
9 loads meadow hay 1809 at £5 10s		49	10	0
10 loads 1809 at £5		50	0	0
First & second crop of 5½ clover 1809		26	0	0
Wheat 1a Wimbush say 4 loads at 60s[6] **See [page] 5**	12 – 0 - 0			
3½ White Joan Biggs Grave[7] say 14 loads at 60s **See [page] 20**	42 - 0 - 0			
6a on the hill 21 loads at 55s[8]	57 – 15 - 0			
		111	14	0
Barley 6½ Brown[9] [Close] 35 qu at 45s	78 - 15			
Benslow Hill 8½[10] say 40 qu at 45s	90			
		168	15	0
Buck Wheat ½ acre & 1 rood sown & at say 18 bushels at 6s		5	8	0
Beans 2½ Starlings Br[idge] say 10 loads at 30s **See page 16**		15	0	0
Peas same field 2½ say 12 loads 35s		21	0	0
Haulm[11] of 10 acres		2	10	0
12 bushels Swedish turnip seed **Upon measuring it now found only 11½ bushels.**		24	0	0
Turnips				
2 acres next Dimsey Sw[edish][12]	12 – 0 - 0			

[5] This was probably the farm bailiff's cottage. For valuation of furniture in 1818 see p113.

[6] When used by Wilshere as a measurement of volume, a 'load' was equivalent to 5 bushels (726 litres). But in some cases, as when discussing meadow hay, he may be using the word in a looser, literal sense, to mean a cart fully loaded.

[7] Joan Biggs' or Briggs' Grave was at the junction of Walsworth Road and Benslow Lane. Who Joan Biggs or Briggs was and why or when she was buried there is unknown. Her grave had become a local landmark by 1676 [Howlett, *Survey of the Royal Manor of Hitchin 1676* (Hertford, 2000) pp5, 20, 95]. Joan Biggs' Close became part of Lower Benslow Hill.

[8] Part of Little Benslow Hill.

[9] One of the fields rented by Wilshere from Thomas Brown. See Biographical Notes.

[10] This was the north side of Great Benslow Hill.

[11] In June 1819 Wilshere paid £2 for haulm for thatching [HALS: 61529 p28].

2 acres Little Wimbush	10 – 0 - 0			
4 acres Pierson's[13]	20 – 0 - 0			
4 acres Waby[14]	10 – 0 - 0			
8½ Benslow Hill[15]	10 – 0 - 0			
1½ Wimbush Sw[edish]	12 – 0 - 0	74	0	0
Wimbush 1½ cabb[age]s £12.10.0, ½ acre beet 2.10.0, 1 acre pot[atoe]s £15, ½ acre carrots £8-0-0		38	0	0
		752	8	0

1809 October 7 Potatoes[16] [p3]

Took up about two thirds of the acre which produced 149 bushels
That is of

The Callico potato	100
Another sort of ditto	15
Old Redrup	15
Mr Maughan's [17]	3
Blood Royal }	
?Pear Cheshire}	2
Another sort of ditto	3
Black Morocco	4
Redfone or yam	1
	143
Taken up before for use	6
	149

Took up the remaining ⅓ of the acre –
which was of the sort called Golden
Drop. Produce   90
                        239

---

[12] Wilshere obtained by exchange an acre of land above the Dell from William Dimsey in 1802. See Biographical Notes. The turnips were planted on Paternoster's Garden.
[13] Pierson's Piece was later called Walsworth Way Close. It was also known as Rail Piece or Stone Piece. Wilshere bought this from Joseph Margetts Pierson in 1810. See Biographical Notes.
[14] This was the Four Acres next Wymondley Road which Wilshere rented from Edward Waby of Stevenage, cousin of Edward Waby (d 1808), a butcher of Hitchin.
[15] This was the south side of Great Benslow Hill.
[16] On 11 October 1809 William Watson was paid £1 10s 4d for beer, inning beans and getting up potatoes [HALS: 61502 p2].
[17] See Biographical Notes for John Maughan.

The quantities stored in the pit are

Callico	50
Golden Drop	80
	130

Carrots 1809 October 12, 13, 14 [p4]

Took up (with forks) half an acre of carrots, employed 2 men & 2 women 3 days.

Produce – 28 bushels as measured by them in baskets.

I found the basket to contain about 80 carrots in number & to weigh about 37lbs. I think that the bushel should weigh at least 40lbs. Thus taken the produce may be considered as 194 bushels on the half acre. The produce is at the rate of about 7 tons per acre.

Mowbray states the proper weight of a bushel of carrots be from 42 to 43 lbs. The wholesale price is now 1s 3d per bushel.[18]

1809 October 14 Wheat [p5]

An acre of wheat sown in Wimbush Field after potatoes produced this year about 20 bushels

Sold October to Ransom at 70s per load & 1 bushel off[al] corn.[19]

This is much the shortest crop I have had after potatoes.

29 & 31 July. It was cut at least a week before any other wheat in the neighbourhood & was considered as very green but the grain is full & not more than one bushel of off[al] corn dressed out of it.

White wheat 3½ [acres] Biggs Grave laid the south end of Wheat Barn, the six acre at the north end.

1809 October Barley [p6]

The produce of Brown's [Close] 6½ acres laid in the west end of Kershaw's Barn.[20]

2 bushels thrashed for fowls 9 October.

Bushel thrashed of which 2 bushels ground for pigs & fowls.

3 November 3½ [bushels] thrashed from the cuttings of this piece.

---

[18] William Mowbray was a Hitchin gardener. See Biographical Notes.

[19] John Ransom of Hitchin, a Quaker farmer and miller. See Biographical Notes.

[20] In 1816 Maria Kershaw occupied part of the large timber framed house owned by Wilshere on the corner of Back Street and Portmill Lane. One of Wilshere's two farmyards was immediately behind this house next to Portmill Lane [NHM: map of Hitchin 1816].

The produce of 8½ the North Side of Benslow Hill laid in the east end of Kershaw's Barn.
3 November 3½ thrashed from the cuttings of this piece.
November 30 began thrashing the remainder of the barley from Brown's Close.

Buck Wheat
The produce of half an acre in Wimbush Field sown in June after tares thrashed 15 October produced 15 bushels.
Another rood sown in July after tares did not ripen sufficiently before the frost came. It was inned October & produced 5 bushels.

Orchard Fruit 1809 very defective [p7]

	Bushels	Pecks
Codlins	3	
Catsheads	2	
Nonpareils	1	2
Golden Pippin old	-	3
Golden Pippin new	-	3
Other apples	1	_
Total bushels	9	

Pears	Bushels	Pecks
Swans Eggs	5	2
Chaumantelle	5	2
Buere	-	1
Burgamot	-	1
baking pears	=	2
Bushels	12	

About 50 quinces.

Garden – Nursery 16 October 1809 [p8]
Mowbray states the larches in the plantation to be worth for sale between 65s to 70 shillings per hundred.

Fencing Joan Briggs' Slipe see [page] 17   **[p9]**
18 October 1809
Twydell Dear states the length of fencing to be nearly 12 chains.[21]

That the labour & nails for a single fence with ditch will be per chain	0	4	6
Posts & stakes	0	5	0
Old rails will be worth per chain 21 rails	0	10	6
Per chain	1	0	0

November 1809 take up and bring home fence set down at Holwell in 1803 – to l[an]d exch[ange]d to Sir F. Willes.[22]
32 chains (about ¹⁄₁₀ taken) & 20 lengths left to mind before plants are ?grown.

>   Useful rails 1100 at 3d, posts 220 at 3d   £11
>   Firewood 2 stacks   £ 2 - 10

15 October 1809   **[p10]**
James Robinson came into my service today as farming man to live in the farm cottage, to go with the horses & with his wife to milk & take care of the cows, pigs & poultry. Wages 12s per week with the usual addition in harvest.[23]

Canary Seed 3 November 1809   **[p11]**
In April 1809 I sowed a small patch of ground with the Canary grass 38 feet by 38 feet amounting to one fortieth part of an acre. It was now thrashed out & produced 1½ pecks being at the rate of 15 bushels per acre. I was told in the Isle of Thanet where this seed is cultivated to a considerable extent that they expect from 20 to 25 bushels per acre and that is worth in price from £3 to £10 per quarter.

---

[21] Twydell Dear was a carpenter. See Biographical Notes. Joan Briggs' or Biggs' Slipe was probably Fells Garden which was incorporated into Waby's Field.
[22] Sir Francis Willes, a government code breaker, who in 1783 bought a substantial estate in Hitchin from Thomas Plumer Byde of Ware Park. He built himself a house called St Ibbs Bush in St Ippollitts. In 1808 he exchanged 22½ acres of land in the parish of Holwell, Bedfordshire, with Wilshere for land near his house. This was Wimbush Field and the adjoining piece containing 12 acres 2 roods. See Biographical Notes.
[23].See Biographical Notes.

Wheat sowing 1809 [p12]

Wrenn's illness & death prevented my sowing wheat early.[24] I then stopped on account of the dryness of the weather, but at length tired of waiting for rain, I began 23rd October & finished 4 November in the following order:
The clover beyond Joan Biggs' Grave south of Benslow Hill road 3 acres was sown with 9 bushels of white wheat **2 acres 3 roods.** [25]
The 3 pieces in Nettledale (clover ley) with 6 bushels of white & 2 of red **2 acres 2 roods.** [26]
Two closes on Benslow Hill (barley stubble) late my brother Thomas' s[owe]d with 9 bushels of burwell **3 acres 1 rood**[27]
An acre in Wimbush after potatoes, half drilled, half broadcast, with three bushels of the same **1 acre.**
I had all the above wheat of Mr Ransom 5 loads 4 bushels £21 – 16 – 3.[28]

Cattle Cabbage [p13]

Sown in August about 2lb of seed.
The last week in October about 10,000 planted out in the asparagus beds - & on the 1st & 2nd November about 6000 in the Nursery part of Wimbush Field.

Beet

A rood (sown for mangel wurzel) began 12 October ended 2nd November keeping 3 cows & principally 13 pigs 3 weeks.

2nd November began an acre of cattle cabbage which was sown in August 1808 & planted out to stand in May last.

Cranberries - or whortle berries [p14]

The plants are to be had at Lee & Kennedy's (Mrs Cuyler).[29] May be sown. The American is the largest but those of England the best.

---

[24] For William Wrenn or Wren see Biographical Notes.
[25] This became part of Waby's Field.
[26] In 1816 Nettledell was divided into seven strips most of which were about an acre. Wilshere then owned and occupied two non contiguous strips about 2½ acres in area, presumably having combined two of the strips. By 1819 he had acquired the whole 10½ acres and enclosed it as one field.
[27] Part of the Slipes above Benslow Hill.
[28] On 24 Nov 1809 Wilshere paid John Ransom £21 16s 3d for seed wheat [HALS: 61502 p14].
[29] Mrs Ann Cuyler was the wife of General Cornelius Cuyler, an American who fought in the British Army and came to live at St John's Lodge (later renamed Danesbury) in

They should be stewed before they are put in a tart.

Beans

In Young's Agricultural Survey of Oxfordshire (page 160) he on the authority of Mr James Welch of Culham to dung for beans to be followed by wheat – that they be cluster planted, that is that 3, 4 or 5 be put in a hole 9 inches asunder, the rows 18 inches apart – this is stated to be much better than planting single beans - it gives good room for the stroke of a hoe between the clusters - hoes twice or thrice.[30]

Carrots (8 November 1809)   [p15]

Mr Whitbread's Bailiff has put up some highland Scotch beasts on carrots.[31] They are small, will not come to much more than 60 stones. They eat each 3 bushels per day of carrots & a small quantity of hay.

	£ - s - d
They were bought in at ?bush fair [32]	
November 1808 at	6 - 6 - 0
11 months on grass at 10s per month	5 – 10 - 0
Say one month on carrots & hay	5 - 0 - 0
	16 – 16 - 0

This is more than they will produce.

Welcome. He was created a baronet in 1814 [W Branch Johnson, *Welwyn By and Large. Historical Gossip from a Hertfordshire Village* (Welwyn, 1967) pp60-61]. Their son, Sir Charles Cuyler, became Wilshere's tenant at The Frythe in Welwyn in 1822 after extensive rebuilding [HALS: 61613 p94]. In June 1811 Wilshere reported on a visit to Lee & Kennedy's nursery in Hammersmith Road. In April 1814 his gardener, James Bowie, made a cranberry bed and obtained plants from London. See pp21-25, 202.

[30] James Welch 'upon the red sand of this district, cultivates beans with much success; usually after barley, so as to enable him to avoid clover in a second round, by which means that grass returns but once in eight years' [A Young, *General View of the Agriculture of Oxfordshire* (1809)]. Some of Wilshere's land between Walsworth and Highbury Roads and on Benslow Hill was on sand.

[31] The bailiff responisble for Samuel Whitbread's home farm at Southill was Thomas Barnes. This was never very profitable (D Rapp, *Samuel Whitbread (1764-1815) A Social and Political Study* (1987) p100.

[32] A bush fair was held on open ground usually in a village, rather than in a market place in a town. See Glossary.

Horses [p16]

The general practice of the best farmers in Oxfordshire is to let the horses lie out in the yard every night – they have sheds to go under.[33]

Beans 1809

November removed from the hovel in the Rickyard to Kershaw's barn & thrashed by Hunt. Produced 10 loads 2 bushels. Many had during Wrenn's illness been eaten by the hogs & the fowls, probably 6 or 8 bushels.

They had been inned before they were dry – 2 loads were spared then to drop on the floor for ?sowing, the remainder 8 loads 2 bushels were kiln dried & reduced to 34 bushels, the whole put in the loft in Smith's yard.[34]

Twydell Dear   November 28 1809 [p17]

Quick per 1000 10s

Had had this month of old rails mine 1254.

Mr Musgrave's 1320 at 4d each.[35]

Taking up & banking at 2/6 per chain. The old pails sold towards the expense. 22,000 taken up January 1810 for Dear.

Folding November 1809 (J Kingsley[36] & others) [p18]

100 Western or about 120 South Down sheep will fold an acre of land in 14 days. If the sheep are well kept, the folding will be worth from 70s to £4 an acre giving about ½d per day as the value of the folding of each sheep (South Down).

Fencing the slipe next Joan Biggs' Grave[37] [p19]
See [page] 9

1809 November 30 began by Twydell Dear. Completed 6 December with posts & rails from Willes' l[an]d Holwell & I found nails & quick. He is therefore to be p[ai]d for labour only 2 men 5 days each.

The same men began 7 December to weed & bank up the quick in Little Wimbush: Chains (*blank*)

Finished (*blank*) - 2 men (*blank*) days each.

---

[33].Oxfordshire farmers claimed this practice kept the horses in a much more healthy state [Young, *General View of the Agriculture of Oxfordshire*, p283].

[34] This may be Samuel Smith, a Hitchin maltster. See Biographical Notes.

[35] For George Musgrave see Biographical Notes.

[36] John Kingsley was a farmer at Pirton. See Biographical Notes.

[37] This was probably incorporated into Waby's Field.

Wheat from the Corner Close next Joan Biggs' Grave 3 acres 2 roods[38]

[p20]

This wheat was thrashed in October & November & produced 15 loads 4 bushels of the best & 6 bushels of off[al] corn, together 17 loads, nearly 5 loads per acre.

The best 8 loads 2 bushels were thrashed in October & November & sold to Mr Ransom at 70s – £29 – 8 - 0.[39]

Due the remaining 7 loads 2 bushels to (*blank*)

1 load of off[al] corn to (*blank*) at (*blank*)

17 January 1810   **[pp21-24]**

A five year old black horse from Mr Hewes sent on trial price £38.[40]

21 January 1810 Plan for the succeeding harvest

	[a] - [r] - [p]
There are sown of wheat in Wimbush Field after potatoes without manure	1 - - - -
In the 3 acres south of Benslow Hill Lane after clover[41]	3 - - - -
In Nettle dale after clover	2 - 2
In the two pieces (taken from my brother at ?M[ichaelma]s last) two pieces north of Benslow Hill Lane, the further piece 2a, the hither piece 1 [acre] 2 [roods][42]	3 - 2
Acres	10 – 0 - 0

For Barley

Pierson's Piece[43]	4 - 0 - 0
Waby's Piece[44]	4 - 0 - 0

---

[38] This became part of Lower Benslow Hill.

[39] John Ransom paid £43 8s for 12 loads 2 bushels of wheat at 70s on 22 Nov 1809 [HALS: 61502 p13].

[40] On 16 March 1810 Wilshere paid Samuel Hewes £38 for a horse [HALS: 61502 p52]. See Biographical Notes.

[41] The close near Joan Biggs' Grave which became part of Waby's Field.

[42] Part of the Slipes above Benslow Hill.

[43] Pierson's Piece was later called Walsworth Way Close. It was also known as Rail Piece or Stone Piece or Dunche's Field.

[44] Four Acres next Wymondley Road.

Little Wimbush		2 - 0 - 0
The piece on the right of Benslow Hill Lane from my		
Brother & that on the left both barley last year[45]		4 - 0 - 0
		14 – 0 - 0

Oats	Paternoster's turnips	2 - - - -
	Shoulder of Mutton[46] old sain foin	3 - - - -
		5
Peas	half the north side of Benslow Hill[47]	4 - 1 - -
Beans	the north piece at Joan Bigg's Grave[48]	3 - 2 - 0
Tares	half the north side of Benslow Hill	4 - 1 - -
Buck	a piece in Benslow Hill new sown with tares	
wheat	with tares [sic] by my Brother	1 - 3 - -
	And a piece of Radcliffe's now held by	
	Watson at the top of Benslow Hill[49]	1 - 1 - -
		5 - - - -[50]

For Turnips

The south side of Benslow Hill now young turnips	8 - 2 - -
Starlings Bridge Close	5 - 0 - 0
The Six of my Brother on Benslow Hill[51]	6 - 0 - 0

Wimbush

Wheat after potatoes	1 a
Tares sown	1 a
For potatoes	1 a
Cabbages	1 - 2
Swedish turnips[52]	2 - 0
1 acre to be cleared for lucerne	

---

[45] Part of Waby's Field.

[46] Little Wimbush, Paternoster's Garden and Shoulder of Mutton were amalgamated into Little Wimbush field in 1815. For Samuel Paternoster see Biographical Notes.

[47] The whole of this field (north end of Pym's) was planted with tares. See p14.

[48] This became part of Lower Benslow Hill.

[49] Part of the Slipes above Benslow Hill.

[50] 5 acres is presumably the area planted with tares.

[51] Little Benslow Hill.

[52] What we would call a swede; not strictly a turnip *Brassica rapa rapa* at all but a separate although related species, *Brassica napus*.

Carrots	- - 3 - -
Mangell Wurzell	- - 2
Sundry garden beds	<u>- - 1</u>
	Acres 9

1 acre to be cleared for lucerne.

17 March 1810   **[p25]**
Barley seed ?home
Began sowing barley, sowed 15 bushels of my own on Pierson's Piece after turnips. Finished with Waby's Piece 5 April.

Swedish Turnip seed   **[p26]**
17 March 1810 weighed a standard bushel & found the weight to be very exactly 48 lb.

30 October 1810   **[p27]**
Hodgson has the following roots & bulbs[53]
Ranunculuses & Anemones
In sorts the R[ununculeses] at about 12 & the A[nemones] about 7s per 100. He says that the 3 last seasons have been very unfavourable for these roots particularly for the Ranunculus's – and there has been little or no increase.

Hyacinths double & single blue & white	4d to 6d per root
Polyanthus narcissus	3s 6d per 100
Jonquils double	3s 6d per 100
single	1s 6d per 100
Tulips mixture	2s 6d per 100

(*The next five pages are blank.*)

Farming Stock 30 September 1810   **[p28]**

	£ - s - d
4 horses £40, 30, 15, 15	100 – 0 - 0
3 cows & a heifer £12, 9, 5, 5	31 –10 - 0
32 hogs, that is one sow with 8 pigs, one with nine not a fortnight old, 6 pigs bought at market about 7 months old & a sow with 6 pigs about 4 months old	30 – 0 - 0
4 carts	40 – 0 - 0

---

[53] Henry Hodgson was a Hitchin nurseryman. See Biographical Notes.

5 ploughs[54] & 3 harrows	20 – 0 - 0
Scuffler £5, ?twitch harrow £5 [55]	10 – 0 - 0
Harness	5 – 0 - 0
Various other implements & barn tackle	5 – 0 - 0
Poultry - 20 turkeys (i.e. 3 old, 14 bought & 3 very young) Guinea fowls 6 of our own old, 4 Miss M[56], 34 young 36 old fowls, 60 chickens, 10 ducks	10 – 0 - 0
23 sacks	5 – 0 - 0
2½ doz[e]n hurdles	1 -- - --
	257 – 10 - 0

Farming Stock 30 September 1810 cont'd   **[pp29-30]**

		[Brought over]		£257-10-0
	12 loads of hay 1809 at 6			72 – 0 - 0
	First & second crop 1810 10 loads} First 3 loads second 7 loads }			50 – 0 - 0
Wheat	In Wimbush		1 a	
	Two closes on Benslow Hill		3½	
	In Neddledale		2½	
	Three acres next Waby's		3	
	The 3 acres [*illeg*] 14 loads of which 1 load off[al] corn			

---

[54] In June 1810 Wilshere paid £8 2s 6d through his brother Thomas for a double furrow plough [HALS: 61502 p68].

[55] Arthur Young reported in 1804 that the first scuffler he saw in Hertfordshire 'was at the Rev. Mr. Keate's, at Hatfield, made by HARDFORD, near Loughborough, in Leicestershire; a very useful and effective tool, far more powerful than a great break, or four-horse harrow.' [*General View*, p42]. It was like a plough with multiple small shares and coulters, usually with a central leading share and coulter and two mounted on a cross-frame, either side of the main beam, behind it, forming a narrow triangle. It was only really effective on light land. A twitch harrow was a type of harrow comprising a framework of heavy planks, in which were set rows of tines. It was designed both to break up the soil after ploughting and uproot twitch grass and similar weeds. Twitch or couch grass (*Elymus repens*) was a serious weed in arable crops before the development of modern herbicides, regenerating easily from root fragments. In July 1810 Wilshere paid William Swain £4 14s 2d for iron work to the twitch harrow made by Wilston in March 1810 [HALS: 61502 p74]. Piggot's *Hertfordshire Directory* 1826 lists William Swaine as a blacksmith at Preston.

[56] Miss Mills, daughter of Mrs Sarah Mills. See Biographical Notes.

		40 loads at 55s	10	110 – 0 - 0
Barley	Little Wimbush		1 - 3	
	Pierson's		4	
	Two closes on Benslow Hill		4	
	Waby's		3 - 3	110 – 0 - 0
		55 quarters at 40s	13 - 2	
Oats	Shoulder of Mutton & a piece below **15 quarters at 30s**		3 - 2	22 – 10 - 0
Peas	T. W.'s 6 acres			
	Bottom of Benslow Hill 2½ a[57]			
		35 loads at 30s	8 - 2	50 – 0 - 0
Beans	In same close	**2 loads**	1	3 – 0 - 0
Buck wheat	In Simpson's 2 acres		1 - 1	
	& in Radcliffe's Benslow Hill[58]		1 - 2	
		12 loads at 25s	2 - 3	15 – 0 - 0
Tares	A miserable crop on 8 [a] 2 [r] the north end of Pym's			
Turnips	South end of Pym's half Swedish		8 - 2	40 - - - -
		Sold [£] 67 – 10 - 0		
	Starlings Bridge Swedish		5	35 - - - -
In Wimbush	Swedish		3 }	
	White & Scotch		1½}	25 - - - -
	Carrots		3 r	10 - - - -
	Cabbages		1 a	
	Ditto		2 r	10 - - - -
	Potatoes		1 a	15 - - - -
Plant of clover in Little Wimbush on lucerne on right hand Benslow Hill piece			8 a	£10
About 3 pecks of Swedish Turnip seeds				
				825 – 0 - 0

Potatoes 1810 [pp31-32]

October took up about ⅔ of the acre in Wimbush Field leaving about ⅓ kidney potatoes not quite ripe, the tops remaining green.

---

[57] Joan Biggs' Close, part of Lower Benslow Hill.
[58] Part of the Slips above Benslow Hill.

17 October took up the remainder, a frosty morning 12th having completely killed the tops. The quantities were

of common White Kidney	33
of a potato called Golden Drop	100
a spotted potato called the Callico Potato	90
of a red potato called the Blood Royal	9
of a black potato called the Emperor of Morocco	9
Harrowed out mixed	_24_
	265
27 on ploughing the land for wheat there got up more of all sorts	_10_
	275

19 October I had two of each of the four sorts, all nearly the same size boiled the same time.

I found the Callico potato the most mealy & fit for immediate use.

The Blood Red - the fullest flavour & sufficiently mealy.

The White Kidney rather waxy & not quite dry enough.

The Black still more waxy but very well tasted.

I did not try the Golden Drop.

October 22nd I tried the Golden Drop & found it scarcely distinguishable from the White Kidney.

Carrots 1810   **[pp33-34]**

October 15 & 16 I ploughed up those in Wimbush Field (nearly 3 roods) **(by measure 2.0.30).** Some thing more than half the ground had been carrots the last year & had no manure. This part of the crop was rather slight, the remainder was on ground on which mangel wurzel grew the last year & it now bore a good crop. The whole quantity was 223 bushels at 45lbs to the bushel.

This I found to be the weight. The number of carrots in a bushel was about 90.

of which reserved for the kitchen & for seed	15 bushels
gave to the Coachman for the horses	131
11 bushels eaten before the end of October.	
120 remain in store	

15

Mrs Mills[59] 1 delivered & one reserved	2
Sent for the farm horses	<u>75</u>
	223
On ploughing the land a second time were	
found	<u>7</u>
	230

I found very few comparatively hurt by the plough. All that were at all broken were put by themselves to be first given to the horses. They amounted to about 10 bushels.

The plough (Yorkshire) went under them & in general brought them up quite hole [sic].[60] After so long a season of drought it would have been very difficult & expensive to have got them up by the fork & much more injurious to them.

Turkies   **[p35]**

1810 November. James Nash[61] informs me that breeding turkies should be kept a short time, the cock not beyond the 2nd year, the hens not more than two or three. None of the eggs which I set this year hatched. They were produced from old hens with an old cock of the 4th year. I bought of him a cock & two hens of this year. He sells them by weight alive – the cocks at 9d & the hens at 10d per lb. Those I bought weigh the cock 18lb, the hens 10lb each.

Digging - Trenching   **[pp36-38]**

21 November 1810 I find by the observation of two men working moderately that in what is called bastard trenching – that is throwing in a moderate spit say 6 inches & throwing on it the next spit say 8 inches without taking out the loose earth (called crumbs) at the bottom, so as to have a depth of 14 inches from the trench, a man will do 90 square feet in an hour or nearly a square perch in 3 hours. Suppose a man therefore to work 7½ hours which is as much as he can do at this season, he should have 10d for a square perch to earn 2s a day - or 8d per perch to earn 20d. I am informed that the work would be better if the crumbs of the lower spit were thrown up & that is worth 2d per perch add[itiona]l. Mr

---

[59] Mrs Sarah Mills was the widow of a plantation owner from Nevis, who lived in Tilehouse Street in Hitchin. See Biographical Notes.

[60] Arthur Young reported that the Yorkshire plough was used by Mr Hale and Mr Roberts of Kings Walden; 'they even break up their land with it, using three horses, and ofter two' [Young, *General View*, p37].

[61] James Nash was the owner of Purwell Mill. See Biographical Notes.

Maughan informs me that he has lately had ground trenched 2 spits & the crumbs of both (in all 2 feet) at 2s 6d per perch.[62]

1 December five men have been digging as above (that is bastard trenching 14 inches deep or about two moderate spits) from the 22nd November to this day both inclusive – but have not been at work the whole time – their united work makes 37 days and the quantity done is 80 rods amo[un]ting at 10d per rod (the price I agreed to pay) to £3 6s 8d or 1s 11d per day.

Poultry 1 December 1810   **[pp39-40]**
For fatting poultry. Mrs Young recommends a paste (not too stiff) of barley meal - that in making it some hot dripping or other sweet fat be poured into it & kneaded up with it. She states that the fowls at Dorking are all so fatted & recommends it for guinea fowl.
That a meal of buck wheat either alone or mixed with barley meal is an excellent food for turkies & almost all poultry.
She sells 2 or if she can three or four hens at the same time with eggs of the guinea fowls that, as they often fail, she may put what are hatched into one or more broods as may be requisite. She states that the only certain criteria between the cock & hen of the guinea fowl is to separate them & observe their note – the cry of the hen is a sound like co-bank, that of the cock a rough chuckle. That they constantly & invariably keep paired though they are gregarious – particularly in winter. She has taken 103 eggs laid by one hen in a season.

20 January 1811   **[pp41-42]**
Robinson informs me that he has thrashed the wheat of the 3 acres ~~next B~~ at Joan Biggs' grave next Wabey's and that it produced 14 loads, of which 1 load off[al] corn, that none of it is sold
That from Waby's Field ~~they~~ he have thrashed 11.6 bushels of which 9.5 sold to Mr Nash at 40s.
& the whole late Willes part of Little Wimbush (which contains of ploughed land about 1 [acre] 3 [roods]) quantity 15 quarters 2 bushels (about 6 bushels was) off[al] corn. 10 quarters sold to Mr Nash 38s. Remainder used for fowls & pigs.[63]
That 2½ part of the three acres & ½ at Joan Biggs' grave turned out a very bad crop producing only 4 loads of which 17 bushels are laid by for seed, the remainder used.

---

[62] See Biographical Notes.
[63] Waby's Field and Willes part of Little Wimbush grew barley.

That they have also thrashed 14 loads 4 bushels out of the six acres next
Nettledale of which 9 or 10 loads have been used & sown. Expects to have 20
loads more from that field.

That he has thrashed 35 bushels of oats, expects to have 11 quarters more.

Buck wheat - all thrashed produced 15 loads of which 3 loads 2 bushels laid by.

20 January 1811   **[pp43-44]**

Robinson states that there is at the farm:

52 fowls of which about 12 are old hens to be sold off & 15 or 16 chickens
& young fowls fit to kill.

20 at Abbis's of which 1 cock & 12 hens to be kept & 7 young fowls for
the table.

22 Guinea fowls	3 p[ai]r old dark ones	6
	Young of the same sort	7
	3 from Miss Mills supposed all cocks	3
	Young ones from Mrs Young pearl colour	6
	to be reduced to 6 pairs	22
Turkeys	3 one cock & two hens from Mr Nash to be kept.	
	1 old hen fatting to be killed	
	8 young ones - 3 cocks are up, 5 hens to put up.	
Ducks	1 old drake & 2 old ducks to be kept.	
	3 young ducks.	

20 January 1811   **[p45]**

I agreed (yesterday) with John Kingsley for the turnips in Starlings Bridge Close
(5 acres very good Swedes) and on Benslow Hill (8½ acres south side ½ Swedes
well planted but small, & ½ white mostly good but rather thin) at £5 an acre.

There is an ag[reemen]t of £4 by Wren's Account in 1808.

I have engaged if he should feed his sheep with corn on the land to make him an
allowance for the manure. I am told that the manure is worth from ⅕ th to ¼ th
of the value of the corn.

I calculated	the 5a at Starlings Bridge at £7 per acre at	35 – 0 - 0
	8 [acres] 2 [roods] at £4	34 – 0 - 0
		69 – 0 - 0
	Abating for some thin places	1 – 10 - 0
		67 – 10 - 0

18

Plants sold from the Nursery (from Grant's Memorandum)
William Lee[64]   **[p46]**

1809 December 12	800 larches 20s [65]	8 - - -
	300 spruce firs	1 – 2 - 6
	200 Scotch	1 - 0 - 0
1810 March 14	100 larch	1 - - - -
	50 spruce	0 - 4 - 0
	70 limes, 10 planes	0 – 16 - 0
1811 February	100 Scotch	0 – 10 - 0
	100 larch	1 - 0 - 0
	200 spruce	1 - 0 - 0
		14 – 12 - 6

Mr Burroughs had March 1810 as a loan 700 Scotch.[66]

1811 February   **[pp47-48]**
Plants from the Nursery sent by desire of Mr Reynolds to Mr Lee Antonie &
L[or]d Tavistock – to be included in Hodgson's bill with plants ordered of him
& to be accounted for by him to me.[67]

---

[64] Thomas Grant was Wilshere's gardener 1806-1810. See Biographical Notes. William Lee changed his name to William Lee Antonie on inheriting the Colworth estate in Bedfordshire. See below.

[65] Presumably 20 shillings per 100.

[66] The Reverend Lynch Salusbury changed his name to Burroughs on acquiring Offley Place and the Offley estate in 1806. In 1805 an Act of Parliament moved the road from Hitchin to Luton to enlarge the park. Lynch Burroughs had the house remodelled by Robert Smirke in 1806-1810 [D C Baines, *'Two Coats Colder'. Chronicles of Offley in Hertfordshire* (Offley, 1994) pp46-48]. Before he inherited the Offley estate Lynch Salusbury lived in Hitchin. In 1801 he sold The Grange in Portmill Lane to Wilshere [TNA: CRES5/37 p125].

[67] In 1800 Samuel Whitbread commissioned Samuel Reynolds, a penniless artist, to improve Southill Park. He recommended him to William Lee Antonie who employed Reynolds to enlarge and improve his house and park at Colworth in Bedfordshire. See M Jones, *Colworth in Context. A History of Colworth Estate, Bedfordshire from 1720 to 1947* (Bedford, 1997) pp100-111. Lord Tavistock was the eldest son of the Duke of Bedford who owned Oakley House in Bedfordshire, a hunting lodge. The Duke of Bedford, Samuel Whitbread and Lee Antonie financed the Oakley Hunt of which Lee Antonie was Master 1798-1809 [Fulford, *Samuel Whitbread,* p84]. Henry Hodgson was a Hitchin nurseryman. See Biographical Notes.

4000 spruce firs	16 - 0 - 0
1000 Scotch	3 - 0 - 0
100 larch	0 - 6 - 0
1000 laurels	12 – 10 - 0
200 lilacs, syringias, and laurentinas}	
50 more laurentinas}	5 - 0 - 0
100 limes	1 – 12 - 6
100 layers of viz 80 limes & 20 planes	0 - 12 - 0
4 large firs	0 - 6 - 0
100 Chinese roses ½ potted	5 - 0 - 0
20 weeping birch	0 - 10 - 0
50 roses	0 - 16 - 8
20 honeysuckles	0 - 5 - 0
2 hicoreys	0 - 1 - 6
20 rosemary	0 - 5 - 0
22 box	0 - 11 - 0
100 laburnums	1 - 5 - 0
2 large cypress	1 - 0 - 0
30 sugar maple	0 - 7 - 6
100 hornbcams	0 - 15 - 0
12 Persian lilac	0 - 6 - 0
12 large abele	0 - 9 - 0
20 large white poplar	0 - 6 - 8
	51 - 4 - 10

24 March 1811 gave copy to Mr Hodgson who is to charge it in his account & to give me credit for the com[missio]n. WW

February 1811 I gave my Brother Thomas 500 plants principally Scotch firs & to Mr Hale Wortham 200 Scotch firs & to Hodgson about 700. [68]

1811 March 11 [pp49-50]

Began sowing barley on the south side of Mr Pym's Benslow Hill piece. I finished Starlings Br[idge] Close the turnips not having been eaten off sooner.

---

[68] Thomas Wilshere had by 1816 established a plantation on part of the Coney Grees to the north of Bearton Green in Hitchin (1 rood 16 perches in area, plot 870 on the map of Hitchin dated 1816). Hale Wortham was the brother of William Wilshere's late wife, Martha. See Biographical Notes.

26 March I killed a pig (one of six produced from a sow given me by Mr Brand[69]) at 10 weeks old. It had been always fat – it weighed 33lbs with & 30 without the head & feet.

1811 May 24 I began sowing Swedish turnips at the south end of the field next Joan Briggs' grave.[70] Continued sowing that field (about 8 acres), in Wimbush nearly 3 acres, Benslow Hill right hand piece 6 acres which was finished 17 June.

My hay

	Mount Garrison	3 acres
	Corner Close & Dimsey's	2
Clover	Pierson's	4
	Little Wimbush	2½
	Upper Benslow Hill south close	2½
		14

All inned without rain between the 8th & the 15th of June.

Cucumbers   [p51]

D Mackintosh[71] raised two pots of a large sort of cucumber one of which was placed in the hot house & the other in the pine fruiting house.
18 June 1811 I cut one 16 inches long weighing 1lb 12 oz.
Pirton Comm[issioners]
& 21 June I cut another 18 inches long weighing 2lb 6oz
Mr Parsons
Both these were young. I cut on the 20th another very young & slender measuring nearly 15 inches.
Mrs Mills[72]

15 June 1811   [pp52-55]

I went to the nursery of Lee & Kennedy on the Hammersmith road, to see their roses & greenhouse plants.[73] They have a printed list of 326 varieties –

---

[69] Thomas Brand (later Lord Dacre). See Biographical Notes.
[70] Lower Benslow Hill.
[71] Daniel McIntosh was Wilshere's gardener. See Biographical Notes.
[72] Probably the Pirton Inclosure Commisioners. Wilshere owned land in Pirton and in 1812 paid £145 towards the cost of enclosure. For Joseph Parsons and Sarah Mills see Biographical Notes.

exclusively of some not in the list. They suppose there may be about 400 – but new varieties are constantly produced from seed. The varieties in many instances are very slight.

Those which appeared to me to be best worth adding to what I have are

No in Cat[alogue]		Prices £	s	d
11	White monthly	0	1	0
47	Scarlet Provence	0	2	6
80	Royal Sweet Briar	0	7	6
89	Imperial blush	0	2	6
92	Shailers Provence	0	10	6
108	Celestial	0	7	6
109	Dutch Provence	0	5	0
111	Burning coal	0	5	0
116	Proserpine	0	5	0
126	Grand purple	0	7	6
130	Invincible Provence	0	7	6
131	Monstrous sweet briar	0	10	6
186	Negro	0	7	6
194	Rosa Peestana	0	5	0
215	Four Seasons	0	5	0
218	Garnet	0	2	6
229	Beetony	0	7	6
232	Margarette	0	7	6
237	Carlile	0	10	6
239	Swiss	0	7	6
287	Malabar	0	7	6
290	Single Provence	0	7	6
291	Yorkshire Provence	0	7	6
302	Double hip	0	2	6

[73] This well known nursery had been established at the Vineyard in Hammersmith in about 1745 by James Lee and Lewis Kennedy. James Lee died in 1795, but the nursery was continued by their sons, James Lee and John Kennedy, until 1817 when James Lee took over the nursery [M Hadfield, *A History of British Gardening* (1960, paperback 1985) pp235-6, 286-7]. Wilshere's cash books do not record any purchases from Lee and Kennedy [HALS: 61503-61504].

The Scotch roses particularly the single & double white
The white moss & the single moss
The Macartney Chinese rose (crimson some double)
The Rosa multiflora Chinensis – this requires a wall.

Amongst their plants are the following which I wish to have:

The Peppermint tree – a Botany Bay plant	0	7	6
A new yellow Japan honeysuckle	0	5	0

For a greenhouse or a south wall.
    Nurphilus Japonica
    Magnolia glauca – flowers abroad in a sheltered situation
    Geranium Hulsearum
    Rubus arcticus
    Camphor tree
    Currida montana
    Currida.

They have about 500 heaths.

At Colville's Nursery Kings Road 15 June 1811 [74]   [pp56-57]

Mysambryanthemums in great variety must have 100. There are from 20 to 30 with very handsome flowers. 1s 6d per pot. They require to be frequently renewed – all strike freely. The earth in which they are planted should be very poor, a great proportion of it may be street dirt.
(Goldfish may be usually purchased in Covent Garden at 7s 6d per pair.)

Double rosa Chinensis nigra	2s 6d
(Macartney Rose) rosa Chinensis milleflora	2s 6d
Calicanthus precox	7s 6d
Olea odoratissimum	5s
Pyrus Japonica	10s 6d
Protea small	2s 6d
Amaryllis speciocissimum	5s

[74] James Colvill established his nursery in the Kings Road, Chelsea in about 1783. He was involved in the early development of the China rose. The nursery was distinguished for hybridization of pelargoniums, gladioli, and hippeastrums; by 1811 it specialized in rare exotics and forced flowers [*VCH* Middlesex Vol 12 pp150-155]. Wilshere's cash books do not record any purchases from Colvill's Nursery.

Amaryllis equestris (the sort which I have from Nevis)[75]	7s 6d
Astanthus major (a bulb)	2s 6d
Antherinum affinum per pot	1s 6d

Pines & Grapes
Colville informs me that Andrews at Lambeth has the best pines & grapes – has the new prov[?idence] pine.[76]

Lee & Kennedy 15 June 1811 continued [p58]
I saw there a beautiful fir from Port Jackson some what like the dark spruce but more feathered – it has grown to the top of the Conservatory & the head had been taken off. (They were propagating it by slips in sand.) The extremities are constantly in a growing state & would therefore be cut off by the frosts of this country. It grows at Port Jackson not uncommonly to the height of 280 feet of the proportionate bulk.
Very few trees in this country grow to 100 feet, few if any to 120 feet.

Strawberries [pp59-60]
by the Revd Robert Painter of Paxton 19 June 1811.
All the large strawberries are better kept cach plant separate – none should remain more than 3 years without transplanting. A good loam well dunged suits them best.

Propagating cuttings
15 June 1811 Mr Lee the Nurseryman states that cuttings of every description are best struck in pure white sand not suffered to get dry, that there are few plants of any description of which the young & tender shoots will not so grow. There is a late publication on the propagation of plants which I have heard well spoken of – memorandum to look for an account of it in the late reviews.

---

[75] Wilshere's friends in Hitchin included the Mills family who owned a sugar plantation in Nevis. In 1813 his gardener James Bowie planted 'West India Seeds' including some collected in Nevis. See pp189-193.
[76] Possibly Isaac Andrew of Lambeth, gardener who died in 1827 possessed of two premises with gardens and hothouses in South Lambeth. In August 1812 Wilshere paid John Proctor £5 10s for pine apple plants [TNA: PROB11/1724/270; HALS: 61504 p64].

[pp61-62]

Mr Sabine recommends the American ?cranberry to be planted where water has full access to the plant – to be had at Lee & Kennedy's – it may also be had at Malcolm's.[77]

A new excellent & free bearing grape is to be had at ?Farmers in Bond Street. White Chelsea grape (Muscat). Transactions of the Horticultural Society 4pts quarto.

Roses 26 June 1811

Mr Sabine recommends the Belladonna or great Maidens blush rose for a trellice – I saw it bloming very finely & very freely at Mr Keet's at Hatfield.[78] (I think I have one in the upper garden immediately before the American ilex). He recommends also the following roses amongst others

	Double Burnet			Scarlet Provence
	Bishop			Shailers Provence
	Brunswick			Invincible Provence
	Carmine			White Provence
	Cardinal		√	Pautana
√	Celestial			Pluto
	York & Lancaster			Proserpine
	Black frizzled			Shell
	Dutch 100 leaved			Spongs
	Lucid			Sarsparilla
	Grand Monarque			Swiss
	Negro			Dutch velvet

June 1811   [pp63-64]

Mottled Lilley immediately above the Althea nearest to the Greenho[use]: it is overshadowed by the Althea & the variegated holly next it.

---

[77] Joseph Sabine, former owner of Tewin House, was honorary secretary of the Horticultural Society from 1810 to 1830. In February 1820 William Wilshere bought £4 7s worth of vegetable seeds from William Malcolm & Co, Nursery and Seedsmen, Kensington. In 1804 Malcolm had taken over Daniel Grimwood's nursery [*ODNB;* HALS: 61481/53; J Harvey, *Early Nurserymen* (Chichester, 1974) p78].

[78] The Reverend John Keet was Rector of Hatfield 1788-1819 [Clergy Database: https://theclergydatabase.org.uk] He/was cited by Young in his *General View of the Agriculture of Hertfordshire* eg p42.

Yellow Lilleys
2 fine bunches in the lower south border of the flower garden – will be better
?bestowed – one about the middle next a double scarlet Lichnis – the other six
yards from the bottom.
There is a fine deep orange lilley in the little garden opposite the turning of the
road to Stevenage.

June 1811 Flowers etc to be procured.
Scarlet zimmia
White campanula (Mr Parsons)
Rose Campion (Mrs Mills or Mr Eade[79])
Monks Hood
Virginian Stock
Single red clematis, single purple ditto – Hodgson
Spigelia Mary Candica

Gooseberries July 1811   [pp65-66]
I weighed an Amber gooseberry from my garden & found it 9 dwts[80] 6 gr[ains].
1814 August I gathered 1 weighing 16 dwts. There were many equal to the
weight of a guinea & ½ that is 8 dwts 2 gr[ains]. Another weighed 11 dwts 6
gr[ains]. I have heard of a gooseberry weighing 18 dwts.
**There is a list in Mcdonald's Gardening dictionary (see for May 12 1811) in
which is one 17 dwts 19 gr[ains] & ?sev[era]l of 17.**

Figs - to get one or two free bearing – the blue is said to be good & to bear
freely.

Dr Dickson's Farmer's Companion ment[ione]d in the Monthly Mag[azine]
February 1811 page 55 as a useful publication.[81]

Haynes on Horticulture Supp[lement] to Monthly Mag[azine] January 1811
page 658.[82]

---

[79] For the Reverend Joseph Parsons, curate of Hitchin, and Joseph Eade, Hitchin
solicitor, see Biographical Notes.
[80] Pennyweights used by apothecaries and jewellers.
[81] *The Farmer's Companion* by Richard Watson Dickson was published in 1810.
[82] Thomas Haynes, *Interesting Discoveries in Horticulture Being an Easy, Rational and
Efficacious System of Propagating All Hardy American and Bog Soil Plants* (1810).

Farm and Garden Memoranda, inspection of orchard trees, 28 August 1811 (*HALS: 61181*).

Harvest 1811 began reaping 24 July
1 acre Wimbush cut 22ⁿᵈ & 23ʳᵈ
Wheat all inned 1 August, harvest completed 21 August.

Orchard Trees [pp67-76]
28 August 1811 **revised 15 September 1814**, on inspection with Hodgson &
McIntosh of the trees in my Garden & Plantation, I find as far as can be
ascertained by them the numbers & sorts to be:

In the border of the Kitchen Garden beginning at the top:
1   Nonpareil
2   ~~Peter Russet~~ **Nonpareil**
3   ~~Unknown~~ **Lemon Pippin**
4   Ribston Pippin
5   Pear unknown
6   Winter Pippin
7   French Pippin
8   Unknown - a smallish red apple before the standard apricot
9   Hollow Crown Pippin
      a very good baking apple in November
10   Russet Nonpareil
11   Norfolk Buffon
12   (next the path below the grass) Nonpareil
13   French Golden Pippin
14   Spice Russet
15   ~~Nearly dead~~ unknown (nearly dead)
16   ~~Unknown~~ **Margill**
17   ~~Chaumontelle (may be given up)~~ **Buffon**
18   Supposed Lemon Pippin
19   Unknown
20   Nonpareil (cut in)

There are 5 damsons of which four are bad (1 the smallest is the ?king
damson & to be saved), 2 or 3 of the others may be given up ?reworked with
better sorts.

28

Orchard of the Kitchen Garden beginning from the bottom:
- A young tree at the north east corner from Murray[83] called the Duncan Apple.
- The tree in the border leading to the bridge next the sweet briar hedge is a French golden pippin.
- The cherry is a ~~Duke Cherry~~ **cut down**,
- Near the path a young Windsor Pear
- Ribston Pippin
- Chaumontelle Pear
- Swans Egg Pear
- **a Catshead in the centre, a Bedford Seedling**
Exclusively of the old trees.
(Damsons of a bad sort - to get some from Shitlington[84])
- another Ribston Pippin next below the standard apricot.

Framing Ground
South side beginning at the Upper End – espaliers (see 2 pages further for standards)
1	Nonpareil
2	Nonpareil
3	Nonsuch
4	Nonpareil
5	French Pippin
6	Nonsuch (to be moved covered by a large pear)
7	Nonpareil next below the gateway

Middle border beginning at the bottom next fence
1	Golden Pippin
2	~~Nonpareil~~ **Ribston Pippin**
3	~~Golden Pippin Pippin~~ **removed**
4	Spice Russet
5	~~Unknown~~ **removed**
6	Golden Pippin (true)
1	Under the Medlar a true Golden Pippin

[83] Robert Murray was a nurseryman in Hertford. See Biographical Notes.
[84] In 1803-1804 William Wilshere purchased land in Shitlington (now Shillington) in Bedfordshire, where his tenant, Cornelius Brookes, had an orchard [HALS: 61613 pp56-58; see pp96, 104 below].

29

2 ~~Nonpareil~~ **Hollow Crown Pippin**
3 ~~Unknown~~ **Oslin**
  Unknown

Border on the north side beginning at the top
  1 ~~Unknown~~ **Golden Pippin (old)**
  2 ~~Hollow Crown Pippin~~ **Nonsuch**
  3 ~~Ribston~~ **Newtown Pippin**
  4 ~~Golden Pippin~~ **removed**
    Martin Seck Pear
  5 Russet supposed Royal
  6 Supposed Russet

Standards in border on the North side
  1 Pear supposed bueré
  2 Ditto Cardillac
  3 Same
  4 ~~Burgamot~~ **Bueré**
  5 Burgamot
  6 Wine Sour Plum
  7 Uvedale St German
with at the bottom of this ground
? 1 a small ?murk pear
& a Purple Magnum Bonum plum
a Jargonelle pear next the ?tool house, a greengage on the other side & a
Colmar on the wall.

Old Orchard
The pear next the Walk & immediately above the pond is a Cresane & next to it
is a Cardillac same as next the drawing room chimney.
Opposite the pond is a French Golden Pippin.
Between the pond and the coach road a true Golden Pippin sickly.
The lowest apple on the right of the walk is called 14 inches.
Burgamots 3 of which 2 want thinning & the 3rd to have the head cut down.
White Nectarine next the fence of Herb Garden.

Plantation divided into 8 quarters
beginning right on entering & next left.
  Quarter 1 A Bueré pear small & sickly

30

An unworked plum on the opposite side

Quarter 2   Only walnuts & 1 ~~unknown apple~~
Holland Pippin

Quarter 3   No 1   Hawthorndeaning a tall young tree[85]
              2   Russet a young tree
              3   Brown Bueré
              4   Whirl Pippin a very round Dutch apple[86]
              5   ~~Brown Bueré~~ **Gansells burgamot**
              6   Swans Egg

Quarter 4   No 1   ~~Wine Sour~~ **Damasine**
              2   ~~Supposed Bedford Seedling~~ **Cats Head**
              3   Golden Pippin
              4   ~~Wine Sour~~ **Damasine**
              5   Nonpareil
              6   Supposed Bedford Seedling

Quarter 5   No 1   ~~nil~~ **unknown**
              2   Norfolk Buffon
               3   Unknown supposed Codlin
              4   French Pippin
              5   ~~Margill~~ **Ribston P[ippin]**
              6   ~~Kentish Cherry~~ **Nonsuch apple**

Quarter 6   No 1   Apple Kentish Fill Basket
              2   Northampton Creeper
               3   ~~Lemon~~ **Gilpins** Pippin
              4   Lemon Pippin
               5   Nonsuch
              6   Nonsuch

---

[85] The Hawthornden, a Scottish culinary variety that probably arose in Midlothian around 1770.

[86] Probably the Whorle or Thorle, a Scottish (not Dutch) dessert variety that arose in the eighteenth century.

Quarter 7	No 1	Swans Egg
	2	French Pippin
	3	Condemned
	4	Jargonelle
	5	~~Duke Cherry sickly to be replaced~~
	6	~~Condemned~~

replaced by 2 apples unknown

Quarter 8	No 1	unknown
	2	supposed Golden Pippin
	3	Bigaron Cherry **condemned G. Pippin**
	4	Duke Cherry
	5	~~Brown Bueré~~ **Chaumontelle**
	6	Ribston Pippin

On the border under the hedge is a Margill apple & a Bigeron cherry. There is another Bigeron cherry near the fence of the Poultry Yard.
I want one two Gansells Burgamots & 2 of the old Burgamots.

September 1811 [p77]
To get the apple called 'Seek no further' the part exposed to the sun is a dark purple covered with down very like a dark plum. It is a sort of Russet.
To take up the carrots north of the Poultry Yard at Abbis's & plant cherries & to take up the variegated elder in that border.

Mangell Worzel [p78]
I planted in my Wimbush field ?600 of the plants of last year for seed in 3 rows. The first row was planted in November & covered over to keep them from the frost. The other two were put in an outhouse & transplanted in February. The row first planted was rather the strongest. The rows were 3 feet asunder, the plants 1½ feet distant in the rows & the whole ground occupied less than 16 perches or one tenth of an acre.
This seed weighs pretty nearly 20 lbs per bushel.
The seed was cut 26 August & produced 7 bushels weighing about 140 lbs. When thoroughly dried & dressed it may perhaps be reduced to about 120 lbs. (I had 12 lbs for 1lb of the seed sown in May last.)
27 February 1812 I found the weight now dressed to be 151 lbs. Sent this day 120 lbs to Murray, Hertford.

32

1812 February 27	Murray	120
	Sold Mr Delroy	6
March 27	Gave Mr Thorpe	4
31	Gave Mr Parsons	2
	Sent to Malcolm	14
March 31	remaining[87]	5 lbs

Potatoes   [pp79-80]

1811 September 12 – I took up half an acre of potatoes in Wimbush Field of different sorts leaving half an acre (not yet ripe) of Whites called the Upright White.

	Bushels	
There was of the Callico Potato	77	**Stored next the barn**
German Kidney	40	**Stored next the ?path to**
Morocco	34	**the herb garden**
Blood Red	1	
	152	

15 September – I had one of each of the above & 1 of the Upright White boiled, those of equal size were selected & all were dressed together. The Callico & German Kidney I found both excellent mealy potatoes, the Callico rather more mealy to the middle. The Kidney remained harder but rather better flavoured. The Upright White was not sufficiently boiled but was a good potato.
The Morocco very moderate (it is likely to be better towards the spring). The Blood Red watery & insipid.
See 7 leaves forward.
Took up the half acre of Upright White which produced 252 bushels.
200 stored in the pit, remainder at the farm. 11 or 12 bushels afterwards ploughed out making 263.
Took up 20 perches on the south side of Wimbush Field of Callico potatoes (sown after turnip seed) produce 45 bushels.

---

[87] For Joseph Parsons see Biographical Notes. Malcolm may be William Malcolm, nursery and seedsman of Kensington, from whom Wilshere bought vegetable seeds in 1820 [HALS: 61481/53]. Mr Thorpe may be Thomas Thorpe of Great Barford, Bedfordshire, who in 1811 was appointed one of the Pirton Enclosure Commissioners [For the process of Parliamentary Enclosure, focusing on Pirton, Hertfordshire see https://pirtonhistory.org.uk/studies/].

| Viz | on 16 perches at bottom | 33 |
| | on 4 perches | 12 |

Placed next to barn.

Carrots 1811   [p81]

½ acre taken up 16 October.

27 perches 24th.

(I found several which went down more than 3ft 6 ins in depth but I could not get any 4 feet, the root at that depth ?becoming so very small it could not be perceived.) They were large, many weighing from 2 to 3 lbs, sev[er]al 4 lbs to 4¼. I had 20 heaped bushels weighed & numbered. I found the n[umber] to be 1050, the weight pretty exactly 8 cwt giving about 14 oz as the weight of each carrot, nearly 45 lbs as the weight of 1 bushel, very nearly 7 tons. *

***some had been drawn for the ?household making full 390 bushels, more than 7 tons.**

		Bushels
Quantity from the ½ acre		347
From the 27 perches sown late		46

	Bushels
Delivered to the Coachman for carriage & riding horses	**160**
To the Gardener for the house & seed	**30**
Remainder for farm horses	**203**

[p82]

The Jessamines proper to plant as climbers in a conservatory seem to be:

The Azorean, which grows very freely

Italian very sweet and climbs to a moderate height

Indian with a bright yellow flower & is pretty hardy

Cape Jessamine is very sweet but is dwarf.

The following are also good plants to climb up the lattice of a conservatory

?Dalleios coronella

Fuschia [sic] ?malsrandia

Garden Wall   [pp83-84]

Mr Whitbread's garden wall at Southill is ?15 feet high from the ground to the top of the coping.

Onions

Directions for growing onions in form & size like those of Spain & Portugal (Month[ly] Mag[azine] October 1811 page 272).

The seeds of the Spanish or Portugal onion should be sown at the usual time in the spring, very thickly & in a poor soil under the shade of the apple or pear tree. In the autumn the bulbs will not be much larger than peas, when they should be taken from the soil and preserved to the succeeding spring and then planted at some distance from each other in a good soil. The bulbs will often exceed 5 inches in diameter, and will keep through the winter much better than those cultivated in the usual manner.

Apples & Pears 1811

October 1811 I had this season 14 bushels of Swans Egg pears, about 3 bushels of the great apple we call Catshead; of all other apples & pears the crop was very deficient.

Farming Stock 30 September 1811   [pp85-86]

	£	s	d
4 horses	100	-	-
?£45, 20, 15, 20. 1 sold in July at £10.			
4 cows & a heifer **3 at 12, 1 at £6, calf 4.**	42	0	0
Hogs 6 at 50s, 5 at 30s, 10 at 15s, sow & 11 pigs £7, ~~boar~~ & an[othe]r sow £3 each	40	-	-
4 carts	30	-	-
4 ploughs & 3 harrows	14	-	-
Scuffler & twitch harrow	10	-	-
Harness	10	-	-
Implements & barn tackle	5	-	-
Poultry	10	-	-
17 sacks	2	10	-
1½ doz[en] hurdles	0	10	-
	264	0	0
Turnip seed Swedish 7 bushels of the best, 1 bushel offal	30	0	0
Hay 3½ hay remainder of crop of 1809 at £6	20	-	-
3 loads of 2nd clover hay 1810	12	-	-

Hay	6 load meadow 1810 at £5-10 s		33	-	-
	14 loads clover at £6		80	-	-
	10 loads 2nd crop ditto at 4s		40	-	-
Wheat	Wimbush	1 a			
	?Paternoster's	2			
	Brown's	6			
		9			
	50 loads at £3		150	-	-
Barley	Benslow	8 - 2			
	Starling's Bridge	5 - -			
		13-2			
	60 quarters at 45s		135	-	-
Peas	Waby's	4			
	Acres 3	3			
	Nettledale	2			
	Beyond Benslow Hill	3			
	36 loads at ?35s	12	63	-	-
			827	-	-

Farming Stock 30 September 1811 [p87]

	B[r]o[ught] over		827	-	-
Turnips	Swedes right of Walsworth Road	8 acres			
	Benslow Hill T. W.'s	6			
	Red – Benslow Hill north side	8 - 2	100	-	-
	Sold 21 November to J Kingsley for £100.				
7 bushels mangel wurzel seed 140 lbs			20		
In Wimbush	4 acres turnips	15 – 0 - 0			
	1¾ cabbages	15 – 0 - 0			
	1 acre potatoes	15 -- ---			
	Nearly 3 roods carrots	12 - - -			
	Nearly 1 ?acre mangel wurzels	3 - - -	60	-	-

Planted of	Clover Starling's Br[idge]	5 a		
	Benslow S[outh] side	8½		
	13 ?acres for wheat			
	Peas 2 acres	10	-	-
Buck wheat 5 loads		5		
		£1022		

Cabbages [p88]

Those sown in the August of 1810, bedded in October & planted out to stand in May 1811 proved very good & mostly of large weights in October 1811. I took one up weighing 42 lbs, others weighed respectively 40, 39 & 38 & many above 30 lbs, few so little as 10 lbs. The average I think about 16 lbs amounting at 5000 per acre to above 35 tons.

Mangel Wurzel 1811 [p89]

1 lb sown at the end of April on 30 perches.
Produce not well ascertained but it was good & the cattle eat it greedily in the last week of February 1812. I planted for seed about 820 roots (which had been taken up in November & laid by).
Produce 6 bush[el]s or 120lbs of seed.

Turnips

Kingsley sent to the turnips on Benslow Hill Piece (8 [acres] 2 [roods] 0 [perches] red) on the 27 November 1811 220 sheep. They remained 3 weeks. The next fortnight there were 200 & the following 11 days to 9 January – 230 being equal to 1360 sheep for one week & valuing the keep at 6d per head per week amounting to £34-0-0.
I sold the turnips at £4 per acre amounting to £34.
See 3 leaves afterwards.

Honeysuckles 7 November 1811 [pp90-91]

I took up the layers of an evergreen honeysuckle amongst the stools in the Frame Ground & had 201 plants from the layers of this year.

Burr Knot apple tree

The nobs [sic] put into the ground will make a long shoot the following spring or knobbed branches with blossom buds upon them will bear the same year. It is uncommonly productive, never misses bearing, is not so liable to blight as other varieties. The fruit is large. It faintly resembles the Ribston Pippin being about its size. For culinary use it is not inferior to the Spanish Codlin and will keep longer. The tree is not liable to canker owing to its not putting out a tap root, but spreading its fibres from the knob horizontally. Monthly Magazine November 1811 page 376.

Reeds 1811
From Rush Mead in Wymondley cut the last week in November - produce 74 trimmed bundles of 3 feet round.[88]

28 December 1811 Bulbs from Mr Desse[89]   **[p92]**

Hyacinths	200
Narcissus	52
Tulips	18
Q. gladiolas	8

(*Inserted in margin*) They turned out badly, hyacinths single white bad blooms.

January 1812
I. Hodgson states his plants at the Folly[90]

	Prices per 100
Oak 4 feet	15s
Ash	10
Birch 2 to 3	5s
Larch 4 feet	15s
Beech 3 feet	8s
English elm 3 to 4	20s
Wych same size	8s
Scotch firs 2 feet	10s
Spruce 1 foot 6	10s
Willows sets	1s

---

[88] Rush Mead is near the River Purwell just beyond the parish boundary of Hitchin. It now forms part of the Purwell Ninesprings Nature Reserve where the reed beds are managed by the Hertfordshire and Middlesex Wildlife Trust. In March 1811 Wilshere paid William Cooper £1 1s for cutting reeds at Purwell Mill. He also paid him £14 13s 3d for thatching work at the British Schools [HALS: 61503 p42]. Houses and ricks in Hertfordshire were usually thatched with wheat straw but reeds were used in a host of other ways, including as stiffening for ceiling plaster.

[89] For John Desse see Biographical Notes.

[90] Isaac Hodgson was the landlord of the White Horse in High Street, but it was Henry Hodgson who in 1816 rented land near the Folly on Stevenage Road [NHM: Map of Hitchin 1816].

Carrots – 19 & 20 February 1812   **[p93]**
I planted 6 bushels for seed.

Planting at Wymondley[91]
15 to 18 February 1812 I planted in that part of the Wymondley field which was
called the Litler common

650	Oaks
300	Ashes
150	~~Alders~~ Larches
50	Spanish chesnuts
	~~Sallows~~
20	Birch
40	Horse chesnuts
200	Poplars
1410	- 30 oaks

29 February Kempston sent 184 willow sets (very good) from Shitlington. I sent
them to the plantation on the common 4th March & they were put in by John
Jeeves on 5th.[92]
**In March I planted about 30 more oaks, 30 more willow sets & about 3000
cuttings of sallow from Shitlington & on the line between me and Adams
120 oaks & about 5000 sallow cuttings.**[93]

~~**Barley 1812**~~   **[p94]**
~~February 29th began sowing – sowed 4-1-0 being the south side of the north
division of Benslow Hill Field. March 13 & 14 sowed the 8 ½ below Benslow
Hill~~. See the next leaf but one.

---

[91] Wilshere bought the Manor of Wymondley in 1806. In 1811 the Wymondley
Enclosure Act was passed. An 1868 map shows six plantations including the Willow
Plantation, and the Upper and Lower Plantations which now form part of Wymondley
Wood. The Upper Plantation includes mature oak, beech, lime, horse chestnut, and ash,
while the Lower Plantation, where there are springs and a pond, has in addition willows
and poplars. The Willow Plantation contains willows, black poplars and beech trees
[HALS: 61047].
[92] For John and James Kempson and John Jeeves see Biographical Notes.
[93] The line was the southern boundary of Wilshere's land in Great Wymondley next to
the ditch from Great Wymondley to Gypsy Lane. There are still oak trees growing here.

39

Daphne Gneorum[94]

13 April – I took up one I had about 16 years since from Mr Walker's garden at Southill[95], which had extended itself in a close circle nearly 6 feet in diameter & was very beautiful till within the last 2 years when it began to decay & was now in a dying state.

Quick   [p95]

Winter 1811-12	sent to Wymondley	20 thousand
		20 ditto
	& afterwards	2 thousand small
		42,000 from my own beds

I bought of Hodgson 93 thousands & Dear supplied some for fencing at Wymondley & fencing at Pirton.

Potatoes 1811 continued

1 April 1812		reserved for seed
I have now left of	Bushels	
Callico	21	7
Morocco	15	3½
Kidney	20	4
Blood Red	1	½
Upright White	13	13
	70	28
For house		**10**
For labourers		**6**
		44

28 April after planting 2 acres & the consumption of the month remain

Kidney	6½
Morocco	4½
Callico	2

---

[94] Probably *Daphne cneorum* introduced to Britain in 1752 from the mountains of southern and central Europe [M Campbell-Culver, *The Origin of Plants* (2001, paperback edition 2004 pp278-9].

[95] P Walker was Samuel Whitbread's bailiff responsible for his Southill estate in 1797 for which he received £150 a year. By 1802 his duties had been taken over by James Lilburne and his son Thomas (Rapp, *Samuel Whitbread,* pp78, 80).

Turnips continued (see 3 leaves ante) **[p96]**

Of 230 sheep which Kingsley had fed on Benslow Hill 130 were taken away 9 January 1812 leaving 100. These remained 4 weeks to 6 February. There were from that time 340 for 7 weeks till 21 March. There were for the last 4 days ?another 100.

		For 1 week
100	4 weeks	400
340	7 weeks	2380
100	4 days	060
		2840
3000 1 week at 6d		£75

They eat 8½ [acres] below Benslow Hill, 3½ in Wimbush, & 3½ in the 6 acres next Nettledale (drew 2½ for cows) together 15½ [acres]. Value at ?£4 about £66.

Barley 1812 **[p97]**

			Acres	Roods
February 29	sowed the north side of Benslow Hill ½ **sown with St Foin, ½ sown with clover**.		8	2
March 13 & 14	sowed the close below **Sown with clover 18 April**.		8	2
April 7	sowed a piece in Wimbush		2	-
April 16	sowed the Benslow Hill 6 acre **Sown with clover**.		6	-
August 17	mowed the 2 acres in Wimbush			
August 20 & 21	mowed 8 ½ in Benslow Hill.			

Potatoes 1812 See 2 leaves forward **[p98]**

		A	R
13 April	Planted in Wimbush Callico potatoes **Taken up 25 September produce 163 bushels. Per McIntosh 138 bushels remain 5 December 1812.**	0	2
	Upright White well dunged **Pitted 164 bushels & for house 40 – 204 bushels**	0	2

28 April	Planted in Nettledale the piece at bottom under the hedge containing about		0	3	10

Kidney	9 bushels
Champion (bo[ugh]t)	3 bushels
Morocco	4 bushels
Blood Red	1 bushel
	3 pecks

A bad crop ploughed up the first time 92, the second time 15. 60 bushels sold to ?Bentley at 20d.[96] See 8 leaves forward.

A bushel of Champion procured by Hodgson as of the best sort planted in the nursery. **Produce 14 October 16 bushels.**

A few of true Buntingford Kidney about a peck.
Produce 3 bushels 1 peck.

Carrots 1812 [p99]

April 15th sowed in Wimbush trenched ground dunged ?lastly for mangel worzel & cabbages 0 – 2 – 20

Produce 24 November 1812 (deferred to this late time by the coldness of the season)		**142 bushels**
Reserved for the house & for seed	**15**	
Farm	**7**	**22**
To Coachman for carriage & riding horses		**120**

Mangel Wurzell 1812 [p100]

21, 23 April I sowed two half acres in Wimbush both well dunged. The seed was steeped 48 hours before the first sowing & 4 days before the 2nd but still continued as hard as at first, the husk only being rendered tough. The furthest (northernmost) half acre was sown broadcast about 2lb of seed, the other half acre dibbled 2 feet asunder & 6 inches in the row.
Began 1 November. From the extreme wetness of the summer it was very difficult to keep the plants alive. The whole was however a good crop, but the

---

[96] Henry and John Bentley were Hitchin gardeners. See Biographical Notes.

drilled was the best in the proportion of about 3 to 2. 2½ square perches of the best produced a ton. The whole quantity upon the drilled half acre was 25 tons - of the other, 16 [tons] as taken up with the leaves. After cleaning & cutting off the leaves a ton produced 17 cwt.

Crop of Wheat 1812 [pp101-103]

Wimbush Field after potatoes	1
Pierson's Close	4
Little Wimbush	2½
Shoulder of Mutton	3
Piece next Reel Shot[97]	2½
	13

I began cutting on Monday 3rd August, but the week being wet, I proceeded very slowly not taking on more than 2 men till Monday 10th or Saturday the 15th. The whole was cut & except 2 acres part of Shoulder of Mutton all bound.

Wednesday 19th I inned the whole Pierson's, Shoulder of Mutton & Reel Close with 18 stacks from Little Wimbush, say 10 acres in the whole, were laid in a cock in Starlings Bridge Close, the remainder in the Wheat Barn. On Tuesday the 18th a few sheaves having been brought home & thrashed, I sold by sample 5 loads at 90 92 to be delivered on Saturday 23. On Friday 21 the harvest thrashed over, we not untying the sheaves, the produce of the acre in Wimbush & 12 sheaves beyond from Little Wimbush. This was dressed by Robinson on Friday 22nd & produced 5 loads 2 bushels including ½ bushel off[al].
I found a bushel to weigh ?6½.

Robinson computes that more than a load remains to be thrashed from the produce of the Wimbush acre.

Thrashed 26 September produce 6 bushels, total 33 bushels.

The number of stacks in each field was as under generally of 10 sheaves to a stack (but a few at the ends of the rows were larger).
21 October the whole of that laid in the Wheat Barn was thrashed out.

Produce from 1 acre Wimbush [6] loads 2 bushels, produce from 2 acres L[ittle] Wimbush 14 loads, = 20 loads 2 bushels, best 19 loads produce £70 – 11s, off[al] corn 1 [load] 2 [bushels] worth £3 – 09s.

---

[97] Next to Little Benslow Hill later absorbed into it.

		Stacks
Pierson's	4 acres	147
Wimbush	1 acre	47
Little Wimbush **eaten down close**	2½	128
by sheep 15 April		
Shoulder of Mutton	3	117
after fallow		
Reel Close	2½	113
	13	552

This, reckoning 16 sheaves to a bushel, would give 69 loads or about 5⅓ per acre.

Crop of Barley 1812   **[pp104-105]**

North side of Benslow Hill	8 - 2	
Close below Benslow Hill	8	
In Wimbush	2	
Close on the south side of		
Benslow Hill Road	6	**producing 34 quarters**
	24 – 2 - 0	

August	17, 18, 19	cut Benslow Hill
	21 & 22	cut the Close below & Wimbush
	24 & 25	cut the 6 acres
	26, 27, 28	inn Benslow Hill & Wimbush
September	2, 3 & 4	inn the Close below
	& 5 & 7	inn the 6 acres

16 November the forestye of the Lower Barn which contained pretty exactly 2 acres has produced

	best	**?[9]**	**6**
	off[al] corn	**1**	**7**
		11 quarters	**5 bushels**

8½ sold at 66s.

Benslow Hill produced	54	one horse loads laid in the Lower Barn
The Six Acres produced	30	such loads also laid there & together filling the barn.

44

The lower 8 acres produced

	69	laid on a rick in the field
and the two acres on Wimbush	13	laid in the Wheat Barn
	166	

I estimate the quantity	Quarters
From Benslow Hill at	42
The Six Acres	28
Lower 8 Acres	50
Wimbush	10
But this will be the utmost	130

Crop of Peas 1812 [p106]

On Brown's Close

Great Clay coloured pea	1 acre	**7 loads laid on barley rick**
Crown pea	1 acre	**4 loads laid in small barn 29 August**
Maple	3 acres	**8 September 2 loads laid on top of barley rick. 10 September (*blank*) loads in the hovel in the rick yard & in the forestye of the Wheat Barn.**

Oats

Dimsey's Close   1 acre

A good deal trodden down & damaged by guinea fowls
4 loads inned 9 September & laid in small barn.

Farming Stock 30 September 1812 [pp107-109]

	£ - s - d
3 horses **45, 20, 15**	80 - - - -
4 cows & heifers **£18 – 12 – 9 – 6 – 6**	50 - - - -
Hogs – 3 sows at £2 10s, boar £2, 3 stores at £3, 10 at 15s	25 - - -- -
4 carts	30

4 ploughs & 3 harrows[98]	15
Scuffler & twitch harrow	10
Harness	10 - 0 - 0
Implements & barn tackle	5
Poultry	10 - - - -
10 sacks	3 - - - -
Hurdles (nil)	
	238 - - - -
Swedish turnip seed 8 bushels	16
Yellow Scotch turnip 3 pecks	
4 loads meadow hay 1811	20
4 loads first clover 1811	22
4 loads second crop ditto	12

54 / 308

Farming Stock 30 September 1812 continued

		Brought forward	Lo	£308 – 0 - 0
Hay 1812	Meadow from 4 acres **from Hollow Lane[99] & ?Home Clo[se]**	8	35 - - - -	
	Clover 1st crop of 13½ acres	27	100 - - - -	
	Second crop of 5 acres	5	20 - - - -	
	Clover seed 8½ acres growing on Benslow Hill **This is a mere guess probably a good deal under the value. From the lateness of the season it turned out not to be worth the labour of ?getting & thrashing.**		25 - - - -	
Turnips	Swedish Waby's & adjoining 3 closes	7 a		
	Wimbush	1 a		
	Small closes above Benslow Hill white & red	7 a		
	Nettledale yellow	1 a	70	
				558 - - - -

---

[98] On 19 Feb 1812 Wilshere paid William Plenty £8 6d for a patent plough [HALS: 61504 p32].
[99] Presumably from Mount Garrison.

Plant of clover	Benslow Hill	4½	
	Close below	7½	
	6 Acres	<u>6</u>	
		18}	
Plant of	St Foin Benslow Hill	4}	**£66**
	Cabbages	2 a	20
	Potatoes 1 a Wimbush 3 roods Nettledale		30
	Mangel wurzell	1 a	10
	Nearly 3 roods carrots		10
Sown	Wheat Starlings Br[idge] Close seed cost	5 a	12
	Buck wheat	1 a	5
	Mangell wurzell seed not cut		<u>10</u>
(This total omits the £66 for clover and sanfoin added later in red ink.)			655 - - - -

Farming Stock 30 September 1812 continued [p110]

	Bro[ugh]t forward		Lo	£655
Corn of the last harvest				
Wheat	Pierson's	4 a	18	
	Hill next Reel Shot[100]	2½	11	
	Little Wimbush	2½	14	
	Shoulder of Mutton	3	<u>15</u>	
	at 12s per bushel		54	160
	Wimbush **Thrashed & 5 loads sold**	1	6½ Lo	
Barley	Benslow Hill	8½		
	Close below	8		
	6 acres	6		
	at 40s		130 qu	260
Oats		1 a	3 qu	5 - - - -
Peas		5 a	12 Lo	20 - - - -
1 acre tares sown				
				1100 - - --

---

[100] This was the piece of land above Little Benslow Hill or TW's Six Acres. The two fields were later amalgamated.

October 1812 Grafts of Mr Knight's apples [p111]

Sir John Sebright will direct his Gardener to send grafts of all the best sorts.[101]

Orchard Fruit 1812

Failed in so great a degree that I had not more than about

	2 bushels	of baking apples
	½ bushel	of Golden Pippins
		of Nonpareils
Pears	2 bushels	Chaumantelle
	4 bushels	Swans Egg
	½ bushel	stewing pears
	½ bushel	Beury
	1 peck	Bergamot

Quick [p112]

In the winter of 1811/12 I took up & planted (with a much
greater no. about 92 thousand which I purchased) for fencing at

Wymondley & Pirton[102]	41,000
In the winter of 1812/13	14,000
Worth 8s per thousand	55,000

Pines 1812

Up to September 3, I have cut in all 50 of which scarcely one half weighed
above a pound – the heaviest 2lb & 10 varying from that to 1½.
I cut afterwards to 28 November 20 more of which 12 were from 2lb to 1.

6 December 1812 [p113]

Agreed with Mr Brown to become the tenant of his two grass closes containing
about 5 acres (taken out of the 12 acres) from M[ichaelmas] last the rent for
these closes & the 7 acres of arable (which I before held at £14) to be £30-0-0.[103]

---

[101] Sir John Sebright (1767-1846) of Beechwood, Flamstead, politician and agriculturist, was MP for Hertfordshire 1807-1834 [*ODNB; History of Parliament*]. For Thomas Andrew Knight, President of the Horticultural Society, see Biographical Notes. One of the new varieties of apples he raised, the Downton Pippin, was producing fruit in Wilshere's garden in 1823. See p163 below.

[102] Wymondley and Pirton had recently been enclosed.

Mangell wurzell seed cut in November & dried with difficulty. From 1000 plants I had 124 lbs prime seed & about 10 lb offal.
12 February 1813 put up 100 lbs for Murray at 1s 9d per pound.

Produce of Potatoes 1812 from Robinson's Account [p114]
exclusively of those planted in different parts of the gardens.

	Bushels
From Wimbush Field half an acre of Callico Potatoes taken up 25 Sept	163
Half an acre of the Upright White from the same field taken up October	204
exclusively of Champion 16, Morocco 9, Kidney Buntingford 3, blood red nearly 1	
About 3 roods in Nettledale taken up Nov with the gleanings 7 Dec	107
	474

Potatoes 1812 continuation 15 January 1813 [p115]
Robinson gives the following account of the application of the produce of Nettledale & of the gleanings of the 2nd half acre of Wimbush:

	Bushels
Bentley[104] has had	60
The garden men & labourers have had	30
Remains in the stable	90
at the lower farm rather more than	30
4 or 5 bushels were spoilt by wet or frost	120

(*Inserted at foot of previous page*)
22 March 1813 remains after early planting

Upright White in the pit		38
Callico in the yard	38}	
Ditto in the small far pit	12}	50
In the tool house Champion	6}	

---

[103] These two closes were on the south east side of Nightingale Road (plots 759 & 760 on the 1816 map; No 6 in colour section). The remaining seven acres from the Twelve Acres lay between these closes and Walsworth Road (plot 757 on the 1816 map).
[104] Henry Bentley and John Bentley were Hitchin gardeners. See Biographical Notes.

Black	12}	
Kidney	2}	20
		108

Barley 1812 in continuation [pp116-117]

16 January 1813 finished the barley in the
Lower Barn which came off the six acres

south west next Nettledale	5 acres	3 [roods]
& of the north side of Benslow Hill	8	2
	14	1

	Quarters	[Bushels]
From the 6 Acres	34	
From Benslow Hill	46	3
	80	3

of which marketable off[al] corn (*blank*)
This gives rather more than 5 quarters 5
bushels per acre.

2 acres in Wimbush dressed 28 January		
1813 produced	10	4

28 January 1813 I sent to Malein's Mill[105] 5 qu of
barley worth 72s. (I sold the remainder of the dressings

to Mr Ransom at that price.)	18 – 0 - 0
I paid for the grinding	1 – 15 - 0
The carr[iage] is worth at least	0 - 5 - 0
	20 - 0 - 0

The produce was	of flour 5 s[acks] 1 B 12 lb	
	Pollard 3 bushels at 5 shillings	0 – 15 - 0
	Bran 6 bushels at 1s	0 - 6 - 0

---

[105] This was Hyde Mill at the confluence of the Rivers Hiz and Oughton on the parish boundary between Hitchin and Ickleford. William Malein of Purwell Mill agreed to buy Hyde Mill in 1775. He died shorly afterwards, but the sale was completed in 1776. Purwell Mill was sold to James Nash in 1804, but William Malein's family still owned Hyde Mill in 1816 [Ickleford Parish Council, *The Mills of Ickleford* (Ickleford, 2014) pp42-43]; William Malein' will [TNA: PROB11/1019/30]; N Farris, *The Wymondleys* (Hertford, 1989) p19; [NHM: map of Hitchin 1816].

I sent for sale to the poor 5 sacks at £3 -12 -6[106]	18 - 2 - 6
I kept 1 [B] - 12 [lbs] worth	0 – 17 - 0
Offal say	1 - 0 - 6
	20 – 0 - 0

1813 January Turnips - Mangell Wurzell - Cabbages & Carrots for seed
[p118]

Planted in Wimbush about 1000 picked Swedish turnips for seed.
Produce ?14 lbs the sheep & horses ate most of it.
& 610 roots of mangell wurzel **Produce 70lbs,**

Turnips

	Acres
November 1812 sold Kingsley	
Benslow Hill Field	7 red
Waby's & adjoining 3 Acres	7 Swedish
Nettledale	1 Scotch
	15 about £75

His sheep came 27 November & continued 7 March (110 days). The shepherd states the average number to have been 250. Their keep came to about 4½ per head per week.
I drew about 1 acre from the 3 Acres next Waby's instead of which Kingsley held 1 acre Wimbush.

Wheat   [p119]
In October 1812 I sowed on an acre of land after potatoes (without any manure ?subsequently to planting the potatoes) 2½ bushels of off[al] corn wheat, first carefully taking out the soil.
Reaped 2nd August 1813
Dressed 3rd October 1813 being very clean & intended for seed no off[al] corn was taken out - produce 39 ⅝ bushels.
Weight per bushel 62 lbs ?bare weight
Value at H[itchin] Market 4 October 12s 6d per bushel
amounting to £24-15-0.

Cabbages (vide in [*illeg*]) 9 October 1813 weighed 6 of the heaviest together 189 lb varying from 40 lb to 30 lb.

---

[106] Wilshere's cash book records £18 2s received from Mr Parsons in February 1813 for five sacks of barley flour for the poor [HALS: 61505 p41].

Mangell Wurzell – I found no root weighing more than from 12 to 13 lb.

Farming Stock 1 October 1813 [pp120-122]

	£ - s - d
4 horses **£50, 50, 20, 20**	140 - - - -
4 cows & a calf **£14, 14, 14, 8, 4**	55 - - - -
Hogs. Sow & 9 pigs **£6**} Sow in pig **£4**} Store hog **£4**} 4 pigs **£6**} 2 smaller **£2**} A boar **£3**}	25 - - - -
4 carts **omitted waggon £20**	40 - - - -
5 ploughs, 7 harrows[107]	25 - - - -
Scuffler, twitch harrow, drill, hoie etc	10 - - - -
Harness	10 - - - -
Implements & barn tackle	5 - - - -
24 sacks	4 - - - -
	314 - - - -
Poultry - 10 turkies, 37 Guinea fowls, 60 fowls	6
Farm	320 - - - -
7 bushels Swedish turnip seed 1812	10

				£ - s - d
Hay	Clover 1812	27 Lo	£70	
	Meadow 1812	4 Lo	18	
			88	
1813	Clover	20 Lo}		
	S. Foine cl[over]	12 - }		
	2nd crop cl[over]	4 - }	212	
	Meadow	12 - }		
		48		300 - - - -
Turnips	Pierson's		4 a	
	In the 12 Acres[108]		6 - 2	
	On the hill next Nettledale		2 - 2	
			13	50 - - - -

---

[107] On 10 September 1813 Wilshere paid James Pain £5 15s 6d for a Norfolk plough from Maulden plus 2s 6d for carriage [HALS: 61505 p94].

[108] Brown's Close.

Plant of clover	3 acres Joan Bigges Grave			
	7 – 2 on Benslow Hill		**20**	
	4 St. Foin Benslow Hill		**10**	
				680 - - - -

				680 - - - -
Wimbush	Cabbages		2 - 1	25 - - - -
	Potatoes		1 - 2	20 - - - -
	Mangel Wurzell		1 - 1	20 - - - -
	Carrots		- - 2	10 - - - -
	Tares sown		2 a	5 - - - -
Corn			Lo	
Wheat	1 acre Wimbush		7	
	5 Starlings Bridge		20	
	8 Benslow Hill		23	
	2 Spring wh[eat]		7	150 - - - -
Barley		[Acres]		
	Closes above Benslow Hill	7 [a]		
	Of the 3 Acres	2		
	Waby's & Nettledale	7		
	80 quarters			175 - - - -
Peas	3 acres Shoulder of Mutton		10 Lo	15 - - - -
Tares	2 roods		9 B	5 - - - -
Buck wheat	1 Lo (*recte acre*) Wimb[ush], 2 acres in Paternoster's			
			15 Lo	15 - - - -
			say £1100	£1120 - - - -

Buck Wheat [p123]

27th May 1813 I sowed on an acre in Wimbush, drilled on the 29th with lucerne (& which had been sown with turnips 2 successive years). It was cut 20 September and produced 52 bushels exclusively of the draggings.

I also had 2 acres of buck wheat on the land which was Paternoster's garden. It was extremely foul & being ready was much eaten by the poultry. It produced 6 loads.

Carrots 1813

Half an acre in Wimbush Field was sown late & the dry weather continuing unusually long, they were small. I took them up 26 October, produce 152 of which reserved for the house 10 bushels, seed 4, Mrs Mills 3, for horses 135.

Potatoes 1813 [pp124-125]

Exclusively of about half an acre in different places.

I sowed in Wimbush Field 1 acre half the Callico & half the Upright White. The Callico were taken up & produced 117 bushels.

The Upright White were taken up 25 October & produced 170 bushels (pitted for the poor).

I had of the	Black	126 bushels
	Champion	13
	Kidney	6

Mangell Wurzell 1813

30 October I weighed 4 perches of an average quality & found rather more than 15 cwt = 40 tons per acre including leaves.

30 October I began taking up the mangell wurzell storing the roots under a hovel in the yard and feeding the cattle with the leaves, taking it up as the leaves (feeding the cattle plentifully) were consumed.

20 November I left two rows of the mangell wurzel for seed, ploughing back a deep furrow upon & between them & ?covering them with ?straw.

26th November I planted a row covering up the crowns.

Scarcely any of either planting survived the severe winter. A ?few remaining which I planted in March produced seed.

Cabbages

26 November I weighed 36 of the early ones taken indiscriminately & found them to amount to 7 cwt 14lbs rather more than 22lbs each without the lower leaves. Given at noon to 4 cows & weaning calf, consumed by 8 the next morning.

(Page 126 is blank.)

August 1814 [p127]

I began cutting wheat of which I had 21 acres (on the 5th) & though this was at least a week before there was a general beginning, I was too late rather than too early – the first cut being better in quality than any other.

The mildew was very general but I had not more than 4 acres (the old part of Joan Bigges' Grave) affected, carted on the 23rd – Benslow Hill 6 acres, that part of Pym's[109] cropped with wheat 4 acres & with the addition of about 30 sheaves of the 8 Acres below set up in a cock there.

Stacks of 10 sheaves each	
Benslow Hill 6 acres (TW's)	264
Spring wheat on the piece above	130
The 8 acres below Benslow Hill	275
The 4 acres Pym	151
Wimbush 1 acre	54
	874

Wheat August 1814 [pp128-129]

I found an average sheaf to measure at the band 32 inches
Weight 16 lbs of which corn 4 14¼ Avoirdupois – approaching one third of the whole weight.

Barley

I had bulky crops in Brown's 7 acres & Pierson's 4 acres together about 10 acres. Actual measure of corn:

From Brown's good one horse loads 46 & drag[gings] 3	49
From Pierson's American wheat 27 & drag[gings] 2	29
	78

Which I estimate at 60 quarters (but this is I think the utmost).

Filled the great barn, the hovel in the rick yard and that in the lower yard. 8 Acres filled the barn & foresty.

Winter Tares from 1 acre Waby's	6 loads
Peas from 2 acres Nettledale	12 loads

---

[109] Reverend Wollaston Pym. See Biographical Notes.

The wheat from TW's 6 acres & from 4 acres Benslow Hill inned Tuesday 23 August & set in a cock at Joan Bigg's Grave with about 30 sheaves from that close. **Stored in there up till July 1815 & then taken in.**
The remainder of the wheat viz. spring wheat from the Benslow Hill 3 acres, the 8 acres Joan Bigg's Grave & 1 acre Wimbush inned Tuesday 30 August, the barley 31 August & 1 September, tares same day, draggings of barley 2 September, peas 3rd.

Farming Stock 1 October 1814   [pp130-131]

	£ - s - d
5 horses including the grey coach horse sent to the farm **£55, 45, 25, 20, 15**	160 - - - -
3 cows, a heifer of the 2nd year & a weaned calf **£14, 13, 10, 10, 3**	50 - - - -
Hogs – 2 sows £5} 1 boar 2} 2 store 6} 8 pigs 16} 7 --- 5} 9 --- 6} 29	40 - - - -
Waggon	20
4 carts	40
6 ploughs & 8 harrows[110]	21
Scuffler, twitch harrow, drill etc.	9
Harness	12
Implements & barn tackle	5
20 sacks (3 old)	3
Poultry - 2 turkies} 25 guinea fowls (12 young) 60 yard fowls} 20 chickens}	7
Old wheat thrashed 35 loads & offal 5 loads at 50s	100 - - - -
Swedish turnip seed 1812 3/2 bushel	10 - - - -

[110] In November 1814 Wilshere paid £6 11s 6d for a one wheeled plough from T Plenty through T Lowden [HALS: 61525 p12]. Thomas Lowden was the tenant of the Angel Inn, Sun Street, Hitchin [NHM: map of Hitchin 1816].

Oats exclusively of 20 quarters for the co[ach] horse stable		
Loads by estimation	Hay	
7	Clover 1812 remainder of rick in Starlings Bridge Close	20
11	Clover 1813 remainder of rick	50
20	ditto 1813 (sold to Brown)	94 – 10 - -
9	Meadow 1813 – in use	40 - 10
13	of 1814 Meadow & St foin	52
16	[of 1814] Clover	64
6	[of 1814] 2nd crop of clover	21
82 loads		£819 - 0

Farming Stock 1 October 1814   [pp132-133]

		Brought over		£819
Corn of 1814 estimated				
Wheat	Wimbush **produce 29 bushels**		1 acre	
	Joan Bigg's Grave		8 – 1	
	Benslow Hill		4 – 1	
	The Six Acres		5 – 3	
	The piece above (spring wheat)		2 – 3	250 - - - -
Barley	Brown's		6 – 2	
	Pierson's		3 – 2	
	of Siberian barley in Wimbush 2 roods		10 - -	
		60 quarters at 35s say [111]		100 - - - -
Peas	Nettledale say 7 loads at 29s		1½	
	of crown pea in Wimbush		1 rood	10 - - - -

---

[111] On 22 March 1815 Wilshere sold 4 quarters of barley to P Mills at 35s per quarter for which he was paid in January 1816 [HALS: 61526 p5]. He was presumably Paitfield Mills of Roxley House, Willian, son of Sarah Mills. See Biographical Notes.

Tares	Winter		1 acre	
	Summer		½	
		Say 4 loads 50s		10 - - - -
Buck wheat	from 3 roods Nettledale 8½ bushels			2
				1191
Plant of clover none.				
Some land ploughed.				
Turnips	Waby's New Close (Sw[edish])		3 – 3	
	Part of Little Wimbush		5	
	Part of Starlings Bridge		1 -1	
	Part of Benslow Hill		2 - -	
			12	
	Scotch Yellow remainder of Little Wimbush		2 - 2	
	Red & White remainder of S. side of Benslow Hill		6 – 1	
	& remainder of Starlings Bridge			
			3 – 2	
			24 - 1	100
Tares	sown (?besides seed)		1¼ a	4
Wimbush		Acres		
	Potatoes	1	£15	
	Cabbages	1	10	
	Many headed ditto after tares	1	5	
	Mangel wurzell	2	25	
	Carrots	1	15	
	Lucerne plant	1 a		
	Siberian barley	½}		
	Crown pea	¼ }	5	75

Estimate of stock 1 October 1814	£1370
Deduct for overcharges	70
Say	1300

Potatoes 1814   [pp134-135]

1 acre in Wimbush taken up 6 & 7 October, half the Callico & the remainder
Champion. Both were exceedingly good but the produce defective. There was
pretty exactly 100 bushels of each sort. See other potatoes on the next page.

Carrots 1814

11 October took up an acre in Wimbush

Produce pretty exactly		300 bushels
Laid by for seed & use	20	
To coachman for his horses	210	230
Not appropriated		70 bushels

Sold J Eade   **40 bushels at 1s 3d**
J Hawkins[112]   **20**
leaving 10 bushels farm horses etc.

Besides the acre of **potatoes** on Wimbush

I have	Morocco	12 bushels
	White Kidney	8
	Blood Royal	2½
	Upright White	½
	Apple (from ?Roxley)[113]	8
		31

Mangel Wurzel 1814

Taken up on & about 31 October. The plants were not so large as usual, many
indeed were very small. They were not weeded so early as they should have
been & stood too close (18 inches between the rows). I compute the whole
quantity on 2 acres as little more then 40 tons.

---

[112] Joseph Eade was articled as a clerk to Wilshere in 1796 and succeeded to his practice.
John Hawkins was articled to Joseph Eade and on Eade's death in 1828 succeeded him
in the legal practice. See Biographical Notes.
[113] Roxley House was in Willian just over the parish boundary with Great Wymondley.
The tenant in 1814 was Paitfield Mills, son of Sarah Mills.

Cultivation of Carrots [pp136-137]
Vide p[art] 2 October 1818.[114]
In the Co[unty] Chron[icle] of 6 December 1814 an acc[oun]t is given of the
cultivation of carrots upon the estate of Walter Cavanagh Esq. in the Co[unty] of
Carlow, in which the soil is stated to be very light, with a substratum at the
depth of 7 inches of yellow sand - & the produce is given at the rate of 1040
bushels (of 50 lbs each) or 23 tons 4 cwt 1 quarter 2 lbs on the English acre.
The seed was about 3 weeks before sowing well rubbed with the hands & mixed
with sand then sprinkled with water until the whole mass was well wetted, and
afterwards spread on a floor for two or three days, and collected into a heap &
turned once or twice a week to prevent heating. On the first symptoms of
sprouting the seed was sown & appeared above ground in a week or ten days.
The seed was drilled, on one bout ridge [115] (after potatoes). The drill should not
be made till the seed be prepared and ready for sowing, & it should be put in, if
possible, the same day the drills are made. A small plough with an expanding
mould board formed the drills (of ridges) & a horse hoe in the form of an
equilateral triangle & a landing hoe, simply formed, to press the earth to the
right & left of the drills – a common hand hoe, a small roller & iron rake. About
the latter end of March the land clean & well pulverised was set into drills of 22
inches, the tops flattened with a light roller – a man followed with a hand hoe &
drew a rut in the top of the drill followed by the sower. A third covered the seed
with an iron rake, levelling the tops of the drills. 1st hand weeding the middle of
May, the intervals horse hoed. 2nd weeding the middle of June. The plants then
thinned to 4 or 5 inches apart. Another hand hoeing the middle of July &
afterwards twice horse hoed & once hand hoed. The tops were cut in October
when the under leaves were getting yellow to soil cattle. Tops worth £2 – 10 – 0.
Expense of culture stated at £13 – 6 – 8, the carrots valued at 1s per bushel.

Blighted Wheat [p138]
January 1815 I bo[ugh]t of Mr Ransom 2 loads of very thin wheat grown by Mr
Curling at Offley Holes.[116] The price was 21s per load. This was ground by Mr
Nash 4 February and produced

---

[114] See pp113-14 below for another method for cultivating carrots.
[115] Arthur Young described, 'cutting up weeds on two bout (or four furrow) Essex
ridges' while '*bouting*' was 'the lapping of two furrows together, by forming narrow
ridges, a *bout* in each' [*General View*, pp39, 59].
[116] Robert Curling, a wealthy London ship owner with a large family, bought Offley
Holes Farm in the parish of Hitchin as well as other estates. When he died in 1809 he
left Offley Holes to his son John who came to live there with his wife and family. John

	B	p	lb
of fine flour	5	1	3
The whole of the offal weighed	2	3	10
Together	8	0	13

I did not weigh the wheat but Mr Ransom supposed it to weigh 18 pecks per load. From the produce he probably overrated it. Mr Ransom states that the usual loss in grinding is about 1 lb per bushel. He thinks that this might lose 1½ which will give the whole quantity. I take the weight of the wheat at 49½ [lbs] per bushel. The waste will not then exceed the usual rate of 1 lb per bushel.

1815 February 10 [p139]

Took up the following plants:

Larch	84	5 feet
Scotch Pine	200	3
Spruce Fir	150	4
Weymouth ditto	7	6
Poplar	100	5
Lime	200	3
Plane	60	3
Elm	150	2
Apples	20	

Sent to The Frith[117]			19 February
12 February	Larch	24	26
	Scotch Pine	200	300 Hodgson

Curling acquired other land in the vicinity and by 1836 moved to Gosmore in the parish of Ippollits. [B Howlett, *Maydencroft. A manor, hunting park, farm and brickworks near Hitchin* (Hitchin, 2012) pp101-102].

[117] Wilshere inherited The Frythe at Welwyn from his father in 1798. His tenant, William Townsend of Staple Inn. Holborn, died in 1814. Townsend's bailiff, Thomas Foxlee, a farmer, then became tenant of the Frythe Farm [TNA: PROB11/1564/249; HALS: 61526 p23]. In about 1845 Wilshere's nephew and heir, William Wilshere, rebult part of The Frythe in neo-Tudor style and moved there from Hitchin. The rebuilding was continued by his younger brother, Charles Willes Wilshere who inherited The Frythe in 1867 [Obituary of William Wilshere 1867, NHM: Lawson Thompson Scrapbooks Vol 1A p2; S Walker, *Saints and Salvation. The Wilshere Collection of gold-glass, sarcophagi and inscriptions from Rome and Southern Italy* (Oxford, 2017) pp19-20, 23-24].

	Spruce Fir	150	
5000 sent in December to	Quick	2000	2000
The Frith			

To Wymondley	Larch	300
	Elm	100
	Apples	20
	Poplars	80
	Sweet briars	30
	Filberts	30
	?Locust	30

200 elms & 100 oak for the hedges in Rawlins[118]

Plants to Mr Brown **[pp140-141]**

1814 December	Spruce	4 feet	200	2 – 16 - 0
	Scotch	2 feet	150	1 - 4 - 0
	Balm Gil[ea]d	18 inches	50	- - 5 - -
	Scotch	7 feet	20	0 – 13 - 4
1815 Feb 13	Spruce	5 feet	30	0 – 15 - 0
	Limes	3 feet	<u>100</u>	<u>- - 6 - -</u>
			550	5 – 19 - 4

Shrubs	Say £5 or 59s
Laurels	50
Dogwood	10
Lilac	40
Honeysuckles	30
Roses	30
Laburnum	10
Syringa[119]	<u>10</u>
	180

---

[118] There are still elm bushes growing in the hedges on the boundaries of Windmill Hill, formerly Rawlins Hill. In March 1815 Wilshere paid Richard Harvey, his gamekeeper, £8 on further account to pay the planters at Wymondley [HALS: 61525 p46].
[119] *Syringa vulgaris*, the common lilac.

Mr Brown paid £4 for L[ad]y Lucas & 2 for Baron Dimsdale 24 February 1815 WW.[120]

1815 March 15 Potatoes remaining

Champion	60 Bushels	
Callico	40	
Black	8	
White Kidney	5	
Apple	6	
Blood Red	2	
White Upright	½	
	121	
Reserve for seed		
Callico	11	
Champion	11	
Kidney	3	
Apple	3	
Black	1½	
Blood Red	½	
White Upright	½	
		30 ½
For the house		20
For the men		17
Send to Mr Mills	5	
Mr Parsons	2	
Mr Eade	2	

---

[120] For Thomas Brown, a Hitchin land surveyor, see Biographical Notes. He was agent for the Wrest Park estate in Bedfordshire owned by Amabel Hume-Campbell, Baroness Lucas, who was created Countess De Grey in 1816. John Dimsdale (1747-1820) inherited the title Baron Dimsdale of the Russian Empire in 1800 from his father Thomas who had inoculated the Empress Catherine the Great against smallpox. John Dimsdale lived in Hampstead, but he also owned the Manor of Willian and land in Great and Little Wymondley and Letchworth [*ODNB; VCH* Hertfordshire Vol 3 pp177-181; TNA: PROB11/1626/280]. It seems probable that Wilshere supplied trees for this neighbouring estate. In 1814 Baron Dimsdale owned a very small plantation near what is now the entrance to Manor Wood, Willian, in the parish of Great Wymondley. In 1839 Thomas Robert, Baron Dimsdale owned six plantations in Willian which he kept in hand [HALS: QS/E80-81; DSA4/119/1-2].

My Brother	2	
Mr Hawkins	1	12
		79 ½
To give away		41 ½

Mushrooms[121]   p142]

16 June 1815 one mushroom taken from the mushroom shed measured 11 inches in diameter weight 12 oz avoird[upois].

19th June 1815 six hautbois gathered this day weighed 1½ oz avoird[upois] the weight of the largest drams 6 grams 4, the girth 3¾.

Robinson gives the following particulars of the expenses of a journey to London with hay waggon in February 1815 [122]

Turnp[ike]	£ - s - d	Other expenses	£ - s - d
Stapleford	0 - 3 - 9	Watton up & down	
Wormley	0 - 2 - 0		0 - 3 - 0
Cheshunt	0 - 2 - 0	Hoddesdon	0 - 9 - 3
Stamford Hill	0 - 2 - 0	London	0 - 4 - 0
Old Str[eet]	0 - 1 - 0	Ponders End	0 - 3 - 0
City toll	0 - 0 - 4		0 – 19 - 3
New Road	0 - 0 - 9	Turnp[ike]	0 – 12 -10
Balls Pond	0 - 1 - 0		1 - 12 - 1
	0 -12 -10		

---

[121] In August 1814 Wilshere paid Mr Nash £1 1s as a subscription for Oldames plan of raising mushrooms [HALS: 61506 p86]. Loudon's *Encyclopaedia of Gardening* describes the German mushroom house introduced to England from Russia by Isaac Oldacre and Oldacre's mode of propagating mushrooms [pp606-6, 806].

[122] Isaac Circuit, a hay salesman of the George Inn, West Smithfield, London, paid Wilshere per TW £8 18s for 1½ loads of clover hay from 1813 sent 23 February1815. He paid £8 for another 1½ loads of clover hay sent 13 March 1815, Wilshere deducted 19s 10d for expenses. [HALS: 61525 p79; Isaac Circuit's will 1833 TNA: PROB11/1822/462]. In December 1807 Thomas Wilshere sold 6 loads of hay in London for his brother William for which he received £32 10s. From this £9 was deducted for carriage and £1 4s 6d for expenses [HALS: 61500 p11].

Potatoes 1815 [p143]

Taken up 9 September	Callico (about ½ the acre)	132
	Champion	77
	Mixed gleanings	64
23 September	Apple (James)	30
	Kidney	27
		330

| | Black | 9 bushels |
| | Blood Red | 5 |

Planted where a hedge had been staked above Wimbush.

Other potatoes might amount to 30 bushels suff[icien]t to the end of October.

Apples (a great failure)

	French Golden	3½ bushels	
	Pippin		
	Red apple	2	
	Nonsuch	½	
	All others	1	7

| Pears | Swans Egg about | 3 bushels | 3 |

Carrots 1815 [p144]

1 acre Wimbush		Bushels
	½ acre drilled	97
	broadcast	153
		250
	Gleanings after a 2nd	
	& 3rd gleaning	46
		296
Gardener laid by		12 bushels
Stored for horses		200

Remainder put in the stable for immediate use.

Farming Stock 30 September 1815 [p145]

5 horses (as good as at the last rest [123] but fallen in value) **£35, 35, 20, 15, 10 = 115**				£ - s - d 115 – 0 - 0
4 cows (2 having calves), 1 heifer, 1 weaned calf **£15, 15, 12, 8, 6, 4 = 60**				60 - - - -
Hogs 2 sows **£5** 1 boar **£2** 2 stores **£5** 6 ditto **£10** 14 pigs **£7** 1 sow Brown **£1 – 15** 1 Foxley [124] **£1 – 15** **32 – 10 – 0**				32 – 10 - 0
Poultry 11 turkies 8 young **£3** 42 Guinea chicks besides 10 young **£4** 40 grown fowls **£4** 40 chickens & some young **£1 - 10**				13 – 10 - 0
			Live stock £	220 – 0 - 0

Farming Stock 30 September 1815 continued [pp146-147]

Implements				£220 - - - --
1 waggon			20	
4 carts			32	
6 ploughs & 5 harrows			16	
Scuffler, twitch harrow etc			7	
Harness			12	
Barn tackle & tools			5	
14 sacks (& 3 or 4 old)			3	95 - - - -
	Old Wheat	Lo	B	
39 – 3 - 0	1813 thrashed **Lower Granary**	39	3	~~50~~ 60
9.3 spring wheat	1814 thrashed **Malting Yard**	34	1	~~35~~ 48

---

[123] Terminology for an annual valuation used in the brewing industry. See Glossary.
[124] Thomas Foxley or Foxlee was Wilshere's tenant at the Frythe Farm and its woodland at Welwyn from 1814 until Michaelmas 1820 [HALS: 61526 pp23, 35; 61530 p77; 61531 pp13, 27].

4.2 offal **20.2 best** **34.1**					
				108	
	Barley 1814 ditto	1		1-10	
Summer 1.3 **Winter 3.2** **5**	Tares summer ~~6 bushels winter~~ ~~11 bushels~~			5-10	
					115 - - - -
Oats bo[ugh]t of Smith [125] **Malting Yard.** **10 quarters to Co[achman]** **Stable 14 October**		Qu 21	B 4	25	
Peas bought[126] **Malting Yard**		12	1	15	
All the above grain screened & laid in the Malting **Yard October 1815.**				40 - - - - £430 [127]	

	Seeds		
Robinson	Swedish 1812	2½ B	£5
	1815 Red	36 lbs}	
Downing	Yellow	50 lbs}	
has these	Swedish	153lbs}	8 - 0
[128]	Mangel wurzel ~~10 B~~	225 lbs	7 -10

[125] In April 1815 Wilshere bought 42 quarters 4 bushels of oats at 24s from Henry Smith and another 2 quarters 2 bushels at 22s from him for a total of £53 15s [HALS: 61525 p50].

[126] In April 1815 Wilshere bought 25 loads of peas at 23s from T Chambers for a total of £28 15s. Thomas Chambers, a Stevenage corn dealer, died in 1829 [HALS: 61525 p50; 31HW27].

[127] This total excludes the £40 worth of oats and peas.

[128] John Downing was Wilshere's gardener. See Biographical Notes.

	Canary	1¾ B	1	
	Carrot 5 B	47 lbs	3 -10	25 - - - -

Hay				
14 loads	1814 St foin & meadow		70	
14 loads	1814 Clover		70	
8 loads	1814 Meadow		40	
				180 - 0 - 0
Wheat 1814 unthrashed in the Wh[eat] Barn the produce of about 10 acres stacked at the harvest & lately brought in as 50 loads				100 - - - -
				735 - - - -

Farming Stock 30 September 1815 continued [pp148-149]

Corn etc of 1815			£ - s - d	£735
a	r	Wheat **about 600 stocks of 10 she[aves]**		
7	2	small closes on the hill[129]		
4	1	P[ym's] north side Benslow Hill		
3	-	Joan Biggs[130]		
1	-	Wimbush		
-	2	Ditto spring wheat		
16	1	say 84 Loads	160 - 0 - 0	
		Barley		
8	2	Benslow Hill south side		
8	-	New 8 acres [131]		
3	-	Worbeys (Wymondley Road)		
5	-	Starlings Bridge		
-	2	Egyptian Wimbush		
25		supposed 125 quarters [132]	200 - - --	

---

[129] The Slipes above Benslow Hill.

[130] Later part of Waby's Field.

[131] The New 8 Acres comprised Little Wimbush (2½ acres), Shoulder of Mutton (3 acres) and two closes of an acre each – see below. The enlarged field became known as Little Wimbush.

		Peas			
4		Pierson	22		
4		Benslow Hill	12	40 - - - -	
			34		
		Crown peas 1 rood	1		
		Tares about 2 loads	2 – 10 - -		
		Buck Wheat 7 bushels	1 – 10 - -		
				£	405

Other crops			£ - s - d
Potatoes - see account of produce 300 bushels [p143]			15 - - - -
Cabbages 1 acre distinct & 1 acre mixed with mangel wurzell			15 - - - -
Mangell wurzell say 1 acre. 2 acres were sown but ?failing from the dry weather cabbages were planted to fill up.			7 – 10 - -
Carrots - see account of produce about 270 bushels			10 - 0 - 0
Turnips			
4 a	Wabys	**Swedish**	
8 -2	opposite 12 Acres[133]	**1 – 2 green, 3 white, 4 Bullock**	
8 - 2	South of Benslow Hill road[134]	**6 Swe[dish], 2 – 2 Bull[ock][135]**	
1 - 2	Nettledale	**red**	
23 - 2[136]			80 - - - -
			1267 –10 - 0

[132] In May 1816 Wilshere sold William and Joseph Lucas 75 quarters of barley at 27s 6d for £103 2s 6d less 8s 6d for the cost of emptying and carrying the sacks [HALS: 61526 p37].
[133] Opposite 12 Acres was Lower Benslow Hill.
[134] Little Benslow Hill.
[135] In May 1815 Wilshere sold George & William Ireland, salesmen, West Smithfield, for £46 12s the two remaining bullocks of six he bought on 17 January 1815 from John Nightingale for £76 10s. He had already received £50 14s for three beasts sold by them in April 1815 [HALS: 61525 pp57, 67; 61481/2].
[136] *Recte* 22 acres 2 roods.

Farming Stock 30 September 1815 continued [p150]

				£1267–10 -0
2 acres tares sown				3 - - -
	Clover sown (a good plant)			
4 - 2	South side of Benslow Hill			
8 - -	New 8 acres (made up of Little Wimbush, Shoulder of Mutton etc)			
5 - -	Starlings Br[idge]			
3 - -	Wabys Wym[ond]ley road			
20 - -				40 - - - -
4	St Foin Benslow Hill			10 - - - -
1	Lucerne			2 - - - -
	Tillage 25 acres broken up			12 – 10 - -
				1335 - 0
Due from Kingsley for turnips		1812/13	70	
		1813/14	50	
		1814/15	100	
				220 - 0 - -
				1555 - 0
Debts	Ransom for seed			
	Nash for seed[137]			
	& Crabb for peas	estimated at		55 - - - -
				1500 - - - -
	Allow for over balance or incidents			150
				1350 - - - -

Potatoes April 13 1816 remaining after providing for seed [p151]

Callico	30 bushels
Champion	20
Apple	23
Kidney	12
Black	7

---

[137] On 16 May 1815 Wilshere paid Charles Nash £11 4s for 3 cwt red clover seed at 73s and sack 5s [HALS: 61525 p64]. See Biographical Notes.

Blood red	3
	95
To be retained for use	20
May be disposed of	75 bushels

Farming Stock 1 October 1816   **[pp152-153]**

		£
5 horses stated on the last rest at £115	say	90
27 December The chesnut horse sold to ?Mr Wells for Lady Ongley at £10.[138]		
5 cows, one heifer		50
2 fatting calves		5
Hogs 3 sows having 27 pigs} 1 boar, 13 store pigs}		25

Poultry turkies 6}
       Guinea fowls 14 & chicks 15}
       3 cocks, 36 hens, 30 chickens}
		10

		140[139]
Implements		
1 waggon	16	
4 carts	28	
6 ploughs & 5 harrows	18	
Scuffler & twitch harrow	5	
Harness	10	
Barn tackle & tools	5	
22 sacks	5	
		87

---

[138] Frances, Lady Ongley, was the widow of Robert Henley Ongley, 2nd Baron Ongley of Old Warden, Bedfordshire, who had died in 1814 [TNA: PROB11/1564/300]. In January 1817 Wilshere received £10 10s from Samuel Wells for a chesnut [sic] horse bought of Daniel Chapman [HALS: 61527].
[139] *Recte* 180.

	Old Wheat thrashed	[Lo]	[B]	
66 [Lo] 1 [B] sold & ackn'd to Mr Nash 24 Oct 1816 at £3 per load.	1813 & ~~1814~~	33	1	
	1815 62 lbs per bushel	18		
	Spring wheat 1814	7		
	Offall ?from all	8		
		66	1	
26 Novr sold to him at the same price loads 5 – 1. Loads 71 – 2 at £3 = £214 – 4	Off[al] corn screened & dressed **55½ per bushel**	5	1	
	Spring wheat 1814 reserved for sowing	0	3	
	estimated 50 shillings per load	72	-	180
See Account of the straw of this wheat cock Common Place 111[140] **& produced £60.**	Wheat of 1815			
	In a cock on Benslow Hill the produce of the 7 acres in small closes & of 4 – 0 north side Benslow Hill & 1½ part of Joan Briggs' estimated at 5 per load [141]			150
	Straw of ditto for plaiting **produced £60**			
	Oats in the Malting Yard [142]		16 Qu	25
	Peas ditto		7 Lo	15
	Tares winter 4 bushels spring 2			8
				605

---

[140] William Wilshere's Commonplace Book is held by North Hertfordshire Musuem [1216]. For a transcript of the entry relating to this straw see Appendix One (pp217-18). Arthur Young reported in 1804 'There is so much plaiting at Hitchin, that they will not go to service; boys are here also employed in it.' [Young, *General View*, p223].

[141] In January 1817 James Nash paid £100 on account of wheat. On 28 February 1817 Wilshere paid him £35 16s for wheat and grinding from 6 April 1816 [HALS: 61527 pp11, 36].

[142] In July 1816 Wilshere paid his brother Thomas £19 4s 10d for 16 quarters of oats from Biggleswade for the farm. He also paid him £5 15s for 5 quarters of oats from Barton for the stable at 23s [HALS: 61526 p52].

Farming Stock 1 October 1816 continued [pp154-155]

	Seeds [143]		£605
Robinson	Clover	3 cwt	10 – 0 - 0
	Swedish turnip old	2½ B	
Downing	ditto of 1815	2½ B	
	~~Red turnip~~ **none**		
	Yellow old	8 lb	
	1815	18	
	Mangel wurzell	cwt 1½	
	Carrot	14	
	Cabbage estimated **36 threshed, 12 more = 48**	~~60~~ 48	20 - - - -
	Hay		
	1814 remnant S foin & meadow	2½}	
	1815 clover remnant	4}	
	1815 meadow a rick	7}	60 - - - -
Produce of about 35 acres.	1816 meadow, St foin & clover in the Rick Yard **Clover 8 acres, san foin 4, meadow 9.**	20}	
	1816 In Starlings Br[idge] Close 13 acres clover **The 2 last injured by the weather.**	20}	140
	Of 2nd Crop injured	3 loads	5 - - - -
	Corn of 1816		
Sown with 1 load of 1815 Produced	2 acres Wheat Wimbush estimated at		
	1 acre **broadcast**	5 – 1	
	1 acre **drilled**	**3 – 3**	25 - - - -
good & well headed	Barley - in the Lower Barn & in a rick in Starlings Bridge Close, the produce of 9 acres, 4	**about 3/5 [ths] 2/5 [ths]**	

---

[143] In February 1817 Wilshere sold Henry Hodgson 88 lbs of 1814 turnip seed at 6d total £2 4s and 48 lbs of 1815 turnip seed at 8d total £1 12s [HALS: 61527 p33].

73

	acres, 8 acres (21) estimated at 80 quarters		200 - - - -
	Egyptian barley 3 roods Nettledale 2 qu		5 - - - -
	Peas – produce of the closes above Benslow Hill together 7 acres in a rick at Starlings Bridge Close & in the small barn. Long & badly ?curved. Estimated 10 loads.		20 - - -
1 – 3 – 6 ____22 1 – 3 – 28 **Produce 15** **Lo 1½ B**	Beans Heligoland seed given by Mr Hale[144] Nettledale 1 [a] – 3 [r], Wimbush 1 rood. Estimated **12 loads at 35s.**		20 - - - -
Produce 14 B	Buck Wheat ½ acre (Wimbush)		3 - - - -
			~~1093~~ 1113

Farming Stock 1 October 1816 continued [pp156-157]

Potatoes			Bushels	1113 - -
Wimbush 1 acre September 1/16 produce			348	
Callico large 106 small 16 together			122	
Champion			135	
Black			20	
Apple			20	
Kidney			21	
Blood red			6	
Early			4	
Gleanings			15	
			343	20 - -
Potatoes remaining 3 April 1817 exclusively of those cut for planting				
Callico	15	**Reserve for use**		
Champion	40	**Apple**	10	
Apple	20	**Callico**	10	
Various	5			
	80	**Sold 60 B £6.**		

---

[144] Probably William Hale of Kings Waldenbury.

Carrots	1 acre	370	
	Gleanings **32 say**	30	
	Sold 63 B [£]3 – 3	400	15 - -
Mangell Wurzell	2 acres & weighing as nearly as could be ascertained on several trials of the weights of given quantities 40 tons. **About 50 roots to a cwt. About 11000 roots per acre. If a cow will eat about 1 cwt of this root per day, say 2 tons per week for 6 cows = 20 weeks consumption.**		27 - -
Cabbages	In Wimbush Manyhead 1 a, Brown's 7 a, Drumh[ea]d 1 a		15 - -
Turnips	Brown's 7 acres Sw[edish]	5½	
	Pierson's 4 acres Sw[edish]	4	
	North side Benslow Hill (Scotch)	8½	
		18	60 - -
Tares sown		1 acre	2 - -
Clover sown	next Nettledale	8	
	Willes	8	
		16	20 - -
Sainfoin	plant per Benslow Hill	4	10
Lucerne		1	2
		£	1284
Tillage	7 acres ploughed		
Due from Kingsley for turnips as per last year's account		220	
add 1815/1816 [145]		80	300
			1584
Deduct for debts - beer, smith etc. etc.		84	
Over valuation		100	0184
			1400

[145] John Kingsley paid Wilshere £300 plus £39 10s interest for turnips 1812-1815 on 11 April 1817 [HALS 61527 p51].

November 1816 [pp158-159]
Minutes of Wheat 1815
I laid at the harvest of 1815 in a cock on Benslow Hill (which I brought into the barn in the last month) the produce of

the small closes above Benslow Hill	7
Half the north division of Benslow Hill	4 – 1
Half the small closes at Joan Biggs' Grave	1 – 1
About 4000 sheaves	12 – 2 acres

I began thrashing it early in November* purposing to lay it up. I did not have it dressed but sent it in the chaff to the granary in Kershaw's Yard.
* 1 load for seed – sown with the produce of 2 acres in Wimbush on 18th.

On the 16 removed 19 five bushel sacks full in the chaff from the barn to the granary. (On dressing 2 bushels with the fan it was found to contain something more than one bushel of wheat about 1.1.)
30 sheaves produced of wheat in the chaff 5 bushels 1 peck.

The 19 bushels 2 men had thrashed in a week, interrupted by drawing the straws) & is supposed to contain of dressed wheat 10 loads.

		Sacks	Bushels
November 16	In the chaff	**19**	95
23	ditto	**23**	115
29	ditto	**16**	80
December 10	ditto	**?[9]**	47
19	ditto	**4**	20
25	ditto	**6**	30
		77	387
1817 January 9		**10**	25
		67	412

Say 25 bushels wh[eat] produce of 320 sheaves 13½ sheaves to the bushel. (1 bushel weighs 34 lbs). Forward

76

Barley 1816

		Qu	Qu	B
10 Dec	dressed up the midstage or middle bay of the barn & found it to contain of the best	11 - 5		
	of off[al] corn	6	12	3
28	dressed the produce of 14 days thrashing by one man – produce of the best	8 - 6	10	-
	off[al] corn	1 – 2		
1817 Jan 9	18 days thrashing (there being two men part of the time) produced	12	13	-
	off[al] corn	1		
18	remainder of the 2 bays at the east end of the barn	6 – 2	7	2
	off[al] corn	1 - -		
25	dressed the produce of 7 days 2 men being about half the 2 west bays	12 – 1		
	off[al] corn	6	12	7
	Put up in the cott[age] late held by Jeeves 50 quarters.			
Feb 1	dressed the last week's thrashing remainder of the barn	10 – 4		
	off[al] corn	1 – 0	11	4
	Total produce of barn		67	0
Draggings thrashed March produced		**3 – 6**		
	& off[al] corn	**3**		
		4 – 1 Qu		

Orchard Fruit 1816   [p160]

		Bushels	Pecks
Apples	French Golden Pippin	6	0
	French Pippin 1	1	0
	Cats Head & large ap[ples]	1	2
	Ribston Pippin	0	1½
	Hollow Crown Pip[pi]n	0	1

Apples	Nonpareil			0	1
	Nonsuch			1	0
	of all sorts			1	0
	I sold 1 bushel 8s			11	1½
From Kemp-son	**Pearman**	**B 1**	**P**		
	Royal Russett	**1**			
		2	**-**		
Pears	Swans Egg	5	2		
	Chaumantelle	2	2		
	Cardillac		1		
	Cresan		1		
				8 [B]	2 [P]

1816 Wheat of 1815 brought two pages forw[ar]d   **[p161]**

		[Sacks]	
	Sown		1 load
	Laid by in the chaff five bushel sacks	87	
1817 January 20	ditto **Remaining unthrashed 451 sheaves**	5	
February 4	ditto	5	
8	ditto	8 – 3	
		105 – 3	

Supposed to amount when dressed to 55 loads.

			Loads	Bushels
23 & 24 May	I dressed the wheat & found it to contain	best	61	1
	besides	offal *	3	1
* reduced a load when redressing it.			64	2

Laid up in the granary in Kershaw's Yard.
I weighed a bushel & found the weight to be 60 lbs.

78

Barley 1816 continued   [p162]

1817 March 7 inned one half of the rick of barley (in the lower barn).
April 14 finished thrashing this.

		Qu		B
There were two dressings	The first	8	& offal	2
	The last	16		7
		24		
		1- 1		
		25 - 1		

April – the remainder of the rick was inned - and three dressings have now (31 May 1817) been thrashed

		Best	Off[al] Corn
amounting to		35 – 1	3 – 5
Kershaw's barn (v[ide] ante)		61 – 2	5 - 6
Draggings		3 – 6	- - 3
		100 – 1	9 – 2
In the straw estimated		**12 - -**	**1 -- -**
			10 – 2
			112 – 1
			122 – 3
Sown		8 – 2	
Remaining	Wheat Barn	30 - 0	
	Cott[age]	20 - -	
	&	3 – 2	
88 – 1	Barley Barn	35 – 1	
		95 – 5	

& off[al] corn 2 quarters.

Heligoland beans 1816 [146] [p163]

I sowed in March 1816 a piece in Nettledale lying for 2 acres but cont[ainin]g
about 7 roods **1 – 3 – 6** & a small piece in Wimbush
0 – 0 - 22 not quite suff[icien]t to make up 2 acres **1 – 3 – 28**
with 4 bushels of these beans given to me by Mr Hale.
1817 January 17 began threshing ?their produce 15 loads 3 bushels.
More than equal to 40 bushels per acre.

		Lo	[B]
5	Mr Brand had	5	
- - 1	Thomas Harwood	-	1
1 B	Mr Rayner of Sandon	-	1
3 B	Mr Foster	-	3
2 Lo 4 B	William Lucas	2	3 *(altered from 4)*
1 B	Farr of Weston	-	1
1 Lo	Mr Sowerby	1	-
2 B	Mr Delme R[adcliffe]	-	2
2 B	Mr Brown	-	2
2 Lo	27, 28, 29 I sowed on 4 - 1 south side of Wimbush		
		2	1
3 Lo		12	4
	Michael Chapman[147]		
	TW		

---

[146] Heligoland beans was a variety of broad bean, *Vicia fabia*, grown in the fields for animal feed. It produced heavy crops of small beans and was a recent innovation in farming. Even on Thomas Coke's famous Holkham estate in Norfolk they were described as 'a new and promising article' as late as 1817 [E Rigby, *Holkham: its Agriculture &c* (1817) p24].

[147] John Sowerby of Hatton Garden bought the Manor of Lilley in 1788. He lived at Putteridge Bury. He paid £2 10s for one load of beans in February 1817. In his will made in 1822 he appointed William Wilshere as one of his executors and trustees [*VCH* Hertfordshire Vol 3 pp37-38; HALS: 61527 p19; TNA PROB11/1671/61]. For Thomas Brand, Thomas Harwood, William Lucas, Elisha Farr of Weston, Emilius Delmé-Radcliffe, Thomas Brown and Michael Chapman see Biographical Notes.

Turnips 1816 [p164]

		Acres	Roods
North side of Benslow Hill yellow Scotch part drilled – part broadcast (the drilled were the best)		8	2
In Brown's Seven Acres Swedish – remarkably good (remainder cabbages)	5½		
Pierson's adjoining ditto	4	9	2
		18	-

Sold to J Kingsley December 1816 at £4 10s 0d per acre - £81.
On 7 January 1817 he sent 240 fatting sheep & that continued 6 weeks to be about the average number. They began with the hill which lasted them to 11 February – 5 weeks. They then began the Swedish turnips. 200 additional sheep came in - they finished 4 April. I drew about ½ Q for the cattle & saved ½ a rood for seed.

1817 Wheat sold to J D Nash [p165]

		Loads		[£]
June	13	5 at	95	23 – 15 - 0
July	11	8 at	70s	28 - 0 - 0
	15	6 at	70s	21 - - - -
	29	6 at	70s	21 - - - -
Augt	10	5 at	65s	16 - 5 - -
	17	5 at	65s	16 - 5 - -
	22	5 at	65s	16 - 5 - -
	29	5 at	65s	16 - 5 - -
Sept	3	2 at	65s	6 – 10 - -
	18	5 at	65s	16 - 5 - -
		52		181 – 10 - 0
		3 at	65	9 - 15
				191 - 5 - -

Edward Burr [148]

5 [loads] at	65s	16 - 5	
3 -1 off[all]	49s	7 - 17	24 - 2
Loads 63 – 1*			215 - 7

---

[148] Edward Burr was a Hitchin miller. See Biographical Notes.

* The quantity put up in May was 64 - 1.

(*Written in pencil on last page of note book*)
At the east end of the Pine Ho[use] an early cluster grape from Mr Townsend ?Probeto form.[149]
At the top of the 7th light from the bottom of Pine House a grape called ?Samers has 2 late clusters. 2 below are Black Hamburgh.
2 above unknown.

---

[149] William Townsend who died in 1814 was Wilshere's tenant at Frythe Farm, Welwyn. He bequeathed £100 to his friend William Wilshere of Hitchin. His nephew, George Townsend, is mentioned in Wilshere's account book in January 1816 [TNA: PROB11/1564/249; HALS: 61526, p16].

NO 2 FARM & GARDEN MINUTES 1 OCTOBER 1817 [HALS 61182]

Land in my occupation Mich[aelmas] 1817 [150]

(*Owner if not Wilshere in red ink*)		Meadow	Quantities including fences and boundaries	Quantities of cultivated land A - R - P
	Home Close	**1 – 1 – 10**	1 – 1 – 19	1 - 1 –10
	Saw Pit Close	**1 – 0 – 14**	1 – 1 – 33	1 – 0 – 14
	Rawlins Hill Sweard	**3 – 0 - 0**	3 – 0 – 21	3 – 0 - 0
	Mount Garrison	**2 – 2 - 20**	2 – 3 – 26	2 – 2 - 30
	Rawlins Hill beyond the Mill (arable)		3 – 2 – 32	3 – 1 - 25
	The Linces		2 – 1 - 1	2 – 0 – 10
	Sweard Slipe	**0 – 3 – 31**	1 – 0 – 10	0 – 3 – 31
	Little Wimbush Field		8 – 1 - 5	7 – 2 – 2
	Great ditto		10- 2 – 29	9 – 1 - 0
Waby	Four Acres next Wym[ond]ley Road		3 – 3 – 24	3 – 2 - 0
	Waby's Field[151]		8 – 1 - 7	7 – 2 - 0
	Little Benslow Hill		10- 0 – 35	9 – 2 - 0
	The Slipes above Benslow Hill		7 – 3 – 24	7 – 1 - 0
Pym	North side of Great Benslow Hill		9 – 0 – 21	8 – 1 - 5

---

[150] See plan 1818, colour section No 7 [HALS: DE/Ws/P16] and The Table of William Wilshere's Fields in Appendix Three.

[151] Waby's Field was an amalgamation of the close owned by a Mr Warbe in *c*1770 comprising 5 acres and the adjoining close comprising 3 acres lower down the hill at the junction of Benslow Lane and Highbury Road next to Joan Biggs' Grave.

	South side of ditto		9 – 0 – 21	8 – 1 - 5
	Lower Benslow Hill		9 – 0 - 0	8 – 0 -35
	Five Acres next Walsworth Way (Starlings Bridge Close)		5 – 0 – 35	4 – 3 - 8
Brown	Brown's Close		6 – 3 – 34	6 – 2 - 0
	First Back Meadow	**2 – 1 - 0**	2 – 2 - 4	2 – 1 - 0
	Second ditto	**2 – 1 - 10**	2 – 2 – 2	2 – 1 - 10
	Walsworth Way Close		4 – 0 -38	3 – 3 - 2
Ransom	Ransom's Meadow	**2 – 0 – 13**	2 – 1 – 33	2 – 0 – 13
Meadow net quantity		**15 - 0 - 18**	116- 0 -39	105- 1 -30
1820 Nettledale (**late** Ransom)	8 – 2 – 8			
(**late** TW)	1 – 3 – 6		10 – 1 –14	9 – 3 -26
			126 –2-13	115–1–16

Minutes on Crops of 1817 [p1]

Wheat in Starlings Bridge Close	213 Sheaves
In the Eight Acres opposite to Wimbush[152]	370
In Waby's Close next Wym[ond]ley Road	140
estimated at 100 loads	723

(Page 2 is blank.)

---

[152] This is Little Wimbush Field.

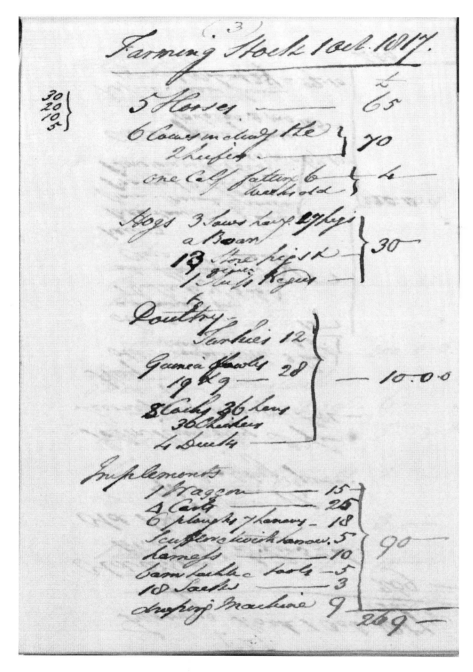

Farm and Garden Minutes: farming stock, 1st October 1817 (*HALS: 61182*)

Farming Stock 1 October 1817 [p3]

	£ - s - d
5 horses £**30, 20, 10, 5**	65
6 cows including the 2 heifers	70
One calf fatting 6 weeks old	4 - -

Hogs - 3 sows having 17 pigs, a boar, 13 store pigs & 1 ?gilt 1 [*illeg*] Negus[153]		30 - -
Poultry - Turkies 12 Guinea fowls 19 & 9 - 28 8 cocks, 36 hens, 36 chickens 4 ducks		10 – 0 - 0
Implements		
1 waggon	15	
4 carts	25	
6 ploughs, 7 harrows	18	
Scuffler & twitch harrow	5	
Harness	10	
Barn tackle & tools	5	
18 sacks	3	
Dressing machine [154]	9	90 - - - -
		269 - - - -

Farming Stock 1 October 1817 continued [pp4-5]

	£269 - - -
Old Wheat Mr Nash D[ebit] for 52 loads	
Old Barley 91 quarters in the Malting Yard	
John Kingsley D[ebit] for turnips of 1816-17 - £81	
Hay	

---

[153] Samuel Negus was a clothier who had acquired though his wife a butcher's stall in Hitchin Market Place [HALS: DE/Ha/B1969 deed 1819].
[154] On 16 June 1817 Wilshere paid Corderoy £1 for a corn cutter [HALS: 61527 p124].

Old	Meadow 1816 good 3 loads at £5	15 - -	
Old	damaged - a remnant in the Rick Yard 5 Lo		
	- at Starlings B[ridge] Close 20 Lo	75 - -	
New	Meadow & St Foin from Mount Garrison		
	Brown's 1 B[?ack Meadow], Slipe & Benslow Hill 15 loads at £4–10– 0	67 - 10	
	Clover from 7 Acres 10 loads at £4–10– 0}	45 - -	
	Trefoil stover from 14 acres about 18 loads at 25s	<u>22 - 10</u>	<u>220 – 0 - 0</u>
			489 - - -
Wheat 1817			
Starlings Br[idge] Close		5 a	
The 8 acres of Little Wimbush		8 - -	
Waby's Wym[ond]ley Road		<u>3½</u>	
Estimated at 90 loads say 45s		16½	202 - 10 - 0
Barley			
Benslow Hill		8½	
Brown's		6½	
Pierson's		<u>3½</u>	
A good crop (estimated 100 qu) say 40s		18½	200 - 0 - 0
Heligoland beans from Benslow Hill 4 acres estimated 16 loads at 30s			6 - - - -
Peas – about ½ acre 2 loads			5 - - - -
Tares – Winter from Wimbush 5 bushels at 8s			2 - - - -
Spring from Nettledale estimated at 8 bushels 7s 6d			3 - - - -
Buck wheat from 1 acre in Wimbush 30 bushels 6s 8d **?q[uery] 3 bushels £1**			<u>10 - - - -</u>
			917 – 10 - -

87

Farming Stock 1 October 1817 continued [pp6-7]

			£ 917 – 10 -
Clover for seed			
On the south side of Benslow Hill road		3 a	
In Waby's		4	20 - - - -
Seeds			
Turnips	1817 Swedish	80	
	Yellow **From ½ rood of 12 acres**[155] **My bro[the]r ?owes me 8 or 9 lbs of Yellow Scotch.**		
	Old Swedish 1815	110 lbs 2 – 10	
Mangel Wurzell	Old 1815	170 lbs	
	New 1817	40 lbs	
Canary	Old	2 pecks	
	New 2 – 2	3 B	
Carrot	Old 1815	18 lbs	
	New 1817	38 lbs	
Cabbage		26	
	Many headed C[abbage]	25	20 - - - -
Trefoil seed produce of 14 acres*			
***Trefoil seed**			
Opposite Brown's 12 Acres		**8**	
Part of the close south of Benslow Hill road		**6**	
		14 a	50 - - - -
Turnips growing			
The close on the north side of Benslow Hill		7½ a	
The 3 acres at Joan Biggs's Grave laid to Waby's Yellow Scotch		3	
		10½	40 - - - -
Potatoes			
1 acre Wimbush			

[155] Brown's Twelve Acres.

88

Produce	Callico	**190**	
	Champion	**121**	
	German Kidney	**15**	
	German Kidney in the whole 23		
	Apple	-	
From ?1 rood of the land which Fells held now laid to Waby's			
	Black	**17**	
	German Kidney	**4**	
	Black ~~Red Kidney~~	**9**	
From the slip on Wimbush			
	Dirk Handle	**3**	
	Asparagus	**1**	
	Red Kidney	**2**	
Total		**6**	
			17 – 10 - -
Carrots	Wimbush 1 acre produce **15 October 272 bushels**		12 -10 - -
Mangel Wurzell	Wimbush 1¾		20 - - - -
Cabbages	Wimbush – Drumhead 1 acre		
	Manyheaded (after tares) 2 acres}		15 - - - -
			1112 -10- 0

Farming Stock 1 October 1817 continued [pp8-9]

			1112 – 10 - 0
Clover sown			
Benslow Hill		8 a	
Brown's		6	
Pierson's		4	
		18	25 - - - -
Sainfoin Plant			
Part of Benslow Hill		4 a	5 - - - -
Tillage			

89

Close at the foot of Benslow Hill part of south Benslow Hill	8 [a]	- - - - -
Tares sown	1 a	- - - - -
Value of clover ley, turnip land etc. in preparation for future crops		- - - -
		1142 - 15
Deduct debts for beer, smith, wheelwright etc etc		73 - 15
Overvaluation		50 - -
Net estimate		1019 - - -
J D Nash d[ebit] for 55 loads & Edward Burr d[ebit] for 5 loads old wheat & 3.1 offal wheat		**210**
Old barley 91 quarters *		**190**
J Kingsley d[ebit] for turnips 1816-17 [156]		**81**
		1500

```
* 1817 10 October sent to Mr Beaver to be malted        15
          4 November                                    32
          5 November                                  40 – 2
                                       Quarters        87 – 2
Ground for pigs etc                       1
Fowls & pigeons have had                - - 6
Remains offal                           - - 3          2 - 1
                                                       89 - 3

Loss – which Robinson states to have arisen from
?strewing & rats                                       1 - 6
                                                       91 - 1
```

October 1817   **[p10]**

Potatoes	Bushels	
from one acre in Wimbush		
Callico	190	
Champion	112	
German Kidney	17	
Apple	20	339

---

[156] Edward Burr paid £25 1s 4d on 6 June 1818 for 5 loads of August 1817 wheat at 65s and 3 loads 3 bushels at 49s [HALS: 61528 p49].

From part of the land which Fells held

Black	17	
Black Kidney	9	
German Kidney	3	29

From other small pieces of Wimbush & in the garden

Champion	9	
German Kidney	5	
Dirk Handle	3	
Asparagus	1	
Red Kidney	2	20
		388

October 1817 [p11]

Canary seed from 18 perches of ground in Wimbush	2 bushels	?1½ pecks
Carrot seed from 3½ of same field	44 lbs	
Mangel wurzell from 4½ of same field	44 lbs	

Pines [157] [p12]

1817 31 October

Fruiting Plants	Stove	69	
	Pit	36	
		105	
Successions, crowns & slips		262	
Crowns & succours of those still in fruit		39	
		406	

41	The no. of pines cut in the last summer & this autumn has been 41. The heaviest weighed	(*blank*)
63	The weight of the whole has been	63 lbs

31 December.

Since the above minute, there have been cut 20 weighing about & 5 still remain.[158]	20 lbs

---

[157] Pineapples.

91

Wheat sowing 1817 [p13]

On account of the dryness of the months of ~~October~~ September & October the land was not in a state to receive the seed till very late, nor had suff[icient] rain fallen when I began on the 20th October.

I first sowed the Bean Etch on the south side of Pym's Benslow Hill	4 – 2
A man employed by Robinson in consequence of his carelessness sowed on this 16 bushels of wheat.	
The lower part of my Bro[ther]'s Benslow Hill a trefoil ley which had been ploughed up in August	4 - -
The close which was Edward Waby's clover ley after seed	4 - -
The remainder of my Bro[ther]'s Benslow Hill & late Sir F. Willes above it by Willes – clover ley 3-2-0	3 - 2
November 4 remainder of my Bro[ther]'s 2	2 - -
November 8 finished my Bro[ther]'s 3 acres next Waby's 4 acres & now laid into it after remarkably good turnips	
Sowed on this 3 acres 9 bushels.	3 - -
	21 - -

The whole quantity sown was 13 loads 3 bushels which grew on the 9 acres of south Wimbush mixed red & white of very good quality.

Wheat thrashed 1817 [p14]

October & November. About half the north ?throw of the Wheat Barn part of the crop of the 9 acre close of south Wimbush produced 12 loads all sown with 1.3 bats egg shell wheat bought of Barnet at 52s. This was sown on 21 ?January on Benslow Hill south of the sainfoin.[159]

				[£ - s]	Loads
	?Bro[ught] down				12
1818 June 10	Nash	17 loads at	56s	47 – 12	
July 20	-----	8	54s	21 - 12	
22	-----	10	58s	29 - -	
Aug 10	-----	13	58s	37 - 14	
		48		135 - 18	48

---

[158] In July 1817 Wilshere received £4 4s from Grant in payment for pines for Mr Smith [HALS: 61527 p123].

[159] For William Barnett see Biographical Notes.

September 1818   Remains in the Lower Barn of the
                        wheat of 1817 about   <u>15</u>

                                                          75

This is very deficient of what it ought to have been & I have no doubt that a considerable quantity has been stolen vide [pages] 1 & 5 per estimate.

~~Heligoland Beans 1817~~   V[ide] p30   **[p15]**
~~On four acres & a rood on Benslow Hill — the crop was exceedingly short. The whole thrashed January 1818 11 loads 2 bushels.~~
     ~~Set in Starlings Bridge Close~~   ~~10 bushels~~
     ~~Mr Crabb~~   ~~16~~
     ~~Farr, Weston~~   ~~5~~

Hen's Egg 2nd April 1818 one was sent me from the farm weighing 3¼ oz.

Mangel Wurzel 1817   **[p16]**
Began to take it up 1 November - finished. The crop is full in point of number but very defective in weight from the drought of May & June which kept it long from growing. The produce of 4 perches of the worst part of the crop when cleaned & the tops taken off left 2 days to dry 8 cwt, & of four perches of the best 10 cwt, giving an average of 18 tons per acre.
Allowing a cow to eat 5 cwt per week an acre furnishes food for one cow 72 weeks.
There ?were two pieces in Wimbush - one containing 1 acre & the other 3 roods. February sent 80 lbs to Murray for sale, ret[urne]d unsold.

Potatoes sold   **[p17]**

1817 October	Mr Eade	30 bushels at 1s 6d	2 - 5 - -
28	Mr Hawkins	25 bushels at 1s 6d	1 – 17 - 6
	Mrs Kimpton	5 bushels	0 – 7 - 6
	Thorpe	2	0 - 3 - 0
	Evered [160]	8 bushels at 1s 8d	0 – 13 - 4

Canary seed sold

| 1817 October | 1 bushel to Draper | 0 – 9 – 6 |
| | 1½ - Farmer[161] | 0 – 14 – 3 |

---

[160] For Joseph Eade, John Hawkins, Mary Kimpton and Richard Thorpe see Biographical Notes. John Evered was the landlord of the Cock Inn, Hitchin.

Fruit [pp18-19]

The orchard fruit of 1817 was exceedingly defective. The whole quantity of apples was 1½ bushels, about half a bushel of pears, besides a few Colmar & Cresan pears.

From the wall trees I had but 2 peaches & about 60 apricots. There was a tolerable crop of Imperatrice plums, but very few of any other sorts. The Peach House ripened about 480 peaches & nectarines mostly very good. The grapes [*illeg*] in the Conservatory ripened well & there was a moderately good crop. A vine in the Pine Pit produced about 60 clusters. There were few grapes abroad & none ripened.

Carrots 1817 [p20]

Produce of 1 acre in Wimbush taken up 15 October 272 bushels.
The crop on about half the ground was thin – the carrots were large.

Turnips 1817 (all yellow Scotch) [p21]

		A	R
October	J Kingsley sent sheep into the 3 acres late my bro[ther]'s with the add[itio]n of that late held by Fells tog[ethe]r about 3 acres 2 roods.[162] The sheep were varied,	3	2
November	The close was eaten & cleaned.		

The following were the numbers kept:

October	9 -14	158 sheep	5 days	= 1 day	790
	14-17	170	3	=	510
	17-21	265	4	=	1060
	21-22	305	1	=	305
	22-29	328	7	-	2296
	29-30	231	1	=	231
Oct 30 – 7 Nov		254	8	=	2032
					7224

about 350 per acre per week 1 week - 1032
The small pieces above Pym's Benslow Hills now laid into
one close 7 - 2

Acres 11

---

[161] Samuel Draper was a grocer in Hitchin Market Place. John Farmer was a Hitchin miller, seeds merchant, mealman and grocer. See Biographical Notes.
[162] This was part of what became Waby's Field.

On the 7th November 250 sheep of which the whole were large & 160 were very large horned sheep were put into the above 7½ [acres] and remained there until 12 December being 5 weeks = nearly to 180 per week. The value of the turnips is £5 per acre or £55 - being nearly 6d per head per week.

Deb[it] for himself of 1816-17 of £81 vide [page] 9.
Tares sown & Peas   **[p22]**
    1817

September 12   Sowed with 3 bushels of winter tares 1 acre at the north
                      east corner of the Nine Acres opposite Wimbush.
3 November   Sowed rather more than 2 bushels more adjoining on
                      about ⅔ of an acre. (The seed was grown by me in
                      Wimbush.)
February 20   Bo[ugh]t of John Watson 7 bushels of spring tares at
                      12/6 per bushel & then sowed 3 bushels in one acre of
                      the same field.
                      4 bushels bo[ugh]t of Watson & 2 bushels grown by me
                      remain to sow about 2 acres.[163]

(About 3 acres of the same field that part which was called the Shoulder of Mutton are sown with 8 bushels of the Clay Pea grown by me & 4 bushels Maples from Hailey.[164])

November 1817   Trees for planting in the Nursery   [p23]
(Remaining after planting those in the next page)

Scotch firs of	2 feet	200
Spruce	1 foot	150
Balm of G[ilea]d	1½ feet	50
Oaks	2 feet	400
Beech	1 foot	100
Ash	1 foot	100
Poplars	3 feet	200
Limes	3 feet	70

[163] John Watson was tenant of the Port Mill in Hitchin [Piggot's *Hertfordshire Directory* 1826].
[164] Thomas Hailey was the tenant of Highover Farm in Walsworth. His wife Elizabeth was Wilshere's niece. See Biographical Notes. In April 1818 Wilshere paid Thomas Hailey £27 for 20 loads of peas December last [HALS: 61528 p34].

Planes	2 feet	25
Elm	1½ feet	450
		1745

See over minute of planting at Wym[ond]ley exclusively of the above.
  Of the above sent to Shitlington [*illeg*] see
  part[icu]lars on the next page   300
  Remain 6 December   1445

Planting 1817 [165]   **[p24]**
November to Shitlington

Oaks	2 feet	150
Elm	2 feet	100
Poplars	3 feet	50
		300

Apple trees	3
from nursery to West's	
Pears from Hodgson	2
Brooks	1
?West[166]	1

November to Wym[ond]ley

Firs	Scotch	1½ feet	150
	Spruce	1¼ feet	100
	Balm of		
	G[ilea]d	2 feet	100
Poplars		3 feet	100
Oaks		2 feet	250
Elm		3 feet	112
Limes		4 feet	50
Beech		1½ feet	50
			912

(*Page 25 is blank.*)

---

[165] In February 1818 Wilshere paid Henry Hodgson nurseryman £42 18s principally for planting at Wymondley and Shitlington [HALS: 61528 p20].
[166] Abraham West was Wilshere's tenant paying £15 a year [HALS: 61525 p75; 61528 p57; 61529 p27]. For Cornelius Brooks or Brookes see Biographical Notes.

96

Cattle [p26]

2 December 1817 J. Kingsley bo[ugh]t for me at Harlow

```
      6 steers at [£]7 – 10 – 0 each      45 - - - -
                          Droving      - -  10 - -
                                        45 – 10 - 0
```

March 1818 Kingsley   had these beasts again the price not settled, supposed £9 each.[167]

24 December 1817

Lord Lynedoch desires that 1 quarter of barley (the best) may be directed to him at Perth.

To the care of Mr Dalgairn's, 36 St Mary's Hill, Tower Street, London.

```
Sent January directed as above      1 quarter        3 - - - -
                                    ?p[ai]d 2 sacks         9
                                                     3 - 9 - 0
```

August last to L[or]d L. 6 March.[168]

24 January 1817[169]   **Trefoil Seed**   [p27]

```
From T. W's Benslow Hill                    6 acres
The close below Pym's Benslow Hill          8_____
                                            14 acres

Produced in the hull    of the best        52 quarters
                        of the inferior        6
                                            58
```

Robinson having now thrashed one bushel from the hull it produced more than a peck of clean seed of a very good quality weighing about 64 lbs supposed now

---

[167] Wilshere's cash book records buying 6 steers from John Kingsley on 29 Nov 1816 for £33 10s which he sold via Kingsley to S Kirkby on 1 April 1817 for £48 [HALS: 61527 pp50-51]. In October 1818 Kingsley owed him £48 for 6 beasts. See p113 below.

[168] Thomas Graham (1748-1843), a successful military commander during the Napoleonic Wars, was created Baron Lynedoch of Balgowan in the County of Perth in 1814. He owned the small estate of Lynedoch in the parish of Methven eight miles from Perth and was an enthusiastic agricultural improver [*ODNB*]. Wilshere's cash book records his receipt of Lord Lyndoch's payment on 7 March 1818 [HALS: 61528 p23].

[169] Presumably a mistake for 1818.

to be worth 40s per cwt. At this rate the total will be about 60 cwt. The price of thrashing is from 3 to 4 sh[illings] per cwt.

February 1818. The best sold in the hull by Mr Hailey to *(blank)* Fordham at 35s per quarter. It measured out 50 quarters 3 bushels losing 1 quarter 5 bushels which I am informed is not more than the usual loss by drying etc.[170]

$$88 - 3 - 6$$

P[ai]d thrashing etc. etc. $\quad \underline{5 - 0 - 0}$

$$83 - 3 - 6$$

About 13 loads of straw worth 45s per load. To [page] 33

Clover Seed of 1817 [p28]

From Waby's Close	4 [acres]
The land late Sir F. Willes above my Bro[the]r's 6 acres[171]	2½

Thrashed February & March 1818		Bushels	Pecks
produced of	The best	11	
	Second sort	2	3
	Offal	3	2½
		17	1½

24 March sold (by Mr Hailey) 2 sacks that is 6 cwt to Dorrington at 67s per cwt. There remains of a second sort worth 58s about 1½ cwt & of what is called offal about as much worth half that price.

Sold 6 cwt at 67s	20 - 2 – 0
Remains 1½ [cwt] at 58s	4 – 7 – 0
1½ [cwt] at 39s	2 – 3 – 6
	26 – 12 – 6
Thrashing at 12s per bushel	10 - 2 – 0
	16 – 10 – 6

---

[170] For Edward and John Fordham see Biographical Notes. On 24 March 1818 Wilshere recived £90 15s from Hailey for 52 quarters of trefoil seed sold to Mr Fordham for £91 less 5s expenses. He then had to credit Hailey for £2 17s because there were only 50 quarters 3 bushels of seed [HALS: 61528 pp29, 33].

[171] Upper part of Little Benslow Hills.

Leaving about £3 per acre, the straw being worth the mowing & inning.

Barley of 1817   **[p29]**

	Thrashing			
14 ½	**29 Nov**	First dressing was that from the south side of Brown's sown last	a	15 - 1
19	**30 Dec**	2 dressing rather better **Laid by for seed. Best of seeds sold.**	b	12 - 7
17	**31 Dec**	3rd from Benslow Hill excellent	c	18 - 6
12	**? Jany**	4th from same	d	17 - -
14-6		5th	e	11
24½	**7 Feby**	6th	f	24 – 4
				99 - 2

19 March 1818 The produce of 1 acre North Side of Benslow Hill about 3:

Sold to W & Joseph Lucas[172]	Qu	B			
1817 Dec 2	14	1	**(a)** at	37s	26 – 1 – 0
1818 Jan 7, 17	29	5	**(c,d)**	60s	88 – 15 – 0
Jan 27	10	-	**(e)**	41s 6d	20 – 14 – 0
Feb 2	25	4	**(f)**	55s	70 – 0 – 0
24	12	2	**(b)**	40s	24 – 9 – 0
					229 - 19 - 0
Lord Lynedoch	1		b[rough]t o[ver]		3
	92	4			
?offall	6	6			
	99	2			

Heligoland Beans of 1817   **[p30]**
From 4 acres south side of Benslow Hill an extremely short crop.

	Bushels	Bushels
Produce		56
Sown in Starlings Bridge Close	10	
Sold to Harwood	2	

---

[172] William and Joseph Lucas were Hitchin brewers and maltsters. See Biographical Notes.

Crabb	14
Farrs[173]	15
My Bro[the]r T.	6
	47
Remain 17 March	9

Potatoes 1817 (vide page 10)   [p31]
18 March 1818.

Besides a very large consumption in the house,
these have been disposed of to:

		Bushels	[Bushels]
	Mrs Mills	4	
	T Mills	1	
	My sisters	9	
	Mrs Dove	1	
	Farming men	20	
	Garden men	27	
	French [174]	4	
This is 10 bushels more than			
Downing has an account of	Sundries	53	
		119	
	Sold	69	
		188	
	Remain about	200	
			388

	Wanted for seed	25	
Consumption	of the house	25	
	for the men	25	
		75	
	May be disposed of	125	

(*Page 32 is blank.*)

---

[173] For Henry Crabb, Farr and Harwood see Biographical Notes.
[174] For Mrs Mills, Harriet Dove and William French see Biographical Notes.

Trefoil Seed (continued from 27)   **[p33]**
18 March 1818

About 5 quarters of inferior seed which remained unsold
was now thrashed & produced   Bushels

good seed	7½
second sort	1¾
offal	2½
	11¾

Bushels

7½	=	4 cwt worth	36s	7 – 4 – 0
1¾		1 cwt	30s	1 –10 – 0
2½		1 cwt	20s	1 – 0 – 0
				9 – 14 – 0

Add from [p] 27 price of 50 Qu 3   88 - 3 – 6
                                                                       97 – 17 – 6

Thrashing (from 27)	5	
As above	1 – 10	
Sundry expenses	1 – 7 – 6	

                                                                7 – 17 – 6
                                                                90 – – –
12½ loads of straw worth at least   25 - - - -
                                                                115

Expenses of mowing & inning 14
acres about   10
Net produce £7 10 per acre   105

TW 2 cwt, T. Hailey 1 cwt[175]

About 2s 6d per bushel thrashing from the hull.
8 days labour of thrashing.

1817 October - Barley of 1816 (from [page] 9)   **[pp34-35]**
Sent to Mr Beaver to be malted 87 quarters 2 bushels.

---

[175] Thomas Wilshere paid £3 10s for 2 cwt of trefoil seed 14 Oct 1818 [HALS: 61528 p73].

January 1818 I paid him

for duty & malting 87 quarters at 24s	£104 – 8 – 0	
for carriage of 78 [Qu] 4 [B] to Ware at 2s	7 – 17 – 0	

I brewed of the above malt   7 – 4 - -
                                              8 – 6 - -

Sold 6 June 1818 (on 4 months credit) by Page at 64s.[176]

Straw of 1817 [177]

1818 August 1	Straw at 1½d per lb	644 lb

Straw 1818   **[pp36-37]**

August	1	Stone had with 644 lbs of 1817 **at 1½ per lb**[178]	70 [lbs]
	8		312
		& left 3 bundles for me	31
	15		170
	22nd		417
	28th		391
From 2 acres white wheat Benslow Hill			1321 [lbs]
1321 [lbs] at 1½d per lb - £8 – 5 –1½			

Or about £4 per acre which is little more if any than the value at the present price of straw for litter (£2 per load) supposing there to be 2 loads per acre, but the tying is saved & the shack & ears are of some value for chaff.

Straw of the other wheat of 1818

August 31		312
September 7		404
so far paid for to Robinson		
September 19		486
26	170 & 31	201
not p[ai]d for.		

---

[176] Joshua Page of Ware was a maltster [TNA: PROB11/1869/237].
[177] On 5 June 1817 Wilshere received £18 8s from James Robinson for straw sold for plaiting [HALS: 61527 p61].
[178] On 2 September 1818 John Stone paid £3 2s 10½d for 503 lbs of straw drawn for plaiting at 1½d [HALS: 61528 p63].

Beans 1818 [p38]

I set the Starlings Bridge Close of 5 acres with Heligoland beans which cost me more than £5 weeding. From the extreme drought of the summer the beans were very short & many were shelled.

August 27 they were thrashed & the whole produce was little more than 18 bushels of which about 1 bushel were dressed out as offal.

Peas 1818

I sowed the upper part of the 9 acres that called Shoulder of Mutton with peas, about 3 acres. From the extreme drought the whole produce was very small.

The last load was a headland, was thrashed August produced	3½ bushels
The supposed quantity remaining is	41½
	45 bushels

Wheat 1818 vide 53 [p39]

I thrashed in August 2 acres of white wheat from the south side of Benslow Hill. It was laid by in the chaff. The quantity is estimated by Robinson at 10 loads. (*Inserted later*) Turned out 8 loads 3 bushels of which 2.2 sown in Starlings Bridge. W[eigh]t per bushel 62½ lbs.

August September thrashed the remainder of the produce of 4 acres on the south side of Benslow Hill, was laid with the above in the Wheat Barn (save that 3 loads of these sheaves were carr[ie]d to the Lower Barn & 7 loads from Waby's Field & the Benslow Hill late TW were laid here.)

28 September	dressed of the remainder	13.3
	weight per bushel 62lbs	22.1

Robinson states that 2 loads of sheaves of this wh[ea]t remain unthrashed about 3 loads.

Straw from the above wheat drawn for platting	1321 lbs
besides 9 [*illeg*] to Abbis	65 lbs

(*Page 40 is blank.*)

Orchard Fruit 1818 [p41]

Pears few

Jargonelle	2 pecks

Swans Eggs	2 bushels	
Chaumontelle	½ peck	
Colmar no. 60		
Cressane no. 12		
Gansells Berg[amot 3		

Apples very plentiful & unusually good.

These were not measured but the whole quantity was estimated at 24 bushels.

	Bushel	Peck
Golden Pippin of which Nonpareils	1	
French Golden Pippin	3	
Nonsuch	-	1
Ribston Pippin	3	
Catshead	2	
Various sorts	15*	

* sold 12 bushels for £3 – 0 – 0

29 Sept	Walnuts from the larger tree	2 B	
	from the young trees about		½ peck

[Bo[ugh]t   Golden Pippins of Fossey   ½ bushel
**   Norfolk Buffon from Arlsey   1 bushel**
I had from Brookes orchard at Shitl[ingto]n about 3 bushels before
they were ripe.[179]

An apple of I. Duncalfe sent for inspection 13 September weighed 17 oz, an oval shape girth the ?lengthy 13½ round 13½ - positive length 5 inches, called the Tankard apple.[180]

Onions 1818

Crop very defective. I had not more than 4 bushels on a share of ground producing in ordinary years at least 20 bushels.

---

[179] William Fossey was a tenant on George Musgrave's estate (which was at Biggleswade and Shillington) while Daniel Fossey was a tenant on the Edwards estate, both managed by Wilshere [HALS: 61529 pp23, 27]. For George Musgrave and Cornelius Brookes see Biographical Notes.
[180] For Isaac Duncalfe see Biographical Notes.

Wall Fruit 1818   [p42]

Very little abroad. An abundant crop in the Peach House & very good.

Potatoes 1818   [p43]

From 1 acre in Wimbush Field

	Bushels	
	Bushels	
Callico	194	laid in the potatoe ho[vel] next the Wood Barn
Champion	41	in potatoe cellar
	235	

Bees 1818   [p44]

One doubled hive taken up 11th September cont[aine]d of honey & wax 42 lbs – the upper hive bright & excellent. I took up another weak hive on the 18th of September. It cont[ained]d about 10lbs of honey. Two hives only remain. They are supposed to be strong enough to support themselves for the winter.

Hitchin Parish Rates   [p45]

1817 I was assessed to the Poors and Church rates
at ⅔ rds of   £299 – 13 – 9   that is   £199 – 15 – 10
Increased by Rawlings Hill
& tithes   11 – 11 – 3   7 - 14 - 2
              311 – 05 – 0   207 – 10 – 0

The Highway rate is calculated at the full estimated rent & the charge is 30 days work with a team. Of this 20 days service performed for 1818 giving an extra day of the team for a deficiency of fillers & I paid a composition at 9d upon £49 – 13 – 9

	amounting to	£1 – 17 – 3
	& for 10 days team at 10s	£5 – 0 – 0
	Comp[ositio]n	£6 – 17 – 3

(from ?referment of St[ephen] Swain 15 September 1818)[181]

---

[181] In 1816 the Hitchin Vestry commissioned a survey and valuation of the parish in order to make an equal rate assessment. In 1818 Wilshere managed to have his new rate assessment reduced [B Howlett, 'Another Early Map of Hitchin', *Herts Past & Present'* 3 12 Autumn 2008 pp10-13]. Stephen Swain was a Surveyor of the Highways [HALS: DP/53/8/3, DP/53/21/7]. He lived in the hamlet of Preston [NHM: 1816 map of Hitchin].

(Page 46 is blank.)

The Suffolk mode of preparing wheat for sowing [p47]
Put a quarter of a peck of unslacked fresh lime into a pail of boiling water to be well stirred & poured hot upon 2 bushels of wheat.
(Mr Brown 22 September 1818)

A Cheap Paint
56 lbs lime 28 lbs Roman cement mixed with as little water as possible to be well beaten & to lie four or five days to be then mixed up with 3 gallons of bullock's blood & 3 gallons of water.
(Mr Brown 22 September 1818)

Minutes from Robinson's inform[atio]n 27 September 1818
vide [pages] 51 & 53 [pp48-49]
Wheat   remains of the year 1817 in the Lower Barn about 15 loads.
[Wheat] of 1818 was laid in the Wheat Barn. The crop of 4.1 the south side of Benslow Hill (with 7 cart loads principally of brown wheat from my Bro[the]r's Benslow Hill & laying two loads of 3 acres 1 rood) to the Barley Barn so that this barn has about 6 acres.
In the Barley Barn about 6 acres.
I do not rely on Robinson's accuracy in this mixture, by Jeeves there was 3 acres 1 rood of South Benslow Hill laid in this barn.[182]
In a rick in Starlings Bridge Close about 9 acres.
Sown 23 September in Stone Piece[183] about 11 bushels of white wheat.

Cows	Gentle	Bull	the beginning of July
	Brown		the beginning of August
	Dun		the end of August
	Kicker		not to be depended upon, should be sold, calved in April
	Alderney		calved in July & has taken the bull 30 September
Hogs	(16 sold)		1 sow will pig early in November
			1 sow took the boar 17th September
			1 boar

---

[182] For Jeeves see Biographical Notes.
[183] Also known as Walsworth Way Close or Rail Piece or Dunche's Field.

	3 large stores for bacon	
	4 smaller stores	
	1 fit to kill (about 7 stone)	
Hay	of 1816 damaged clover fit to cut into chaff	about 4 loads
	Meadow of 1817	about 4½ loads
	Meadow of St Foin 1818	20 loads
	Clover of 1818	20 loads
	A few cwts cut off for the horses	
Land for Peas	South side of Benslow Hill was peas in 1808	
	Waby's – Nettledell 4 acres in 1813	
	The 3 acres now laid to it lower)	
	The Slipes above Benslow Hill in 1810	

Carrots 1818   [p50]

19 October took up 3 roods in Wimbush Field south end. Produce - 300 bushels.

Wheat sown 1818   [p51]

	Net Quantity Acres			Bushels
Sept 23	4 – 0 – 0	On Stone Piece (clover ley) white wheat}		12
Oct 6 & 7	8 - - - -	On 8 acres on the north side of Benslow Hill (clover ley) leaving about 2 roods which had been sown with buck wheat left for partridges		24
(north side)		Bo[ugh]t of Kempston	15	
		Bo[ugh]t by TW part of 3 loads	9	
6 to 10	6 - 2	Dibbled on Brown's Piece (ley) on the north side of my own white wheat	2½	
		next to this Talavera wheat from Brown	5	
		then Talavera wheat from Crowther	5	

107

		Remainder of the close 2 acres south side white wheat[184]	1½	
				14
Novr 3		Drilled on 1 acre of Wimbush after		
	1 -	potatoes		3
	19 - 2		[altered from 52]	53
	2	Remainder of the north side of Benslow Hill		

Potatoes 1818 [p52]

I had in different parts of the Garden suff[icien]t to last from the time they became fit for use in July, till the end of October & suff[icient] of the early ?kinds for seed.

In the third week of October an acre of Wimbush Field was taken up & produced

	Bushels	
Callico	194	**Laid in the Potato Ho[vel] next Wood Barn**
Champion	41	**in Potato cellar**
German Kidney	5}	
Apple	3}	**at home**
Black	3}	
Mixed harrowed out	13	**from Potato cellar**
	259	

Sold	**Mr Eade**	**Call[ico]**	**20**	
		Ch[ampion]	**5**	**25**
	Hawkins	**Callico**		**10**
	Churchilll[185]	**Callico**		
Gave	**Mrs Mills**	**Callico**		**2**

---

[184] Wilshere's cash book for 1818-1819 records payments of £3 to Thomas Brown for 1 load of Talavera wheat, £3 10s to T Crowther for a load of seed wheat, £8 14s to James Kempson for 3 loads of seed wheat at 58s and £8 17s to his brother for 3 loads of seed wheat at 59s. Thomas Crowther was a tenant on the Edwards estate managed by Wilshere [HALS: 61528 pp7, 15, 74, 84, 86, 100].

[185] Smyth Churchill was a surgeon who lived in Bancroft opposite Wilshere. He had retired to Ramsgate by 1842 [NHM: 1816 map of Hitchin; TNA: PROB11/2077/371].

(continued [page] 54)

Wheat thrashed 1818 vide [page] 39 [p53]

			Bushels
August	White wheat 2 acres from the south side of Benslow Hill		43
	Sown on Stone Piece	**11 B**	
	On the north & south of Brown's Piece	<u>**4**</u>	
		15	
Sept 28	of mixed wheat from the 2 [acres] 1 [rood] adj[oining]		68
		111	
	Bo[ugh[t] of Kempson for seed	**15**	
	By T.W	**15**	
	Brown Talavera wh[eat]	**5**	
	Crowther ditto	<u>**5**</u>	
	[altered from 151]	**152**	
	Sown (vide parts 51)	<u>**52**</u>	
Oct 6	**Sold to Mr Nash at 59s**	**100**	
	No offell made		

	Bushels
There has been sown of Benslow Hill wheat	19
Sold to Nash with 6 bushels remainder of 15 from T.W	<u>94</u>
	113
There remains about 2 loads of sheaves supposed at least	14
Stolen about	<u>3</u>
Produce of 4 acres 1 rood about 30 bushels per acre	130

(to[page] 61)

Potatoes 1819 continued from 52 [p54]

April 9 remains after setting about 30 bushels in Wimbush & the Garden 64 bushels

Farming Stock taken 1 October 1818 [p55]

Horses	Gilbert		30	£ - s - d
	Smug		20	
	Tommy		15	
	Dimond		--	65
Cows	Gentle			
	Brown			
For times of	Dun			
calving see	Kicker			
[page] 48	Alderney			50
Hogs	* 2 sows			
	1 boar			
* for times of	3 stores for bacon			
pigging vide	4 smaller stores			
[page] 49	1 fit to kill (7 stone)			15
Poultry	Turkies 4			
	Guinea fowls 27			
	Cocks & hens 36			
	Chickens 25			10
Implements	Waggon with tilth & ladders[186]		20	
	Carts 4, one bad		25	
	Ploughs	3 Plentys[187]		
		wheel plo[ugh]		
		Yorksh[ire] plo[ugh]		
		double plo[ugh]	18	
	Harrows 7		5	
	Harness		10	

---

[186] Wilshere paid John Farmer £5 14s for a waggon tilt and sacks on 3 August 1818 [HALS: 61528 p60].

[187] On 19 February 1812 Wilshere paid William Plenty £8 6d for a patent plough [HALS: 61504 p32]. William Plenty of Newbury, Berkshire, won a prize for ploughs offered by the Earl of Bridgwater at Ashridge in 1805. In 1815 he fitted a wheel behind his patent plough [Grace's Guide to British Industrial History https://www.gracesguide.co.uk/William_Plenty]. In November 1814 Wilshere paid £6 11s 6d for a one wheeled plough from T Plenty through T Lowden [HALS: 61525 p12].

Implements	Dressing mach[ine]	8	
	Sacks 27	2 -10	
	Barn tackle & tools }		
	Scuffler & twitch harrow }	6 -10	95
			235

Farming Stock 1 October 1818 continued [pp56-57]

				Bro[ugh]t forward	£235 - -
Old Wheat	Remaining 15 loads together				45 – 0 - 0
	Mr Nash d[ebit] for 48 loads **vide [page] 14**				135 -18 – 0
Wheat 1818	Produce of 21 acres estimated at 500 bushels at 10s per per bushel. **I have taken this as it stood before any was thrashed for sowing or sale.**				250 – 0 – 0
For sowing **vide [page] 13**		A	R		
	Benslow Hill	4	1		
	Opposite	9	1		
	Waby's	7	2		
	Acres	21	-		
Barley 1816	G. Beaver d[ebit] for 78 quarters of malt (estimated) .				240 – 0 – 0
	Produce of 1818 – 15 acres estimated at 40 quarters & 60s per quarter **Turned out 39 quarters 6 bushels at 62s.**				
	Upper Benslow Hill		**8**		
	Little Wimbush & the 3 acres		**7** **15 a**	120 – 0 – 0	
Heligoland beans	17 bushels **Mill Lane**[188]		**[£]** **8**		
Peas	30 bushels **(vide [page] 38)**		**12**	20 – 0 - 0	

---

[188] Mill Lane was Portmill Lane where Wilshere had a granary and other farm buildings.

111

Hay	damaged clover of 1816 3 loads at 40s	6	
	1817 Meadow 4 loads at 120s	24	
	1818 Clover 20 loads at 130s	130	
	S Meadow & Sainfoin 20 loads at 110s	110	270 – 0 - 0
Clover Seed	Brown's & Stone Piece & a small part of North Benslow Hill estimated at 15 cwt		50 - - - - -
Turnips	Due from Kingsley for 1816/1817	81	
	for 1817/18 **vide page 21**	49	130 - - - - -
Turnips 1818 growing	Stevenage Waby's[189] **Scotch**	3½ [acres]	
	Rawling's Hill **Scotch**	6½ [acres]	
	Wimbush **3 acres Swedes**	4 [acres]	70 - - - - -
Turnip Seed	33 Scotch new 33 **sown 1819 Little Wimbush**		
	1817 Swedes 3 bushels fine **grown in Brown's**		
	1813 3 bushels not so good **given to Robinson**		
Clover seed	dressed 1cwt		
Trefoil	dressed ½ cwt		5 - - - - -
Mangel wurzle seed	old 5 bushels, 1817 1 bushel		- - - - - -
Carrot seed	1 bushel		- - - - - - -
Cabbage	Scotch 10 lbs, - manyheaded 15		- - - - - - -
			1570 -18-0

---

[189] Edward Waby of Stevenage was the cousin of Edward Waby, butcher of Hitchin, who died in 1808.

Farming Stock 1 October 1818 continued [p58]

				£1570 -18-0	
Wimbush Field exclusively of turnips	Cabbages	1 a	10		
	Potatoes	1 a	20		
	Carrots	0 – 3 r	15		
	Mangel Wurzell	1 a	10		
In Little Wimbush Cabbages			5	60 - - - - -	
Kingsley for 6 beasts[190]				48 - - - - -	
Tillage etc	Ley for wheat Brown's & Stone Piece		10 a		
	Clover for the Slipes above Benslow Hill		7 a		
	Broke up for wheat		20 a	30 - - - - -	
Furniture in Bailiff's ho[use][191] £10 **Bed, bedstead, bolster & pillows, 2 blankets, coverled, 2 tables, 5 chairs, clock, grate**					
				1708 –18 - 0	
Deduct for over val[uatio]n		120			
For debts to brewer, smith & wheelwright		[8]8 – 18		208 – 18 - -	
				1500 – 0 - 0	

Carrots – cultivation of [p59]
(vide part 1 1814)[192]
In the Monthly Rev[iew] for October 1818 there are some extracts from a paper of Mr Burrows published in the proceedings of the Board of Agriculture stating an average produce of £27 18s 3½d at an expense of 10 13 2½.
The carrots are sown on wheat stubble ploughed 1 in autumn, 2 in February, 16 loads of dung in the last week in March, ploughed the 3rd time & sown the first week of April. 10 lbs of new seed mixed a fortnight before is used with fine mould or sand turned over daily, the outside being previously sprinkled with water. In six weeks the carrots are ready for the first hoeing with a four inch hoe succeeded immediately by a six inch hoe. The carrots to be left 9 inches apart to a foot. 3 or 4 hoeings may be necessary – 30s per acre. Crop 700 to 800 bushels.

---

[190] Kingsley bought 6 beasts from Wilshere in March 1818. See p97 above.
[191] This was presumably on the vacation of the house by James Robinson.
[192] See p60 above for another method of cultivating carrots.

113

70 lbs daily to a horse.

(*in margin*) q[uery] if not worth the trial with turnip seed.

(*Page 60 is blank.*)

Wheat thrashed 1818-1819   (from [page] 53)   **[p61]**

		Lo	B	
1819 January 22				
Thrashed the remainder of the wheat in the Wheat Barn		12	0	
	Offal	-	2	62

Straw tied up for platting 336 lbs

from [page] 53	**White wheat from Benslow Hill**	**43**
	Mixed wheat	**68**
		173
	Stolen about	**3**

This will give for the produce of 7 acres 2 roods (vide 48) as 24 bushels per acre.   **176**

		Loads	Bushels
February 22	To Mr Nash at	11	2
	Sown on Benslow Hill		
	where buck wheat grew		1½
	Remains		3½
			62 bushels

1 March Crawley began thrashing wheat in the Lower Barn (part the remains of 1817)

		Lo	B	Lo	B
March	dressed old		19		
27 March	dressed new	16			
	& offal	1			
		17			85
31 March	dressed new	5			
	& offal		1		27
					112
					288

21 loads 1 bushel put into the granary over Eade's brewho[use].[193]

(to page 65)

Barley thrashed 1818-1819   **[p62]**

		Best	Offal
1818 Nov 22	by Jeeves[194]	5 - -	0 - 6
	Some had previously been		
	thrashed for fowls.		
1819 Jan 22	by Taylor	10 – 4	1 - -
	Olney states that he has thrashed		
	at different times since harvest		
	besides the above[195]	0 – 3	
24th	**10 quarters sent to Mr Beaver to**		
	be malted for my own use.		
	Val[ued] 75s per quarter.		
Jan 30	by Taylor	5 - -	
Feb 14	by Taylor	10 – 3	- - 7
22	by ditto	5 – 1	- - 3
		36 – 3	3 - -
		3	
* I had estimated it (page 56) at 40 quarters. *		39 – 3	

	[acres]
This was the whole produce of the Slipes above Benslow	
Hill cont[ainin]g of ploughed land about	7
& of Lower Benslow Hill about	9
About 2½ quarters per acre	16

27 January 1819   **[p63]**

H[enr]y Hodgson states the price of digging as under:

For ground which works kindly & clears the spade – digging one	
full spit with a spade No 5 10 inches in depth per pole	3d
For strong or stony ground	4d
Two spits (no crumbs thrown out 20 inches deep)	7d
For trenching 3 spits deep & the crumbs so as to move the ground to	
the depth of 3 feet (proper for apples & other fruit trees)	2s

---

[193] This was in Portmill Lane opposite the Grange House, both of which Joseph Eade
rented from Wilshere.
[194] For John Jeeves see Biographical Notes.
[195] For Joshua Olney see Biogaphical Notes.

Clover Seed of 1818 [p64]

Olney began thrashing the seed.

		[cwt qu lb]
March	delivered to Mr Beaver at 108s per cwt 3 sacks	2 – 3 – 12
	?cont[ainin]g exclusively of the weight of the	2 – 3 – 13
	sacks[196]	2 – 3 – 14
		8 – 2 – 11
March	finished – further produce	1 sack net
		1 [ditto]
		5 – 3 – 0

2 bushels dressed out & reserved for myself & about 3 bushels of best & light seeds taken out which were sown on the sweards.

Wheat Acco[un]t continued from [page] 61 [p65]

				Bushels
			brought forward	**288**
1819 April 17	Olney dressed of 16 loads the wheat of 1818 from the rick	Loads	Bushels	
	best	16		
	offal		4	84
	16 loads to the granary over Eade's brewho[use].			
[April] 21	Crawley dressed the remainder of the wheat of 1817			
	best	11		
	offal	1		
	Granary	12		60
				432
	Estimated page 56 at 75 bushels of 1817			87
	Remains in sacks in the barn			345
1819 May 4	Olney dressed of the wheat of 1818 from the rick			
	best	13	3	
	offal	0	4	72

---

[196] On 16 February 1820 George Beaver paid Wilshere £44 13s for 8 cwt 2 quarters 26 lbs clover seed at 102s 6d [HALS: 61529 p71].

						417
	Put in the granary over Eade's brewho[use]					417
14	He finished thrashing & dressed					
		best	9	2		
		offal		3		
	Put into the same granary		10	-		**50**
						467

		[Lo]	[B]
June in the granary over Mr Eade's brewho[use]		60	2
	offal good	3	-
	1 bad		1
		63	3

21 acres at 4½ loads	**473½ B**	
21 acres 22 bushels per acre	**462 B**	**To pa[ge] 81**

(*There is no p66.*)

Oranges [p67]

1819 April 28 amongst 17 I have gathered to prevent their injuring the trees was one of a fine form & colour meas[ur]ing 12¾ inches round.

1819 Straw

April sold 10 loads to J Marshall at 45s.[197]

£22 10s paid 14 September 1819.

5 May delivered	5 loads
	3
& for Crabb	2
	10

7 June I have in store about 10 loads exclusively of about 2 loads residue of 4 loads from Hewes.

Malt [p68]

24 January 1819 I sent to Mr Beaver to be malted for me · · · 10 Qu

barley **then worth 75 [shillings per quarter].**

Of the malt made of the above I brewed[198] · · · April 1 · · · 1 – 4

---

[197] Hitchin brewer in partnership with Henry Crabb. See Biographical Notes.

117

3	1 – 4
6	1 – 4
9	1 – 4
May 13	<u>1 – 4</u>
	7 - 4
Remains	2 – 4

Fetched home & deposited in seed room 5 June 1819.

I bought on the same day of Richard Watson 10 quarters at 72s.[199]   10

[*illeg*] **same time vide p[age] [*illeg*].**

Minutes 6 June 1819 Barley – malt & seed   [p69]

George Beaver D[ebit]

1819 January 24	10 quarters barley	at 75s	£37 – 10
February 22	15 - 7	at 61s	<u>48 – 8</u>
			85 - 18
Clover seed	8 – 2 - 26	at 102s 6d	<u>44 – 13</u>
			130 – 11

Cr[edit] making 10 quarters for my use with duty at 25s   12 - 10

Beer for the Hay time & Harvest of 1819   [p70]

1819 May 13	brewed for the above purposes with 12 bushels malt & 12 lbs hops		[Hogsheads]
		Ale	2 Hds
		Smaller beer	3 Hds
	August in add[itio]n to the above took from the cellar		
		Ale	1⅔ Hds
		Small beer	½ H

Calculation of the above

20 bushels malt at 66s	8 – 5 - 0
20 lbs hops at 1s 9d	1 – 15 – 0

---

[198] On 29 October 1819 Wilshere paid Robert Rose, a Hitchin cooper, £4 18s 9d for brewing for his house and farm [HALS: 61529 p44]. See Biographical Notes.

[199] On 5 June 1819 Wilshere paid Richard Watson £36 for 10 quarters of malt [HALS: 61529 p118]. Watson was a Hitchin malster and a neighbour of Wilshere's at what became 102-103 Bancroft. He died in 1838 [NHM: 1816 map of Hitchin; HALS: will of Richard Watson 150HW71].

Brewer's fuel etc		2 – 4 – 10		
		£12 - 4 – 10		
3 H[ogshea]ds ⅔	**=**	**198 gall[ons]**	**at 11d**	**9 - 1 – 6**
3 H[ogshea]ds ½	**=**	**190 g[allons]**	**at 4d**	**3 - 3 – 4**
				12 - 4 – 10

Estimate of Labour for Harvest of 1819 [p71]

Jeeves}	Harvest men at £5 for the month each to have 5 pints of ale
Olney}	per day & small beer.
Froy }	
Gray }	
Abbis	To have harvest wages & to work harvest hours that is from morning to sunsetting. To go into the field when wanted for carting etc.
French	To go into the field when wanted & to have harvest wages for harvest
Knightley[200]	To cut 4 acres of oats & may cut wheat & hoe turnips by the acre.

Reaping	14 acres	wheat	28 days
Mowing	10	barley	10
	8	oats	5
Pulling up	5 ½	beans	13
		rye tares	1
Carting		wheat	11
		barley	18
		oats	21
		beans	3
			110
Hoeing	8 acres	turnips	20
			130

4 men each 28 days	96
3 men each 11 days	34
	130

---

[200] James Abbis and William Knightley were 'garden men'. William French was Wilshere's carpenter. See Biographical Notes.

Potatoes in Wimbush Field 1819

1 acre taken up 13 September produce

Callico	198	say	190
Champion	45	say	42
of various sorts	10	---	10
gleanings	9	say	8
	262		250

I grew in other places from 50 to 60 bushels.

I found a bushel (that is the corn bushel ?filled heaped up as long as the potatoes would lie on) to weigh 63 lbs, level with the top of the bushel 51 lbs.

September 1819

Peas

Sown in Wimbush Field 5 bushels of marrow fat peas which promised extremely well for a crop till they were stop[pe]d by a frost in the night of 29 May which so far destroyed them that the produce was only

1 bushel 3 pecks.

Winter Tares & Rye

		Bushels	
I sowed nearly an acre in Starlings Bridge Close			
proving much affected by the same frost - produce			Pecks
	Rye	7	3
	Tares	1	1

Rye sown 19 September with 1 bushel from Dimsey on 1 acre of Brown's Close.

Spring Tares

I sowed about half an acre in Waby's field – produce   2 bushels   3 pecks only

Canary Seed

About 10 poles in Wimbush produced   1 bushel   1 peck

Wall Fruit 1819

A very abundant crop in & out of the House.

Grapes

Very productive & good abroad.

A fair crop in the Conservatory & in the Pine Pit.

None in the fruiting ho[use] – the vines to be taken up.

Onions
More than 20 bushels very fine.

Orchard Fruit 1819   **[p75]**

		Bushels	Pecks
Apples	Ribston Park Pippin	3	
	Nonpareil	4	
	French Golden Pippin	3	
	Holloweyed Pippin	2	
	Tankard Apple	2	
	Golden Pippin	0	1
	Sundries	1	
		15	1

Exclusively of harvest & other

		Bushels	Pecks
early apples	2		
Codling	1	3	
Total apples		18	1

Pears	Buere	0	1
	Gansells Burgamot		½
	Burgamot	2	
	Chaumontelle	3	
	Swan's Egg	4	2
	St German	1	
	Cardillac	1	
	Cresane No 9 [&]		
	Colmar No 40		½
	exclusively of Jargonelle	12	--

| **Quinces** | | 2 | |

121

Farming Stock 1 October 1819 [p76]

			£ - s - d
Horses	Gilbert	30	
	Smug	20	
	Tommy	15	
	Captain	25	
	Old co[ach] horse	--	90 - - -
Cows 5	Gentle		
	Brown		
	Dun		
	Kicksey		
	Alderney died 1820		60 - - -
Hogs	2 sows	7	
	1 boar	2	
	2 large stores	3	
	10 smaller	8	20 - - -
Poultry	4 old and 21 young turkies		
	20 Guinea fowls		
	36 fowls		
	20 chickens		12 - - --
Implements	Waggon with tilt & ladders	20	
	4 carts	25	
	6 ploughs & 3 out of use	18	
	Scuffler	5	
	6 harrows & ?thill	10	
	Twitch harrow	3	
	Harness	10	
	2 drags	2	
	42 sacks	7	
	Barn tackle, rakes, forks etc.	5	
	Dressing machine	10	<u>115</u>
			297 - - -

Farming Stock 1 October 1819 continued

			£297 - - -
Old wheat thrashed 63 loads **Eade's and 14 loads over Olney's ho[use] 25**			120
J D Nash d[ebit] on balance for wheat		104 – 2 - 6	
out of which he is to retain Robinson's bal[ance]		46 –11 – 1	
			56 -11 -5
G Beaver d[ebit] for barley & clover seed			130 -11- 0
J Kingsley d[ebit] for turnips	1816-17	81	
	1817-18	49	
Paid December 1819	1818-19	70	
			200 - - - -
Wheat produce of 1819			
20 acres	Brown's, Stone Piece, north, south Pym's Benslow Hill & north side of Wimbush estimated 80 loads at 37s 6d		150 - - - -
Barley – produce of 1819			
9 acres	Waby's & Benslow Hill estimated 40 quarters at 40s		80 - - - -
Oats white			
8½	the close under Benslow Hill[201] estimated 30 quarters at 24s		36 - - - -
Produce	Part Benslow Hill 4 acres Siberian estimated 24 at 25s		30 - - - -
Peas			
4 acres	Part Benslow Hill 4 acres estimated 10 loads at 30s		15 - - - -
Heligoland Beans			
5 acres	next Benslow Hill Way (bad) estimated 20 bushels at 10s		10

---

[201] Lower Benslow Hill.

	Thrashed July 1820 produce 20 bushels of wh[ich] 3 bushels offal br[ough]t to house stables for carr[iage] horses & pigeons.		
Buck Wheat same close			
1 acre	estimated 20 bushels		5
Rye & Tares from about 1½ estimated			3
Hay of 1818	Clover 10 loads at £5	50	
	Meadow 12 [loads] at £4.10	54	
of 1819	Clover from 7 acres above Benslow Hill estimated 8 loads at £5	40	
	Meadow estimated 12 loads at £4 10s	54	
			198
Clover seed from 7 acres above Benslow Hill			15
Produce of Wimbush			
1 acre	potatoes 250 bushels	15	
3 acres	cabbages estimated at	30	
1 acre	carrots	15	
3 roods	mangel wurzell	10	
1 acre	stubble turnips at	- -	70
Clover seed of 1818			
Turnip seed			
Canary seed			
Spring tares			<u>10</u>
			1426 – 2 -5

Farming Stock 1 October 1819 continued [p79]

		£1426 – 2 -5
Turnips growing		
Little Wimbush [*illeg*] Swedish 7½ acres		
T. W.'s Benslow Hill principally Scotch 9 acres at £4		68 - - - -
Tillage	1 acre winter tares sown	
	7 acres ley for wheat	
	1 acre Wimbush for wheat	
	20 fallow broken up	20 - - - -

Furniture in Bailiff's House	20 - - - -
	1534 – 2- 5
Deduct for errors in balance & debts	
£25 added to wheat	134 – 2 –5
Net value	£1400 - - - -

Barley 1819 [p80]

Waby's Close by Wymondley Way

Rawling Hill & the Linces

		Qu	B	P
Sept 25	Thrashed the draggings in the fore sty of Lower Barn	2	0	2
Nov 23	Thrashed of the barley in Waby's Close next the Wym[ond]ley Road a parcel which being laid was there carried under the hovel in the Rick Yard.	2	7	0
1820 Jan 8	--	12	1	2
[Jan] 26	--	9	1	-
March 7	--	17	4	:
		43	6	0

Some was sent in the straw to Wym[ond]ley about 2
quarters for game.   **2**
From 9 acres rather than 5 quarters per acre.   **45   6   0**

	Sown on 7 acres of		
	Little Benslow Hill	3	4
	On Little Wimbush	3	1
	On 1 acre in Wimbush		2

		6	7
		36	7
April 11	Sold to Nightingale at 40s [202]	20	
		16	7

24 April remains 3 quarters

---

[202] On p128 below Wilshere states that he sold 20 quarters of barley at 40s to Smith in May 1820. However on 18 May 1820 TW paid Wilshere for 20 quarters of barley sold to Thomas Chambers, a Stevenage corn dealer, at 40s a quarter [HALS: 61530 p13].

Wheat continued from page 65 vide 96 continued [p81]

Bushels

17 Jan 1820   I removed the wheat of 1818 from the granary
over Mr Eade's brewho[use] p.65 & from the
bin over Olney's ho[use] (of 1817) & found in
the whole   389

                                Dressed out refuse   __4
                                                                          385

Off[al] corn left in sacks in the Lower Barn   __10
Laid in a barley loft in the Malting Yard   375

24 Apr 1820   **Sold the above 385 bushels of wheat at 10s per bushel
to Mr Nash to be taken as he wants to use it.**

1820 June   Thrashed the Talavera wheat grown on 4 acres of
Brown's Close produce 77 bushels, **best
72, offal 4, waste 1**, exclusively of 3 bushels
planted on Little Benslow Hill together 80 bushels. It had
been much injured by the vermin.

1820 July 17   Dressed the wheat from the remainder of Brown's
Close & from the adjoining close – produce 52
bushels, **best 47, offal 5**. This had also
been very much lessened by rats.

18 July   **Sold together to Nash at 49s 23 loads 4
bushels, 9 bushels offal remaining.**

Wheat sowing 1819 [p82]

Oct 18 – 23   Dibbled the Slipes above Benchlow[203] Hill with white
wheat bo[ugh]t by my Brother in the market. The quantity
of ground is 7 acres 1 rood 0 perches, of wheat dibbled 12
bushels.
(Another bushel was limed & was sent to my Brother.)

Novr   Drilled one acre in Wimbush – 3 bushels sown viz. 2
bushels left of the above & 1 bushel rep[ai]d by my
Brother.

1820 Feby 29   I attempted to dibble an acre & a half in Little Benslow
Hill with Talavera wheat, but the weather being
unsuitable, the men could put in only about 3 roods. The

---

[203] Alternative form of Benslow.

remainder was sown broadcast.

Carrots of 1819 [p83]

From 1 acre in Wimbush taken up 12 & 13 October 284 bushels.

Mangel Wurzel 1819

From 3 roods in Wimbush 50 rows of which I weighed 3 of average appearance 1 on each side & one of the middle.

Sheared of & taken up October & in November the tops were eaten, the last 18 November.	Roots			Tops					
	cwt	q	lbs	cwt	q	lbs			
	8	1	21	2	0	19	10	2	12
	8	2	12	2	-	-	10	2	12
	6	2	19	1	1	7	7	3	26
	23	2	24	7	1	26	29	0	22
Per acre	31	2	24	7	1	6	38	3	20

Deposited under the shed in the upper farm yard.

1819 November Minutes for planting at Wymondley[204] [p84]

Orchard	Fruit trees	9
	Damsons	6
Home Plant[atio]n	Scotch & spruce	
	Fir & larch	100
South boundary next Adams	Larch	300
Hanging Plantation	Oak, ash & elm	400
Hill Plan[tatio]n	Ditto	500
Spring Grove	Ditto	200
Furze Plant[atio]n	Fir & larch	300
Willow Plant[atio]n	Black poplar	200
		2000

Began planting 17 November 1819.

---

[204] The orchard and Home Plantation were presumably close to Manor Farm. There is still a belt of trees along the southern boundary of Wilshere's land in Great Wymondley but these are mostly oaks. The Hanging and Hill Plantations now form part of Wymondley Wood. The Spring Grove and Furze Plantation probably bordered Willian Road; the larger of the two still exists. The Willow Plantation with its hybrid black poplars adjoins the Letchworth Garden City Greenway between Purwell and Willian.

Turnips of 1819 [p85]
TW's Benslow Hill
Swedish 1 acre.
Green tops 4 acres, Scotch 5½, together 9 acres 2 roods.
(Saved about half a rood for seed).
To Kingsley at £31 – 10.
Began 18 November 1819, ended 5 January 1820.
Fed 140 sheep per week per acre, the price being 66s per acre.
The keep of each sheep was 5.65d per week.
(*in margin*) Kingsley states the keep to be worth 6d per week per head.

123 sheep	**18 – 23 November**
203	**23 – 30 November**
183	**30 November – 5 January**

Little Wimbush
Swedish turnips 7 acres 2 [roods]. Sold to Kingsley at £50.
These turnips turned out all having been a good deal injured by the frost.
They did not keep 200 sheep more than 28 days.

Cabbages in Wimbush Field [p86]

Drumhead   2 acres
Manyheaded   1 acre

Began the drumhead 22 November taking up 2 rows for a cart path.
Those which have burst or are likely to burst to be first used. Alternate
rows to be left for sheep if they can be spared from the cows.

Barley of 1819

		Qu	B
(produce of 9 acres Wym[ond]ley Way Close &			
Rawlings Hill)	1819 Nov 19	2	7
	1820 Jan 10	12	1½
	26	9	1
	Mar 17	<u>17</u>	<u>4</u>
		41	5½
I sent to Wymondley in the straw for game estimated		<u>1</u>	<u>1½</u>
		43	-

**May I sold to Smith 20 quarters at 40s. I sowed about 8 quarters. The
remainder was consumed by pigs & poultry.**[205]

---

[205] See p125 and fn 202 above. For Samuel Smith see Biographical Notes.

Ice House [p87]

Filled 25 November 1819 from Mr Pierson's pond at Ickleford with 30 cart loads of ice.[206]

Clover Seed March 1820

			remains
Clover seed from the Slipes above Benslow Hill 1819		2 – 3 – 17	
	of which TW had	1 - 2 - 0	
besides some offall included in 6 – 2 – 8 below			1 – 1 – 17
The second cut added to the offal of the last year		6 – 2 - 8	
To TW	1 – 2		
Sown on barley land Little Wimbush & Little Benslow Hill	1 – 2 – 8	3 – 0 – 8	
			3 – 2 – 0

		[£ s d]
TW D[ebit]	1½ cwt cl[over] seed at 75s	5 - 12 - 6
vide [page] 106	1½ old at 60s	4 – 10 – 0
		10 – 2 – 6
Cr[edit]	3 quarters trefoil seed at 80s	3 - - - - -
	Bal[ance] due from TW	7 – 02 – 6

P[ai]d with other articles 18 May 1820.

Oats 1819 [p88]

Produce from 4 acres 0 roods 22 perches on the south side of Benslow Hill path –Siberian.

Thrashed	Bushels	How disposed of	
Oct 2	17½	27 Oct rep[ai]d my Bro[the]r borr[owe]d	
16	29	of him	40
27	51	October, November & December	
Nov 10	28	To coach horse stable	43
24	4	To farm horses	76½

---

[206] The location of William Wilshere's ice house is unknown. Payments relating to ihe ice house are recorded from Nov 1802 to at least Jan 1827 [eg HALS: 61495 p56; 61496 p57; 61497 p55; 61544 p157]. For Joseph Margetts Pierson see Biographical Notes.

29	42	To fowls & turkies off[al] corn	10
Dec 15	_89_	Dec 15 to my Bro[the]r in exch[ange] for	
	260½	the same quantity for coach horse stable	
			80
Qu 32 – 4½		Remains for farm horses & fowls	_11_
Nearly 8 quarters per acre			260½

White oats from Little Wimbush & trefoil ley 7 [a] 2 [r] 0 [p] of ploughed land.

Thrashed		How disposed of	
In the winter by			
Jeeves	60	To coach horse stable	24
Mar by Olney	44	Retained on the farm for farm horses	80
Apr & May by		To co[ach] horse stable	92
Olney	_136_	Farm **gone 17 June**	40
		Fowls etc	_4_
	240		240

Salt sown 1819 & 1820 [207]   **[p89]**

1819 October 17

On dibbled wheat on the Slipes above Benslow Hill on 3 patches
staked out of half an acre each   Bushel

On half an acre	south	3
	middle	2
	north	1

1820 April 19

On grass Mount Garrison on three patches of a rood each staked
out & marled   1½

                                                                            1

                                                                            ½

Each 1 rood   3

And on 3 patches in the north of Mr Brown's grass closes   1½

                                                                            1

                                                                            ½

                                                                            3

---

[207] In October 1819 Wilshere paid John Fordham £1 11s for 6 lbs of crushed salt and carriage [HALS: 61529 p40].

July 1820
I have not been able to observe any difference in the wheat or grass
between the spots sown with salt & the adjoining parts of the closes.

Weight of fire wood & faggots [p90]

1820 April. The wood of my hedges when cut for sale is divided into fire wood
& faggot wood, the fire taking all the strait & lower parts of the wood cut into
lengths of 4½ to 5 feet then made into bundles. The remainder of the wood is
made into bush faggots. They are sold at 15s for 120 called an hundred, that is
1½d each faggot. A bundle of fire wood is considered as equal to & sold at the
price of 2 faggots. I found them when made up to weigh the fire wood per
bundle about 28 lbs & the faggots about 18 lbs. The length of the fire wood 4½
feet, circumference of the bundle 2 feet 3 inches. Length of the faggot 4½ -
circumference about 3 feet.

> I cut of fire wood this year from the so[uth] side of Starlings Bridge Close,
> and the east and south of the Slipes in faggots & fire wood 12 hundred
> which sold 7 hundred & 80 (vide Gray's ac[coun]t) at 15   5 – 15 - -
> I had home 4 [hundred] & 20 value   3 – 2 – 6
>   8 – 17 – 6

Drilling [pp91-92]

20 June 1820 Minutes from the inform[atio]n of John Smith, Hitchin Str[eet],
Baldock. (Makes drills & dressing machines, keeps drills for hire)
Charge for drilling turnips with manure 3s per acre, without manure 2s.
He brings the drill, the employer finds (2) horses for working it at 8 acres per
day from 2 lb to 3 lb seed per acre, rows 12 inches apart.

> From 6 bushels to a quarter or 2 sacks of
> malt dust   12s per quarter   per acre
> 10 bushels soot
> 10 bushels salt
> 5 to 8 bushels oil dust with about the
> same quantity of cinders
> (11½ quarters called a thousand now £13)

1820 June & July

I drilled (by Smith) turnips on the south side of Benslow Hill 8 [acres] 1 rood & Waby's Field 7 [acres] 2 [roods], the former on the 26th of June & the latter on the 1st of July.

On Benslow Hill by mismanagement about 32 lbs of seed were sown, that is on the upper part 15 lbs of the Yellow Scotch saved by me & on the bottom & headlands 17 lbs of green top'd bo[ugh]t of Farmer.[208]

On Waby's Field were sown 20 lbs of green top from Farmer.

On Benslow Hill 6 quarters of oil dust was drilled with the seed, a small patch being drilled with crushed salt & ashes with an interval on each side with[ou]t any manure.

Bo[ugh]t of Croft at 30s 6d per quarter £9-3-0 being about £1 3s per acre.
[209]

On Waby's 6 quarters of malt dust was drilled with the seed. The above pieces were prepared by the scuffler & the shim with[ou]t the plough.[210]

Bo[ugh]t of S. Smith at 12s per quarter £3-12 being 10s 3d per acre drilling.
[211]

See over turnips continued.

Turnips 1820 (for those drilled see the preceding page)   [p93]

14 June sowed Starlings Bridge with Swedish turnips (my own seed).

Hoed 12-15 July.

On 2 acres on the south side were laid & ploughed in 20 loads of yard dung. The remainder was prepared by the scuffler & shim. On the 2 acres on the north side I laid 2 cwt of salt petre with 40 bushels of cinder ashes. On the middle acre no manure was laid.

20 June sowed that part of Lower Benslow Hill south of the gate (6 acres 2 roods) with Swedish turnips. 2 acres on the south & 1 acre on the north side were manured with about 10 loads of yard dung per acre & 2 acres 3 roods in

---

[208] John Farmer was a Hitchin corn and seed merchant. See Biographical Notes.

[209] John Croft was a seed, corn and coal merchant in Cock Street, Hitchin [NHM: 1816 map of Hitchin; Piggot's *Hertfordshire Directory*; HALS: 61530 p75].

[210] Arthur Young gave a drawing and description of a shim used for cutting up weeds on ridges or furrows and cleaning land without ploughing or burying the soil [*General View*, p39].

[211] Samuel Smith was a Hitchin maltster. See Biographical Notes.

the middle with 2¾ cwt of salt petre & 45 bushels of cinder ashes, about a rood on each side being left unmanured.
3 July sowed the 2 acres of this close north of the gate with with [sic] red turnip with[ou]t manure prepared by the scuffler.

Haymaking 1820 [p94]

Clover	Rawlings Hill[212]	3 – 1 – 25	
	Lower [Rawlings Hill][213]	2 – 0 – 10	
	Waby's Field by Wym[ond]ley Way	3 – 2 – 0	8 – 3- 35
Meadow	M[oun]t Garrison	2 – 2 – 20	
	Rawlings Hill	3 - - - - -	
	Sweard Slipe	0 – 3 – 31	
	Brown's Meadow	4 – 2 – 10	
		11 - 0 – 21	
	Garden Close & hedge greens about	1 - - - - -	12 – 0 - 21
			21 - 0 –16

Began mowing the clover 19 June. Finished the meadow 29[th]. Finished carting 6 July. About 3 acres of the clover had a little rain & about 4 acres of the meadow, but too little to injure either.

The clover rick estimated about	16 loads.
The meadow about	14

The expense of mowing & inning was nearly this:		£ - s - d
Mowing at 3s per acre	3 – 3 – 0	
Beer ?bo[ugh]t	0 – 12 – 0	3 – 15 – 0
Making 40 days men & boys, 46 women cost about		6 – 15 – 0
Beer 1 h[ogshea]d ale, 1 h[ogshea]d small		4 - - - - - -
4 days carting		4 - - - - - -
Thatching Straw load		18 – 10 – 0

---

[212] Rawlings Hill beyond the Mill.
[213] The Linces.

Wheat of 1819 continued from page 81 [p95]

July I inned a wheat cock from Little Wimbush, the produce of 8 acres the north side of Benslow Hill & of something more than an acre of Brown's. It was thrashed immediately, produce 36 (*altered from 35*) loads 1 bushel **vide [page] 110.**

of which 35 (*altered from 34*) loads prime 6 bushels offal. The 34 loads laid in the granary over Mr Eade's brewho[use] & the offal remaining in a sack there.

Harvest 1820 [pp96-98]

July 31	Began to reap an acre of drilled wheat in Wimbush. It Was green when begun. I had 1 rood per day cut for 4 days. Inned 14 August. Thrashed immediately. Produce (*blank*)
August 3	Began cut & on this & the two following days cut 8 acres Siberian oats on the north side of Pym's Benslow Hill. Inned 10th. Laid in a rick in the rick yard.
Augt 7 to 12	Was consid[ere]d the regular commencement of the harvest. Began with cutting pease in Pierson's Close & on the 10th wheat in the Slipes above Benslow Hill. (2 [acres] 2 [roods] of this wheat remaining on the 14th cut by Lane.)
14	Began cutting barley in TW's Benslow Hill.
16	Inned 4 acres of the barley
August 17	Carted the pease to the small barn & some more barley.
18	Carried the wheat from Benslow Hill Slipes to a cock at the bottom of Benslow Hill topped by about 3 loads remaining of the pease.
19	Stopped in carrying barley by slight rain. Continue cutting.
21	Continue cutting barley. Prevented by slight showers from carrying.
22, 23	Cut & carry barley. Fill the barn in the lower yard into which about 12 acres have been put.
24	Cut an acre of Heligoland beans on TW's Benslow Hill & carry the remainder of the barley cut. Fill the two side bays of the Upper Barn.
25	Cut & carry about 5 roods of Talavera wheat from TW's Benslow Hill about half dribbled. Laid in the forestye of the Upper Barn. **1 acre 1 rood 9 perches.**
26	Cut & carry to the hovel of the Rick yard an acre of barley

134

	sown (with lucerne) in Wimbush & carry & lay over the barley about half an acre of winter tares cut by French 17th.
Evg of 26th	Nothing remains abroad except the beans (cut 24th), about a rood & ½ summer tares (cut this morning), about 5 roods sown for ?fodder which remains for seed & about 1½ of buck wheat & about 7 acres clover left for seed. The harvest men having served 3 weeks had their supper and were dismissed.
Sept 2	Inned the winter tares, thrashed 8th, produce 7½ bushels. Cut the rood & ½ of summer tares. 9th inned & thrashed them, produce 2½ bushels.
14	Cut buck wheat.
26	Thrashed in the field, produce 33 bushels.
(*in margin*)	Clover seed cut 25 & 26 September & carried 4 October. Laid in the Rick Yard.

See over for exp[ense]s of harvest.

Expenses of Harvest 1820 [p99]

Wages		£	
	Robinson	5	
	Olney	5	
	Jeeves	5	
	Silsby	3	
	boys	2	
		2	22

An acre of wheat in Wimbush cut before the regular
harvest began   0 – 10   0 – 10

		Cutting oats	0 – 10
French	7½ days		
Abbis	6 days		
Chapman	1 days [sic]		4 - - - -
Beer - ale, small, cost			7 - - - -
Exclusively of horses worth			16 - - - -
			50

The quantities being   acres

			acres
	Wheat	nearly	10
	Barley	nearly	16
	Oats		8

135

Peas	4
Tares	2
Buck wheat say	2
Clover seed sold say	8
	50 being 20
	shillings per acre

Wheat of 1820 [p100]

			B	B
August 26 laid in granary over Mr Eade's brewho[use]	I thrashed (Chapman) in the harvest one acre of drilled wheat from Wimbush which disappointed me having produced only	Prime Offal	18 1	19
September 7 laid in granary over Mr Eade's brewho[use]	Finished thrashing the Talavera wheat produce of 1 acre 1 rood 9 perches produce 36 bushels 2 bushels offal. **Nearly 30 bushels per acre. Vide [page] 110.**			38

Barley of 1820 [p101]

			Qu	B
	Sept 23rd	Thrashed in the Lower Barn for fowls		3
	Oct 16	Finished thrashing an acre of barley sown on Wimbush with lucerne produce	5	
Froy	Dec 2	Dressed the north bay of the Small Barn about half the produce of 3 [acres] 3 roods, the lower of TW's		
10 quarters sent to Beaver for malting		Benslow Hill best 10 Qu		
		off[al] corn 1 - 5	11	5
(Froy)	[Dec] 15	Dressed the south bay of the same barn Produce 12 - 4 best		
12 - 4 sent to Beaver for malting.		off[al] corn 1 – 7	14	3
		26 quarters from less than 4 acres		

136

1821	Dressed the midsty of the				
Jan 2	Lower Barn				
	best		10 – 2		
		off[al] corn	3 - 3	13	5
To Beaver at 26s				45	
Jan 22	Dressed the western bay of				
	the Lower Barn				
	best		19 - -		
		off[al] corn	3- 6	22	6
To Beaver at				67	6
Feb 5	Dressed about ½ the eastern				
	bay				
		best	12 - -		
To Beaver at		off[al] corn	4 - -	16	-
				83	6
[Feb] 23	Finished the eastern bay				
10 quarters to		best	17 - -		
Beaver		off[al] corn	6 - -	23	
for malting.				106	6
Remainder for	The barley to Beaver wanted				2
sowing & fowls.	**6 [quarters] 5 [bushels] per acre.**				

Potatoes 1820
August 28 & 29

[p102]

Took up an acre in Wimbush one half of which Champion & the other half Callico, except that about 1/20 part of the latter half had small quantities of the other sorts ment[ione]d at the foot. They were very ripe & good, but from the season smaller than usual.

	Bushels
Champion laid in the pit in the Plant[atio]n	118
Callico laid in the building in the Dog Yard	113
	231
Gleaned	9
	240

137

Specimens of various sorts laid separately in the Dog
Yard

German Kidney	
Blood Royal	
Asparagus	
?Frorroges Purple	
Black Read	
Upright White	2
Callico White from Plant[atio]n	18
	260

Potatoes continued from 102 [p103]

1821			B	B
February	remains			158
	For seed		**25**	
	Ho[use] consumption		**20**	
			45	

Beans 1820 [p104]

September 29 Thrashed an acre of Heligoland beans. Produce 30 bushels.
Brought to the coach horse stable except about 3 pecks of offal given to the
hogs.

Buck Wheat 1820

1½ in Brown's Close after wheat cut 14 September thrashed in the field 26th.
Produce 33 bushels, 3 bushels being offal bro[ugh]t to the stable for pigeons.[214]
Remaining 30 bushels.

Tares 1820 [p105]

About half an acre of winter tares in Brown's Field remainder of an acre sown
for fodder cut 17 August, carried 26th, thrashed 2 September. Produce 7½
bushels.

October sown on an acre in Wimbush 3 bushels, on 1½ acres in Nettledale 4½ [bushels].

1. Summer tares left of those sown for fodder in Brown's Close 1½ roods cut 2
September, inned 9th & thrashed immediately. Produce 2¾ bushels.

---

[214] Wilshere had a dovehouse. See cash book 1808 [HALS: 61500 p42].

2. Summer tares remainder of another sowing in the same field 1 acre 1 rood cut
25 & 26 September, inned 4 October, laid in the Rick Yard.

Clover Seed 1820   **[p106]**

    Waby's Close next Wym[ond]ley Way about   1 - 2
    The rest cut green for horses.
    Rawling Hill & the Linces cut 25 & 26 September,
    inned 2 October laid in the Rick Yard.   5 - 2

1821 April 6 Minute of some remaining clover seed of 1818 & 1819

    Left with my brother 15 April 1820   of 1818   4 C[wt]
                                of 1819   1   - 1 - 17

Thus disposed of TW		4 C[wt]	at 50s	£10 - -- - -
	&	0 – 3 – 17	at 60s	£ 2 – 14 - -
Sown by me		- - 2 - --		£12 – 14 - -
		5 – 1 – 17		

Carrots 1820   vide [page] 116   **[p107]**
                                                                B

October 19 &   Ploughed up an acre of carrots in Wimbush
20   (the acre at the south next the Garden).
                Ploughed over a second time. Produce

                                                            376

                6 February 1821 remains for seed
                & ?h[ou]se about   **17**
                for horses   **113**

October 20   Laid in a stall in the Lower Stable for
                immediate use   100
                In the Wood Yard   226
                Pitted   20

Mangell Wurzell 1820   **[p108]**
One acre in Wimbush (about half the land has a defective crop & is filled up
with cabbages.) (Taken up (*blank*) about (*blank*) cart loads. Part laid in the hovel
in the Upper & the remainder in the stable of the Lower Yard.)

Farming Stock 1 October 1820   **[pp109-110]**

				£ - s - d
4 horses				90 – 0 – 0
3 cows	1 sold, 1 dead			40 – 0 – 0
Hogs	1 boar, 2 sows, 8 pigs			15 – 0
Poultry	turkies 2 old[215], 7 young			
	guinea fowls 7 & 3 young			
	cock & hens 30, at Abbis 13, young 27			10 - - - -
Implements	1 waggon, 4 carts (1 new)[216]			
	6 ploughs			
	2 sets of harrows			
	1 twitch harrow			
	1 scuffler			
	Harness for 5 horses			
	Dressing machine			
	40 sacks			
	2 shovels, 5 rakes, 7 forks, 2 drags			
	3 gathering forks			
	3 dung forks, 6 cart ropes			
	2 fans, 4 sieves, 3 skips			120 - - -
				275 - - -
Wheat		B		
thrashed	In the granary over Mr Eade's brewhouse of 1819	181	**vide 95**	
	of 1820 produce of 5 roods Talavera	38	**vide 100**	
	of an acre in Wimbush	19	**vide 100**	
		238		100 - - -
	A rick on Benslow Hill produce of 7 - 1 (The Slipes) **inned July 1821**			60 - - - -

215 On 1 January 1821 Wilshere paid W Harvey £1 10 for 4 turkeys for the house [HALS: 61530 p56].
216 On 28 June Wilshere paid William Watson, a Hitchin wheelwright, £15 for a new iron armed cart. £5 was deducted from the price of £20 in exchange for an old cart [HALS: 61530 p28].

Barley	Produce of part	Acres	Roods	
	of TW Benslow Hill	7	2	
	of Little Wimbush	7	2	
	in Wimbush	1	-	
		16	-	100 - - -
Beans	Produce of 1 acre - 30 bushels			6 - - -
Peas	Produce of Rail Close[217] 3 [a] – 3 [r]			20 - - -
Oats	A rich produce of north side of Benslow Hill 8 acres 1 [rood]			50 - - -
Tares	(vide 105) Produce of about 2 acres			10 - - -
				621

Farming Stock 1 October 1820 continued   [pp111-112]

			£621 - - - -
Hay	Meadow remainder of 1818	1¾	
	Clover of ditto	¾	
	Meadow 1819	12	
	Meadow 1820	12	
	Clover 1820	13½	
	Loads	40	180 - - - -
Clover seed	Produce of 7 acres (vide 106)		30
Turnips	J Kingsley for (vide 85) 17 acres		81 – 10 - 0
Turnips growing (vide 92-93)	South side Benslow Hill 8–1 acres being 0-3 roods defective	7- 2	
	Starlings Br[idge] Swed[ish]	4 -3	
	Lower Benslow Hill Swed[ish]	6 -2	
	Ditto green	1 -3	
	Waby's with add[itio]ns	7 -2	
		28	100 - - - -
Platting straw	about 3000 lbs		12 -10 - 0
Potatoes (vide 102)	260 bushels produce of 1 acre Wimbush		15 - - - -
Carrots	1 acre Wimbush **produce 341 bushels**		10
Mangell wurzell ditto 1 acre			10

---

[217] Rail Close was also known as Stone or Pierson's Piece and as Walsworth Way Close.

Cabbages ditto 2½	20 - - - -
Newly sown lucerne 1 acre	5
Cabbages in Brown's 2 acres	5 - - - -
Clover sown TW's Benslow Hill 9 acres	9
Clover ley for wheat 9.2	20 - - - -
Potatoes l[an]d for wheat 1	1 - - - - -
Fallow- north side of Benslow Hill, Rail Piece & part of Brown's 16 acres[218]	10 - - - - -
	1130

Wheat sowing 1820 [p113]

October 9 to 23. The following land was dibbled with 18 bushels of mixed wheat white & Lammas produced on an acre in Wimbush with the add[itio]n of 3 bushels of the same seed bought of Farmer:

	[a]	[r]	[p]
Waby's next Wym[ond]ley Road	3	2	0
Rawlings Hill	3	1	25
Linces	2	0	10
In Wimbush	1	-	--
	10	0	35

1821 March

		[a]	[r]	[p]
Dibbled in Waby's Field	Talavera at bottom	3	1	-
	of mixed wheat	4	1	-
		17	2	35

Haws [p114]

1820 October 14. Sowed on beds in the north eastern quarter of the Plantation Garden the haws pitted the last season ((*blank*) bushels),

Carrots

1820 October. Produce of 0 acres 3 [roods] 20 [perches] in Wimbush 341 bushels **besides about 14 gleaning.**

Orchard Fruit 1820 [pp115-116]

Apples	Bushels	Pecks
Harvest App[le]	6	

---

[218] These fields were all planted with turnips.

Codlins	3	-
French Codlin	1	2
Ribston Pippin	6	-
Winter Pearmain	8	1
French Golden Pippin	10	-
Hollow Crown Pippin	2	2
King of Pippins (called Catshead)	2	2
Nonsuch	-	2
Spice Russet	-	1
Golden Rennet	-	2
Minshaw Crabb	-	1
Nonpareils	2	2

	Pecks		
Bedford Seedling	½		
Golden Pippin	¼		
various	1¼	-	2
		44	**1**

1820 October 26 deliv[ere]d to Hodgson

French Golden Pippins	**5 bushels**	
Ribston Pippins	**2 bushels**	
Gansells Berg[amo]t No. 100		

	Pears	Bushels	Pecks
	Jargonelle	1	0
	Cressan	0	0½
No 257	Brown Bueré	-	3
	Grey Bueré (growing near the pond)	1	-
	A pear growing near the gate of the Lower Yard – q[uery] whether a Bueré or a Cressan	0	2½
	~~Golden~~ Orange Burgamot	-	2
No 357	Gansells Burgamot	2	-
	Autumn Burgamot	1	2
No 180	Colmar	-	2

Swans Egg	3	
Black Worcester	2	
Cadillac	-	2½
Uvedale's St Germain	-	3
Chaumontelle	-	1
	16	**1½** [219]
	60	**2**
Quinces	1	
Medlars	-	3
	1	**3**
Bushels	**62**	**1**

Grapes both in the houses & abroad very slight.

Peaches & nectarines in the house abundant & fine & abroad a good crop.

Plums abundant except damsons.

21 October sent pears to TW, Sisters, Eade, Niblock, Kimpton, Gibbon, Bentley, ?Willding. [220]

Turnips 1820   (vide 92, 93, 111)   [p117]

7 December 1820 sold J Kingsley my turnips with the cabbages in Brown's 30 acres at £130, that is 10 acres Swedish at £5 & 20 acres at £4. I promised if they should be found too dear to make some abatement.

On Sat[urda]y 9th December 247 sheep came into the 8 acres at Joan Biggs' Grave.

19 January 1821 Kingsley delivers the following account:

11 to 27 Decr	16 days	247 sheep
27 to 3 Jany	7	229
Jan 3 – 6	3	293
6 - 18	12	333
18 – 20	2	501
Jan 20 to Feby 15	26	441
		11th 100 were sent to Benslow Hill

[219] This total includes not only the pears but also the quinces and medlars, to which was then added the 44 bushels 1 peck of apples, then the 1 bushel of quinces and 3 pecks of medlars were included a second time to make the total of 62 bushels and 1 peck.

[220] For Joseph Eade, Joseph Niblock, Mary Kimpton, C W Gibbon, William Bentley and John Willding see Biographical Notes.

20 – 22		eating the ?shalls on Waby's Piece 8 acres 100
4 ~~February~~		~~3 part of~~ the 441 removed to Starlings Br[idge] & remainder to the north of Lower Benslow Hill.
Feb 15 to 20	5	304
20 to 26	6	262 **25 Feb Starlings Br[idge] finished & all except 6 acres of Lower B[enslow] Hill**
26 to Mar 26	28	15
Mar 26 to 28	2	100
28 to 29	1	290
Mar 29 to Apr 6	7	525
Apr 6 to 9	3	425
9 to 10	1	235
10 to 21	11	106

?B[oar]d per week per head amounting to about £120.

On the means of giving Vigour to old Apple and Pear Trees   **[p118]**
From a French work "Archives des découvertes" reviewed M[onthly] R[eveiw]
App. to Vol 92 N.S.
In order to give vigour to old apple & pear trees, and to make them bear fine
fruit, a method is employed in some parts of France which does not appear to be
generally known. It consists in cutting off all the small branches, & inserting
grafts in the places from which these are cut of about an inch or an inch & a half
in circumference. A tree thus ?charged with 100 or 150 grafts is in full vigour at
the end of 2 y[ea]rs & begins to give fine fruit.

13 November 1820   **[p119]**
I agreed with my brother TW that he should have the Slipes above Benslow Hill
for the current year for sowing tares. I am to pay the tithes & taxes & he is to
give me 24 quarters of good oats in the course of the year.

    13 April 1821   Put by for me in a loft of his.
    7 May   Began for farm horses
    2 July   7 quarters have been carr[ie]d to farm
    I found 3 July a bushel to weigh 40 lbs.

145

Winter tares

1821	3 July	Bought 2 loads of his winter tares to be put by for me price 27s 6d.
	Aug	B[ough]t 20 ?quarters of oats put by for me in his loft in Crabb's Yard at 21s.

Cabbages 1820 [p120]

After eating in November some planted where the mangel wurzel missed, began 18 November with 2 acres Scotch in Wimbush. The 3 cows eat about 100 in the day. (100 found to weigh about 500 lbs. These taken from the worst part.)

4 February   The first acre finished.

Peas 1820 [p121]

Rail Close 3 [acres] 3 [roods] – greater part laid in the Little Barn, part upon the wheat cock and part upon the oat rick.

Those in the Little Barn were thrashed out as they were wanted, the last on Thursday 4 January 1821.

Amount from that barn	47½ bushels
Remains 6 January	6 bushels

Oats of 1820 [p122]

1821 January   Inned about one third of the rick produce of the north side of Benslow Hill – thrashed by Jeeves 7 quarters 7 bushels

Pork for Salting 1821 [p123]

		Stones	lb
Jan 10	1 for bacon	22	3
-	1 for pickled pork	15	3
15	1 for ditto	15	-
Feb 8	1 for bacon	24	4

9 January 1821   Oil Cake (& Bones)

(from the inform[atio]n of John Foreman)

The cakes should weigh from the mill 3 lbs each. They are often found to weigh less, but if bought by n[umber], the deficiency of weight is made up by n[umber]. 1½ ton may be about & usually is consid[ere]d a thousand cakes. Oil cake is of two kinds. That from rape seed is not used in England for food, but very much as manure now worth £7–10 per ton. Linseed cake is that used

146

for food now worth about £10 per ton. 1000 of oil dust is consid[ere]d as 11 quarters.
(*added in margin*) 2½ quarters per acre is a good dressing. Some lay near 3 quarters ?measured as corn.
Crushed bones worth about £6 or 6 guineas per ton suff[icien]t for an acre, excellent & very lasting.

To preserve apples   **[p124]**
It is recommended that they should never be plucked till <u>quite ripe</u>, always gathered by hand, laid carefully & thinly on clean fresh straw, moved as little as possible & guarded ag[ains]t frost.
Month[ly] Mag[azine] February 1821 page 44

Beer from a mixture of one half or a greater proportion of barley stated to be as good as that made wholly of malt.
Labourer's Friend   June 1821 page 90

Onions to produce them very large by transplanting.
Cottager's Monthly Visitor June 1821 page 287

Nepaul Cucumber   **[p125]**
1 September 1821	One preserved for seed which was this day cut
	Measured in length	16¾ inches
	& in girth	12 [inches]
	& weighed	lbs 4½

26 April 1821 3 roots of a red potatoe from the Horticultural Society sent from Holland called Lanckmann's Potatoe said to be from South America planted in the Nursery Garden. **The 3 potatoes were not weighed but were not of a size to exceed 1 lb each**.
Taken up 27 October. Produce 3½ bushels. Number rather more than 700. Weight 215 lbs.

Wheat of 1819 & 1820 remaining September 1821   **[p126]**
I had at October 1820 in the loft over Eade's brewhouse

	Bushels
of 1819	181
of 1820 Talavera	38
of an acre in Wimbush	<u>19</u>
	238

A rick on Benslow Hill produce of 7 acres 1 rood The Slipes
Br[ough]t into the Wheat Barn July 1821.

		Bushels	
Sowed	October 1820 9 to 23	18	
	March 1821	15	<u>33</u>
Mrs Dove had (*blank*) bushels.		205	

16 April removed from above loft to a loft of my Brother's in
Crabb's Yard

of mixed	165
Talavera	22
off[al] corn	<u>10</u>
	197

Some bushels lost by vermin & screening.

1821 September 10 Malt [p127]

1821 September 10

	[Qu]	[B]	[Qu]	[B]
1820 December				
Sent to Beaver to be malted for me	10	-		
&	<u>12</u>	<u>4</u>	22	4
Ret[aine]d by him – in return for the same quantity borrowed in November 1820 for brewing	5	-		
1821 April 3 brewings	<u>4</u>	4	<u>9</u>	<u>4</u>
In the loft in Back Street yard		Qu	13	-

10 September upon measuring the malt store found 102 bushels instead of 104 bushels. Some had been destroyed by vermin while it lay in a loft in Smith's yard.

1821 January. Sent to Beaver to be malted & remains with him	10

Removed 6 October 1821 to the same loft in Back Street yard.

Salt for Cattle [p128]

30 October 1821 Mr Fordham recommends that salt be put in lumps before the horses & cows who will lick it when they require it. He puts about a lb of the crushed salt to a pan (6 bushels) of chaff & puts it together in the Chaff House.

It will heat & comes out like hay. More proper for farm horses & for cows than for riding or carr[iage] horses, but salt lumps may be put with advantage before them.

The market gardeners about London strew it in their alleys to destroy slugs & worms.

November 1821 [p129]

> To send Mrs Lautour[221]
>> Seed of the single anemony
>> Plant of the winter cherry
>> 2 kinds of double yellow dahlias & single yellow
>> Plant of winter cherry
>> Cuttings of variegated box
>> Seeds of myrtle

Orchard Fruit 1821

Apples	27 bushels of which 8 the Ribston Park Pippin & 7 the French Golden Pippin
Pears	7 bushels of which 4 bushels ?Wonton pears

Potatoes 1821	1 acre Wimbush Field - something more than 200 bushels.
Carrots 1821	about 3½ roods of Wimbush – 396 bushels

Mangel Wurzell 1821 [p130]

An acre in Wimbush Field taken up from the beginning to the end of November in order that the tops might be eaten. The roots were rather small but pretty uniform. Three parcels from different parts of the acre were separately weighed after the tops cut off.

	Tons	Cwt
The best gave at the rate per acre of	24	7
The next	21	4
The worst	17	10
	3/63	1
Giving an average of	21 tons	

---

[221] Owner of Hexton Manor. See Biographical Notes.

?Packed in the shed in the farm yard except about 600 roots reserved for seed put under MacIntosh's care.

Potatoes cultivation of [p131]

In the Cottager's Monthly Visitor for December 1821 (No. 557) are the following minutes of the manner of cultiv[ation]n in a cott[age] garden. The writer states the produce of 3½ poles of ground to have been 12½ bushels. Dig a trench, put the dung in the trench and lay the sets on the dung with the eye uppermost 2 feet distant in the row & the rows 2 feet apart. ("I plant a few beans not less than 6 feet apart each way.") Never allow a bad sort of potatoe. The sets are cut out of the largest potatoes never more than 2 from one potato & those from the middle refusing both ends, laid till wanted in a hole guarded from frost & wet.

Farming Stock 1 October 1821 [p132]

		£ - s - d
4 horses[222]		80
4 cows		50
26 hogs		25
7 turkies, 4 ducks, 27 hens, 2 cocks & at ~~Abbis's~~ 16 pullets & at Abbis's 7 turkies, 28 fowls		10 - - - -
Implements	1 waggon	
	4 carts	
	? ~~ploughs~~ old	
	2 sets of harrows	
	A five beamed harrow	
	Twitch harrow	
	Scuffler	
	Cow crib	
	4 hog troughs	
	Harness for 4 horses	

---

[222] In Nov 1820 Wilshere sold a black horse to James Nash for £20 10s. In Jan 1821 he bought a horse from Charles Kingsley for £30 for the farm. Charles Kingsley was a son of John Kingsley who became tenant of Walnut Tree Farm, Pirton [HALS: 61530 pp45, 68, https://pirtonhistory.org.uk/; J Wayne ed *A foot on three daisies. Pirton's Story* (Pirton, 1987) p62].

Implements	30 sacks	
	3 wheel ploughs, a dray plough, a double plough, & 3 others	
	Corn screen, a bushel, barley chopper, 2 pails, hay knife	
	6 sieves, 2 fans, 3 dung forks, an iron shovel, 2 ?carting shovels, 2 drags, 3 gath[er]ing forks	
	4 pea hooks, chaff box & knife	
	3 hoes, cart ropes	100 - - - -
		265

Farming Stock 1 October 1821 continued [pp133-134]

		Loads	£265
Wheat thrashed	Loft Mr Crabb's yard	33	
	Offal	2	
	Talavera	4 – 2	
		39 - 2	60 - - - -
Summer tares in the loft in Portmill Lane		3 loads	5 - - - -
A wheat cock in Starlings Br[idge] Close produce of about 10 acres Rawlings Hill, the Slipes & 1 acre part of Waby's Field			70 - - - -
Wheat in the barn the produce of 7 acres Waby's Field, 3 acres being Talavera wheat			50 - - - -
Oats in the straw remainder of a rick of 1820			10 - - - -
Barley produce of 21 acres - south side of Benslow Hill, 8.1, Starlings Br[idge] 4.3 Swed[ish], Lower B[enslow] Hill 6.3 Sw[edish], 1.2 Green[223]			100 - - - -
Peas	2 ricks one on Nettledale produce of about 4 acres & another in Little Benslow Hill produce of about 3 acres		
	In the small barn the produce of 2 acres		50 - - - -

---

[223] Swedish and Green are the types of turnip grown on this land in 1820 and eaten by sheep the following winter.

Hay	Remainder	of meadow of 1819	3½	
		of clover 1820	3	
		meadow 1820	10	
		meadow 1821	11	
		clover 1821	8	
	Estimated quantity	Loads	35½	120 - - - -
Buck wheat & tares				------
Clover seed of 1820				10 - - - -
Potatoes	1 acre			
Cabbages	3 acres			
Mangel wurzell	1 acre			
Turnips Wimbush	2 acres			60 - - - -
Turnips growing		North Benslow Hill	8 [a]	
		Brown's	6½	
		Stone Piece	3½	
		Wimbush	1	30
				830

Farming Stock 1 October 1821 continued   [p135]

		Balance	£830
Tillage including clover & sainfoin			50
J Kingsley for turnips	1818-1819	31 – 10	
	1819-1820	130	
		161 – 10	
	Abate	11 – 10	150
			1030 - - -
	Allow for overcharges & debts		30
	Leaving the net value		1000 - - -

31 December 1821   J Kingsley owes for

Turnips 1819 9 a 2 r		31 - 10
1820 10 a Swedish at £5	50	
20	at £4	80	130

If he found them too dear, I consented to make some abatement.

1821 agreed for 9 acres north side of Benslow Hill

6 - 2	Brown's
3 - 2	Stone Piece
1	Wimbush

He to pay what he should find them worth.

At 3d per head per week for the sheep J. K. makes the am[oun]t £26 – 7 –7.
Kingsley states that he has an acc[oun]t of some peas not paid for by me at the time of our last settlement.

Swedish Turnip Seed [p136]
24 June 1822 I thrashed the seed of 10 perches of transplanted Swedish turnips - produce 49 lbs.

27 June MacIntosh Cucumber
Cut a cucumber of this sort young with the flower still remaining at the point – length 1 foot 6 inches, weight 1 lb 7 oz. It was eaten at the dinner of the Book Society & found to be a very good one, few seeds & those scarcely formed.[224]

29 June cut a Sucade Melon.
Seed from Mr Griffin, Woodhall, weight 3 lbs 13 oz. I had cut two before, one eaten on 27 June – pale greenish flesh, melting & well flavoured.[225]

Tares [p137]

		Bushels	Pecks
In Wimbush Field self sown, cut 5 June, inned 10th, thrashed the 12, produce			
	of the best	9	2
	of off[al] corn	1	=
		10	2

Pine [Apple]
31 July 1822 - Cut a New Providence Pine weighing 4½ lbs. Sent to Mr Delmé Radcliffe.

---

[224] Wilshere was a member of the Hitchin New Book Society established in 1813 [HALS: 61506 p82; 61527 p124; 61529 p118]. Catalogues of the Society's Library for 1819 and 1824 can de found in the Lawson Thompson Scrapbooks [NHM: Vol 1A p7].
[225] William Griffin was Samuel Smith's gardener at Woodhall Park, Hertfordshire. See Biographical Notes.

Dahlias – to propagate by cuttings (H. Hodgson 22 August 1822)
Take as early in the season as the plant is in suff[icien]t forwardness, the side
shoots to be cut off smoothly below the 2nd joint from the extremity. Trim the
leaves & insert the cuttings at the edge of a pot of light earth. A moderate hot
bed will forward their striking. The cuttings will soon make roots & be fit to
plant out & will blow the same year.

Potatoes 1822   [p138]
17 September   Took up an acre of potatoes in Wimbush Field.

	Produce	Callico	131 bushels
		Champion	115
		Sundries	6
			252

Carrots
12 October   Took up an acre of carrots in Wimbush Field
                Quantity   430 bushels

Mangel Wurzel
3 roods 20 perches (a bad crop from the dry summer)
Took up 15 October. The whole weighed calculating by the weight of a row in
the middle about 15 tons.

Turnips 1822   [p139]
19 November   Agreed with J. Kingsley for mine at £4 per acre. (He represents
this to be a high price. If I find it to be so, I propose to make him some
reduction, but have ent[ere]d into no agreement for this purpose. His first offer
was £3 – 10 which I rejected.

Nettledale	8 - - (*altered from 10*)
The close hired of Waby next	
Wym[ond]ley Way	3 - 2
Rawlings Hill & ~~Slipes~~ Linces	5 - 2
	17 - - (altered from 19)
~~Wimbush~~ Slipes	7 - 1
	24 - 1

Wimbush 3 acres eaten by bullocks.

24 acres at £3 - 10s = £72 + £12   + 1 [rood] = £1 = £85.

1822 November 26   **to Mr Brown, Willian**   **[p140]**

			£ - s
Lady De Grey	{1000	oaks (3 feet) 200 of them	
	{	American	3 – 10
£8	{1000	larch (5 feet)	3 - - -
	{300	elm (5 feet)	1 - - -
	{200	ash (4 feet)	- - 10
£1 - 15	{200	Spanish chestnut (4 feet)	- - 15
	{100	horse chestnut (5 feet)	- - 5
	{25	limes (6 feet)	- - 5
	{100	spruce fir (3 feet)	- - 5
	{100	Scotch fir (3 feet)	- - 5

	30000	quick	
L[ad]y De Grey	**20000**	£8 + £8 = £16	
T ?Dimsdale[226]	**10000**	£4	<u>12 - - -</u>
			21 -15

For Mr Brown personally deduct <u>1 - 15</u>

[*illeg*] Paid 30 May 1823   **20 - - -**

Plants in the Nursery fit for
planting

150	Spanish chestnut
180	larch
150	spruce
(*blank*)	oaks
70	black poplars
50	ash
25	elms
20	limes
10	oriental planes

---

[226] Amabel, Lady Lucas, owner of Wrest Park, was created Countess De Grey in 1816 [*ODNB*]. When John, 2nd Baron Dimsdale died in 1820, he left the manor of Willian to his brother, Thomas Dimsdale [TNA: PROB11/1626/280].

Barley 1822 [p141]

North side of Benslow Hill					9 – 0 – 21
Brown's Close					6 – 2 - - -
Walsworth Way Close					3 – 3 – 2
					19 – 1 – 23

	Qu	B	Qu	B	
1822 Dec 7	24				**Malted by Beaver**
& off[al] corn			2	7	**produced 24 – 4**
1823 Jan 1	22		3		**22 Qu sold to Beaver**[227]
25	15	4	3	1	
Feb 8	16		3		
Draggings			3		
	77	4	15	-	
	15				
	92	4			

June 1823 [p142]

Mr Griffin's recipe for destroying the white bug in pines.[228]

Flour of sulphate	2 lbs
Scotch snuff or tobacco pounded & ?dried	4 oz
Camphor grated	4 oz

To be put with the finger & thumb or puff a small quantity at a time on the plant infected which after putting on the lamp once or twice, should be slightly watered.

1 July 1823 [p143]

Agreed with (*blank*) Gray & (*blank*) to continue to hoe turnips for me till harvest at 4s 6d with 2 quarts of beer per acre.
To go over them a second time at half the price.[229]

---

[227] George Beaver paid £35 15s for 22 quarters of barley at 32/6 25 January 1823 [HALS: 61532 p71].
[228] Probably William Griffin. See Biographical Notes.
[229] For the possible identity of Gray see Biographical Notes.

Farming Stock 1 October 1822 [p144]

		£ - s - d
	4 horses	
	4 cows [230]	
	10 hogs	
	16 turkies	
	4 ducks	
	10 guinea fowls	
	65 fowls & 24 at Abbis's	150 - - - - -
Implements	Waggon	
	6 carts	
	Harness 4 horses	
	8 ploughs, a potatoe plough	
	3 sets of harrows	
	Twitch harrow	
	? Thill	
	Dressing machine	
	26 sacks	
	Corn screen, 2 fans	
	Barn tackle	
	Shovels, forks etc.	100 - - - - -
Wheat thrashed	64 loads	100 - - - - -
Barley thrashed	3 quarters	3 - - - - -
Peas thrashed	11 loads 3 bushels	12 - - - - -
Tares	9 loads	11 - - - - -
Tares	10 bushels	2
Buck wheat	13 loads	13
		391

Farming Stock 1 October 1822 continued [pp145-146]

	Balance	£391 - - - -
Wheat in the straw		

---

[230] In March 1824 Wilshere bought a new cow from Taylor through Mr Hailey for £14 10s and sold him the old dun cow for £9 [HALS: 61535 p96].

Produce 1821 of Little Wimbush 3 acres, (5 acres) Rawlings Hill & The Linces, Waby's 4 acres & about 1 acre of Waby's Field – 13 acres		75 - - - -
& produce 1822 of Little Benslow Hill 9 [a] 2 [r] & part Little Wimbush 4 [a] - 13 [a] 2 [r]		75 - - - -
Barley		
Produce of the north side of Benslow Hill, Brown's Close, Walsworth Way Close 18 acres		100 - - - -
Peas		
Produce of 4 acres Nettledale, of 6 acres Little Benslow Hill 1821		30 - - - -
& produce 1822 of Waby's Field & of 4 acres Lower Benslow Hill		30 - - - -
Clover seed 1821 of Rawlings Hill		5 - - - -
		706
Hay	Loads	
Meadow 1820	6	
Meadow 1821	11	
Meadow 1822	16	
Clover 1821	3	
Sainfoin & clover of 1822	17	
	53	175 - - - -
Potatoes	1 [acre]	
Cabbages	3	
Mangel Wurz[el]	1	
Carrots	1	60
Turnips growing 24a 1[r] - part of Nettledale 8a, Waby's Wym[ond]ley Close 3[a] 2[r], Rawlings Hill & The Linces 5[a] 2[r], The Slipes 7 [a] **Vide minute of sale [page] 139. 3 acres Wimbush eaten by bullocks.**		60 - - - -
Tillage including clover & sainfoin		50 - - - -

Due from Kingsley for turnips			
	1819-20	31 – 10	
	1820-21	130 - -	
	1821-22	30 - - -	
		191 – 10	
	Deduct	11 – 10	
		180 - - -	180 - - - -
			1231 - - - -
	Allow for overcharges & debts		131 - - - -
			£1100 - - -

(*Page 147 is blank.*)

Farming Stock 1 October 1823   [p148]

(*added later*)		£ - s - d
1824		
3	4 horses	
3	4 cows	
2 pigs	2 sows, 2 hogs, 5 pigs	
	21 turkies, 11 guinea fowls, 5 ducks, 45 fowls & at Abbis's 24	120 - - -
	Implements	
	Waggon & tilt, 5 farm carts, 1 light cart	
	Harness for 4 horses	
	8 ploughs & a potatoe plough	
	2 sets of four beamed harrows & 1 of five beamed, twitch harrow, scuffler, 4 hog troughs, 2 pails, chaff box & knife, hay knife,	
3 fans	corn screen, 2 fans, 7 sieves,	
2 gath[er]ing forks	dressing machine, bushel measure, barley chopper, iron shovel & 2 carting shovels	
5 rakes	3 dung forks, 5 ?bean forks, 2 pitch forks, 2 drags, 3 gath[er]ing forks, 7 rakes, 3 scythes	
3 p[ea] hooks	4 peas hooks, 4 beer bottles, 2 wheel hoes, 3 bean hoes, 2 milk pails, seed skip, gun & measuring chain	100 - - -
		220 - - -

159

Farming Stock 1 October 1823 continued

			Lo	B	£220 - -
Wheat thrashed			Lo	B	£220 - -
See	Cott[age] in Lower Yard best		30	4	
min-	mixed		9	-	
ute	**mixed together**				
page	In loft above		10	-	
158	**& some off[al] corn**				
	Malting Yard	6 - -			
	In bad condition	3	9		
	In Crabb's loft 1821	13 - 1			
	& offal 1	2 - 1	15	2	
	Old Talavera bad		3	-	
	Off[al] corn		3	-	100 - - -
The value of the wheat is under rated.			80	1	
Wheat unthrashed					
(Rick)	Part of produce of 1821 north end of wheat barn				
	Produce 1822 of Little Benslow Hill 9 [a] 2 [r]				
	& part Little Wimbush 4a.				
Over	**Taken into the barn January 1824.**				
rated	Produce 1823 of 4a part Great Benslow Hill & 2a				
	part of Wimbush south end of wheat barn				150 - - -
Barley					
See minute	Produce 1823 of Nettledale	10 - -			
[page] 164	The Slipes	7 - -			
Injured by	Waby's 4 acres	3 - 2			
rabbits	Rawling Hill & Linces	3 - 1			130
Peas thrashed					
	Produce of 1821 in loft over		Lo		
	brewho[use] in Portmill Lane				
See minute	**damaged by rain**		22		
page 162	Ditto in a loft in the Malting Yard				
	damaged by rain		8		
	& not damaged		3		
	In Mr Crabb's loft produce of 1822		22		
			55		55 - - --

Tares in loft over brewho[use] in Portmill Lane	Spring	5 - 2	
	Winter	1 - 4	
		7 - 1	
3 loads sold to [*illeg*] Roberts 10 February at 44s. **Measured 13 February 1824.**[231]			10 - - - -
Platting straw			1 - - - -

			B	P	
Clover seed (1820)			5	3	
		Offal	1		
			6	3	5 - - - -
Tares 1823 **over stable**			5	2	
Buck wheat 1823 **over stable**			14	-	4 - - - -
Wimbush		Potatoes	1 acre		
		Carrots	1		
		Mangel wurzel	1		
		Cabbages	2		
		Winter tares	1		50 - - -
					£725

Farming Stock 1 October 1823 continued   **[p151]**

		Brought forward	£725 - - -
Hay		Lo	
	Meadow of 1821	3	
	Meadow 1822	16	
	Meadow 1823	4	
	The quantity is considerably understated. It is nearly if not quite 8 loads. **Began upon 23 March 1824.**		
	Clover sain foin 1822	6	
	1823	9	
	Began 1 March 1824.		
		38	130 - - - -

[231] Wilshere's cash book records the sale of 3 loads of tares to 'Tho Robards' in February 1824. The same month he bought Swedish turnip seed from Thomas Roberts and James Roberts [HALS: 61535 pp68, 81].

Turnips growing		a	[r]	
	Little Benslow Hill	9	2	
	Waby's Field	7	2	
Sweeds	Little Wimbush	7	2	
	Lower Benslow Hill	6	-	
		30	2	70 - - - -
Remains due from Kingsley **B. 615 & bal[ance]** ~~of account of bullocks~~ cattle 1822 **£110 - 8 – 1**[232]				100 - - - -
Tillage including clover & sainfoin				50 - - - -
				1075 - - -
Allow for debts etc				75
				£1000 - - -

(*Loose sheet of paper enclosed between pp149-150. See pp159-165.*)

March 1824

Loads	Wheat	
14	1 [*illeg*]	27 – 3
40	11 February	92 – 12
		119 – 15
	?remains	180 – 5
		300 - --

Quarters	Barley	
19	Williamson[233] Nov 11	28 – 8
20	Malted	35 - -
15	Bell[234] 26 February	27
10	Beaver 8 March	19 – 15
34	Carter 14 March	64 - 5
		174 – 8
Sown – ?seed corn & remains		25 – 12
		200 - --

---

[232] On 16 June 1823 John Kingsley paid Wilshere £360 on account recorded in his cash book with the reference 'B615' probably to his Ledger B [HALS: 61535 p23].

[233] John Williamson was a Hitchin malster living in Cock Street (now High Street) [Piggot's *Hertfordshire Directory* 1826]

[234] This sale is recorded on **p165** of the Memoranda Book where the purchaser is described as 'Bell of Ware'. Piggot's *Hertfordshire Directory* for 1823 lists Charles Bell of Water Row as a maltster in Ware. Carter was also 'of Ware'.

Add May 7 - 4

Orchard Fruit 1823 [p152]

Many of the apples were so much injured by the frosts & by insects in the early part of the season as to be extremely small & imperfect & of very little value, though there was in point of numbers an abundant crop, & upon the whole, I had as many as in ordinary years of such as were good.

Apples		Bushels	Pecks
	King Pippins	3	
	Ribston Pippin	2	
	Hollow Crown Pippin	6	2
	Downton Pippin	3	
	French Golden Pippin	6	
	Golden Rennet	1	1
	Nonsuch	0	3
	Lemon Pippin	0	2
	Monstrous Rennet	0	2
	Cheshire	0	2
	Bedford Seedling	0	2
	Keswick Codlin	0	2
	Old Golden Pippin	0	3
	New Town Pippin	1	
	Minshaw Crab[235]	1	
		27	3
Codlins[236] not measured about		1	1
Harvest Apples about		6	
		35 bushels	

See pears on the next page & cont[inuatio]n of apples.

Orchard Fruit 1823 continued [p153]

Pears		Bushels	Pecks
	Chaumontelle	1	2

[235] Presumably the Minshull Crab, a late-season cooking apple that arose in the Cheshire village of that name, likewise in the eighteenth century.

[236] Codlin was a general term for a culinary apple that cooked to a smooth mash.

Brown Bueré	1	
Cresan	1	
Gansells Burgamot		1
Grey Bueré		2
Colmar		2
Bergamot	1	2
Swans Egg	2	-
Cardilliac	-	2
Black Worcester	1	-
	9	3

Apples	Brought over	35 Bushels	
continued	Margil	1	
	Golden Drop	-	3
	Nonpereals	4	2
		41	1

Potatoes 1823   [p154]

(on 1 acre in Wimbush Field taken up 6 & 7 October.)

			Bushels
Callico	half an acre		115 - -
Champion	half an acre (less one row)		99 - -
One row of various			
Black Morocco	3		
Blood Red	2		
Shaw	1		
German Kidney	1		
Early King	-	1	
Prince Regent	-	1	
Blue Kidney	-	2	
Upright White	1	0	
Painted Lady	1	0	
Fox's Seedling	1	-	
Asparagus potato	-	2	
			11 - -
		Bushels	225

24 March Remain	Champion	sorted	40
		small	12
	Callico	sorted	30
		small	20
	of the other sorts		8
			110

For seed	**20**
For the house	**20**
For sisters, men etc	**20**
	60
May be disposed of	**50**

Carrots 1823 [p155]

0 [acres] 3 [roods] 20 [perches] in Wimbush Field the southern plot.
   Taken up 23 & 24 October   304 bushels

Mangel Wurzell 1823

1 acre in Wimbush Field. Taken up November & December. Finished 10 December.
There were 48 rows of which I weighed 6 taken from different parts, the tops being cut close off. The average weight was 8 cwt 16 lbs a row giving exactly 20 tons per acre.

Drumhead Cabbages

1 acre Wimbush. The heaviest weighed about 25 lbs. I compute the weight of the acre at something more than 20 tons, but I consider them to be much inferior to the mangell wurzell.

1823 December   Sale of Turnips [p156]

The two closes of green topped turnips were sold to Mr Kingsley at 50s per acre.
He agreed that Mr Chapman should take part to be settled between them.

(*Note in pencil*)	Bens[low]	9 - 2
		5 - -
(*Note in pencil*)	Lower Benslow Hill	7 - 0
		9 - 2

165

1824 January 9 Agreed with J Kingsley for my Swedish turnips Little Wimbush & Garden Close at £3 – 10 – 0 agreeing to reduce it to £3 – 5 – 0 or £3 if the times should require it.

(*Note in pencil*)	Little Wimbush	9 - 2
	Waby's or Garden Close	3 - 2
		13

(*Loose piece of paper enclosed between pp155-156.*)

Wheat	In the cottage	45 – 0
	Great Barn	18 - 1
	Mr Crabb's Loft	30 - 1
		93 - 2
	Loft over cottage	10 - -
		103 - 2

Barley   In the Little Barn   5½ quarters

Samples to Mr Chapman 29 June 1824.

(*Page 157 is blank.*)

Wheat   [p158]

(See estimate of stock page 149)

1824 3 February

Michael Chapman sold for me to James Dupin Nash the wheat in the Lower Barn and the cottages 40 loads at 46s 6d and as 15 loads the wheat [*illeg*] of 1822 last thrashed (there are but 14 besides 3 loads of offal) at 39s.

There appears to be but 14 loads.

14 loads delivered at various times as sent for, the last 4 loads 20 March.

11 February.

Delivered to Mr Nash's loft in Hitchin[237]	Loads	Bushel
from the cott[age]	39	1
and from new wheat	--	<u>4</u>
	40	-

The quantity put in was 39 – 4. Some which had got a little damp by lying against the wall was separated. The whole quantity as measured was nearly 39 – 3, rather more than one bushel deficient.

11 October

Thrashed part of the produce of 2 acres Wimbush 1823

laid in the Little Barn	4	4
of which was sown in the Walsworth Way Close & Great Wimbush*	1	<u>4</u>
Leaving	3	-

***Stone Close & ½ acre Great Wimbush. Of this 4 bushels [*illeg*].
October1813 [sic] I had of Ransom 2 loads Dantzick wheat sown (dibbled) in Starlings Br[idge] Close & on ½ of an acre of Great Wimbush.**

January 1824	Thrashed of 1822	14
	& offal	<u>3</u>
		17

Delivered 20 March the 14 loads sold to J D Nash 3 February at 39s.

Wheat continued　　　　　　　　　　　　　　　　　　　**[p159]**

12 & 13 February 1824

I had all my remaining thrashed wheat measured & all which required it well dressed some of it having become very dusty & foul - & injured by vermin. The quantity in the estimate of October last & that since thrashed are stated at the foot.

---

[237] James Dupin Nash owned Purwell Mill on the parish boundary between Hitchin and Great Wymondley. His father Daniel owned and occupied a house, maltings and outbuildings in Cock Street on the corner of Pound Lane. On Daniel's death in 1810 his wife Esther inherited the property and occupied the house while James occupied the maltings [TNA: PROB11/1511/496; NHM: map of Hitchin 1816; HALS: D/P53/11/7]. The house and buildings were demolished in the 1830s to widen Pound Lane (now Brand Street) [T Crosby, P Douglas, S Fletcher et al, *Jeeves Yard. A dynasty of Hitchin builders and brickmakers* (Hitchin, 1993) pp32-33].

Thrashed wheat by valuation of 1 October 1823 (page 149)

	61 lbs per bushel				Lo	B
A	Cott[age] in Lower Yard				39	4
B	In Loft above				10	-
C	In Malting Yard	Tal[avera]		6		
D		Off[al] corn		3	9	-
E	In Crabb's Y[ar]d	old Tal[avera]		3		
F		Off[al] corn		3	6	-
G	Of 1822 thrashed					
		April 1823		13 - 1		
H		Off[al] corn		2 - 1	15	2
	Stock of thrashed 1 October		Loads		80	1
I	Thrashed October 1823 part of produce of 2 acres Great Wimbush 1823 **about ½ remainder in Wheat Barn**				4	4
K	Thrashed January 1824	of produce 1821		14 – 0		
L		Off[al] corn		3 - 0	17	0
					102	-
	61 lbs per bushel				Lo	-
A	1824 February 11 Delivered to Mr Nash **39 loads 1 bushel, off[al] corn 4 bushels**				40	
K	Laid in the cott[age] for Nash				14	
B	Remains in the loft above the cottage **60 lbs**				10	
G	At Mr Crabb's yard of 1822 **55 lbs bushel**				13	
	Old red **56 lbs the bushel**				3	
	Old Talavera **56 lbs the bushel**				5	2½
Part I	of 1823 ½ load taken out to grind. ½ bushel **dressed out**				2	1
D, F, H, L	Offals mixed **½ load taken out to grind 17 February. About 4 bushels dressed out 3 March**				8	2½
Part I	Sown				1	4
					98	-

Bad offal dressed out	1		
Rubbish & chumblings	2	3	-
		101	-
Deficient		1	
		102	

Wheat continued [p160]

1824 February 17 I sent to be ground 2½ bushels of the mixed offals at Mr Ransom's mill.[238] It weighed 121 lbs.

    Produced flour   104
        bran etc.   17
                    121

Baked 35 lbs. Gave French 14 lbs.

1824 March 6 I sent to be ground 2½ bushels of the old Talavera wheat. It weighed 139 [lbs].

    18th Produced flour   97
        bran etc.   35
                    132

27 March 1824 I thrashed 2 acres grown 1823 in Wimbush. Produce best 10 loads **A**, off[al] corn 3 bushels **E**.

April from the stack of Red of 1822			**B**	2 loads
	off[al] corn		**F**	0 - 2

May 13 from rick 1822	Best	33	**C**	
	off[al] corn	2	**G**	
	d[resse]d very bad	2 – 2		
appropriated to fowls				37- 2

June 8 from **G[rea]t Benslow**			**D**	
Hill 1823	Best	18 - 1		
	off[al] corn	1 - -		
	1st bad (in barn	1 – 3		
				20 – 4

---

[238] Grove Mill in Hitchin. See Biographical Notes.

9 June	Loads	
A	10	
B	2	
C	33	45 in cottage
D	<u>18 – 1</u>	on the barn floor
	63 - 1	
E, F, G	2 - -	in cott[age] [*illeg*] taken in sacks

(*Page 161 is blank.*)

Peas and Hogs [p162]
See min[ute] of quantities [page] 149.

Having in November 1823 bought 16 pigs they were immediately fed with peas and sold as they became sufficiently fat for market. Therefore cost prices, the quantity of peas consumed & the produce are intended to be stated at the foot. The peas turned out much less in quantity than had been laid by – in fact about 11 loads had been stolen.

	Loads
There were over the brewho[use] in Portmill Lane	22
In the Malting Yard	8
&	3

Of these there was a deficiency of 11 loads.

In Mr Crabb's loft	22

15 loads of the above were bought of Edward Fordham February 1822 at 15s per load.
The whole of those over the brewho[use] & in the
malting yard being   22 loads
And from Mr Crabb's loft   <u>2</u>
     24

were given to the above hogs. See acc[ount] of
produce on next page.

1824 February 4 Sold to Thomas Jeeves at 25s per Mr
Ch[apman] **del[ivere]d 7th**.[239]   14
February 11 Removed to loft over the brewho[use]

                                                                                            6

Continued on the next page.

Peas and Hogs continued   [p163]

1823 November 11	8 pigs at 28s	11 – 4 – 0
12	8 - at 22s 6d	9 – 0 – 0
		20 – 4 – 0
December 11	2 to London produce	2 – 12 –10
20	3 ditto ~~for the House~~	4 - 4 – 10
1824 January 28	1 for the house (bacon)	3 – 19 – 7
	1 Bentley	2 – 13 –7½
30	3 for Carter [240]	10 – 7 – 3½
February 4	1 for the house	2 – 13 – 6
6	3 Carter	9 – 19 – 6
16	1 for the house	2 – 12 – 2
18	1 ditto for bacon	4 – 2 – 2
	6 plucks sold separately	- - 11 – 7
		43 - 17 - 1
	Costs as above	20 – 4 – 0
		23 – 13 – 1
	Butcher	- - - 10 - --
Leaving for 24 loads of peas consumed		23 – 3 – 1

19s 3½d per load

Supposing the dung to be worth the labour, the peas were discoloured by rain, they were about 20 sh[illings] or a guinea per load, it was therefore a losing trade.[241]

---

[239] Wilshere's cash book records £17 8s paid by T Jeeves by Mr Chapman for 14 loads of peas at 25s [a load] with 2s deducted [HALS: 61535 p77]. For Thomas Jeeves and Michael Chapman see Biographical Notes.
[240] John Carter became Wilshere's gardener in June 1823. See Biographical Notes.

Barley of 1824 [p164]

1824 February 11

It appears from the account of farming expenses etc. kept by John Willding that there has up to this time been thrashed:

	Best	Off[al] Corn
That is by Clemens	19 - -	3 - 2
by Jeeves & Silsby	7 - 4	- - 4
by Roberts & Tuffnell	12 – 6	2 – 2
	39 - 2	7 - - *(recte 6)*
And in small parcels	2 – 0	1 – 2
	41 – 2	8 – 2
		41 – 2
		49 – 4 *(recte 48-4)*

Quarters sold to Williamson at 30s 4 Nov[242]		19
Sent to Mr Beaver to be malted for me 31 Jany		20
		39 qu

Malt 20 quarters 6 ½ rec[eive]d 5 March.

		Quarters
Sold as above		19
Malted		20
Delivered to French for fowls & pigs	2 - 2	
To Abbis for fowls	1 - 1	
To Dines[243] for dogs	2 - 4	
Remains in granary **only 12 bushels**	1 – 7	7 - 6
		46 - 6
Not accounted for		3 - 6
		49 - 4

Over

---

[241] Despite this conclusion, on 27 April 1824 Wilshere bought 9 pigs from William Roberts for £5 8s [HALS: 61535 p102].

[242] For Willding, John Jeeves, Silsby and Tuffnell see Biographical Notes. Wilshere's cash book records the sale of 19 quarters of barley to J Williamson, a Hitchin maltster, by [Robert] Rose [HALS: 61535 p49].

[243] George William Dines, William Wilshere's gamekeeper. See Biographical Notes.

Barley 1823 continued [p165]

			Best	Off. Corn
49 – 4 15 - -- 3 - --	1824 February 16. Dressed the barley thrashed by Tuffnell & Roberts in the last 10 days		15	3
15 – 4 3 - - 86	17th The 15 quarters above sold by Chapman to Bell of Ware at 36s. Delivered at Chapman's Yard the 18th			
15 101 25	28 dressed the barley thrashed by Tuffnell & Roberts to this time leaving only the 2 west bays.		15 - 4	3
126 7 – 4 133 - 4	28 February. Sown on the upper three acres ½ of Waby's Field	Qu 1 - 3		
	3 & 4 March on Little Benslow Hill	3 - 7		
	March 5. 10 quarters to Mr Beaver at 39s 6d.	10 - - 15 - 7		
	Mar 20. Dressed a thrashing - put to it		12 - 4	2 - 4
	remainder of the last thrashing not sown		- - 2	
	Remained in the Little Barn		- - 2	
		13 quarters		
	March 31. Dressed		21 - 4	4
	April 6 34* quarters sold by Mr Chapman to Carter of Ware at 38s.			
* On measuring there proved to be 5 bushels short either by error in reckoning the last dressing or by stealing. This 5 bushels was made up out of the off[al] corn.				
	May 28. Dressed draggings		5 - 4	2 - 0

(The next page is blank. The few remaining pages which have been used are not numbered.)

M[onthly] Rev[iew] May 1823 Phillips' History of Cultivated Vegetables.
[p167]

Asparagus
May be produced till late in September by cutting down the stalks towards the end of July, forking & raking the beds &, if dry, watering them with the drain of a dung hill or water wherein horse or cow dung has been steeped. The prejudice against the use of dung is unfounded. The sweetest asparagus is that raised on the richest soil.

Beans
"We have found it an excellent plan in procuring late beans to cut down the stalks after the crop has been gathered for the kitchen. They will soon sprout out again & if the weather be showery, yield a better supply than late planting. Some blighted Windsor beans cut down yielded an excellent crop in November.

Wheat Season 1823 [p168]
October
I bought of J Ransom 10 bushels of Dantzwick wheat which was dibbled 13-18 October in Starlings Bridge Close & on the half of an acre in Great Wimbush. The other half acre was planted at the same time with a bushel of my own red wheat.
October 6 – 11
Walsworth Way Close dibbled with 7 bushels of my own red wheat.

1824 February
I bought of J Ransom 10 bushels of Talavera wheat of which I planted the lower 4½ acres with 7 bushels 28 February to 6 March. Returned to Mr Ransom the remaining 3 bushels.

Barley Season 1824 [p169]
February 28
Sowed the upper three acres of Waby's Field with 11 bushels of my own barley.
March 4 – 6
Sowed Little Benslow Hill with 31 bushels of my own growth.
8 March 1824
Received from Nicholas Francis, Cambridge, 4 quarters of fen barley for seed at 40s - intended for Little Wimbush. The upper part sown 19 & 20 March, the lower part 26th. The quantity sown was 3 quarters 1 [bushel] on 7 [acres] 2 [roods], remains 7 bushels.

Garden Minutes 1824   **[p170]**
Cucumbers

January	2 or 3 small ones were cut from vines in the Pine House.
February	4 or 5 were cut from the frame autumn sown plants but not regular or well formed.
March 10	Cut one of a better form & good size.
11	Cut a handsome one 8½ inches in length 6½ oz weight.

Ice plants grow to great perfection on small hillocks of rich mould supported by stakes put together in imitation of rock work – 2 or 3 feet high with a base of about 4 feet diameter.   Hert[fordshire] Trans[actions] Vol 5 p275

(*The rest of the memoranda book is unused.*)

Catalogue of William Wilshere's Farming Stock December 1824 (HALS 60351)

(*In manuscript*) Catalogue of Farming Stock etc. Late W.W.

A CATALOGUE OF THE LIVE AND DEAD FARMNG STOCK, COMPRISING,

7 Ricks of Meadow, Clover, and Cinquefoin Hay,
4 USEFUL DRAFT HORSES,
A remarkably fine grey seasoned Carriage Horse,
And a Clever stout bay Cob,
THREE FINE MILCH COWS,
Two handsome Yelts, 18 Guinea Fowls, 14 Turkeys,
Ducks, Fowls, and Chickens,
WAGGONS, CARTS, PLOUGHS, AND OTHER EFFECTS
Of W. Wilshere, Esq. decd,

WHICH WILL BE SOLD BY AUCTION, BY MR. STANTON, [244]
ON THE PREMISES IN BACK STREET, HITCHIN,
On FRIDAY, December 17th, 1824, AT ELEVEN O'CLOCK.

CATALOGUES my [sic] be had at the Principal Inns in the Neighbouring Towns, and of the Auctioneer, Hitchin.
PATERNOSTER, PRINTER, HITCHIN

Conditions of Sale

1. The highest bidder to be the buyer, and if any dispute arise between two or more bidders, the lot to be put up again and re-sold.
2. No person to advance less than sixpence at each bidding; above one pound, one shilling; above five pounds, two shillings and six-pence; and so on in proportion.
3. The purchaser to pay a deposit of five shillings in the pound, in part of payment, and the remainder on or before delivery.
4. The lots to be taken away with all faults and defects on the next day after the sale is ended.

---

[244] William Stanton was a Hitchin auctioneer who lived in Cock Street (now High Street) [NHM: map of Hitchin 1816; Piggot's *Hertfordshire Directory* 1826].

5. Upon failure of complying with the above conditions, the deposit money shall be forfeited, and the proprietor be at liberty to re-sell such lot, by private or public sale, and if any deficiency shall happen on such re-sale, the same shall be made good by the defaulter at this sale, together with all charges attending the same.

CATALOGUE, &C

On FRIDAY, December 17th, 1824 AT ELEVEN O'CLOCK

BARN AND GRANARY

LOT		(*ms notes*)
1	Three hay forks, pitching fork, gathering fork, dung fork, and 3 rakes	
2	Ditto and ditto	
3	Haum rake, 3 peasehooks, dock iron and 3 hoes	
4	Docking iron, 2 dung hooks, 2 wheat hoes, scythe and 2 sickles	
5	Two scythes, iron shovel and barley chopper	Not to be sold
6	Four wood bottles	
7	Corn screen and bushel	Barley chopper
8	Two pair of cart ropes	
9	Two light drags	
10	Twelve corn sacks	Not to be sold
11	Ditto	Not to be sold
12	Old wagon tilt	0 – 5 – 0
13	Old gun	
*14	A malt screen	0 – 5 - 0
*15	Old corn screen	0 – 2 - 6
16	Chaff-box and knife	
17	A good dressing machine	6 – 5 – 0

STABLE.

18	Thill harness for 1 horse	
19	Ditto	
20	Ditto	
21	Fore-horse harness for 1 horse	

22	Ditto	
23	Ditto	
24	Two pair hames and 2 pair plough chains	
25	Ditto	
26	Four headstalls and reins	
27	Two leathern wanties and 2 bearing chains	
28	Corn-bin, lantern, sieve and whip	

YARD AND SHEDS.

29	Three hen-pens,	Not to be sold
	yoke, 2 pails and skip	
30	Two pig-troughs	
31	Ditto and cow-crib	
*32	Two lamb-troughs	0 – 7 – 0
*33	Two long sheep-troughs	0 – 11 – 0
*34	Two sheep troughs on wheels	0 – 12 – 0
*35	Ditto	0 – 10 – 0
*36	Ditto	0 – 9 – 0
*37	Ditto	0 – 14 – 0
38	A Hertfordshire wheel plough[245]	
39	A Hampshire ditto	
40	A dray plough	
41	A Hampshire plough	
42	Ditto	
43	Ditto	
44	A Suffolk plough	
45	A Norfolk ditto	
46	A double-furrow plough	
47	A potatoe-moulding plough	
48	A good drill plough	TW 2 – 0 – 0
49	Old plough-beams, &c.	
50	A good scuffler	
51	A large twitch harrow	TW 1 – 7 – 0

---

[245] Arthur Young considered the great Hertfordshire wheel plough to be 'exceedingly well calculated' for 'breaking up strong flinty fallows in a dry season', but 'for all other works it is a heavy, ill-formed, and ill-going plough'. About Hitchin it was used for breaking up land [Young, *General View*, pp36, 59].

52	A set of three 4-beamed harrows	
53	Ditto	
54	A 5-beamed harrow and plough slide	
55	A good narrow-wheel dung cart	
56	Ditto with iron arms	4 – 12 – 6
57	Ditto	10 – 10 – 0
58	A light cart, with ditto	1 – 13 – 0
59	A 6-inch wheel mould cart, wood arms	
60	A narrow-wheel waggon, with iron arms}	14 – 5 – 0
61	Old tilt for ditto}	
*62	Old 6-inch wheel waggon, with iron arms	11 – 0 – 0
*63	Old tilt for ditto	0 – 18 – 0
64	An old cart	
65	A frame roll	

LIVE STOCK.

66	A handsome yelt	2 – 18 – 0
67	Ditto	3 – 6 – 0
68	A fine milch cow in full profit, *Gentle*	12 – 5 – 0
69	A fine white short-horned cow in profit	12 – 5 – 0
70	Ditto Yorkshire ditto, *Beauty*	11 – 10 –0
71	Useful grey carriage-horse, aged, *John*	Not to be sold
72	Ditto, ditto, *Tom*	Not to be sold
73	Useful black draft-horse, aged, *Gilbert*	10 – 0 – 0
74	Ditto bay ditto, blind	13 –10 – 0
75	A remarkably fine grey carriage-horse, 8 years old	66 – 0 – 0
76	A useful stout bay cob	15 – 0 – 0
77	Eight guinea fowls, at (*blank*) per head	Not to be sold
78	Ten young ditto, at ditto	Not to be sold
79	Three Spanish ducks	Not to be sold
80	Five old Turkies	Not to be sold
81	Five young ditto	Not to be sold
82	Four ditto	Not to be sold
83	Thirty fowls, at (*blank*) per head	Not to be sold
84	Sixteen chickens, at ditto	Not to be sold
85	White fowls and chickens, at (*blank*) per head	Not to be sold

HAY.
In Stack-Yard.

86	A rick of good old meadow hay, about 16	3 - 0 – 0 sold at 41 – 0 – 0
87	A rick of new ditto, about 12 loads	3 - 0 – 0 at 24 – 0 – 0
88	Part of a rick of old hay	4 – 5 – 0
89	A rick of second crop of clover, the produce of 17 acres	2 - 10 – 0, 25 – 0 – 0
90	~~A stack of haum~~	

In a Field called Nettle-Dell.

91	A rick of clover hay, the produce of 10 acres	2 - 0 – 0 , 35 – 0 – 0

In Lower Bensley Hill Field.

92	A rick of clover hay, the produce of 10 acres	2 - 0 – 0, 15 –0 – 0
93	A rick of cinquefoin hay, the produce of 4½ acres	3 - 10 – 0, 21 –10 – 0
94	A rick of old clover and cinquefoin hay, about 7 loads	3 - 10 – 0, 30 – 0 – 0

95	Sundries	
96	Ditto	
97	Ditto	
98	Ditto	

THE END

(*Labelled*) T. Wilshere Esque.

List of seeds of greenhouse plants sown by James Bowie, 1813 (*HALS: 61598*)

Lists of Trees, Seeds &c Sown, Planted &c, in the Garden of Wm Wilshere Esq. at Hitchin, Herts. by James Bowie (HALS: 61598)

(*Note inside front cover of book*)

		Peaches Budded
	8 (*deleted*)	Avant ?
	8 (*altered from 9*)	E[arly] Purple
	9 (*altered from 10*)	Catherine
		Plumbs
	1	Early Tours
	2	Green

Maiden Trees planted in Boxes for forcing 1st January 1813

1	Noblesse Peach 2 trees
2	French Mignon peach
3	Early Purple ditto
4	Red Magdalen ditto
5	Brunion Nectarine
6	Elruge ditto
7	Temple's ditto

7th

1	Long Cucumber / Vine Place
2	-------------------- Douglass Clap
3	Fine Long / Wells /
4	This did not grow. Allen / Kensing[to]n
5	-------------------- McIntosh[246]
6	Early Cantaloupe Mellon

---

[246] Daniel McIntosh was Wilshere's gardener from February 1811 to December 1812. See Biographical Notes.

LIST OF TREES ETC PLANTED BY JAMES BOWIE

2nd February 1813 Sowed

HP	{No 7	Southgate Cu[cumbe]r	/10
	{ 8	Early ditto	/9
	{ 9	Early frame	/10
	10	H.P. favourite Cantaloup	

4 Mar.

11	Southgate Cucumber
12	Very Long Lumsden
13	Long prl[?] Ridges McIn[tosh]
14	H.P. fav[ourite] Cant[aloupe] Mellon
15	Persian ditto
16	Polinac ditto
17	Romana ditto
18	Long ribbed ditto
19	Scarlet Rock
20	Green Flesh D Sussex
21	Large Green rock
22	Bossey Rock
23	Golden Rock
24	White Turkey Cuc[umbe]r

25 March

25	Knights White Melon
26	Salonica Mellon
27	Ispahan Mellon
28	Favourite -----
29	Scarlet Flesh from Oatlands
30	Black Rock Cantaloupe
31	Large Rock Mellon
32	Romanna Mellon
33	Large Black Rock
34	Green Flesh Mellon (*There is no 35*)
36	Netted Cantaloupe Mell[on]

	{37	Snake Mellon
Fultons	{38	Cobels Rock Mellon
	{39	White Prickley Cuc[umbe]r
	{40	Green Prickley ditto

7 Ap[ril]

41	Prolific McIn[tosh]	
42	Long Ridge	
43	Stewart 1811	
44	---------- 1812	

List of Seeds of G[reen] House Plants sowed 1813

No	1	Mimosa elegans	
	2	---------- longifolia	M
	3	---------- microphylla	M
	4	---------- myrtifolia	M
	5	---------- suaveolens	M
	6	---------- saligna	
	7	Myrica obcordata	
	8	Mimosa verticillata	
	9	Diosma imbricata	
	10	Entaxia myrtifolia	
	11	Diosma serratifolia	
	12	Billadiera scandens	
	13	Lavatera Thuringiacca ?	
	14	Pultenea sp---	
	15	---------- sp	
	16	Pomaderris sp	
	17	Loddigessia Oxalidifolia	
	18	Dolichos lignosus	
	19	Lupinus arboreus	
	20	Indigofera australis	

Seeds of Greenhouse Plants

21	Cytissus proliferus
22	Cobeaea scandens
23	Goodia lotufolia
24	Pultenea sp
25	Euphorbia mellifera
26	Chorizema illicifolia
27	Mimosa simplicifolia
28	Platylobium formosum

LIST OF TREES ETC PLANTED BY JAMES BOWIE

29	Pultenea linophylla
30	Polygala myrtifolia
31	Mixt Sps
32	Pultenea
33	Lobelia stricta
34	
35	
36	(*Unused numbers continue to 49.*)

Stove Plants

50	Lagostroemia regina
1	Hibiscus salidariffa
2	Crotolaria pulchella
3	Crotolaria elegans
4	Asclepias currassavica
5	Hibiscus sp
6	Myrtus tormentosus
7	Thunbergia fragrans
8	Cassia alata
9	------- marginata
60	Diospyros chloroxylon
1	Clitoria ternatea
2	Costus speciosus
3	Clitoria ternatea China
4	Pentapetes Phoenicia ?lanerifer toro.
5	Sida tormentosa
6	Bixa orelana
7	Oveidia verticilata
8	Melia azaderach
9	Ardisia solonacea
70	Croton sebiferum
1	Arbor grandis leguminosus shun-yeni-ying
72	Crotolaria verucossa
3	Arbor grandis shun ying-tchui
4	Melastoma
5	Mimosa lucida
6	Celosia coccinia nov. var.

7	Poiniciara pulcherima

Perenial Plants

100	Veronica crenulata[247]
1	----------- glomerata
2	Astrantia major
3	Gentianna cruciata
4	Delpinium hybridum
5	Astrantia carniolica
6	Stoechas rubra
7	Aconitum uncinatum
8	Melitis grandiflora
9	Scabiosa lutea
110	---------- alpina
1	Delpinium urceolatum
2	Allium angulosum
3	Delphinium grandiflorum
4	Aconitum anthora
5	Rudbekia hirta
6	Delphinium intermidium
7	Alchemilla alpina
8	Scabiosa atropurpurea
9	Veronica gentianoides
120	Delphinium aconitum
1	Aconitum album
122	Gnaphalium foetidum
3	Prunella laciniata
4	Phlomis tuberosus
5	Saxafraga densa
6	------------ groenlandia
7	------------ cotyledon
8	------------ muscoides
9	------------ palmata

[247] Although many of the Latin names Bowie used for garden plants are still employed today, a significant minority have been superceded. *Veronica Crenulata* (longleaf speedwell) is now usually termed *Veronica longifolis* subs.*longifolia.*

130	------------ Lyons
1	------------ punctata
2	------------ mixture
3	Orobus purpureus
4	Cheledonium glaucum
5	Papaver cambricum
6	Erinus alpinus
7	Iberis aliata
8	Antirrhinum pictum

Bienials

150	Chieranthus	Purple queen stock
1	---------------	White ditto ditto
2	--------------- beinis	
3	Fumaria fungosa	
4	Digitalis orientalis	
5	---------- fine white	
6	---------- lutea	
7	---------- purpurea	
8	---------- thapsi	
9	Campanula latifolia ? N.W.	
160	Campanula latifolia / Kew /	
1	Ferula sp	
2	------- sp	
3	Althea sp Bltz holyhock	

Hardy Annuals

1	Delphinium ajacis
2	Iberis pinnata /alba
3	Androsace septentrionale
4	Blitum virgatum
5	Lathyrus aphaca
6	Heliophilla pinnata
7	Polygonum orientale
8	Trifolium messiniense
9	Vicia Bythinica
10	Silene viridiflora
1	Agrostemna coelirosa

LIST OF TREES ETC PLANTED BY JAMES BOWIE

2	Astragalus pamosus
3	Astragalus boeticus
4	Calceolaria pinnata
5	Argemone Mexicana
6	OEnothra dentate
7	------------ rubra
8	Amaranthus sanguineus
9	-------------- grezicans
20	-------------- oleraceus
1	-------------- hypochondriacus
2	-------------- cordata
3	-------------- flava
4	-------------- erectus
25	Amaranthus orientalis
6	-------------- coronarius
7	-------------- gangetrius
8	-------------- cordatus
9	-------------- sp
30	Xeranthemum lucidum
1	Reseda odorata
3	

3rd April

1	Red celery
2	North's
3	Solid
4	E[arly] Purple Broccoli

7th April

1	Balsam /Dimsey own/[248]
2	ditto ditto very good
3	--------- /JB
4	Dw[ar]f Coxcomb
5	best dw[ar]f ditto
6	Yellow ditto
7	Tricolor
8	Bicolor

[248] David Dimsey and William Dimsey were Hitchin gardeners. See Biographical Notes.

188

	9	Purple Globes
	10	Stript ditto
	11	White ditto
	12	Virginian Tobacco
	13	Patagonian Cuc[umber]
	14	Love Apple
	15	Long Capsicum Bentley's[249]
	16	Sweet Scented Marygold
	17	Humble plant
	18	Ice plant
	19	Purple Egg plant
	20	Patagonian Cuc[umbe]r 1811
	21	Purple browallia
	22	White ditto
	23	Purple Convolvulus
	24	Stript ditto
	25	Yellow Chrysanthum [sic]
	26	White ditto
	27	China pink
	28	Pompion
20 April	1	White Broccoli
	2	Early purple ditto
	3	Syberian ditto
	4	Shining leav'd ditto
	5	Late Cauliflower
	6	Brussells Sprouts
	7	Early Dw[ar]f Cabbage
	8	Early York ditto
	9	Savoy
	10	Scots Cale [sic]

West India Seeds 18 May 1813

No 1	-----------------	Sponge cucumber
2	Cucumis anguira	Mutton cuc[umber]

---

[249] Henry Bentley was a Hitchin gardener who sold Wilshere seeds in 1796-1798 [HALS: 61479/19]. See Biographical Notes.

3	Calotropis gigantea	Auricula tree
4	Helenium	Sunflower
5	Bryonia	Sherise of Surinam
6	Poncianna pucherimma	Flowerfers
7	Anona sp.	
8	------------	Tonquin Bean[250]

Pencil drawing of a leaf and stem labelled 'Trapen' (*HALS: 61598*).

---

[250] Tonka beans *Dipteryx odorata.* See Wilshere's Commonplace Book p210 below.

LIST OF TREES ETC PLANTED BY JAMES BOWIE

West India Seeds

	arrived	**July 1813**	**sow'd**
1	Sweet lemon		
2	Meringo		
3	Physic nut		
4	Unknown		
5	Gum Arabic		
6	Cabbage Tree		
7	Sappadilla		
8	Lime		
9	Unknown	Pitcarinia ? J B	
10	Velvet Vine		
11	Unknown	Papaio ? J B	
12	Bell Apple		
13	Rattle plant		
14	Otahite Shade Tree		

These collected by William Hamilton at Nevis.[251]

15	Capsicum frutescens
16	Passiflora suberosea
17	Mimosa punctata ? Yellow flo[wer] sensitive
18	Mimosa tortuosa Common cashew
19	A beautiful climber unknown
20	Acacia vera Gum Arabic
21	Worm Seed
22	Stachylarpheta Jamaiciensis

---

[251] It is not clear whether the seeds collected by Mr Hamilton were nos, 1-14 or nos 15-23. They were probably sent to Wilshere through his friend, Mrs Sarah Mills of Hitchin. See Biographical Notes. Her son, John Colhoun Mills, was living in Nevis by 1796. William Hamilton may have been the Revd William Vaughan Hamilton who went to Nevis in 1807. His stepmother, Martha Hamilton, inherited the Montpelier Plantation in Nevis from her father, John Richardson Herbert, who had managed the Mills' family's plantation for John Mills. Mrs Mills was a friend of Martha Hamilton's cousin, Frances Lady Nelson [David Small, 'Montpelier Estate. St John Figtree, Nevis. Contrasting Legacies on a Sugar Plantation' May 2010 https://seis.bristol.ac.uk/~emceee/montpelier.pdf; Revd William Vaughan Hamilton, Legacies of British Slave Ownership: https://www.ucl.ac.uk/lbs/person/view/2146633319].

23   Cassia occidentalis

1813 List of Trees in the Peach House

Back Trellis

No	1	French mignonne	Peach
	2	Nobblesse	Peach
	3	Elruge	Nectarine
	4	Roman	Nectarine
	5	La Teton de Venus	Peach
	6	Van Gard	Peach
	7	Clermont	Nectarine
	8	Early Avant	Peach

No		Front Trellis	
	1	La Teton de Venus	Peach
	2	French Mignonne	Peach
	3	Brugnon	Nectarine
	4	Galland	Peach
	5	Montaubon	Peach
	6	Elruge	Nectarine
	7	French Mignonne	Peach
	8	Brugnon	Nectarine
	9	Red Magdalen	Peach
	10	Violet Hative	Nectarine
	11	La Teton de Venus	Peach
	12	Red Roman	Nectarine
	13	Noblesse	Peach

A List of the Peaches in Pots

No 1	Early Avant
No 2	La Teton de Venus
No 3	Cha
No 4	Grimwood's Royal George[252]

---

[252] Bills survive for bulbs bought by Wilshere in October 1796 from Grimwood & Wykes, Nursery & Seedsmen, at The Pine Apple, Kensington. This nursery taken over by Daniel Grimwood in 1783 continued with variouse partners until 1804 when it was taken over by William Malcolm from whom Wilshere bought vegetable seeds n 1820 [HALS: 61480/172-173; 61481/53; Harvey, *Early Nurserymen* p78].

LIST OF TREES ETC PLANTED BY JAMES BOWIE

No 5	Red Magdalen
No 6	Galland
No 7	Nobless

(Entries started from the back of the book in a different handwriting presumably by James Gray.)

1818 November 17   Vines Planted in Pots

No 1	Black Hamburgh
2	Royal Muscadine
3	White Sweetwater
4	Black Muscadine
5	White Frontinac

30   Maiden Trees Planted

1	Brunion nectarine
2	Roman Red ditto
3	Grimwood Royal George peach
4	Elruge nectarine
5	Peach Nobless
6	ditto French Minion

Same time in Peach House

4	Brunion nectarine stan[ar]d
5	Elruge ditto dw[ar]f

1818 November 30   Planted in Pots

6 Kalmia glauca
1 Fine rose azalia
1 Scarlet ditto
1 Purple magnolia, ha-ha
1 Fine new Rododendron katawbiense

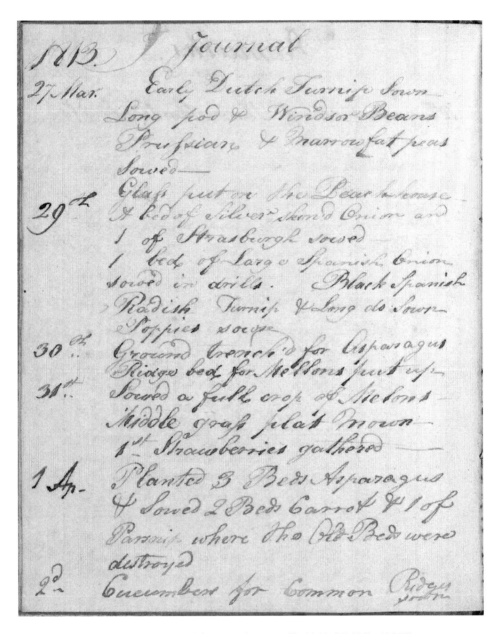

Page from James Bowie's Journal for March to April, 1813 (*HALS: 60158*).

Journal kept in the Garden of William Wilshere Esq. Hitchin, Herts. By James Bowie gardener (HALS 60158)

1812	Journal
20ᵗʰ Dec	Vines in the Conservatory pruned.

1812   Journal

20th Dec — Vines in the Conservatory pruned.

22nd — Standard and espalier fruit trees, currant & gooseberry bushes pruned, in the Forcing Quarter.

28th — South border in the plantation manured & dug,

31st — Put up and planted a 2 light bed for forcing asparagus.

[Remarks.] 10 January 1813 Began to push quick. Cut a dish on the 18th. Good. Dark hazy black frost. No sunshine

French beans sown in pans in the Hot House.

[Remarks.] 14th Planted out in pots. Flower 24 Feb & began to set 27.

Lettuce, radish & carrot sown

1 Jany 1813 — Planted 8 maiden peach & nectarine trees in boxes for forcing.

Likewise some of the Syringa Chinense pot[te]d.

2nd — The first, or left hand quarter in the plantation dunged & dug, likewise part of the first right hand quarter dug.

7th Jany — Put up a seed bed & sowed some cucumber & melon seeds.

Remarks. The bed being 5 ft high & 4 ft wide the width of the frame. Seeds up 18. Black frost. Wind SE to NE. Thermometer in bed 70º. Potted off 25th. Wind E. Fruit out in April.

9th — 48 pots of strawberries put into the great Stove. N.B. the plants extremely weak & some of them had been forced before.

Remarks. Some of these shewed flower 24th. Some few fruit set 27th. Feb 6 weather favourable.

Grape vine on the front of the study pruned & nailed.

16th — Currant & gooseberrys and raspberries pruned, and standard fruit trees in the north quarter of the Home Garden pruned. Ground dug.

Plants in the Conservatory cleaned & turned round.

	Espalier fruits in home border pruned & tied.
20th	Shrubs in the south border of the home quarter pruned.
29th	The above border turned in.
30th	Bed for cucumbers of 3 lights put up. Dung rather rank especially at the west end.
	Remarks. The middle hole shewed fruit 20 March, cut 7 April.
1 Feb	Sowed 5 rows round spinach on the first quarter of the plantation.
1 Feb	Planted 7 rows shallots and 3 rows garlick on the Cypress quarter in the plantation ten inch between the rows & six between setts.
6th	Transplanted early peas from the forcing quarter to the south border in the plantation. Sowed at the same time 2 rows peas along the border & 4 rows beans across it.
	Cucumbers ridged out in 3 light box.
7th	Began to dig, stopped 14th for the foundation of a Peach House.
13th	Planted out the Scots cabbage Stumpy for seed.
	Sowed a few early dw[ar]f cabbage in pans.
	[Remarks] Planted out in April.
15	Sowed a row of sweet peas in the Home Quarter near the strawberries.
16 & 17	Border on the grass plot dug.
17	Sowed some cattle cabbage & thousand headed ditto on south border of the plantation.[253]
	[Remarks] Pricked out 3rd May.
17 Feb	Sowed a little solid celery (on asparagus bed) for the first crop.
	[Remarks] Pricked out 27 April.
	Put up a slight 1-light hot-bed & sowed thereon some early cauliflower and Cape Broccoli for successional crops.

---

[253] A bill from the Hertford nurseryman Robert Murray for Janaury to March 1813 includes thousand headed cabbage seed, mushroom spawn and rhodendrons ponticum, maximum and ferragenia [HALS: 61479/31].

	[Remarks] 22 Mar pricked out. Planted 7 May.
28th	Sowed 6 rows of long-pod beans & 4 rows spinage on the first quarter of the plantation. 4 rows early peas sown on the Cypress quarter. Upper part – larkspur & candytuft sown.
1st Feb [sic]	A bed of larkspur sown.
2nd	A bed of onion and a few leeks with them sown in the home quarter.
	[Remarks] Crop of onions very thin.
	Radish & lettuce sown at the same time.
	Annuals on the borders of the grass plat sown.
	[Remarks] The annual flower seeds eat off greatly.
3rd	York cabbage sown.
4th	Edges of the grass plat cut.
7	Main crop of cucumber & mellon sown.
7 Mar	Concluded the nailing wall trees.
10	Clean'd the pines & new tan'd the pit in the Fruiting House.
	Remarks. 18th About 18 of those started kindly.
14	About half a rood of potatoes planted for an early supply.
17th	Cauliflower planted out in s[outh] border of the plantation. The bed had been well dunged & dug. 2 doz[e]n roses potted for forcing.
18	Some rhododendrons potted for forcing.
20	Early potatoes planted upon dung heat. The last forcing of asparagus planted.
22d	Cauliflower pricked out in a cold 3-light box. Ten weeks stock in pans up. Sowed a pan of mignonette.
23rd	Succession House shifted & dress'd. N. B. The plants good but very foul some being literaly eat thro'.
27 Mar	Early Dutch turnip sown, Long pod & Windsor beans, Prussian & marrow fat peas sowed.

	Glass put on the Peach House.[254]
29th	A bed of silver skin'd onion and 1 of Strasburgh sowed.
	1 bed of large Spanish onion sowed in drills.
	Radish, turnip & long ditto Black Spanish sown.
	Poppies sown.
30th	Ground trench'd for asparagus.
	Ridge bed for mellons put up.
31st	Sowed a full crop of melons.
	Middle grass plat mown.
	1st strawberries gathered.
1 Ap	Planted 3 beds asparagus & sowed 2 beds carrot & 1 of parsnip where the old beds were destroyed.
2d	Cucumbers for common ridges sown.
2d Ap	Bed of Reading onions sown where the beds had been dunged after cabbages.[255]
3d	American squash, gourd, and Patagonian cucumber sown.
	India wheat & a full collection of tender annuals sown.
	Red beet, red cabbage, Brussels sprouts & Scots cale sown.
	Marjoram and bazil sown.
4th	3 holes of mellons ridged out. French beans planted in Peach House.
5	Ten week stock pricked out.
	Mushroom bed put up & spawned. Moulded on the 10th.
9th	An acre of potatoes planted by plough.
10	Half acre of carrots sown. Cuttings of wallflower & hydrangea put out.
13th	Artichokes dress'd & 4 rows newly planted. Spinage sown between the rows in drills.
14	Bed of cabbage, broccoli, Scots cale & savoy sown. 2 beds of radish sown.

---

[254] Wilshere paid William Stanton £100 for the Peach House in May 1813 and a further £100 that September [HALS: 61505 pp68, 94].

[255] The 'Reading onion' was a strongly flavoured variety with a large oval bulb. See J Abercrombie, *The Complete Kitchen Gardener and Hot-Bed Forcer* (1789) p80.

16	2 beds coss lettuce planted out.
	Migonette planted upon the open border.
17 Ap	Vines in the Conservatory stopped having shewn fruit.
18th	Stool quarter in the forcing ground dug & plants layed.
19	Layers of laurestinus & bays planted out.
	Asparagus sown in drills.
20th	Row of scarlet runners sown & some early yellow & black negro beans sown.
22d	Isaphan mellon ridged out.
	[Remarks] Not worth cultivating.
	Knights white mellon & white Turkey cucumber ridged out.
	[Remarks. Not worth cultivating] (Smyrna or Salonica)
	Celery prick'd out in beds.
23	A rood of cattle cabbage planted out they being 4 feet square. Ten loads dung upon the rood.
24th	Black, kidney & champion potatoes planted.
	[Remarks] Black potatoe turned out best.
26	An acre of cattle cabbage planted 3 feet square.
	[Remarks] Some of these weighing from 30 to 40 lbs.
27th	Cattle cabbage prick'd out from the seed beds.
	First gathering of gooseberries.
3d May	1 rood of mangel wurzel sown for experiment with 5 loads dung. An acre for a full crop sown of mangel wurzel after wheat.
	Remarks. Sown in drills 2 feet apart.
4th	Cucumbers ridged out. Fine, mild, showery day.
	Remarks. Cut first fruit 11 June.
5, 6, 7 to 13	Laying gravel.[256]
14	Sowed 2 rows Knight's peas & 4 rows Windsor beans & 6 ditto Glory of England peas.[257]

---

[256] In January 1813 Wilshere paid Stephen Swain, Surveyor of the Highways £1 for digging gravel for the garden [HALS: 61505 p34].

199

	Remarks. Those [Knight's] peas excellent. Wants very rich soil. Grow very tall.
	Parsnips & curious stone turnips sown.
	Scorzenera & salsaffi sown.
	China aster & other tender annuals planted out.
	Large rock mellons were ridged out on the 10th.
16	Cuttings of various greenhouse plants made & planted.
17	Seeds of greenhouse seeds sown.
20th	Some of the greenhouse plants taken out.
	Large rock mellon in flower and impregnated with the scarlet flush for want of a male blossom of the former.
	Strasburg onion & purple speckl'd beans sown.
	Red celery, cauliflower & broccoli sown.
23d to 30th	Green beet sown. Broccoli & cabbage sown.
	½ acre of the 100 head cabbage planted.
	Lucerne sown 28 – 9 - 30.
4 June	Greenhouse plants taken out.

(There is a gap in the Journal here. James Bowie left several pages blank before resuming his Journal on 1 January 1814. Some of the blank pages were used in 1821 and 1822 by a later gardener. These entries have been transcribed at the end in chronological order.)

1814 1 Jany	Bed for cucumbers made up and seeds sown. [Remarks] Weather extremely dark, frost. Kept very backward.
3d	Early peas transplanted into the Peach House. Very hard frost continued without intermission for 6 weeks, then a few days thaw. Frost not quite out of the ground.
22d Feb	Fresh tann'd pine pits.
28 Feb	Ridged out 3 lights cucumber and one light Persian

---

[257] Possibly the Champion of England pea, although this only appears in nursery catalogues from the 1840s. It is described by G W Johnson, *The Cottage Gardener and Country Gentleman' Companion* (1854) p455.

	melon.
2ᵈ Mar	Sowed some cauliflower & Cape broccoli in pans.
5ᵗʰ	Second crop of early peas and Mazagan beans sown.[258]
	Garlic & shallots planted.
	Onions for seeds planted.
	Frost & snow. Wind N E cutting.[259]
1814	Acorns sown in drills.
Mar 14ᵗʰ	Long pod beans sown.
	Hotts peas ditto.
20	Onion for full crop sown.
	Mellons potted off.
	Radish & E Horn carrot sown.
24ᵗʰ	A 2ᵈ crop of Hottspur peas sown.
	Mushroom bed put up.[260]
25	Early Dutch turnips sown.
26	Parsnips sown.
	6 rows bog or fan beans sown.
	Chief of the hardy annuals sown in the borders.
	9 rows of Spanish drop peas sown.[261] Spinage, Hambro parsley & burnet sown.
30ᵗʰ	Half acre of carrot sown.
~~1 April~~	Canary seed sown.

---

[258] A small, delicately flavoured and early variety of the broad bean, *Vicia fabia*.

[259] Joseph Ransom, a Hitchin farmer, eldest son of John Ransom, recorded on 1 March 1814 'We have had such remarkable sharp weather with very deep snow these 10 weeks past that every Spring production is exceeding backward. The above sort of weather continued with but little alteration until 20ᵗʰ inst when the wind changed & the weather became quite mild.' [V Campion, *Joseph Ransom's Naturalist's Notebook 1804-1816 The Nature Notes of a Hitchin Quaker* (Hitchin, 2004) p39].

[260] In August 1814 Wilshere paid Mr Nash £1 1s as a subscription for Oldames plan of raising mushrooms [HALS: 61506 p86]. Loudon's *Encyclopaedia of Gardening* describes the German mushroom house introduced to England from Russia by Isaac Oldacre and Oldacre's mode of propagating mushrooms, pp606-6, 806.

[261] Perhaps the Spanish morotto pea, a large variety which was widely cultivated in the eighteenth century.

31st	Dw[ar]f imperial & blue Prussian peas sown.[262] Bog beans sown.
1814 2d April	Knight's peas sown. Cabbages planted out in the old quarter. Red beet sown.
4 – 5 – 6	Limes, elms & maple layers taken off and stools layed.
7 & 8	Laurels layed.
9th	Orange trees shifted.
11th	Dw[ar]f marrow peas & Windsor beans sown in the field.
12th	Two asparagus beds planted. Silver skin'd & Strasburg onion sown in them
13th	Zinnia revoluta planted on the borders.
14,15,16	Mangel wurzel sown.
19th	Artichokes dress'd.
20th	Strawberrys in front of Summer House planted the ground having been trenched. Scarlet runners sown in boxes.
1814 April	Early Dutch turnips, radishes and parsley sown.
21	Thousand head cabbage & early York cabbage sown Succession House shifted.
22d	Snowing
23	Cranberry border made & partly planted. Large rock mellon sown. Persian mellon beds lined & moulded.
25	Black, Upright White, Peach, Blood Red, Large & German Kidney potatoes planted.
26th	Cattle cabbage pricked out.
27	Dahlias planted on the borders.
28	Rock mellons ridged out.
29	Half acre mangel wortzel sown.
30	Cranberrys from London planted.
2d May	Mowing.

---

[262] The Prussian Blue was a popular type of pea with blue-green seeds which was developed in Germany in the eighteenth century. It was grown in the gardens of Thomas Jefferson at Monticello in Virginia.

3ᵈ	6 classes cucumbers ridged.
4ᵗʰ May	Salsaffee & scorzenera sown.
	Early purple, late ditto, White, Syberian, & Brimstone broccoli, cauliflower, cabbage, savoy & lettuce sown.
5	Marseilles & green coss lettuce planted out.
	Pompion²⁶³ & squash ridged out.
6 & 7	Mowing plantation walkes & edgeing.
9ᵗʰ	Hoeing.
9ᵗʰ to 11	Hoeing lucerne.
	White blossom beans sown after broccoli without manure.
	Row of early peas sown in field.

(The rest of this page is blank. In October 1814 James Bowie sailed on a plant hunting expedition to Brazil organised by Sir Joseph Banks. The Journal resumes in October 1814 in a different handwriting presumably by John Downing.)

1814 [changed to 1815] Journal

11 Octr	Made mushroom bed.
12	Planted out cabbage plants.
24	Poted bulbs for forceing.
29	Made up the asparagus bed.
14 Nov	Sowed early peas.
24	Put up two lite box for asparagus.
1 Decr	Put up two lite box for cucum[be]r.
	Sowed horse chesnut and acorns.
13	Planted turnips for seed.
	Sowed radish on a s[outh] border.
2 Jany 1815	Sowed second crop e[arl]y peas.
9	Sowed radish carrot on a border.
	[Remarks] 27 May Take carrot.
11	Sowed early Mazagan beans.
28	Put up two lite box cucum[be]r.
	Sowed melon seed.

---

²⁶³ Pumpkin.

1 Feby	Put the [sic] in Peach House.
	Sowed cattle cabbage.
7 Feby	Sowed cauliflower & Cape brocoli.
	Sowed springs. Ditto radish & lettuce.
8	Ditto dw[ar]f pan peas.
9	Planted shallots & garlic.
18	Put a three lite box for potatoes
22	Sowed cattle cabbage.
	Planted early potatoes on s[outh] b[order].
25	Sowed thousand headed cabbage. Ditto Windsor beans.
	Planted fir seedling.
1 Mar[c]h	Sowed larkspur & candytuft.
2	Ditto onion & carrot.
4	Ditto tender anuals.
12	Potted moss roses. Sow'd asparagus.
17	Planted cauliflower in the open ground.
20	Sow'd hardy anuals.
20 Mar	Sowed early turnips. Ditto savoys.
	[Remarks] 5 June took up turnips.
23	Forked asparagus beds.
31	Sowed half an acre carrots in drills.
	Cut a dish of asparagus on open ground.
1 Ap	Sowed half acre carrot broadcast.
	[Remarks] 21 Sepr plough up the carrot. Very good.
	256 bushels.
3	Ditto early turnip. Ditto solid celery. Ditto savoy & broccoli.
4	Artichoakes dress'd.
6	Sowed peas & beans. Ditto French beans. Salsafy & scorzanera.
	Sowed squash. Ditto red beet.
8	Made border for rhododendron.
13	Sowed turnip radish.
	Planted one acre potatoes.
15 Ap	Planted half acre cattle cabbage.
18	Sowed two acres mangel wurzel.
22	Ditto broccoli & cauliflower.
	Made cucum[be]r ridgh (*ridge*).

26	Began to lay gravel on the G[arden] walks.[264]
13 May	Ridgh (*ridge*) out squash.
15	Sowed peas & beans. Ditto spinage.
17	Ditto endive.
22	Planted spring sowing cattle cabbage.
12 June	Ditto spring & 100 headed cabbage betwixt the rows of mangel wurzel.
13	Ditto brocoli.
29 July	Sowed spinage.
20 Augt	Ditto cauliflower & onion. Ditto cattle cabbage.

(The entries stop here. A few entries in another hand, presumably that of Daniel McIntosh, for November 1821 to January 1822 were made on the pages left blank for the second half of 1813.)

28 Novr 1821	McIntosh sowed one row of pease against the Carpenter shop. Same day a patch of Mazagan beans west end of the border from the west end as far as the 2^d white nectrine. White blossom'd beans the east end broad Windsor.
14 Jany 1822	Sowed 1 row of pease against the east end of the Peach House when the other sowing had been up above 10 days.

1822 Jany 21st	Narcisses planted.	
	No 1	Narcisses incomparabils
	2	ditto pleno
	3	ditto calathinus precox
	4	ditto bifions
	5	ditto incomparabiles
	6	ditto spe
	7	ditto jonquilla
	8	ditto jonquilla long stigma
	9	ditto propinquis

---

[264] In July 1815 Wilshere paid the Revd W Pym £1 10s 3d for 121 loads of gravel from Benslow Hills in March 1815 for the paths in Wimbush Field [HALS: 61525 p74]. This was presumably from the land rented by Wilshere.

	10	ditto	tubiflorus
	11	ditto	orientalis[?]
	12	ditto	bicolor
	13	ditto	mercurusfolius
	14	ditto	proculiformis
	15	ditto	mazalis semi double
	16	ditto	biflorus
Jany 21 1822	No 1	Paonea	molan rubra
	2	ditto	papavaracea
	3	ditto	offincinalis canescans
	4	ditto	paradoxa dimbriata
	5	ditto	albiflora siberica
	6	ditto	pumilus
	7	ditto	decora elatior
	8	ditto	albifolia vestigus
	9	ditto	albiflora fragrens
	10	ditto	officinalis rosea abo
	11	ditto	peregrina grevilla
	12	ditto	albiflora whitlesa

APPENDIX ONE

WILLIAM WILSHERE'S COMMONPLACE BOOK 1814-1824
(NHM 1216)
Entries selected for their agricultural or horticultural interest

Orchards [pp3 – 7]

Extracts from an 'Essay on the Science of Orcharding' by Thomas Skip Dyot Bucknall Esqr. (in the Transactions of the Society of Arts Vol 12) taken from the Annual Reg[iste]r of 1796.

The gum found on fruit trees is produced by a sudden check which stops the pores, & obstructing the perspiration it forces a fissure through the bark, out of which ouzes the almost stagnated sap, which there condensing becomes gum. The bark, wanting its due proportion of nourishment, begins to crack & split, and from that time the tree runs fast into ruin.

Therefore any smearing or other cause, which may impede circulation & perspiration, must injure the tree. A plaster is then recommended not to extend beyond the bare wood or torn bark. (The composition of the plaster is referred to as I wrote in a former paper *; it is stated to be from its drying qualities extremely salutary.)

- There is afterwards a reference to the Ann[ual] Reg[iste]r for 1793 page 82 for Mr Bucknall's first paper.

It is a mistake to cut off the heads of trees & engraft them merely to procure young wood, pruning being better, as an old tree cannot continue in health after such loppings, for the head being gone, the roots become inactive, and more mischief takes place out of sight than can be repaired in years.

Do not attempt to force a tree higher than it is disposed to grow. Keep the branches out of the reach of cattle then let them follow their natural growth. Prune as soon as the fruit is off, that the wounds may tend towards healing before the frost comes on, but do not suffer a broken or decayed branch to continue at any time. The substantial form of the tree should be the same before & after pruning, and all extreme shoots keep the same distance as in pruning wall trees.

In planting choose young trees properly pruned, with heads of 3 or 4 good leading shoots, which will not require pruning for some time, & having no wounds to heal in the y[ea]r in which they are transplanted, their growth will be accelerated. Do not plant galled, fretted, or cankered plants – there is a vapour arising from cankered trees which affects the sound ones. (*in margin*) **q[uery] WW.**

APPENDIX ONE

In planting keep the roots as long as you conveniently can – which will give them a disposition to run horizontally.

The plantation should be screened on the east, north & west, & open on the south, the strongest growing trees should be on the outsides, & the more delicate in the centre & south.

Do not plant too deep. More mischief arises from that than from all the other combined causes. When trees are too deep, they may be raised, if in high health, if not, grub them up.

Avoid planting too thick – sunshine & shade are the cause of sweet & sour fruits.

Extracts from a concluding Essay in the same Annual Reg[iste]r (extracted from the Transactions of the Society of Arts Vol. 14).

(This essay refers to Mr Bucknall's first paper on orcharding in A[nnual] Reg[iste]r 1793 p82 & to Instr. Vol 13 of Transactions & in Annual Reg[iste]r 1795 p77.)

It is asserted that trees of the age of 20 years and upwards may with care be safely removed to supply vacancies.

Great stress is again laid on judicious pruning. When perfectly understood, the whole will, except from accident or neglect, be little other than penknife pruning.

Mr B. undertakes to produce 4 apple trees, within the same inclosure, each covering 10 poles of ground, before they fall into decay – and proposes 4 trees on the north side of Sittingbourne, if the owner will submit them to his management. He describes them as being at least 100 y[ea]rs old, & overrun with stumps, dead wood, & moss. In pruning, if a tree be very old & much incumbered, do not let in the cold wind, but with care take off the stumps with all the decayed, rotten & blighted branches.

(Reference to a process for preventing destruction by insects Transactions Vol 11 & Ann[ual] Reg[iste]r 1793 p85 & A[nnual] R[egister] 1795 p80). Washing with soap suds & with oil recommended referring to A[nnual] R[egister] 1795 p80.

Oak Timber - whether it succeeds when transplanted
(from Qu[arterly] Review Oct. 1813 p9 -10)   **[pp33 – 34]**

It is a general idea that transplanted oaks do not thrive so well as those raised from the acorn, on account of the taproot being cut or injured. This appears to be disproved by the Appendix to the 1ˢᵗ Rep[ort] of the Comm[issioners] of Woods & Forests printed by order of the Ho[use] of Commons 13 June 1812.

A field in Dean Forest of several acres was sown with acorns about 1783 - at the age of 14 y[ea]rs 40 or 50 trees were transplanted into the open forest & afterwards sev[era]l thousands. In 1809 three of the trees first transplanted, 3 transplanted 1807, & 6 which remained in their orig[ina] places (not left too close) were carefully measured in the presence of the Surveyor General, at the height of six feet from the ground. They were again measured in the foll[owin]g y[ea]r, when it appeared that those which had been transplanted first had increased the most, those transplanted in 1807 the next, & of those which remained in their original place, 2 had not increased at all & the other 4 not so much as any of those transplanted. (App[endi]x 154)

Mr T A Knight[265] asserts that the taproot is of consequence only during the first year's growth of the tree, and that shortening the tap & the lateral roots of young trees tends much to increase their future growth, by increasing the number of roots.

Potatoes for the London Market   [pp40 – 41]
16 August 1814
John Burgess, a grower at Enfield,[266] states, that the Champion is their principal crop – some earlier potatoes are ?sought but not many. They are called shaws & have but little top – sell well by weight but the quantity is deficient – 126 lbs is called an cwt & 20 of those hundreds to a ton – which varies in price from £3 to £9 – (now £4). The produce is divided into

Ware	the market term for the best
Midling	usually sold to cowkeepers at about 1s the bushel
& Chats	the smallest given to pigs, sometimes saleable to the cowkeepers at about 6d per bushel.

8 tons per acre are reckoned a good crop – often not more than 5 – about 40 bushels per ton

---

[265] Thomas Andrew Knight (1759-1838) horticulturist and plant physiologist, and one of the original members of the Horticultural Society. He was the author of *Pomona Herefordiensis* as well as papers on the grafting of fruit trees. See Biographical Notes.
[266] John Burgess was a tenant of Mrs Sarah Mills of Hitchin whose property was managed by Wilshere [eg HALS: 61528 pp31, 123]. For Sarah Mills see Biographical Notes.

APPENDIX ONE

The Ware is ordinarily sold at Spitalfields Market (sometimes to the retailers). At the market the sale is by factors or salesman who warrant the money & have a comm[ission]n of 5s per ton.

Orange trees – produce of [p42]

The average produce of a full grown tree in the Island of St Michael is from 1000 to 5000. A tree belonging to the Prior of del Gada is said to have yielded one y[ea]r the extraordinary number of 20,000 oranges, but that was looked upon as a prodigy.

From the Qu[arterly] Rev[iew] April 1814 No 21 p200.

Wheat – comparative weight of Straw & Corn [p45]

8 October 1814. I found the weight of a wheat sheaff of the average size of this County (32 inches at the band) to be 15 lbs (probably 16 lbs when it was first brought in). It was this day thrashed & the produce was of clean corn 4 lbs 14¼ oz avoirdupois, the chaff & cavings about 1 lb 2 oz, leaving 9 lbs of straw. (Of such sheaves I had about 42 per acre which would give 18 cwt of corn equal to 31½ per acre of wheat weighing 64 lbs the bushel.

Taking the straw at 3/5th of the whole weight of the crop, there will be 105 trusses of 36 lbs or nearly 3 loads, but this is a great crop. I conceive an average acre giving 20 bushels of wheat will produce 2 loads of straw.

Hay – weight & bulk compared [p46]

11 October 1814. I measured some trusses of clover hay (with trefoil) of 1813 - - - weighing 56 lb and found the average bulk to be length feet 2.75, breadth 2.25, thickness 10½ to 11 inches = 5.6 cubic feet or 10 lb the cubic foot giving pretty exactly 200 cubic feet for a load of hay.

Tonquin Beans[267] [p46]

Galt[268] in his Letters from the Levant page 59 says "One of my fellow passengers was a Corsican going to Tripolizza to sell Tonquin beans to the Turks – that kind of beans which some of your snuff takers are so foolish as to buy although <u>Woodruffe</u>, a weed common enough in their own neighbourhood, has the same perfume & even more delicately."

---

[267] Tonka beans *Dipteryx odorata*. In May 1813 Wilshere's gardener, James Bowie, sowed tonquin beans. See p190 above.

[268] John Galt, *Letters from the Levant: containing views of the state of society, manners, opinions and commerce in Greece and several of the principal islands of the Archipelago - - -* (1813).

APPENDIX ONE

Trees forest pruning [p56]

A correspondent of The Gentleman's Mag[azine] (July 1814 page 20 recommends from experience the pruning forest trees in the last week of July & thro[ugh] August & September that the wounds may heal before the winter. His trials were on young trees. The branches were cut close & smooth – where of 10 feet the stem was cleared 6 feet, of 12 feet 7, of 14 feet 8. He states that the bark had closed over every wound before the month of June in the next y[ea]r. That for 1 y[ear] this ?compas was applied to the ?service of the trees and he thought it impeded the growth of the bark.

Oak Pales & Laths [pp63 – 64]

7 February 1815 from the information of Creasy, lathrender[269].
100 laths of 4 feet are a bunch
Of other lengths so many as will make up 400 feet in the whole.

The hundred of pales consists of 100 at five feet & of other lengths of so many as will make up 500 feet in the whole.
The prices of rending are –   {lath 1s per bunch
                                {pales

In rending timber for the proprietor's own use a foot of timber makes little if any more than 400 feet or a bunch of tiling lath.
In rending for sale about a fifth more are made & in timber of a moderate size as 12 inches girth – they expect to make about half as much sap as heart lath - & still to have as many bunches of heart as there are feet of timber.
Of oak pales for the proprietor's use a foot is usually rent into a 100 feet in length, that is 25 four feet pales or, if not wanted very stout, it will make 400 feet.
For sale, 500 feet are made of a foot.

The present prices are
Pales per 100   40s
Laths per bunch
- heart tiling   7s
- heart plaister   5s

---

[269] John Creasy the elder was a lathrender who lived at Gosmore in the parish of Ippollitts. He died in 1824 leaving four sons, James, John, Henry and George [HALS: 31HW16]. In October 1818 Wilshere paid James Creasey £1 18s 6d for rending laths and pales [HALS: 61528 p72].

APPENDIX ONE

- sap plaister   3s 6d

Vide 27 & 129 of preceding book.

Apples – directions for selecting the seed   [p76]
(Gent[leman]'s Mag[azine] March 1815 page 215)
In every perfectly ripe apple will be found one & sometimes two round seeds,
the others will have one or more flatted sides. The round seeds will produce the
improved fruit from which they are taken, & those with flatted sides will
produce the fruit of the crab upon which the graft was inserted. If the seeds are
sown together, the variation will be discovered in 2 or 3 years. The plants from
the flat seeds will throw out the leaves of a crab & the other those of an
improved tree distinguished in shape, fibre & a lanuginous appearance.

Mutton – price of – butcher's profits of   [p82]
28 October 1815. I purchased of Joshua Ransom a South Down wether sheep of
[blank] years at £2 – 6 – 0 which was killed by Bernard the butcher.[270]

The carcase weighed	73½ lb
Suet	4¼ lb
Gut fat (tallow)	3¼ lb
Total	81 lb
Cost of sheep	2 – 6 - 0
Butcher	1 - 5
	2 – 7 - 5
The skin sold for	0 – 3 - 0
Tallow 3¼ at 4¾	0 – 1 - 5
Value of the head	0 – 1 - 0
Carcase & suet 77¾	
at 6½ 2 – 2 – 1 say	2 – 2 - 0
	2 – 7 - 5

Mr Parsons had a fore quarter weighing -   16
Mr Eade a fore quarter [271]   -   20

---

[270] Joshua Ransom (1789-1863) was the third son of John Ransom of Hitchin, a farmer,
miller and mealman. See Biographical Notes.
[271] For Joseph Eade and the Revd Joseph Parsons see Biographical Notes.

APPENDIX ONE

I kept the remainder.

I killed the sheep to see the profits made by the butchers who now (at H[itchi]n) sell mutton of this description at 7½ (to which it has been lately reduced from 8d). The profit appears to be 1d per lb after all[owin]g for the labour of killing which I think a reasonable profit.

Corn prices of December 1815 & January 1816 [p84]

4 January 1816. John Kingsley of Pirton[272] states the following to have been the average prices of corn taken by him for the purpose of fixing the payments for crops of corn approved at the last harvest.

Hitchin December 26	Wheat per load	34s
	Barley per quarter	24s
	Oats ditto	22s 6d
	Peas per load	21s
	Peas & beans per load	17s
	Tares per load	19s
St Albans December 30	Wheat	36s
	Barley	25s
	Oats	23s
	Peas	23s
	- - - - & beans	19s
	Tares	20s
Royston 3 January 1816	Wheat	30s
	Barley	22s
	Oats	18s 6s
	Peas	18s
	Beans	15s
	Tares	20s

Wheat [p87]

1816 I counted the grains in two good ears of 1815 & found 88.

Straw for platting - Minutes November 1816 [pp104 – 105]

3 sheaves of wheat straw (of 1815) of an average quality weighed 42 lb.

---

[272] For John Kingsley see Biographical Notes.

The ears when cut off	23
The straw drawn for platting	
(after cutting off the ears)	13
Flag & other refuse	6

The produce, when cut into lengths & prepared for platting, was

	£ - s - d
3 lb coarse, some worth six pence, some 9d	
per lb, & on average 7½	- - 1 - 10½
1¼ lb fine at 1s 6d	- - 1 - 10½
	0 – 3 - 9

Three other sheaves, which were selected as of better quality, weighed 35 lb

	Ears	19
	Straw	11
	Refuse	5

Produce		£ - s - d
	2½ lb at 7½ (say)	0 – 1 - 7
	1½ at 1s 6d	0 – 2 - 3
		0 – 3 - 10

One other sheaf which had been rejected by the dealers as unsaleable weighed 8 lb of which

Ears	4
Straw	2¼
Refuse	1¾
	8

Produce		
	5 oz at 7½	2d
	4½ at 1/6	5
		- /7

A woman (the wife of Abbis)[273] was employed about 3½ days – her work may be valued at 4s. The account will then stand thus

---

[273] She was the wife of James Abbis, one of Wilshere's garden men. See Biographical Notes.

	£ - s - d
Value of the straw when prepared	0 – 3 - 9
	0 – 3 - 10
	0 – 0 - 7
	- - 8 - 2
Labour	- - 4 - -
Leaving	0 - 4 - 2

26 lb of straw (drawn from 7 sheaves) at about 19/- per cwt – rather more than 5d per sheaf.

The finest straw, fit for platting without being split, is worth 2s 6d per lb, but the proportion of this is very small, not more than 1/20th. It has not therefore been taken into this account.

[pp106-107]

A man used to the work will easily draw 8 lb of straw in a rough state in an hour, or 64 lb will be an easy day's work, and a woman with a child of 10 or 11 years of age will prepare it in 2 days. The produce may be stated at 20 lb of which

		£ - s - d
1 lb finest		0 - 2 - 6
6	at 1/6	0 - 9 - 0
6	at /9	0 - 4 - 6
7	at /6	0 - 3 - 6
20 [lbs]		- - 19 - 6

		£- - 19s - 6d
Allow for the labour & the skill of the man	0 – 5 - 0	
For 2 days work a woman & child	0 – 3 - 0	- - 8 - -
Remains as the value of 64 lb of straw		0 – 11 - 6

or about 24s per cwt. I sold mine at 20s per cwt. W.W.

From 8 lb rejected by the straw drawers Mrs Abbis ?obt[aine]d

	£ - s - d
2¼ at 6d	- - 1 - 1½
¼ at 1s 6d	- - - - 4½
	0 – 1 - 6

APPENDIX ONE

I learn upon enquiry from the persons buying straw prepared for platting, that Mrs Abbis has valued the produce much under the market price & from the sellars that she has put far too great a proportion at the lowest price. The result is that the drawers sell good straw as drawn at 4d or 5d per lb, & that even after reserving the finest which will sell at 2s 6d, that from 20 lb of straw as drawn they obtain

	£ - s - d
1 lb at	0 – 2 - 6
3 lb at	0 – 4 - 0
2½ at 8d say	0 – 1 - 6
	0 – 8 - 0

The profit is therefore much more considerable than I have stated it.

Vide 110   **[pp108-109]**
2 of my own labourers in 2½ days drew 76 sheaves which produced pretty exactly 2 cwt of straw - & very nearly 3 lb per sheaf. This straw is worth at market 4d per lb or 37s 4d per cwt.

Taking it 3d per lb (28s per	£ - s - d
cwt) the value is	2 – 16 - 0
The labour	0 – 10 - 0
	2 - 6 - 0

This gives more than 7½d per sheaf for the 76 sheaves.
Vide page 110 where it will appear that this calculation is too low.

In preparing the straw (after it is drawn for platting) the thumb nail is pressed against the straw a little above a joint so as to separate the straw itself which is then drawn out of the flag by which it is ?enveloped. (Some straws are sufficiently long & good to give two lengths.) It is then cut to lengths of about 11 inches. Such as have spots or soils are thrown out or put by for the coarser work. The rest are in a box with the lid closed, exposed to the fumes of burning brimstone, & sometimes this operation is repeated. This assists very much in improving the colour. It is again looked over & that which is fit for use is tied up in bundles of a pound weight for sale. Scarcely one third of this straw actually goes into the plat, only about 3 or 4 inches being fit for the work & the rest is cut off from the platted part. Only the very fine is used whole, the other is split by an instrument drawn through it into 4, 5, 6 or 7 breadths.

A pound of split straw of good quality is sufficient for from 80 to 100 yards of plat which will make 2 bonnets weighing 2 to 3 ounces each. Many are much finer & lighter - & more are much coarser. 10 yards per day of good plat is a fair day's work. It now sells at 2/6 per score giving the platter something more than 1/- per day net. Some earn double & others not above half so much.

Vide 108   [pp110 – 111]

2 December 1816[274] Two labourers (the same) began at 9 this morning & before dark had drawn 30 sheaves of an average bulk & appearance as to goodness (2 of them being rejected as not worth the labour). The 28 produced 95 lb of drawn straw – considerably more than 3 lb per sheaf.

28 December. The same men have continued drawing straw for several weeks (with some interruptions) and have drawn at the rate of 30 sheaves a day producing 90 to 100 lb of straw which sells readily to the straw dealers as well as to platters at 3½ per lb.

For the last week sev[era]l of the men who had declined the bargain at 20s per cwt bought it at the rate of 9d per sheaf drawing it themselves. They got something more than 3 lb per sheaf about equal to 27s per cwt.
In January 1817 the remaining sheaves were sold to them at £10 being nearly 6d per sheaf including those before refused.

The whole produce of the straw of 12 acres of wheat has been

To 18 December 1816	cwt	qr	lb		£ - s - d
	24	3	7	at 20/-	24 – 16 - 0
	5	1	4	at 31/6 (averages)	8 - 6 - 0
12 sheaves at 9d					0 - 9 - 0
					33 – 11 - 0
January 1817	2	2	4	at 32/8	4 - 2 - 10
224 sheaves				at /9	9 - 3 - 0
	6	0	0	at 28/-	8 - 8 - 0

---

[274] In December 1816 Wilshere recorded, 'Joseph Rowley and others by James Robinson for 24 cwt 3 qrs 7 lbs straw drawn for platting from the rick of 1815 brought from Benslow Hill at 1£ per cwt £24 16. James Robinson on account of straw drawn by him & sold at 3d ½ per lb equal to 32s 8d per cwt £8 15.' [HALS: 61526 p87]. Straw plaiters from Essex travelled to Hitchin to buy straw [J G Dony, *A History of the Straw Hat Industry* (Luton, 1942) p41].

Residue of straw at					10 - 0 - 0
[Total]					65 - 4 - 10
Remains	1	2	01	Value	2 - 2 - -
Gave Knightley[275]	-	1	10		
					67 - 6 - 10
The expenses of drawing & of some allowance to my own men & the buying have been less than					7 - 6 - 10
Profit from the straw of 12 acres					60 - 0 - 0

Musty Wheat (or other corn) to make sweet Vide 142 **[p124]**
From Annual Reg[iste]r for 1816 page 604
Put the wheat into any convenient vessel capable of containing at least three times the quantity and the vessel must be subsequently filled with boiling water. The grain should then be occasionally stirred and the hollow and decayed grains (which will float) may be removed; when the water has become cold or in gen[era]l when half an hour has elapsed, it is to be drawn off. It will be proper then to rince the corn with cold water in order to remove any portion of the water which had taken up the must; after which the corn being completely drained without any loss of time to be thinly spread on the floor of a kiln & thoroughly dried care being taken to stir & to turn it frequently during this part of the process.

This is all that is required & I have constantly found that even the most musty corn (on which ordinary kiln-drying has been tried without effect) thus became completely purified whilst the diminution of weight caused by the solut[io]n of the tainted part was very inconsiderable.

Straw Platting (continued from 110) **[p142]**
1818 August 3. Two sheaves of new wheat were delivered to Abbis's wife to prepare the straw for platting. Weight of the two 18 lb.

Ears when cut off	8½
Straw drawn	5½
Refuse	4
	18

---

[275] William Knightley was one of Wilshere's garden men. See Biographical Notes.

Produced 2 lb prepared for platting worth 1/2 or 1/3 per lb. (Q[uery] if more than 1s). She was employed in this work 4 hours.

Heat by Thermometer 5 August 1818 per Fa[h]r[en]h[eit]   [p143]

	In the Sun	N. of the box room abroad	Shade N. side the Garden	Libr-ary	Draw-ing Room west end	My Bed Room	Entr. Hall	Open Air
At Noon	118	86	80	77	73	76		
One pm	123	87	81	77	74	78		
Two	123	89	84	77	76			
Three	124	89	84	79	78			
Four	121	88	82	79	78	77		
Five	108	87	79	78	78	78		
Six	94	85	78	77	77	79		
Seven	92	82	72	76	76	77		
Eight	-	-	-	76	76	76		
Ten	-	71	-	74	72	76	72	65
Eleven	-	70	-	73	72	74	70	63

I placed one of Six's therm[omete]rs in the garden at night of the 5th & found in the morning of the 6th that it had been at 63½. By ano[the]r of the same desoner in the Library the lowest had been 71½.
21 August 9 am Entrance Hall 52.

Mildew in Wheat   [p157]

Sir Joseph Banks certainly mistook an effect for a cause, or at least a proximate cause for a remote one, when he attributed the mildew of wheat to the attachment of parasitic fungi, for it is tolerably well ascertained that these fungi affix themselves only to those plants of wheat which are already diseased, while the healthy stems resist their insidious and deadly entrance.
M[onthly] R[eview] August 1818 N.S. Vol 86 p362

Liver of a Fowl – extraordinary size of   **[p160]**
27 April 1819 Mr Mills[276] sent me from Roxley the liver of a common hen –
appearing to be old, & which had been found dead in the yard. A greater weight
than the appearance indicated led to her being opened. The liver was found so
preternaturally large as to fill almost the whole cavity of the body – both lobes
appeared to have increased in similar proportion. The weight was 1 lb 3 oz
avoirdupois.

Box Trees on the south side of my Garden   **[p162]**
56 in n[umber]. Of the large trees the highest 35 feet – the others varying from 1
to 4 feet.
The girth of the largest 2 feet 11 inches, many above 2 feet.
24 June 1819 [277]

Partridges – weight of   **[p162]**
I found the weight of a full grown partridge to vary from 14 to 13 oz September
1819. Reduced 3 oz when picked & drawn and further reduced about 2 oz when
dressed so as to weigh when brought on the table about 9 oz.

24 December I killed in Hitchin Field a cock partr[idge] weighing 16¼ oz.

Brick Work   **[p174]**
Value per rod at Hitchin 1820

	£ - s - d	£ - s - d
4500 47s 6d per 1000 & adding **If of proper size 4200 or even 4100** **suff[icien]t**	2 – 7 - 6	
for carriage **5s per mile**	0 – 5 - 0	
	2 – 12 - 6	12 - 1 - 3
4 quarters of lime at 8s		1 - 12 - 0

---

[276] Paitfield Mills was the son of Mrs Sarah Mills. See Biographical Notes.
[277] The box trees were originally part of a hedge which in 1728 was described as being
over a hundred years old. The owner of the neighbouring property claimed they were too
close to his house and cut down six of the largest trees which were then over 10 feet tall
[HALS: 60327]. The remaining trees survived the demolition of part of William
Wilshere's house in 1874 to become Hitchin's famous old box trees featured in many
postcards growing on the south side of Hermitage Road. They were cut down by Hitchin
Urban District Council in 1919 [newspaper cuttings 1914 & 1919 NHM: Lawson
Thompson Scrapbooks Vol 3 p11, Vol 3B p244].

Labour (may be done for £2 – 5 – 0)	2 - 10 - -
Sand & carr[iage] } Scaffolding etc }	- - 6 - 9
	16 - 10 - 0

Usually charged from £17 to £18.

Cottages – Expense of building at Hitchin as estimated by Joshua Ransom June 1820
A row of 6 cottages each 16½ by 11½ feet lath & plaister & slated with water pipes from the room to the ground £84 each.
-         6 of stud & clay called wattle & dab thatched – £68 - 5s each.

July 1818 I paid Waller for 5 at Wym[ond]ley considerably larger including privy & pump £258 = stud & clay thatched.[278]
July 1820 I paid Ransom for 3 cott[ages] & a shop about equal to ano[the]r at Hitchin – lath & plaister tiled including privy £340. These are 43½ feet by 18.[279]

[Preserving Fruit]   [p199]
Journal of Science No 22 page 395
Fruits picked a few days before they would be ripe may be preserved
            peaches, plums & apricots -   a month
            apples & pears   -   3 months
by putting at the bottom of a bottle a paste of lime, sulphate of iron & water. The fruit to be kept from touching the bottom or each other & the bottle closed by a cork or cement.
Refers to a prize paper of M. ?Benerd published by the French Academy of Sciences & in the Annales de Chemie XVI p152-235

---

[278] These cottages are now 1-5 Hornbeam Court, Wymondley Arch Road, which were renovated, rethatched and extended at the rear in 1974 by the Hertfordshire Buildings Preservation Trust. They are listed Grade II (https://historicengland.org.uk/listing/the-list/list-entry/1347443?section=official-list-entry). Joseph Waller was a Hitchin carpenter who was also landlord of the Dial Public House in Bridge Street [Piggot's *Hertfordshire Directory* 1826].
[279] In his Minutes of Property Wilshere recorded a payment of £389 15s in August 1820 for building cottages at The Biggin [HALS: 61613 p90]. These four cottages on the corner of Back Street and Biggin Lane (now demolished) were part of the property which he bequeathed as an endowment to the British Schools [TNA: PROB11/1692/97]. HALS holds plans and estimates for cottages in Biggin Lane to be built by Wilshere [61026-61029; 61207].

Beer of Barley [p210]

19 January 1822 I tasted beer brewed by Robert Rose[280] for himself of the
following materials

		Value	£ - s - d
Barley	10 bushels	cost	1 - - - -
Malt	2 B		15 - 6
Molasses	4 lb		1 - 6
Liquorice	1 lb		2 - -
Hops	8 lb		6
Firing & labour beyond the value of			5 - -
the grains			2 - 10 - -

The quantity brewed was 128 gallons for something less than 5d per gallon. It
was pleasant beer & of sufficient strength.

6 November 1821 I brewed 8 bushels malt & 4 bushels barley which made 3
hogsheads.

21 February 1822 2 bushels malt & 12 bushels barley made 3 hogsheads.

Both were pleasant beers, the last evidently the weaker – and not I conceive
such as would keep for any considerable time.

Turf or Peat for Fuel [pp211 – 212]

26 January 1822 I purchased 7,200 (called six thousand) of the small brick
formed pieces in which it is dug, at 10s for ten hundreds of 120 each being at the
rate of ten for a penny. The men who brought it stated it to have been dug at or
near Warboys in Huntingdonshire.

That after the surface is taken off, the peat is found about 2 feet in depth. It is
dug with a narrow spade in a brick like shape. It is laid in rows to dry, this may
take a year. It is then put under cover where it should remain about a year more
before it is fit for use. That a man may dig about 3000 in a day. That when dry it
makes 8s per 1000 on the spot (this I doubt). Each piece is about 9 inches in
length, 2 inches in breadth & 2 inches thick. A bushel packed [illegible] &
heaped contains 45 in number, weighing about 15 lb.

Comparison of turf with coals
A bushel of coals weighs 75 lb costs   18d
Peat - - -   15   - -   4½

---

[280] For Robert Rose see Biographical Notes.

APPENDIX ONE

The peat is therefore ¼ of the price of coals by measure & 5/4 by weight.

One of the pieces weighing 7 oz was dried in an iron oven till the weight was reduced to 3 oz 14 drams and there being after a long exposure to the height of the oven no further reduction, it was put into an iron ladle and burned to ashes which weighed 6,200 drams.
I put into water 4 of the pieces weighing [blank]. They took up in [blank] so much water as to increase the weight to [blank].

Taxes upon the articles consumed by an agricultural labourer and his family supposed to consist of himself, his wife and 4 children [p213]

	£ - s - d
Beer 54 gallons excise on malt, hops & beer	1 - 7 - 0
Salt 26 lb	0 - 6 - 0
Leather 12 p[ai]rs of shoes	0 - 6 - -
Candles 24 lb Soap 12 lb	0 - 4 - 0
Tea 4 lb	0 - 12 - 0
Sugar 52 lb	0 - 15 - 0
	3 - 10 - 0

The excise on malt & hops for the beer found by the Master in harvest, hay time & turnip hoeing estimated at 36 gallons – excise 12s.
Reckoning 1 labourer to 25 acres the above tax[atio]n will amount to about 3s/3d per acre.

Teasel - Cultivation of [p 229]
Minutes made at Harptree, Somersetshire August 1822[281]
Sown in March in a good loamy soil. Requires to be carefully thinned and to be kept very thin by the hoe, is a biennial plant – usually ripe early in August of the 2nd year. The heads cut with knives at 3 or 4 times as they get ripe, that is as the petals fall off, the flower is white. The spines are curved or hooked downwards & are somewhat elastic.
20,000 heads are a pack, an acre will sometimes produce 10 packs or more – now worth from £3 to £5 per pack when cut, tied in bunches of 20 heads & fastened round poles to be carried & dried which is done under a shed or other cover & requires 8 to 14 days according to the weather, will not bear rain.

---

[281] Wilshere's cash book confirms that he visited Harptree in August 1822 [HALS: 61532 p88].

APPENDIX ONE

Cutting 7 sh[illings] per pack or 2s per day mostly by women. (See this article Rees Cyclop[aedia].)

THREE NURSERYMEN'S BILLS

Robert Murray of Hertford 1813-1814 (HALS 61479/31)

Wm Wiltshire Esqr. Bo[ugh]t of Robt Murray   **Hertford Nursery**

			£	s	d
1813	Jany23	1 lb Thousand Headed Cabbage	-	7	6
	Mar 4	To 3 bu[shells] Mushroom Spawn 8s 6d			
		P[er] Hampr 3s	1	8	6
	18th	18 Rhoddodendron Ponticum 2s 6d P	2	5	-
		6 Rhoddodendron Maximums 3 Pr	-	18	-
		150 2 Years Seedlings Ponticums	-	18	-
		2 Rhoddodendron Ferragenia 3s 6d Pr	-	7	-
		2 Andromeda Pulverulenta 5s P	-	10	-
		2 Kalmia Latifolia 7s Pr	-	14	-
		2 Kalmia Angustifolia 2s P	-	4	-
		4 Kalmia Glaucca 2s 6d P	-	10	-
		2 Azalia Pontica 5s	-	10	-
		2 Ditto Calondulaccia 8s	-	16	-
		[Total]	9	8	-

Feby 19th By 100 lb Mangel Wurzel at 1s 9d per lb - £8 15s

Wm Wiltshire Esqr. To Robt Murray

		£	s	d
	To goods as p[e]r Bill deliver[e]d last Summer			
		9	8	-
Cr[edit]	By goods as p[e]r Acc[oun]t deliver[e]d ditto			
		8	15	-
	Balance due last Summer	0	13	0
1813	2 Azelia Nudiflora Rubra 4/- P	-	8	-
Octr 19				
	2 Early White ditto 6s, 2 Late Red ditto 8s	-	14	-
	1 Sewartia Malacodenderon	-	6	-
	1 Sterax Lavigatum 5s, 4 White Azelias 12s	-	17	-
	Matt, Basket & Package	-	6	-

			£	s	d
1814 May 23	1 Ludum Thymifolia 3s 6d, 1 Goltheria procumbens 1s 6d		-	5	-
	1 Gum Cistus 2s, 2 Erica Mediterania 4s, 1 Cylipus purpurea 2s 6d		-	8	6
	1 Phlox Stolinifera 2s, 1 Ditto Subilata 2s		-	4	-
	A Pott of Erica Daboesia 5s, 1 Scarlet Arbutis 6s		-	11	-
	1 Arbutis Andrachne 8s, 2 Rhoddn. Rosea 10s		-	18	-
	1 Rhoddn. New Variety or Magnoliafolia		-	6	-
	1 Lobelia fulgens 5s 1 Fothergilla alba 3s		-	8	-
	1 Magnolia Glaucca 6s, 1 Azelia Pontica 5s		-	11	-
	2 Orange Azelia 16s, 1 Daphne Alpina 3s 6d		-	19	6
	1 Daphne tartonraria 2s 6d, 1 ditto Pontica 5s 1 ditto Colina 3s 6d		-	11	-
	2 Genesta triquetra 5s, Basket & Package 6s		-	11	-
		[Total]	8	17	-
1813 Decr 18	Cr[edit] By 26 lb Mangel wurzel at 3s 0d per lb		3	18	-
	Balance du this year		4	19	-
1814 Aug 11	Cr[edit] By Cash		4	19	-
	Settled Rob Murray		£0	0	0

Thomas Gibbs & Co of London 1814 (HALS 61479/29)

William Wilshere Esq.   **London September 3rd 1814**
Thomas Gibbs & Co, Nursery & Seedsmen to the Honourable Board of
Agriculture, Corner of Half Moon Street, Piccadilly

> Grass seeds for 1 Acre consisting of Meadow Foxtail,
> Fescue, Cocksfoot, Impr[ove]d perennial Rye Grass,
> Tall Oat Grass, Dogstail, Meadow Catstail, Yarrow,
> Cow Grass, White Clover, Trefoil, Rib grass, great
> Meadow grass, Sweet Vernal & Red Suckling

		£2 – 16 - -
1 2 Bushel Bag		- - 2 - 6
1 Peck	Ditto	- - - - 9
Cartage & Booking		- - - - 6
		£2 – 19 - 9

London October 5th 1814
Received of Wm Wilshere Esq. the sum of Two pounds 19s 9d for goods as per Bill
£2 – 19 - 9   For Thomas Gibbs & Co   Andr, Murray[282]

Henry Hodgson of Hitchin 1823 (HALS 61479/44)

Hitchin 1823   Wm Wilsher Esqr
To Henry Hodgson, Nursery & Seedsman

		£	s	d
Jany 6th	1 Pint Reddish 2s, 20 Large Matts 33s 4d	1	15	4
	½ Peck Best early Pease 2s, 1 Peck Prusion 4s	-	6	-
	1 Peck Charlton Pease 4s, 1 Peck Marrow Pease 4s	-	8	-
	3 Canvers Baggs 1s 6d	-	1	6
Jany 16th	10 Large Matts 16s 8d, 3 Strong Moss Roses 2s 3d	-	18	11
	6 Com[mo]n Provence Roses 3s	-	3	-
	4 Pruning Knives 8s	-	8	-
Feby 20th	1 lb Shallots 1s 6d, ½ lb Garlick 7d	-	2	1
	1 Peck early Kidney Potatoes 2s	-	2	-
	2000 Larch fir 2 years old Seedlings	-	16	-
	1000 Scotch 2 years old Seedling	-	4	-
	1000 Spruce 2 years old seedlings	-	8	-
	1 oz Salsifi 9d, 1 oz Salsizanero 9d	-	1	6
March 21st	4 oz Turnip 9d, 9 oz Brocoli in sorts 9s	-	9	9

[282] Wilshere's cash book shows that the grass seed was for Dimsey's Close above Rawlings Dell [HALS: 61525 p110].

227

	4 oz Endive 4s, ½ oz Sweet Bassel 9d	-	4	9
	4 Qu[art]s early Pease 2s, 1 oz early Carrot 3d	-	2	3
	2 Muscat of Alexander Vines 6s	-	6	-
	1 ?Qu[art] Spinach 1s 6d, 2 Syclamon Coum 3s	-	4	6
	4 Rododendorens in Potts Large 8s	-	8	-
	4 Double yellow Primroses 2s	-	2	-
May 14th	1 Peck Patagonian Pease 5s	-	5	-
	1 Pint Dw[ar]f French Beans 6d	-	-	6
July 3rd	1 Pruning Knife 2s. 4 oz Cabbge 4s	-	6	-
	2 oz Lettuce 2s, 4 oz Endive in sorts 4s	-	6	-
	2 oz Spanish Raddish 1s	-	1	-
	10 Papers of New Sorts of Stocks	-	3	4
	4 oz Hardy Winter Lettuce in sorts 4s	-	4	-
	1 Matt 1s 8d, 2 Qu[art]s Spinach 3s	-	4	8
	1 Pint Scarlet Reddish 2s	-	2	-
	½ Pint White Turnip Reddish 1s	-	1	-
	400 Cape Brocolc Plants 5s	-	5	-
	800 Collard Plants 3s 4d	-	3	4
Augt 24th	4 Cast of Potts 60 to a Cast 20s	1	-	-
	1 Cast of 32 & 48 to a Cast 5s	-	5	-
	2 Bushl Mushroom Spawn 16s	-	16	-
	1 Qu[art] Mustard 1s 6d, 2 oz Onion 1s, 2 oz Carrot 6d	-	3	-
	20 Large Matts 33s 4d	1	13	4
Octr 21st	1 Bushl Mushroom Spawn 8s	-	8	-
	2 Pecks early Pease 8s, 1 Qu[art] Beans 6d	-	8	6
	12 Moss Roses in Potts for Forsing 12s	-	12	-
	12 Com[mo]n Provence in Potts for Ditto 12s	-	12	-
	20 Matts 33s 4d, 3 D[o]z[en] Hyacinths 36s	3	9	4
	½ Peck Mustard 6s	=	6	=

228

APPENDIX TWO

	Over	19	7	7
Decr 1st	2 St[andar[d] Appels 3s, 1 St[andard] Prune Damsine 2s 6d	-	5	6
	1 Nobless Peach, 1 Chansler, 1 Galland	-	6	-
	1 Violet Hative Peach, 1 Temple Nect[ari]n[e]	-	4	-
	1 Moor Park	-	2	-
		-	17	6
	Brou[gh]t forward	<u>19</u>	<u>7</u>	<u>7</u>
	[Total]	20	5	1

	£	s	d
Matts	5	18	4
Seeds	5	11	1
Trees, plants, pruning knives & Garden potts	<u>8</u>	<u>15</u>	<u>8</u>
	20	5	1

APPENDIX THREE

WILLIAM WILSHERE'S FIELDS

WW = William Wilshere, TW = Thomas Wilshere, FW = Sir Francis Willes, JR = John Ransom senior

Name	Area	Owner *c1770*	Plot number & owner 1816	When & how acquired
Home or Barn Close (meadow)	1a 1r 19p	1a 2r 0p Richard Tristram	409 WW	1785 will of Richard Tristram
Saw Pit or Back Gate Close (meadow)	1a 0r 33r	1a 2r 0p Mrs Simpson	410 WW	1795 Elizabeth Simpson left her Hitchin property to WW senior who exchanged with WW two closes of 5½ acres in the tenure of Samuel Paternoster east of Walsworth Road.
The Lodge and Kitchen Garden	1a 3r 8p	1a 2r 0p Mrs Simpson	411 WW	1795 Elizabeth Simpson left her Hitchin property to WW senior. He exchanged with WW a close of 1½ acres west of Walsworth Road.
Rawlins or Rawlings Hill (grass)	4a 1r 21p	Part of 5a 0r 0p Richard Tristram	418 WW 419 JR - site of windmill	418 1785 will of Richard Tristram 419 WW bought the windmill by 1816.

APPENDIX THREE

Name	Area	Owner c1770	Plot number & owner 1816	When & how acquired
Mount Garrison (meadow)	2a 3r 26p	1a 0r 0p Thomas Whitehurst	424 WW	Before 1808
Rawlings Hill beyond the Mill or Windmill Piece (arable) The first reference to this being cropped is with turnips in 1818.	3a 2r 32p	1a - H Carter 2a 2r - John Foster 0a 2r - Mrs Barrington 1a 2r - H Carter	420 & 421 WW	1799 Wollaston Pym sold his 2 strips (inherited from Elizabeth Carter) to WW. By that date WW had already acquired the other 2 strips.
The Linces The first reference to this being cropped is with turnips in 1818.	2a 1r 1p	Part of 5a 0r 0p Richard Tristram	415 & 416 WW	1785 will of Richard Tristram
Sweard Slipe or Dimsey's Slipe or Garden or Close In 1814 sown with meadow grass	1a 0r 10p	1a H Carter	414 WW	1795 owned by Sarah Dimsey who died by 1802. Her son William exchanged an orchard and a garden (1 acre) shooting upon Rawlings Dell lying between the Linces with WW for 2½ acres of other land.

Name	Area	Owner *c*1770	Plot number & owner 1816	When & how acquired
Little Wimbush Field- formed 1815 amalgamating: Paternoster's Garden (1½ acres)	8a 1r 5p	2a – Mrs Simpson	413 WW	1795 Elizabeth Simpson left a close of 2 acres in the tenure of Samuel Paternoster to WW senior, exchanged with WW.
Little Wimbush (2 acres)		3a –Thomas Byde		1808 FW exchanged Wimbush Close 2½ acres with WW.
Dobbs Close (meadow 2 acres)		2 closes each 1a – Widow Dobbs		One merged with Little Wimbush and the other with Shoulder of Mutton
Shoulder of Mutton Piece (2 acres)		1a – William Lucas, brewer 1a – Mr Lane		Shoulder of Mutton WW by 1809

Name	Area	Owner c1770	Plot number & owner 1816	When & how acquired
Great Wimbush Field (Wimbush Field)	10a 2r 29p	12a 0r 0p Thomas Byde	412 WW	1783 bought by FW. 1808 FW exchanged Wimbush Close and the adjoining piece containing 12a 2r with WW for 22½ acres of land in Holwell, Bedfordshire. They were in the occupation of John Wilshere. In 1804 W W paid John £30 on quitting Wimbush Close.
Four Acres next Wymondley Road	3a 3r 24p	4a Thomas Goldsmith	673 WW Nettledell	Rented by WW from Edward Waby. The 1816 map is incorrect.
Waby's Field Close near Joan Biggs Grave Combined with Wabey's Nettledell (3½ acres)	8a 1r 7p	3a - Mrs Simpson 5a – Mr Warbe	676 WW	Close at Joan Biggs grave - TW inherited 1798. Exchanged with WW part of 7a 1r 20p WW occupied it by 1806. The owner, Edward Waby, butcher, died in 1808. In 1814 trustees for his heir Edward Crawley sold 4 acres in 1 piece near Nettledell to WW.

Name	Area	Owner c1770	Plot number & owner 1816	When & how acquired
Fell's Garden (2r 32p)		1a – late William Lucas	675 (2r 32p) WW occupied by John Fells	
Little Benslow Hill Includes T.W.'s Six acres Reel Close	10a 0r 35p	Lower part 8a – Mrs Simpson Upper part 1a 2r – Mrs Ann Newman Also parts of strips owned by Widow Paternoster and Thomas Byde.	677 WW	TW inherited 1798. Exchanged with WW 6a 1r 14p. FW acquired 1½ acres from executors of Samm Newman in 1791. The additional 2½ acres higher up the hill WW acquired from FW by exchange – final payment made Jan 1817.
The Slipes above Benslow Hill	7a 3r 24p	2a – Mrs Simpson 1a 2r – Mrs Simpson Between above 1a 2r – John Radcliffe 0a 1r –John Radcliffe 4a – Thomas Byde	747 WW	TW inherited Mrs Simpson's pieces in 1798 and in 1809 exchanged with WW 3a 1r 3p who at the same time seems to have acquired Radcliffe's pieces. WW noted in November 1817 'The small pieces above Pym's Benslow Hills now laid into one close'.

Name	Area	Owner *c*1770	Plot number & owner 1816	When & how acquired
The Slipes above Benslow Hill	7a 3r 24p	2a – Mrs Simpson 1a 2r – Mrs Simpson Between above 1a 2r – John Radcliffe 0a 1r –John Radcliffe 4a – Thomas Byde	747 WW	TW inherited Mrs Simpson's pieces in 1798 and in 1809 exchanged with WW 3a 1r 3p who at the same time seems to have acquired Radcliffe's pieces. WW noted in November 1817 'The small pieces above Pym's Benslow Hills now laid into one close'.
North Side of Great Benslow Hill	9a 0r 21p	Part of 20a H Carter	755 part Wollaston Pym	WW rented this land by 1806 (also known as Great Benslow Hill) from the Reverend Wollaston Pym whom had inherited almost 200 acres of land in Hitchin, from his cousin, Elizabeth Carter of Charlton Abbots, Gloucestershire, who had inherited it from her great grandfather, Simon Lucas of Hitchin.

Name	Area	Owner *c1770*	Plot number & owner 1816	When & how acquired
South Side of Great Benslow Hill	9a 0r 21p	Part of 20a H Carter	755 part Wollaston Pym	As above
Lower Benslow Hill Amalgamation of Joan Biggs' Close and rest of land	9a 0r 0p	4a – Mrs Simpson next to Benslow Lane 5a – Thomas Byde	756 WW	Close at Joan Biggs grave - TW inherited 1798. Exchanged with WW In 1783 FW bought an enclosure 4a 2r 32p. Exchanged with WW. Was in the occupation of John Wilshere, but WW by 1806.
Five Acres next Walsworth Way (Starlings Bridge Close)	5a 0r 35p	5a 2r Mrs Simpson	758 Trustees of Back Street Meeting	TW inherited 1798 Exchanged with WW
Brown's Close (part of Brown's Twelve Acres)	6a 3r 34p	Part of 12a William Thomas	757 Thomas Brown	Rented by WW by 1806.
First Back Meadow (part of Brown's Twelve Acres)	2a 2r 4p	Part of 12a William Thomas	759 Thomas Brown	Rented by WW from Michaelmas 1812.

Name	Area	Owner *c*1770	Plot number & owner 1816	When & how acquired
Second Back Meadow (part of Brown's Twelve Acres)	2a 2r 24p	Part of 12a William Thomas	760 Thomas Brown	Rented by WW from Michaelmas 1812.
Walsworth Way Close (Pierson's, Stone or Rail Piece or Dunche's Field)	4a 0r 38p	4a Thomas Whitehurst	761 TW	1810 Stone Piece 4a Joseph Margetts Pierson sold to WW. WW already occupied it by 1806.
Ransom's Meadow	2a 1r 33p	Not shown on map	JR 210	Rented from John Ransom.
Nettledale (Nettledell) By 1820 WW had acquired all these strips starting at the top of the hill:	10a 1r 14p		667-672 see below	
	0a 2r 0p	0a 2r – Mr Cooper	667 owned FW occupied TW	TW exchanged with WW
	1a 1r 6p	1a – Mrs Simpson	667a Town Land occupied TW	TW exchanged with WW

Name	Area	Owner *c1770*	Plot number & owner 1816	When & how acquired
	0a 2r 9p	0a 3r – H Carter	668 owned TW occupied JR	TW exchanged with WW
	3a 2r 31p	1a – William Lucas brewer 1a – Mr Lane 1a – William Lucas brewer 1a – Mr Lane	669 owned & occupied by JR	Acquired from John Ransom
	1a 3r 6p	1a – Thomas Byde 1a – Mrs Simpson	670 owned & occupied by WW	FW bought 1783 3r 5p. Exchanged with.WW –final payment made Jan 1817. TW inherited 1798
	1a 3r 13p	1a 2r – Mr Capreol 0a 1r - H Carter	671 owned & occupied by James Watson	? acquired from John Ransom
	0a 3r 29p	1a Mrs Simpson	672 owned & occupied by TW	TW inherited 1798 Exchanged with WW

APPENDIX THREE

Name	Area	Owner *c1770*	Plot number & owner 1816	When & how acquired
Gray's Garden	1a 2r 14p	1a 2r Mrs Ann Newman	674 WW Occupied by John Gray	1791 trustee of will of Samm Newman sold garden in occupation of James Gray to William Mowbray, gardener. In 1803 he mortgaged and in 1805 sold it to WW.
Brown's Pightle	0a 2r 13p	1a Mrs Ann Newman	422 WW Occupied by Daniel Brown	1791 trustee of will of Samm Newman sold pasture to William Mowbray, gardener. In 1803 he mortgaged and in 1805 sold it to WW.

Sources: Map of Purwell Field *c*1770 [HALS: DZ/72/P121605], 1816 map and assessment of the parish of Hitchin [NHM], plan of an estate of William Wilshere *c*1808 [HALS: 58869], plans of fields occupied by William Wilshere 1806 and 1819 [HALS: DE/Ws/P15-16]; Wills of Richard Tristram 1785, Elizabeth Simpson 1795 and William Wilshere 1824 [TNA: PROB11]; Hitchin Manor court books 1785-1824 [TNA: LR3/29, CRES5/37]; Sale particulars for Thomas Plumer Byde's estate 1783; Lovell Papers [Wiltshire & Swindon Archives: 161/57] and Information from James Carter 1856 [HALS: 60597].

BIOGRAPHICAL NOTES

Abbis or Abbiss, James (*c*1780-1845)
James Abbis was employed by William Wilshere to work in his garden from 1802 onwards. In 1805 he was paid 10s 6d a week. He and his wife probably lived in the ornamental thatched cottage built by Wilshere in the corner of Walsworth Road and Whinbush Road next to his poultry yard. In 1816 and 1818 Wilshere paid Mrs Abbis to prepare straw for plaiting. In a codicil to his will dated 26 March 1824 Wilshere left £15 to James Abbis, one of his garden men. He also left £5 to James Abbis' wife.[283]
James Abbis probably continued in the employment of William Wilshere's nephew. The 1841 census records him as a garden labourer aged about 60 living with his wife Ann in one of the Whinbush Cottages, apparently Wilshere's ornamental thatched cottage. His daughter, Elizabeth, was married at St Mary's Hitchin on 25 April 1829 to William Scott of Hitchin, a basket maker. The administration of the estate of James Abbiss of Hitchin, gardener, was granted to his only child, Elizabeth Scott, in 1845.[284]

Barnett, William
Hitchin farmer. William Barnett was a tenant on Sir Francis Sykes' estate in Walsworth, probably occupying Walsworth Old Farm, from 1811 to 1817. He sold Wilshere white oats in January 1817. He also sold him bats egg shell wheat which was harvested in 1817. In April 1818 the household furniture and farming stock of William Barnett of Hitchin were auctioned to pay his creditors.[285]

Beaver, George (*c*1785-1875)
Hitchin maltster and basketmaker. In 1806 he married his cousin, Amy Crofts, in St Mary's Church, Hitchin. She inherited from her father Robert Crofts, a basketmaker and maltster (who was George's uncle), his house on the north side of the Market Place (now no 3), his two ozier grounds, and half a share of his barley, malt and stock in trade as a maltster. Robert Crofts rented a maltings behind the houses on the corner of Bancroft and Pound Lane, which was widened in the 1830s to become Brand Street. In 1813 George Beaver bought the whole property including the Brotherhood House (now 2-6 Bancroft). He continued to live in the Market Place where by 1855 two of his sons, William and John, were grocers and basketmakers. George died in 1875 aged 90.

---

[283] Wilshere's cash books [HALS: 61495 p56; 61497 p55); Common Place book [NHM: 1216 pp104-107, 142]; William Wilshere's will [TNA: PROB11/1692/97].
[284] Hitchin marriage register [HALS: DP/53/1/15]; grant of administration [HALS: H23/89].
[285] Cash books [HALS: 61504 p25; 61527 pp16, 53; 61526 p83]; *County Chronicle* 7 April 1818, 12 May 1818.

Another son George born in 1809 became a land surveyor. North Hertfordshire Museum has a copy of his journal.[286]

Bentley, Henry (c1752-1818)
Hitchin gardener. In 1773 John Radcliffe's gardener regularly employed Francis Bentley to work at Hitchin Priory. He also occasionally employed 'Young Bentely' or H Bentely. In 1778 Henry Bentley was married in St Mary's Church Hitchin to Catherine, daughter of John Alldridge of Martley in Worcestershire. Their son John was baptised at St Mary's on 29 June 1785 and their son William (see below) on 31 July 1791. Henry Bentley was listed as a gardener in the *Universal British Directory* for 1794. Wilshere paid him for seeds and work between 1796 and 1805. The family lived in a house on the south side of the churchyard, part of the Parsonage House site which was owned by Trinity College Cambridge. Henry Bentley also rented a shop in the Great Yard and a large garden (2 roods 35 perches in extent) between the Great Yard, the River Hiz and the Sun Inn. He died in 1818 and was buried in St Mary's churchyard. His widow, Catherine, continued to live in the same house which comprised a kitchen, pantry and three bedrooms for which she paid Trinity College £6. She paid the College an additional £8 for the large garden at the back of The Sun. She died in 1840 aged 87.[287]

Bentley, John (1785-1830)
Henry Bentley's son John also became a gardener selling Wilshere trees worth 16s in 1824. John Bentley paid Wilshere 16s for 12 bushels of potatoes in July 1823. He had married Ann Chalkley at Hitchin in 1809. He died in 1830 aged 45 and was buried at St Mary's with his brother Henry who died in 1814 aged 31 and his children, William Henry who died in 1832 aged 20 and Jane who died in

---

[286] Hitchin marriage register [HALS: DP/53/1/14]; Will of Robert Crofts 1809 [TNA: PROB11/1497/7]; deeds and papers relating to the Brotherhood House (BLARS Z937/15/17, Z937/33/1; Map of Hitchin 1816 [NHM]; George Beaver's Journal [NHM: M265]
[287] John Radcliffe's Garden book 1773 [HALS: DE/R/F204]; Hitchin parish register [HALS: DP/53/1/4]; cash books [HALS: 61489 p8; 61494 pp112,120; 61498 p20]; bill [HALS: 61479/19]; Hertfordshire Family History Society, *Hertfordshire Monumental Inscriptions Hitchin The Parish Church of St Mary* (2007) pp20, 22; map of Hitchin 1816 [NHM]; plan of Impropriate Estate of Trinity College Cambridge 1822 [HALS: DP/53/29/1]; reference book 1822 Trinity College Archives [42 Hitchin 52].

1847 aged 29. Jane Bentley had continued to occupy the house in churchyard and the garden behind The Sun.[288]

Bentley, William (1791-1861)
Hitchin solicitor. William Bentley was the son of Henry and Catherine Bentley (see above). In December 1805 Wilshere paid Henry Bentley & Son 5s for 'writing letters and forwarding same & for many other attend:'. By 1807 William Bentley was employed in Wilshere's office and remained there until 1817. In his will made in March 1824 Wilshere left William Bentley £200. In a codicil dated 31 July 1824 Wilshere stated that in March 1824 'I was at that time engaged in the revision of all my accounts and I then gave directions in regard thereto in case I should not live to complete the revision in which I have made considerable progress, but I still find old unclosed accounts on which balances appear against me of about £3,700 or thereabouts'. Mr Bentley was now examining and making up these accounts to facilitate which Wilshere had allocated £5,000. He left an additional legacy to William Bentley of 100 guineas for his trouble.[289]
William Bentley married Jane Primett in 1817 and lived in Sun Street (in the house now 9 Sun Street). In 1825 he bought the house in Tilehouse Street (now 88) formerly owned by Wilshere's mother in law, Martha Wortham. Reginald Hine, Hitchin's local historian, described Bentley as 'a man of considerable abdominal dignity' reproducing a sketch of him by Samuel Lucas. William Bentley died in 1861. His son Robert, born in 1821, became a botanist and pharmacognosist and Fellow of the Linnaen Society.[290]

Bowie, James (c1789-1869)
Gardener and botanist. James Bowie was born in London, the son of a seedsman based in Oxford Street. From 1810 he was employed in the Royal Botanic Gardens at Kew. In December 1812 he took charge of William Wilshere's garden where he kept a garden journal and compiled a list of trees and seeds sown and planted which have been transcribed as part of this volume. The

[288] Hitchin marriage register [HALS: DP/53/1/14]; Hertfordshire Family History Society, *Hertfordshire Monumental Inscriptions Hitchin The Parish Church of St Mary* (2007) pp20, 22; cash book [HALS: 61535 pp31, 70]; Hitchin tithe map and apportionment 1841-1844 [HALS: DSA4/53/1-2].
[289] Cash book [HALS: 61498 p20]; cash books 1807-1817 [HALS: 61500-61506; 61525-61527]; William Wilshere's will [TNA: PROB11/1692/97].
[290] Hitchin marriage register [HALS: DP/53/1/17]; agreement for sale 1824 [NHM]; R L Hine, *Hitchin Worthies. Four Centuries of English Life* (1932, reprinted 1974) pp389, 391; G S Boulger, revised J K Crellin, 'Robert Bentley', *ODNB* (2004).

journal breaks off in June 1813, but was resumed on 1 January 1814 until May 1814.

James Bowie left Wilshere's employment in August 1814 and by that autumn was on his way to Brazil with Allan Cunningham to collect plants for Sir Joseph Banks for Kew. He was sent from there to South Africa, arriving in November 1816 the first botanical collector from Kew since Francis Masson in 1795. He undertook four long journeys and collected and despatched to Kew many plants and seeds, particularly mesembryanthemums, aloes, and euphorbias, including many succulent species new to Kew. Bowie was summoned home in 1823 and dismissed. He arranged his herbarium at Kew, but he returned permanently to the Cape in 1827 as a commercial plant collector. From 1838 to 1842 he was superintendent of Baron Heinrich von Ludwig's garden. His entry in the *Oxford Dictionary of National Biography* concludes:

> 'Bowie wrote the earliest guide to the Cape flora printed in South Africa (1829), and his botanical knowledge was famous: he was thought able to identify any plant presented to him, giving its local and Latin names, history, and uses. He advised on gardens, notably Baron Ludwig's botanical collection, and hunted plants with such success that W H Harvey considered him to have enriched Europe's gardens with more succulents than any other individual. His feats were honoured in the genera *Bowiea*, named by Harvey, and *Bowiesia*, named by R K Greville, but he enjoyed few more tangible rewards, growing old in poverty, an alcoholic dependent on charity. He died at Claremont, outside Cape Town, Cape Colony, on 2 July 1869.'[291]

Brand, Thomas, Lord Dacre (1774-1851)

Thomas Brand inherited The Hoo at Kimpton from his father, Thomas Brand, in 1794. He served as MP for Hertfordshire from 1807 until 1819 when he inherited the title 20th Baron Dacre from his mother, Gertrude. He became one of the foremost Whig supporters of the agricultural interest. In August 1814 he published a pamphlet in the form of a letter to William Wilshere in defence of the Corn Laws in which he argued that landowners and farmers needed a fair return for their crops and stressed the dangers of relying on imports.[292]

In 1824 William Wilshere made Lord Dacre one of his trustees and executors of his will. He devised the Hitchin British Schools with additional property

---

[291] R Drayton, 'James Bowie', *ODNB* (2004); S2A3 Biographical Dictionary of South African Science https://www.s2a3.org.za.

[292] R G Thorne, 'Hon Thomas Brand (1774-1851), History of Parliament Online; letter on Corn Laws [HALS: 61708].

intended as an endowment for the school to Lord Dacre, who in 1826 set up a trust to run the school.[293] Their names are commemorated in Wilshere-Dacre School built in Hitchin in the 1920s by Hertfordshire County Council. On Lord Dacre's death in 1851 William Lucas of Hitchin, a Quaker brewer, described him as:

> 'a fine specimen of our best old nobility, so accessible, so simple, so well informed in all public and political matters, a most reasonable landlord, a very influential and useful man in the county, truly liberal in sentiment and action, unostentatious to a degree that was almost quizzical - - - ; very hospitable, passionately fond of the country with all its sports and rural pursuits, yet not neglecting his senatorial duties.'

Lord Dacre had married Barbarina Wilmot, née Ogle, a poet and playwright, in 1819. He had no children; his heir was his nephew, Thomas Brand.[294]

Brookes, Cornelius

Cornelius Brookes was William Wilshere's tenant at Shitlington (now Shillington) in Bedfordshire, where he had an orchard. In Wilshere's will he stated:

> 'Cornelius Brooks is in the occupation of a cottage in Shitlington and in receipt of the rent of another and of some land adjoining which are mortgaged by him to me for more than their value. It is my desire that he and his wife shall be permitted to possess the same during their lives and the life of the survivor without any payment in respect thereof on condition that he shall release and convey the equity of redemption to my Trustees - - -.'[295]

Brown, Thomas

Land surveyor of Hitchin. Thomas Brown was the son of Thomas Brown, land surveyor of Luton. Shortly before 1804 Thomas Brown junior of Luton, married Mary Margaret Thomas, only surviving child of William Thomas, maltster of

---

[293] William Wilshere's will [TNA: PROB11/1692/97]; British Schools Museum, *Educating Our Own. The Masters of Hitchin British School 1810 to 1929* (Hitchin, 2008) p29.

[294] G E Bryant & G P Baker ed, *A Quaker Journal Being the Diary and Reminiscences of William Lucas of Hitchin (1804-1861)* (1934) vol II p447; T Cooper, revised R Mills, 'Barbarina Brand [née Ogle], Lady Dacre' *ODNB* (2004).

[295] See pp96 and 104 above. William Wilshere's will [TNA: PROB11/1692/97].

Hitchin, a Baptist, who had died in 1781 just before the birth of his daughter. On the death of her half brother in 1791, she inherited all her father's property in Hitchin including the Swan Inn and 12 acres of land between Walsworth Road and Nightingale Road known as The Twelve Acres which Thomas Brown rented to Wilshere. In 1806 Brown bought the house on the corner of Bancroft and Portmill Lane (now occupied by Marks and Spencer).[296]

Thomas Brown was appointed surveyor to the Pirton Enclosure Commissioners in 1811 while his father was one of the Commissioners. On his father's death he replaced him as a Commissioner. Thomas Brown became agent to the Wrest Park Estate, but continued to live in Hertfordshire moving from Hitchin to the nearby village of Willian, then returning to Hitchin. He died in 1849. His wife died in 1853.[297]

Burr, Edward (c1786-1863)

Hitchin miller and a Quaker, who was tenant of the Port Mill in Portmill Lane which adjoined William Wilshere's garden. By 1830 he had moved to Charlton Mill in the hamlet immediately to the south of Hitchin. He bought Charlton Mill in 1838 together with the windmill on the hill above the hamlet. When the old post mill burnt down in the same year, he replaced it with a tower mill. He lived at Charlton Mill with his sister, Mary, where they were painted outside the mill by Samuel Lucas. He died in 1863 aged 77.[298]

Carter, James (?1781-1858)

William Wilshere's gardener from July 1810 until February 1811. It is possible that he was the James Carter born in Hitchin in about 1781 who by 1841 was an agricultural labourer living in a cottage belonging to William Wilshere in Back Street with his wife Elizabeth and seven children. In 1851, now a widower aged 69, he was described as a retired farm bailiff, living in Dead Street with four of his children. In 1856 James Carter or 'old Carter' provided a detailed description

[296] Deeds to the Swan Inn [HALS: DE/Ha/T103]; Wills of William Thomas maltster 1781 and of William Thomas gentleman 1791 [TNA: PROB11/1079, PROB11/1202]; map of Hitchin 1816 [NHM]; Manor of Hitchin court book [TNA: CRES5/37 p408].
[297] 'The process of Parliamentary Enclosure focussing on Pirton, Hertfordshire' see https://pirtonhistory.org.uk/studies/; wills of Thomas Brown 1849 and Mary Margaret Brown 1853 (HALS: 20HW88, 20HW95).
[298] Map of Hitchin 1816 [NHM]; D Rance, *St Ippolyts A country parish in the nineteenth century* (Baldock, 1987) pp105-108; C Moore, *Hertfordshire Windmills & Windmillers* (Sawbridgeworth, 1999) p23.

of small pieces of land held by William Wilshere in the vicinity of Walsworth Road which had been amalgamated into larger fields. He died in 1858.[299]

Carter, John (c1777-1857)

Gardener. John Carter was born in Tamworth, Staffordshire. By 1817 he was living in Putney where his daughter Mary was born. He was appointed William Wilshere's gardener in June 1823. After Wilshere's death in 1824 he continued in charge of the garden. The 1841 census described him as a gardener aged about 60, living with his wife Mary aged about 50 in Back Street in the gardener's cottage which Wilshere's nephew and heir had built in the frame garden at the corner of Back Street and Portmill Lane. In January 1842 John Carter made his will leaving all he possessed to his daughter, Mary. When William Wilshere moved to The Frythe at Welwyn in about 1846, he took John Carter with him to take charge of the gardens. The 1851 census described him as a widower living with his unmarried daughter Mary aged 43. John Carter died in 1857. His estate was valued at under £600.[300]

Chapman, Daniel (c1744-1821)

Hitchin banker. His father, Thomas Chapman who died in 1767 was a bricklayer and Daniel initially followed his father's occupation, being employed by John Radcliffe in the 1770s in rebuilding part of Hitchin Priory and improving the park.[301] In a 1794 Directory Daniel Chapman was listed as a Distributor of Stamps. He became one of William Wilshere's partners in the Hitchin and Hertfordshire Bank which they founded in 1789 and in the purchase of the lease of Hitchin Rectory in 1790. He lived in the Bull House, on the corner of Bridge Street and Dead Street. He died in January 1821 aged 78. His heir was his daughter, Ann Marsh of Offley. He directed his executors to sell his share in the bank and the Rectory lease.[302]

---

[299] Cash books [HALS: 61502 p86; 61503 p38]; 1838 rate assessment [HALS: DP/53/18/9]; 1841 and 1851 censuses; Information from James Carter 1856 [HALS: 60597].

[300] 1841 and 1851 censuses; cash book [HALS: 61535 p24]; John Carter's will [HALS: 31HW94].

[301] B Howlett, *Hitchin Priory Park, The history of a landscape park and gardens* (Hitchin, 2004) pp27, 35, 83.

[302] Wilshere's Minutes of Property [HALS: 61613 pp28, 30, 52]; map of Hitchin 1816 [NHM]; Daniel Chapman's will [TNA: PROB11/1639/339].

BIOGRAPHICAL NOTES

Chapman, Michael (*c*1774-1859)
Hitchin cornfactor, yeoman and stamp distributor. He was one of the three sons of William Chapman, a Hitchin builder and yeoman, who died in 1803. Daniel Chapman (see above) was his uncle. Michael Chapman owned and occupied a farmyard and barn at the corner of Back Street and Biggin Lane. He lived in High Street and in 1810 bought the premises between Cock Street and Churchyard including his home, corn lofts and granaries. Arthur Young described him as 'a very intelligent farmer' and frequently cited his opinions in his *General view of the Agriculture of the County of Hertfordshire*.[303]

Crabb, Henry (*c*1796-1830)
Younger son of John Crabb, brewer and farmer of Hitchin who died in 1811. John Crabb senior was one of William Wilshere's partners in the Hitchin and Hertfordshire Bank which they founded in 1789 and in the purchase of the lease of Hitchin Rectory in 1790. His elder son, John, died unmarried in 1813 leaving his younger brother Henry as his heir. Henry Crabb became partner in the bank with Joseph Margetts Pierson. He inherited his father's brewery in Sun Street which he operated in partnership with John Marshall, who lived in the brewery house. He also owned a maltings in Bridge Street and leased from Trinity College Cambridge their recently built farm buildings in West Lane (now Paynes Park). For many years Wilshere bought beer for harvest from Crabb's brewery. Henry Crabb lived at Temple Dinsley, near Preston. He died in 1830 aged 34 and his will directed his executors to sell his interest in both the bank and the brewery.[304]

Dacre, Lord – see Brand, Thomas

Dear, Twydell
Carpenter of Shillington in Bedfordshire. Twydell Dear married Ann Olive of Hatfield in 1800. In 1819 his uncle, Twydell Dear of Shillington, gentleman, bequeathed him a share of property in Dunstable as well as all his household goods. Wilshere made payments to Twydell Dear, carpenter, for work on behalf

---

[303] Manor of Hitchin court book 1803 [TNA: CRES 5/37]; map of Hitchin 1816 [NHM]; deeds to 22-24 High Street [HALS: DE/Ha/T99]; Young, *General View,* pp71, 82, 93-95, 108, 113-114, 135, 163, 169, 173, 184.
[304] Wilshere's Minutes of Property [HALS: 61613 pp28, 30]; wills of John Crabb 1811, John Crabb 1813 and Henry Crabb 1830 [TNA PROB11/ 1525/512, PROB11/1546/210, PROB11/ 1773/268]; A Whitaker, *Brewers in Hertfordshire. A historical gazetteer* (Hatfield, 2006) p143; map of Hitchin 1816 [NHM]; cash books eg [HALS: 61506 p2; 61527 p34; 61528 p104].

of Samuel Whitbread 1804-1806 including 'weeding quick on tithe allotments' and paid him 16s for 30 bushels of haws in 1817. In 1811 he paid him £500 for building work on the British Schools in Dead Street. In 1815 he loaned Dear £100.[305]

Delmé-Radcliffe, Emilius (1774-1832)

Owner of the Hitchin Priory estate including much of Pirton, which was managed by Wilshere. Emilius was the younger son of Peter Delmé of Cams Hall, Hampshire, and his wife, Lady Betty Delmé. His aunt, Lady Frances Howard, had married John Radcliffe, who rebuilt Hitchin Priory in the 1770s and enlarged the park. Emilius was friendly with John's nephew and heir, Charles John Clarke, and lived in one of the Radcliffe family properties at Highdown, near Pirton. After Charles John Clarke's death in an accident in Paris, in 1802 Emilius married Charles' elder sister Anne, who had inherited the Radcliffe and Clarke estates and changed his name to Delmé-Radcliffe. Anne died in 1808 after giving birth to four children. Emilius lived at Hitchin Priory in possession of the estate until his own death in 1832, when he was succeeded by his second son, Frederick Peter Delmé-Radcliffe.[306]

Desse, John

London lawyer. John Desse of Desse and Dendy, Breams Buildings, Westminster, was a trustee with William Wilshere of the Radcliffe estates. Wilshere's ledger records a payment from the Radcliffe estate to Mr Desse of £1 1s for bulbs in February 1802. Wilshere also bought bulbs from him for himself, but those he purchased in December 1811 turned out badly. However he paid Mr Desse £1 10s in 1817 for bulbs bought in 1814. John Desse died in 1822.[307]

Dimsey, David

Several members of the Dimsey family of Hitchin were gardeners. In 1792 Wilshere bought quick thorn from Dimsey for Rawlings Dell.[308] David Dimsey

---

[305] Hatfield marriage register [HALS: DP/46/1/47]; Twydell Dear's will 1819 [TNA: PROB11/1614/305]; ledger D [HALS: 61543 p32]; cash book 1817 [HALS: 61527 p122]; British Schools Museum, *Educating Our Own,* p24; cash books [HALS: 61525 p42; 61527 p122].
[306] Howlett, *Hitchin Priory Park,* p45.
[307] Letters to Emilius Delmé-Radcliffe 1805-1806 [HALS: DE/R/C402/1-5]; accounts of the Radcliffe settled estates 1798-1824 [HALS: DE/R/F266]; Wilshere ledger D [HALS: 61543 p3], cash books [HALS: 61494 p126; 61527 p122]; John Desse's will [TNA: PROB11/1665/57].
[308] Cash book [HALS: 61484 p68].

rented a garden around the fish pond west of Bancroft until about 1780 when the land was acquired by Isaac Sharples and made into a pleasure ground and plantation for his house, The Woodlands. By 1784 David Dimsey was landlord of the Three Horse Shoes in Cock Street. He occupied a garden next to the churchyard until this was purchased as an extension to the burial ground in 1809. In 1810 Wilshere appointed David's son, Thomas Dimsey (born in 1782) as the first master of the British Schools. He also became parish clerk. Thomas Dimsey rented the garden behind the British Schools in Storehouse Lane.[309]

Dimsey, William (c1765-1844)
In 1801 William Dimsey, gardener, was living in Back Street in Hitchin, near Widow Dimsey, presumably his mother. His father, William Dimsey of Hitchin, gardener, brother of David Dimsey (see above), died in 1775 aged 40. His mother Sarah died in 1801 aged 63. The following year William exchanged with Wilshere one acre of land above the Dell described as an orchard and garden, which he had inherited from his parents. He received in return two closes of land containing 2½ acres next to Stevenage Road near the Folly, one of which was occupied as a garden by Henry Bentley. In 1816 he also owned two houses in Storehouse Lane, and five houses in Back Street next to Thorpe's Yard. William Dimsey, gardener, died in 1844 aged 79. His first wife Sarah died in 1830 aged 64. His second wife Martha died in 1856 aged 80.[310]

Dines, George William (1800-1863)
George William Dines was baptised in Luton in 1800, the son of William Dines, a gamekeeper. William Dines was employed by Sir Robert Salusbury, then by the Revd Lynch Burroughs, for Wellbury and Offley in 1805 and 1806, by Richard Oakley at Cockernhoe in 1814, by Lord Melbourne at Brocket Hall in 1816 and by Lord Dacre for Codicote in 1828. Many members of the Dines family were gamekeepers including Charles Dines, Samuel Whitbread's gamekeeper who was killed by poachers at Southill in 1815, and George Dines, who from 1802 was employed by Emilius Delmé-Radcliffe of Hitchin Priory for his manors of Charlton and Maydencroft and by Anthony Rhudde for Hitchin

---

[309] Isaac Sharples' will 1806 [TNA: PROB11/1450/233]; P Gadd, 'Hitchin Inns etc.' (typescript, 1987); *An Account of the Hitchin Charities extracted from the further report of the Commissioners appointed to continue the Inquiries concerning Charities 1836* pp.20-21, 31; British Schools Museum, *Educating Our Own*, pp32-34.
[310] Photocopy of 1801 census [NHM]; William Dimsey's will 1775 [HALS: 35HW68]; *Hertfordshire Monumental Inscriptions Hitchin The Parish Church of St Mary,* p22,70; Manor of Hitchin court book 1802 [TNA: CRES 5/37 p151]; map of Hitchin 1816 [NHM]; William Dimsey's will 1844 [HALS 36HW19].

BIOGRAPHICAL NOTES

Portman and Foreign. On 26 August 1820 George William Dines was registered as William Wilshere's gamekeeper for the Manors of Great and Little Wymondley to replace Richard Harvey and also for Hitchin Portman and Foreign. In 1822-3 he was paid 21s a week (£54 12s a year) and lived in the Keeper's Cottage at Wymondley. When Wilshere died in 1824, he left George William Dines 19 guineas and mourning.

William Wilshere's trustees appointed George William as gamekeeper for the Wymondleys and George Dines as gamekeeper for Hitchin. Both appointments were renewed by Wilshere's nephew and heir in 1830. However in September 1831 Emilius Delmé-Radcliffe appointed George William as his gamekeeper for his Pirton Manors. William Wilshere replaced him with John Ellerd. In September 1832 Emilius' son and heir, Frederick Peter Delmé-Radcliffe, appointed George Dines as gamekeeper for all his Hertfordshire manors where he stayed until 1840.[311]

While living in the keeper's cottage at Great Wymondley, George William and his wife Elizabeth had three children, Charles Edward, George William and Martha baptised at Willian parish church between 1824 and 1829. Martha died just five days after her baptism. When he was employed by the Delmé-Radcliffes, George William Dines lived in Ickleford where his daughter, Elizabeth Barbara, was baptised in January 1833. In 1841 George Dines, gamekeeper, was living in Wimpole, Cambridgeshire, with his wife, Elizabeth, and their daughter, Elizabeth Barbara. His widowed mother, Barbara, had joined them there by 1851. Barbara died in 1853 and by 1861 George William had lost his wife and moved to Bedford with his daughter and grandson. He was now working as a gardener. He died in 1863.[312]

Dove, Harriet
Harriet Dove was the daughter of the Revd Thomas Dove of Gosmore in the parish of Ippollitts, whose advice on the cultivation of sainfoin was quoted by Arthur Young in his *General view of the Agriculture of the County of Hertfordshire*. Thomas Dove's home is now called Gosmore House. On his death in 1808 he left his real and personal property in Gosmore to his wife Elizabeth for her life, then to his daughter Harriet. Wilshere bought a load of

---

[311] Luton parish register [BLARS: P85/1/9]; S Whitbread and S Bunker, 'Southill – A Sporting Estate' in P Bell ed, *Southill and the Whitbreads 1795-1995* (Biggleswade, 1995) pp48-49; register of gamekeepers [HALS: QS/Var/5]; Wilshere cash book [HALS: 61532 p82]; William Wilshere's will [TNA: PROB11/1692/97].
[312] Willian parish registers [HALS: DP/125/1/4 and 11]; Ickleford baptism register [HALS: DP/58/1/2]; 1841, 1851 and 1861 censuses.

tares from her in 1818 for £4. In Wilshere's will he left Mrs Harriot Dove 19 guineas for a ring or other memorial. She died in 1842.[313]

Downing, John (c1790-1861)
John Downing was born about 1790 in Halkin in Flintshire. In October 1814 he was appointed Wilshere's gardener in succession to James Bowie and was paid £47 5s a year. He would have been responsible for the entries in the garden journal from October 1814 to August 1815. He left Wilshere's employment in August 1818.[314]
By 1827 John Downing had married and moved to Chicksands in Bedfordshire where his daughter Lucy was born. His wife came from nearby Southill. In 1841 John Downing was living in the neighbouring town of Shefford with his wife and two children. In 1851 he was gardener at Chicksands Lodge. His daughter Lucy was now a teacher aged 23 while his son Henry aged 14, born while his parents were living in Shefford, was a gardener. *The Gardeners' Chronicle and Agricultural Gazette* for 9 June 1859 recorded the election of John Downing as one of the pensioners of the Gardeners' Royal Benevolent Institution. By 1861, now aged 70, he had returned with his wife and daughter to Shefford where he was employed as a domestic gardener. He died later that year.[315]

Duncalfe, Isaac
Hitchin stone mason whose house and yard were on the corner of Dead Street (now Queen Street) and Lyle's Row. Reginald Hine, the Hitchin historian, described him as an unbeliever and 'a red republican'. His first wife, Lydia, died childless in 1791. His second wife died in 1815 or 1816. In February 1812 Wilshere paid him £55 6s 6d for mason's work on his house, greenhouse, tank and the British Schools where he presumably carved the foundation stone with the initials 'W.W.' and the date 1810. Wilshere also commissioned him to provide memorial stones for some of his clients. When Duncalfe died in 1819, he left the bulk of his property to Mrs Jane Mount, formerly Goodship, otherwise called Jane Duncalfe, spinster. His journeyman, William Warren, continued the stone mason's business as Mrs Mount's tenant. Isaac Duncalfe was responsible for the memorials to Edward Young and John Twydell in St

---

[313] Young, *General View*, pp121, 124; Rance, *St Ippolyts*, p18; wills of Thomas Dove 1808 and Harriet Dove 1842 [TNA: PROB11/1480/276, PROB11/1969/121]; William Wilshere's will [TNA: PROB11/1692/97].
[314] 1851 census; cash books [HALS 61525 p10; 61528 p62].
[315] 1841, 1851 and 1861 censuses.

BIOGRAPHICAL NOTES

Mary's Church Welwyn while William Warren was paid for carving the Wilshere family monument at Welwyn in February 1820.[316]

Eade, Joseph

Hitchin lawyer. Son of Jonathan Eade esquire, he was articled to William Wilshere as a clerk for five years on 13 October 1796. In 1801 Wilshere handed over to Joseph Eade his practice in the Common and Crown Law and in 1805 his practice in the Court of Chancery. In 1808 when Wilshere was called to the Bar, Joseph Eade succeeded to such of his business as was incompatible with the character of a barrister. He lived in the Grange House in Portmill Lane, owned by Wilshere, the further part of the garden of which Wilshere had appropriated as his Frame Garden. Their office was in the adjoining house in Portmill Lane also owned by Wilshere. In his will he left Joseph Eade £250 and 19 guineas to his wife. Joseph Eade died in 1828 and was succeeded in the practice by John Hawkins.[317]

Farmer, John

Hitchin corn and seed merchant, miller and grocer. John Farmer owned and occupied two houses on the east side of Hitchin Market Place. He also rented a yard behind them from Wilshere and the other lessees of Hitchin Rectory. In 1815 he leased Port Mill from its new owner, William Bodger. John Farmer also rented the windmill on Rawlings Hill (now Windmill Hill) from Wilshere who had bought it from John Ransom by 1815. In 1816 Wilshere paid for a flour mill and sack tackle. John Farmer sold Wilshere wheat seed in 1820. He died in 1823 leaving his wife, Sarah, and his son, John, to carry on his trade.[318]

Farr, Elisha

Elisha Farr of Weston was a farmer. In 1811 he obtained a licence for one of his buildings to be used for Methodist services. He died in 1826.[319]

---

[316] Hine, *Hitchin Worthies,* pp389-390; A Crosby, P Douglas, S Fletcher et al, *Jeeves yard. A dynasty of Hitchin builders and brickmakers* (Baldock, 2003) p13; cash books [HALS: 61504 p34; 61502 p86; 61528 p66]; J Bettley, N Pevsner and B Cherry, *The Buildings of England Hertfordshire* (2019) p620; cash book [HALS: 61529 p78].

[317] Minutes of Property [HALS: 61613 pp46, 60, 66]; William Wilshere's will [TNA: PROB11/1692/97]; Joseph Eade's will [TNA: PROB11/ 1752/433].

[318] Map of Hitchin 1816 [NHM]; draft lease of Port Mill [HALS: 57885]; cash books 1816-1823 [HALS: 61526 pp47-48; 61528 p77; 61535 p7]; John Farmer's will 1823 [TNA PROB11/1673/2].

[319] R L Hine, *The Story of Methodism at Hitchin* (1934) p4; Elisha Farr's will [HALS: 45HW104].

BIOGRAPHICAL NOTES

Fells, Abraham (1792-1845)

Hitchin nurseryman. Abraham Fells was baptised in St Mary's Hitchin in November 1792, the son of John Fells (see below) and his wife Elizabeth. Mrs Fells was admitted into communion of the Back Street Independent Church in June 1803. Abraham married Hannah Ray in 1813. When their sons John and William were baptised in 1814 and 1816 at St Mary's Church, Abraham was described as a gardener living in Dead Street. Abraham's daughters, Eliza and Jessica, and his son Frederic Gallaher were baptised at Back Street Independent Church in 1819, 1823 and 1821. Abraham Fells was listed in the 1826 Directory as a Hitchin seedsman and nurseryman. In 1816 he was renting a garden at the top of Hitchin Hill, but in the mid 1820s this was being developed as Hitchin New Town. By 1838 Abraham was cultivating two small fields on the upper side of Storehouse Lane which belonged to the trustees of the British Schools. In 1841 Abraham, described as a nurseryman aged 49, was living in Back Street on the corner of Biggin Lane with his wife Hannah and three younger children.[320] One of Abraham's sons, William joined his father's business while his eldest son, John, established his own nursery. Abraham Fells & Son supplied plants to Mrs Delmé-Radcliffe of Hitchin Priory in the early 1840s. Abraham died in 1845. His son, John, supplied a long list of plants to William Wilshere at The Frythe in 1859. The Fells' nurseries flourished into the early twentieth century.[321]

Fells, John

Gardener. John Fells, then a gentleman's servant, was married in St Mary's Church, Hitchin, on 8 October 1780 to Elizabeth Picking. He was listed in a 1794 Directory as a grocer. However from January 1790 he was employed by Wilshere to take charge of his garden. He was also responsible for Wilshere's limited farming activities. The growth of the agricultural enterprise led to this responsibility being shared with Richard Smith from November 1803, then in late 1804 William Wren took over the farm. John Fells remained in charge of Wilshere's garden until July 1806 when Thomas Grant succeeded him. John Fells then assisted in the management of Wilshere's farm until the end of

---

[320] Hitchin parish registers [HALS: DP/53/1/4,6,15]; Back Street Meeting Church Book [HALS: NR8/1/1]; Back Street baptism register [TNA: RG4/743]; D Howlett & P Ellis, 'Hitchin Hill – a first "New Town"' in B Howlett & P Humphries ed *Discovering More About Hitchin* (Hitchin, 2018) p25; Hitchin rate assessment [HALS: DP/53/18/9]; 1841 census.

[321] Howlett, *Hitchin Priory Park,* pp56-59; V Taplin and A Stewart, *Two Minutes to the Station* (Hitchin, 2010) pp97-100; John Fells' bill [HALS: 61480/139].

September 1806. His son William was also employed in Wilshere's garden at this time.[322]

In 1801 John Fells lived in Bridge Street where he occupied cottages and barns in the Boot Yard. His household comprised 5 males and 5 females. He rented 3 roods of land next to Highbury Road which Wilshere had incorporated into Waby's Field by 1817. In his will in 1824 William Wilshere left £10 to John Fells 'an old servant'. John's son Abraham became a nurseryman in Hitchin (see above).[323]

Fordham, Edward King, and Fordham, John
John Fordham and his brother Edward King Fordham established the Royston Bank in 1806 in partnership with Richard Flower. Another brother, George Fordham of Ashwell, was a brewer.[324] Edward King Fordham of Royston died in 1848.

French, William
William French was a carpenter employed by Wilshere from 1809 onwards. He was paid 15s a week in 1822. Wilshere also paid him for harvest work in 1816, 1817, 1819 and 1820 and in 1824 to look after his fowls and pigs. William French, carpenter, and his wife Martha had a son Charles baptised at St Mary's, Hitchin, in 1812 and a daughter Martha baptised in 1817 when they were living in Biggin Lane in a cottage for which they paid rent to Wilshere. By the time their son, George, was baptised in 1824 they had moved to Back Street. In a codicil to his will dated 26 March 1824 Wilshere left 19 guineas to William French, his carpenter. In a later codicil dated 30 July 1824 he gave him an additional legacy of £20. Wilshere's brother Thomas continued to employ William French both as a carpenter and to care for his poultry. In 1838 William French was living in a cottage in Back Street owned by William Wilshere MP backing on to his farmyard. In 1841, aged about 50, he was still in Back Street, but now as part of the household of John Seymour, a carpenter, who had been his neighbour in 1838.[325]

---

[322] Hitchin parish register [HALS: DP/53/1/14]; cash books 1790-1806 [HALS: 61482-61497].
[323] Photocopy of 1801 census and map of Hitchin 1816 [NHM]; Isaac Sharples' will 1806 [TNA: PROB11/1450/233]: 1818 plan [HALS: DE/Ws/P16]; William Wilshere's will [TNA: PROB11/1692/97].
[324] Whitaker, *Brewers in Hertfordshire,* p41.
[325] Cash books [HALS: 61501-61506; 61525-61535]; Hitchin parish registers [HALS: DP/53/1/5-6]; William Wilshere's will [TNA: PROB11/1692/97]; cash book 1825 [HALS: 61512]; 1838 rate assessment [HALS: D/P53/18/9]; 1841 census.

BIOGRAPHICAL NOTES

Froy, John, and Froy, William

Hitchin labourers. John was employed by Wilshere from 1788 to 1800. In 1801 he lived in Bancroft in a household of one male and two females. In 1798 Wilshere paid Froy 2s 6d for mending the hedge of Pym's Close. In February 1814 Wilshere paid W and J Froy for faggoting wood from his garden for use in his house. Froy was employed for harvest work in 1819. William Froy, a labourer, lived in Tilehouse Street from 1801 to 1817, then in Boot Yard in Bridge Street by 1818.[326]

Gibbon, Charles Warren

Charles Warren Gibbon was employed in Wilshere's office from at least 1806 until May 1821. In 1820 his salary was £110 a year. In 1814 Wilshere paid for the education of his son Henry at the Reverend John Dyer's school in Tilehouse Street, which according to another pupil William Lucas, 'was considered a first-rate concern in those days, and many of the little gentry, clergy and principal farmers sent their sons to it'. Charles Gibbon lived in a house in Tilehouse Street rented from Martha Wortham's heirs. He died in 1826 leaving a wife Hannah, and children Henry Wortley Gibbon, Robert Gibbon and Ann Gibbon.[327]

Grant, James

James Grant was Samuel Whitbread's gardener at Southill, Bedfordshire, where Wilshere was a regular visitor. In his will made in 1810 Samuel Whitbread recommended that during the minority of his elder son, William Henry Whitbread, Southill House should be kept in hand and that the park and plantations and land around the house including the kitchen garden should be let, 'and that the Kittchen Garden and Gardener's House therein be offered to my present Gardner, James Grant, with a reasonable allowance for keeping up the Flower Garden and grass walks now under his care'. The plantations, nursery and wood ground were under the management of William Ireland. James Grant was to receive a legacy of £100. In a codicil to his will dated August 1813 Samuel Whitbread left James Grant an annuity of £75 for his natural life, then to his wife for her life, if she survived her husband. On Samuel Whitbread's death in 1815, his son William Henry was aged 20.[328]

---

[326] Cash books 1789-1800, 1814 [HALS: 61482 - 61492; 61506 p36]; photocopy of 1801 census [NHM]; St Mary Hitchin baptism register [HALS: DP/53/1/6]; 1838 rate assessment [HALS: DP/53/18/9].

[327] Cash books [HALS: 61499 p12; 61506 p26; 61531 pp18-19]; Bryant & Baker ed, *A Quaker Journal Vol I* p31; map of Hitchin 1816 [NHM]; agreement for sale 1825 [NHM]; C W Gibbon's will [TNA: PROB11/1710/369].

[328] Samuel Whitbread's will [TNA: PROB11/1578/124].

BIOGRAPHICAL NOTES

Grant, Thomas (*c*1777-1859)

Thomas Grant was born in Elgin in Scotland in about 1777. From August 1806 he was employed as Wilshere's gardener earning £35 a year. He left Wilshere's employment in July 1810. On 27 October 1810, now living in Fulham, an area noted for its nurseries, he returned to Hitchin to marry Esther Higgason, a widow. Her first husband, John Higgason, a gardener, was licensee of the Three Moorhens at the top of Hitchin Hill with its 1½ acres of land. John Higgason died in November 1808 leaving all his property to his wife Hester. Thomas Grant became landlord of the Three Moorhens and took over the cultivation of the land and another half acre of land between the Stevenage and London Roads, all of which were owned by the brewer, John Izzard Pryor of Baldock. In September 1814 Wilshere paid Grant £2 2s for superintending his garden for two weeks after the departure of James Bowie. Grant paid Wilshere £4 4s in July 1817 for pines [pineapples] supplied to Mr Smith. In the 1841 census Thomas Grant gave his occupation as a gardener. He was living with his wife Esther and a female servant at Hitchin Hill. Esther died in 1846. In the 1851 census Thomas Grant, a widower aged 73, was described as a gardener and publican. He died in 1859.[329]

Gray, James

In 1801 James Grey, gardener, lived in Back Street in Hitchin as head of a household of 3 males and 4 females. In 1791 he occupied a piece of land next to Highbury Road which was called Gray's Garden. A man named Gray was employed periodically by John Fells to work in Wilshere's garden 1803-1806, but it is not clear whether this was James Gray or John Gray (see below).[330] In 1816 James Gray owned and occupied a house in Back Street opposite Biggin Lane. He succeeded John Downing as Wilshere's gardener in August 1818. In November 1818 he recorded vines, peaches, nectarines and other trees and shrubs planted in pots in the List of Trees Seeds etc sown and planted in William Wilshere's Garden started by James Bowie. In January 1819 he also became farm bailiff. He was paid £52 a year and lived in a cottage belonging to Wilshere. He left Wilshere's employment in June 1820.

---

[329] Cash books [HALS: 61498 p101; 61502 p78]; St Mary Hitchin marriage register [HALS: DP/53/1/14]; Harvey, *Early Nurserymen* p128; photocopy of 1801 census [NHM]; John Higgason's will [TNA: PROB11/1490/105]; Victuallers recognizances 1806 [HALS: QS/VAR/434-493]; map of Hitchin 1816 [NHM]; cash books [HALS: 61506 p80; 61527 p123]: 1841 and 1851 censuses.

[330] Photocopy of 1801 census [NHM]; Hitchin manor court book 1791 [TNA: LR3/29 p382]; cash books [HALS: 61495 p90; 61497 pp8, 63, 81].

BIOGRAPHICAL NOTES

Administration of the estate of James Grey, yeoman of Hitchin, was granted in June 1834 to his daughter, Susan Gray, spinster, one of the next of kin of James Gray, labourer. In 1838 his cottage in Back Street was occupied by Isabella Gray. Susan Grey of Back Street, Hitchin, daughter of James Grey gardener, was married in 1839 in St Mary's Church, Hitchin, to William Honeybone, a shoemaker, who lived in Lyles Row, close to her father's cottage.[331]

Gray, John

John Gray, employed in husbandry, was living in Back Street in 1801 as head of a household of 2 males and 2 females. John Gray, gardener, married Ann Hooper at St Mary's Hitchin in 1809. Wilshere bought seed potatoes from him in 1810 and in February 1812 paid him for planting at Wymondley and for faggoting for the house. John Gray owned and occupied a house, barn and yard at the corner of Back Street and Hollow Lane. In 1816 he rented from Wilshere a cottage in Portmill Lane and a piece of land next to Highbury Road which was called Gray's Garden, previously occupied by James Gray in 1791. John Gray died in 1821 leaving £10 to his sister, Arabella Gray, and the rest of his estate to his wife Ann.[332]

Gray, Edward or George

A man named Gray was employed by Wilshere for the 1819 harvest and for hoeing turnips in 1823. He may have been Edward Gray, a labourer, who lived in Back Street in 1816 and 1818 or George Gray, also a labourer, who lived in Back Street in 1822.[333]

Griffin, William

William Griffin was gardener to Samuel Smith at Woodhall Park, Watton at Stone. He was renowned for his fruit growing, especially pineapples. He gave Wilshere 'as a token of gratitude and esteem' a copy of a paper he had read to the Horticultural Society 'On the Management of Grapes in Vineries' on 22 February 1820. Joseph Paxton at the age of 17 was employed as a gardener at Woodhall in 1818 where he was trained by William Griffin for three years. In

[331] Map of Hitchin 1816 [NHM]; See p193 above; cash books 1818-1820 [HALS: 61528-61530]; Grant of administration [HALS: H23/1064]: St Mary, Hitchin marriage register [HALS: DP/53/1/17].
[332] Photocopy of 1801 census [NHM]; St Mary Hitchin marriage register [HALS: DP/53/1/14]; cash book [HALS: 61504 pp30, 32]; map of Hitchin 1816 [NHM]; Hitchin manor court book 1791 [TNA: LR3/29 p382]; John Gray's will 1821 [HALS: 53HW67].
[333] St Mary Hitchin baptism register [HALS: DP/53/1/6].

Samuel Smith's will made in 1830 he left William Griffin £50 if he was in his service at the time of his death.[334]

Hailey, Thomas (c1782-1861)
Hitchin farmer. Thomas Hailey was born in Pirton in about 1782. In 1804 he married Elizabeth Wilshere, daughter of John Wilshere, William's brother. He took over the tenancy of Highover Farm near Walsworth after the death of John Pettengell in 1807. This was part of the Sykes estate managed by William Wilshere who bought Highover from Sir Francis Sykes in 1822. In his will Wilshere left £1,000 to his niece Elizabeth Hailey and £50 to Thomas Hailey. Hailey was still tenant of Highover Farm in 1851, but by 1841 his wife was living with her brother William in Bancroft. Thomas Hailey died in 1861 and Elizabeth died in 1863.[335]

Harwood, Robert (c1765-1843)
In 1806 Robert Harwood was tenant of Poynders End Farm in the parish of Ippollitts which belonged to Joseph Darton of Temple Dinsley. By 1839 Robert aged about 75 was living with his brother in law, Charles Nash, in Silver Street in Hitchin. He died in 1843.[336]

Harwood, Thomas
Thomas Harwood may have been a nephew of the Thomas Harwood who inherited Temple Dinsley at Preston in 1767, which on his death in 1786 he left to another nephew, Joseph Darton.[337]

Hawkins, John (1791-1877)
Hitchin lawyer. John Hawkins was the eldest of eight sons and one daughter of Henry Hawkins of Lawrence End, Kings Walden, by his second marriage to

[334] 'On the Management of Grapes' [HALS: 63744]; F Davison, *The Hidden Horticulturalists* (2019) pp23, 298; Samuel Smith's will 1834 [TNA: PROB11/1830/332].
[335] Wilshere Family Tree [HALS: ACC 6412]; B Howlett and J Walker, 'Highover and Farming in Walsworth' in Howlett & Humphries ed *Discovering More About Hitchin,* p112; cash book [HALS: 61505 p83]; 1841 and 1851 censuses; William Wilshere's will [TNA: PROB11/1692/97].
[336] Rance, *St Ippolyts,* p25; 1841 census; Charles Nash's will 1841 [TNA: PROB11/1958/154]: Robert Harwood's will [HALS: 68HW1].
[337] Thomas Harwood's will [TNA: PROB11/1151/44].

Ann Gurney. Henry Hawkins' first wife, by whom he had one son, Henry, was Charlotte Wortham, sister of William Wilshere's wife Martha. When Henry Hawkins made his will in 1803, he appointed Wilshere one of his executors and guardians of his children. Wilshere did not have to take on this responsibility in respect of John Hawkins, as Henry lived until 1813, but was no doubt instrumental in his being articled to Joseph Eade.[338]

John Hawkins married Susanna, daughter of Theed Pearse, clerk of the peace for Bedfordshire. By 1816 they were living near Wilshere in Bancroft in the house which became 101 Bancroft. In Wilshere's will he left John Hawkins £250, with 19 guineas to his wife, 19 guineas each to his mother and her five other children, and 19 guineas to his father in law Theed Pearse esquire.

When Joseph Eade died in 1828, John Hawkins succeeded him both in the legal practice and as steward of the Manor of Hitchin. He moved to the Grange House in Portmill Lane where he lived for the rest of his life, while his brother, Dr Frederick Hawkins, took over his former home in Bancroft. John Hawkins became a dominant personality in Hitchin, known as the 'King' of Hitchin. He is the subject of a biographical sketch by Reginald Hine in *Hitchin Worthies*. His son, Henry Hawkins, Baron Brampton (1817-1907) is commemorated in the *Oxford Dictionary of National Biography*.[339]

Hewes, Samuel (*c*1782-1862)
Samuel Hewes was born in about 1782 in Great Wymondley. He became a farmer owning land in Great Wymondley and Ippollitts. In 1811 he married Mary Adams who had inherited a house and maltings in Bancroft (later 36-40 Bancroft) from her father, Walter Adams, yeoman of Great Wymondley. Hewes sold Wilshere a horse in 1810. Wilshere lent him £100 and bought land from him in Great Wymondley for £925 in 1815. By 1838 Samuel Hewes was living with Mary and their daughters in one of his wife's houses in Bancroft. He was described as of independent means.[340]

---

[338] Wills of Martha Wortham and Henry Hawkins [TNA: PROB11/1413/200, PROB11/1541/65].

[339] Hine, *Hitchin Worthies,* pp201-208; map of Hitchin 1816 [NHM]; William Wilshere's will [TNA: PROB11/1692/97]; S Herbert, revised P R Glazebrook, Henry Hawkins, Baron Brampton, *ODNB*.

[340] Walter Adams's will [TNA: PROB11/1437.274]; Great Wymondley marriage register [HALS: DP/128/1/4]; cash books [HALS: 61502 p52; 61525 p44]; minutes of property [HALS: 61313 p80]; 1841 and 1851 censuses.

BIOGRAPHICAL NOTES

Hodgson, Henry (c1769-1858)

Hitchin nurseryman. Henry Hodgson was born in Staindrop, County Durham. In 1802 or 1803 he settled in Hitchin and established a nursery garden. In 1804 he accompanied John Fells to inspect Samuel Whitbread's greenhouse at Southill on William Wilshere's behalf. Wilshere made purchases from him for his garden in 1805 and 1806. In 1811 he assisted Wilshere with the inspection and identification of his fruit trees. By 1816 he occupied a garden of 2½ acres on a steeply sloping site above Park Street between Taylors Hill and Standhill Road as well as other land in the parish of Hitchin. Wilshere paid him £47 1s 9d for plants and seeds supplied from 1812 to 1816 as well as for expenditure on behalf of Emilius Delmé-Radcliffe of Hitchin Priory and George Musgrave esquire. Hodgson bought turnip seed from Wilshere in 1814 and 1815. A bill listing plants Hodgson supplied to Wilshere in 1820 including vegetables, roses, fruit trees, and conifer seedlings has been transcribed as part of Appendix Two. In 1823 Wilshere loaned him £50 with his title deeds as security.[341]

In 1831-1832 Henry Hodgson was able to supply Emilius Delmé-Radcliffe with an impressive range of trees, shrubs, roses, fruit trees and vegetable seeds as well as almost 16,000 quick thorns and 250 privets. In 1851 aged 80 and retired from the nursery business he was living with his wife Sarah in one of Skynners' almshouses in Bancroft. His son Henry, who was unmarried, had taken over his nursery, but seemed to be running it on a much smaller scale. Henry Hodgson died in 1858.[342]

Jeeves, John

A man named Jeeves was employed by Wilshere possibly for tree planting in 1812 and certainly for farm work between at least 1818 and 1824. There were several men called Jeeves living in Hitchin at this time, but it was probably John Jeeves, a labourer, who worked on Wilshere's farm. In 1813 John and his wife Edith were living in Tilehouse Street when their son John was baptised at St Mary's. Between 1820 and 1824 they were living in Back Street when three more children, Martha, Betsey and George were baptised.[343]

---

[341] 1851 census; cash books [HALS: 61496 p103; 61498 p12; 61499 p4]; map of Hitchin 1816 [NHM]; cash books [HALS: 61504 p58; 61525 p40; 61527 pp33-34]; See pp28, and 227-9; cash book [HALS: 61535 p50].

[342] Howlett, *Hitchin Priory Park,* pp50, 56-57; D Wheeler, *Hodgson & Hankin. A Fishy Tale of Old Hitchin* (Hitchin, 2005) pp24-26.

[343] Hitchin baptism register [HALS: DP/53/1/6].

BIOGRAPHICAL NOTES

Jeeves, Thomas (*c*1764-1824)
Hitchin seedsman. In 1801 he bought a house, workshops, out buildings, yard and garden on the west side of the Market Place next to the Red Lion. His wife Hannah died in 1805. Thomas Jeeves died intestate in 1824 leaving as his heir his daughter Mary. In 1825 she married William Bowyer who built a large house which he called Mount Pleasant on land formerly owned by Thomas Jeeves on the west side of Hitchin between Offley and Pirton Roads.[344]

Kempson or Kempston, John and James
John Kempson was a yeoman of Shillington, Bedfordshire, and Wilshere's tenant. Wilshere bought 14 lbs of Swedish turnip seed from John Kempson in July 1811. Kempson provided him with willow sets from Shillington in 1812 and apples in 1816. John Kempson had four sons. In his draft will drawn up in 1808 he left his real estate to his eldest son William and his farming stock to be divided between his four sons. However if his son James succeeded him as tenant of his farms and land, then he was to be able to buy out his brothers' shares of the farming stock. John Kempson died in 1815 or 1816. James Kempson succeeded him as Wilshere's tenant and sold Wilshere seed wheat in 1818.[345]

Kershaw, Jonas, John and Maria
In 1764 Mr Kershaw and his wife were admitted into the Back Street Independent Church as occasional communicants. In 1784 Jonas Kershaw, a stage coachman, leased for 12 years a large timber framed house at the corner of Back Street and Portmill Lane with the barns, stables and cottages adjoining. He became licensee of the Swan Inn in Hitchin Market Place in 1794 and ran a stage coach service from there to London in partnership with his brother, John, and then after John's death in 1792, with John's children. Jonas died in 1798. In 1804 his son George Kershaw, a victualler in Clerkenwell, leased the Swan Inn in Hitchin from Thomas Brown, and continued the stage coach service with Richard Kershaw who died in 1810. George bought the Swan in 1813.[346]
John Kershaw, yeoman, lived in Back Street in 1801. Wilshere paid John for oats and for dung and carting in 1802. John Kershaw paid him £6 for one year's

---

[344] Deeds to the Red Lion 1801-1851 [HALS: DE/Ha/B1967]; B Howlett, 'The Fields Beneath' in Howlett & Humphries ed, *Discovering More About Hitchin* p9.
[345] Cash books [HALS: 61503 p64; 61528 p100], draft will [HALS: DE/Ha/B63/102].
[346] Church book [HALS: NR8/1/1]; lease [HALS: 60534]; Hitchin Historical Society, *Hitchin Arcade Then and Now* (Hitchin, 2007) pp12-13; Hitchin parish register [HALS DP/53/1/4]; Jonas Kershaw's will [HALS: 78HW45]; deeds to The Swan Inn [HALS: DE/Ha/T103]; Richard Kershaw's will [TNA: PROB11/1510/119].

rent in February 1802. He died in 1804. Wilshere bought the premises on the corner of Back Street and Portmill Lane in 1807. Maria Kershaw lived in a house here in 1816. One of Wilshere's two farmyards was immediately behind Maria Kershaw's house next to Portmill Lane.[347]

Another John Kershaw continued the family's coaching business. In 1822 Wilshere paid John Kershaw £2 12 8d for carriage and in 1823 £2 11s for bringing fruit from London.[348]

Kimpton, Mary

Daughter of Elizabeth Kimpton, who was the sister of Richard Tristram, whose home and legal practice Wilshere had inherited. Mary Kimpton was a beneficiary of Richard Tristram's will receiving a share of the rents from his lands. She was Wilshere's tenant in the adjoining house to his in Bancroft. She lent £525 to Samuel Whitbread in 1791 for which she received payments of interest. In 1796 she was admitted into the communion of the Back Street Independent Church. In his will William Wilshere left her £10. She died in 1842.[349]

Kingsley, John (c1758-1839)

Farmer of Pirton. John Kingsley was the tenant of Middle Farm which was one of the two largest farms on the Delmé-Radcliffe estate in Pirton. John Kingsley contracted with Wilshere to feed his sheep on turnips growing in Wilshere's fields from at least 1805 onwards. He also rented a two acre meadow in Hitchin next to Ickleford Road. A sheep fair was held twice a year in Pirton in April and October.[350] Wilshere's cash book for April 1817 records purchases from John Kingsley of sainfoin seed and oats in 1815-1816 and six steers in November 1816 for £33 10s which he sold via Kingsley to S Kirkby on 1 April 1817 for £48. Wilshere sold six heifers to him in 1819.[351] John Kingsley died in 1839

---

[347] Photocopy of 1801 census [NHM]; cash book [HALS: 61494 pp51, 108]; Hitchin parish register [HALS: DP/53/1/5]; deed 1807 [HALS: 60536]; map of Hitchin 1816 [NHM].

[348] *Hitchin Arcade Then and Now* p13; cash books [HALS: 61531 p64; 61535 p30].

[349] Wills of Richard Tristram, Elizabeth Kimpton and William Wilshere [TNA: PROB11/1136/42, PROB11/1203/335, PROB11/1692/97]; map of Hitchin 1816 [NHM]; ledger A [HALS: 61542 p69, 116]; cash books [eg HALS: 61502 p32; 61525 p32; 61526 pp16, 58]; Church book [HALS: NR8/1/1].

[350] J Wayne ed *A foot on three daisies. Pirton's Story* (Pirton, 1987) pp17, 26, 29; cash book [HALS: 61500 p7]; Plot 1037 map of Hitchin 1816 [NHM].

[351] Cash books [HALS: 61527 pp50-51; 61529 p17].

aged 81. More information about him can be found on the Pirton Local History Group website at https://pirtonhistory.org.uk/.

Knight, Thomas Andrew (1759-1838)
Born into a wealthy land and mine owning family in Herefordshire, Thomas Knight became a horticulturist and plant physiologist. By 1809 he had moved to Downton Castle in Herefordshire owned by his older brother. In 1811 he became President of the Horticultural Society of which Wilshere was a member. Knight grew and exhibited specialist fruit and vegetables. He was the author of *Pomona Herefordiensis* as well as papers on the grafting of fruit trees. One of the new varieties he raised, the Downton pippin, was producing fruit in Wilshere's garden in 1823.[352]

Knightley, William
In a codicil to his will dated 26 March 1824 Wilshere left £15 to William Knightley, one of his garden men. William Knightley married Sarah Cannon in 1811. They were living in Churchyard when their son Joseph was baptised at St Mary's in 1813. William was described as a labourer. By the time their son George was baptised in 1815 they had moved to Hollow Lane. They had moved again to Back Street to a cottage owned by Wilshere when their daughter Sarah was baptised in 1817. William Knightley was tenant of one of the potato gardens in the Chalk Dell. On 19 July 1824 William married Ann Pollard at St Mary's Hitchin. He died in 1838. In 1841 Widow Knightley aged 42 was living in Back Street with six children aged between 4 and 18. In the 1851 census Ann Knightley was described as a charwoman and pauper living in Back Street with her youngest daughter, Charlotte, aged 13.[353]

Lautour, Caroline Young de (1793-1869)
Mrs Caroline Young de Lautour inherited Hexton Manor from her father, William Young who died in 1824. She married Joseph Andrew de Lautour in 1809.[354]

[352] J Brown, 'Knight, Thomas Andrew' *ODNB* (2022); [HALS: 61529 p118]; J C Loudon, *An Encyclopaedia of Gardening* (1835) pp823, 891. See pp48 and 163 above.
[353] William Wilshere's will [TNA: PROB11/1692/97]; Hitchin parish registers [HALS: DP/53/1/6, 14-15]; cash books [HALS: 61525 p7; 61512]; 1838 rate assessment [HALS: D/P53/18/9]; 1841 and 1851 censuses.
[354] A Ashley Cooper, *A Harvest of Hexton* (Hexton, 1986) pp151-152; William Young's will [TNA: PROB11/1686/256].

BIOGRAPHICAL NOTES

Lucas, Joseph (1771-1832)
Quaker brewer of Hitchin. His father, William Lucas (who died in 1819), inherited the brewery at the corner of Sun Street and Bridge Street and bought several public houses as well as acquiring land in Hitchin, which Joseph and his brother William inherited. They also owned maltings behind 11 High Street and at the Wratten behind Tilehouse Street. Joseph and his family lived at the brewery house in Sun Street. His daughter, Phebe Glaisyer, recorded her memories of her childhood.[355]

Lucas, William (1768-1846)
Quaker brewer and farmer of Hitchin. The elder brother of Joseph, he lived in Tilehouse Street. His unpublished diaries are held by North Hertfordshire Museum. Extracts from his eldest son's diary have been published. His second son Samuel was a noted amateur artist who exhibited at the Royal Academy.[356]

McIntosh or MacIntosh, Daniel
Daniel McIntosh took charge of Wilshere's garden in February 1811 and assisted with the inspection of his fruit trees in the August of that year. He may be the Daniel McIntosh, gardener, whose son Daniel was born in Elford in the parish of Bamburgh, Northumberland, in April 1788 and was baptised in the Scotch Presbyterian Church in Alnwick on 1 May 1788. On 12 November 1811 Daniel Macintosh of Hitchin, widower, married Elizabeth Pearson at Stevenage. He relinquished charge of Wilshere's garden on 8 December 1812.[357]
On 8 December 1819 Wilshere paid McIntosh £10 for work in his garden and in July 1820 he again took charge of Wilshere's garden in succession to James Gray and was paid £38 11s a year. He was responsible for entries in the garden journal from November 1821 to January 1822. He left Wilshere's employment in May 1823.[358]
At the beginning of March 1824 Daniel McIntosh was appointed gardener to the Countess de Grey at Wrest Park on the recommendation of Thomas Brown, Wrest Park steward (see above). A letter from Thomas Brown to the Countess dated 30 March 1824 stated that the new gardener, Daniel McIntosh, had been

---

[355] J Lucas, *Phebe's Hitchin Book* (Hitchin, 2009).
[356] Hine, *Hitchin Worthies* pp194-200, 218-240; William Lucas's diaries [NHM: 492]; G E Bryant & G P Baker ed, *A Quaker Journal Being the Diary and Reminiscences of William Lucas of Hitchin (1804-1861)* (1934).
[357] Cash books [HALS: 61503 p42; 61505 p12]; See pp21 and 28 above; Alnwick Scotch Church register of births and baptisms [TNA: REG4/2479]; Stevenage marriage register [HALS: DP/105/1/11].
[358] Cash books [HALS: 61529 p120; 61530 p26; 61535 p16].

installed, though the pleasure gardens had been put in charge of a foreman. An undated letter to the Countess from the wife of her nephew and heir, comments that she was 'delighted with Macintosh and all he has done. The laurels will be a great improvement; those planted last year have grown much, and less than may have been expected dead from drought'.[359]

When Daniel McIntosh made his will in 1831 he described himself as gardener at Wrest Park. He left everything to his wife, Jane, who had been born in Allendale, Northumberland in about 1776. A Daniel McIntosh had married Jane Ward on 27 December 1819 at St Andrew's Church, Holborn. He died in 1837. His widow Jane continued to live in Silsoe as an annuitant. She was still alive in 1861 aged 84.[360]

Marshall, John

Hitchin brewer and liquor merchant. John Marshall was clerk to John Crabb the elder. After Crabb's death in 1811 Marshall took on the superintendence of his brewery in Sun Street during the minorities of his sons, John (who died in 1813) and Henry. He then became Henry Crabb's partner in the brewery. After Henry Crabb's death in 1830, Joseph Margetts Pierson became John Marshall's partner in the brewery. John Marshall died in 1836.[361]

Maughan or Maugham, John

Land surveyor of Luton, Bedfordshire 1798-1802, 1810-1820, of Hitchin 1810, of Oswestry, Shropshire 1821-c1830, and of Barnt Green, Worcestershire 1831-1846. John Maughan was involved in the enclosure of Offley and Kings Walden. Wilshere's ledger D records that John Maughan had £3 credit from Colonel Wishaw for 2,000 larches and that Michael Coak was charged £12 19s 11d for hedges and trees under the Kings Walden inclosure in 1812-1813. In 1821 John Maughan gave evidence to the Parliamentary Committee on the Depressed State of Agriculture. He died in 1846.[362]

---

[359] Correspondence to Countess de Grey [BLARS: L30/11/40/31, L30/11/236/3].

[360] Daniel McIntosh's will [TNA: PROB11/1875/53]; St Andrew Holborn marriage register [LMA: P82/AND/A/005/MS06672/003]; 1851 and 1861 censuses.

[361] Whitaker, *Brewers in Hertfordshire,* pp142-143.

[362] S Bendall, *Dictionary of Land Surveyors and Local Mapmakers of Great Britain and Ireland 1530-1850* (2nd edition, 1997) p347; Survey of the Parish of Kings Walden 1802 [HALS: DE/X783/E2]; Ledger D [HALS: 61543 p98]; John Maughan's will [TNA: PROB11/2049/37].

BIOGRAPHICAL NOTES

Mills, Mrs Sarah (1743-1819)

Sarah Mills was the daughter of James Paitfield, a City of London merchant. Her mother came from Dunton, near Biggleswade. In 1769 she married John Mills, a London sugar merchant and owner of a plantation in Nevis. By 1778 she had moved to Hitchin with her young family. At the time of his death in Grenada in 1784 John Mills appears to have been in serious financial difficulties with a commission in bankruptcy against him. When his widow, Sarah, made her will in 1812 she explained 'What I have to give has arisen out of the savings I have been able to make from my narrow income, the dwelling house I inhabit in Tylehouse Street I purchased with my own money'. However she was still receiving an income from the plantation in Nevis, and by 1796, her eldest son, John Colhoun Mills, had gone out to Nevis to manage the family interests there. He was joined by his brother, Paitfield. John Colhoun Mills returned home to Hitchin for a visit in 1803 when he appears to have brought his mother a very young black servant, Jeanette Eve, 'a Negress Aged 11 Years', who was baptised at St Mary's Church on 14 October 1803. Sarah Mills wrote in her will dated 1812 'to my negro Girico Jennette I give £20 as a token of my regard for her and I hope she will remain with my daughter and let her keep her money'. Unfortunately nothing more is known about Jeanette.

John Colhoun Mills made at least one more visit to Hitchin in 1813, but he had married a member of a Nevis planter family, Anne Maynard, and he continued to live in Nevis until his death in 1828 in financial difficulties. His younger brother, Paitfield, returned to settle in England in about 1813 and rented Roxley House in the parish of Willian (now the site of Roxley Court). In 1814 Sarah Mills sold her house in Hitchin and went to live with Paitfield at Roxley House. When she died in 1819, she was buried in Hitchin with her 'dear and highly valued daughter Elizabeth', who had died in 1811.

Her younger daughter, Sarah Pittman Mills, returned to Hitchin to live in a smaller house in Tilehouse Street. Her financial situation was improved by legacies not only from her mother, but from William Wilshere. On his death in 1824 he had left her 100 guineas and during her life, the dividends of £1,250 new 4% bank annuities. He also bequeathed to her £300 of which £250 was in trust for the education of his godson, William Wilshere Mills, son of John Colhoun Mills, and the other £50 was in trust for his goddaughter, Hester, daughter of Thomas Mills. When Sarah died in 1827, her bequests included a picture of William Wilshere. Records of the Mills' family plantation and enslaved Africans are on display in the Sugar and Slavery Gallery in the Museum in Docklands in London.[363]

Mowbray, William

Hitchin gardener, who in 1801 lived in Bucklersbury in Hitchin. Ann and William, children of William and Mary Mowbray, were baptised at Back Street Independent Church in 1790 and 1791. Hannah, Sarah, Susanna and Grace, daughters of William and Susanna Mowbray, were baptised at Back Street in 1802, 1803, 1805 and 1807. Their sons, John, Robert, Thomas and Andrew were baptised in 1801, 1808, 1810 and 1812. In 1791 William Mowbray bought two pieces of land on opposite sides of Highbury Road, about 2 acres in total, the larger piece of which was described as a garden. In 1803 he mortgaged them to William Wilshere and in 1805 he sold them to Wilshere. In 1816 he was renting from Isaac Duncalfe a garden just over an acre in extent between Dead Street and Storehouse Lane just north of the British Schools. By 1838 this garden was occupied by John Warren who had taken over Isaac Duncalfe's stone mason's yard.[364]

In April 1806 Wilshere paid Mowbray £2 16s 6d for pine apple plants purchased from W Ironside. In 1812 Wilshere paid him £2 11s 8d for seeds for his garden. In February 1817 Wilshere paid William Mowbray £2 8s for planting on his Wymondley estate.[365]

Murray, Robert

Robert Murray owned an 'important tree nursery' in Hertford from 1807 to 1823. Mr Murray sold John Carrington of Bramfield six trees in 1810.[366] He sold Wilshere plants on several occasions between 1808 and 1821 when Wilshere paid £15 12s 6d 'principally for American plants'. Bills for plants sold by Murray to Wilshere in 1813-1814, including many headed cabbages, mushroom spawn and rhododendron ponticum, have been transcribed in Appendix Two. Wilshere sold Murray mangel wurzel seed which partly covered the costs of his plants. Auctions of Robert Murray's nursery stock were advertised in the *County Chronicle* for 31 October 1820 and 14 January 1823. On 8 December 1827 a

---

[363] B Howlett, 'Hitchin, Sugar and Slavery', *Hitchin Historical Society Journal* Vol 18 no 2 Oct 2008.
[364] Photocopy of 1801 census [NHM]; Back Street Independent Church register of baptisms [TNA: REG4/743]; Hitchin Manor court books 1785-1824 [TNA: LR3/29, CRES5/37]; map of Hitchin 1816 [NHM]; 1838 rate assessment [HALS: D/P53/18/9].
[365] Cash books [HALS: 61498 p73; 61504 p8; 61527 p20).
[366] J Harvey, *Early Nurserymen*, p98; S Flood, *John Carrington, Farmer of Bramfield His Diary Vol 2 1805-1810* (Hertford, 2022) p223.

notice to the creditors of the late Robert Murray nurseryman appeared in the *Hertfordshire Mercury.*[367]

Musgrave, George

George Musgrave inherited an estate including property in Biggleswade and the manors of Shillington Bury and Apsley Bury in 1806 from his brother, Joseph Musgrave of St George Hanover Square. William Wilshere managed his estate. In 1822 Wilshere bought Furzen Hall Farm, Biggleswade, from George Musgrave.[368]

Nash, Charles

There were two men called Charles Nash farming near Hitchin. One Charles Nash was the son of George and Mary Nash of Wellbury. When he made his will he described himself as yeoman of Hitchin. He was then living in Silver Street in Hitchin with his brother in law, Robert Harwood. He died in 1842 aged 86.[369]

The eldest brother of James Dupin Nash (see below) was also called Charles Nash. In 1822 William Wilshere entered into an agreement to let Furzen Hall Farm at Biggleswade to Mr Charles Nash for 8 years with his consent to underlet 50 acres each year for gardening. Charles Nash bought a water mill in Biggleswade from George Cooper. Charles Nash, gentleman of Biggleswade, died in 1836.[370]

Nash, James Dupin

Hitchin miller. He was one of the three sons of Daniel Nash of Hitchin who owned two malthouses. In his will proved in 1810 Daniel Nash left his friend, William Wilshere, a mourning ring. James Dupin Nash bought Purwell Mill on the parish boundary with Great Wymondley in 1804. He also bought a windmill at Walsworth. In addition he continued to use the maltings behind his mother's house on the corner of Cock Street and Pound Lane until her death in 1825 or

---

[367] Cash books [HALS: 61500 p82; 61503 p79; 61504 p59; 61506 p76; 61528 p60; 61531 p80]; bill [HALS: 61479/31]. See pp29, 32-3, 49, 93, 225-6 above.

[368] *VCH* Bedfordshire Vol 2 pp293-299; Joseph Musgrave's will [TNA: PROB11/1463/251]; Ledger D [HALS: 61543 p26]; minutes of property [HALS: 61613 p94].

[369] Hertfordshire Family History Society, *Hertfordshire Monumental Inscriptions Hitchin The Parish Church of St Mary* p73; Charles Nash's will 1841 [TNA: PROB11/1958/154]; Robert Harwood's will [HALS: 68HW1].

[370] Wills of Daniel Nash, William Wilshere and Charles Nash [TNA: PROB11/1511/496, PROB11/1692/97, PROB11/1859/264].

1826. In March 1816 Wilshere paid James Dupin Nash for malt supplied in 1814 as well as for grinding wheat, barley and beans. Nash died in 1829 leaving a wife, Elizabeth, and two children, William Minior Nash and Esther Elizabeth Nash. William Minior Nash died in 1851 aged 38. Esther Elizabeth Nash married John Gurney Hawkins, son of John Hawkins, and died in 1877 aged 61.[371]

Niblock, Joseph White (1786-1842)
The Revd Joseph White Niblock was born in Liverpool in 1786, the son of a linen draper, who after being made bankrupt in 1791 moved to Bristol. Despite being christened in an Independent chapel, Joseph Niblock graduated from Oxford in 1808 and was ordained deacon in 1811 and priest in 1812. In 1817 he became curate of Hitchin where he was also employed in the Registry of the Archdeaconry of Huntingdon, William Wilshere being Deputy Registrar. Joseph Niblock was highly esteemed as a classics scholar. In 1819 he was appointed master of the Hitchin Free School where he taught private pupils including Wilshere's nephew, Charles Willes Wilshere. He chaired a committee which established a Girls School at the British Schools in 1819 which Wilshere had founded in 1810. In 1826 he became curate of Newnham. He left Hitchin in 1830 after a dispute with the trustees of the Free School who insisted that Latin and Greek should only be taught as an extra if required.[372]

Olney, Joshua
A man named Olney was employed on Wilshere's farm in 1819 and 1820. Joshua Olney lived in one of Wilshere's houses in Portmill Lane or Back Street. In January 1820 Wilshere recorded Joshua Olney had paid him 1s 6d for 52 weeks through James Gray, and in June 1820 another 24 weeks rent, but he owed £3 18s for a year's arrears 1817-1818.[373]

---

[371] Wills of Daniel Nash and James Dupin Nash [TNA: PROB11/1511/496, PROB11/1762/14]; Farris, *The Wymondleys* p19; map of Hitchin 1816 [NHM]; cash book [HALS: 61526 p26]; rate assessments 1825-1827 [HALS: D/P53/11/7]; *Hertfordshire Monumental Inscriptions Hitchin The Parish Church of St Mary* pp71, 73.
[372] N Wilson, 'John Clare's Contemporaries: The Anonymous Versifier', *John Clare Society Journal 40 July 2021* pp35-46; https://theclergydatabase.org.uk/jsp/search/index.jsp; R L Hine, *History of Hitchin Grammar School* (Hitchin, 1931, revised 1951) pp35-46.
[373] Cash books [HALS: 61529 p57; 61530 p17].

BIOGRAPHICAL NOTES

Parsons, Joseph
The Revd Joseph Parsons was ordained deacon in 1784 and priest in 1785. According to the Clergy Database he served as Vicar of Shopland in Essex from 1799 to 1803. However the 1801 census records him as living in Churchyard in Hitchin. In November 1806 he became curate of Hitchin and Rector of Caldecote, an almost deserted Hertfordshire parish. In March 1808 he was instituted Rector of Holwell, then in Bedfordshire, the advowson of which belonged to Emilius Delmé-Radcliffe of Hitchin Priory. In September 1815 he was appointed Prebendary of Peterborough Cathedral retaining the Rectory of Holwell. The grateful inhabitants of Hitchin presented him with a tea tray worth £84 'In testimony of his able & zealous services, as a minister & a magistrate, to the Parish of Hitchin'. Joseph Parsons was one of William Wilshere's executors and trustees. On his death in February 1829 he bequeathed his real estate in the Counties of Hertford, Northampton and Huntingdon to his son, the Revd Henry Parsons of Godmanchester.[374]

Paternoster, Samuel
Samuel Paternoster was listed in a 1794 Directory as a Hitchin fruiterer and in the 1801 census as a fishmonger living in Bucklersbury. In 1795 Elizabeth Simpson left her Hitchin property to William Wilshere senior who exchanged with his son William two closes of 5½ acres in the tenure of Samuel Paternoster east of Walsworth Road. Wilshere referred to one of these closes as 'Paternoster's garden.'[375]

Pierson, Joseph Margetts (c1722-1809)
Joseph Margetts Pierson, originally a grocer, was one of Wilshere's partners in the Hitchin and Hertfordshire Bank which they founded in 1789 and in the purchase of the lease of Hitchin Rectory in 1790. Pierson married twice. Both wives, Ann Reading and Mary Squire, brought him property in Hitchin. He died in 1809 aged 87. His only surviving child was his son by his second marriage, also called Joseph Margetts Pierson.[376]

---

[374] https://theclergydatabase.org.uk/jsp/search/index.jsp; photocopy of 1801 census [NHM]: Wilshere's Common Place book [NHM: 1216 p85]; William Wilshere's will [TNA: PROB11/1692/97]; Joseph Parsons' will [TNA: PROB11/1752/23].
[375] Photocopy of 1801 census [NHM]; Hitchin manor court book [TNA: LR3/29 p471].
[376] Minutes of property [HALS: 61613 pp28, 30]; *Hertfordshire Monumental Inscriptions Hitchin The Parish Church of St Mary* p52.

BIOGRAPHICAL NOTES

Pierson, Joseph Margetts (1783-1842)

He inherited his father's share in the Hitchin bank and the lease of Hitchin Rectory. Wilshere bought Walsworth Way Close (also known as Rail Piece or Stone Piece) from him in 1810. In 1816 Joseph Margetts Pierson was living in Woodlands in Bancroft rented from Joseph Sharples. In 1823 he bought the substantial and impressive Lewesford House in Tilehouse Street, formerly owned by the Revd Lynch Salusbury and moved there with his large family. After Henry Crabb's death in 1830 Joseph Margetts Pierson acquired his share in the Sun Street brewery in partnership with John Marshall. Joseph Margetts Pierson's speculative investment in an alkali works in Brussels ended in his bankruptcy and that of his bank and brewery in 1841. He died suddenly the following year.[377]

Pym, Wollaston

The Revd Wollaston Pym was ordained deacon in 1785 and priest in 1786 when he became Rector of Radwell near Hitchin, holding also from 1792 to 1803 the Vicarage of Willian. In 1787 he inherited almost 200 acres of land in Hitchin, from his cousin, Elizabeth Carter of Charlton Abbots, Gloucestershire, who had inherited it from her grandfather, Simon Lucas of Hitchin. Wilshere rented from Pym 18 acres 1 rood of land known as Great Benslow Hill for which in 1815 Wilshere paid him £31 10s for a year's rent and £1 10s 3d for 121 loads of gravel for the paths in Wimbush Field. Wollaston Pym resigned his living in 1834 and retired to London. On his death in 1846 his Hitchin estates were inherited by his nephew, Francis Pym of Hazells Hall, Sandy, Bedfordshire, who sold them in 1852.[378]

Ransom, John (1749-1828)

Hitchin farmer, miller and mealman, a Quaker, who lived in the red brick house next door to Wilshere (later 107-109 Bancroft). His father, Joseph Ransom who

---

[377] Hitchin manor court book [TNA: CRES5/37 p372]; map of Hitchin 1816 [NHM]; Mary Squire's will [TNA: PROB11/1054/186]; Abstract of title and sale particulars for Lewesford House [HALS: DE/Sb/T46]; Whitaker, *Brewers in Hertfordshire,* p143; A M Foster and L M Munby, *Market Town* (Hitchin, 1987) pp172-175; *Hertfordshire Monumental Inscriptions Hitchin The Parish Church of St Mary* p51.
[378] https://theclergydatabase.org.uk/jsp/persons/index.jsp; *Hertfordshire Monumental Inscriptions Hitchin The Parish Church of St Mary* p51; cash book [HALS: 61525 p74]; wills of Elizabeth Carter and Wollaston Pym [TNA: PROB11/1152/193, PROB11/2033/115]; N Sayany, 'Gaping Hills Lane: a foot in town and country' in Howlett & Humphries ed *Discovering More About Hitchin* p17; sale particulars 1852 [NHM: 7752/7].

died in 1779, had acquired a lease of Port Mill on the River Hiz next to Portmill Lane and Shotling Mill (usually called Burnt Mill) at the confluence of the Rivers Hiz and Purwell. Joseph Ransom also owned a windmill which he moved from the top of Hitchin Hill near The Three Moor Hens to the top of Rawlings Hill (now known as Windmill Hill). When the Crown Estates sold the two water mills in 1814, John Ransom bought Shotling Mill. His sons, John and Joshua, pulled down the old mill and built a new one which they called Grove Mill. Though John Ransom did not buy Port Mill, he retained a yard, barn, outbuildings and cottages in Portmill Lane. By 1816 William Wilshere had bought the windmill at the top of Rawlings Hill.[379]

John Ransom was described by his fellow Quaker William Lucas as 'a portly man with large wig & dark brown top-boots, usually seen on horse-back & was in that position said to resemble the old king'. He died in 1828 aged 79. His grandson, William Ransom, founded a pharmaceutical company in premises (later 105 Bancroft) which John Ransom had bought next door to his home.[380]

Robinson, James (c1780-1849)

James Robinson was employed by Wilshere as his 'farming man' in October 1809. He was paid 12s a week (£30 4s a year) plus extra at harvest and was to live in the farm cottage and 'with his wife to milk and take care of the cows, pigs & poultry'. The 'farm cottage' was probably one of the houses owned by Wilshere in Back Street on the corner of Portmill Lane or on the other side of the road next to his farmyard there. He and his wife Elizabeth had three children, William, John and Elizabeth, baptised at St Mary's Church between 1810 and 1812. James was described in the parish register as a bailiff. Then tragedy struck the family. Their daughter Elizabeth died in August 1813 aged one year. The following January, their baby son James, died, followed less than three months later by his mother. Like many widowed fathers with young children, James remarried. His second wife was Amelia Smith, a spinster, whom he married at St Mary's Hitchin on 19 April 1815. Surprisingly he signed the register with his mark, though his bride signed her name.

A new wife seems to have led to a new occupation. When their son, George Smith Robinson, was baptised on 19 January 1817, James Robinson was

[379] Ransom family tree [NHM: Lawson Thompson Scrapbooks Vol 2A p73]; V Campion, *Joseph Ransom's Naturalist's Notebook 1804-1816 The Nature Notes of a Hitchin Quaker* (Hitchin, 2004) pp6-7; Joseph Ransom's will [TNA: PROB11/1050/166]; map of Hitchin 1816 [NHM]; cash book [HALS: 61526 pp47-48].
[380] Campion, *Joseph Ransom's Naturalist's Notebook,* pp6, 9; John Ransom's will [TNA: PROB11/1742/368].

described as a shopkeeper. In September 1818 he ceased to be Wilshere's bailiff, though he was paid for harvest work in 1820. In October 1818 the furniture in the bailiff's house was valued at £10 after its vacation by James Robinson. Rate assessments show that by 1816 James occupied a house further along Back Street (later 100 Queen Street, now demolished) which was not owned by Wilshere. This was a grocer's shop and James Robinson was listed in a Directory of 1826 as a grocer. In 1836 Robinson, 'a respectable man', was engaged by Hitchin Board of Guardians at 10s a week to superintend the paupers digging the foundations for the new union workhouse at Chalkdell. In 1841, aged about 60 and a grocer, he was living in Back Street with George Robinson aged 24 and Amelia Robinson aged 58. He died in 1849.[381]

Rose, Robert
Robert Rose was a cooper who occupied a house and premises in the corner of Bancroft and Pound Lane (now Brand Street) which he later bought from George Beaver. A boundary stone with his initials and the date 1829 can still be seen in the rear wall. From 1819 Wilshere regularly employed Rose to brew beer for his household and at harvest time on his farm. In his will Wilshere bequeathed Robert Rose £10. He died in 1843 leaving his property to his wife Mary and his three sons.[382]

Silsby, William
Agricultural labourer. In November 1818 Wilshere paid John Cooper 14s for a pair of shoes for William Silsby to be reclaimed from his wages. Silsby was employed by William Wilshere to assist with the harvest in 1820 and thrashing in 1824 and by Thomas Wilshere to cleave wood in 1828. William Silsby lived in Hollow Lane with his wife Elizabeth. Their daughter Harriet was baptised at St Mary's in 1815 followed by two more daughters, Hannah in 1820 and Fanny in 1823.[383]

---

[381] See pp6, 106-7, 113, 135 above; Hitchin parish registers [HALS: DP/53/1/5-6, 15, 27]; map of Hitchin 1816 [NHM]; rate assessment 1838 [HALS: DP/53/18/9]; Foster, *Market Town*, p26; 1841 census.

[382] Robert Rose's will [TNA: PROB11/1984/27]; rate assessment 1838 [HALS: DP/53/18/9]; cash books [HALS: 61529 p44; 61530 p10; 61532 p64]; William Wilshere's will [TNA: PROB11/1692/97].

[383] Cash books [HALS: 61528 p80; 61512 p88]; Hitchin baptism register [HALS: DP53/1/6].

BIOGRAPHICAL NOTES

Smith, Samuel
Hitchin maltster who bought barley from William Wilshere and sold him malt dust. He was the tenant of a maltings owned by Wilshere next door to his house in Bancroft. In 1826 he became a trustee of the British Schools founded by Wilshere.[384]

Thorpe, Richard
Richard Thorpe was a Hitchin butcher and the grandson of Elizabeth Kimpton, the sister of Richard Tristram, who left him £150. John Kimpton Thorpe and Thomas Pattenden Thorpe, sons of Richard and Ann Thorpe, were baptised in the Back Street Independent Church in 1805 and 1810. Richard Thorpe owned Thorpe's Yard in Back Street. In 1818 he bought a calf from Wilshere for £4. In his will William Wilshere left him £10.[385]

Tuffnell, ? James
Tuffnell was employed on Wilshere's farm in 1824. Wilshere's brother, Thomas, paid him for thrashing in January 1825. James Tuffnell married Charlotte Pestell at St Mary's Hitchin on 19 June 1824. Sarah, daughter of James and Charlotte Tuffnell of Walsworth, was born in August 1824 and baptised at Back Street Independent Church on 19 September 1824. Another daughter, Susanna, was baptised in 1828.[386]

Whitbread, Samuel (1764-1815)
Samuel Whitbread was probably a distant cousin of William Wilshere, whose great grandmother, Dorothy, was the daughter of William Whitbread of Cardington, Bedfordshire. Samuel Whitbread's father, who established the Chiswell Street Brewery, rented a maltings in Hitchin for a few years from 1748 and continued to purchase malt from Hitchin. He bought an estate at Bedwell in Essendon and his son and his family lived nearby at Woolmers until they moved to Southill in Bedfordshire in about 1800. By 1789 Wilshere was lending money to Samuel Whitbread junior. He became Samuel Whitbread's legal and business advisor and friend.[387]

---

[384] Map of Hitchin 1816 [NHM]; British Schools Museum, *Educating Our Own,* p29.
[385] Richard Tristram's will [TNA: PROB11/1136/42]; Back Street Independent Meeting register of baptisms [TNA: RG4/743]; map of Hitchin 1816 [NHM]; cash book [HALS: 61528 p57]; William Wilshere's will [TNA: PROB11/1692/97].
[386] Cash book [HALS: 61512 p2]; Hitchin marriage register [HALS: DP/53/1/15]; Back Street Independent Meeting register of baptisms [TNA: RG4/743].
[387] Wilshere family tree [HALS: Acc 6412]; Mathias, *Brewing Industry in England 1700-1830* p467; Ledger A [HALS: 61542 p69].

Samuel Whitbread senior died in 1796 leaving the brewery to his only son. Samuel junior took two of his clerks and Timothy Brown, a banker, into partnership. In 1801 William Wilshere agreed to take £33,333 6s 8d part of Samuel Whitbread's share in the stock and trade of the Chiswell Street brewery for which he had paid him £26,666 13 4d in stages by February 1803. The remaining £6,666 13 4d was charged to him from the profits of the trade over the two subsequent years.[388]

Samuel Whitbread proposed to Parliament a far reaching scheme for the reform of the Poor Laws in 1807. Whitbread's biographer wrote, 'Much of the foundation of facts, on which the speech rested, was prepared by his friend and neighbour William Wilshere'. His proposal included the establishment of a school in every parish.[389]

In April 1815 Whitbread was seized with anxiety about sending his sons back to the University of Cambridge after the Easter vacation because he believed that the town was unhealthy. Wilshere sent Dr Oswald Foster of Hitchin to Cambridge to investigate. Wilshere dined with Samuel and Lady Elizabeth Whitbread the evening before Whitbread's suicide on 6 July 1815. With Charles Grey, Lady Elizabeth's brother, he went through Whitbead's correspondence and destroyed much of it. Although Samuel Whitbread had appointed Wilshere one of his executors, he and his fellow executor, Robert Sangster, partner and clerk in the brewery, renounced the administration of his estate. With the reordering of the partnership of the brewery he became a formal partner with a share of £35,000. He sold £10,000 of this to Whitbread's younger son, Samuel Charles, in 1819. Whitbread's elder son, William Henry, owed him an additional £30,000.[390] In his will William Wilshere directed that the mortgage debts due to him from William Henry Whitbread should not be demanded for five years and the same might remain as much longer as Mr Whitbread should choose and his executors find convenient. If none of Wilshere's nephews or nieces had any legitimate descendants, the ultimate heir to his estates would be 'my highly esteemed cousin Elizabeth the wife of the Honourable William Waldegrave her heirs and assigns'. She was the elder daughter of Samuel Whitbread.[391]

---

[388] R Fulford, *Samuel Whitbread 1764-1815. A Study in Opposition* (1967) pp94-96; minutes of property [HALS: 61613 p54].

[389] Fulford, *Samuel Whitbread,* pp176-180.

[390] Fulford, *Samuel Whitbread* ppx, 304-306; cash book [HALS: 61525 p112]; Samuel Whitbread's will [TNA: PROB11/1578/124]; Mathias, *The Brewing Industry,* pp312, 441; minutes of property [HALS: 61613].

[391] William Wilshere's will [TNA: PROB11/1692/97].

BIOGRAPHICAL NOTES

Willding, John (1798-1864)
Land surveyor. John Willding was born in Kettering, Northamptonshire in 1798, the son of William Willding, a draper. The family moved to Hitchin where William Willding is listed in a directory dated 1826 as a straw hat maker in Bucklersbury. By October 1814 John Willding was employed in William Wilshere's office. In June 1820 he took over in addition the management of Wilshere's farming activities. In Wilshere's will he received a bequest of £50. By 1838 John Willding was living in a newly built semi-detached house in Tilehouse Street (now part of no 28). By 1844 he had bought his father's former house and shop in Bucklersbury where his name and the date 1845 can still be seen on the wall separating nos 8 & 9. In 1851, now married and described as a land surveyor, John Willding was living in Stevenage. He died at Albert Villa, Stevenage in 1864.[392]

Willes, Sir Francis (c1735-1827)
Sir Francis Willes was a government code breaker, who in 1783 bought 200 acres of arable land in Hitchin from Thomas Plumer Byde of Ware Park, which made him the second largest landowner in Hitchin (excluding Walsworth). He purchased additional land in Hitchin and the neighbouring parish of Ippollitts where he built himself a house called St Ibbs Bush. In 1807 he acquired the Manor of Biggleswade. His code breaking activities meant much of his time was spent in London or at his house in Hampstead. His property in the Hitchin area was managed by William Wilshere's father then by his brother, Thomas. Most of it was tenanted by Thomas Wilshere, John Wilshere and members of the Ransom family. In 1808 Sir Francis Willis sold William Wilshere 12½ acres bordering Walsworth Road which had been let to John Wilshere in exchange for 22½ acres of land in the parish of Holwell, Bedfordshire.[393]

Wilshere, Ann (1766-1843)
William Wilshere's sister. She and her sister Mary lived in a house in Bancroft (later 30 Bancroft) owned by their brother Thomas with an additional garden owned by their brother William. William bequeathed his sisters Ann and Mary

---

[392] Kettering baptism register; cash books [HALS: 61525 p4; 61530 p20]; William Wilshere's will [TNA: PROB11/1692/97]; rate assessment 1838 [HALS: DP/53/18/9]; Hitchin tithe map and apportionment 1841-1844 [HALS: DSA4/53/1-2]; 1851 and 1861 censuses.

[393] B Howlett, 'Sir Francis Willis and Francis Lovell – from code breaker to landowner' in Howlett & Humphries, ed *Discovering More About Hitchin*, pp116-119; sale particulars for Thomas Plumer Byde's estate 1783, Lovell Papers [Wiltshire & Swindon Archives: 161/57].

articles of furniture and plate to the value of £200, to each of them £1,000 in money, and during their joint lives an annuity of £200 with an annuity of £150 to the survivor.[394]

Wilshere, John (1755-1836)

William Wilshere's brother. In 1780 he bought a house and malting in the town centre (later known as Church House or 19 Churchyard) previously rented by his father where he made his home. John Wilshere became a maltster in partnership with his father and brother and also managed a farm in partnership with his brother. In July 1787 all joint accounts with his brother were closed.[395] An 1826 directory listed John Wilshere as a maltster, corn and seed merchant, coal merchant and wine merchant. He rented a farm in Walsworth from Sir Francis Sykes which he purchased in 1822. The front of the house was rebuilt as a gentleman's residence. This became Walsworth House which is now part of North Hertfordshire College.[396]

John Wilshere became estranged from both his father and his brother William. William Lucas, the Quaker brewer, wrote in his dairy in 1838:

> 'Old John Wilshere was perhaps the most singular and original character in our Town. Early in life a spendthrift, out of spite to his Father and Brother Wm. he turned over a new leaf and became extremely penurious. His temper was most violent and such was his tenacity of resentment that he attended and publicly rejoiced both at his Father's and Brother's funeral. At the latter I saw him dressed as usual in rags on his old pony and attended by all his spaniels and greyhounds, watching for the coffin to be brought out and endeavouring, though in vain, to conceal by bitter jests, the turbulent conflict of his own feelings. At his Father's funeral he gave the death halloo. When not irritated he appeared the mildest of men and his gentle silver voice and venerable countenance contrasted strangely with the roughness of his costume. Before his death a long illness appeared to have brought about a change of heart and his end was peace. He acquired large property and was an honourable man in business.'[397]

---

[394] Wilshere family tree [HALS: Acc 6412]; map of Hitchin 1816 [NHM]; wills of Thomas Wilshere and William Wilshere [TNA: PROB11/1807/146, PROB11/1692/97].
[395] Hitchin manor court book [TNA: LR3/29 p56]; Ledger A [HALS: 61542 pp31-34].
[396] Map of Hitchin 1816 [NHM]; John Wilshere's will [TNA: PROB11/1870/452].
[397] Bryant & Baker ed, *A Quaker Journal* Vol I pp143-144.

BIOGRAPHICAL NOTES

John Wilshere married three times and had two children, Elizabeth born in 1783 who married Thomas Hailey, and William born in 1785, known as William Wilshere of Walsworth to distinguish him from his cousin of the same name, son of his uncle Thomas. Their uncle William bequeathed each of them £1,000. William Wilshere of Walsworth married Louisa Croft in 1836, but she soon separated from him. William then lived with his sister Elizabeth in Church House. After the deaths of William in 1854 and Elizabeth in 1863, John Wilshere's estates were inherited by Thomas Wilshere's son, William. John Wilshere and both his children were buried in Back Street Independent Church burial ground.[398]

Wilshere, Mary (1768-1861)
WilliamWilshere's sister. In 1793 she briefly kept house for her widowed brother, but by 1794 a paid housekeeper took over. She was admitted to full communion of the Back Street Independent Church in 1796, the only one of William's brothers and sisters to be so admitted apart from their sister Sarah who was admitted in February 1773 and died later that year aged 16. After the deaths of her parents in 1798 and 1800 Mary and her sister Ann lived in a house in Bancroft (later 30 Bancroft) owned by their brother Thomas with an additional garden owned by their brother William.[399]

Wilshere, Thomas (1775-1832)
William Wilshere's youngest brother referred to as 'TW' in his memoranda books. Thomas farmed the land in Hitchin he had inherited from Mrs Elizabeth Simpson and other land which he rented from Sir Francis Willes whose local estates he managed. In 1816 he owned 156 acres in Hitchin, slightly more than his brother William's 152 acres. Thomas lived in Bancroft in the house later known as The Croft formerly owned by Elizabeth Simpson. He married Lora Beaumont and had five children, William born 1804, Laura born 1806, Elizabeth Simpson born 1808 who died aged three years, Thomas born 1811, and Charles Willes Wilshere born 1814. His first four children were baptised at Back Street Independent Church. Thomas was clearly on good terms with his brother William who made Thomas' eldest son his heir, regarding him as his adopted son. William bequeathed Thomas articles to the value of £500, £2,000

---

[398] Wilshere family tree [HALS: Acc 6412]; wills of William Wilshere and John Wilshere [TNA: PROB11/1692/97, PROB11/1870/452]; Bryant & Baker ed, *A Quaker Journal* Vol I p143; 1851 and 1861 censuses; will of William Wilshere of Walsworth [TNA: PROB11/2185/16].
[399] Wilshere family tree [HALS: Acc 6412]; cash books [HALS\; 61485-61486]; Back Street Independent Church Book [HALS: NR8/1/1]; map of Hitchin 1816 [NHM].

278

BIOGRAPHICAL NOTES

in money and an annuity of £500. Thomas' wife Laura was to have an annuity of £100 for her own use and an annuity of £200 if she outlived her husband. Thomas died in 1832 when he was thrown out of a carriage when the horses bolted. He was buried in the Back Street Independent Church burial ground.[400] Neither of Thomas' two elder sons married. Consequently on William's death in 1867 (his brother Thomas having died in 1840), Charles Willes Wilshere inherited the estates of all three Wilshere brothers, William, John and Thomas. In 1873 Charles Willes Wilshere of The Frythe at Welwyn owned 3,342 acres in Hertfordshire and Bedfordshire worth £6,339 a year. He was a passionate supporter of the Oxford Movement and formed an important collection of early Christian art and archaeology which he bequeathed to Pusey House, Oxford. His collection is now in the Ashmolean Museum.[401]

Wortham, Hale
Hale Wortham of Royston esquire was the elder brother of William Wilshere's wife Martha. His mother, also called Martha Wortham, bought a house in Tilehouse Street in Hitchin in 1795 where she lived until her death in 1804. Wilshere left Hale Wortham £100 and 19 guineas to his wife. When Hale Wortham died in 1828, he left his estates to his wife Mary, his brother George, George's son Hale Wortham, his nephew, Henry Hawkins, and his brother, James Wortham.[402]

Wren or Wrenn, William
William Wren was in charge of William Wilshere's farming activities from August 1804 until his death in the autumn of 1809. No record of his burial has been found so far.[403]

---

[400] Elizabeth Simpson's will [TNA: PROB11/1254/33]; Howlett, 'Sir Francis Willis and Francis Lovell' in *Discovering More About Hitchin* pp119-120; map of Hitchin 1816 [NHM]; Wilshere family tree [HALS: Acc 6412]; William Wilshere's will [TNA: PROB11/1692/97]; Hine, *Hitchin Worthies* p202 note; Thomas Wilshere's diary, 1832 [HALS: 61177].
[401] *The New Domesday Book of Hertfordshire compiled from the Official Return of Owners of Land 1873* (Hertford, *c*1873) p63; S Walker ed *Saints and Salvation. The Wilshere Collection of gold-grass, sarcophagi and inscriptions from Rome and Southern Italy* (Oxford, 2017).
[402] Wills of Martha Wortham, William Wilshere and Hale Wortham [TNA: PROB11/1413/200, PROB11/1692/97, PROB11/1741/206].
[403] Cash book [HALS: 61496 p101]. See pp7 and 9 above.

GLOSSARY

Wilshere Farm and Garden Memoranda

(All definitions are taken from The Oxford English Dictionary (on-line edition) or The Oxford Companion to Local and Family History. Any other sources are given in square brackets after the entry).

acre: the area that could be ploughed by a team of eight oxen in one day; standardized by Edward I (1272-1307) as a plot of land measuring 4,840 square yards and traditionally 40 poles long by 4 poles wide (220 yards x 22 yards; 0.4047 hectares).

ashes and soot: used for fertiliser. In Hertfordshire used to top-dress wheat in the spring [Young, *Agriculture of Hertfordshire*, p82].

avoirdupois: a system of weights based on a pound of 16 ounces or 7,000 grains, widely used in English-speaking countries.

blanching pans: '*Blanchers* are any close utensil that, when whelmed over a plant, will exclude the light. The most common is the *blanching-pot*, which is used to exclude light from sea-kale and rhubarb-stalks and some other culinary vegetables, where the green colour is to be avoided.' [J C Loudon, *An Encyclopaedia of Gardening* (1835) p546].

bran(n): the husk of wheat, barley, oats or other grain separated from the flour after grinding. The coarsest portion of the ground husk.

bushel: the Imperial bushel was not established in Great Britain until 1824; prior to that it could be smaller and could vary in local use according to the kind or quality of goods in question. 4 pecks or 8 gallons (56 lbs; approx 27 kg).

bush fair: a fair held on open ground usually in a village, 'in the bush', rather than a market place in a town.

chaff: a collective term for the husks of corn or other grain separated by threshing or winnowing. Also the cut hay or straw used for cattle feed.

copyhold: a form of customary tenure by which a tenant held a copy of the entry made in the records of the manorial court. In return for the land holding a tenant performed services to his manorial lord. By the sixteenth century the performance of services had largely been replaced by the payment of a fixed annual sum known as a quit rent. Changes in ownership occasioned the payment of entry fines.

draggings: possibly daggin' meaning trailing [M Ward ed, *Hertfordshire Dialect and Country Sayings* (Newbury, 2003) p33].

GLOSSARY

faggots: A bundle of sticks, twigs, or brushwood tied together for use as fuel.

harrow: heavy frame of timber or iron set with iron teeth. It is dragged over ploughed land to break up clods, turn the soil, root up weeds or cover the seed.

haulm: the stalks or stems collectively of peas, beans, or potatoes without the pods or tubers, as used for animal bedding.

hovel(l): an open shed or lean-to building; an outhouse used as a shelter for cattle, a receptacle for grain or tools.

hurdle: used to form temporary fences, sheep pens etc. They are made from interwoven withes of hazel, willow etc over a portable, rectangular frame.

in: to bring in, to carry 'In the corn and in the barley' [Ward, *Hertfordshire Dialect and Country Sayings,* p58].

inning: inning the corn – harvest home [Ward, *Hertfordshire Dialect and Country Sayings,* p58].

lath: A thin narrow strip of wood used to form a groundwork upon which to fasten the slates or tiles of a roof or the plaster of a wall or ceiling, and in the construction of lattice or trellis work.

load: a unit of capacity or weight that can vary by locality and substance. John Carrington of Bramfield states that in Hertfordshire a load of wheat is 5 bushels. Wilshere also reckons 5 bushels to a load of wheat. [Flood, *John Carrington, Farmer of Bramfield, His Diary, 1798-1810 Volume 1, 1798-1804* (HRS Vol 26, 2015) p69].

malt dust: refuse which falls from the grain in the process of malting. In Hertfordshire this is used as manure. [Young, p170].

meal: the finer part of the ground grain, as opposed to the bran (qv).

meal man: one who deals in meal.

messuage: a legal term for a dwelling house and its surrounding property.

Michaelmas: 29 September; one of the 'quarter' days when traditionally tenants paid their rent. The Quarter Sessions held around this date was known as the Michaelmas Sessions.

midsty: the threshing floor or space between two mows in a barn [Ward, *Hertfordshire Dialect and Country Sayings,* p68].

offal: that which falls or is thrown off from some process, as husks from milling grain, chips from dressing wood, etc; residue or waste products. [R HOLLAND *Gloss. Words County of Chester* (1886) (at cited word) *Offal corn, offal wheat*, the lighter grains winnowed from the marketable samples, and used for feeding fowls].

pales: a pointed piece of wood intended to be driven into the ground, especially as used with others to form a fence; a stake. Now usually any of the bars or strips of wood fixed vertically to a horizontal rail or rails to form a fence.

GLOSSARY

peck: a measure of capacity used for dry goods - a quarter of a bushel; a liquid measure of two gallons.

pole: linear measurement of 5½ yards; 4 poles = 22 yards; 40 poles = one furlong.

pollard: the bran sifted from the flour; also, relating to a tree, cut back or lopped.

quick: live slips or cuttings of plants, set in the ground to grow especially those of whitethorn or other shrub of which hedges are made.

rest: at the end of the annual brewing season in early June larger breweries with more than one owner drew up a Rest Book or annual balance in which everything was valued and outstanding debts and liabilities noted. [Matthias, *The Brewing Industry in England* p29].

rood: a unit of land area equal to 40 square rods (a quarter of an acre, approx. 0.1012 hectare), but varying locally.

sanfoin: a low-growing perennial herb, *Onobrychis sativa* (formerly *Hedysarum Onobrychis*), much grown as a forage plant. 'It is the best hay to sell or use' [Young, p122].

score: twenty.

seedsman: a sower or dealer in seed.

small beer: beer of a weak, poor or inferior quality.

tares: common cultivated vetch grown as a natural manure and for the feeding of livestock. In Hertfordshire most farmers 'have tares for soiling their horses' [Young, pp125-6].

thill: the shaft of a cart or wagon; thill harness – cart harness [Ward, *Hertfordshire Dialect and Country Sayings,* p99].

tithe: the payment of one tenth of one's produce, or profits, to the support of the church and clergy. Originally tithes were payable in kind eg the tenth sheaf of corn. Over time many landowners agreed on a fixed money payment instead. Demands from the clergy to increase the amounts paid often led to disputes as here demonstrated in the diaries.

vide: See; consult (used as an instruction in a text to refer the reader to a specified passage, book, author, etc, for further information).

yelt: young sow, gilt [J L Fisher, *A Medieval Farming Glossary of Latin and English Words* (2nd edition, Chelmsford, 1997) p20].

BIBLIOGRAPHY

Manuscripts
Hertfordshire Archives and Local Studies
Wilshere Papers
61181-61182 Farm and garden memoranda books 1809-1824
60351 Sale catalogue of William Wilshere's farming stock Dec 1824
61598 List of trees, seeds etc sown and planted etc 1813-1814, 1818
60158 Garden Journal 1812-1822
61479-61481 Bills and receipts
57765 Lease of Church House, Hitchin 1759
57885 Draft lease of Port Mill, Hitchin 1815
58871-58873 Sketches of property in Biggin Lane, Hitchin 1819
60314-60318, 60337-60343, 60359, 60497-60498 Deeds to the Hermitage,
 Hitchin
60325 Case for opinion with sketch plan 1707
60327 Case for opinion concerning overgrown hedge 1728
60356-60362 Deeds to the Grange House, Hitchin 1584-1620
60534-60536 Deeds to former tan house in Back Street 1784-1807
60597 Information from James Carter 1856
60618 Draft lease of the Hermitage 1863
60637 Copyhold lands of William Wilshere 1864
60649 Schedule of title deeds to the Hermitage 1864
60985 Carpenters and Bricklayers work to be performed at Mr Tristram's House
 1763
60994 Appointment as steward of manor of Hitchin 1785
61026-61029, 61207 Plans and estimates for cottages and barns in Biggin Lane,
 Hitchin 1818, 1823
61101 Election to the Fellowship of the Society of Antiquaries 1817
61171 School exercise book 1766-1767
61173 Diary of William Wilshere's actions consequent to the death of Richard
 Warbuton Lytton Dec 1810 – Jan 1811
61482-61506 Cash books 1789-1814
61525-61532 Cash books 1814-1823
61535 Cash book 1823-1824
61512 Thomas Wilshere's cash book 1825-1829
61515 Thomas Wilshere's account with Trustees 1824-1825
61542-61543 Ledgers A and D
61520 Richard Tristram's inventory 1785
61613 Minutes of Property 1824
61708 Letter from Thomas Brand on the Corn Laws 1814
63744 'On the Management of Grapes' by William Griffin 1820

BIBLIOGRAPHY

64356 Terrier of the Manor of Hitchin 1727

58869 Plan of estate in Hitchin belonging to William Wilshere *c*1801-1807

67196 Plan of land in Hitchin occupied by William Wilshere 1819

DE/Ws/P15 Plan of several fields in the Parish of Hitchin occupied by William Wilshere 1806

DE/Ws/P16 Plan of land in Hitchin occupied by William Wilshere 1818

DE/Ws/P22-P23 Plans of property conveyed to Mr Prime 1865-1866

61407 Plan of the estates of Charles Willes Wilshere in the parishes of Hitchin, Great Wymondley, Ickleford & Ippollitts 1868

Hawkins Family of Hitchin including solictors' papers
DE/Ha/B63/102 Draft will of John Kempson 1808

DE/Ha/B570 Papers re will of Elizabeth Constance Gainsford 1939-1940

DE/Ha/B1967 Deeds to the Red Lion, Hitchin 1801-1851

DE/Ha/T99 Deeds to 22-24 High Street, Hitchin

DE/Ha/T103 Deeds to the Swan Inn, Hitchin

DE/Ha/T111 Deeds to Lodge Cottage and land between Walsworth Road and Whinbush Road, Hitchin 1795-1865

Radcliffe Family of Hitchin Priory
DE/R/C402/1-5 Letters to Emilius Delmé-Radcliffe 1805-1806

DE/R/F204 John Radcliffe's garden book 1773

DE/R/F266 Accounts of the Radcliffe settled estates 1798-1824

St Mary Hitchin Parish Records
DP/53/1 Parish registers

DP/53/8/3 Vestry minute book 1811-1828

DP/53/11/7 Rate assessments 1825-1827

DP/53/18/9 Rate assessment 1838

DP/53/21/7 Highway rate book 1808-1818

DP/53/29/1 Plan of Impropriate Estate of Trinity College Cambridge 1822

Registers of other Parishes
DP/46/1/47 Hatfield marriage register

DP/58/1/2 Ickleford register of baptisms

DP/105/1/11 Stevenage marriage register

DP/125/1/4, 11 Willian registers of baptisms and burials

DP/128/1/4 Great Wymondley marriage register

BIBLIOGRAPHY

Diocesan and Archdeaconry Records
DSA4/53/1-2 Hitchin tithe map and award 1841-1844
DSA4/119/1-2 Willian tithe map and award 1837-1839
HW Wills proved in the Archdeaconry Court of Huntingdon

Back Street Independent Church, Hitchin
NR8/1/1 Back Street Independent Church Book 1715-1822

Hertfordshire Quarter Sessions
QS/E80-81 Great and Little Wymondley enclosure award and map 1814-1819
QS/Var/5 Register of Gamekeepers 1789-1859
QS/VAR/434-493 Victuallers' recognizances 1806

Hitchin Urban District Council
UDC/10/1/10-17 Minutes 1919-1929

Miscellaneous
ACC/6412 Wilshere Family Tree
87587-87834 Miscellaneous deeds and papers relating to Hitchin and District
   deposited by R L Hine
DE/Sb/T46 Abstract of title and sale particulars for Lewesford House, Hitchin,
   1842
DE/X783/E2 Survey of the Parish of Kings Walden 1802
DZ/72/P121605 Plan of Purwell Field *c*1770

North Hertfordshire Museum
1216 William Wilshere's commonplace book 1814-1824
492/7 William Lucas' diary 1824
1203 William Dunnage's manuscript History of Hitchin 1815
7752/7 Sale particulars for land owned by Francis Pym 1852
M265 George Beaver's journal
Map and survey of Hitchin 1816
Merrett's map of Hitchin 1820
Lawson Thompson scrapbooks
Loftus Barham scrapbooks
Photocopy of 1801 Hitchin census
Agreement for sale of 88 Tilehouse Street 1824

The National Archives
E315/391 Survey of the Manor of Hitchin 1556
SC12/8/29 Rental of the Manor of Hitchin 1591

BIBLIOGRAPHY

LR3/29 Hitchin Manor court book 1779-1796
CRES5/37 Hitchin Manor court book 1797-1815
PROB/11 Wills proved in the Prerogative Court of Canterbury
RG4/743 Back Street Independent Church, Hitchin: baptism register
REG4/2479 Alnwick Scotch Church register of births and baptisms

Trinity College Cambridge
42 Hitchin 52 Reference book to the College estate in Hitchin 1822
42 Hitchin 74. Letter form John Hawkins as to arrears of tithe rentcharge at
  Hitchin upon allotment gardens enclosed out of the common. 1861

Bedfordshire and Luton Archives
L30/11/40/31, L30/11/236/3 Letters to Countess de Grey
Z937/15/17, Z937/33/1 Deeds and papers relating to the Brotherhood House,
  Hitchin
P85/1/9 Luton parish register

Wiltshire and Swindon Archives
Lovell Papers 161/57 Sales particulars for Thomas Plumer Byde's estate 1783

Online Resources
Clergy of the Church of England Database https://theclergydatabase.org.uk /
FruitID: https://www.fruitid.com/#main.
Grace's Guide to British Industrial History https://www.gracesguide.co.uk
Historic England https://historicengland.org.uk/listing/the-list/list
The History of Parliament https://www.historyofparliamentonline.org/
Legacies of British Slave Ownership www.ucl.ac.uk/lbs
Oxford Dictionary of National Biography
Oxford English Dictionary
Pirton Local History Group https://pirtonhistory.org.uk
S2A3 Biographical Dictionary of South African Science https://www.s2a3.org.za
Small, D, *Montpelier Estate. St John Figtree, Nevis. Contrasting Legacies on a
  Sugar Plantation.* May 2010 https://seis.bristol.ac.uk/~emceee/montpelier.pdf
*The Victoria History of the Counties of England: Bedfordshire, Hertfordshire
  and Middlesex* at www.british-history.ac.uk

Secondary Sources
*An Account of the Hitchin Charities extracted from the further report of the
Commissioners appointed to continue the Inquiries concerning Charities 1836*
Abercrombie, J, *The Complete Kitchen Gardener and Hot-Bed Forcer* (1789)
Agar, N E, *Behind the Plough. Agrarian society in nineteenth-century*

286

BIBLIOGRAPHY

Hertfordshire (Hatfield, 2005)

Aiton, W, *Hortus Kewensis; or, a catalogue of the plants cultivated at the Royal Botanical Gardens in Kew*, Vol. 4 (1812)

anon., *Hints Concerning the Cultivation and Use of the Potato* (1795)

Ashley Cooper, A, *A Harvest of Hexton* (Hexton, 1986)

Austin, T G, *The Straw Plaiting and Straw Hat and Bonnet Trade* (Luton, 1871)

Baines, D C *'Two Coats Colder'. Chronicles of Offley in Hertfordshire* (Offley, 1994)

Barnes, G, Dallas, P, and Williamson, T, 'The Black Poplar in Norfolk', *Quarterly Journal of Forestry* 103 (2009) pp31–8

Barnes, G, and Williamson, T, *Trees in England: management and disease since 1600* (Hatfield, 2017)

Barnes, G, and Williamson, T, *The Orchards of Eastern England: History, Ecology, Myth* (Hatfield, 2021)

Barnes, G, and Williamson, T, *English Orchards: a Landscape History* (Oxford, 2022)

Beavington, F, 'The development of market gardening in Bedfordshire, 1799-1939', *Agricultural History Review* 23, 1 (1975)

Beckett, J V, *Agricultural Revolution* (1990)

Belcher, J, *The Foldcourse and East Anglian Agriculture and Landscape, 1100-1900* (Woodbridge, 2020)

Bellamy, L, *The Language of Fruit: literature and horticulture in the long eighteenth century* (|University of Pennsylvania Press, Philadelphia, 2019)

Bendall, S, *Dictionary of Land Surveyors and Local Mapmakers of Great Britain and Ireland 1530-1850* (2nd edition, 1997)

Bettley, J, Pevsner, N, and Cherry, B, *The Buildings of England Hertfordshire* (2019)

Blackburne-Maze, P, *The Apple Book* (1986)

Blanc, R, *The Lost Orchard: A French Chef Rediscovers a Great British Food Heritage* (2020)

Branch Johnson, W, *Welwyn By and Large. Historical Gossip from a Hertfordshire Village* (Welwyn, 1967)

British Schools Museum, *Educating Our Own. The Masters of Hitchin British School 1810 to 1929* (Hitchin, 2008)

Brooks, C W, *Pettyfoggers and Vipers of the Commonwealth. The 'Lower Branch' of the Legal Profession in Early Modern England* (Cambridge 1986, paperback edition 2004)

Brown, J, *The Forester* (1847)

Brown, P, *The Apple Orchard: the Story of Our Most English Fruit* (2016)

Bryant, G E, & Baker, G P, ed, *A Quaker Journal Being the Diary and*

BIBLIOGRAPHY

Reminiscences of William Lucas of Hitchin (1804-1861) A Member of the Society of Friends (1933)

Campbell, S, *A History of Kitchen Gardening* (2005)

Campbell-Culver, M, *The Origin of Plants* (2001, paperback edition 2004)

Campion, V, *Joseph Ransom's Naturalist's Notebook 1804-1816 The Nature Notes of a Hitchin Quaker* (Hitchin, 2004)

Chauncy, H, *The Historical Antiquities of Hertfordshire* (1700)

Cirkett, A F, ed, *Samuel Whitbread's Notebooks, 1810-11, 1813-14* (Bedford, 1971)

Clarke, M, *Apples: a Field Guide* (revised edn. Tewin, 2015)

Cobbett, W, *Cottage Economy* (1822)

Common Ground, *Orchards: a Guide to Local Conservation* (1989)

Cooper, F, *The Black Poplar: History, Ecology and Conservation* (Oxford, 2006)

Copas, L, *A Somerset Pomona: the Cider Apples of Somerset* (Wimbourne, 2001)

Crawley, B, ed, *Wills at Hertford 1415-1858* (2007)

Crawley, L, 'The Growth of Provincial Nurseries: Norwich Nurserymen, c.1750-1860', *Garden History* 48, 2 (2020) pp119-34

Crosby, T, Douglas, P, Fletcher, S, et al., *Jeeves Yard. A dynasty of Hitchin builders and brickmakers* (Hitchin, 2003)

Davison, F, *The Hidden Horticulturalists* (2019)

Defoe, D, *A Tour through the Whole Island of Great Britain* (Penguin edition 1971, repr 1983)

de Rougemont, G M, *Collins Field Guide to the Crops of Britain and Europe* (1989)

Dony, J G, *A History of the Straw Hat Industry* (Luton, 1942)

Douglas, P, and Humphries, P, *Discovering Hitchin* (Baldock, 1995)

Drake, L J, *Wood & Ingram: Huntingdon Nursery: 1742–1950* (Cambridge, 2008)

Drayton, R, 'James Bowie', *Oxford Dictionary of National Biography* (2004)

Duchenne, C, 'Hawkins Russell Jones, 1591 to 1991' in S Walker, ed, *Hitchin Glimpses of the Past* (Hitchin, 2020)

Ellis, W, *The Practical Farmer, or, the Hertfordshire Husbandman* (1732)

Ellis, W, *The Practical Farmer: or, the. Hertfordshire husbandman: containing many new improvements in husbandry* (1736)

Ellis, W, *The Timber-Tree Improved* (1738)

Ellis, W, *The Modern Husbandman or, the Practice of Farming* (1744)

Eyre, S R, 'The Curving Plough-Strip and its Historical Implications', *Agricultural History Review* 3, 2 (1955) pp80-94

BIBLIOGRAPHY

Farris, N, *The Wymondleys* (Hertford, 1989)

Finch, J C, 'A Transatlantic Dialogue: The Estate Landscape in Britain, the Caribbean, and North America in the Eighteenth Century', *Huntington Library Quarterly* 84, 3 (2021) pp491-515

Fisher, J L, *A Medieval Farming Glossary of Latin and English Words* (2nd edition, Chelmsford, 1997)

Flood, S, ed, *John Carrington, Farmer of Bramfield, His Diary, 1798-1810 Volume 1, 1798-1804* HRS Vol 26 (Hertford, 2010)

Flood, S, ed, *John Carrington, Farmer of Bramfield, His Diary, 1798-1810 Volume 2, 1805-1810 and John Carrington Junior's Diary May 1810-December 1812* HRS Vol 33 (Hertford, 2022)

Flood, S, and Williamson, T, ed, *Humphry Repton in Hertfordshire: Documents and Landscapes* (Hatfield, 2018)

Floud, R, *An Economic History of the English Garden* (2019)

Foster, A M, and Munby, L M, *Market Town. Hitchin in the Nineteenth Century* (Hitchin, 1987)

Fulford, R, *Samuel Whitbread 1764-1815. A Study in Opposition.* (1967)

Gadd, P, 'Hitchin Inns etc.' (typescript, 1987)

Gee, M, *The Devon Orchards Book* (Wellington, 2018)

Gerish, W B, *Sir Henry Chauncy, Kt; Serjeant-at-Law and Recorder of Hertford* (1907)

Glendinning, D R, 'Potato introductions and breeding up to the early 20th century', *New Phytologist* 94 (1983) pp479-505

Goose, N, 'Straw-plaiting and hat-making', in D Short, ed, *An Historical Atlas of Hertfordshire* (Hatfield, 2011) pp90-92

Gordon, J, *Planters, Florists and Gardeners Dictionary* (1774)

Hadfield, M, *A History of British Gardening* (1960, paperback 1985)

Harvey, J, *Early Nurserymen* (Chichester, 1974)

Harvey, N, 'The coming of the Swede to Great Britain: an obscure chapter in farming history', *Agricultural History* 23, 4 (1949) pp286-88

Hertfordshire Family History Society, *Hertfordshire Monumental Inscriptions Hitchin The Parish Church of St Mary* (2007)

Hickman, C, *The Doctor's Garden: Medicine, Science, and Horticulture in Britain* (2022)

Hine, R L, *The History of Hitchin Volume I* (1927) *Volume. II* (1929)

Hine, R L, *History of Hitchin Grammar School* (Hitchin, 1931, revised 1951

Hine, R L, *Hitchin Worthies. Four Centuries of English Life* (1932, reprinted 1974)

Hine, R L, *The Story of Methodism at Hitchin* (1934)

BIBLIOGRAPHY

Hine, R L, 'Hitchin and the Threatened Invasion of 1806' in Hine, R L, *Relics of an Un-Common Attorney* (1951)

Hitchin Historical Society, *Hitchin Arcade Then and Now* (Hitchin, 2007)

Hodge, C, Burton, R, Corbett, W, Evans, R, and Scale, R, *Soils and their Uses in Eastern England* (Harpenden, 1984),

Hogg, R, *British Pomology* (1851)

Howlett, B, ed, *Survey of the Royal Manor of Hitchin, 1676* HRS Vol 16 (Hertford, 2000)

Howlett, B, *Hitchin Priory Park. The history of a landscape park and gardens* (Hitchin, 2004)

Howlett, B, 'Hitchin, Sugar and Slavery', *Hitchin Historical Society Journal* Vol 18 no 2 Oct 2008

Howlett, B, 'Another Early Map of Hitchin', *Herts Past & Present'* 3 12 Autumn 2008 pp10-13

Howlett, B, *Maydencroft. A manor, hunting park, farm and brickworks near Hitchin* (Hitchin, 2012)

Howlett, B, and Humphries, P, ed, *Discovering more about Hitchin* (Hitchin, 2018)

Ickleford Parish Council, *The Mills of Ickleford* (Ickleford, 2014)

Jacson, M, *The Florist's Manual; or Hints for the Construction of a Gay Flower Garden* (1816)

James, J, and Bettey, J H, ed, *Farming in Dorset: James Warne's Diary, 1758 and George Boswell's Letters 1787-1805*, Dorset Record Society (1993)

Johnson, G W, *The Cottage Gardener and Country Gentleman's Companion* (1854)

Jones, J, *Seedtime and Harvest: The Diary of An Essex Farmer, William Barnard of Harlowbury, 1807-23* (Chelmsford, 1992)

Jones, M, *Colworth in Context. A History of Colworth Estate, Bedfordshire from 1720 to 1947* (Bedford, 1997)

Kain, R J P, *An Atlas and Index of the Tithe-Files of Mid Nineteenth Century England and Wales* (Cambridge, 1986)

Kerridge, E, *The Common Fields of England* (Manchester, 1993)

King, A, and Clifford, S, 'The Apple, the Orchard, the Cultural Landscape, in Clifford, S, and King, A, ed, *Local Distinctiveness: Place, Particularity and Identity* (1993) pp37-46

Knight, T A, 'On raising of new and early varieties of the potato Solanum tuberosum', *Transactions of the Horticultural Society of London*, 1 (1807) pp57-59

Knight, T A, 'On Potatoes', *Transactions of the Horticultural Society of London*, 1 (1810) pp187-193

BIBLIOGRAPHY

Knight, T A, 'On the culture of the potato in hotbeds', *Transactions of the Horticultural Society of London*, 1 (1810) pp213-4

Knight, T A, 'On some early varieties of the potato and the best method of forcing them', *Transactions of the Horticultural Society of London*, 1 (1811) pp244—247

Knight, T A, 'Some Remarks *on the* supposed Influence of the Pollen, in cross breeding, upon the Colour of the Seed-coals of Plants, and the Qualities of their Fruits', *Transactions of the Horticultural Society* 5 (1824) pp377-80

Knight, T A, 'On the potato', *Transactions of the Horticultural Society of London*, Series 2 1 (1831) pp93-100

Knight, T A, 'On the culture of the potato', *Transactions of the Horticultural Society of London* Series 2, 1 (1833) pp415-18

Laird, M, *The Flowering of the Landscape Garden: English Pleasure Grounds, 1720-1800* (University of Philadelphia Press, Pennsylvania, 1999)

Letters and Papers on Agriculture, Planting &c. Selected from the Correspondence of the Bath and West of England Society for the Encouragement of Agriculture, Arts, Manufacture and Commerce (Bath, 1802),

Loudon, J C, *An Encyclopedia of Gardening* (1822)

Loudon, J C, *An Encyclopedia of Agriculture* (1825)

Loudon, J C, *An Encyclopaedia of Gardening* revised ed (1835)

Lucas, J, *Phebe's Hitchin Book* (Hitchin, 2009)

Masset, C, *Orchards* (Princes Risborough, 2012)

Mathias, P, *The Brewing Industry in England 1700-1830* (Cambridge, 1959)

Meager, L, *English Gardener* (1683)

Mitchell, A, *Trees of Britain and Northern Europe* (1978)

Mitchell, B R, and Deane, R, *Abstract of British Historical Statistics* (Cambridge, 1962)

Moore, C, *Hertfordshire Windmills and Windmillers* (Sawbridgeworth, 1999)

Morgan, J, and Richards, A, *The New Book of Apples* (Revised edn, 2002)

Muggleton, W, *The Apples and Orchards of Worcestershire* (Malvern, 2017)

Newbold, D, 'A Historical Note on the Guinea Fowl', *Sudan Notes and Records* 9, 1 (1926) pp125-129

Overton, M, *Agricultural Revolution in England* (Cambridge, 1996)

Parker, J, *'Nothing for Nothing for Nobody' A History of Hertfordshire Banks and Banking* (Stevenage, 1986)

Pieris, M, *Take 6 Carrots, 4 Heads of Celery, 8 Large Onions - - -The Receipts of a Hertfordshire Family* (Hitchin, 1994)

Preston, J, *That Odd Rich Old Woman. Elizabeth Barbara Bulwer-Lytton of Knebworth House 1773-1843* (1998)

BIBLIOGRAPHY

Quinion, M, *Cider Making* (Princes Risborough, 2008)

Rance, D, *St Ippolyts. A country parish in the nineteenth century* (Baldock, 1987)

Ranger, W, *Report to the General Board of Health – Hitchin* (HMSO, 1849)

Rapp, D, *Samuel Whitbread (1764-1815) A Social and Political Study* (1987)

Rigby, E, *Holkham: its Agriculture &c* (1817)

Romans, A, *The Potato Book* (2005)

Rotherham, I D, ed, *Orchards and Groves: their History, Ecology, Culture and Archaeology* (Sheffield, 2008)

Rowe, A, ed, *Garden Making and the Freman Family: a Memoir of Hamels* HRS Vol 17 (Hertford, 2001)

Rowe, A, and Williamson, T, *Hertfordshire a landscape history* (Hatfield, 2013)

Royal Commission on Historical Monuments (England), *An Inventory of the Historical Monuments in Hertfordshire* (1911)

Salaman, R N, *Potato Varieties* (Cambridge, 1926)

Salaman, R N, *The History and Social Influence of the Potato* (Cambridge, 1949; revised edn 1984)

Sanders, R, *The Apple Book* (2010)

Seebohm, F, *English Village Community* (1883)

Short, B, May, P, Vine, G, and Bur, A-M, *Apples and Orchards in Sussex* (Lewes, 2012)

Slater, G, *The English Peasantry and the Enclosure of Common Fields* (1907)

Slater, T, and Goose, N, 'Panoramas and microcosms: Hertfordshire's towns through both ends of the telescope', in T Slater and N Goose, ed, *A County of Small Towns. The development of Hertfordshire's urban landscape to 1800* (Hatfield, 2008) pp1-26

Spooner, S, *Regions and Designed Landscapes in Georgian England* (2018)

Taplin, V, and Stewart, A, *Two Minutes to the Station. The Tale of Hitchin's Victorian Triangle* (Hitchin, 2010)

Thaer, A, D, *The Principles of Agriculture*, 2 Vols. (1844)

The Repertory of Arts, Manufactures and Agriculture 4 (1804)

Turner, M E, 'Arable in England and Wales: estimates from the 1801 Crop Return', *Journal of Historical Geography* 7 (1981), pp291-302

Turner, M E, *Volume 190: Home Office Acreage Returns HO67. List and Analysis*, three parts, part 1 (1982)

Turner, M E, Beckett, J V, and Afton, B, *Farm Production in England 1700-1914* (Oxford, 2001)

Wade Martins, S, and Williamson, T, ed, *The Farming Journal of Randall Burroughes of Wymondham, 1794-99*, Norfolk Record Society Vol 58 (Norwich, 1995)

BIBLIOGRAPHY

Wade Martins, S, and Williamson, T, 'Labour and Improvement: Agricultural Change in East Anglia c.1750-1870', *Labour History Review* 62, 3 (1997)

Wade Martins, S, and Williamson, T, 'The lease and East Anglian agriculture, 1660-1870', *Agricultural History Review* 46, 2, (1998)

Wade Martins, S, and Williamson, T, *Roots of Change: farming and the landscape in East Anglia, c.1700-1870* (Exeter, 1999)

Wadsworth, A, *The Farming Diaries of Thomas Pinniger, 1813-1847*, Wiltshire Record Society Vol 74 (Gloucester, 2021);

Walker, S, *Underground Hitchin. A look at what's under our feet* (Hitchin, 2000)

Walker, S, ed, *Saints and Salvation. The Wilshere Collection of gold-grass, sarcophagi and inscriptions from Rome and Southern Italy* (Oxford, 2017)

Ward, M, ed, *Hertfordshire Dialect and Country Sayings* (Newbury, 2003)

Warde, P, *Energy Consumption in England and Wales, 1560-2000* (Rome, 2007)

Watkins, C, *Trees, Woods and Forests: a Social and Cultural History* (2014)

Waugh, E, *Rivers Nursery of Sawbridgeworth: the Art of Pomology* (Ware, 2009)

Waugh, E, Planting the Garden: the Nursery Trade in Hertfordshire' in Spring, D, ed, *Hertfordshire Garden History Volume 2: Gardens Pleasant, Groves Delicious* (Hatfield, 2012) pp177–201

Wayne. J, ed, *A foot on three daisies. Pirton's Story* (Pirton, 1987)

Whately, T, *Observations on Modern Gardening* (1770)

Wheeler, D, *Hodgson & Hankin. A Fishy Tale of Old Hitchin* (Hitchin, 2005)

Whitaker, A, *Brewers in Hertfordshire. A historical gazetteer* (Hatfield, 2006)

Whitbread, S, and Bunker, S, 'Southill – A Sporting Estate' in P Bell ed, *Southill and the Whitbreads 1795-1995* (Southill, Biggleswade, 1995)

Whitmore, R, *Didn't you use to be Richard Whitmore? Memoirs of a TV newsreader and reluctant drawing room lady killer* (2015)

Willes, M, *The Gardens of the British Working Class* (Yale, 2014)

Williamson, T, *The Archaeology of the Landscape Park: garden design in Norfolk, England, c.1680-1840* (British Archaeological Reports, Oxford, 1998)

Williamson, T, *The Transformation of Rural England: farming and the landscape 1700-1870* (Exeter, 1999)

Williamson, T, 'Production, power and the natural: differences between English and American gardens in the eighteenth century'; *Huntington Library Quarterly* 84, 3 (2021) pp 467-90

Wilson, N, 'John Clare's Contemporaries: The Anonymous Versifier', *John Clare Society, Journal 40, July 2021* pp35-46

BIBLIOGRAPHY

Young, A, *Gleanings from Books on Agriculture and Gardening* (1802)
Young, A, *General View of the Agriculture of Hertfordshire* (1804; reprint
  1971)
Young, A, *General View of the Agriculture of Oxfordshire* (1809)

HERTFORDSHIRE RECORD SOCIETY

The Hertfordshire Record Society exists to make Hertfordshire's historical records of all kinds more readily available to the general reader. Since 1985 a regular series of texts has been published.

ALAN THOMSON, Chairman
HEATHER FALVEY, Hon. Secretary
PAUL CASSIDY, Hon. Treasurer
SUSAN FLOOD, Hon. General Editor

Membership enquiries and orders for previous publications to the Hon. Treasurer, Revel's Hall, St Leonard's Road, Bengeo, Hertford, SG14 3JN

Annual Subscription (2023-2024)   £17.50

Previous publications:

I: *Tudor Churchwardens' Accounts*, edited by Anthony Palmer (1985) O/P

II: *Early Stuart Household Accounts*, edited by Lionel M Munby (1986) O/P

III: *'A Professional Hertfordshire Tramp' John Edwin Cussans, Historian of Hertfordshire*, edited by Audrey Deacon and Peter Walne (1987) O/P

IV: *The Salisbury-Balfour Correspondence, 1869-1892*, edited by Robin Harcourt Williams (1988) O/P

V: *The Parish Register & Tithing Book of Thomas Hassall of Amwell* [1599-1657], edited by Stephen G. Doree (1989) Price £6.00

VI: *Cheshunt College: The Early Years*, edited by Edwin Welch (1990) Price £6.00

VII: *St Albans Quarter Sessions Rolls, 1784-1820*, edited by David Dean (1991) O/P

VIII: *The Accounts of Thomas Green, 1742-1790*, edited by Gillian Sheldrick (1992) O/P

IX: *St Albans Wills, 1471-1500*, edited by Susan Flood (1993) O/P

X: *Early Churchwardens' Accounts of Bishops Stortford, 1431-1538*, edited by Stephen G. Doree (1994) Price £6.00

XI: *Religion in Hertfordshire, 1847-1851*, edited by Judith Burg (1995) O/P

XII: *Muster Books for North & East Hertfordshire, 1580-1605*, edited by Ann J. King (1996) O/P

XIII: *Lifestyle & Culture in Hertford: Wills and Inventories, 1660-1725*, edited by Beverly Adams (1997) Price £6.00

HERTFORDSHIRE RECORD SOCIETY

XIV: *Hertfordshire Lay Subsidy Rolls, 1307 and 1334*, edited by Janice Brooker and Susan Flood, Introduction by Mark Bailey (1998) Price £6.00

XV: *'Observations of Weather': The Weather Diary of Sir John Wittewronge of Rothamsted, 1684-1689*, edited by Margaret Harcourt Williams and John Stevenson (1999) Price £6.00

XVI: *Survey of the Royal Manor of Hitchin, c1676*, edited by Bridget Howlett (2000) Price £6.00

XVII: *Garden-Making and the Freeman family A Memoir of Hamels, 1713-1733*, edited by Anne Rowe (2001) Price £6.00

XVIII: *Two Nineteenth Century Hertfordshire Diaries, 1822-1849*, edited by Judith Knight and Susan Flood (2002) Price £6.00

XIX: *"This little commonwealth": Layston parish memorandum book, 1607-c1650 & 1704-c1747*, edited by Heather Falvey and Steve Hindle (2003) Price £6.00

XX: *Julian Grenfell, soldier and poet: letters and diaries, 1910-1915*, edited by Kate Thompson (2004) Price £6.00

XXI: *The Hellard Almshouses and other Stevenage Charities, 1482-2005*, edited by Margaret Ashby (2005) Price £6.00

XXII: *A Victorian Teenager's Diary: the Diary of Lady Adela Capel of Cassiobury, 1841-1842*, edited by Marian Strachan (2006) Price £5.00 (pbk)

XXIII: *The Impact of the First Civil War on Hertfordshire, 1642-1647*, edited by Alan Thomson (2007) Price £6.00

XXIV: *The Diary of Benjamin Woodcock Master of the Barnet Union Workhouse, 1836-1838*, edited by Gillian Gear (2008) Price £6.00

XXV: *Datchworth Tithe Accounts, 1711-1747*, edited by Jane Walker (2009) Price £6.00

XXVI: *John Carrington's Diary*, I, *1798-1804*, edited by Susan Flood (2010) Price £22.00 (members £17.50)

XXVII: *Humphry Repton's Red Books of Panshanger and Tewin Water, 1799-1800*, with an Introduction by Twigs Way (2011) Price £30.00 (members £17.50)

XXVIII: *The Receipt Book of Baroness Elizabeth Dimsdale, c.1800*, edited Heather Falvey (2012) Price £22.00 (members £17.50)

XXIX: *Records of the Manor of Norton, 1244-1539*, translated by Peter Foden (2013) Price £22.00 (members £17.50)

XXX: *Weston School Log Books, 1876-1914*, transcribed by Joan Amis, Margaret Bowyer and Janet Gunn; edited and with an Introduction by Margaret Ashby (2014) Price £22.00 (members £17.50)

XXXI: *Lord Fordwich's Grand Tour, 1756-60*, translated and edited by Sheila White and Philip Sheail (2015) Price £22.00 (members £17.50)

XXXII: *St Albans Wills, Inventories and Probate Accounts, 1600-1615*, edited by Pat Howe and Jane Harris (for 2016) Price £22.00 (members £17.50)

XXXIII: *The Diaries of John Carrington, farmer of Bramfield (part 2) 1805-1810 and John Carrington, junior, 1810-1812*, edited by Susan Flood (2022) Price £22.00 (members £17.50)

XXXIV: *Walter Morrell's 'Manufacture for the New Draperie' (1616)*, edited by Michael Zell and Heather Falvey (2018) Price £22.00 (members £17.50)

XXXV: *Hertford Gaol Records, 1834-1844*, edited by Eileen Wallace (not yet published)

XXXVI: *The Third Earl Cowper and his Florentine Household, 1760–90*, edited by Philip Sheail (2020) Price £22.00 (members £17.50)

XXXVII: *Ashwell Overseers' Accounts, 1676-1722*, edited by David Short (2021) Price £22.00 (members £17.50)

XXXVIII: *Berkhamsted St Peter Churchwardens' Accounts, c1584-1660*, edited by Nick Brown and Christine Whittingham (2022) Price £22.00 (members £17.50)

Maps:

The County of Hertford From Actual Survey by A Bryant In the Years 1820 and 1821 (2003; reprinted 2012) Price £8.00 (members £5.00)

A Topographical Map of Hartford-Shire by Andrew Dury and John Andrews, 1766 (2004) Price £9.50 (members £8.50)

Barnet Enclosure Award Map and Schedule, 1818 (2016) Price £8.50 (members £6.00)

Special publication:

Hertfordshire Population Statistics 1563 to 1801 (2nd edition), first edition (1964), by Lionel Munby, updated by Heather Falvey (2019) Price £5.00

INDEX OF NAMES

INDEX OF NAMES

INDEX OF NAMES

INDEX OF NAMES

302

INDEX OF NAMES

INDEX OF NAMES

INDEX OF NAMES

INDEX OF PLACES

INDEX OF PLACES

INDEX OF PLACES

INDEX OF PLACES

INDEX OF PLACES

INDEX OF PLACES

INDEX OF SUBJECTS

INDEX OF SUBJECTS

INDEX OF SUBJECTS

INDEX OF SUBJECTS

INDEX OF SUBJECTS

INDEX OF SUBJECTS

INDEX OF SUBJECTS

INDEX OF SUBJECTS

INDEX OF SUBJECTS

INDEX OF SUBJECTS

INDEX OF SUBJECTS

INDEX OF SUBJECTS

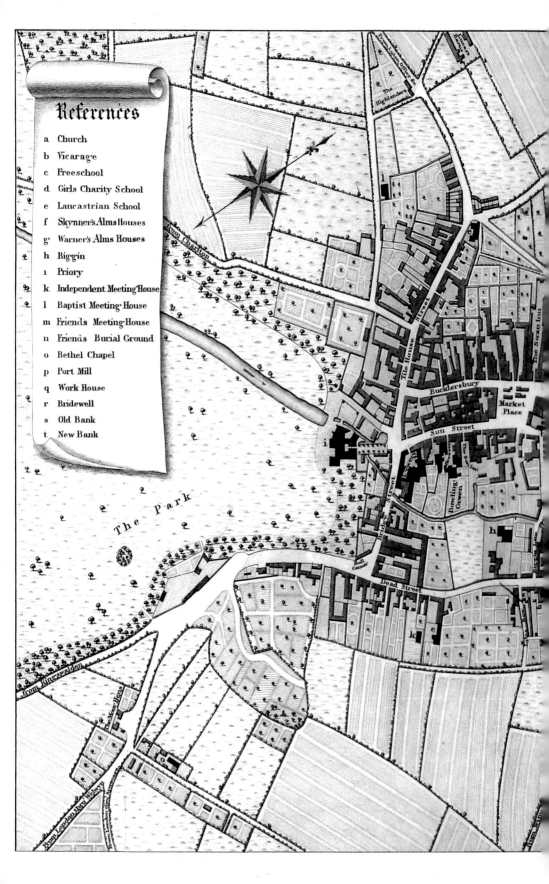

References

a   Church
b   Vicarage
c   Freeschool
d   Girls Charity School
e   Lancastrian School
f   Skynner's Alms Houses
g   Warner's Alms Houses
h   Biggin
i   Priory
k   Independent Meeting House
l   Baptist Meeting House
m   Friends Meeting House
n   Friends Burial Ground
o   Bethel Chapel
p   Port Mill
q   Work House
r   Bridewell
s   Old Bank
t   New Bank

The Park

Tile House Street

Bucklersbury

Market Place

Sun Street

Bowling Green

Dead Street

The Swan Inn

Bridge Street

from Charlton

From Kingswalden

From London via Welwyn

The Highlanders